The Law of Investor Protection

Second Edition

AUSTRALIA
Law Book Co.
Sydney

CANADA and USA
Carswell
Toronto

HONG KONG
Sweet & Maxwell Asia

NEW ZEALAND
Brookers
Wellington

SINGAPORE and MALAYSIA
Sweet & Maxwell Asia
Singapore and Kuala Lumpur

The Law of Investor Protection

Second Edition

by

JONATHAN FISHER Q.C.
B.A., LL.B. (Cantab.), of Gray's Inn, Barrister
Senior Visiting Fellow, City University Business School (PMV)

JANE BEWSEY
M.A. (Cantab.), of Inner Temple, Barrister

MALCOLM WATERS Q.C.
M.A., B.C.L., (Oxon.), of Lincoln's Inn, Barrister

and

ELIZABETH OVEY
B.A., (Oxon.), of Middle Temple, Barrister

Published in 2003 by
Sweet & Maxwell Limited of
100 Avenue Road, Swiss Cottage,
London NW3 3PF
Typeset by LBJ Typesetting Ltd
of Kingsclere
Printed and bound in Great Britain
by TJ International Ltd, Padstow, Cornwall

No natural forests were destroyed to
make this product: only farmed
timber was used and re-planted

ISBN 0 421 67300 1

A CIP catalogue record for this book is available from the British Library

Foreword

When the authors of the first edition of Fisher and Bewsey on Investor Protection hung up their pens with a sigh of relief in July, 1996, they may have seen the looming portents of a change in structure on the financial services regulatory front. They can scarcely have foreseen how radical the reform of the entire industry has been in the seven years that have followed, how much new and complex legislation in this field has been passed and how very necessary the new edition of this excellent book has become.

The second edition of what we must now call Fisher, Bewsey, Waters and Ovey is a comprehensive guide through a very dense and fertile forest. Swathes of legal timber have had to be chopped out, replaced by totally fresh chapters of greenwood, much of it as yet untested in the courts.

As markets and those who participate in them, whether as traders or customers, become more sophisticated, so the laws necessary to regulate the one and protect the other need to develop at a similar rate. The Financial Services and Markets Act regime has now been in force since December, 2001. Its scope is breathtakingly wide but the Financial Services Authority which it has created has scarcely bared its teeth in anger. The foreboding which greeted the new Act has subsided as trader and investment houses have taken stock and have now got to grips with the requirements to train their staff, to have in place adequate controls and reporting mechanisms and explaim the changes to their clients. This book will be of immense help in setting out clearly and concisely the changes that FSMA has introduced.

Investor protection is the central plank in the evolving law of financial services. New markets are opening up and an ever-growing number of investment vehicles are devised to entice envestors and make money for those who promote them. Investors need all the help they can get to educate them, to give them a real choice, to tell the worthwhile from the dangerously speculative and to guide them where they can get relief when things go wrong. The new edition of "Investor Protection" pulls together the strands that make up the intricate and complex web that is the financial services sector today.

The reader will learn about the different regulations that cover the professions, the investment houses and pensions and mortgage providers. The book covers the new regulations embracing market abuse and money laundering. There is a full account of the criminal offences which can be commited all too commonly in this area, where the rewards are very large and the prospects of detection, still less of successful prosecution and an eventual penalty very small. Most importantly, in a book directed at the protection of investors, the reader will want to know about the various systems for complaints and compensation, including the Financial Services

Ombudsman Scheme and the Investors' Compensation Scheme, both key features of effective investor protection and redress.

The book is intended primarily as a text for the student of investment law; this edition will be welcomed by student and lecturer in this field alike. But the book will be a "must-have" for all who practice in this ever expanding area of law and those who are not lawyers but who are brave enough to dip their toes into the deep and sometimes treacherous waters of financial investment. If I have been able to encourage such brave souls to read Fisher on Investor Protection before they part with much larger sums by way of speculative investments, I will be satisfied.

ROSALIND WRIGHT CB
Chairman, Fraud Advisory Panel
(Director, Serious Fraud Office, 1997–2003)

Preface

The last 15 years have witnessed a change in our attitude towards the use of money. Whereas during the years of high inflation people came to the view that it was sensible to spend money on consumer goods before inflation ravaged the value of their money, the contemporary attitude towards money is quite different. Successive Conservative administrations have encouraged people to save money, through a variety of investment schemes. Investment opportunities have multiplied and often these have been laced with tax incentives. Thrift has become a fashionable virtue.

Associated with the growth of investment opportunities, the Thatcher years witnessed a revolution in the provision of financial services, as "Big Bang" in the City heralded a new era of the small investor in which the ordinary and the meek were invited to accumulate wealth by prudent investment in the financial markets. New types of investment vehicles developed, as small shareholders were encouraged to participate in capital ventures. The size of the world shrank, as computer technology enabled money to be transferred across international boundaries instantaneously at the press of a button. The time of the financial entrepreneur had arrived. Instead of acting as the intermediary between capital and labour, which was the role ascribed to the entrepreneur in classical Marxist theory, the entrepreneur acted as the intermediary between capital and investor. The investor varied in degrees of sophistication from the City meritocrat who was investing his large annual profit bonus to the ordinary man on the Clapham omnibus who had some money to invest but was uneducated in the skills of financial investment.

Legal headlines in the past 15 years have been dominated by the casualties of the changes and innovations which have occurred in the investment world, as Parliament and the Courts have struggled to protect the interests of investors. Investors lost money which they had invested, sometimes at the hands of dishonest men who set out to defraud their victims of their savings, but more often at the hands of the incompetent or the reckless, who were trying to accumulate wealth for themselves and their clients by taking risks which the more prudent could not justify. Barlow Clowes, the Levitt Group, BCCI, the Lloyd's insurance market, and Barings Bank, have become household names associated with the dishonest or reckless loss of investor's money.

It was unfortunate, though perhaps inevitable, that before sponsoring this change in attitude in favour of saving and investment the Government did not ensure that there were sufficient legal protections in place to protect the investor. In order to afford investors some protection the courts have sought to rely upon the traditional common law principles enshrined in the law of contract and the law of tort. In some areas the courts have successfully assimilated the changes and innovations within the boundaries of established legal norms and principles, but in other areas the task has been too great. Parliament has responded to investor related problems by amending existing post-war legislation in some areas and enacting fresh legislation in others, and different Acts of Parliament apply to different spheres of investment activity. A burgeoning jurisprudence is developing in each of these spheres of activity, as cases under the new statutory regimes, such as the Financial Services Act 1986, the Pensions legislation and the new Company and Insolvency legislation have started to come through the courts, with increasing frequency in recent years.

There is no shortage of written material on each of these areas, and there are good texts on the subject matter of each area which is covered in this book. The problem lies not with the absence of comprehensive texts on each subject, but rather in the fact that the statutory and non-statutory systems for investor protection, together with the established areas of criminal and civil law, are so unwieldy and fragmented that it is difficult to take an overall view. There is no book which pulls together the disparate threads into one readable and coherent text.

It is the object of this book to undertake this somewhat Herculean task and provide readers with a coherent account of the law which protects investors and regulates those involved in the investment industry. At the present time the law of investor protection is not a recognised subject in its own right. We hope that this book will stimulate interest in the development of this area of the law in academic as well as legal circles.

Notwithstanding the depth of the recession, investment activity has continued. New challenges continue to confront the legal system. We hope that in meeting these challenges this book will, by drawing together disparate strands and presenting an overall approach to the subject, provide a useful companion to legal practitioners, compliance officers and all those who work in the field of investment.

Above all, we hope that the production of a coherent text which concerns itself with an overall picture of investor protection will assist in efforts to improve the present state of the existing law. There can be little doubt that fragmentation of investor protection and regulation has hindered the development of the law in this area.

Similar problems have arisen in other jurisdictions, not just in Europe, the United States, Canada and Australia, but also in Pacific Rim countries and countries which have seen a rapid growth in investment markets. Experiences in former Commonwealth countries, the East European countries, and the Middle East, particularly in Israel, come to mind. We hope that this book will also be of interest and assistance to legislators, legal practitioners and academic lawyers in these jurisdictions.

In undertaking this work we have not sought to analyse investor protection in jurisprudential or socio-economic terms. Our focus is confined to a consideration of the provisions of the substantive law.

There are bound to be errors and omissions in a book of this kind. We hope that readers will point them out to us, for correction in the next edition. We also hope readers will let us know where they would like to see changes in content or scope. We have avoided the use of footnotes in the hope that the text will flow more freely.

The book deals with the law relating to England and Wales. The law is stated as at July 31, 1996.

Preface

The idea to write this book arose from the need to provide a text for Masters degree students who study Investment Law at City University Business School (PVM). Jonathan Fisher would like to thank all at City University for their encouragement with this work.

Both authors wish to acknowledge with grateful thanks the support they have received from their families, their clerks, and our publishers, Sweet and Maxwell, at all times during the writing of this book.

Jonathan Fisher
Jane Bewsey
5 King's Bench Walk
Inner Temple
London

July 31, 1996

Preface to Second Edition

It is hard to believe that six years have elapsed since the publication of the first edition. In the preface to the first edition we anticipated that new challenges would continue to confront the legal system, and in presenting a text which drew together many disparate strands of investor protection, we suggested that fragmentation had hindered the development of the law in this area.

Shortly after publication, the incoming Labour Government announced that it was introducing a new system to regulate the provision of financial services by bringing the multiplicity of regulatory bodies under the auspices of a single regulator. Even the regulatory functions discharged by the Bank of England would be embraced by this new regulator, to be established by Parliament as an independent non-governmental body with statutory powers.

The first stage of the reform was completed in June 1998 when responsibility for banking supervision was transferred to the new regulator, known as the Financial Services Authority or by its acronym, the FSA. The Financial Services and Markets Act, which received Royal Assent in June 2000 and came into force on December 1, 2001, transferred to the FSA the responsibilities of several other organisations, including:

- Building Societies Commission;
- Friendly Societies Commission;
- Investment Management Regulatory Organisation;
- Personal Investment Authority;
- Register of Friendly Societies;
- Securities and Futures Authority.

The new legislation also introduced some additional responsibilities for the regulator involving, in particular, the regulation of certain aspects of mortgage lending, and the setting up of, and monitoring of compliance with, a Code of Market Conduct.

These changes rendered the need to produce a second edition very obvious, and whilst we described the writing of the book in the preface to the first edition as a Herculean task, we recognized that we were now faced with a task of truly gargantuan proportions. The new Financial Services and Markets Act 2000 contained 433 sections and 22 schedules. Over 100

Statutory Instruments have already been made under the Act. At the time of writing the FSA has published somewhere in the region of 200 consultation papers; and the new FSA Handbook of Rules and Guidance is an impressive tome which, due to its size and the availability of a search facility, is best accessed on the FSA's website.

Other developments also needed to be addressed in a second edition. There have been significant developments in the areas of public interest disclosures, obtaining of information from sources abroad, the application of the principles of constructive trust to investor cases and, more recently, the confiscation of criminal assets under the new Proceeds of Crime Act 2002.

Additionally, September 11, 2001 brought in its wake further significant changes. A new European Directive on Money Laundering was agreed by the European Council in November 2001. The Amending Directive has been implemented in the UK by the Money Laundering Regulations 2003.

Swamped by so many different developments, it was plain that a mere up-dating of the first edition would not suffice, and Jonathan Fisher and Jane Bewsey were delighted (and much relieved) when two additional partners, Malcolm Waters QC and Elizabeth Ovey, were recruited to collaborate in the production of the second edition.

Jonathan Fisher and Jane Bewsey believe that Malcolm and Elizabeth's involvement has immeasurably strengthened the quality of the second edition. The law of investor protection crosses legal boundaries; in some areas it is necessary to look to the criminal law in order to identify the way in which investor interests are protected, whilst in other areas one has to look to the civil law to discover the ways in which investor rights and entitlements are safeguarded. We hope that the different professional experiences of the authors, coming from both the Criminal Bar and the Chancery Bar, will serve readers well.

In this fast moving area of law, further legislative changes will unquestionably take place. The UK Government has only recently responded to the challenges presented by the corporate scandals in America, with a promise of "Enron style" legislation to reform company law. We address the implications for UK investor protection law in the final chapter of this book.

As before, we recognize that there are bound to be errors and omissions in a book of this kind. We hope that readers will point them out to us, for correction in the third edition. We also hope that readers will let us know where they would like to see changes in content or scope.

The book deals with the law relating to England and Wales. The law is stated as at the June 30, 2003.

The relevance of the book to those studying Investment Law at Cass Business School, City University London, remains extant, and Jonathan Fisher renews his thanks to all at City University for their encouragement with this work.

With the production of the second edition, the authors wish to acknowledge with grateful thanks the support they have received from their families, their clerks and, above all, from Kate Hayes of Sweet and Maxwell at all times during the writing of this book.

Jonathan Fisher, QC
Jane Bewsey
18 Red Lion Court
London

Malcolm Waters, QC
Elizabeth Ovey
11 Old Square
Lincoln's Inn, London

August 31, 2003

Contents

PART 3—MARKET MANIPULATION AND MARKET ABUSE

PART 4—ENFORCING THE NEW REGIME

PART 5—INVESTOR PROTECTION IN CRIMINAL LAW

PART 6—INVESTOR PROTECTION IN CIVIL LAW

PART 7—CONCLUSION

PART 8—APPENDIX

Table of Cases

Table of Statutes

All references are to paragraph numbers

1985 Companies Act—*cont.*
ss.156–158 24–030
s.156(1) 24–031
s.156(4) 24–032
s.156(5) 24–031
s.156(6) 24–031, A–005
s.156(7) 24–032, A–005
s.157 24–029
s.157(2) 24–033
ss.159–181 24–007
s.160(4) 24–007
s.163(2)(b) 7–027
s.169 .... A–005
s.169(6) A–005
s.169(7) A–006
s.173 .... A–006
s.173(6) A–006
s.175(7) A–006
s.176 .... A–006
s.176(4) A–006
s.183(6) A–006
s.185(1) A–006
s.185(5) A–006
s.189(1) A–006
s.189(2) A–006
s.191(4) A–006
s.198 14–049
s.210 .... 23–015, 23–018
s.210(3) A–007
s.211 .... A–007
s.211(10) A–007
s.212 .... A–007
s.214(5) A–007
s.215 .... A–007
s.215(8) A–007
s.216(3) 23–015, A–007
s.217(7) A–007
s.218(2) A–007
s.218(3) A–007
s.219(3) A–007
s.221 ..... 23–020, 23–021, 23–024
s.221(5) 23–020
s.222 .... 23–021, 23–024
s.222(4) A–008
s.222(5) 23–021
s.223(1) A–007
s.223(2) A–008
s.231(3) A–008
s.231(4) A–008
s.235(7) A–008
s.238(2) A–008
s.240(5) A–008
s.242(1) 23–022
s.242(2) 23–022
s.242(4) 23–022
s.243(1) A–008
s.245(1) A–020
s.245(2) A–020
s.246(2) A–008

1985 Companies Act—*cont.*
s.254 .... A–008
s.254(6) A–008
s.288 .... A–009
s.288(4) A–009
s.291(5) A–009
s.294(3) A–009
s.303 29–057
s.305 .... A–009
s.305(3) A–009
s.306(4) A–009
s.309 29–007
s.310 29–021
s.310(1) 29–020
s.310(3)(a) 29–020
ss.311–322 23–003
s.314 .... A–009
s.314(3) A–009
s.317 .... 23–004, 29–010
s.317(1) 23–003
s.317(7) 23–003, A–009
s.318(1) A–009
s.318(5) A–009
s.318(7) A–009
s.318(8) A–009
s.319(4) A–009
s.322B(4) A–009, A–020
s.323 .... 13–018, 29–070
s.323(1) 23–006
s.323(2) A–009
s.323(5) 23–006
s.324 .... 23–007, 23–008, 23–018, 29–070
s.324(7) A–010
s.324(7)(a) 23–007
s.324(7)(b) 23–007
s.325 23–008
s.326(2), (3), (4), (5) 23–008, A–010
s.327 23–006
s.328 23–007
s.328(6) 23–007, A–010
s.329 23–018
s.329(3) A–010
ss.330–347 23–009
s.330 .... 23–009, 23–010, 23–011, A–010
s.330(2)(a) 23–009
s.330(2)(b) 23–009
s.330(3)(a) 23–009
s.330(3)(b) 23–009
s.330(3)(c) 23–009
s.330(4)(a) 23–009
s.330(4)(b) 23–009
s.330(5) 23–010
s.330(6) 23–009
s.330(7)(a) 23–009
s.330(7)(b) 23–009

Table of Statutory Instruments

All references are to paragraph numbers

Table of Rules of the Supreme Court

All references are to paragraph numbers

Table of Treaties and Conventions

All references are to paragraph numbers

Table of EC Directives

All references are to paragraph numbers

Part 1

Introduction

Chapter 1

Investor Protection in Context

Before embarking upon a study of the way in which the interests of an investor are protected by the law, it is necessary to ask one or two preliminary questions. Who is an investor, and what is an investment? Like so many questions in the discipline of law, the questions are easier to ask than answer. In this chapter the different attempts to reach a comprehensive definition of these terms are explored. As a working definition, this book proceeds upon the basis that an investor is a person who uses money for the purchase of some species of property from which interest or profit is expected. **1–001**

In the second part of this chapter, consideration is given to the way in which investor interests have come to be recognised in law.

Definition of an Investor

Definitions in the Courts

In *Inland Revenue Commissioners v Rolls Royce Ltd* [1944] 2 All E.R. 340 Macnaghten J. offered a general definition in the following terms: **1–002**

> "The word 'investment', though it primarily means the act of investing, is in common use as meaning that which is thereby acquired; and the meaning of the verb 'to invest' is to lay out money in the acquisition of some species of property".

That said, the Courts have been reluctant to qualify the definition of an investment by reference to the nature of property which is acquired. For as Lord Greene MR noted two years later in *Inland Revenue Commissioners v Desoutter Brothers* [1946] 1 All E.R. 58:

> "the question whether or not a particular piece of income received from an investment must, in my view, be decided on the facts of the case . . . [Investment] is not a word of art but has to be interpreted in a popular sense".

There are two problems with a qualified definition of an investment. First, there are too many different species of property in English law. Any attempt to define the meaning of an investment by reference to the nature of the property acquired would be unworkable. Secondly, the purpose for **1–003** which property is acquired may be quite different. One man's investment may be another man's indulgence. One man may purchase diamonds to leave in his Bank Security Box for the benefit of his grandchildren in 50 years time. Another man might purchase the same diamonds to use in his wife's eternity ring, with no intention of investment in mind. Also, the prevailing state of the economy can affect the motive with which a particular type of property is acquired. When considering the scope of an investment clause in a deed of trust, P O Lawrence J. in *Re Wragge* [1919] 2 Ch.58 noted that "the expression 'investing in house property' is one which every lawyer must frequently have heard, and who could doubt that in such a case the house property purchased is properly described as 'an investment'". There are few lawyers today who would not entertain such doubts!

Tax Legislation

1–004 There have been many cases in which the meaning of "investment income" has been discussed within the context of the tax legislation, but following the abolition of the surcharge on investment income as from 1984/85, the distinction between earned and investment income is relevant only in relatively few situations. The juristic task of attempting to find a definition of an investment is not advanced by a consideration of the old cases on this point.

Construction of Deeds of Trust

1–005 The law reports contain a number of reported cases in which the Courts have considered the meaning of an investment within the confines of an investment clause in a deed of trust. Each case turns on the particular language which was used by the trust draftsman, and the unhelpful nature of these cases can be demonstrated by a consideration of the decision in *Re Price* [1905] 2 Ch.55, where Farwell J. held that the phrase "pecuniary investments" did not include money placed on deposit at a bank. According to the Judge:

> "the money that is deposited with a man's banker is money that awaits investment—it is not, in fact, already invested. Whether or not it produces interest by being put on deposit account is immaterial".

The financial world has advanced significantly since this case was decided.

The Financial Services and Markets Act 2000

1–006 A glimpse at Sch.2, Pt II of the Financial Services and Markets Act 2000 reveals the variety of investments which were identified by Parliament as constituting investments for the purposes of that legislation. The provisions of the Financial Services and Markets Act 2000 are considered in

Part 2 of this book at some length. Suffice it to note here that instead of defining the scope of investment generically, Parliament chose to list fourteen different species of investment in the Schedule.

The Dictionary Definition

The word "invest" derives from the Latin verb "investire", which means to clothe or adorn, in the sense that powers may be invested in a body, or a person may be invested with the insignia of office. A secondary meaning which developed in the use of the English language bore a financial connotation, and the Oxford Shorter English Dictionary notes that by 1613 the verb "to invest" was used to indicate the employment of money from which interest or profit is expected. This secondary meaning presents an appropriate working definition for the purposes of this book. The obtaining of interest or profit is the defining characteristic of an investor. **1–007**

Recognition of Investor Interests

Sources of law

Having identified a working definition of an investor, the next question to consider is this: are the interests of investors recognised in English law? The answer, again, is not susceptible to a simple statement. Essentially, English law recognises investor interests in four principal ways.

Civil Law

The interests of an investor are recognised in the application of civil law which governs the particular arrangement into which the investor has entered. So, for example, if an investor has purchased shares in a company, his rights and obligations will be governed by principles of company law. If the investment involves the deposit of funds in a bank account, the rights and obligations of the parties will be determined by the law of contract. If an investor has purchased property, his landowning interests will be determined by the law of property, etc. **1–008**

Statutory Systems of Regulation

In some cases the interests of an investor are recognised in Acts of Parliament which have been passed to regulate the provision of investment services in different areas. The Financial Services and Markets Act 2000 is a primary example, since this Act was passed to regulate the conduct of investment business. **1–009**

It is important to stress that, in contrast to the first way in which investor interests may be protected, Acts of Parliament tend to be directed at the regulation of investment dealings and not the rights and obligations of the particular investment arrangement which continue to be determined by the incidence of the general law.

Non-statutory Systems of Regulation

1–010 Investor interests may be recognised under systems of self-regulation. The Panel on Takeovers and Mergers is a classic example of a truly self-regulatory system, because unlike the bodies set up under the auspices of the Financial Services Act 1986 which embody a large element of self-regulation, the powers of the Panel are derived exclusively from the voluntary arrangement made between the people who agreed to be bound by a code of conduct of their own devising—*R v Panel on Takeovers and Mergers Ex p. Datafin* [1987] 1 All E.R. 564.

Criminal Law

1–011 English law also recognises investor interests through the mechanism of the criminal law. In addition to the creation of various criminal offences to support prohibitions which have been included in Acts of Parliament passed to regulate commercial dealings in a particular area, for example s.19 of the Financial Services and Markets Act 2000 which makes it a criminal offence for an unauthorised person to conduct investment business, the criminal law can operate more generally to protect the interests of an investor. Unauthorised movement of funds from a company's bank account may, if undertaken dishonestly, amount to an offence of theft contrary to s.1 of the Theft Act 1968. Also, on occasions Parliament has created criminal offences directed at the protection of investors' interests which stand independently from any regulatory system. The legislation which criminalises insider dealing comes to mind. Additionally, there are an array of criminal offences not drafted specifically with the investor in mind which may be utilised in cases in the investment context, where the unfortunate investor stands as a victim of a fraud.

The problems encountered in the prosecution of investor fraud cases often reflect the practical problems of prosecuting serious fraud as much as some deficiency in the criminal law. For instance, it is not uncommon for prosecutors to meet investor witnesses who, having lost money in some investment swindle, are reluctant to testify against the perpetrators because the invested funds had been concealed from the attentions of the Inland Revenue in the first place!

It follows, therefore, that English law does recognise investor interests. There are legal provisions directed at the protection of these interests, but for a variety of different reasons these provisions are diverse and can be found only on a consideration of disparate areas of substantive law and in an eclectic collection of Acts of Parliament passed since the Second World War. There is no generic, coherent code of investor protection law. The relevant law has developed slowly, without the benefit of any grand overview, and above all, the development has been responsive to advances made in the investment sector.

Re-active Recognition of Investor Interests

By definition the legal system is re-active and not pro-active, and traditionally there is lengthy delay before the legal system responds to changes and innovations in commercial activity. This is certainly true in the field of investor protection. A consideration of legal developments in the field of property investment well demonstrates the point. **1–012**

In the eighteenth and nineteenth centuries an investor who purchased property invariably would have done so without assistance from any third party. Investor protection was rooted in the rights and incidents of property ownership. As Milsom noted in the Historical Foundations of the Common Law, 1969, from the earliest settlements until the industrial revolution the economic basis of society was agrarian. Land was wealth, livelihood, family provision, and the principal subject-matter of the law. "Lordship was property, the object of legal protection from above, just as it was the source of legal protection for rights below" (at p.88).

Complications started to occur when other investors sought to join an investment proposition. Lordship, to use Milsom's word (derived from the Latin "dominium"), was difficult to divide. Where property was purchased in the name of more than one person, under the provisions of the Law of Property Act 1925 the law deemed that the owners held the property as joint tenants in law. Severance of joint tenancies into tenancies in common, whereby the equitable interests of each owner could be identified, was a cumbersome procedure, and there were obvious problems where one or more of the co-owners wished to realise his investment in the property. The concept of joint ownership in law was not easily adapted to multiple ownership of property in the investment sector. In recent times, following the heady days of property market boom in the 1970s and 1980s, the value of "blue-chip" property increased beyond the reach of the non-institutional investor. Even large pension funds thought twice before committing substantial funds to the purchase of a large single building in the City of London. **1–013**

It was against this background that the financial services sector sought to create mechanisms which would enable investors to acquire a part interest in a single property, and to be able to trade the part interest separately on a secondary property market. Various complicated mechanisms have been devised, such as the Single Asset Property Company ("SAPCOs"), Single Property Ownership Trust ("SPOTs"), and Property Income Certificates ("PINCs"). For a number of reasons PINCs appeared to be the most attractive vehicle for investors. The scheme involves the establishment of a specially formed vehicle company, the granting of a headlease and an underlease, and the issue of certificates which would be similar to bonds. Under the scheme the investor is afforded two principal rights—the right to receive income and rents from an intermediary, and the right to receive shares in a vehicle company. **1–014**

In the event, for a variety of reasons these schemes have not caught the imagination of the investing public. In legal terms, this was probably just as well. Whilst the Financial Services and Markets Act 2000 and delegated legislation made under that Act permits this sort of investment mechanism to be regulated as a collective investment scheme in certain cases, there is some doubt as to the precise status of the scheme. To take just one issue, the Financial Services and Markets Act 2000 does not apply where the participant carries on a non-investment business and enters into the arrangement for commercial purposes relating to that business. In what circumstances would a participant who is entering a property transaction for the first time or is merely a landowner be deemed to be carrying on non-investment business? This sort of question, together with clarification of the rights and obligations of the investor, would fall to be determined by the Courts with reference to the provisions of the Financial Services and Markets Act 2000 and the application of existing principles of company law, land law and the law of contract, to which this investment device would have been completely unknown.

Thus, the Courts must respond to developments in the financial services sector but inevitably protection of investor's interests falls to be considered *ex post facto*, in this discursive and piece-meal way.

The European Influence

1–015 The influence of the European Community should not be overlooked as a catalyst in the development of the law in this area. The emphasis of the Community has focused on the need for harmonisation, but not by the imposition of a single set of rules which would be directly applicable throughout the Community. Rather, the Community has endeavoured to promote harmonisation by mutual recognition of domestic systems of regulation, particularly with regard to company law, banking and investment services. Reference to the role and influence of the European Community will be made at various stages in this book.

Striking a Balance

1–016 Protection of investors' interests has to be balanced against the needs and demands of the financial markets. The market-place is essentially pragmatic, and whilst the protection of investors' interests are paramount, the realities of commercial life must not be eclipsed. As Professor Gower wrote in his Discussion Document on Investor Protection:

> "it would be lamentable if our regulations were so strict in comparison with those of other countries that London ceases to be the world's centre for financial services as it still is. If the constraints imposed here are unduly severe, market makers will move elsewhere" (at para.7.01).

Concern for the protection of investors' interests has to be balanced against the need to maintain international competitiveness. There was considerable turbulence generated by the voluminous rule books which were created by the self regulatory organisations (SROs) recognised under the Financial Services Act 1986, as investment businesses contended that the extent of regulation was overburdensome. The Securities and Investments Board subsequently promulgated a series of principles (known as the 10 commandments) and 40 core rules in an effort to simply the regulatory requirements and focus on the critical areas of attention. Today, the regulatory regime established by the Financial Services and Markets Act is far from straight-forward. Part 2 of this book is designed to lead the reader through the regulatory morass in a manageable way.

Part 2

The New Regime

Chapter 2

An Overview

Introduction

In Ch.1 we noted that English law has historically recognised investor interests in four principal ways: by the substantive determination of rights and obligations under civil law; by the protection derived from statutory systems of regulation; by the terms of voluntary systems of regulation; and by the provisions of the criminal law. This still remains the case, but with the advent of the Financial Services and Markets Act 2000 (FSMA 2000) the range of statutory provisions relating to investments has become overwhelmingly the most obvious feature of the law relating to investor protection. Parts 2 to 5 of this work are therefore concerned primarily with areas substantially affected by FSMA 2000. Investor protection in criminal law is considered in Part 6 and investor protection in civil law in Part 7. We begin this Part with an overview of the 2000 Act. **2–001**

Background to the Financial Services Act 1986

The first attempt at regulation in the City of London of what is now known as investment business was in 1697, when an Act was passed requiring those who worked in the City and were engaged in dealings in Government securities and the shares or stock of companies (not, of course, the limited liability companies which are such a dominant feature of the modern scene) to be licensed annually by the Court of the Aldermen of the City. The licensed brokers were required to take an oath to transact business honestly and without fraud. However, this effort at regulation lapsed early in the eighteenth century. **2–002**

Further efforts towards market regulation were not attempted until the middle of the nineteenth century, which saw the passage of a series of Companies Acts concerning the setting up and running of limited companies. The pace of company legislation increased as time went on and this was the main source of what little regulation of the investments markets there was before the enactment of the Financial Services Act.

The only exception to this general laissez-faire approach to regulation began with the Prevention of Fraud (Investments) Act 1939, which was the first major piece of legislation in the United Kingdom to deal specifically with the protection of the interests of the individual investor. The Act was concerned with regulating unit trusts and introducing a system of licensing **2–003** and regulating individuals, firms and companies carrying on the business of dealing in securities. Unlicensed dealing became a criminal offence under the 1939 Act, as did distributing circulars containing information or invitations calculated to induce investment through a unit trust. Under the Act the Board of Trade (later the Department of Trade and Industry) issued Conduct of Business Rules for licensed dealers in securities. These rules were periodically updated, most recently (and finally) in 1983, but they were of limited application.

The 1939 Act was followed by the Prevention of Fraud (Investments) Act 1958, a consolidating Act which amended the 1939 Act and included various provisions of the Companies Acts 1947 and 1948. Under the 1958 Act the Board of Trade was also given the power to appoint inspectors to investigate the administration of unit trusts. The Act remained in force (as amended by the Protection of Depositors Act 1963) until the Financial Services Act 1986 came into force on April 29, 1988. However, the Prevention of Fraud (Investments) Acts were of very limited scope in practice, regulating only a fraction of investment business, by imposing criminal sanctions on those who, as principals or agents, dealt in securities without being duly licensed.

2–004 In the 1980s there was a growing appreciation of the need for comprehensive regulation of investment business following a number of financial scandals. Professor L.C.B. Gower was commissioned by the Government to undertake a review intended to consider and advise upon what statutory protection was required by both private and business investors, and on the need for statutory control of dealers in securities, investment consultants and investment managers. His report was published in January 1984 and expressed the view that the Prevention of Fraud (Investments) Act 1958 no longer provided a proper foundation for regulation. The report in turn led to a White Paper setting out the Government's proposals for legislation on financial services in the United Kingdom, which eventually took shape as the Financial Services Act.

2–005 Professor Gower had been conscious of the need to balance on the one hand regulation of the domestic financial services market and the need to protect United Kingdom investors from concerns based in foreign jurisdictions without the same degree of regulation and on the other the United Kingdom's obligations under the Treaty of Rome to allow freedom of establishment and the supply of services by concerns based in other Member States. He recommended that legislation should empower the Secretary of State to recognise that firms established in countries which have comparable controls should be treated as complying with United Kingdom investment law.

This was entirely consistent with the European Union's own approach, which was to harmonise the regulation of financial services across Europe through the implementation in domestic law of European Directives. As will be seen later, such Directives now play a very significant part indeed in the law of investor protection. This is to be viewed in the context of the consideration of the principle of freedom of establishment by the European Court in *Alpine Investments BV v Minister van Financien* [1995] All E.R. (EC) 543. The European Court was asked to decide whether Netherlands law regulating financial services, which restricted the cold calling of customers both in Holland and other Member States, constituted a restriction of the freedom to provide services within the meaning of Art.59 of the Treaty of Rome. The court held that investor confidence and the maintenance of the good reputation of the national financial sector could constitute an imperative reason of public interest capable of justifying restrictions on the freedom to provide financial services. In particular, the court held that the smooth operation of financial markets was largely contingent on the confidence they inspired in investors. That confidence depended in particular on the existence of professional regulation serving to ensure the competence and trustworthiness of the financial intermediaries on whom investors were particularly reliant.

The Financial Services Act 1986

The 1986 Act covered all those "carrying on investment business in the United Kingdom" and also extended to certain managers of occupational pension schemes. Any person carrying on investment business (or purporting to do so) had to be authorised or exempted from authorisation. It was a criminal offence to carry on investment business without being authorised. Authorisation was normally to be achieved by membership of one of four self-regulatory organisations: the Securities and Futures Authority (the SFA); the Investment Management Regulatory Organisation (IMRO); the Financial Intermediaries, Managers and Brokers Regulatory Association (FIMBRA); and the Life Assurance and Unit Trust Regulatory Organisation (LAUTRO). FIMBRA and LAUTRO were later replaced by the Personal Investment Authority (the PIA). The various self-regulatory bodies were themselves regulated by the Securities and Investment Board (the SIB). **2–006**

Accountants, actuaries and lawyers engaged in investment business were separately regulated under the Act through membership of recognised professional bodies and the SIB had certain powers of regulation in respect of recognised investment exchanges and recognised clearing houses, which were exempted persons in relation to activities which constituted investment business.

This framework operated by reference to the key concepts of "investments", "investment business" (*i.e.* certain activities relating to investments), "excluded activities" (*i.e.* certain activities excluded from the scope of investment business) and "carrying on investment business". The Act contained specific provisions in relation to life insurance, collective investment schemes and unit trusts and investment trusts.

The Financial Services Act also contained restrictions on the promotion and advertisement of financial services. In general, it was an offence to issue or cause to be issued an investment advertisement the contents of which had not been approved by an authorised person. Civil consequences also followed; subject to a discretionary power to vary those consequences given to the court, the person issuing or causing the advertisement to be issued could not enforce an agreement to which the advertisement related and the other party was entitled to recover any money or property **2–007** transferred by him under the agreement. Similar civil consequences applied in respect of an agreement entered into as the result of an unsolicited ("cold") call.

The investor was also protected by the creation of two further criminal offences. The 1986 Act broadly speaking made it an offence: (1) knowingly or recklessly to make a misleading, false or deceptive statement for the purpose of inducing, or being reckless as to whether it might induce, another person to make or refrain from making an investment agreement; and (2) to do any act or engage in any course of conduct which created a false or misleading impression as to the market in or the price or value of any investments with the purpose of creating that impression and thereby inducing another person to deal with or refrain from dealing with such investments.

Other Regulatory Systems

2–008 As appears from the foregoing, the Financial Services Act had within its purview a large number of activities relating to the provision of financial services. Many other such activities, however, were not regulated by that Act. Banks were subject to supervision under the Banking Act 1987 (and previously under the less extensive provisions of the Banking Act 1979), first by the Bank of England and then by the Financial Services Authority, as the SIB became, while building societies were regulated by the Building Societies Commission under the Building Societies Act 1986. (Unlike banks, building societies had a long history of some degree of statutory regulation; the first Building Societies Act was passed in 1836.) By the time FSMA 2000 came into force, there were close similarities between the statutory regime applicable to banks and that applicable to building societies, not least because in each case the regime had been amended from time to time to reflect the European law, contained in various Directives, relating to credit institutions, which applies to both types of body. Friendly societies were subject to supervision under the Friendly Societies Acts 1974 and 1992 by the Friendly Societies Commission, which also had responsibilities in relation to industrial and provident societies. Credit unions were also subject to statutory provisions contained in the Credit Unions Act 1979. The Department of Trade had responsibilities as respects insurance companies under the Insurance Companies Act 1982.

2–009 In addition, Lloyds's of London, although the subject of Acts of Parliament from 1871 onwards, remained largely self-regulated under structures established by the Lloyd's Act 1982, and take-overs and mergers were required to be conducted in accordance with the City Code on Take-overs and Mergers administered by the Panel on Take-overs and Mergers, yet another self-regulatory body.

Moreover, in case the position was not otherwise sufficiently complicated, a body was liable to be regulated by different authorities in connection with different activities; there were in existence eight relevant Ombudsman schemes for dealing with complaints, some of which were statutory and some of which were voluntary; and there was also a range of compensation schemes to prevent or reduce loss in cases in which a body had insufficient funds to satisfy the claims of investors.

The Financial Services and Markets Act 2000

In 1997 the Labour Manifesto promised that if Labour were returned to power it would bring self-regulation in the investment business sector to an end and would make the SIB the direct regulator in that field. In fact, in May 1997, the new Government announced that it proposed to go a great deal further and to introduce "one stop regulation". The existing arrangements were understandably described as not only confusing, but also costly and inefficient. The emphasis was to be shifted from the constitutional nature of the body engaging in an investment-related activity to the nature of the activity itself. The 2000 Act accordingly replaces all the forms of regulation considered above and extends statutory regulation in some areas. The SIB itself has been renamed the Financial Services Authority (the FSA). **2–010**

In dealing with FSMA 2000 in this work we will consider first in the chapters succeeding this one the regime applicable to certain bodies and certain forms of financial services under the auspices of the single regulator (Part 2); then issues of market manipulation and market abuse (Part 3); then enforcement (Part 4); and finally the difficult subject of money laundering. In the remainder of this chapter, we will look at some matters of more general application. **2–011**

Regulation under the New Legislation: General

One Stop Regulation

The description "one stop regulation" is a helpful pointer to a principal feature of FSMA 2000. It builds on a lot of the work previously done in establishing the regulatory systems referred to above, but seeks to draw them together in a more coherent, efficient and effective form. Therefore, although the system of regulation itself is new, many of the underlying features have strong similarities to one or more of the previous systems. This in part accounts for the fact that although the Act is a lengthy and complicated measure, its long title reads simply: **2–012**

> "An Act to make provision about the regulation of financial services and markets; to provide for the transfer of certain statutory functions relating to building societies, friendly societies, industrial and provident societies and certain other mutual societies, and for connected purposes".

The single regulator under the new regime is, of course, the FSA (the renamed SIB). Pt I of the Act contains general provisions relating to the regulator. S.1 states simply that the FSA has the functions conferred on it by or under the Act and introduces Sch.1, containing requirements as to its constitution. It is a body corporate with a chairman and governing body, the chairman being appointed by the Treasury and the governing body containing a majority of non-executive members (Sch.1, paras 2 and 3), and **2–013** is under annual reporting obligations, both to Parliament through the Treasury and to the public, by means of a public meeting to be held within three months of the making of any report to enable the report to be considered (Sch.1, paras 10 and 11). Under s.7 the FSA is under a duty to have regard to such generally accepted principles of good corporate governance as it is reasonable to regard as applicable to it.

2–014 Having introduced the single regulator, FSMA 2000 goes on to set out in s.2 four regulatory objectives, as follows:

- the market confidence objective (maintaining confidence in the financial system, defined to mean the financial system operating in the United Kingdom and to include financial markets and exchanges, regulated activities and other activities connected with financial markets and exchanges: s.3);
- the public awareness objective (promoting public understanding of the financial system, including in particular promoting awareness of the benefits and risks associated with different kinds of investment or other financial dealing: s.4);
- the protection of consumers objective (securing the appropriate degree of protection for consumers: s.5(1)). "Consumers" means, broadly speaking, persons who use, have used or may be contemplating using financial services; persons who have rights or interests derived from or attributable to the use of financial services by others; and persons who have rights or interests which may be adversely affected by the use of financial services by persons acting on their behalf or in a fiduciary capacity in relation to them: s.138, applied and extended by s.5(3). In other words, direct consumers, persons deriving rights from direct consumers and persons on whose behalf direct consumers act are all consumers for these purposes;
- the reduction of financial crime objective (reducing the extent to which it is possible for a business carried on by a regulated person or in contravention of the general prohibition (discussed in para.2.023 below) to be used for a purpose connected with financial crime: s.6(1)).

Of these various objectives, the third is the one most overtly directed to investor protection, but the other three objectives clearly have a role to play as means towards achieving that end.

Functions, Powers and Duties of the FSA

2–015 The FSA has a number of general functions, listed in s.2(4) as: making rules under FSMA 2000; preparing and issuing codes under the Act; giving general guidance; and determining the general policy and principles by reference to which it performs particular functions. In discharging those functions it is expressly required, by s.2(1), to act, so far as is reasonably possible, in a way which is compatible with the regulatory objectives set out above and which the FSA considers most appropriate for the purpose of meeting those objectives. It must also, by virtue of s.2(3), have regard to:

- the need to use its resources in the most efficient and economic way;
- the responsibilities of those who manage the affairs of authorised persons;
- the principle that a burden or restriction should be proportionate to the expected benefits, considered in general terms;
- the desirability of facilitating innovation in connection with regulated activities;
- the international character of financial services and markets and the desirability of maintaining the competitive position of the United Kingdom;
- the need to minimise the adverse effects on competition which might arise from anything done in discharge of those functions;
- the desirability of facilitating competition between those who are subject to any form of regulation by the FSA.

The particular functions of the FSA will be considered in the context of in which they are exercisable and no attempt is here made to list them. We do, however, draw attention briefly to certain further provisions in Pt I of and Sch.1 to the Act relating to the FSA's powers and duties. **2–016**

S.8 imposes on the FSA a specific obligation to make and maintain effective arrangements for consulting practitioners and consumers on the extent to which its general policies and practices are consistent with its general duties under s.2. Those arrangements must include, by virtue of ss.9 and 10, the establishment of two panels, one to be known as "the Practitioners' Panel" and to represent the interests of practitioners and the other to be known as "the Consumers' Panel" and to represent the interests of consumers. Each Panel has a chairman, whose appointment or removal must be approved by the Treasury. The FSA is obliged to have regard to representations made by either Panel. Some teeth are given to that requirement by the provisions of s.11, under which not only must the FSA consider any such representation, but also, if it disagrees with a view expressed or a proposal made in the representation, it must give the relevant Panel a written statement of its reasons for disagreeing. The arrangements neatly illustrate the possibilities of tension between various of the matters to which the FSA is required to have regard. **2–017**

The Treasury has power under s.12 to appoint an independent person to conduct a review of "the economy, efficiency and effectiveness" with which the FSA has used its resources in discharging its functions. The scope of the review may be, but need not be, limited to functions specified when the appointment is made, but cannot in any case extend to the merits of the FSA's general policy or principles. The person conducting the review must **2–018** produce a written report to the Treasury, which is to be laid before Parliament and published in such manner as the Treasury considers appropriate. S.13 gives the person conducting the review a right to obtain documents in the custody or control of the FSA which are reasonably required and information from a person holding or accountable for such a document which is reasonably necessary. Obligations arising from the exercise of powers under s.13 are enforceable by court order. The review procedure is clearly a useful control but does not deal directly with investor protection.

2–019 By contrast, the Treasury has a separate power under s.14 to arrange for an independent inquiry to be held in two particular cases. The first is where events have occurred in relation to a collective investment scheme or a person carrying on a regulated activity which posed or could have posed a grave risk to the financial system or caused or risked causing significant damage to the interests of consumers, and the events might not have occurred, or the risk or damage might have been reduced, but for a serious failure in the system of regulation or in its operation. The second is where events have occurred in relation to listed securities or an issuer of listed securities which caused or could have caused significant damage to holders of listed securities and those events might not have occurred but for a serious failure in the regulatory system or its operation. S.15 provides that the Treasury may give directions to the person appointed to carry out the inquiry as to its scope, the period during which it is to be held, its conduct and the making of reports.

The person appointed is enabled by s.16 to obtain information from such persons and in such manner as he thinks fit, to make such inquiries as he thinks fit and to determine the procedure to be followed in connection with the inquiry. He may require any person who, in his opinion, is able to provide any information or produce any document relevant to the inquiry to do so, and he has the same powers as the High Court (in Scotland, the Court of Session) in respect of the attendance and examination of witnesses and the production of documents. On completion of the inquiry, the person appointed must make a written report to the Treasury setting out the result and making such recommendations as he considers appropriate (s.17), and the Treasury may publish the whole or any part of the report. A copy of the published material must be laid before Parliament. Under s.18, failure to comply with a requirement imposed under s.17, or obstruction of the inquiry in some other manner, may be treated as a contempt of court.

Clearly one of the purposes to be served by the exercise of this power is the future protection of investors. This is no doubt why the powers of a person appointed to conduct an inquiry are wider than those of a person appointed to carry out a review and why non-compliance with requirements may lead straight to the sanction of punishment for contempt of court.

2–020 As mentioned in para.2–013 above, a majority of the members of the governing body of the FSA must be non-executive members. The FSA must also establish a non-executive committee of the governing body, which must keep under review the question whether the FSA is discharging its functions in accordance with decisions of the governing body, the question whether its internal controls secure the proper conduct of its financial affairs and the remuneration of the chairman and executive members of the governing body: Sch.1, paras 3 and 4. A report on those matters by the non-executive committee is to be included in the FSA's annual report. The functions of the non-executive committee cannot be delegated.

Para.5 contains a general power to delegate other functions of the FSA, but subject to the provision that its legislative functions must be exercised through the governing body. Those functions are defined in para.1 as: making rules, issuing codes under specified provisions; issuing statements under specified provisions; giving directions under specified provisions; and issuing general guidance.

The FSA is under a specific duty, imposed by para.6 of Sch.1, to **2–021** maintain arrangements to monitor compliance with requirements imposed by or under the Act and to enforce the provisions of, or made under, the Act.

It is also under a duty to set up a complaints scheme under which complaints arising in connection with the exercise of or failure to exercise any of its functions other than its legislative functions may be investigated: para.7. A scheme has now been established, following the procedure set out in that paragraph, and is to be found under the title "Complaints against the FSA" in Block 4 of the *FSA Handbook* (discussed at para.2–035 and following below).

It will be recalled that much of the long title to the FSMA 2000 refers to **2–022** the transfer of functions relating to mutual societies. The relevant provisions in the Act itself are brief (Pt XXI and Sch.18), although they are elaborated by means of delegated legislation. The functions in question are essentially the registration functions which used to be carried out by the central office of the Registry of Friendly Societies. The central office has now ceased to exist, following the completion of the transfer. The significance of the registration functions from the point of view of investor protection is that they are the means by which important information as to the constitution and governance arrangements of the mutual societies concerned is made available to the public generally.

Elements of Regulation: Essential Definitions

At the centre of the provision for regulation of financial services made by **2–023** FSMA 2000 is s.19, which contains what is called "the general prohibition". That is a prohibition on any person's carrying on a regulated activity in the United Kingdom, or purporting to do so, unless he is an authorised person or an exempt person. The prohibition is, of course, a primary plank in the regime for ensuring the protection of investors. It follows that the meaning of the expressions "regulated activity", "authorised person" and "exempt person" is of crucial importance, and to that question we now turn.

Regulated Activity

2–024 The Act itself has a very open-ended definition of "regulated activity" in s.22. It requires simply that the activity should be one of a kind specified in an order made by the Treasury, that it should be carried on by way of business and that it should either relate to an investment of a kind specified in such an order or, if so specified, should be carried on in relation to property of any kind. That section is supplemented by Sch.2, giving an inclusive rather than exhaustive list of activities and investments with respect to which provision may be made. The Treasury exercised its power by making the Financial Services and Markets Act 2000 (Regulated Activities) Order 2001 (SI 2001/544), which, as amended by the Financial Services and Markets Act 2000 (Regulated Activities) (Amendment) Order 2002 (SI 2002/682), specifies the following activities:

- accepting deposits;
- issuing electronic money;
- effecting and carrying out contracts of insurance;
- dealing in investments as principal;
- dealing in investments as agent;
- arranging deals in investments;
- managing investments;
- safeguarding and administering investments;
- sending dematerialised instructions;
- establishing, operating or winding up a collective investment scheme;
- establishing, operating or winding up a stakeholder pension scheme;
- advising on investments;
- advice on syndicate participation at Lloyd's;
- managing the underwriting capacity of a Lloyd's syndicate;
- arranging deals in contracts of insurance written at Lloyds;
- entering as provider into a funeral plan contract;
- entering into or administering a regulated mortgage contract;
- agreeing to engage in any of the above activities, save for accepting deposits, issuing electronic money, effecting or carrying out contracts of insurance and the activities relating to collective investment schemes and stakeholder pension schemes.

It is proposed that when mortgages come to be regulated, the Order should be amended to cover also advising on and arranging regulated mortgages.

The structure of the Order is to specify in Pt II (which comprises the bulk of the Order) an activity and then the exclusions applicable to that activity. All the activities are ones which are regulated if carried on by way of business and in relation to specified investments (which are listed in Pt III of the Order) and the activities relating to collective investment schemes and stakeholder pension schemes are also regulated activities if carried on by way of business and in relation to property of any kind. There are also a number of exclusions which apply to several types of activity. The specified investments are closely related to the specified activities and are: deposits, electronic money, contracts of insurance, shares or stock in the share capital of any body corporate and any unincorporated body constituted under the law of a country or territory outside the United Kingdom, instruments creating or acknowledging indebtedness, government and public securities, instruments giving entitlement to investments, certificates representing certain securities, units in a collective investment scheme, rights under a stakeholder pension scheme, options, futures, contracts for differences or with a purpose similar to that of such contracts, Lloyd's syndicate capacity and syndicate membership, funeral plan contracts, regulated mortgage contracts and rights to or interests in investments. **2–025**

Many of these activities are considered in detail in subsequent chapters and so the particular activities are not considered further at this point. By way of general comment, it may be noted that the bulk of the activities are investment activities which were regulated under the Financial Services Act 1986. There are, however, important new regulated activities in the form of activities concerned with stakeholder pension schemes, Lloyd's, the provision of funeral plan contracts and regulated mortgages. **2–026**

Authorised Person

An authorised person is defined in s.31 as: **2–027**

- a person who has a permission under Pt IV of the Act ("a Part IV permission") to carry on one or more regulated activities;
- an EEA firm qualifying for authorisation under Sch.3;
- a Treaty firm qualifying for authorisation under Sch.4;
- a person who is otherwise authorised by a provision of or made under the Act.

EEA and Treaty firms are both persons who do not have their head office in the United Kingdom. The primary means by which an individual or body based in the United Kingdom will become authorised is therefore by obtaining a Pt IV permission. It follows that the grant or refusal of Pt IV permission is a very significant element in the system of regulation, and it will be considered separately below. As that decision is heavily dependent on the questions who will conduct the business and how they will do so, the discussion ranges well beyond Pt IV itself.

2–028 It should be noted that in addition to its power to grant or refuse permission, the FSA has power to vary permission, either on the application of the body concerned or on its own initiative, and to cancel permission in certain cases. These powers give the FSA forceful arguments with which to encourage authorised persons who are found, in the course of supervision or otherwise, to be conducting their affairs in a way which does not commend itself to the FSA to return to more satisfactory ways of carrying on business. They will therefore be considered in Ch.15, dealing with enforcement and sanctions.

Exempt Person

2–029 Again, delegated legislation is very important in defining "exempt person". S.38 of FSMA 2000 simply enables the Treasury by order to provide for specified persons or specified classes of persons to be exempt from the general prohibition. That power has been exercised primarily in the Financial Services and Markets Act 2000 (Exemption) Order 2001 (SI 2001/1201), although that Order was then amended in minor respects by the Financial Services and Markets Act 2000 (Exemption) (Amendment) Order 2001 (SI 2001/3623). Under the Order some bodies are exempt in respect of any regulated activity other than insurance business (for example, the Bank of England, the central banks of other EEA States and certain development banks); some are exempt in respect of accepting deposits (for example, certified school banks, local authorities, industrial and provident societies to the extent of deposits in the form of withdrawable share capital and credit unions); some are exempt in respect of a wider range of regulated activities (for example, the Tourist Boards for the constituent parts of the United Kingdom) and some are exempt as respects other particular regulated activities (for example, bodies engaged in certain enterprise schemes). The list is detailed and the Order should be consulted for further particulars.

2–030 In addition, there are certain exemptions in the Act itself. S.39(1) exempts an appointed representative of an authorised person, "appointed representative" meaning a person who:

(a) is a party to a contract with an authorised person (called "the principal") which permits or requires the representative to carry on business of a prescribed description and complies with prescribed requirements; and

(b) is someone for whose activities the principal has accepted responsibility in writing.

The exemption is in relation to any regulated activity comprised in the carrying on of the business for which the principal has accepted responsibility. Where the exemption applies, regulatory control is thus exercised through the control of the principal. A similar exemption was available under the Financial Services Act 1986 and was introduced primarily to cover the large number of self-employed sales persons who traditionally sold life policies, pensions and unit trusts. The relevant statutory instrument is the Financial Services and Markets Act 2000 (Appointed Representatives) Regulations 2001 (SI 2001/1217). Consistently with the underlying rationale for this exemption, the types of business prescribed by the Regulations are: arranging deals in investments, safeguarding and administering investments, advising on investments and agreeing to carry on any of those activities. The Regulations require that the contract should either prohibit the appointed representative from acting for other potential principals or should give the principal power to prohibit him from doing so or to restrict the potential other principals or the types of investment in relation to which other principals may be represented.

The other exemptions in FSMA 2000 itself apply to recognised invest- **2–031**
ment exchanges and recognised clearing houses and are contained in s.285. In each case, "recognised" means that a recognition order is in force in relation to the particular investment exchange or clearing house. The exemption for investment exchanges covers regulated activities carried on as part of the exchange's business as an investment exchange or for the purposes of, or in connection with, the provision of clearing services by the exchange. The exemption for clearing houses covers regulated activities carried on for the purposes of, or in connection with, the provision of clearing services by the clearing house. The recognition regime is considered further in Ch.5.

Elements of Regulation: Structure of FSMA 2000

It will be appreciated from the foregoing that, as already noted, the vast **2–032**
bulk of the work of investor protection in the United Kingdom is now carried out by the FSA through the authorisation and permission regime and its ramifications. That is the concern of much of the Act, building on the groundwork laid by the initial provisions establishing the regulator (Pt I), setting out the general position with regard to regulated activities (Pt II) and relating to authorisation and exemption (Pt III). In addition to the provisions in Pt IV dealing directly with the grant, variation and cancellation of permission, FSMA 2000 contains a mixture of substantive and administrative provisions covering the following areas:

- control of the individuals or other persons engaged in regulated activities at a senior level, including those who control authorised persons, and of the manner in which they carry out regulated activities: see Pt V (performance of regulated activities), Pt XII (control over authorised persons), Pt XIV (disciplinary measures) and Pt XXVII (offences);
- fair dealing: see Pt VIII (market abuse) and Pt XXV (injunctions and restitution);
- establishing the framework within which authorised persons are to operate: see Pt X (rules and guidance);
- financial failure by an authorised person: see Pt XV (the Financial Services Compensation Scheme) and Pt XXIV (insolvency);

- persons not based in the United Kingdom: see Pt XIII (incoming firms: intervention by FSA);

- procedural and administrative matters: see Pt IX (hearings and appeals), Pt XI (information gathering and investigations), Pt XXI (mutual societies) Pt XXII (auditors and actuaries), Pt XXIII (public record, disclosure of information and co-operation, Pt XXVI (notices) and Pt XXVIII (miscellaneous).

2–033 There are also to be noted areas within the scope of FSMA 2000 in which the FSA's role is slightly different. Reference has been made in para.2–031 to the exemption from the requirement of authorisation given to recognised investment exchanges and recognised clearing houses. It does not follow that the FSA is not concerned with the affairs of such bodies. In fact, Pt XVIII gives the FSA extensive powers in relation to recognition. Similarly, Pt XX provides that the general prohibition in s.19 does not apply to the carrying on of a regulated activity by a person subject to the supervision of a recognised professional body, if certain requirements are satisfied, but nevertheless in effect requires the FSA to keep under review the way in which recognised professional bodies are operating in relation to financial services and gives the FSA certain powers of intervention.

The FSA also has rather different responsibilities under Pt VI (official listing), by which it is made the competent authority in relation to the official list of securities, Pt XVII (collective investment schemes), by which it is given various responsibilities in relation to various types of collective investment schemes, and Pt XIX (Lloyd's), by which it again has a supervisory role in relation to Lloyd's, together with powers of intervention.

Many of the provisions mentioned in the preceding paragraph extend to aspects of the work done in these contexts also.

2–034 Finally, the work of three other bodies which relate closely to the FSA should be mentioned. First, FSMA 2000 makes provision in Pt XVI for a single ombudsman scheme in relation to financial services. Although the FSA has the task of establishing the scheme operator which administers the scheme and of making some of the rules relating to the scheme, the Financial Ombudsman Service, as the scheme is known, operates independently of the FSA. Nevertheless, codes and guidance from the FSA are highly material to the determinations which the Financial Ombudsman Service is required to make. Secondly, the Office of Fair Trading, in the person of the Director-General of Fair Trading, features with particular regard to competition scrutiny and Consumer Credit Act business. Both the Office of Fair Trading and the FSA have a concern with fair treatment of customers by providers of financial services and close liaison is required in certain areas: for example, in relation to the impact of the Unfair Terms in Consumer Contracts Regulations 1999 (SI 1999/2083) on mortgage conditions and on terms in unsecured consumer credit loans. Thirdly, the presence of the Treasury, which has many rule-making powers, is pervasive throughout the Act.

The *FSA Handbook*

Legislative Background, Structure and Status

As mentioned in para.2–032, Pt X of FSMA 2000 is particularly concerned with rules and guidance from the FSA. That Part contains a general rule-making power in s.138, a procedural code involving consultation and notification to the Treasury in ss.152 to 156 and a power under s.157 to give guidance consisting of information and advice on matters there specified. It also contains important provisions as to the effect of contravention of FSA rules: **2–035**

- a rule may be expressed to be an evidential provision only, in which case it must also provide that contravention may be relied on as tending to prove a contravention of another specified rule or that compliance may be relied on as tending to establish compliance with another specified rule (s.149);
- subject to the previous point, a contravention of a rule is actionable in effect as a breach of statutory duty, unless otherwise expressly so provided (s.150);
- a person is not guilty of an offence by reason of a contravention of a rule, and the contravention does not make any transaction void or unenforceable (s.151).

Further rule-making powers for the FSA may be found throughout the Act.

This is the basis on which the FSA has built the *FSA Handbook*, which **2–036**
is a very substantial work. It is available on the Internet, CD-ROM and on paper and has been produced after a substantial consultation period. It is likely to undergo fairly frequent updating, particularly while it is still relatively early days for the new regime. In particular, the prudential regime is still only in interim form at the time of writing, and so consists of five interim prudential sourcebooks rather than the single integrated sourcebook which the FSA intends eventually to achieve. The FSA describes the *Handbook* as consisting of material of two different kinds: sourcebooks, which provide sources of the FSA's requirements and guidance, and manuals, which contain processes to be followed. Each sourcebook or manual is identifiable by a reference code of two or more letters. The FSA also produces a reader's guide to help the reader to grapple with the *Handbook*.

The sourcebooks and manuals are, as appropriate, divided into chapters and subdivided into sections and then paragraphs. The start of a sourcebook, manual, chapter or section consists of an application provision which indicates to whom the following material applies. A chapter, and sometimes a section, will then contain a statement of the purpose of the provisions within that chapter or section, and a chapter may be accompanied by an annex setting out supplementary material. Where there is supplementary material affecting the whole of a sourcebook or manual, or more than one chapter, it takes the form of an appendix.

The use of schedules in relation to sourcebooks or manuals has also been standardised. A schedule of transitional provisions appears after the Contents page and after the text there appear the following schedules: 1 (record-keeping requirements), 2 (notification requirements), 3 (fees and other required payments), 4 (statutory powers exercised by the FSA in making the *Handbook*), 5 (rights of action for damages: see s.150) and 6 (rules that can be waived).

The *Handbook* includes a glossary of definitions, which is extremely extensive, and an index, which is not to be regarded as comprehensive. Defined terms appear in italics throughout the *Handbook* It may be helpful to note that the word "firm" is used to denote any authorised person; the expression is not limited to partnerships, as is usually the case in English law. Electronic links are available in addition to the index.

2–037 The status of different provisions in the text of the *FSA Handbook* varies, as may be inferred from the reference above to rules and guidance and to evidential provisions. The status of any particular provision is indicated by the presence of an icon beside it containing one of the letters R, G, E, D, P, or C, the first three letters mentioned being those of most general application. Their meaning is as follows:

- R: general rules made under s.138 and specialised rules made under ss.140 to 147 and other powers. The legal effect depends on the power under which the rule is made and the language in which it is expressed, but most of the rules create obligations binding on authorised persons
- G: normally, guidance given under s.157. Guidance is not binding and does not have an evidential effect. It is generally designed to throw light on a particular aspect of regulatory requirements and is not intended to be an exhaustive statement of obligations. If, however, a person acts in accordance with general guidance in the circumstances contemplated by that guidance, the FSA will proceed on the footing that the person has complied with the aspects of the rule or other requirement to which the guidance relates. Rights conferred on third parties cannot be affected by guidance, and guidance does not bind the courts. The letter G may also identify statements of policy by the FSA
- E: evidential provisions falling within s.149. E is also used for the paragraphs in the Code of Practice for Approved Persons, which may be relied on as tending to establish whether or not the conduct of an approved person complies with the Statements of Principle for approved persons, and for certain paragraphs in the Code of Market Conduct, which specify descriptions of behaviour which in the opinion of the FSA amount to market abuse and factors which in the opinion of the FSA are to be taken into account in determining whether or not behaviour amounts to market abuse
- D: directions and requirements given under various powers conferred by the Act, such as directions about the form and content of applications for Pt IV permission. Directions and requirements are binding upon those to whom they are addressed

- P: Statements of Principle for approved persons made under s.64 of the Act. The Statements of Principle are binding on approved persons. Other material (for example, the threshold conditions for the grant of Pt IV permission) also carries the P icon.
- C: conclusive descriptions of behaviour which, by virtue of s.122, is not to be taken as amounting to market abuse.

Contents

The contents of the *FSA Handbook*, with the code references for the sourcebooks and manuals, are as follows: **2–038**

Block 1—High Level Standards

Principles for Businesses (PRIN)
Senior Management Arrangements, Systems and Controls (SYSC)
Threshold Conditions (COND)
Statements of Principle and Code of Practice for Approved Persons (APER)
The Fit and Proper test for Approved Persons (FIT)
General provisions (GEN)

Block 2—Business Standards

Interim Prudential sourcebooks (IPRU)
  for banks (IPRU(BANK))
  for building societies (IPRU(BSOC))
  for friendly societies (IPRU(FSOC))
  for insurers (IPRU(INS))
  for investment businesses (IPRU(INV))
Conduct of Business (COB)
Market conduct (MAR):
  Code of market conduct
  Price stabilising rules
  Inter-professional conduct
  Endorsement of the Takeover Code
  Alternative Trading Systems
Training and Competence (TC)
Money Laundering (ML)

Block 3—Regulatory Processes

Authorisation (AUTH)
Supervision (SUP)
Enforcement (ENF)
Decision making (DEC)

Block 4—Redress

Dispute resolution: complaints (DISP)

Compensation (COMP)
Complaints against the FSA (COAF)

Block 5—Specialist Sourcebooks

Collective Investment Schemes (CIS)
Credit Unions (CRED)
Electronic Commerce Directive (ECO)
Electronic money (ELM)
Lloyd's (LLD)
Mortgages (later) (MORT)
Professional firms (PROF)
Recognised Investment Exchanges and Recognised Clearing Houses (REC)
United Kingdom Listing Authority (later) (UKLA)

Block 6—Special Guides

Energy Market Participants (EMPS)
Small Friendly Societies (FREN)
Oil Market Participants (OMPS)
Service companies (SERV)

2–039 In the remainder of this Chapter we consider further the FSA's Principles for Businesses, the authorisation and permission regime, the approved persons regime and certain other provisions of the *Handbook* dealing with high level standards and business standards which have considerable impact in relation to authorisation and approval. Matters relating to the interim prudential sourcebooks and the specialist sourcebooks will in general be considered in subsequent Chapters of this Part. Market manipulation and market abuse, an area of FSMA 2000 which attracted considerable comment before the Act reached the statute book, forms the subject matter of Part 3, while enforcement (including supervision), compensation and the Financial Ombudsman Service are covered in Part 4. Finally as respects FSMA 2000, money laundering receives separate treatment in Part 5.

Principles for Businesses

2–040 We begin with the FSA's Principles for Businesses because the Principles are a general statement of the fundamental obligations of firms under the regulatory system and they apply in whole or in part to every firm, albeit with some modification for incoming EEA firms, incoming Treaty firms and UCITS (undertakings for collective investment in transferable securities) qualifiers: see the *Handbook* at PRIN 1.1.1 and 1.1.2. The three categories of firm in relation to which the Principles are modified are discussed further at paras 2.066 and following of this Chapter and at this stage it need be noted only that in each case the firm has rights under

European legislation. As respects United Kingdom firms, with which we are primarily concerned, the Principles are of general application, and those interested in the particular modifications should consult the *Handbook* at PRIN 3.1.1. The FSA regards being ready, willing and organised to comply with the Principles as a critical factor in applications for Pt IV permission: PRIN 1.1.4. They therefore set the scene for the regulatory work of the FSA.

The Principles themselves are to be found at PRIN 2 and are as follows: **2–041**

(1) A firm must conduct its business with integrity.

(2) A firm must conduct its business with due skill, care and diligence.

(3) A firm must take reasonable care to organise and control its affairs responsibly and effectively, with adequate risk management systems.

(4) A firm must maintain adequate financial resources.

(5) A firm must observe proper standards of business conduct.

(6) A firm must pay due regard to the interests of its customers and treat them fairly.

(7) A firm must pay due regard to the information needs of its clients, and communicate information to them in a way which is clear, fair and not misleading.

(8) A firm must manage conflicts of interest fairly, both between itself and its customers and between a customer and another client.

(9) A firm must take reasonable care to ensure the suitability of its advice and discretionary decisions for any customer who is entitled to rely upon its judgment.

(10) A firm must arrange adequate protection for clients' assets when it is responsible for them.

(11) A firm must deal with its regulators in an open and cooperative way, and must disclose to the FSA appropriately anything relating to the firm of which the FSA would reasonably expect notice.

In considering the Principles, it may be helpful to bear in mind that the expressions "client" and "customer" do not bear the same meaning. "Client" includes "customer", but it also includes market counterparties (an expression which has a lengthy and complex definition but broadly refers to governments, central banks, other national monetary authorities and those engaged in aspects of the financial services industry when acting in that capacity). Clearly the application of the Principles to clients who are customers and clients who are market counterparties is likely to impose different requirements.

It is evident that the Principles, as one would expect, are at a high level **2–042**
of generality, and much of the *Handbook* is concerned with the detail of what compliance with their spirit involves. Further guidance as to their relevance can be found in PRIN generally, but we draw attention to a

number of features. First, although the Principles apply with respect to regulated activities generally, in applying the Principles with respect to the activities of accepting deposits, issuing electronic money, general insurance business and long-term insurance business involving pure protection contracts or reinsurance contracts, the FSA will proceed only in a prudential context. That is, the FSA would not expect to exercise the powers brought into play by a contravention of a Principle unless the contravention amounted to a serious or persistent violation with implications for confidence in the financial system (PRIN 1.1.3).

Secondly, Principles 3, 4, and 11 take into account the activities of the other members of a firm's group. Inadequacy of risk management systems or resources on the part of another member of the group will not necessarily involve a firm in contravention of one of the Principles, but the potential impact of the member's inadequacy will be considered (PRIN 1.1.5). Principle 3 is further amplified in SYSC, which considers the proper apportionment of responsibilities within a firm and identifies the main areas to be considered in looking at a firm's systems and controls.

Thirdly, the Principles are relevant to the FSA's powers of information-gathering and of investigation and intervention, as well as to its powers in relation to Part IV permission, and provide a basis on which the FSA may apply to a court for an injunction or restitution order or require a firm to make restitution (PRIN 1.1.8). These matters are considered further in Ch.15. The Principles do not, however, give rise to an action for damages by a private person.

2–043 The territorial application of the Principles should also be observed. Principles 1, 2 and 3, in a prudential context, apply with respect to activities wherever they are carried on. Principles 4 and 11 apply generally with respect to activities wherever they are carried on. Principle 5 applies with respect to activities wherever they are carried on if the activities have, or might reasonably be regarded as likely to have, a negative effect on confidence in the financial system operating in the United Kingdom. Otherwise, the Principles apply to activities carried on from an establishment in the United Kingdom, unless, as respects principles 1 to 3 and 6 to 10, the activity is affected by another applicable rule which has a wider territorial scope, in which case the wider scope applies.

Authorisation and Permission

Threshold conditions

2–044 Against that background, then, we turn to consider questions of authorisation and permission. (The interrelation of these two matters has already been discussed in para.2–027.) Under s.40 of FSMA 2000, an application for a Part IV permission may be made by an individual, a body corporate, a partnership or an unincorporated association, except that:

- a person with an existing Pt IV permission cannot make such an application, but must instead apply under s.44 to vary the existing permission

- an EEA firm may not make an application for permission to carry on a regulated activity which it is, or would be, entitled to carry on in exercise of an EEA right.

The former prohibition avoids the confusions which might arise if a particular firm (to use the FSA's expression) had multiple permissions, while the latter ensures that all EEA firms with relevant EEA rights are subject to the EEA regime in respect of their regulated activities where that regime is applicable. (The European dimension is discussed in paras 2–059 and following.) Once the application is made, the FSA's first task, under s.41, is to consider whether the threshold conditions set out in Sch.6 to FSMA 2000 and introduced by that section are satisfied.

Legal Status

Under the first threshold criterion, applications for permission to carry on certain regulated activities may be made only by persons of certain legal status. If the activity concerned is the effecting or carrying out of contracts of insurance, the authorised person must be a body corporate, a registered friendly society or a member of Lloyd's. If the person concerned appears to the FSA to be seeking to carry on or to be carrying on a regulated activity constituting accepting deposits or issuing electronic money, it must be either a body corporate or a partnership. These restrictions are derived from provisions of European legislation now contained in Art.8 of the First Non-life and the First Life Insurance Directives (respectively Dir.73/239 [1973] O.J. L228/3, and Dir.79/267 [1979] O.J. L63/1) and Art.1 of the Banking Consolidation Directive (Dir.2000/12 [2000] O.J. L126/1). The reference to electronic money was introduced by amendment effected by the Financial Services and Markets Act 2000 (Regulated Activities) (Amendment) Order 2002 (SI 2002/682). **2–045**

Location of Offices

The second criterion requires that if the applicant is a body corporate constituted under the law of any part of the United Kingdom its head office and, if it has a registered office, its registered office must be in the United Kingdom. If the applicant has its head office in the United Kingdom but is not a body corporate, it must carry on business in the United Kingdom. Again the criterion has a European background; it is derived from Art.6 of the Prudential Supervision ("post-BCCI") Directive (Dir.95/26 [1995] O.J. L126/1), although under FSMA 2000 it is applied generally and not only to the extent that the Directive would require. **2–046**

Neither the Directive nor the Act defines "head office". The FSA indicates in the *Handbook* (COND 2.2.3) that the key issue is the location of the central management and control of the applicant.

Close Links

The post-BCCI Directive also forms the basis for the third criterion, although again the criterion ranges more widely than the Directive requires. That criterion requires that if the applicant has close links with **2–047** another person, the FSA must be satisfied that those close links are not likely to prevent the effective supervision of the applicant and, if it appears to the FSA that the person with whom the applicant is so linked is subject to the laws, regulations or administrative provisions (defined as "the foreign provisions") of a territory which is not an EEA state, that neither the foreign provisions, nor any deficiency in their enforcement, would prevent the FSA's effective supervision of the applicant. The words "close links" have a detailed definition covering parent and subsidiary relationships and relationships where one person controls 20 per cent or more of the voting rights of another. The existence of parent and subsidiary relationships is to be determined by reference to the Seventh Company Law Directive (Dir.83/349), which has the effect that the questions whether a person has the right to appoint or remove a majority of the board of directors or a right to exercise a dominant influence, or actually exercises such an influence, must be considered.

In considering whether it is satisfied as the criterion requires, the FSA will look at whether it is likely to receive sufficient information for effective supervision, whether the structure and geographic spread of the applicant may present difficulties in the flow of information, whether consolidated supervision of group activities is possible and whether it is possible to form a fair view of the consolidated financial position (see the *Handbook* at COND 2.3.3). The *Handbook* makes clear that the FSA's consideration of relevant matters will not be limited to matters occurring in the United Kingdom.

Adequate Resources

2–048 The statutory criterion itself is fairly short and straightforward. It requires that in the opinion of the FSA the resources of the applicant should be adequate in relation to the regulated activities he seeks to carry on or carries on in fact. Sch.6 goes on to provide that in reaching that opinion the FSA may take into account the fact that the person is a member of a group and any effect which that may have, and may have regard to the provision which he makes, and any group members make, for liabilities (including contingent and future liabilities) and the means by which he manages, and any group members manage, the incidence of risk in connection with his business.

2–049 Not surprisingly, the FSA gives some fairly detailed guidance about the approach which it will take to this criterion. It interprets the word "adequate" to mean sufficient in terms of quantity, quality and availability, and "resources" to include all financial resources, non-financial resources and means of managing the applicant's resources (see the *Handbook* at COND 2.4.2). This means that an applicant's senior management arrangements, systems and controls will come under scrutiny, as well as its ability to satisfy the detailed financial resources and systems requirements set out in the relevant Interim Prudential sourcebook. The latter requirements are considered in the context of the particular type of applicant later in this Part; certain of the *Handbook* provisions relating to senior management arrangements, systems and controls are considered in the course of this

Chapter. The FSA will also look at the persons connected with the applicant, in accordance with the statutory requirement to that effect in s.49.

The FSA further states by way of guidance that it will have regard to whether there are any indications that the applicant may have difficulties if the application is granted, at the time of the grant or in the future, in complying with any of the FSA's prudential rules; whether there are indications that the applicant may not be able to meet its debts as they fall due; whether there is anything in the history of the applicant which points to financial difficulties; whether it has taken reasonable steps to identify and measure any risks of regulatory concern that it may encounter in conducting its business and has installed appropriate systems and controls and appointed appropriate human resources to measure them prudently at all times; whether it has sufficiently investigated the financial resources required for the field of activity in which it intends to engage; and whether it has taken adequate steps to satisfy itself and, if necessary, the FSA that it has a well-constructed business plan which has been sufficiently tested and that its financial and other resources are commensurate with the likely risks it will face (see the *Handbook* at COND 2.4.4). Again, the FSA does not limit its consideration to matters arising in the United Kingdom. **2–050**

Suitability

The final criterion is that the applicant must satisfy the FSA that it is a fit and proper person having regard to all the circumstances, including its connection with any person, the nature of any regulated activity that it seeks to carry on and the need to ensure that its affairs are conducted soundly and prudently. The "main dimensions" of this standard are set out in the Principles for Businesses considered earlier in this Chapter (see the *Handbook* at PRIN 1.1.4). The condition is concerned with the applicant itself rather than the individuals by whom the applicant's operations are to be conducted. Their suitability is assessed separately under the approved persons regime considered in para.2–073 and following of this Chapter. Serious doubt as to the suitability of individuals, either as individuals or collectively, may, however, be relevant to the FSA's consideration of whether the applicant itself is suitable. **2–051**

The *Handbook* (COND 2.5.4) identifies three broad headings to be looked at in relation to this criterion:

- whether the applicant conducts, or will conduct, its business with integrity and in compliance with proper standards;
- whether it has, or will have, a competent and prudent management;
- whether it can demonstrate that it conducts, or will conduct, its affairs with the exercise of due skill and diligence.

The *Handbook* goes on to consider in more detail aspects of those headings, making clear that the FSA will be concerned, among other matters, with the extent to which the applicant has been open and co-operative with the regulator, the people with whom the applicant is connected, its past history in relation to regulation, the range of skills and experience among those controlling its affairs, its internal controls and information and reporting procedures. In relation to this criterion also, the FSA does not limit its consideration to matters arising in the United Kingdom.

2–052 It will be evident that concern for the protection of investors has a substantial part to play in the way in which the FSA approaches the criteria. Investors are to be protected not only through the emphasis on both adequate planning and financial resources and competent and honest management but also through the requirements directed to ensuring that the applicant is amenable to effective regulation by the FSA. Some further comments on the criteria may be found in AUTH 3.8 of the *Handbook*.

Scope of Permission

2–053 While clearly an applicant who does not satisfy the threshold conditions will not obtain a Pt IV permission, there is no express provision that an applicant who does will obtain such a permission. This may appear to be implied, but it should be noted that:

- the FSA may grant permission to carry on some, but not all, of the regulated activities to which the application relates (s.42(2) of FSMA 2000)
- the FSA must not only specify the permitted regulated activity or activities, but also describe it or them in the manner the FSA thinks appropriate (s.42(6) of the Act).

This latter requirement enables the FSA to incorporate limitations on the scope of the permission as well as to give permission ranging more widely or narrowly than that sought in the application. A permission will also identify the specified investments involved in the regulated activity. Generally speaking, the FSA has adopted the descriptions in the Regulated Activities Order (see para.2–024) both for the regulated activity itself and for the investments involved in that activity.

Examples of possible limitations (which may be applied for by the applicant as well as imposed by the FSA) are limitations as to: the type or number of clients in respect of whom the regulated activity is carried on; the type of specified investments in relation to which the regulated activity is carried on; and the type of specified insurance business in relation to which the regulated activity is carried on (see the *Handbook* at AUTH 3.6.3).

2–054 Under s.43 of FSMA 2000, the FSA may also include "requirements" when framing a permission. A requirement:

- may, in particular, be imposed so as to require the applicant to take or to refrain from taking specified action;
- may extend to activities which are not regulated activities;

- may be imposed by reference to the applicant's relationship with its group or other members of its group.

A requirement will expire at the end of such period as the FSA may specify.

The difference between a limitation and a requirement is explained by the FSA in the *Handbook* at AUTH 3.7.2 as being that a limitation will be specific to a particular regulated activity but a requirement may be unrelated to a regulated activity or related to a range of regulated activities. Suggested requirements include submission to periodic independent compliance reviews, or submission of financial returns more frequently than normal, in the early days of the applicant's business (AUTH 3.7.6). Again, the applicant can apply for an appropriate requirement to be included.

S.48 of FSMA 2000 makes specific provision for a particular class of **2–055**
requirements, known as assets requirements. Such a requirement is one by which an authorised person is prohibited from disposing or otherwise dealing with assets in the United Kingdom or elsewhere, or restricting such disposals or dealings, or by which an authorised person is required to transfer to a trustee approved by the FSA all or any of that person's assets, or all or any assets belonging to customers but held by that person or to his order. The section contains provisions designed to ensure that third parties cannot be required by a person subject to an assets requirement to act in such a way as to put the effectiveness of the requirement at risk.

Connected Persons

FSMA 2000 imposes on the FSA a specific requirement, in considering an **2–056**
application for permission, to have regard to any person "appearing to it to be, or likely to be, in a relationship with the applicant or person given permission which is relevant": see s.49. Guidance on this section appears in the *Handbook* at AUTH 3.9.22. Persons falling within this category include the directors of an applicant, a controller of the applicant and any other person who may exert influence on the applicant which might pose a risk to the applicant's satisfying or continuing to satisfy the threshold conditions. This formulation indicates what sort of relationship is "relevant" for the purposes of the section. "Controller" has a complex definition in s.422 of the Act which reflects the requirements of Art.1 of the Banking Consolidation Directive in respect of a qualifying holding. It includes a holding which represents 10 per cent or more of the shares in a body corporate or its parent, or which entitles the holder to exercise or control the exercise of 10 per cent or more of the voting power at any general meeting of the body or its parent, or which enables the holder to exercise a significant influence over the management of the body or its parent. In considering whether those requirements are satisfied, the holder of the shares is to be treated as one person with his associates, who are defined to include spouses and children, the trustees of certain settlements, certain companies (and in relation to companies, directors and some other companies or undertakings) partners and employees, and persons with

whom certain types of agreement or arrangement exist relating to the shares of the relative voting power.

Public Information

2–057 The FSA is required by s.347 of FSMA 2000 to keep a public record of, among other matters, every person who appears to the FSA to be an authorised person and of every approved person. The record as presently kept shows the limitations on an authorised person's permission, but does not show any requirements which the FSA may have imposed.

Procedure

2–058 The procedure for making an application for Pt IV permission is sketched out in ss.51 and 52 of the FSMA 2000 and is covered in detail in the Authorisation Manual which forms part of the *Handbook*. The Manual explains what material must be included in an application and the time limits within which the FSA must reach a decision. Applicants are in fact encouraged to have a pre-application meeting with the FSA (see AUTH 3.9.1 and 3.9.2), which should benefit both parties by helping to ensure that applications are properly prepared and presented.

If the application for permission is granted as made, the FSA is simply required to give notice to the applicant accordingly, stating the date from which the permission is to run. If the FSA proposes to impose a narrowing limitation or a requirement or to refuse the application, it must give the applicant a warning notice. Such a notice is governed by a detailed code under s.387 of the Act, which essentially gives the applicant a reasonable period within which to make representations on the basis of access to the relevant material. After the representation period, the FSA must decide, within a further reasonable period, whether to proceed to issue a decision notice or a notice that it is discontinuing the course of action it was undertaking. Decision notices are the subject of s.388 of the Act and notices of discontinuance appear in s.389. A decision notice must inform the person concerned of his right to have the matter referred to the Financial Services and Markets Tribunal, which is considered in further detail in Ch.15.

The European Dimension

2–059 As mentioned in para.2–005 above, it has been the policy of what is now the European Union, in association with the EFTA states which are not members of the EU but form part of the EEA (currently Iceland, Liechtenstein and Norway), to seek to harmonise financial services regulation through a number of European Directives. The Directives in question are identified collectively in Sch.3 to the FSMA 2000 (as amended by the Banking Consolidation Directive (Consequential Amendments) Regulations 2000 (SI 2000/2952)) as "the single market directives" and consist of the Banking Consolidation Directive (Dir.2000/12 [2000] O.J. L126/1), the First, Second and Third Non-life Insurance Directives (Dirs 73/239 [1973] O.J. L228/3, 88/357 [1988] O.J. L172/1 and 92/49 [1992] O.J. L228/1), the First, Second and Third Life Insurance Directives (Dirs 79/267 [1979] O.J. L63/1, 90/619 [1990] O.J. L330/50 and 92/96 [1992] O.J. L360/1) and the Investment Services Directive (Dir.93/22 [1993] O.J. L141/27). The effect of the single market directives is to establish a regime, made effective in the United Kingdom by Sch.3, under which a body with a head office in any of the EEA states and accordingly regulated by the relevant regulator of that state in respect of activities falling within one or other of the single market directives has what is known as a "passport" to carry on those activities in the other EEA states.

Pt I of Sch.3 consists of definitions relevant in relation to passport rights. **2–060**
As well as defining "the single market directives" and identifying EEA states, it covers the following:

- "EEA firm": a body which does not have its head office in the United Kingdom and which is an investment firm (as defined by Art.1 of the Investment Services Directive) authorised by its home state regulator, a credit institution (as defined by Art.1 of the Banking Consolidation Directive) authorised by its home state regulator, a financial institution (also as defined by Art.1 of the Banking Consolidation Directive) which fulfils certain conditions or an undertaking pursing the activity of direct insurance (within Art.1 of the First Life Insurance Directive or the First Non-life Insurance Directive) authorised by its home state regulator;

- "EEA authorisation": authorisation granted to an EEA firm by its home state regulator for the purpose of the relevant single market directive;

- "EEA right": the entitlement of a person to establish a branch, or to provide services, in an EEA state other than that in which he has his head office in accordance with the Treaty establishing the European Community (defined by FSMA 2000, s.417, as "the Treaty") and subject to the conditions of the relevant single market directive;

- "home state regulator" means the competent authority (within the meaning of the relevant directive) of an EEA state other than the United Kingdom in relation to the EEA firm concerned;

- "UK firm": a person whose head office is in the United Kingdom and who has an EEA right to carry on activity in an EEA state other than the United Kingdom;

- "host state regulator": the competent authority of an EEA state other than the United Kingdom in relation to a UK firm's exercise of EEA rights there.

2–061 As those definitions suggest, the single market directives are crucial to establishing the nature of EEA rights. It is the directives which specify which activities may be carried on in exercise of passport rights and the machinery for the exercise of those rights, although it is Sch.3 which makes the machinery effective in domestic law. The effect from the point of view of EEA and UK firms is that they need obtain authorisation once only rather than in every EEA state in which they wish to carry on activities. The position of the investor is protected by the requirements imposed by the various directives as to conditions which must be satisfied before the regulator may grant authorisation.

It should nevertheless be noted that Sch.3 does not give a UK firm power to do things it could not otherwise do, nor do the Schedule and Directives dispense with the need for compliance with any separate regulatory regime in the UK.

2–062 The Treaty itself distinguishes between carrying on activities through the establishment of a branch and carrying on activities through the provision of services without a branch. The procedural requirements differ in the two cases. As respects UK firms, the requirements are contained in Pt III of Sch.3; as respects EEA firms, the requirements are contained in Pt II.

UK Firms Carrying on Activities in other EEA States

2–063 A UK firm wishing to establish a branch must first give notice to the FSA of its intention to do so. The FSA is then required to give notice to the proposed host state regulator unless:

- where the EEA right is derived from the Banking Consolidation Directive or the Investment Services Directive, it has reason to doubt the adequacy of the firm's resources or its administrative structure;
- where the EEA right is derived from an insurance directive, it has reason to doubt the adequacy of the firm's resources or its administrative structure or to question the reputation, qualifications or experience of the directors or managers of the firm or the person proposed as the branch's authorised agent.

The host state regulator then has two months in which to give the firm in question, or the FSA if the EEA right derives from one of the insurance directives, notice of the host state rules with which the firm will be required to comply, and the right then becomes exercisable. Where notice is given to the FSA, the FSA must inform the firm of the relevant host state rules. If the host state regulator does not give notice within the two month period, the firm may proceed to exercise its EEA right.

Sch.3 provides for further specification as respects notices of the first two kinds and the relevant details are to be found in the *Handbook* at SUP 13, as are further provisions relating to the exercise of EEA rights by UK firms. The Schedule also provides a warning and decision notice procedure if the FSA is minded not to give notice to the host state regulator, with a provision for appeal to the Financial Services and Markets Tribunal.

The procedure where the UK firm proposes only to provide services is much shorter and simpler. Before the firm may exercise its EEA right, it must give the FSA notice of its intention to provide services. If the EEA right derives from the Investment Services Directive or the Banking Consolidation Directive the FSA must, within a month, send a copy of the notice to the host state regulator and give notice to the firm that it has done so. Since the FSA cannot refuse to send a notice to the host state regulator in such cases, there is no need for a warning and decision notice procedure or for a right of reference to the Tribunal. Following an amendment made to Sch.3 by the Financial Services (EEA Passport Rights) Regulations 2001 (SI 2001/1376), if the right derives from an insurance directive, the FSA must, within a month, either give notice to the host state regulator or give notice to the firm of its refusal to give notice to the host state regulator and of the reasons for that refusal. In such a case there is a right of reference to the Tribunal. A firm may not exercise an EEA right under any of the insurance directives until it has received notice that the FSA has sent a notice to the host state regulator. In other cases, there is no such delay. Again, further details are to be found in the *Handbook* at SUP 13. **2–064**

Sch.3 also contains some provisions for continuing regulation of UK firms. First, where the details given on the establishment of a branch are to be changed, prior notice must again be given to the FSA, with consequences similar to those applying on initial notification, except that the host state regulator has only one month in which to give its notice: see the Financial Services and Markets Act 2000 (EEA Passport Rights) Regulations 2001 (SI 2001/2511), setting out the detailed requirements. The FSA, however, may refuse consent only on prescribed grounds, and there is a right to refer any refusal to the Financial Services and Markets Tribunal. Secondly, if a UK firm with a Pt IV permission is exercising an EEA right to carry on any Consumer Credit Act business in an EEA state other than the United Kingdom, and if the Director of Fair Trading informs the FSA that the firm or certain other persons have done one of a number of things specified in s.25 of the Consumer Credit Act 1974 as relevant to the question whether the firm is a fit person to hold a standard licence for Consumer Credit Act activities, the FSA may exercise the power given to it by s.45 of FSMA 2000 to vary the firm's Pt IV permission. Thirdly, if a UK firm which does not need a Pt IV permission for the relevant activity is exercising a right under the Banking Consolidation Directive, and if the host state regulator so requests, the FSA may impose any requirement in relation to the firm which it could impose if the firm had a Pt IV permission in relation to the business and the FSA was entitled to exercise its power of variation. **2–065**

EEA Firms Carrying on Business in the UK

The provisions in Pt II of Sch.3 mirror those of Pt III from the point of view of the host state regulator. An EEA firm seeking to exercise an EEA right qualifies for authorisation if it satisfies either the establishment or the **2–066** service conditions. The establishment conditions are that the FSA has received a proper notice from the firm's home state regulator and that either the firm has been informed of the rules with which it must comply or two months have elapsed since the FSA received the notice. The Schedule in fact obliges the FSA to prepare for the supervision of the firm, to notify the firm of those rules and if the firm is exercising a right under an insurance directive, to notify the home state regulator of those rules also. This is an automatic process; the FSA could not, consistently with the aim of dealing with matters of authorisation in the home state, exercise any judgment or discretion in relation to an EEA firm. Similarly, the service conditions are that the firm has given its home state regulator notice of its intention to provide services in the UK and, if the EEA rights are being exercised under the Investment Services Directive or one of the insurance directives the FSA has received notice from the home state regulator. Additionally, if the rights are being exercised under one of the insurance directives, the firm must have been informed by the home state regulator that notice has been sent to the FSA. The FSA must prepare for the firm's supervision and notify it of any host state rules with which it will have to comply.

When an EEA firm qualifies for authorisation it has, in respect of each permitted activity which is a regulated activity, permission to carry it on through its United Kingdom branch or by providing services in the United Kingdom (as the case may be). The permission is treated as being on terms equivalent to those appearing from the notice given by the home state regulator or the notice of intention, as the case may require.

As with UK firms, notice must be given of changes in the details notified. The relevant requirements are in the Financial Services and Markets Act 2000 (EEA Passport Rights) Regulations 2001 (SI 2001/2511). Detailed guidance for EEA firms wishing to exercise EEA rights is to be found in the *Handbook* at AUTH 5.

Treaty Rights

2–067 A Treaty firm is defined in Sch.4 to FSMA 2000 as a person whose head office is situated in an EEA state other than the UK and which is recognised under the law of that state as its national. A Treaty firm qualifies for authorisation if it has received authorisation under the law of its home state to carry on the regulated activity in question, the relevant provisions of the law of the home state either afford equivalent protection or satisfy the conditions laid down by a Community instrument for the co-ordination or approximation of laws, regulations or administrative provisions of member states relating to the carrying on of that activity and the firm has no EEA right to carry on that activity in the manner in which it is seeking to carry it on. Provisions afford equivalent protection if, in relation to the carrying on of the permitted activity, they afford consumers protection which is at least equivalent to that afforded by or under FSMA 2000 in relation to that activity (a state of affairs of which a certificate to that effect issued by the Treasury is conclusive evidence). A firm is not to be regarded as having home state authorisation unless its home state regulator has so informed the FSA in writing. A firm which qualifies for authorisation has permission to carry on the permitted activities through its United Kingdom branch or by providing services in the United Kingdom. The permission is treated as being on terms equivalent to those to which the firm's home state authorisation is subject. The only formality required is that the Treaty firm must give written notice of its intention to carry on the regulated activity or activities in question at least seven days before beginning to do so. Again, detailed guidance is to be found in the *Handbook* at AUTH 5.

UCITS Qualifiers

A UCITS is an undertaking for collective investment in transferable **2–068**
securities within the meaning of the UCITS Directive (Dir.85/611). The purpose of the Directive was to enable a UCITS formed in one member state, and complying with the rules of that state as required by the Directive, to be sold freely in any other Member State. "Member State" for this purpose currently means EEA state. A UCITS may be a trust, an investment company or a common fund constituted by contract, but must be open-ended, and the Directive imposes limitations on its investments, both as to percentages of assets and as to type of investment. In pursuance of the United Kingdom's obligations under the Directive, FSMA 2000 contains special provisions as respects UCITS situated within other EEA states. These will be considered later in Ch.6, dealing with collective investment schemes generally. For present purposes it is necessary to note only that a UCITS may become a recognised scheme under s.264 of FSMA 2000 and that by Sch.5 to the Act a person who for the time being is an operator, trustee or depositary of such a scheme is an authorised person. The permission covers any activity, so far as it is a regulated activity and is appropriate to the capacity in which he acts in relation to the scheme, of the kind described in the activity of establishing collective investment schemes as set out in Sch.2 to the Act.

Variation and Cancellation of Permission

As has already been mentioned in para.2–028, FSMA 2000 provides for the **2–069**
variation of a Pt IV permission, either on the application of the authorised person or on the initiative of the FSA, and for its cancellation in some circumstances. In so far as the FSA acts on its own initiative, its powers are clearly part of the regulatory, supervisory and disciplinary weapons available to it, and are discussed in Part 4 of this work, dealing with enforcement of the FSMA 2000 regime. At this point, however, we deal briefly with voluntary variation and cancellation.

The Act gives an authorised person power under s.44 to apply to the **2–070**
FSA to vary the permission by:

- adding a regulated activity to those for which it gives permission;
- removing a regulated activity from those for which it gives permission;

- varying the description of a regulated activity for which it gives permission;
- cancelling or varying a requirement.

The authorised person may instead apply for cancellation of the permission. The FSA may refuse the application if it takes the view that the interests of consumers, or potential consumers, would be adversely affected if the application were granted and that it is desirable in the interests of consumers, or potential consumers, for the application to be refused. When an application is made, it is necessary to look at the implications, if the grant were to be made, for matters such as the firm's ability to continue the activities it wishes to continue, any effect on the firm's activities in other EEA states, the implications for financial and human resources, whether the change would affect the firm's prudential category and whether it would affect the arrangements in place to comply with the approved persons regime: see the *Handbook* at SUP 6.3 for a discussion of matters to be considered. When an application is made, the FSA may include any provision which it could have included if a fresh permission were being given on an application under s.40. If the effect of the variation is that there are no longer any regulated activities for which the authorised person has permission, the FSA must, once it is satisfied that it is no longer necessary to keep the permission in force, cancel it.

2–071 The procedure for making an application under s.44 is very similar to the procedure for making an initial application for permission. If the application is granted, the FSA must give the applicant written notice, stating the date from which the variation has effect. If the FSA proposes to grant an application for variation but with a limitation or requirement, or to refuse an application, it must give the applicant a warning notice and, if it proposes to continue with that course of action, a decision notice. The applicant may then refer to the matter to the Financial Services and Markets Tribunal.

Transitional Provisions

2–072 As discussed at the beginning of this Chapter (see in particular paras 2–006 to 2–008), authorisation as a concept was by no means new when FSMA 2000 was introduced. Various regulatory processes involving some form of authorisation had been in force for nearly 30 years before, in some areas of the financial services field. Further, the requirements for authorisation had been developed so that when the FSA acquired its full powers at N2, there were many firms whose authorisation had been granted applying criteria derived from the European Directives which are also the foundation of the permission regime in the Act. In those circumstances, it was not surprisingly decided to adopt the pattern followed when previous authorisation regimes were introduced and to make transitional provisions by virtue of which persons with an existing authorisation would be treated as having an appropriate Pt IV permission. This process is commonly known as "grandfathering". It is not necessary for our purposes to engage in a detailed discussion of the operation of the grandfathering process. The details are contained in the Financial Services and Markets Act 2000 (Transitional Provisions) (Authorised Persons etc.) Order 2001 (SI 2001/2636), made under ss.426 to 428 of the Act.

Carrying on Business

The Approved Persons Regime

We have noted in para.2–047 that one of the threshold criteria for obtaining permission is that the applicant must satisfy the FSA that it is itself a fit and proper person to be granted permission. The approved persons regime is directed towards ensuring that important functions in the running of the applicant's affairs are carried out by individuals whose suitability for their role has itself been considered by the FSA. The primary statutory provision by which this is effected is s.59 of FSMA 2000, which places two obligations on an authorised person, called in the Act "A". A must: **2–073**

- take reasonable care to ensure that no person performs a controlled function under an arrangement entered into by A in relation to the carrying on by A of a regulated activity unless the FSA approves the performance by that person of the controlled function to which the arrangement relates;
- take reasonable care to ensure that no person performs a controlled function under an arrangement entered into by a contractor of A in relation to the carrying on by A of a regulated activity unless the FSA approves the performance by that person of the controlled function to which the arrangement relates.

Although this language may seem a little obscure, the picture becomes clearer when it is observed that, by s.59(10), an "arrangement" means any kind of arrangement for the performance of a function of A which is entered into by A or any contractor of his with another person, and includes in particular that other person's appointment to an office, his becoming a partner or his employment (whether under a contract of service or otherwise). Practically speaking, then, the approval of the FSA must be obtained for the performance of a controlled function by anyone involved in the management of the business of an authorised person. The only case in which the obligations set out above do not apply is where the question whether the person concerned is a fit and proper person is reserved under any of the single market directives (for which see para.2–059) to an authority in a country or territory outside the United Kingdom: s.10(8).

It is therefore crucial to know what a controlled function is, and for this purpose the Act directs the reader to rules to be made by the FSA. The FSA's rule-making power is, however, circumscribed by the requirements **2–074** that a function may only be specified as a controlled function if one of three conditions is met, namely:

(1) that the function is likely to enable the person responsible for its performance to exercise a significant influence on the conduct of the authorised person's affairs, so far as relating to the regulated activity;

(2) that the function will involve the person performing it in dealing with customers of the authorised person in a manner substantially connected with the carrying on of the regulated activity; or

(3) that the function will involve the person performing it in dealing with property of customers of the authorised person in a manner substantially connected with the carrying on of the regulated activity.

In determining whether the first condition is satisfied, the FSA may take into account the likely consequences of a failure to discharge the function properly.

2–075 The controlled functions which the FSA has specified are to be found in the Supervision Manual of the *Handbook* at SUP 10.4.5. (The whole of Ch.10 of the Supervision Manual is concerned with the approved persons regime.) There are 27 controlled functions, the majority of which are specified under the first condition as "significant influence functions." The remainder are specified under either the second or the third condition and are described as "customer functions". The list of functions is as follows:

Significant Influence Functions

A. Governing functions, comprising: director function, non-executive director function, chief executive function, partner function, director of unincorporated association function, small friendly society function and sole trader function;

B. Required functions, comprising: apportionment and oversight function, EEA investment business oversight function, compliance oversight function, money laundering reporting function and appointed actuary function;

C. Systems and controls functions, comprising: finance function, risk assessment function and internal audit function;

D. Significant management functions, comprising: significant management (designated investment business) function, significant management (other business operations) function, significant management (insurance underwriting) function, significant management (financial resources) function and significant management (settlements) function.

Customer Functions

Investment adviser function, investment adviser (trainee) function, corporate finance adviser function, pension transfer specialist function, adviser on syndicate participation at Lloyd's function, customer trading function and investment management function.

As respects the list, it is to be noted, first, that it is clear that not every authorised person will need to have an approved person performing each of those functions. Indeed, the governing functions which require to be performed inevitably depend upon the constitutional arrangements of the authorised person and there could be no question of an authorised person's having to secure the performance of each of those functions. In relation to other categories, the need will naturally depend on the nature of the business undertaken. Every authorised person must, however, have at least one approved person to perform each of the required functions: see the *Handbook* at SUP 10.7.2. Secondly, the apportionment and oversight function itself reflects the further FSA requirement that an authorised person must appropriately allocate to one or more individuals the function of dealing with the apportionment of responsibilities under its provisions relating to senior management arrangements, systems and controls: the *Handbook* at SYSC 2.1.3. Further detailed guidance appears at SYSC 2.1.6, which includes the points that the apportionment and oversight function ought to be one of the chief executive's functions unless it is allocated to someone of greater seniority and that there is no upper limit on the number of individuals to whom the function is entrusted, although the allocation must be "appropriate", and the arrangements must not be such that responsibility falls between two stools (the FSA's view being that usually one or two individuals would be the appropriate number to whom to entrust the function). The compliance oversight function is also an FSA requirement (SYSC 3.2.8) and may be carried out by more than one person (SUP 10.7.11). It should be observed that as far as the *Handbook* is concerned, the compliance oversight function is limited to compliance with the conduct of business and collective investment scheme rules, although a firm might choose to allocate further compliance functions to the individual given the compliance oversight function. **2–076**

Procedure

The making of an application for approval is governed by s.60 of FSMA 2000. The application may be made by the authorised person concerned (including a person who has applied for Pt IV permission and will be the authorised person if permission is given), and must be made in such manner as the FSA may direct and contain or be accompanied by such information as the FSA may reasonably require. S.61 requires that the FSA may grant an application only if it is satisfied that the person in respect of whom it is made is a fit and proper person to perform the function to which the application relates. In deciding that question, the FSA may have regard to whether the candidate for approval, or any person who will perform a function on his behalf, has obtained a qualification, or undergone or is undergoing training, or possesses a level of competence, in each case **2–077** required by general rules in relation to persons performing functions of the kind to which the application relates. In line with the approach noted previously, there is a warning notice and decision notice procedure if the FSA does not grant the application and the applicant, the person concerned and the person by whom that person is to be retained, if not the applicant, may each refer an adverse decision to the Financial Services and Markets Tribunal: see s.62. The details of the application procedure may be found in the *Handbook* at SUP 10.12.

Criteria for Assessment

2–078 Since the approval of persons performing controlled functions is clearly a major plank in the regulatory framework, it is not surprising to find that a separate section of the *Handbook* is given over to the assessment of whether an individual is a fit and proper person to perform a particular controlled function. While the FSA naturally does not exclude from its consideration any matter which it may consider relevant in a particular case, the three most important considerations are listed in the *Handbook* at FIT 1.3.1 as the person's:

- honesty, integrity and reputation;
- competence and capability;
- financial soundness.

The application is, of course, to be considered in the context of the activities of the firm for which the controlled function is to be performed, the permission held by the firm and the markets in which it operates.

2–079 The *Handbook* offers guidance in relation to the main assessment criteria at FIT 2. The criterion considered in the most detail is the first, as to which it is said that the FSA will have regard, in summary, to the person's previous history as respects criminal proceedings and convictions, civil proceedings and disciplinary and regulatory proceedings, whether he has been the subject of any justified complaint relating to regulated activities, whether registration, authorisation, membership or a licence has been refused to him or a business in which he has worked, whether such a business has become insolvent while he was working there or within a year afterwards, whether he has been dismissed or asked to resign from a fiduciary position, whether he has been disqualified from acting as a director or in a managerial capacity and whether he has been candid and truthful in his dealings with regulatory bodies in the past (FIT 2.1.3).

In considering the second criterion, the FSA will have regard to matters including whether the person satisfies the requirements of the Training and Competence Sourcebook (referred to further at para.2.124) in relation to the particular controlled function and whether he has demonstrated by experience and training that he is able to perform that function (FIT 2.2.1).

Under the third criterion, the specified matters to which the FSA will have regard are whether the person has been the subject of a judgment debt or award, in the United Kingdom or elsewhere, which remains outstanding or was not satisfied within a reasonable period, and whether, in the United Kingdom or elsewhere, he has made any arrangement with his creditors, filed for bankruptcy, been adjudged bankrupt, had assets sequestrated or been involved in proceedings relating to any of these (FIT 2.3.1). The point is made that the FSA will not normally require the person to supply a statement of assets or liabilities and the fact that he may be of limited financial means will not in itself affect his suitability to perform a controlled function.

Controllers

We have referred in para.2–056 to "controllers", who may be considered as **2–080** connected persons of an authorised person. It is not necessary that a controller should be an approved person simply because he is a controller. FSMA 2000 does, however, require that the FSA should know not only who is a controller of an authorised person, but also of any proposed or actual significant increase or reduction in the extent of control and, in the case of acquisition of or an increase in control, should have an opportunity to object. The statutory provisions are to be found in Pt XII of the Act (ss.178 to 192). In the case of an acquisition or increase, there is a procedure for notification, consideration and approval, with or without conditions, or, if objection is taken, warning and ultimate decision. The imposition of conditions is also subject to a warning and decision procedure. In either case, if the decision is adverse, the matter may be referred to the Financial Services and Markets Tribunal. Under s.191, non-compliance with the various requirements is an offence.

The subject of changes in control is covered in the *Handbook* at SUP 11. The requirements there set out range more widely than those in FSMA 2000, since the *Handbook* provides for notification of changes in control of overseas firms, as well as United Kingdom companies or unincorporated associations. The FSA also requires to be notified of changes in the persons with whom a firm has close links (SUP 11.9).

Withdrawal of Approval

Not surprisingly, the FSA has a power to withdraw approval as well as a **2–081** power to approve. The power of withdrawal is given by s.63 of FSMA 2000 and is exercisable if the FSA considers that the person in respect of whom the approval was given is not a fit and proper person to perform the function to which the approval relates. When considering whether to exercise the power, the FSA may take into account anything which it could take into account when considering whether to grant approval. Clearly withdrawal is likely to be a serious matter, as is recognised by the FSA in the *Handbook* at ENF 7.5, where its policy is set out. The factors which the FSA will take into account include: the honesty, integrity and reputation of the person concerned; his competence and capability; his financial soundness (all of which matters have been considered above in relation to the criteria for initial approval); any non-compliance with the Statement of Principle or knowing involvement in the contravention of a requirement of or under FSMA 2000; the relevance, materiality and length of time since the occurrence of any matters indicating unfitness; the severity of the risk posed by the person; and his previous disciplinary record and general compliance history. The FSA may have regard to the cumulative effect of a number of factors and may take account of the particular controlled functions which the person concerned is carrying out, the nature and activities of the authorised person for whom he so acts and the markets within which the authorised person operates.

The usual warning notice and decision notice procedure applies if the FSA is contemplating withdrawing approval and if approval is withdrawn the person on whose application the approval was given, the person approved and the person by whom that person's services are retained, if not the original applicant, may refer the matter to the Financial Services and Markets Tribunal.

Prohibition Orders

2–082 A prohibition order may be seen as the opposite of approval under the approved persons regime. It is an order under s.56 of FSMA 2000 prohibiting an individual from performing a specified function, any function falling within a specified description or any function. The FSA's power to make such an order arises when it appears to the FSA that an individual is not a fit and proper person to perform functions in relation to a regulated activity carried on by an authorised person. The Act goes on to provide that the section applies to the performance of functions in relation to a regulated activity carried on by a person who is an exempt person in relation to that activity or to whom the general prohibition under s.19 does not apply because of the provisions of Pt XX dealing with the provision of financial services by members of professions as it applies to the performance of functions in relation to a regulated activity by an authorised person. The individual who is the subject of the order may be, but need not necessarily be, an approved person.

A prohibition order may relate to a specified regulated activity, any regulated activity falling with a specified description or all regulated activities, and to authorised persons generally or to any person within a specified class of authorised persons. The FSA may revoke or vary a prohibition order on the application of the person named in it.

An individual who performs or agrees to perform a function in breach of a prohibition order is guilty of an offence and liable to a fine. It is a defence for an individual to show that he took all reasonable precautions and exercised all due diligence to avoid committing the offence. An authorised person must take reasonable care to ensure that no function of that person's, in relation to the carrying on of a regulated activity, is performed by a person who is prohibited from performing that function by a prohibition order.

2–083 The FSA has stated in the *Handbook* at ENF 8.4.2 that the scope of a prohibition order will depend on the range of functions which the individual concerned carries out in relation to regulated activities. It takes the view that a prohibition order is a more serious penalty than the withdrawal of approval, because it will usually be much wider in scope (ENF 8.4.4). The FSA will therefore consider whether the particular unfitness can be adequately dealt with by withdrawing approval or other disciplinary sanctions (such as public censure or financial penalties, discussed at paras 2–092 and following) or by issuing a private warning. It will consider making a prohibition order only in the most serious cases of lack of fitness and propriety. It follows that where the person in question is an approved person, the list of factors which the FSA will consider is virtually the same as that applying in cases where the FSA is considering withdrawal of approval.

Under ss.57 and 58 of FSMA 2000, the warning notice and decision **2–084** notice procedure must be gone through before a prohibition order is made and before the FSA refuses an application for the variation or revocation of a prohibition order. If the FSA does decide to proceed with the making of an order or the refusal of an application, the person affected may refer the matter to the Financial Services and Markets Tribunal.

Breach of Statutory Duty

A contravention of the provisions of s.59 set out in para.2–073 or of the **2–085** terms of a prohibition order made under s.56 is actionable at the suit of a private person who suffers loss as a result, subject to the defences and other incidents applying to actions for breach of statutory duty: s.71 of FSMA 2000. "Prescribed" here means prescribed by the Treasury, which has exercised its power to make the Financial Services and Markets Act 2000 (Rights of Action) Regulations 2001 (SI 2001/2256). Broadly speaking, under the Regulations a private person is an individual who is not engaged in a regulated activity or a person who is not an individual and who is not engaged in business: regs 3 and 5. The Act enables the Treasury to extend the right of action in prescribed cases to a person who is not a private person, again subject to the defences and other incidents applying to actions for breach of statutory duty. Under the current Regulations, a person who is not a private person will have a right of action only if he is acting in a fiduciary capacity for a private person.

Statements of Principle and Code of Practice

S.64 of FSMA 2000 empowers the FSA to issue statements of principle **2–086** with respect to the conduct expected of approved persons and provides that if the FSA does so, it must also issue a code of practice for the purpose of helping to determine whether or not a person's conduct complies with the statement of principle. The mechanics of issuing a statement or code are set out in detail in s.65, which requires the publication of a draft accompanied by a cost benefit analysis and a notice of the period within which representations about the draft may be made to the FSA. The FSA must have regard to any such representations and, if it issues the statement or code, must publish an account, in general terms, of the representations made and its response. The cost benefit analysis may be dispensed with if, in effect, the FSA considers that there will be no significant cost impact. The procedure as a whole may be dispensed with if the FSA considers that the delay involved in compliance would prejudice the interests of consumers.

A statement or code issued under s.64 may be altered or replaced and a similar procedure then applies.

When the FSA issues a statement or code, it must publish it in the way which appears to the FSA to be best calculated to bring it to the attention of the public. A code which has been published and is in force at the time when any particular conduct takes place may be relied on so far as it tends to establish whether or not that conduct complies with a statement of principle. Failure to comply with a statement of principle does not of itself give rise to any right of action by persons affected or affect the validity of any transaction.

2–087 Not surprisingly, the FSA has exercised its power under s.64 and the Statement of Principle and Code of Conduct are to be found in Block 1 of the *Handbook*. The Statement of Principle itself is at APER 2 and provides as follows:

(1) An approved person must act with integrity in carrying out his controlled function.

(2) An approved person must act with due skill, care and diligence in carrying out his controlled function.

(3) An approved person must observe proper standards of market conduct in carrying out his controlled functions.

(4) An approved person must deal with the FSA and with other regulators in an open and cooperative way and must disclose appropriately any information of which the FSA would reasonably expect notice.

(5) An approved person performing a significant influence function must take reasonable steps to ensure that the business of the authorised person for which he is responsible in his controlled function is organised so that it can be controlled effectively.

(6) An approved person performing a significant influence function must exercise due skill, care and diligence in managing the business of the authorised person for which he is responsible in his controlled function.

(7) An approved person performing a significant influence function must take reasonable steps to ensure that the business of the authorised person for which he is responsible in his controlled function complies with the relevant requirements and standards of the regulatory system.

2–088 The Code of Conduct begins with an introduction (APER 3.1) which sets out the background to the Code and makes the following points:

- the significance of conduct identified in the Code as tending to establish compliance with or breach of a Statement of Principle will be assessed only after all the circumstances of a particular case have been taken into account;
- an approved person will only be in breach of a Statement of Principle where he is personally culpable: *i.e.* his conduct was deliberate or his standard of conduct was below that which would be reasonable in all the circumstances;
- the Code is not exhaustive of the kind of conduct that may contravene the Statements of Principle. Its purpose is to help determine whether or not a person's conduct complies with a Statement of Principle;
- Statements of Principle 1 to 4 apply to all approved persons;
- in applying Statements of Principle 5 to 7, the nature, scale and complexity of the business under management and the role and responsibility of the individual performing a significant influence function with in the firm will be relevant in assessing whether an approved person's conduct was reasonable (so that, for example, the smaller and less complex the business, the less detailed and extensive the systems of control need to be).

In relation to all the Statements of Principle, the FSA will take into account whether the particular conduct relates to activities which are subject to other provisions of the *Handbook* and whether that conduct is consistent with the requirements and standards of the regulatory system relevant to the person's firm (APER 3.2). In relation to Statements of Principle 5 to 7, the FSA will take into account whether the person exercised reasonable care when considering the information available to him; whether he reached a reasonable conclusion which he acted on; the nature, scale and complexity of the firm's business; his role and responsibility as an approved person performing a significant influence function; and the knowledge he had, or should have had, of regulatory concerns, if any, arising in the business under his control.

The Code deals with the various Statements of Principle separately and **2–089** in some detail at APER 4. Although we shall not set out the entire Code, its provisions helpfully illuminate the Statements of Principle and so we give the basic evidentiary provisions without the supplementary explanations which the Code contains. It is to be recalled that the evidentiary provisions may be evidence of either a breach of or compliance with a Principle.

The evidentiary provisions as to breach are that conduct of the following **2–090** types by an approved person does not comply with the relevant Principle:

Principle 1: deliberately misleading (or attempting to mislead) by act or omission a client, the firm (or its auditors or appointed actuary) or the FSA;
deliberately recommending an investment to a customer, or carrying out a discretionary transaction for a customer where

the person knows that he is unable to justify its suitability for that customer;
deliberately failing to inform, without reasonable cause, a customer, the firm (or its auditors or appointed actuary) or the FSA of the fact that their understanding of a material issue is incorrect, despite being aware of their misunderstanding;
deliberately preparing inaccurate or inappropriate records or returns in connection with a controlled function;
deliberately misusing the assets or confidential information of a client or the firm;
deliberately designing transactions so as to disguise breaches of requirements and standards of the regulatory system;
deliberately failing to disclose the existence of a conflict of interest in connection with dealings with a client.

Principle 2: failing to inform a customer or the firm (or its auditors or appointed actuary) of material information in circumstances where he was aware, or ought to have been aware, of such information, and of the fact that he should provide it;
recommending an investment to a customer, or carrying out a discretionary transaction for a customer, where he does not have reasonable grounds to believe that it is suitable for that customer;
undertaking transactions without a reasonable understanding of the risk exposure of the transaction to the firm;
failing without good reason to disclose the existence of a conflict of interest in connection with dealings with a client;
failing to provide adequate control over a client's assets;
continuing to perform a controlled function despite having failed to meet the standards of knowledge and skill set out in the Training and Competence Sourcebook for that controlled function.

Principle 4: failing to report promptly, in accordance with the firm's internal procedures (or if none exist direct to the FSA), information which it would be reasonable to assume would be of material significance to the FSA, whether in response to questions or otherwise;
where he is, or is one of the approved persons who is, responsible within the firm for reporting matters to the FSA, failing promptly to inform the FSA of information of which he is aware and which it would be reasonable to assume would be of material significance to the FSA, whether in response to questions or otherwise;
failing without good reason to inform a regulator of information of which he was aware in response to questions from the regulator, to attend an interview or answer questions put by a regulator, despite a request or demand having been made, or to supply a regulator with appropriate documents or information when requested or required to do so and within the time limits attaching to that request or requirement.

Principle 5: failing to take reasonable steps to apportion responsibilities for all areas of the business under his control;
failing to take reasonable steps to apportion responsibilities clearly amongst those to whom responsibilities have been delegated;
if he is responsible under SYSC 2.1.3 for dealing with the apportionment of responsibilities under SYSC 2.1.1, failing to take reasonable care to maintain a clear and appropriate apportionment of significant responsibilities among the firm's directors and senior managers;
failing to take reasonable steps to ensure that suitable individuals are responsible for those aspects of the business under the control of the individual performing a significant influence function.

Principle 6: failing to take reasonable steps adequately to inform himself about the affairs of the business for which he is responsible;
delegating the authority for dealing with an issue or a part of the business to an individual or individuals (whether in-house or outside contractors) without reasonable grounds for believing that the delegate had the necessary capacity, competence, knowledge, seniority or skill to deal with the issue or to take authority for dealing with part of the business;
failing to take reasonable steps to maintain an appropriate level of understanding about an issue or part of the business that he has delegated to an individual or individuals (whether in-house or outside contractors)
failing to supervise and monitor adequately the individual or individuals (whether in-house or outside contractors) to whom responsibility for dealing with an issue or authority for dealing with a part of the business has been delegated.

Principle 7: failing to take reasonable steps to implement (either personally or through a compliance department or other departments) adequate and appropriate systems of control to comply with the relevant requirements and standards of the regulatory system in respect of the firm's regulated activities or, if he is responsible under SYSC 2.1.3 for overseeing the firm's obligation under SYSC 3.1.1, failing to take reasonable care to oversee the establishment and maintenance of appropriate systems and controls;
failing to take reasonable steps to monitor (either personally or through a compliance department or other departments) compliance with the relevant requirements and standards of the regulatory system in respect of the firm's regulated activities;
failing to take reasonable steps adequately to inform himself about the reason why significant breaches (whether suspected or actual) of the relevant requirements and standards of the regulatory system in respect of the firm's regulated activities may have arisen (taking account of the systems and pro-

cedures in place);
failing to take reasonable steps to ensure that procedures and systems of control are reviewed and, if appropriate, improved, following the identification of significant breaches (whether suspected or actual) of the relevant requirements and standards of the regulatory system;
if he is the money laundering reporting officer, failing to discharge the responsibilities imposed on him in accordance with Ch.8 of the Money Laundering Sourcebook;
if he is responsible for compliance under APER 3.2.8, failing to take reasonable steps to ensure that appropriate compliance systems and procedures are in place.

2–091 The evidentiary provisions as to compliance are brief. Compliance with MAR 3 (Inter-Professional Conduct) or the Code of Market Conduct (MAR 1) or relevant market codes and exchange rules will tend to show compliance with Principle 3.

Misconduct

2–092 S.66 of FSMA 2000 enables the FSA to take action against a person if it appears to the FSA that he is guilty of misconduct and it is satisfied that in all the circumstances it is appropriate to take action against him. Despite the generality of those words, a person may only be guilty of misconduct for these purposes in respect of conduct occurring while he is an approved person. "Misconduct" consists of his failing to comply with a Statement of Principle issued under s.64 or having been knowingly concerned in a contravention by the relevant authorised person of a requirement imposed on that authorised person by or under the Act. The sanctions available to the FSA are the imposition of a financial penalty or the publication of a statement of his misconduct. There is a limitation period for action under s.66 of two years from the day on which the FSA knew of the misconduct, unless proceedings in respect of the misconduct were begun against the person concerned within that period. S.67 applies the usual warning notice and decision notice procedure to any proposal by the FSA to take action under s.66 and provides for the person concerned to refer to the Financial Services and Markets Tribunal any decision to take action against him.

If the FSA does take action and that action consists of the publication of a statement, the FSA is required by s.68 to send a copy of the statement to the person concerned and to any person to whom a copy of the decision notice was given.

2–093 The FSA is required by s.69 of the 2000 Act to prepare and issue a statement of its policy with regard to the imposition of penalties under s.66 and the amount of penalties under that section. It is, however, statutorily obliged to include in its policy, in determining what the amount of a penalty should be, having regard to: the seriousness of the misconduct in question in relation to the nature of the principle or requirement concerned; the extent to which that misconduct was deliberate or reckless; and whether the person on whom the penalty is to be imposed is an individual. The statement may be altered or replaced at any time, but must then be issued in the replaced or altered form. The FSA must give the Treasury without delay a copy of any statement published under the section and must publish it in the way appearing to the FSA best calculated to bring it to the attention of the public. Not surprisingly, in exercising or deciding whether to exercise its power under s.66 in any particular case, the FSA must have regard to any statement published and in force at the time the misconduct occurred. S.70 contains provisions for the publication of a draft on which representations may be made before a statement under s.69 is published.

The current statement of policy may be found in the *Handbook* at ENF 11, 12 and 13. It is made clear that action will be taken against approved persons only on the basis of personal culpability and not on the basis of vicarious liability (ENF 11.5.3 and 11.5.6). A public statement is regarded as a serious sanction, but one which may have value in showing what standards are expected and that enforcement is taken seriously, thus contributing to the regulatory objectives of market confidence and the protection of consumers (ENF 12.2.2). If a financial penalty is under consideration, the factors to which the FSA will have regard, in addition to those specified in s.69, are identified in ENF 13.3.3 as: **2–094**

- the amount of profits accrued or loss avoided;
- the person's conduct following the contravention;
- his disciplinary record and compliance history;
- previous action taken by the FSA against other approved persons;
- action taken by other regulatory authorities.

The factors which may influence the FSA in deciding whether (assuming that formal disciplinary action is to be taken at all) to impose a financial penalty or to make a public statement are considered in ENF 12.3. They are as follows: **2–095**

- if the approved person has made a profit or avoided a loss, that may point to a financial penalty;
- the more serious the breach, the more likely the FSA is to impose a financial penalty;
- if the approved person admits the breach, gives full cooperation to the FSA and takes steps to ensure that consumers are compensated for any loss, that may point towards a public statement rather than a financial penalty;
- a poor disciplinary record or compliance history may be a factor in favour of a financial penalty;
- the FSA's approach in similar previous cases;
- if the approved person has inadequate means to pay a penalty of the amount the breach would usually attract, that may be a factor in

favour of a lower penalty or a public statement, but only in exceptional cases will the FSA make a public statement instead of imposing a financial penalty where a financial penalty would otherwise be the appropriate sanction.

It will be seen from this list that some matters may fall to be considered at more than one stage in the disciplinary process.

Business Standards

Conduct of Business

2–096 The Conduct of Business (COB) provisions of the *Handbook* are of considerable length and are only considered in a summary way in this work. The main contents section of COB lists the following Chapters:

- application and general provisions;
- rules which apply to all firms conducting designated investment business;
- financial promotion;
- accepting customers;
- advising and selling;
- product disclosure and the customer's right to cancel or withdraw;
- dealing and managing;
- reporting to customers;
- client assets;
- operators of collective investment schemes;
- trustee and depositary activities;
- Lloyd's.

There are also detailed transitional provisions, reflecting the fact that in many areas previous regulators operated conduct of business rules which have some correspondence to the rules made by the FSA.

We shall consider first the general provisions at the beginning of COB and then draw attention to the general areas falling within more particular Chapters.

2–097 COB applies to every firm, subject to limited exceptions in relation to an incoming EEA firm with respect to its passported activities; a UCITS qualifier and a service company (a company whose permission covers only making arrangements with a view to transactions in investments and agreeing to do so) except as regards financial promotion; an investment company with variable capital (an ICVC); and an authorised professional firm with respect to its non-mainstream regulated activities (explained in PROF 5.2) except as regards clear, fair and not misleading communication, financial promotion and terms of business and client agreements with customers: see COB 1.2.1.

It applies with respect to the carrying on of all regulated activities, except to the extent that a particular provision provides for a narrower application, and to unregulated activities to the extent specified in any provision: COB 1.3.1. In practice, most of COB applies to regulated activities falling with the definition of designated investment business; its application in relation to deposits, pure protection contracts (certain policies offering payment on death or incapacity due to injury, sickness or infirmity) and general insurance contracts (listed in Pt I of Sch.1 to the Regulated Activities Order) is limited (COB 1.3.2). "Designated investment business" means the regulated activities of dealing in investments as principal (without the limitation as to holding out found in art.15 of the Regulated Activities Order), dealing in investments as agent, arranging deals in investments (in relation to designated investments), managing investments (in relation to designated investments), safeguarding and administering investments (in relation to designated investments), sending dematerialised instructions, the specified activities in relation to a collective investment scheme or a stakeholder pension scheme, advising on investments (in relation to designated investments) and agreeing to carry on any of those activities except activities relating to a collective investment scheme or stakeholder pension scheme. "Designated investments" means most of the specified investments set out in Pt III of the Regulated Activities Order, but excludes deposits, electronic money and contracts of insurance other than life policies.

The application of COB is limited to the provisions relating to Chinese walls, client classification and personal account dealing as respects inter-professional business (an expression considered further in para.2.120).

Detailed provisions for the territorial application of COB are contained in COB 1.4. In brief, COB applies in full to activities carried on from an establishment maintained by a firm or its appointed representative in the United Kingdom and to a more limited extent in other cases. There are further particular provisions relating to occupational pension scheme firms, stock lending activity, corporate finance business, oil market activity and energy market activity. COB does not apply directly to appointed representatives, but it is to be recalled that in determining whether a firm has complied with any provision of COB, anything done or omitted by its appointed representative will be treated as having been done or omitted by the firm: see para.2–030.

The second Chapter of COB is concerned with provisions which apply to **2–098** all firms carrying on designated investment business. It contains the following rules:

- when a firm communicates information to a customer, the firm must take reasonable steps to communicate in a way which is clear, fair and not misleading;

- a firm must take reasonable steps to ensure that it, and any person acting on its behalf, does not offer, give, solicit or accept an inducement, or direct or refer any actual or potential item of designated investment business to another person on its own initiative or on the instructions of an associate, if it is likely to conflict to a material extent with any duty that the firm owes to its customers in connection with designated investment business or any duty which such a recipient firm owes to its customers;
- a firm must not deal in investments as agent for a customer, either directly or indirectly, through any broker, under a soft commission agreement (that is, an agreement to receive goods or services in return for putting designated investment business through or in the way of another person), except on specified conditions;
- a firm may accept goods or services supplied under a soft commission agreement, and the goods or services will not constitute an inducement subject to specified conditions;
- before a firm enters into a client agreement authorising it to deal for a customer, either directly or indirectly, with or through the agency of another person, under a soft commission agreement which the firm has, or knows, or ought reasonably to know, that another member of its group has, with that other person, the firm must inform the customer in writing of the existence of the soft commission agreement and the firm's or, when relevant, its group's policy relating to soft commission agreements;
- if a firm has, or knows, or ought reasonably to know, that another member of its group has a soft commission agreement with another person under which either the firm or that other member of its group deals for a customer, the firm must give the disclosure specified;
- a firm must keep the records specified;
- a firm will be taken to be in compliance with any rule in COB that requires a firm to obtain information to the extent that the firm can show that it was reasonable for the firm to rely on information provided to it in writing by another person;
- when a firm establishes and maintains a Chinese wall (explained as being an arrangement that requires information held by a person in the course of carrying on one part of its business to be withheld from, or not to be used for, persons with or for whom it acts in the course of carrying on another part of its business) it may withhold information as specified and the further provisions set out apply;
- when any of the COB rules apply to a firm that acts with knowledge, the firm will not be taken to act with knowledge for the purposes of

that rule if none of the relevant individuals involved on behalf of the firm acts with that knowledge as a result of proper Chinese wall arrangements;

- a firm must not, in any written or oral communication, seek to exclude or restrict, or to rely on any exclusion or restriction of, any duty or liability it may have to a customer under the regulatory system;
- a firm must not in any written or oral communication to a private customer seek to exclude or restrict, or to rely on any exclusion or restriction of, any other duty or liability unless it is reasonable for it to do so.

Financial Promotion

Although this Chapter is described as applying generally to firms in relation to all financial promotions (that is, invitations or inducements to engage in investment business), its application is in fact limited as set out in COB 3.1 in respect of financial promotions for deposits, general insurance contracts, pure protection contracts and reinsurance contracts, financial promotions within specified exempting provisions and financial promotions to persons outside the United Kingdom. The provisions distinguish between a "real time financial promotion", which is a promotion communicated in the course of some form of "interactive dialogue" and a "non-real time financial promotion" (COB 3.5.5) and separate requirements as to form and contents in relation to the two types of promotion are set out in COB 3.8. There are further requirements in COB 3.9 in relation to direct offer financial promotions (non-real time financial promotions which include an offer or invite a response and which indicate how the response is to be made or provide a response form). Unsolicited real time financial promotions (defined as not being solicited real time financial promotions, a carefully limited expression) are subject to strict limits under COB 3.10. **2–099**

There is a general statutory prohibition in s.238 of FSMA 2000 as respects financial promotions of unregulated collective investment schemes, but that prohibition is subject to exemptions as set out in COB 3.11. COB 3.12 contains provisions relating to the approval by an authorised person of a financial promotion to be undertaken by an unauthorised person, which would otherwise involve a contravention of s.21 of the Act. A real time financial promotion cannot be approved under those provisions. There are particular restrictions on the approval of non-real time promotions for overseas persons. Additional requirements apply in respect of financial promotions for an overseas long-term insurer, as set out in COB 3.13.

Guidance on the use of the internet and other electronic media to communicate financial promotions is contained in COB 3.14.

Accepting Customers

The first important requirement of Ch.4 is that before conducting designated investment business with or for any client, a firm must take reasonable steps to establish whether that client is a private customer, an **2–100** intermediate customer or a market counterparty (COB 4.1.4). A private customer is essentially a client who is neither an intermediate customer or a market counterparty. An intermediate customer is, broadly speaking, a local or public authority, a publicly quoted company, a substantial company, partnership or trust, certain other bodies which might be expected to have a degree of expertise and a private customer who under the provisions of COB 4.1.9 becomes an intermediate customer. (A firm may so classify a private customer if it has taken reasonable care to determine that he has sufficient experience and understanding for that purpose, it has given him written warning of the regulatory effect and sufficient time to consider the implications and it can show that he has given informed consent.) The expression "market counterparty" is considered at para.2–041, but it should be noted in addition that a large intermediate customer may in certain circumstances, and subject to a warning and consent procedure, be classified as a market counterparty (COB 4.1.12). If advantage has been taken of COB 4.1.9 or 4.1.12, the firm must review the classification annually, except that if no designated investment business has been conducted for the client over the last 12 months, the review may be deferred until business is next conducted (COB 4.1.15). Appropriate records must be kept, which will include sufficient information to support a classification where necessary (COB 4.1.16). The object of this classification is of course to identify clients most in need of regulatory protection and to focus regulatory requirements accordingly.

2–101 The second part of Ch.4 generally requires a firm to provide a customer (of either class) with its terms of business within certain time limits and, if the business is of certain kinds, set out in COB 4.2.7, the terms of business must take the form of a client agreement, unless the customer is a private customer habitually resident outside the United Kingdom and the firm has taken reasonable steps to establish that he does not with to enter into a client agreement. "Client agreement" means simply terms of business signed by the client or to which the client has consented in writing. The terms of business must set out in adequate detail the basis on which designated investment business is to be conducted (COB 4.2.10), a provision which is clarified by the table of general requirements to be found in COB 4.2.15 and the following table applicable where the firm is to manage investments on a discretionary basis. If the terms can be amended without the customer's consent, at least 10 business days' notice must be given before the firm conducts designated investment business on the amended terms, unless it is impracticable to do so (COB 4.2.13). Again there are record-keeping requirements.

Advising and Selling

2–102 The provisions of COB 5.1 give effect to what is called the policy of polarisation, under which a firm advising a private customer on packaged products must either act independently for the private customer or act on a tied basis, its advice then being restricted to its own products, those of its marketing group and adopted packaged products. A "packaged product" is a life policy, a unit in a recognised collective investment scheme, an interest in an investment trust savings scheme or a stakeholder pension scheme. An "adopted packaged product" is a stakeholder pension scheme not produced by the firm or a member of its marketing group but on which the firm has taken a decision that it will provide advice. The basic obligation on the firm is set out in COB 5.1.7 and is that a firm which provides packaged products, except when acting as the manager of designated investments on a discretionary basis, must take reasonable steps to ensure that neither it nor any of its employees or representatives gives advice to a private customer about the purchase of a packaged product unless the product is issued by the firm itself or by another member of its marketing group or is an adopted packaged product. Under COB 5.1.8, a provider firm must also take reasonable steps to ensure that each of its appointed representatives complies with those requirements. Further rules are intended to secure that the customer is not led reasonably to believe that the firm is in a position to advise or procure advice on investments which are packaged products other than those of its marketing group or its adopted packaged products; that its representatives are able to sell the products they are authorised to sell with competent advice; that its representatives are not likely to be influenced by the structure of their remuneration to give unsuitable advice; that where advice is given about an adopted packaged product any charges imposed by the firm in addition to those of the original producer are disclosed; and that private customers are informed whether any advice given will be independent or restricted to a particular range of products or given for the purposes of managing a portfolio with discretion. Where the firm advises as an independent intermediary, it must act in the best interests of its private customers, it must not enter into commercial arrangements with other persons which might be likely adversely to affect its ability to advise on an independent basis and it must take steps to ensure that its appointed representatives comply with those requirements (COB. 5.1.16).

COB 5.2 gives substance to the "know your customer" policy. It applies **2–103** to a firm which gives a personal recommendation about a designated investment to a private customer, or acts as an investment manager for a private customer or arrange a pension opt-out or pension transfer from an occupational pension scheme for a private customer. The requirement is that the firm should take reasonable steps to ensure that it is in possession of sufficient personal and financial information about the customer relevant to the services which the firm has agreed to provide (COB. 5.2.5). Appropriate records must be made and kept (COB 5.2.9). A table offering guidance on the collection of information appears at COB 5.2.11.

The next part of Ch.5, COB 5.3, is concerned with the suitability of **2–104** investments for the particular customer. It requires the firm to take reasonable steps to ensure that it does not make a personal recommendation to a private customer to buy or sell a designated investment or effect a discretionary transaction for a private customer unless the recommendation or transaction is suitable for the customer having regard to the facts disclosed by him and other relevant facts about him of which the firm is, or reasonably should be, aware (COB 5.3.5). (Where the customer has pooled his funds with those of others, the firm's task is to take reasonable steps to ensure that a discretionary transaction is suitable for the fund, having regard to the stated investment objectives of the fund.) By way of natural consequence, where the firm is tied to a particular range of products, it must take reasonable steps to ensure that no recommendation is made if the range does not contain a suitable product (COB 5.3.6). Further detailed provisions as to suitability follow, and there is extensive guidance on matters to be taken into account when making personal recommendations.

2–105 COB 5.4 tackles the subject of customers' understanding of risk. The principal provision is that a firm must not make a personal recommendation of a transaction, act as a discretionary investment manager, arrange or execute a deal in a warrant or derivative or engage in stock lending activity with, to or for a private customer unless it has taken reasonable steps to ensure that the private customer understands the nature of the risks involved (COB. 5.4.3). There are evidential provisions as to the reasonable steps to be taken in relation to certain specified types of investment or activity.

2–106 The next three sections are concerned with information about the firm and with charges and remuneration. COB 5.5 deals with information required to be disclosed; COB 5.6 obliges a firm to ensure that its charges to a private customer made in connection with the conduct of designated investment business are not excessive and COB 5.7 requires that before a firm conducts designated investment business with or for a private customer, it must disclose in writing to the customer the basis or amount of its charges and the nature or amount of any other income receivable by it or, to its knowledge, by its associate which is attributable to that business. Particular requirements apply in relation to packaged products. The remaining short sections are concerned with customers introduced to clearing firms by introducing brokers and overseas introducing brokers (COB 5.8) and with giving information about stakeholder pension schemes (COB 5.9).

Product Disclosure and the Customer's Right to Withdraw

2–107 The earlier sections of Ch.6 are directed to ensuring that customers' information needs are satisfactorily met. The first step is to require product providers or stakeholder pension scheme operators to produce "key features" for each packaged product offered and to require a firm offering a cash deposit ISA to produce an appropriate information document (COB 6.1.4). "Key features" are defined by reference to the requirements of COB as to the contents of key features information, which are to be found in COB 6.5, as are the information requirements for cash deposit ISAs. Key features must be produced in printed hard copy format, with electronic format an optional extra, unless the relevant activities are intended to be conducted solely through electronic media. The topic of projections for life policies, schemes and stakeholder pension schemes is dealt with in COB 6.6, the principal requirement being that a firm must not provide such a projection unless it is calculated and presented in accordance with the rules in that section (COB 6.6.4)

Questions of cancellation and withdrawal are covered in COB 6.7, which applies to product providers, an insurer which provides pure protection contracts, an independent intermediary in specified circumstances, a deposit-taking firm in specified circumstances and the operator of a stakeholder pension scheme. Under COB 6.7.7, a customer who is an individual has a right to cancel certain investment agreements and a variation of certain life policies, pension contracts or stakeholder pension schemes. Trustees of an occupational pension scheme and trustees and managers of a stakeholder pension scheme have the same right to cancel as an individual customer (COB 6.7.8). The right is exercisable within the period specified in COB 6.7.10 or 6.7.11, whichever may be applicable. The circumstances in which there is a right to withdraw are to be found in COB 6.7.14, which explains that the right to withdraw procedures are that the offer made by the customer to enter into the agreement cannot be accepted by the firm until at least seven days after the offer is made. Where there is a right to cancel, the firm which enters into the agreement with the customer must give the customer, in writing, clear and prominent notice of the right both before and after the agreement has been concluded (COB 6.7.30), and such notices must comply with the further requirements of COB 6.7. **2–108**

Particular disclosure requirements in relation to life and generally insurance contracts are contained in COB 6.8, and COB 6.9 requires long-term insurers issuing with-profits life policies, with the exception of some friendly societies, to produce and make available a with-profits guide. There are detailed requirements as to the content of such a guide. **2–109**

Dealing and Managing

This Chapter begins by looking at issues of conflict of interest and material interest, and the provisions of COB 7.1 apply to a firm when it is conducting designated investment business with or for a customer. If a firm has or may have a material interest (broadly, any interest of a material nature) in a transaction to be entered into with or for a customer, or a relationship that gives or may give rise to a conflict of interest in relation to such a transaction, or an interest in a transaction that is, or may be, in conflict with the interest of any of the firm's customers, or customers with conflicting interests in relation to a transaction, the firm must not knowingly advise or deal in the exercise of discretion in relation to that transaction unless it takes reasonable steps to ensure fair treatment for the customer (COB 7.1.3). An evidentiary rule provides that a firm may manage a conflict of interest by taking one or more of a number of reasonable steps, namely: disclosure of an interest to a customer; relying on a policy of independence; establishing internal arrangements (Chinese walls); declining to act for a customer (COB 7.1.4). Further guidance then follows. **2–110**

COB 7.2 similarly applies to a firm that conducts designated investment business with or for a customer. It prohibits dealing and switching unless the firm has taken reasonable steps to ensure that the deal or switch is in the customer's best interests, both when viewed in isolation and when viewed in the context of earlier transactions (COB 7.2.3).

2–111 Ch.7 then turns to deal with some more specific situations. In the interests of dealing fairly with customers, a firm is required to postpone to a limited extent transactions on its own account at the point when it is intending to publish a written recommendation or a piece of research or analysis to customers relating to a designated investment (COB 7.3.3); to execute customer orders and own account orders in designated investments fairly and in due turn (COB 7.4.3); in general, provide best execution (in effect, obtain the best price available) (COB 7.5.3); in general, execute an order as soon as reasonably practicable (COB 7.6.4); allocate designated investments acquired upon the execution of aggregated orders in accordance with a written policy that is consistently applied and fulfils the requirements of COB 7.7 (COB 7.7.3); realise a private customer's assets in order to discharge an obligation only in accordance with the provisions of COB 7.8; lend money or grant credit to a private customer only in accordance with the provisions of COB 7.9; obtain the required margin from a private customer entering into a transaction which exposes him to a contingent liability (COB 7.10.3); and give appropriate notice on the sale of non-exchange traded securities to a private customer (COB 7.11.3). Record keeping requirements are contained in COB 7.12.

Reference has already been made to specific requirements in relation to own account dealing. Under COB 7.13.4, a firm must take reasonable steps to ensure that a personal account transaction in a designated investment undertaken by any of its employees does not conflict with the firm's duties to its customers under the regulatory system, and that when it gives permission to any of its employees to undertake a personal account transaction, it receives prompt notification of, or is otherwise able to identify, that transaction. "Employee" here includes appointed representative and the employee or appointee of an appointed representative (COB 7.13.5). Again there is further guidance as to reasonable steps and record-keeping requirements. The final sections of the Chapter deal with programme trading (*i.e.* a single transaction or series of transactions executed for the purpose of acquiring or disposing, for a customer, of all or part of a portfolio or a large basket of securities) and non-market-price transactions.

Reporting to Customers

2–112 Under COB 8.1, a firm which executes a sale or purchase of a designated investment with or for a customer must promptly send the customer a written confirmation recording the essential details of the transaction (COB 8.1.3). Those requirements are expanded upon in the remainder of COB 8.1. A firm which acts as an investment manager or administers any other account or portfolio which includes designated investments for a customer, or operates a customer's account containing uncovered open positions in a contingent liability investment must promptly and at suitable intervals provide the customer with a written statement containing adequate information on the value and composition of the customer's account or portfolio with the firm as at the end of the period covered by the statement (COB 8.2.1 and 8.2.4). Again, further detail follows.

Client Assets

COB 9.1 applies to a firm when it is safeguarding and administering investments, and sets out the custody rules which must be observed (COB 9.1.1). The rules are designed primarily to restrict the commingling of client and firm's assets and to minimise the risk of the client's custody investments being used by the firm without the client's agreement or contrary to the client's wishes, or being treated as the firm's assets in the event of its insolvency (COB 9.1.12). Under COB 9.2.5 a firm holding written authority from a client under which it may control a client's assets or liabilities in the course of or in connection with the firm's designated investment business is specifically required to establish and maintain adequate records and internal controls in respect of its use of the mandate, which must include an up-to-date list of the mandates and any applicable conditions, a record of all transactions entered into using the mandate and internal controls to ensure that they are within the scope of the authority of the person and the firm entering into the transaction, the details of the procedures and authorities for the giving and receiving of instructions under the authority and internal controls for the safeguarding of such documents as passbooks. **2–113**

Client money is dealt with in COB 9.3, which sets out what it describes as "the client money rules". Not surprisingly, solicitors will comply with the client money rules if they comply with the applicable professional rules (COB 9.3.25). Client assets held as collateral in connection with an arrangement to secure the obligation of a client in the course of, or in connection with, its designated investment business are dealt with specifically in COB 9.4. Provision for the return of client money in the event of the failure of a firm or third party holding client money is made by COB 9.5 ("the client money distribution rules").

Operators of Collective Investment Schemes

The application of COB to operators of collective investment schemes is extremely limited in relation to scheme management activity, as set out in COB 10.2. This is because such activity is principally regulated by other provisions in the *Handbook*, and in particular by the Collective Investment Schemes Sourcebook. Collective investment and unit trust schemes are discussed in Ch.6 and accordingly this part of COB is not further considered here. **2–114**

Trustee and Depositary Activities

Again, COB is modified in its application to such activities. The effect of the Chapter, as set out in COB 11.1.12, is to redefine "customer" so that it applies meaningfully in the trustee firm/depositary context (for example, a trustee firm could be both the customer and the firm), to recognise that some trustee firms may not be experts in investment and should be allowed to delegate regulatory responsibility for compliance with COB to other suitable firms, to apply different rules to different types of trustee and to apply rules specifically devised for trustee firms and depositaries. **2–115**

Lloyd's

2–116 As might be assumed, Ch.12 contains specific provisions relating to advising on syndicate participation at Lloyd's, management of the underwriting capacity of a Lloyd's syndicate, carrying on designated investment business in relation to funds at Lloyd's and communicating or approving a financial promotion in relation to the underwriting capacity of a Lloyd's syndicate, membership of a Lloyd's syndicate, effecting or carrying out contracts of insurance at Lloyd's or any of the activities previously specified (COB 12.1.1). The purpose of the Chapter is explained as being to protect the interests of members or potential members and policyholders or potential policyholders (COB 12.1.5). Lloyd's is discussed in Ch.8, and so COB 12 is not further considered here.

Interim Prudential Sourcebook for Investment Business

2–117 Although this Chapter does not deal in general with the various interim prudential sourcebooks, the conduct of investment business is not dealt with as a whole elsewhere in this work and it is therefore appropriate to follow our discussion of COB, which has such a significant application in relation to investment business, by a brief consideration of the relevant interim prudential sourcebook. Its purpose is to set out the detailed financial resources and prudential standards which the FSA applies to the relevant firms pending the introduction of a single prudential sourcebook (IPRU (INV) 1.1.1). It sets minimal capital and other risk management standards with a view to reducing the possibility that firms will be unable to meet their liabilities and commitments to consumers and counterparties (IPRU (INV) 1.1.2).

2–118 At first sight, the arrangement of IPRU (INV) seems eccentric. The basic compliance obligation as set out in IPRU (INV) 1.2.4 and the accompanying table is as follows:

- a professional firm must comply with the provisions of Chs 1 and 2;
- a securities and futures firm which is not an investment firm or a firm carrying out limited investment services and not holding client money (a "Category D" firm) must comply with the provisions of Chs 1 and 3;
- the Society of Lloyd's (in relation to underwriting agents) and members' advisers must comply with the provisions of Chs 1 and 4;
- an investment management firm must comply with the provisions of Chs 1 and 5;
- a service company must comply with the provisions of Chs 1 and 6;
- a securities and futures firm which is an investment firm or a Category D firm must comply with the provisions of Chs 1 and 10;
- a personal investment firm must comply with the provisions of Chs 1 and 13.

The explanation for the unusual numbering system is that the underlying scheme of the sourcebook is, wherever appropriate, to apply the financial and other prudential standards which applied to a firm immediately prior to its becoming authorised by the FSA under FSMA 2000, and that the Chapter numbers correspond with those of the rulebooks of previous regulators (IPRU (INV) 1.1.3). Consistently with this approach, there are certain transitional provisions of general application enabling certain types of borrowings or facilities which were capable of being treated as part of a firm's capital resources under the regime governed by the Financial Services Act 1986 still to be treated in such a way, subject to certain conditions (IPRU (INV) 1.2.7). The most common example of such borrowing is a subordinated loan which meets specified conditions.

The various Chapters in IPRU (INV) vary considerably in length and **2–119** complexity. Chs 2 and 4 are both short and will be considered in the context of professional firms and Lloyd's respectively. The shortest Chapter is Ch.6, which simply requires a service company to be able to meet its liabilities as they fall due and provides that in complying with that requirement a firm may use any assets which are available to meet any of its liabilities (IPRU (INV) 6.1.2). This reflects the fact that a service company will only make arrangements for transactions in investments and its permission will be subject to a limitation substantially to the effect that it can only deal with market counterparties and intermediate customers (as to which, see para.2–100 above). The provisions applicable to each of the other types of firm are well over 100 pages in length (over 200 in the case of the second class of securities and futures firms) and cannot practicably be discussed in this work. The essential point to note is that there are extensive financial resources and record-keeping provisions, intended to ensure the protection of consumers and the maintenance of market confidence (IPRU (INV) 1.1.2).

IPRU (INV) also contains a lengthy section containing forms referred to in the substantive provisions.

Inter-professional Conduct

Also included in the business standards section of the *Handbook* and of **2–120** general application is that part of the market conduct regulations which concerns inter-professional dealing. (The remaining market conduct provisions, namely, the Code of Market Conduct, the price stabilising rules and the endorsement of the Takeover Code are considered in Chs 14, 5 and 7 respectively). The inter-professional rules apply to every firm except a service company (for which see para.2–119 above), certain friendly societies and insurers (*i.e.* "non-directive" friendly societies and insurers, which are defined by reference to their carrying out relatively limited business) and a UCITS qualifier (for which see para.2–068) (MAR 3.1.1). They apply when the firm carries on regulated activities or related ancillary activities involving dealing in investments as principal or agent, acting as an arranger or giving advice in connection with a specific transaction, but only if the activity concerns an inter-professional investment and is undertaken with or for a market counterparty (MAR 3.1.2). "Professional" in this context may be understood broadly as meaning involved professionally in some form of financial services activity rather than as meaning connected with a professional firm regulated as such. It can readily be appreciated that requirements which are properly to be applied when a firm deals with an individual investor may not be required or even helpful when a firm deals with a person who may be supposed to be on an equal footing in terms of expertise. The rules are intended to secure good market practice by firms undertaking inter-professional business (MAR 3.2.1).

2–121 Much of the meat of the rules is to be found in MAR 3.4, which offers guidance on the applications of Principles 1 (integrity), 2 (skill, care and diligence), 5 (market conduct) and 7 (communications with clients) in the inter-professional context. In such circumstances, a firm is not required to assess the suitability of a particular transaction for the client or to provide best execution or other dealing protections (MAR 3.4.3). Giving information does not amount to an assumption of responsibility for giving advice and the only requirement of Principle 7 as respects counterparties is that information must be communicated in a way which is not misleading (MAR 3.4.4 and 3.4.5). If a firm does provide information, it is not obliged to keep the counterparty informed of any changes in the information and the more limited nature of its obligations will mean that there is often no conflict of interest and thus no requirement to make disclosure of the firm's interest, although where there is a conflict, it must of course be managed appropriately (MAR 3.4.7). A firm should take reasonable steps to ensure that it is clear to a market counterparty in what capacity the firm is acting in relation to a particular transaction, and should not, following agreement to a particular capacity, act in a different capacity without obtaining consent (MAR 3.4.11). Further specific provisions deal with marketing incentives, inducements and payments in kind (MAR 3.4.14 and 3.4.15) and firms must adopt appropriate systems, controls and policies to that end (MAR 3.4.16).

2–122 Non-market-price transactions have a separate chapter in recognition of the fact that they give rise to particular issues. The FSA observes in MAR 3.5.1 that experience shows that the fact that a transaction is carried out at a price other than the prevailing market price is often a good indicator that the purpose of the transaction is improper, and of course a firm should not enter into a transaction which it knows to be improper or which it ought reasonably to have realised to be improper. Firms must therefore take reasonable steps to check whether there is a legitimate reason for a counterparty's entering into such a transaction (MAR 3.5.4) and must keep records of the steps it has taken in that connection (MAR 3.5.5). It follows that a firm must be able to identify non-market-price transactions and have in place policies and procedures for reviewing such transactions (MAR 3.5.7). There is detailed guidance on whether a transaction is to be considered a non-market-price transaction (MAR 3.5.8 and following) and whether it is to be considered to be for improper purposes (MAR 3.5.13 and following). There is also detailed guidance on the appropriate procedures (MAR 3.5.17 and following).

2–123 MAR 3.6 deals with record-keeping requirements in relation to transactions entered into by a firm and MAR 3.7 is concerned with the specific activity of acting as a wholesale market broker.

Training and Competence

The remaining area of business standards to be considered in this Chapter is the training and competence requirements. Those requirements are described as "general, high level, commitments" which every firm should make, subject to some limitations in connection with incoming EEA firms, incoming Treaty firms and UCITS qualifiers (TC 1.1.1). Compliance with the requirements is seen by the FSA as an element of compliance with Principle 3 of the Principles for Business (reasonable care to organise and control the firm's affairs responsibly and effectively) and as a criterion relevant to the suitability of the firm to carry on a regulated activity for the purposes of threshold condition 5 of the conditions for permission. It follows that training and competence matters may also be relevant under SYSC, which amplifies Principle 3, and in connection with the approval of persons to perform controlled functions: see TC 1.1.3 and following. **2–124**

The commitments are as follows (TC 1.2.1): **2–125**

- that the firm's employees are competent;
- that they remain competent for the work they do;
- that they are appropriately supervised;
- that their competence is regularly reviewed; and
- that the level of competence is appropriate to the nature of the business.

Further details are set out in TC 2, which contains rules and guidance relating to recruitment, training, attaining competence (which may involve acting under supervision, satisfying assessment procedures and passing approved examinations), approved examinations, maintaining competence, supervising and record-keeping. Breach of the rules in TC does not, however, give rise to an action for damages by a private person under s.150 of the FSMA 2000.

Chapter 3

The Professions

Statutory Context

The 1986 Act

Under the Financial Services Act, professional persons such as solicitors, accountants and actuaries could become authorised persons for the purpose of carrying on investment business by obtaining a certificate issued by a recognised professional body. The recognition in question was recognition by the Securities and Investment Board (later renamed the FSA, as noted in Ch.2). The bodies in question were standard professional bodies (for example, the Law Society, the Institute of Chartered Accountants in England and Wales and the Institute of Actuaries) and certificates could be issued to members: that is to say, any person entitled to practise the relevant profession and subject to the rules of the relevant professional body. The underlying assumption was that the general objects of investor protection could be sufficiently achieved by the use of the existing regulatory framework to which such professionals were subject, and it was in fact a condition that a professional body seeking to become recognised should offer protection at least equivalent to that which would be offered by a self-regulatory organisation. **3–001**

Although the primary task of regulating members of professional bodies was thus given to the bodies themselves, there were many requirements of the 1986 Act which extended to authorised professionals or their professional body, both to ensure that the existing framework was adequate for the purpose and to make available a sufficiently wide range of powers and remedies, so that an investor would not be disadvantaged by the fact that the person by whom financial services had been provided to him was regulated by a professional body and not by one of the self-regulatory organisations. Not surprisingly, the Act required recognised professional bodies to have adequate arrangements and resources for the effective monitoring of compliance by its members and those arrangements had to include provision for the withdrawal or suspension of certification in the event of breaches of the rules of the body concerned. The powers of requiring information and conducting investigations which were given to the Securities and Investments Board extended to recognised professional bodies, and members of such bodies fell within the categories of those from whom a private investor who had suffered loss as a result of contravention of any rules or regulations under certain provisions of the 1986 Act might **3–002** claim compensation. Recognised professional bodies were also required to have effective arrangements for the investigation of complaints relating to the carrying by authorised professionals of investment business in respect of which they were authorised through their professional body and the relevant body's own regulation of investment business. The Securities and Investments Board could exercise its powers of intervention in relation to a professional authorised through a recognised professional body, but only if requested to do so by the body itself.

3–003 It should be noted that it was not invariably a requirement that professionals should obtain authorisation if their only relevant activities were arranging deals in investments or giving investment advice. An exemption in relation to those activities was available if the services in question were provided in the course of carrying on any profession not otherwise constituting investment business and the provision of the services was "a necessary part" of other advice or services given in the course of carrying on that profession. In practice, however, it was rare for professional firms to rely on the exemption, not least because of the apparently stringent nature of the test imposed by the words "a necessary part". The appropriate certificate was sought and the firm's notepaper bore a statement to the general effect that the firm was authorised under the Financial Services Act and was regulated in the conduct of the relevant business by a specified professional body.

FSMA 2000

3–004 The overall scheme of the 2000 Act as respects the provision of financial services by members of the professions is similar to the scheme under the 1986 Act, although it does not lead to the result that such professionals are authorised under the later Act. The first question is, of course, whether the activities which the professional person proposes to carry on are regulated activities. The answer to this question is to be found by reference to the Financial Services and Markets Act 2000 (Regulated Activities) Order (SI 2001/544). As noted in Ch.2, the activities of dealing in investments as agent, arranging deals in investments, safeguarding and administering investments and advising on investments are regulated activities. By art.67 of the Order, however, there is excluded any activity which:

- is carried on in the course of carrying on any profession or business which does not otherwise consist of the carrying on of regulated activities in the United Kingdom; and
- may reasonably be regarded as a necessary part of other services provided in the course of that profession or business; and
- is not remunerated separately from the other services.

It will be seen that the exclusion is similar to the previous exemption, but the words "a necessary part" have been subjected to some qualification and there is a further condition that separate remuneration may not be charged.

(It seems that additional, but not separate, remuneration is permitted.) Although the intended effect of introducing the words "may reasonably be regarded as" was to reduce the number of firms who obtained precautionary authorisation, it seems unlikely that the new phrase will have done much to encourage firms to abandon the precaution, and the authorisation provisions of the Act in relation to members of the professions will therefore continue to be significant. The principal provisions are to be found in Pt XX, containing ss.325 to 333.

By s.327, the general prohibition on the carrying of regulated activities by a person who is neither authorised nor exempt (s.19, discussed in Ch.2) does not apply if certain conditions are satisfied and no relevant direction under s.328 or order under s.329 is in force. In the Act the professional person in question is called "P" and it is convenient to follow that usage. The conditions to be satisfied are set out in s.327 itself and are as follows: **3–005**

(1) P must be a member of a profession or controlled or managed by one or more such members;

(2) P must not receive from a person other than his client any pecuniary reward or other advantage which arises out of his carrying on a regulated activity and for which he does not account to the client;

(3) the manner of the provision by P of any service in the course of carrying on the activities must be incidental to the provision by him of professional services;

(4) P must not carry on or hold himself out as carrying on a regulated activity which is not one which rules made pursuant to s.332(3) of the 2000 Act allow him to carry on or one in relation to which he is an exempt person;

(5) the activities must not be of a description, or relate to an investment of a description, specified in an order made by the Treasury for the purposes of s.327;

(6) the activities must be the only regulated activities carried on by P, with the exception of regulated activities in relation to which he is an exempt person.

The expression "professional services" is defined to mean services which do not constitute the carrying on of a regulated activity and the provision of which is supervised and regulated by a designated professional body.

The Treasury has exercised its power to specify activities in respect of which the exemption does not apply in the Financial Services and Markets Act 2000 (Professions) (Non-Exempt Activities) Order 2001 (SI 2001/1227, as amended by SI 2001/3650 and SI 2002/682), which lists the activities of accepting deposits, issuing electronic money, effecting and carrying out contracts of insurance, dealing in investments as principal, establishing, operating or winding up a collective investment scheme, establishing, operating or winding up a stakeholder pension scheme, managing the **3–006** underwriting capacity of a Lloyd's syndicate and providing funeral plan contracts. The activities of managing and advising on investments, providing regulated mortgage contracts, advising a person to become a member of a particular Lloyd's syndicate and agreeing to carry on listed activities are also covered by the Order in certain circumstances. There is thus a substantial number of regulated activities in relation to which a professional person will remain subject to the general prohibition.

3–007 A body becomes a designated professional body if it is designated in an order made by the Treasury under s.326 of FSMA 2000. The Treasury may only exercise that power in relation to a body if it is satisfied that the body meets the basic condition and one or more of the additional conditions. The basic condition is that the body has rules applicable to the carrying on by members of the profession in relation to which it is established of regulated activities which, if the body were to be designated, would be exempt regulated activities. The additional conditions are that the body has power under legislation of the United Kingdom or any part of it to regulate the practice of the profession, or being a member of the profession is a requirement under any such legislation for the exercise of particular functions or the holding of a particular office, or the body has been recognised for the purpose of any other such legislation and that recognition has not been withdrawn, or the body is established in another EEA State and in that State the situation corresponds to one of the other additional conditions.

The designation power was exercised by the Financial Services and Markets Act 2000 (Designated Professional Bodies) Order 2001 (SI 2001/1226) to designate professional bodies governing solicitors, accountants and actuaries.

3–008 Under s.332 of the FSMA 2000, the FSA has power to make rules applicable to persons to whom the general prohibition does not apply by virtue of s.327. The power is to be exercised for the purpose of ensuring that clients are aware that such persons are not authorised persons. The rules in fact made are contained in the *FSA Handbook* at PROF 4 and are considered further at para.3–16 below. A designated professional body must itself make rules applicable to members of the relevant profession who are not authorised persons governing the carrying on of regulated activities by such persons, with the exception of any regulated activities in relation to which they are exempt persons: see s.332(3). The purpose of such rules is to secure that the only regulated activities carried on by a member in providing a particular professional service to a particular client are ones which arise out of or are complementary to the provision of that service to that client (s.332(4)) and the rules must be approved by the FSA (s.332(5)).

3–009 A direction under s.328 (which prevents the benefit of s.327 from being available) is a direction by the FSA which, if given, must be in writing and may be given in relation to different classes of person or different descriptions of regulated activity. The power is exercisable only if the FSA is satisfied that it is desirable in order to protect the interests of clients (s.328(6)). Any direction must be published in the way which appears to the FSA best calculated to bring it to the attention of the public and a copy must be given to the Treasury without delay. In deciding whether to make a direction, the FSA must have regard to the effectiveness of the compliance, complaints, redress and co-operation arrangements of any relevant professional body. "Clients" essentially means past, present and potential users of services by a professional, those who have rights or interests derived from other users and those who have rights or interests which may be adversely affected by the use of such services by another on their behalf. The beneficiaries under a trust of which a professional person providing exempt regulated services is a trustee are to be treated as persons who use the professional's services. S.330 contains a procedure for the FSA to consult and to receive representations on a published draft of any proposed direction before it is made. Those requirements do not apply, however, if the FSA considers that the delay in compliance would prejudice the interests of consumers: s.330(6).

By contrast with the generality of the direction provisions in s.328, s.329, **3–010**
an order under which again prevents s.327 from applying, tackles the problem of particular persons who, in the view of the FSA should not enjoy the benefit of s.327. It enables the FSA to make an order if it appears to the FSA that a person currently entitled to that benefit is not a fit and proper person to carry on regulated activities in accordance with that section. If made, the order disapplies s.327(1) in relation to that person to the extent specified (s.329(2)). There is provision for the person affected to apply to the FSA to vary or revoke the order. The "person" may be a partnership and provision is made to ensure that changes in the membership of the partnership do not affect the continuance of the order and that the order continues to bind a successor to the business of a dissolved partnership (provided that the members of the new partnership are substantially the same as the members of the old and the succession is to the whole or substantially the whole of the business). As might be expected, s.331 provides for a warning and decision notice procedure (as to which see ss.387 and 388 of the FSMA 2000 and para.2–058 of Ch.2) to apply in relation to the making of such an order. The FSA's approach to the exercise of its s.329 power is set out in ENF 18. It should be noted that the FSA's register will include a record of persons against whom a s.329 order has been made (ENF 18.8.2).

The FSA is itself under a general duty, imposed by s.325 of the 2000 Act, **3–011**
to keep itself informed about the way in which designated professional bodies supervise and regulate the carrying on of exempt regulated activities by members of their respective professions, and the way in which members in fact carry on such activities. "Exempt regulated activities" are of course regulated activities which may be carried on by members of the professions without breaching the general prohibition. "Members" are persons who are entitled to practise the profession in question and who, in practising it, are subject to the rules of the body designated in relation to that profession, whether or not they are in fact members of that body. The FSA is further obliged to keep under review the desirability of exercising any of the powers given to it by Pt XX (s.325(3)). Each designated professional body is in turn obliged to co-operate with the FSA by sharing information and otherwise in order to enable the FSA to perform its functions under that Pt (s.325(4)).

3–012 A person who describes himself as a person to whom the general prohibition does not apply as a result of Pt XX, or who behaves or otherwise holds himself out in a manner which indicates or is reasonably likely to be understood as indicating that he is such a person, is guilty of an offence if he is not such a person in fact: see s.333(1). It is a defence for the person to show that he took all reasonable precautions and exercised all due diligence to avoid committing the offence. The maximum potential fine for such an offence is increased in cases in which the conduct in question involved or included a public display of material.

The *FSA Handbook*

The Specialist Sourcebook for Professional Firms

3–013 The sourcebook, which is contained in Block 5 of the *FSA Handbook*, applies to professional firms which can take advantage of s.327 of the 2000 Act (called "exempt professional firms"), to professional firms which are authorised and to designated professional bodies (PROF 1.1.1). In large part it repeats the statutory material considered above, but it also casts light on the FSA's understanding of certain statutory provisions and on its approach to the exercise of certain powers.

3–014 The provisions of s.327 itself are considered in PROF 2. The FSA expresses the view that the obligation to account to the client, noted in para.3–05 above, requires that an exempt professional firm must hold any pecuniary reward or other advantage received from anyone other than the client to the order of the client (PROF 2.1.12). To satisfy the requirement that the provision of any service in the course of carrying on regulated activities is incidental to the provision of professional services, regulated activities cannot be a major part of the practice of the firm. It is also relevant to consider the scale of regulated activities in relation to other professional activities, whether and to what extent regulated activities are held out as separate services and the impression given of how the firm provides regulated activities (for example, through advertising or other promotions of its services) (PROF 2.1.14). The conditions in s.327 are not interpreted by the FSA as imposing any restriction on the regulated activities which an exempt professional firm may carry on outside the United Kingdom (PROF 2.1.15).

3–015 The FSA proposes to perform its duty under s.325 to keep itself informed by making arrangements with the designated professional bodies, pursuant to their duty of co-operation, to obtain information about complaints and redress arrangements, complaints volumes and their analysis, disciplinary action, supervisory action and the activities carried on by exempt professional firms, the risks arising from them and how they are mitigated (PROF 3.1.2). Information may also be obtained from firms themselves, government departments, trade bodies, consumer organisations and clients, and the FSA may commission reviews or research (PROF 3.1.3).

The disclosure rules in PROF 4.1 are, as already noted, made pursuant to the FSA's power under s.332 of the 2000 Act. An exempt professional firm must, before providing a service which includes the carrying on of a regulated activity in the United Kingdom, disclose to the client in writing, in a manner which is clear, fair and not misleading, that the firm is not authorised under the Act: see PROF 4.1.3. The information may, however, be included in engagement or client care letters (PROF 4.1.4). The FSA expects that designated professional bodies will require firms to state: **3–016**

- that the firm is not an authorised person;
- the nature of the regulated activities carried on by the firm and the fact that they are limited in scope;
- that the firm is regulated for those activities by the relevant body, identifying the body concerned;
- the nature of the complaints and redress mechanisms available in respect of those activities.

The FSA also requires firms to ensure that any statement referring to the FSA itself does not lead a client to suppose that the FSA has direct regulatory responsibility for the firm.

It is a consequence of these provisions that the letterheads of firms which had been authorised under the 1986 Act but became exempt under the 2000 Act were liable to involve a breach of the prohibition on making a representation of authorisation, at least if the word "authorised" appeared in a statement of the kind referred to in para.3–003 above. By PROF TP 1, firms were allowed to use up existing stocks of notepaper and other similar material provided that any such statement was struck through.

One possible, although undesired, effect of s.327 is liable to be the distortion of competition between exempt professional firms and authorised professional firms carrying on regulated activities in respect of which the benefit of s.327 would be available if the firms in question were not in fact authorised. The FSA's policy is to avoid such a situation (PROF 5.3.1). The *FSA Handbook* therefore identifies a class of "non-mainstream regulated activities" and disapplies or modifies provisions of the *Handbook* as in respect of such activities when carried on by authorised professional firms. As might have been expected, non-mainstream regulated activities are designed to mirror as far as possible the conditions which an exempt professional firm has to satisfy in order to obtain the benefit of s.327: see PROF 5.2. Provisions of the *Handbook* which are disapplied or modified are identified in PROF 5.3 and include certain provisions in the Conduct of Business, Training and Competence, Money Laundering, Complaints and Market Conduct Sourcebooks and in the Supervision Manual. The need to include such provisions is an indication that the Pt XX regime is less onerous than the full regime usually applicable to authorised persons, no doubt because of the incidental nature of exempt regulated activities. A private person who suffers loss as a result of a breach by an authorised professional firm of the conditions on which it can follow the provisions for non-mainstream regulated activities has a cause of action against the firm: s.157 of FSMA 200 and PROF Sch.5. **3–017**

Chapter 4

Banks and Building Societies

The Old Regime

The Supervision of Banks under the Old Regime

Until June 1, 1998, banking in the United Kingdom was supervised by the Bank of England under the Banking Act 1987. The function of supervising banks was transferred to the FSA, with effect from that date, by the Bank of England Act 1998. The 1987 Act, however, remained the source of the FSA's supervisory powers until N2 (December 1, 2000), when the FSA assumed the wider powers conferred on it by FSMA 2000. 4–001

S.3 of the Banking Act 1987 generally made it a criminal offence for anyone otherwise than an authorised institution to accept a deposit in the United Kingdom in the course of carrying on a deposit-taking business. The prohibition did not, however, apply to persons falling within one of the exempt categories set out in Sch.2 to the Act. These included bodies regulated under other statutory regimes, such as building societies, friendly societies and authorised insurers. The prohibition was also qualified by the Banking Coordination (Second Council Directive) Regulations 1992 (SI 1992/3218) to take account of the "passport rights" enjoyed by other European institutions. The effect of the change was that, subject to complying with the necessary formalities, a European institution was free to carry on any "listed activity" in the United Kingdom if it was authorised or permitted to carry on that activity in its home state. A "listed activity" was an activity listed in the Annex to the Second Council Directive, the first item on the list being the acceptance of deposits from the public. 4–002

One of the main features of the 1987 Act was that it did away with the distinction between recognised banks and licensed deposit takers, which had existed under earlier legislation (the Banking Act 1979) and which allowed for less rigorous supervision of recognised banks. This was a factor in the failure in 1984 of Johnson Matthey Bank (a recognised bank), which was found to have substantially misreported large loans to selected customers. Investigations revealed that Johnson Matthey's assets were not sufficient to cover these loans. Before the news broke, the Bank of England felt impelled to take over the bank as a matter of urgency because it was considered that the failure of an institution which was then one of the five participants in the London bullion market could have undermined the stability of the whole banking system. Under the 1987 Act, the relaxed regime of supervision for recognised banks, which had allowed the position 4–003 at Johnson Matthey to remain undetected, was replaced by a unitary system of supervision for all authorised institutions.

4–004 Authorisation was the central feature of the system of regulation under the 1987 Act. The minimum criteria for authorisation were set out in Sch.3 the Act. These criteria were supplemented by a statement of principles, which the Bank of England (later the FSA) was required to publish under s.16 of the Act.

Sch.3 to the 1987 Act set out six criteria for authorisation. In summary, they were as follows:

(1) Every director, controller or manager of the institution had to be a fit and proper person to hold his position.

(2) There had to be at least two individuals effectively directing the institution's business.

(3) Where the institution was incorporated in the United Kingdom, the directors had to include such number of non-executive directors as the Bank of England (or later the FSA) considered appropriate.

(4) The business of the institution had to be conducted in a prudent manner. Among other things, this required the institution to:

- maintain its own funds and other capital resources at a level commensurate with the nature and scale of its operations and of an amount and nature sufficient to safeguard the interests of depositors;
- maintain its own funds at not less than five million ecus;
- maintain adequate liquidity;
- make adequate provision for depreciation or diminution in the value of its assets, including provision for bad or doubtful debts;
- maintain adequate accounting and other records of its business, and adequate systems of control of its business and records.

(5) The business of the institution had to be carried on with integrity and with the professional skills appropriate to the nature and scale of its activities.

(6) At the time of authorisation, the institution had to have initial capital amounting to not less than five million ecus.

Where an applicant for authorisation had its principal place of business outside the United Kingdom, the Bank of England (or later the FSA) had a discretion under s.9 of the Act to regard criteria (1), (4) and (5) as fulfilled if it was informed by the applicant's home supervisor that the supervisor was satisfied with respect to the prudent management and overall financial soundness of the applicant.

4–005 Although the above criteria were framed with reference to the grant of initial authorisation, they had a continuing role to play in the supervision of institutions to which authorisation had already been granted. The reason for that was that the Bank of England (or later the FSA) had power under ss.11 and 12 of the 1987 Act to revoke or restrict authorisation if it appeared to it that any of the criteria in Sch.3 had not been, or might not have been, fulfilled. There was a wide range of other cases in which authorisation might be revoked or restricted. These included cases where the institution had failed to comply with its obligations under the 1987 Act, and cases in which interests of depositors, or potential depositors, were threatened in any other way. The circumstances in which the powers could be exercised were extended between 1992 and 1996, by successive amendments to s.11 of the 1987 Act.

The definition of a "deposit-taking business" lay at the heart of the supervisory regime set up by the 1987 Act. The definition had many similarities to the way in which the activity of accepting deposits is now defined under FSMA 2000. The new definition is considered below.

The Position of Building Societies under the Old Regime

Until N2, building societies were supervised by the Building Societies Commission under the Building Societies Act 1986. With effect from N2, the function of supervising building societies passed to the FSA, so that both banks and building societies are now subject to the common regulatory regime established by FSMA 2000. **4–006**

Despite the common scheme of regulation which now applies to banks and building societies, building societies remain distinct from banks in being mutual institutions whose powers and purposes are subject to constraints imposed by the 1986 Act, as amended (in particular) by the Building Societies Act 1997.

Prior to the enactment of the 1986 Act, building societies were limited to the single statutory purpose of raising funds from their shareholding members (*i.e.* savers with share accounts in the society) for the purpose of making mortgage advances to their borrowing members. Societies had a small range of additional powers available to them by statute (*e.g.* to borrow and receive deposits from non-members), and such further powers as could fairly be regarded as reasonably incidental to their express statutory powers. **4–007**

The 1986 Act, and the statutory instruments made under it, conferred a greatly increased range of powers on building societies to carry on new activities, either on their own account or through "associated bodies" (normally, subsidiaries or other bodies in which the society had invested). The new powers included powers to engage in activities traditionally carried on by banks, such as the making of unsecured loans to individuals and the provision of credit and debit cards. However, it remained necessary for a society's principal purpose to be that of raising funds from shareholding members to lend on mortgage to its borrowing members, and that requirement was reinforced by various statutory limits on the composition of a society's balance sheet.

Despite the wider powers made available by the 1986 Act, it remained true to say that (in contrast, for example, to banks) building societies continued to be tied to a primary purpose defined by statute, and to a range **4–008** of specific powers conferred by the Act or by statutory instruments made under it. Any activity which went beyond what was expressly or impliedly permitted by the prescribed purpose and powers was *ultra vires* and prohibited. The restrictive nature of the statutory regime was one factor which led a number of the larger building societies to convert to banks during the 1980s and 1990s.

Following a review of the 1986 Act by the Treasury, the Government decided that the regime under which building societies operated was too restrictive, and needed to be liberalised. That objective was achieved by the enactment of the Building Societies Act 1997, which made extensive amendments to the 1986 Act.

4–009 The present position can be summarised as follows. The principal purpose of a building society continues to be defined by statute, though the 1997 Act has simplified the definition of that purpose so that it now refers to "making loans which are secured on residential property and are funded substantially by its members" (see s.5(1) of the 1986 Act, as amended). The 1997 Act has also replaced the complex balance sheet restrictions which applied under previous legislation by two limits, known respectively as the lending limit and the funding limit. The effect of the lending limit (imposed by the new s.6 of the 1986 Act) is that at least 75 per cent of the society's trading assets must be made up of loans which are fully secured on residential property. The effect of the funding limit (imposed by the new s.7) is that at least 50 per cent of the society's funds must be made up of investment shares in the society held by individuals. The combined effect of the redefined principal purpose and the two limits is to ensure that building societies will retain their traditional character as mutual institutions focused on retail savings and residential mortgage lending. Outside this core area, however, the 1997 Act greatly increased the freedom of societies to carry on other activities. Societies are now free to carry on any additional activities specified in its memorandum, with the exception of a small number of financial transactions which are excluded by the new s.9A (*e.g.* acting as a market maker in securities). It can be seen, therefore, that the 1997 Act has moved societies from a regime under which everything was prohibited unless expressly permitted to one under which everything is permitted unless expressly prohibited.

4–010 Turning now to the regulation of building societies, the position under the 1986 Act was that the function of supervising building societies was entrusted to the Building Societies Commission, a new regulatory body which enjoyed wider and more sophisticated powers than those exercisable by the former regulator (the Registry of Friendly Societies). S.9 of the 1986 Act provided that, with limited exceptions, it was a criminal offence for a building society to raise money from members or to accept deposits of money unless the society had been authorised by the Commission, or was treated as so authorised because it had received authorisation under the previous regime (established by the Building Societies (Authorisation) Regulations 1981 (SI 1989/1488)). In its original form, s.9 required the Commission to grant unconditional authorisation if it was satisfied of the following:

(1) The society had qualifying capital of not less than £100,000 (increased in 1992 to 1 million ecus).

(2) The chairman, executive directors, chief executive, secretary and managers were each fit and proper persons to hold their respective positions in the society.

(3) The directors, with the chief executive and secretary, had the capacity and intention to direct the society's affairs in accordance with the "criteria of prudent management" (as to which, see below).

(4) The investments of shareholders and depositors would be adequately safeguarded without the imposition of conditions on the society's authorisation.

The Commission had power under ss.42 and 43 of the 1986 Act to **4–011**
impose conditions on a society's authorisation, or to revoke its authorisation, if it considered it expedient to do so in order to protect the investments of the society's shareholders and depositors. For these purposes, s.45(1) provided that the Commission would be entitled to assume that a failure to satisfy the criteria of prudent management would prejudice the security of the investments of shareholders or depositors.

The criteria of prudent management therefore lay at the heart of the **4–012**
system of prudential supervision set up by the 1986 Act. As amended by the 1997 Act, s.45(3) of the 1986 Act specified eight criteria of prudent management, the majority of which performed a similar role to the criteria for authorisation for banks set out in Sch.3 to the Banking Act 1987. In summary, the eight criteria were as follows:

(1) Compliance with the principal purpose, the lending limit and the funding limit mentioned above.

(2) Maintenance of adequate reserves and capital resources, and maintenance of own funds of at least one million ecus.

(3) Maintenance of adequate assets in liquid form.

(4) Maintenance of a system for managing and containing risks to the net worth of the business and risks to its net income, whether arising from fluctuations in exchange rates or from other factors.

(5) Maintenance of suitable arrangements for assessing the adequacy of the security for mortgage loans and the borrower's willingness and ability to repay the loan.

(6) Maintenance of suitable accounting records and systems for the control of its business and for inspecting and reporting on those systems.

(7) Direction and management by a sufficient number of persons who were fit and proper to be directors or officers of the society, such direction and management being carried out by them with prudence and integrity.

(8) Conduct of the business with adequate professional skills.

These criteria were fleshed out by detailed prudential notes issued by the Commission.

The Transition to FSMA 2000

4–013 As we have seen in Ch.2, the effect of the general prohibition imposed by s.19 of FSMA 2000 is that no person may carry on a regulated activity in the United Kingdom, or purport to do so, unless he is an authorised person or an exempt person. Many of the activities carried on by banks and building societies are activities which are now regulated by FSMA 2000 (the most obvious example being the acceptance of deposits). To ensure that banks and building societies authorised under the previous legislation could lawfully continue those parts of their businesses which involve the carrying on of regulated activities, the Financial Services and Markets Act 2000 (Transitional Provisions) (Authorised Persons, etc.) Order 2001 (SI 2001/2636) provided as follows:

(1) Any institution which was authorised under s.9 of the Banking Act 1987 immediately before N2 (*i.e.* December 1, 2001, being the date on which s.19 of FSMA 2000 came into force) was to be treated as having permission under Pt IV of the FSMA 2000 to carry on any regulated activities which, by reason of such authorisation, it was able to carry on in the United Kingdom without contravening s.3 of the 1987 Act (art.11(1)).

(2) A building society which was authorised for the purposes of the Building Societies Act 1986 immediately before N2 was, similarly, to be treated as having a Pt IV permission to carry on any regulated activities which, by reason of such authorisation, it was able to carry on in the United Kingdom without contravening s.9(1) of the 1986 Act (art.22(1)).

Further provisions were included in the Order to extend the scope of the Pt IV permission to enable banks and building societies to carry on activities which they were lawfully carrying on prior to N2, but which were not directly covered by their authorisation under the previous legislation (*e.g.* deposit-taking businesses being carried on overseas).

Authorisation under the Current Regime

Acceptance of Deposits by Way of Business

4–014 Banks and building societies are likely to carry on a number of different activities which are regulated under FSMA 2000. The acceptance of deposits is, however, one form of regulated activity which is central to the businesses of both types of institution. We shall therefore begin our consideration of the current position of banks and building societies by looking at the way in which FSMA 2000 deals with the acceptance of deposits.

The activity of accepting deposits is "specified" by art.5 of the Financial Services and Markets Act 2000 (Regulated Activities) Order 2001 (SI

2001/544) (the RAO 2001). That has the consequence that, under s.22(1) of FSMA 2000, the activity will be regulated if it is carried on by way of business.

In more detail, art.5(1) of the RAO 2001 provides that accepting deposits is a specified kind of activity if: **4–015**

> "(a) money received by way of deposit is lent to others; or
> (b) any other activity of the person accepting the deposit is financed wholly, or to a material extent, out of the capital of or interest on money received by way of deposit."

Art.5(2) goes on to provide that, with certain exceptions, "deposit" means a sum of money paid on terms "under which it will be repaid, with or without interest or premium, and either on demand or at a time or in circumstances agreed by or on behalf of the person making the payment and the person receiving it". However, the effect of art.5(2)(b) is that a payment will not fall within the definition of "deposit" if it is made on terms which are "referable to the provision of property (other than currency) or services or the giving of security". That means, in summary, that a payment will not be a "deposit" if it is a contractual advance payment or part payment, which is repayable if there is a failure to provide property or services under the contract; or if is paid by way of security for the performance of a contract, or to cover loss caused by the non-performance of a contract (art.5(3)).

As noted above, an activity cannot constitute a regulated activity under s.22(1) unless, in addition to being "specified", it is "carried on by way of business". The latter requirement is amplified by the Financial Services and Markets Act 2000 (Carrying on Regulated Activities by Way of Business) Order 2001 (SI 2001/1177) (CRAWBO 2001). Art.2(1) of that Order provides that a person who carries on the activity of accepting deposits is not to be regarded as doing so by way of business if — **4–016**

> "(a) he does not hold himself out as accepting deposits on a day to day basis; and
> (b) any deposits which he accepts are accepted only on particular occasions, whether or not involving the issue of any securities."

Art.2(2) elaborates art.2(1)(b) by providing that, in determining whether deposits are accepted only on particular occasions, regard is to be had to the frequency of those occasions and to any characteristics distinguishing them from each other.

Some assistance in applying these provisions can be gained from the Court of Appeal's decision in *SCF Finance Co. Ltd v Masri (No. 2)* [1987] 1 All E.R. 175, although it is important to bear in mind that that case was dealing with the meaning of the expressions "deposit" and "deposit taking business" in s.1(3) of the Banking Act 1979. While s.1(3) was in similar terms to art.2(1) of CRAWBO 2001, the 1979 Act did not elaborate the concept of accepting deposits "on particular occasions" in the way that art.2(2) now does. **4–017**

4–018 The facts of the case were that SCF carried on business as licensed brokers in commodity and financial futures. They held themselves out as willing to deal in the market on a client's behalf and for this purpose required clients to place funds with them to cover the transaction as well as "margins" to cover the risk of loss on the transactions. The margins proved inadequate in Masri's case and SCF incurred substantial losses in the course of trading on his behalf. Masri failed to settle his account and SCF brought an action against him for the amount due. Masri argued that this agreement with SCF contravened the prohibition in the 1979 Act on the acceptance of "deposits" in the course of an unauthorised "deposit taking business". Accordingly, he claimed that the transactions were illegal and that SCF was not entitled to sue him on the agreements. Masri's arguments were rejected both at first instance and in the Court of Appeal. The Court of Appeal considered the meaning of "deposit" and "deposit taking business". On the first question, the court held that the amounts paid by Masri had been paid by way of security for payment for the provision of property or services to be provided by SCF and were thus not deposits for the purposes of the 1979 Act: the decision on this point would no doubt go the same way under art.5(2)(b) and (3) of the RAO 2001. On the meaning of "deposit-taking business", the Court of Appeal held that:

> "in our judgment, on the ordinary meaning of the words, a person 'holds himself out to accept deposits on a day-to-day basis' only if (by way of an express or implicit invitation) he holds himself out as being generally willing on any normal working day to accept such deposits from those persons to whom the invitation is addressed who may wish to place moneys with him by way of deposit" (*per* Slade L.J. at 190).

4–019 The Court of Appeal held that a request by SCF for specific payments to be made by a client did not come within this concept. No doubt that part of the decision would also go the same way under art.2(1)(a) of CRAWBO 2001. On the question whether SCF accepted deposits "on particular occasions", the Court of Appeal said:

> "The particular occasions will be those occasions on which SCF find it necessary or advisable for their own protection to demand deposits, having regard to the course of the trading carried out and to be carried out by them in accordance with their clients' instructions. The mere fact that these occasions may be numerous does not render them any less 'particular' within the meaning of s.1(3)(b)."

It is less clear that this point would be decided in the same way under CRAWBO 2001, since art.2(3) expressly emphasises the need to have regard to the frequency of the occasions on which deposits are accepted. As against that, however, art.2(3) also requires one to have regard to any characteristics distinguishing the occasions from one another. So the more the characteristics of each occasion can be distinguished from one another, the less significant will be the fact that the occasions are frequent.

Obtaining Authorisation: General

4–020 If a person carries on the activity of accepting deposits by way of business within the meaning of the above provisions, then the activity (if carried on in the United Kingdom) will be a regulated activity for the purposes of s.22(1) of FSMA 2000. It follows that, to avoid placing himself in breach of the general prohibition in s.19(1), the person must either be an authorised person or an exempt person.

A bank or building society which accepts deposits within the United Kingdom will almost invariably do so by way of business. It will thus need to be authorised or exempt in order to avoid infringing the general prohibition.

The general rule is that an agreement made by a person in the course of carrying on a regulated activity in contravention of the general prohibition is unenforceable against the other party (FSMA 2000, s.26(1)). The general rule is, however, excluded in cases where the regulated activity is accepting deposits (s.26(4)). In such a case, the depositor has the right to apply to the court for an order for the return of the money deposited by him, unless he is already entitled to its immediate return under his agreement with the deposit-taker (as he would be if the deposit were credited to a current account, or instant-access savings account). The court has a discretion not to make such an order if it is satisfied that it would not be just and equitable for the money to be returned, having regard to the issue whether the deposit-taker reasonably believed that he was not contravening the general prohibition by making the agreement (s.29). **4–021**

Obtaining Authorisation: Banks

There are two routes by which a bank may become authorised. **4–022**

The first will apply if the bank has its head office in the United Kingdom. In such a case, authorisation will depend on the bank's obtaining permission from the FSA under Pt IV of FSMA 2000 to accept deposits and to carry on any other regulated activities falling within the scope of its business (or alternatively on its being treated as having the necessary permission under the transitional provisions noted above). In giving permission, the FSA will need to ensure that the person concerned will satisfy, and continue to satisfy, the threshold conditions in Sch.6 to the FSMA 2000 in relation to all of the regulated activities for which he will have permission (FSMA 2000, s.41(2)). The threshold conditions apply generally to applicants for permission, and have already been considered in Ch.2. It should, however, be noted that an applicant for permission to accept deposits will need to be either a body corporate or a partnership (Sch.6, para.1(2)). The procedure for obtaining permission from the FSA is set out in the Authorisation Manual. This, too, is of general application, and is discussed in Ch.2.

Secondly, a bank may be an EEA firm, which qualifies for authorisation by virtue of its single market "passport". Sch.3 to FSMA 2000 gives effect to these passport rights. The purpose of these provisions is to ensure that a firm which is authorised in another EEA state may set up branches or provide services in the United Kingdom without the need to obtain fresh authorisation from the FSA. In the present context, the relevant type of EEA firm will be a credit institution which does not have its head office in the United Kingdom and is authorised by the competent authority of **4–023** another EEA state (its "home state regulator"). Sch.3 lays down different procedural requirements for cases in which an EEA firm wishes to establish a branch in the United Kingdom (para.13) and for cases in which such a firm merely wishes to provide services here (para.14):

(1) In the first type of case, the FSA must receive a notice (called a "consent notice") from the home state regulator giving its consent to the firm establishing a branch in the UK. The FSA then has two months in which to inform the firm of any "applicable provision"—these being any rules which the firm must comply with when carrying on the activities identified in the consent notice through a branch in the United Kingdom. Once these requirements have been met, the firm will have permission to carry on, through its United Kingdom branch, each activity described in the consent notice which is regulated activity under FSMA 2000 (para.15).

(2) In the second type of case (where the firm is seeking to provide cross-border services), the institution does not require consent from its home state regulator, but merely has to give that regulator a notice (called a "notice of intention") stating its intention to provide services in the United Kingdom. As before, the FSA then has two months in which to notify the firm of any "applicable provisions". The firm will then have permission to provide, in the United Kingdom, each of the services described in its notice of intention which is a regulated activity under FSMA 2000.

4–024 It should be noted that an EEA firm which qualifies for authorisation will still need to apply to the FSA for a Part IV permission (referred to in the *FSA Handbook* as a "top-up permission") if it wishes to carry on any regulated activity which falls outside the scope of its "passport" rights. This situation could arise either because the regulated activity is not covered by the single market directives, or because the activity is not covered by the firm's home state authorisation (see AUTH 5.7.1G).

Obtaining Authorisation: Building Societies

4–025 A building society must be established under the Building Societies Act 1986, and must have its principal office in the United Kingdom (see s.5(1) of the 1986 Act). It follows that the only route by which a building society may become authorised is by obtaining (or by being treated under the relevant transitional provisions as having obtained) a Pt IV permission which covers the acceptance of deposits and any other regulated activities which fall within the scope of the society's business.

It should be noted that building societies may accept funds from investors in the form of subscriptions for shares, as well as in the form of ordinary deposits. There is, however, no doubt that money subscribed for shares in a building society (other than deferred shares) constitutes a "deposit" within the meaning of art.5(2) of the RAO 2001, since, unlike shares in a company, they are withdrawable by the investor. A building society which accepts money for investment in a share account will, therefore, be carrying on a regulated activity and will require authorisation to do so.

Accepting Deposits by Exempt Persons

The general prohibition in s.19 of FSMA 2000 prevents a person carrying on a regulated activity in the United Kingdom unless he is *either* an authorised person *or* an exempt person. It follows that an exempt person is free to accept deposits in the United Kingdom by way of business, even though he is not authorised to do so. **4–026**

A person who carries on a regulated activity as principal will only be an exempt person if an exemption order made under s.38(1) of FSMA 2000 exempts him from the general prohibition in relation to that activity (s.417(1)). The exemption order currently in force is the Financial Services and Markets Act 2000 (Exemption) Order 2001 (SI 2001/1201) (the Exemption Order).

Pt I of the Schedule to the Exemption Order contains a list of bodies which are exempt in relation to any regulated activity (other than effecting and carrying out contracts of insurance). These bodies include the Bank of England, the other central banks of the EEA states, the European Central Bank, the European Community, the IMF and a number of overseas development banks. **4–027**

Pt II of the Schedule lists various categories of bodies which are exempt from the general prohibition specifically in relation to the acceptance of deposits. These include:

(1) a municipal bank (*i.e.* a bank whose shares are held by members of a local authority and whose funds are lent to, and whose deposits are guaranteed by, that authority: see s.103 of the Banking Act 1987);

(2) a school bank certified by the National Savings Bank or by an authorised person which has permission to accept deposits;

(3) a local authority;

(4) a body which has a statutory power to issue a precept to a local authority;

(5) a charity, but only insofar as it accepts deposits (a) from another charity or (b) in respect of which no interest or premium is payable; and

(6) an industrial and provident society, insofar as it accepts deposits in the form of withdrawable share capital.

Prudential Standards for Banks

The FSA's detailed prudential standards for banks are set out in the Interim Prudential Sourcebook for Banks (IPRU (BANK)). As its name suggests, the sourcebook has been prepared on an interim basis, pending **4–028** the transition to an Integrated Prudential Sourcebook (to be known as PSB), which will apply to all firms regulated by the FSA. The Integrated Prudential Sourcebook is currently expected to be introduced in stages, between 2004 and 2006.

4–029 The prudential standards set out in IPRU (BANK) reflect the fact that the nature of a bank's business exposes it to a range of risks, including credit, market, liquidity and operational risks. Against that background, the FSA has explained (in IPRU (BANK) Chapter GN, s.2.4) that the purpose of the prudential standards is:

> "to ensure that banks maintain capital resources commensurate with their risks and appropriate systems and controls to enable them to manage those risks. The FSA requires in particular that banks maintain adequate capital against their risks: capital enables banks to absorb losses without endangering customer deposits; that they maintain adequate liquidity; and that they identify and control their large credit exposures — which might otherwise be a source of loss to a bank to a bank on a scale that might threaten a bank's solvency."

4–030 The essential elements of the prudential scheme are set out in the form of rules in s.3 of the first chapter of IPRU (BANK) (known as "Chapter GN"). A number of the rules are elaborated by detailed guidance in the following chapters of the Sourcebook.

Most of the material in IPRU (BANK) applies only to UK banks (*i.e.* banks formed under the law of any part of the United Kingdom). However, the rules in s.3 of Chapter GN also apply to overseas banks (*i.e.* banks formed under the law of a country or territory outside the EEA) and the rules and guidance on liquidity also apply to EEA banks (*i.e.* EEA credit institutions exercising their "passport" rights to establish a branch or provide services within the United Kingdom).

Unless otherwise stated, references in the following summary are to s.3 of Chapter GN of IPRU (BANK).

Four Eyes

4–031 The first rule (in 3.3.1R) provides that a UK bank and an overseas bank must ensure that at least two individuals effectively direct its business (3.3.1R). This rule reflects the requirement in art.6(1) of the Banking Consolidation Directive.

The object of the rule is to ensure that at least two independent minds are being applied to both the formulation and implementation of the bank's policies. In a case where only two individuals are nominated to direct a bank's business, the FSA will expect each to play a part in the decision-making process on all significant decisions affecting the business. In a case where the business is directed by more than two individuals, there must still be at least two individuals who are involved in all decisions affecting the strategy and general direction of the business.

Capital Requirements

4–032 The bare bones of the capital requirements for UK banks and overseas banks are set out in the next set of rules in s.3. These rules are to the following effect:

(1) The bank must have initial capital amounting to at least five million euros when it obtains a Pt IV permission to carry on regulated activities which include accepting deposits (3.3.9R).

(2) The general rule is that the bank must maintain own funds which amount to at least five million euros (3.3.11R). The general rule is, however, relaxed in the case of a UK bank which was authorised under the Banking Act 1987 immediately before January 1, 1993. Such a bank is required to maintain the own funds which it had on January 1, 1993, or at any higher amount (not exceeding five million euros) at which its own funds have stood at any time since January 1, 1993. If, however, there is a change in the bank's parent undertaking, then the requirement for own funds of five million euro will apply in place of any requirement for own funds of a lesser amount which applied until then (3.3.12R.).

(3) The bank must maintain capital resources which are commensurate with the nature and scale of its business and the risks inherent in that business. If the bank is a member of a group, its capital resources must also be commensurate with the risks inherent in the activities of other members of the group insofar as those risks affect the bank (3.3.13R).

The last of these rules is elaborated in detailed guidance contained in no **4–033**
less than fifteen of the later chapters of IPRU (BANK). Ch.CO is particularly useful in giving an overview of the underlying policy. As is apparent from that chapter, the FSA assesses the adequacy of a bank's capital by using a framework derived from the Basel Accord 1998. There are three main elements to the framework:

(a) The first element defines the characteristics which an instrument must have in order to qualify as capital. For these purposes (as explained in Ch.CA), capital is divided into three tiers, according to the ability of each type of instrument to absorb losses without affecting the interests of depositors, and to provide the bank with a cheap and flexible funding source on which the bank can draw in times of difficulty. In summary, the three tiers are as follows:

   (i) *Tier 1.* This forms the bank's core capital. It is perpetual and its returns are non-cumulative. It may be issued (as with share capital) or internally generated (as where retained profits are added to the bank's reserves or dividends are capitalised).

   (ii) *Tier 2.* This is split into upper and lower tiers.
   Upper Tier 2 capital is perpetual, but is generally cumulative. It may be issued (as with perpetual subordinated debt and cumulative preference shares) or internally generated (as with general provisions and reserves arising from the revaluation of certain fixed assets).
   Lower Tier 2 capital consists of term subordinated debt with a minimum original maturity of over five years.

   (iii) *Tier 3.* This consists of short-term subordinated debt, having a minimum maturity of over two years. It may only be used to support market risk in a bank's trading book, and is thus only of relevance to banks which have a trading book (such banks being subject to the requirements of the Capital Adequacy Directive).

(b) The second element in the framework is to weight the risks associated with different categories of asset held by the bank and the activities in which it engages. This enables a bank to hold less capital backing for assets with lower risk weights than for those with higher risk weights. This element in the framework will produce a notional weighted risk asset figure for the bank's risk. The level of capital which the bank should maintain can then be calculated by multiplying this figure by the trigger or target ratio described in (c) below.

(c) The third element in the framework comprises the trigger and target capital ratios which the FSA sets for the bank. The "trigger ratio" is the minimum capital ratio which the FSA considers the bank should maintain. A failure to meet this ratio will be a serious matter and will act as the trigger for an obligation on the bank to notify the FSA of the fact immediately. The absolute minimum trigger ratio which the FSA considers to be appropriate is the figure of eight per cent, set out in the Banking Consolidation Directive. In practice, however, the FSA expects banks to work to a trigger ratio significantly above that level. The FSA sets the "target ratio" some way above the trigger ratio. A failure to meet the target ratio acts a warning light that the cushion of capital resources normally considered adequate to prevent an accidental breach of the trigger ratio is being eroded.

Liquidity

4–034 The next rule in s.3 (3.3.15R) deals with liquidity. It provides that a bank must maintain adequate liquidity, taking into account the nature and scale of its business so that it is able to meet its obligations as they fall due. This rule applies not only to UK banks and overseas banks, but also to any UK branch of an EEA bank. It should be noted that, in the case of UK banks and overseas banks, the policy on the management of the bank's liquidity must be set out in a written policy statement. The policy in the statement must be such that compliance with it will enable the bank to maintain adequate liquidity in conformity with 3.3.15R (3.4.3R).

Guidance on the above rules is given in Chs LM and LS of IPRU (BANK). Ch. LM contains a helpful outline of the rationale underlying the treatment of liquidity. The reason why liquidity gives rise to prudential concerns is that banks typically use short-term deposits to make comparatively long-term loans. This so-called maturity transformation exposes the bank to the risk that depositors' demands for repayment might outstrip its ability to transform assets into cash. The bank therefore needs to maintain a prudent liquidity policy in order to ensure that it has adequate funding capacity to enable it to meet its obligations as they fall due. It is essential that the bank should be able to do that if confidence in it is to be maintained.

Adequate Provisions

A UK bank and an overseas bank must maintain adequate provisions for the depreciation or diminution in value of its assets (including provisions for bad and doubtful debts), for liabilities which will or may fall to be met by it and for losses which it may incur (3.3.17R). The bank must set out its policy on provisioning in a written policy statement. The policy in the statement must be such that compliance with it will enable the bank to comply with 3.3.17R, except that an overseas bank need only cover such provisions as are made in the accounts of its operations in the United Kingdom (3.4.5R). **4–035**

Guidance on the above rules is given in Ch.PN of IPRU (BANK). The FSA there states that it regards the prudent valuation of assets and the establishment of provisions as being of fundamental importance, and that it expects contingent liabilities and anticipated losses to be recognised in accordance with accepted accounting standards.

Large Exposures

The next set of rules relate to large exposures—an "exposure" being the maximum loss which a bank might suffer if (a) a counterparty or group of closely related counterparties fails to meet its obligations or (b) the bank realises assets or off-balance sheet positions. **4–036**

A UK bank and an overseas bank must have adequate systems and controls to enable it (a) to monitor and control its large exposures in conformity with its policy statement on large exposures (as to which, see below) and (b) to calculate its large exposures accurately and promptly (3.3.19R). A UK bank is also required to notify the FSA if it proposes to enter into a transaction or transactions which would result in its having an exposure which exceeds 25 per cent of its capital (3.3.21R). The bank's policy on large exposures must be set out in a written policy statement, covering how the bank controls its exposures to ensure compliance with its large exposure limits and the reporting of its large exposures to the FSA (3.4.1R).

Guidance on the above rules is given in Chs LE and TL of IPRU (BANK). Ch.LE explains that excessive exposure to a single customer, or to a group of customers operating in the same economic sector, is a significant risk incurred by banks. While the risk cannot be eliminated, it can be contained by ensuring that the bank's exposure is diversified, *e.g.* by customer, geographical spread or economic sector. The FSA states that, for this reason, safeguarding against excessive concentration is one of the most important components of any system of supervision for banks. The FSA's policy builds on the limits initially introduced by the Large Exposures Directive, which is now consolidated into the Banking Consolidation Directive.

Audit

4–037 A UK bank and an overseas bank should have an internal audit function, which may either be in-house or outsourced to a third party (3.3.23E). This is an evidential provision (as opposed to a rule), whose contravention may be relied on as tending to establish a breach of SYSC 2.1.1R (which requires firms to take reasonable care to maintain a clear and appropriate apportionment of significant responsibilities among its directors and senior managers).

A UK bank should have an audit committee, which should either be chaired by a non-executive director of the bank, or be an audit committee of non-executive directors of the bank's holding company. This, too, is an evidential provision. Its contravention may be relied on as tending to establish a breach of SYSC 3.1.1R (which requires a firm to take reasonable care to maintain systems and controls appropriate to its business).

Guidance on these two evidential provisions is given in Ch.AR of IPRU (BANK). The purpose of internal audit is to provide independent assurance over the integrity and effectiveness of the bank's systems for the control of its business. The position of head of internal audit should be a key role within the bank, to be undertaken by an experienced and skilled individual who will normally be expected to report to the chief executive officer and to have access to the bank's audit committee through its non-executive chairman.

Prudential Standards for Building Societies

4–038 The FSA's detailed prudential standards for building societies are set out in the Interim Prudential Sourcebook for Building Societies (IPRU (BSOC)). Like the equivalent sourcebook for banks, it will in due course be replaced by the Integrated Prudential Sourcebook (PSB) which will apply to all firms regulated by the FSA.

4–039 Like the high street banks, building societies provide deposit and savings accounts to members of the public. It is not surprising to find, therefore, that many of the prudential issues covered by IPRU (BANK) are also dealt with by IPRU (BSOC). However, IPRU (BSOC) differs from its banking counterpart in including material which reflects:

(1) the different constitutional structure of building societies—notably, the fact that their principal purpose is limited by statute to that of making loans which are secured on residential property and are funded substantially by its members, and that they are subject to statutory lending and funding limits designed to ensure compliance with that purpose;

(2) the consequent need to set prudential standards relating to societies' core activity of mortgage lending;

(3) the different capital structure of building societies—notably, the fact that they are not able to issue equity shares and that an ordinary

share in a building society (while conferring membership and voting rights on the holder) is withdrawable and thus has the economic characteristics of a deposit rather than permanent capital;

(4) the special responsibilities which the mutual nature of building societies imposes on their boards and management; and

(5) the special statutory provisions governing building society mergers and transfers of business, which have no counterpart for banks.

In contrast to IPRU (BANK), the rules which apply to building societies are not collected together at the beginning of IPRU (BSOC), but are included in the chapters containing the subject-matter to which the rules are relevant. Unless otherwise stated, references in the following summary are to paragraphs in IPRU (BSOC).

Capital Requirements

Ch.1 of IPRU (BSOC) (Solvency) provides that a society must maintain **4–040** own funds of at least £1 million (1.2.2R). It will be noted that this figure is lower than the limit of five million euros which normally applies to banks: in specifying the limit for building societies, the UK has taken advantage of the option allowed to member states by art.5(1) of the Banking Consolidation Directive to grant authorisation to particular categories of credit institutions with initial capital of at least one million euros.

As indicated above, a building society's capital will not include the ordinary shares which it issues to investing members. Its own funds will comprise the following tier 1 and tier 2 capital resources:

(1) *Tier 1.* This tier consists primarily of the reserves which the society has accumulated out of retained profits. The other principal source of tier 1 capital is a form of deferred shares known as permanent interest bearing shares (PIBS). As their name suggests, these are perpetual instruments which offer a (non-cumulative) return in the form of interest.

(2) *Tier 2.* This tier includes subordinated debt, which may either be undated (*i.e.* permanent) or issued for an initial term of more than five years. Interest on subordinated debt may be cumulative. Tier 2 capital also includes a society's general provisions for bad debts and revaluation reserves.

Ch.1 also provides that a society must maintain adequate capital **4–041** resources commensurate with the nature and scale of its business and the risks inherent in its business. If the society has subsidiaries, it must also maintain capital resources commensurate with the scale and nature of the activities of the whole group (1.2.1R).

The FSA will notify each society of a "threshold ratio" which it is expected to maintain. This will be based on the FSA's assessment of the society's risk profile, and will be set so as to provide against the risk of a society inadvertently breaching the minimum solvency ratio of eight per cent set out in the Banking Consolidation Directive. It is the society's responsibility to ensure that it has sufficient capital at all times to avoid breaching its threshold ratio (Ch.1, s.5).

As for banks, a society's assets must be weighted for risk before its solvency ratio can be calculated. The ratio can then be worked out by expressing the society's own funds as a percentage of the sum of its risk weighted assets. Each society's solvency ratio can then be monitored against the threshold ratio set by the FSA and the eight per cent minimum which applies under the Banking Consolidation Directive.

Financial Risk Management

4–042 The core business of building societies involves the use of short-term personal savings to fund long-term residential mortgages. This subjects building societies to an even higher degree of maturity transformation than typically applies to banks. Ch.4 of IPRU (BSOC) contains rules and guidance for the management of the risks created by this feature of the business. The essential requirement is that each society must have an adequate system for managing and containing financial risks to the net worth of its business, and risks to its net income, whether arising from fluctuations in interest or exchange rates or from other factors (4.2.1R). The society must maintain, and submit to the FSA, a board-approved policy statement on financial risk management (4.2.5R).

Liquidity

4–043 Liquidity is dealt with in Ch.5 of IPRU (BSOC). The basic requirement is that each society must maintain adequate liquid resources, including prudential liquidity, appropriate to the scale and nature of its business to enable it to meet its obligations as they fall due (5.2.1R). The expression "prudential liquidity" refers to cash and bank deposits, together with instruments and other assets that are marketable or have three months or less to run to maturity. The society must maintain, and submit to the FSA, a board-approved policy on liquidity (5.2.7R).

The rule stated in para.5.2.1 is coupled with an evidential provision that a society should keep an amount equal to at least 3.5 per cent of its share and deposit liabilities in the form of eight day liquidity (*i.e.* cash, current account balances and other assets which can be realised within eight days). Contravention of this requirement may be relied upon as tending to establish a breach of 5.2.1R. (See 5.2.4E.)

The need for a society to maintain an appropriate amount and mix of liquid resources stems, once again, from the mismatch between the long-term nature of its mortgage lending and the short-term nature of the savings products which are the primary source of funds for that lending. Adequate liquidity is essential to ensure that the society can meet the full range of its liabilities as they fall due, and thereby maintain the confidence of the investing public.

Lending

As we have seen, at least 75 per cent of a society's trading assets must be made up of loans fully secured on residential property. The crucial importance of mortgage lending to a society's business is reflected in Ch.6 of IPRU (BSOC), which contains rules and guidance relating to the risks associated with lending, including, in particular, the risk that the security will prove to be inadequate for the money lent, and the risk that the borrower will be unable to meet his personal liability to repay the loan. **4–044**

The principal requirement imposed by Ch.6 is that each society must have adequate systems for managing and controlling risk arising from lending, including systems for assessing both the adequacy of security for loans and the ability and willingness of borrowers to repay their loans (6.2.1R). The society is required to maintain, and submit to the FSA, a board-approved policy statement on lending, which must include plans for management of arrears, and the procedures for making specific and general provisions against impaired loans (6.2.2R).

Ch.8 of IPRU (BSOC) lays down further requirements for cases in which a society undertakes new lending with a loan-to-value ratio of more than 80 per cent. Societies must have an adequate policy in place to provide protection against the greater risks arising from this type of lending (8.2.1R). This may include the provision of mortgage indemnity cover, either through an outside insurer or through a "captive" mortgage indemnity insurer.

Large Exposures

The risks to building societies arising from large exposures are similar to those faced by banks. For building societies, the topic is dealt with in Ch.7 of IPRU (BSOC). The essential requirements are that each society must: **4–045**

(1) give prior notification to the FSA before committing itself to a new exposure which will exceed 20 per cent of own funds, or will exceed that figure when added to any existing exposure to the same counterparty or group of connected counterparties (7.6.2R);

(2) report exposures of between 10 and 20 per cent of own funds to the FSA on a quarterly basis (7.6.3R);

(3) maintain adequate systems and controls which will enable it to monitor and control its large exposures in accordance with its large exposures policy and must make timely and accurate reports to the FSA on its large exposures (7.7.1R); and

(4) set out its policy on large exposures as part of its policy statements on financial risk management, liquidity and lending (7.7.3R).

Systems and Audit

Ch.9 of IPRU (BSOC) contains rules and guidance on societies' systems of business control and accounting records, as well as evidential provisions relating to the audit function. **4–046**

The basic requirement relating to a society's systems is that the society must have a fully-documented system of control (9.2.1R). The society's systems should enable its directors to control the conduct of its business and its accounting and other records. The requirement for the systems to be fully-documented means that the documents setting out the systems should be available to the board at all times. It should also be noted that a society is also required to maintain, and submit to the FSA, a board-approved corporate plan (9.2.7R).

As with banks, a building society should have an internal audit function, which may either be in-house or outsourced to a third party (9.2.3E). A society should also establish an audit committee consisting of at least three members who are also non-executive directors (9.2.5E). These are evidential provisions, whose contravention may be relied upon as tending to establish a contravention of the society's obligation under SYSC 3.1.1R to take reasonable care to establish and maintain such systems and controls as are appropriate to its business.

Enforcement

4–047 The techniques available to the FSA for enforcing compliance with the threshold conditions and the prudential standards in IPRU (BANK) and IPRU (BSOC) are those which apply generally to the enforcement of the obligations imposed by FSMA 2000 and the rules made under it. They are therefore considered as part of the discussion of enforcement and sanctions in Ch.15.

The FSA's Own-initiative Power to Vary or Cancel a Pt IV Permission

4–048 In the present context, it is sufficient to draw attention to the FSA's power under s.45 of FSMA 2000 to vary or cancel an authorised person's Pt IV permission on its own initiative. This power is referred to as the own-initiative power, to distinguish it from the FSA's comparable power under s.44 to vary a permission on the application of the authorised person.

The own-initiative power may be exercised in a number of circumstances which could be relevant to the enforcement of the regulatory requirements imposed on banks and building societies. These include cases in which it appears to the FSA that an authorised person is failing, or likely to fail, to satisfy the threshold conditions in Sch.6 to FSMA 2000. They also include cases in which it appears to the FSA to be desirable to exercise the power in order to protect the interests of consumers or potential consumers. The power may also be exercised at the request of, or for the purpose of assisting, a regulator who is outside the United Kingdom and exercises a function corresponding to any function of the FSA (see FSMA 2000, s.47 and the Financial Services and Markets Act 2000 (Own-initiative Power) (Overseas Regulators) Regulations 2001 (SI 2001/2639)).

As noted, the power enables the FSA either to cancel or vary a permission. Cancellation speaks for itself. The variation of a permission covers (among other things) the removal of a regulated activity from those covered by the permission (s.44(1)(a)), and the inclusion of any provision that could be included on the grant of a fresh permission under s.40, *e.g.* the incorporation of a limitation in the description of the permission under s.42(7), or the imposition of a requirement under s.43 (see s.45(4)). **4–049**

Guidance on the FSA's policy for the exercise of its power to vary or cancel a permission is given in the *FSA Handbook*, at ENF 3.5 and 5.5 respectively. **4–050**

As regards the use of the own-initiative power to vary a permission, the FSA will proceed on the basis that the authorised person itself is primarily responsible for ensuring that it conducts its business in compliance with the Act, the Principles and the rules. The FSA may therefore make clear to that person that it expects certain steps to be taken, and envisages that normally that will take place without the need for any formal exercise of its powers. Formal exercise will be considered if the informal route does not succeed, and the FSA may take into account the fact that a formal requirement may assist the person to take steps which might otherwise be difficult because of legal obligations owed to third parties. Examples of circumstances in which the FSA might have concerns serious enough to warrant the variation of an authorised person's permission, but not such as to suggest that the permission should be cancelled include: apparent inadequacy of resources; failure to conduct its business in accordance with high standards; lack of competent and prudent management; and breaches of requirements under the Act, the Principles or the rules which are material in number or individual seriousness.

The use of the own-initiative power to cancel a permission will be considered where the FSA has very serious concerns about a firm or the way its business is being conducted, or where the firm's regulated activities have come to an end but it has not applied for cancellation of its permission. It should be noted that, under s.54 of FSMA 2000, permission may not be cancelled with immediate effect. Where the matter is serious and urgent, therefore, the FSA may first vary the authorised person's permission so that there is no longer any regulated activity for which it has permission. **4–051**

Other Investigatory and Enforcement Powers under FSMA 2000

There are a number of other investigatory and enforcement powers which may be relevant in policing the obligations imposed on banks and building societies under the regulatory system set up under FSMA 2000. These powers apply generally to authorised institutions and are considered in Ch.15. Here, we need simply note that they include power: **4–052**

(1) to require an authorised person to provide information or documents reasonably required in connection with the exercise of the FSA's functions (s.165);

(2) to require an authorised person to appoint a "skilled person" to provide the FSA with a report on any matter relating to the exercise of its functions (s.166);

(3) to appoint persons to carry out a general investigation into the business of an authorised person (s.167) or an investigation into a suspected contravention of specified regulatory requirements or other statutory provisions (s.168);

(4) to censure publicly an authorised person which the FSA considers has contravened a requirement imposed on it by or under FSMA 2000 (s.205);

(5) to impose a financial penalty on an authorised person which the FSA considers has contravened such a requirement (s.206); and

(6) to require an authorised person to make restitution in the event that it has made a profit, or caused loss to another person, as a result of a contravention of a requirement imposed by or under FSMA 2000 (s.384).

Other Regimes for the Protection of the Consumer

4–053 In the conduct of their business, banks and building societies are subject to a number of other regimes, both statutory and non-statutory, which have been set up for the protection of the consumer. The following call for comment in this connection.

The Consumer Credit Act 1974

4–054 The Consumer Credit Act 1974 imposes exacting formal and procedural requirements on persons who, in the course of business, enter into "regulated agreements". In summary, these comprise agreements, other than exempt agreements (as to which, see below), which fall within either of the following two categories (set out in ss.8 and 15 of the 1974 Act):

(1) credit agreements under which a person provides an individual with credit not exceeding a specified limit (currently £25,000); and

(2) hire agreements under which a person agrees to bail goods to an individual by way of hire, being an agreement which:

- is not a hire-purchase agreement;
- is capable of subsisting for more than three months; and
- does not require the hirer to make payments exceeding a specified limit (currently £25,000).

4–055 Exempt agreements are defined partly in s.16 of the 1974 Act and partly in Regulations made under it (currently, the Consumer Credit (Exempt

Agreements) Order 1989 (SI 1989/869) as amended). In the present context, the most important exemption to note is that covering credit agreements under which a bank or building society provides credit under a mortgage to finance or re-finance the purchase of land or the provision or improvements of buildings it.

Where an agreement is regulated, the Act lays down detailed procedural requirements for the conclusion of the agreement (see ss.58, 61(2) and (3), 62 and 63), and for the form and content of the agreement (see ss.60 and 61(1)). These requirements are further elaborated in Regulations made under the Act, the most important being the Consumer Credit (Agreements) Regulations 1983 (SI 1983/1553, as amended) and the Consumer Credit (Cancellation Notices and Copies of Documents) Regulations 1983. These Regulations are the source of the prescribed statements of the customer's statutory rights, which are a characteristic feature of agreements regulated by the 1974 Act. **4–056**

Failure to comply with these requirements will have the consequence that the agreement is not "properly executed", and can only be enforced against the debtor or hirer on an order of the court (see ss.65 and 127 of the 1974 Act). Normally, a court may only dismiss an application for the enforcement of an improperly executed agreement if it considers it just to do so having regard to the prejudice caused by the contravention, and to the extensive powers which the court has under the Act to reduce the amount payable by the consumer or to suspend or vary the terms of the agreement (s.127(1) and (2), and ss.135 and 136). In certain cases, however, the court is debarred by s.127(3) and (4) from making an enforcement order, so that the agreement will be irredeemably unenforceable. These include cases where the basic information prescribed in Sch.6 to the Consumer Credit (Agreements) Regulations 1983 is not included in the agreement or in any other document signed by the consumer. **4–057**

The Court of Appeal has, however, held that s.127(3) is incompatible with the creditor's rights under the European Convention on Human Rights in imposing an inflexible prohibition on the making of an enforcement order in any case where the prescribed information is not included: see *Wilson v First County Trust Ltd (No. 2)* [2002] Q.B. 74. S.127(3) will, however, remain in force unless and until the Government acts to remedy the incompatibility found by the Court of Appeal: see s.4(6) of the Human Rights Act 1998. It should be added that, at the time of writing, an appeal against the Court of Appeal's decision in the *Wilson* has been heard by the House of Lords, but the speeches determining the appeal have not yet been delivered. **4–058**

The Unfair Terms in Consumer Contracts Regulations 1999

The Unfair Terms in Consumer Contracts Regulations 1999 (SI 1999/2083, as amended) replaced the Unfair Terms in Consumer Contracts Regulations 1994 (SI 1994/3159), which implemented the EC Directive on Unfair Terms in Consumer Contracts (93/13) ([1993] O.J. L95/29). **4–059**

The 1999 Regulations apply to unfair terms in contracts concluded between a seller or a supplier and a consumer (reg.4(1)). For these purposes, a "consumer" means any natural person who, in contracts covered by the Regulations, is acting for purposes which are outside his trade, business or profession and a "seller or supplier" means any natural or legal person who, in such contracts, is acting for purposes which do relate to his trade, business or profession (reg.3(1)). A bank or building society supplying banking services, including the making of making a loan (whether secured or unsecured), will clearly constitute a "supplier" for these purposes.

4–060 Reg.5(1) of the 1999 Regulations provides that a contractual term which has not been individually negotiated is to be regarded as unfair if, contrary to the requirement of good faith, it causes a significant imbalance in the parties' rights and obligations arising under the contract to the detriment of the consumer. The width of that provision is, however, qualified to some extent by the so-called "core terms" exemption in reg.6(2), which provides that, insofar as it is in plain intelligible language, the assessment of the fairness of a term shall not relate (a) to the definition of the main subject matter of the contract or (b) to the adequacy of the price or remuneration, as against the goods or services supplied in exchange. Guidance on the meaning and effect of the corresponding provisions in the 1994 Regulations has been given in *Director General of Fair Trading v First National Bank plc* [2002] A.C. 481 (in which the House of Lords rejected a challenge to the fairness of a term in a bank's regulated loan agreement which provided that interest would continue to be charged at the contract rate, notwithstanding that the bank had obtained judgment for the amount due under the agreement).

4–061 A term which is found to be unfair is not binding on the consumer (reg.8(1)). That is not, of course, the same thing as saying that the term is void: while the consumer will be freed from any obligations imposed on him by an unfair term, the supplier will remain bound by it. Both parties will, however, be released if the contract is incapable of remaining in existence without the unfair term (reg.8(2)).

4–062 Two types of challenges may be made to an unfair term. First, an individual consumer who has entered into a contract containing an unfair term may rely on the Regulations to establish the unfairness of the term in ordinary civil proceedings between him and the supplier. Secondly, the Director General of Fair Trading and the various "qualifying bodies" set out in Sch.1 to the Regulations have power under reg.12 to apply for an injunction against any person using, or recommending the use of, an unfair term drawn up for general use in contracts concluded with consumers. In other words, they have power to launch a general challenge to the fairness of a particular standard term which may be incorporated in a very large number of individual contracts (*e.g.* a term in a set of standard mortgage or investment conditions used by a bank or building society). The FSA is one of the "qualifying bodies" specified in Sch.1 to the Regulations, and has assumed lead responsibility for enforcing the Regulations for most contracts in the areas of investments, pensions, life and general insurance, mortgages and banking. Contracts concerning products covered by the Consumer Credit Act 1974, particularly personal loans and credit cards, remain the responsibility of the OFT.

While the 1999 Regulations apply generally to standard terms in contracts with consumers, they have had a major impact on the drafting of standard form documents used by banks and building societies to offer investment and lending products to their non-business customers. A topic which has attracted particular concern is the application of the Regulations to terms which confer power on the bank or building society to vary the interest rate payable on such products—an issue which is clearly of key importance to the retail savings and lending businesses of both banks and building societies. The source of the problems generated by the Regulations in this area is that a term which has the object or effect of enabling the supplier to alter the terms of the contract unilaterally "without a valid reason which is specified in the contract" will be treated as "indicatively" unfair under para.1(j) of Sch.2 to the Regulations (reg.5(5)). Para.1(j) is then qualified by the obscurely worded para.2(b) of Sch.2. This states that para.1(j) is: **4–063**

> "without hindrance to terms under which a supplier of financial services reserves the right to alter the rate of interest payable by the consumer or due to the latter, or the amount of other charges for financial services without notice where there is a valid reason, provided that the supplier is required to inform the other contracting party or parties thereof at the earliest opportunity and that the latter are free to dissolve the contract immediately."

The combined effect of paras 1(j) and 2(b) is controversial, but it appears that a unilateral power to vary the interest rate will not be regarded as indicatively unfair if either: **4–064**

(1) "valid reasons" for the exercise of the power are specified in the contract (no guidance, however, being given in the Regulations on the kind of reasons will be regarded as "valid" for this purpose); or

(2) in cases where the supplier has power to vary the rate without prior notice, the contract requires the supplier to have a valid (though not necessarily specified) reason for making the change and to notify the consumer of the change at the earliest opportunity, and the consumer is then "free" to dissolve the contract immediately (which presumably means that the consumer must not only be able to terminate the contract without notice, but must also be able to do so without incurring any "exit penalty", such as a loss of interest or a redemption fee).

The OFT's guidance note, *Interest Variation Terms* (OFT 297), February 2000, contained guidance for mortgage lenders and deposit-takers on what it considered to be unfair terms for interest variation in mortgage and savings contracts. The OFT's guidance note has since been withdrawn, and new guidance from the FSA is currently awaited.

The Financial Ombudsman Service

As we shall see in Ch.16, the Financial Ombudsman Service (FOS) was established under Pt XVI of FSMA 2000 to resolve disputes between all types of authorised persons and persons who constitute "eligible **4–065** complainants"—being, in the main, individuals or small businesses who are customers or potential customers of the authorised person. In the case of banks and building societies, the FOS takes the place of the previous voluntary scheme which applied to banks (the Banking Ombudsman scheme) and the previous statutory scheme which applied to building societies (the Building Societies Ombudsman scheme).

4–066 The scheme is intended to provide for the resolution of disputes quickly and with the minimum of formality (FSMA 2000, s.225(1)). It has both a compulsory and a voluntary jurisdiction. A complaint will fall within the compulsory jurisdiction if it relates to an act or omission by an authorised firm in carrying on any of the following: any regulated activity (which of course includes the acceptance of deposits); mortgage lending (which is not yet a regulated activity); certain types of unsecured lending; paying money by plastic cards (other than store cards); and the provision of ancillary banking services (such as the provision and operation of cash machines and safe deposit boxes): DISP 2.6.1R and 2.6.6G. Complaints about activities which are ancillary to any of the above (such as the provision of advice about them) are also covered by the compulsory jurisdiction: DISP 2.6.2R. The voluntary jurisdiction only applies to activities falling outside the compulsory jurisdiction; as the name suggests, a complaint will not fall within the voluntary jurisdiction unless the firm has chosen to participate.

4–067 A complaint under the compulsory jurisdiction must be determined by reference to what, in the opinion of the ombudsman, is fair and reasonable in all the circumstances: FSMA 2000, s.228(1) and (2) and DISP 3.8.1R. The complainant is free either to accept or reject a determination by the ombudsman, but, if he accepts it, it will become final and binding on both the complainant and the firm: DISP 3.8.3R. If a complaint is determined in favour of the complainant, the determination may include a money award against the firm of such amount (not exceeding £100,000) as the ombudsman considers fair compensation for financial loss and for any pain and suffering, damage to reputation or distress and inconvenience which the complainant has suffered: DISP 3.9.1(1)G, 3.9.2R and 3.9.5R. The determination may also include a direction that the firm take such steps in relation to the complainant as the ombudsman considers just and appropriate: DISP 3.9.1(2)R.

4–068 The decisions of the FOS may have far-reaching implications for banks and building societies. The point can be illustrated by reference both to the treatment of complaints relating to the interest rate paid on variable rate TESSAs in the run-up to N2, and the FOS's treatment of post-N2 complaints relating to the introduction of dual variable mortgage rates.

4–069 To begin with TESSAs, changes in the tax legislation resulted in these accounts becoming unavailable to new savers with effect from April 6, 1999. They were replaced with ISAs. Although TESSAs and ISAs were similar in offering savers the ability to make tax-free savings, the statutory provisions governing the two accounts meant that they were subject to significantly different conditions. In particular, a TESSA had to be held for a five year term before the interest would qualify for tax relief (though transfers of the account to another TESSA provider were permitted). By contrast, withdrawals could be made from an ISA at any time, without affecting the tax-free status of the account. In an effort to attract new savers into ISAs, many banks and building societies paid interest at very competitive rates on their ISAs. Often, the institution set its ISA rate significantly higher than the rate which it was paying to existing customers with TESSAs. In may cases, too, the launch of the ISA heralded the gradual downgrading of the interest rate on the institution's TESSAs.

Prior to N2, the Banking Ombudsman Scheme and the Building Societies Ombudsman Scheme received numerous complaints from customers with TESSAs. At one point, the complaints were said to be running at 18,000 per week. In September 2000, the two schemes issued guidance about their approach to complaints regarding the interest rate paid on variable rate TESSAs. The essence of the guidance was as follows: **4–070**

> "In relation to a complaint about the interest rate on a variable rate TESSA, we will consider two questions:
>
> - Did the bank or building society pay a "fair" rate of interest on the TESSA?
>
>   For this purpose, we will treat the effective interest rate on the TESSA as "fair" if it is at least as good as the interest rates available on any other accounts with less onerous features in that bank or building society's current range. . . .
> - If the bank of building society did not pay a "fair" rate of interest on the TESSA, did it tell the investor by 5 May 1999 that the TESSA could be moved freely?
>
>   Because of government tax changes, TESSAs could not be opened after 5 April 1999. From that date they became "superseded" accounts. We consider that, within 30 days (by 5 May 1999), the bank or building society should have told the investor that the account was superseded — but could be transferred to another bank or building society without any notice period or additional charge."

The second element in the above Guidance was said to be based on ss.2.17 and 2.18 of the then current edition of the Banking Code, though those sections contained nothing which would oblige the bank or building society to offer its customers the opportunity to transfer an account to a rival institution.

One of the many complaints dealt with under the above guidance was brought by a Mr Jones, who had a TESSA with the Norwich & Peterborough Building Society. The Society had introduced a TESSA-only ISA (a form of ISA for investors with matured TESSAs), which paid interest at a higher rate than its TESSA. But, unlike many institutions, it had not reduced the interest rate on the TESSA following the introduction of the ISA. The Society's TESSA rate remained among the best in the market and there was no evidence that Mr Jones could have done any better by moving his account elsewhere. The Building Societies Ombudsman decided that, nevertheless, the Society had treated Mr Jones unfairly because the TESSA not only paid interest at a lower rate than the ISA but was subject to more onerous terms than the ISA—in particular, a term requiring the saver to give notice before transferring the TESSA to another provider, and to suffer a 60 day interest penalty even after giving notice. **4–071**

4–072 The Ombudsman's final decision became binding shortly after N2. The Society challenged it by bringing proceedings for judicial review against the FOS. Ouseley J. held that the challenge failed: see *R v Financial Ombudsman Service, on the application of Norwich & Peterborough Building Society* [2002] EWHC 2379 (Admin); [2003] 1 All E.R. (Comm) 65. Although he found that the Ombudsman had misconstrued the relevant provisions of the Banking Code, he accepted that the decision could be independently supported by reference to the principle of "relative onerousness" (*i.e.* the principle summarised in the first bullet point in the above extract from the Guidance), which the Ombudsman had applied in reaching the decision.

4–073 The decision is important in showing that the courts will adopt a light touch in reviewing the Ombudsman's decisions as to what is unfair. At paras 77 and 78 of the judgment, Ouseley J. said that:

> "The Ombudsman is entitled, and consistency in decision-making probably obliges him to develop criteria as to what constitutes unfairness. Those criteria are a matter for him. The very concept of "unfairness" is very wide, and permits reasonable people to disagree. But its very width serves as a caution against over-active judicial intervention in the approach adopted by the Ombudsman, in the criteria which he develops or in the application of those criteria or of the concept of unfairness to the circumstances of the case.
>
> It is only if the Ombudsman has committed such errors of reasoning as to deprive his decision of logic that it can be said to be legally tainted. The Court should be very wary of reaching such a conclusion. Its own views as to what would be fair are not to be substituted for the Ombudsman's views when what is at issue is a question of the substantive merits of a decision as to unfairness."

While those remarks were directed to a decision of the Ombudsman reached under the terms of the former Building Societies Ombudsman Scheme, it seems quite clear that they would be equally applicable to a decision reached under the new scheme set up under FSMA 2000.

4–074 Turning now to complaints about dual variable mortgage rates, these were prompted by the decision taken by a number of major banks and building societies early in 2001 to move from having a single variable mortgage rate to having two such rates—one higher than the other. Typically, the lower rate would be made available both to new borrowers and to existing borrowers with variable-rate loans which could be repaid without incurring any early repayment charge. Where, however, existing borrowers were "locked-in" by the obligation to pay such a charge, they would be denied the opportunity to switch from the higher to the lower rate unless they were prepared to pay the charge.

4–075 In a series of decisions involving lenders who introduced dual mortgage rates, the FOS has found that this practice was unfair on existing 'locked-in' borrowers. The earlier decisions are summarised in the March 2002 issue of *Ombudsman News*; later decisions upholding complaints against Halifax plc and Abbey National plc are summarised on the FOS's website. On first reading, it may appear that the decisions are based on the premise that, on the introduction of the lower variable rate, references in the complainant's mortgage documentation to the lender's "standard variable rate" or "base rate" came to have effect as references to the new rate. That, however, would have led to the conclusion that all "locked-in" variable-rate borrowers were automatically entitled to be charged interest by reference to the lower rate as soon as it was introduced. In fact, however, the FOS only reached that conclusion in cases where existing borrowers who were not "locked-in" were switched automatically to the lower rate. In cases where such borrowers had to apply to the lender before they were switched to the lower rate, the FOS has only upheld complaints from "locked-in" borrowers in cases where the complainant applied to be switched to the lower rate at a time when it continued to be available to borrowers who were not "locked-in". In effect, therefore, the FOS has approached these cases on the basis that "locked-in" borrowers were entitled to be treated no worse and no better than borrowers who were not "locked-in".

The Ombudsmen's decisions in the TESSA cases and in the dual variable mortgage rate cases have had far-reaching financial implications for the institutions concerned, and for banks and building societies as a whole. The point was recognised by Ouseley J. in the *Norwich & Peterborough* case (at para.111): **4–076**

> "Although the Ombudsman correctly disclaimed any regulatory role, the impact of a decision that Mr Jones had been treated unfairly will inevitably constitute a decision that in such circumstances, which must be very widespread, a TESSA holder should receive the same interest as an ISA holder, if that account is still available, or as a [TESSA-only ISA] holder, in the alternative. More precisely, the account holder should do so until informed that the account can be transferred without notice or penalty to another account. But I do not consider that the general application of the conclusion means that the Ombudsman should be seen as having moved from a consistent adjudicator to industry regulator."

Nonetheless, the potential for cases with wider implications to impact on the regulatory function of the FSA has been recognised in a Memorandum of Understanding between the FSA and the FOS concluded in August 2002 and published on the FSA's website. The Memorandum provides for the sharing of information between the two bodies in cases where (among other things) a complaint may give rise to regulatory issues or where it may be desirable for the FSA to consider using its regulatory tools, including the exercise of its investigative and other enforcement powers, the making of rules or the giving of guidance. The FSA and the FOS will decide how best to communicate with consumers and with firms in cases where it is likely that regulatory action by the FSA will lead to steps being taken to address the generality of the problems which may have arisen; the object of any such communication will be to ensure that consumers and complainants are at least made aware of the time scale within which action may be taken and can remain confident that their concerns will be appropriately addressed. **4–077**

The Banking Code and Business Banking Code

The Banking Code and the Business Banking Code are both voluntary codes and accordingly apply only to those banks and building societies which have subscribed to them. The Codes both set standards of good **4–078** banking practice for banks and building societies to follow in their dealings with customers in the United Kingdom. The Banking Code covers dealings with personal customers while the Business Banking Code covers dealings with business customers.

The present editions of the Banking Code and Business Banking Code became effective on March 1, 2003. The subscribers to the Banking Code currently comprise some 120 banks and building societies, accounting for over 99 per cent of the market place. The Business Banking Code currently has 30 subscribers.

4–079 Both Codes begins by setting out a number of key commitments. These include promises: to act fairly and reasonably in all dealings with customers; to help customers understand how the subscriber's financial products and services work (*e.g.* by giving information about them in plain English and explaining their financial implications); to deal with things that go wrong quickly and sympathetically; and to publicise the Code, have copies available and make sure that the subscriber's staff are trained to put it into practice. The Codes then go on to set out a number of detailed obligations in specific areas, including the notification of changes in interest rates and the imposition of charges for banking services.

4–080 It is important to note that, while the Banking Code generally covers loans and overdrafts to personal customers, it does not apply to mortgages. The reason for that exclusion is that mortgages entered into by personal customers are separately covered by the Mortgage Code (discussed below).

Compliance with the Banking and Business Banking Codes is monitored by the Banking Code Standards Board, which has power to impose sanctions on subscribers for breaches of the Codes. The sanctions available to the Board include: the issue of directions as to future conduct; the issue of recommendations on the remedy of past conduct; the cancellation or suspension of a subscriber's registration; and the public censure of a subscriber in the media.

The Mortgage Code

4–081 The Mortgage Code is a voluntary code followed by lenders and mortgage intermediaries in their relations with personal customers in the United Kingdom. It sets standards of good mortgage lending practice which are followed as a minimum by those subscribing to it.

The main provisions of the current edition of the Code came into effect for lenders from July 1, 1997 and for mortgage intermediaries March 31, 1998. The subscribers to the Code comprise some 150 lenders, covering virtually the whole market, and 13,000 intermediary firms.

Like the Banking Codes, the Mortgage Code begins with a statement of ten key commitments, and then sets out more detailed provisions relating to particular aspects of the mortgage transaction. These include provisions relating to: the level of service provided to the customer when choosing a mortgage; taking guarantees or security from a third party; notification of changes in the interest rate which applies to the mortgage; and information about charges which the lender may impose.

Compliance with the Mortgage Code is monitored by the Mortgage Code Compliance Board. Complaints of breaches must first be referred to the subscriber's internal complaints procedure. If they cannot be dealt with by that route, they must be referred either to the Mortgage Code Arbitration Scheme or to the FOS.

Chapter 5

Exchanges and Clearing Houses

The Regulatory Framework

Recognised Investment Exchanges and Recognised Clearing Houses

Those who buy and sell investments on a market (such as the London Stock Exchange) have an interest in ensuring that the market functions in a fair and orderly manner and that proper arrangements are in place to enable transactions to be settled promptly. Pt XVIII of FSMA 2000 gives the FSA power to recognise investment exchanges and clearing houses which meet requirements intended to ensure that those objectives will be achieved. The process of recognition involves the making of a recognition order by the FSA. The expressions "recognised investment exchange" (RIE) and "recognised clearing house" (RCH) refer respectively to an investment exchange or clearing house in respect of which a recognition order is in force, and the expression "recognised body" refers to a body which has been recognised as an RIE or an RCH. The requirements which a UK body must meet before it can be recognised in this way are set out in the Financial Services and Markets Act 2000 (Recognition Requirements for Investment Exchanges and Clearing Houses) Regulations 2001 (SI 2001/995) (the RIE Regulations 2001), which were made by the Treasury under the FSMA 2000, s.286. 5–001

As we saw in para.2–031, recognised bodies, when acting as such, are exempt persons and are therefore free to carry on regulated activities for which they would otherwise need authorisation in order to avoid infringing the general prohibition imposed by s.19. The scope of the exemption is set out in FSMA 2000, s.285. In the case of RIEs, it covers regulated activities carried on as part of the exchange's business as an investment exchange or for the purpose of, or in connection with, the provision of clearing services by the exchange. In the case of RCHs, it covers regulated activities carried on for the purposes of, or in connection with, the provision of clearing services by the clearing house. In either case, therefore, the exemption will permit the body (for example) to arrange deals in investments, or to deal in investments as principal, without the need for authorisation.

The exempt status accorded to recognised bodies reflects the fact that they are themselves regulatory bodies, which make and enforce the rules governing their own members. Correspondingly, the control which the FSA exerts over recognised bodies is looser and less direct than the control which it exerts over authorised persons. The main elements of the FSA's control over such bodies are to be found in the following powers conferred on it by FSMA 2000:

(1) the power to make orders (with Treasury consent) recognising a body as an RIE or RCH (s.290);

(2) the power to make rules requiring the body to supply the FSA with specified information relevant to the FSA's statutory functions (s.293);

(3) the power, where a recognised body is failing to meet the requirements for continued recognition, or is failing to comply with any other obligations imposed on it by the Act:

- to require the body to take steps to put right or avert the failure (s.296); or
- to revoke the order by which the body was recognised (s.297).

These elements are considered in turn, below.

Requirements for Recognition

5–002 The requirements which a UK body must meet in order to be eligible for recognition as an RIE are set out in Pts I and II of the Schedule to the RIE Regulations. Those which such a body must meet in order to be eligible for recognition as an RCH are set out in Pts III and IV of that Schedule.

The requirements for the two types of body are similar. So, for example, the body is required in each case to have sufficient financial resources, to be a fit and proper person, and to have adequate systems and controls (including those concerning the transmission of information). Each type of body is also required to promote high standards of integrity and fair dealing by persons using its facilities, and to co-operate (*e.g.* by sharing information) with the FSA and other regulatory bodies. The body must have effective arrangements for monitoring and enforcing compliance with its rules, and for investigating and resolving complaints. It must also ensure that proper protection is afforded to investors and that (in the case of an RIE) business is conducted in an orderly manner.

The key requirement for the proper protection of investors is supplemented, in each case, by a number of specific obligations. Those applicable to RIEs include the duty (set out in para.4(2) of Pt I of the Schedule to the RIE Regulations) to ensure that:

(1) access to its facilities is subject to criteria designed to protect the orderly functioning of the market and the interests of investors;

(2) dealings in investments on the exchange are limited to investments in which there is a proper market;

(3) appropriate arrangements are made for price-sensitive information to be made available to persons dealing in investments on the exchange;

(4) satisfactory arrangements are made for the recording and timely settlement of transactions effected on the exchange; and

(5) appropriate measures are adopted to reduce the extent to which the exchange's facilities can be used for a purpose connected with market abuse or financial crime.

Where the body enters into market contracts (within the meaning of s.155(2)(b) or (3) of the Companies Act 1989), it must also have rules (known as default rules) which regulate the position in cases where a member of the body is unable to meet his obligations under such a contract. In the case of an investment exchange, the default rules must comply with Pt II of the Schedule to the RIE Regulations; in the case of a clearing house, the rules must comply with Pt IV of that Schedule. The purpose of the rules is to ensure that rights and liabilities between the defaulter and any counterparty to an unsettled market contract are discharged and that payment of a single net sum should be made by or to the defaulter in respect of all such contracts with the same counterparty.

Guidance on the FSA's interpretation of the recognition requirements for UK applicants is given in the *FSA Handbook* at REC 2.

The procedure governing applications for recognition is set out in FSMA 2000, ss.287 and 288. The application may be made by any body corporate or unincorporated association, and must be accompanied by a copy of the applicant's rules and of any guidance which it has issued. It must also be accompanied by particulars of any clearing arrangements to be provided by the applicant, and by such other information as the FSA may reasonably require for the purposes of determining the application. **5–003**

Guidance on the application process for UK applicants will be found in the *Handbook* at REC 5.

The following UK bodies have been recognised as RIEs:

- LIFFE Administration and Management;
- London Stock Exchange plc;
- OM London Exchange Limited;
- The International Petroleum Exchange of London Limited;
- The London Metal Exchange Limited;
- virt-x Exchange Limited.

In addition, two UK bodies have been recognised as RCHs, namely, CRESTCo Limited and The London Clearing House Limited.

The FSA also has power to recognise an overseas investment exchange or clearing house (that is to say, an investment exchange or clearing house which neither has its head office nor its registered office in the United Kingdom: see FSMA 2000, 313(1)). In the case of an application for recognition by an overseas body, the requirements for recognition are modified by FSMA 2000, s.292. This enables the FSA to make a recognition order in respect of such a body if it satisfied that the requirements set out in s.292(3) are met. Those requirements are that: **5–004**

(1) investors are afforded protection equivalent to that which they would be afforded if the body were required to comply with the recognition requirements in the RIE Regulations;

(2) there are adequate procedures for dealing with a person who is unable, or likely to become unable, to meet his obligations under any market contract connected with the investment exchange or clearing house;

(3) the applicant is willing and able to co-operate with the FSA by the sharing of information and in other ways;

(4) adequate arrangements exist for co-operation between the FSA and those responsible for the supervision of the applicant in the country or territory in which its head office is situated.

Guidance on the recognition requirements and application process for overseas applicants will be found in the *Handbook* at REC 6.

Twelve bodies (including NASDAQ, NYMEX and the Swiss Stock Exchange) have so far been recognised as overseas investment exchanges in accordance with s.292. No bodies have so far been recognised as overseas clearing houses.

5–005 A recognition order may only be made with the approval of the Treasury under the FSMA 2000, s.307. The requirement for Treasury approval is part of the statutory machinery for ensuring that applications for recognition are subject to scrutiny on competition grounds. That machinery includes the following elements:

(1) The FSA must supply the Director General of Fair Trading (the DGFT) with copies of the applicant's rules, any guidance which the applicant has issued and its clearing arrangements (which are together referred to as the applicant's "regulatory provisions"), along with any other relevant information in its possession. The DGFT must then issue a report on whether the regulatory provisions have a significantly adverse effect on competition, and must send a copy of the report to the FSA, the Competition Commission and the Treasury. (See s.303).

(2) The Competition Commission must normally make its own report on the matter if either the DGFT's report concludes that the regulatory provisions do have a significantly adverse effect on competition or, while the DGFT's report does not reach that conclusion, the DGFT nevertheless asks the Commission to consider his report. If the Commission's report concludes that the regulatory provisions have a significantly adverse effect on competition, the report must also state whether the Commission considers that that effect is justified. (See s.306.)

(3) In a case where the Competition Commission produces a report which concludes not only that the regulatory provisions do have a significantly adverse effect on competition, but also that that effect is not justified, the Treasury must refuse to approve the making of

the recognition order unless it considers that there are exceptional circumstances which make it inappropriate to refuse its approval. In any other case, the Treasury may only refuse its approval if it considers that there are exceptional circumstances which make it inappropriate to give its approval. (See s.307.)

The above provisions apply just as much to overseas bodies seeking recognition as they do to UK bodies.

5–006 If the FSA decides to refuse to make a recognition order (otherwise than in a case where the Treasury has refused its approval under s.307), it is required by s.290(5) to take the same steps as it would have to take in a case where it had decided to revoke an existing recognition order. Those steps are set out in s.298 (discussed in para.5–013, below). Their purpose is to ensure that the applicant, its members and any other persons affected by the decision will be informed of the FSA's reasons for refusing recognition and will have a period of at least two months in which to make representations to the FSA.

Requirements for the Supply of Information to the FSA

5–007 FSMA 2000, s.293(5) to (7) require a UK recognised body to notify the FSA of any change in its rules, guidance or clearing arrangements. In addition, s.293(1) to (4) confer power on the FSA to make rules requiring a recognised body to give it notice of specified events relating to the body, and such other information relating to the body as may be specified. The rules currently applicable to UK recognised bodies are set out in the *FSA Handbook* at REC 3, which also contains the FSA's guidance relating to the rules. The rules require the body to supply the FSA with information on a wide range of matters, including: changes in the persons appointed as its "key individuals" (*e.g.* its chairman and chief executive, and the members of its governing body); changes to its memorandum and articles of association; a change in its auditors; any complaint which is upheld against it in relation to its regulatory functions; changes in the products and services provided (*e.g.* a change in the type of security which an RIE admits to trading), and any suspension of its services. The body is also required to provide the FSA with copies of its annual report and accounts, and of its quarterly and monthly management accounts.

5–008 The notification requirements which apply to overseas recognised bodies are less exacting. S.295 provides that, at least once a year, such a body must provide the FSA with a report stating whether any events have occurred which are likely either to affect the FSA's assessment of whether the requirements in s.292(3) are met (as to which, see para.5–004, above) or to have any effect on competition. The report must, in addition, contain such information as may be specified in rules made by the FSA. The rules currently in force are set out in the *Handbook* at REC 6.7 and they require the report to include (among other things): particulars of any changes to its constitution, its regulatory provisions or its chairman or chief executive; particulars of any disciplinary action taken against it by any supervisory authority in its home territory; a copy of its annual report and accounts; and particulars of the actual or threatened revocation or restriction of any licence, permission or authorisation which the body requires in order to conduct any regulated activity in its home territory.

5–009 S.294 gives the FSA power to waive or modify the application of any rules which it has made under ss.293 or 295 in relation to a recognised body. The power may be exercised either on the application of the body concerned or with its consent, but the FSA may only exercise the power if it is satisfied that compliance with the rules (or with the rules as unmodified) would be unduly burdensome or would not achieve the purpose for which the rules were made, and that the waiver or modification would not result in undue risk to persons whose interests the rules are intended to protect. Guidance on the procedure for applying for a waiver of modification is given in the *Handbook* at REC 3.3.

The FSA will periodically review any waiver or modification which it has given. The FSA may revoke a waiver or modification at any time. It may also vary a waiver or modification, but only on the application or with the consent of the body to which it relates.

The FSA's Power to Give Directions or Revoke Recognition

5–010 Once it has been recognised, an RIE or RCH must ensure that it continues to satisfy the requirements for recognition summarised in para.5–002, above, and to comply with the other obligations imposed on it by or under FSMA 2000 (*e.g.* the requirements for the supply of information noted in paras 5–007 to 5–009). If it fails to do so, then, as noted below, the FSA has power either to direct the body to take appropriate remedial steps or to revoke the body's recognition. The recognition requirements therefore represent a key element in the FSA's ongoing supervisory functions in relation to RIEs and RCHs.

5–011 The FSA's power to give directions is contained in FSMA 2000, s.296. The section applies if it appears to the FSA that a recognised body has failed, or is likely to fail, to satisfy the recognition requirements or has failed to comply with any other obligation imposed on it by or under the Act. Where the section applies, the FSA may direct the body to take specified steps for the purposes of securing the body's compliance with the recognition requirements or with its statutory obligations. Any such direction is enforceable on the FSA's application by an injunction.

5–012 S.297 confers power on the FSA to make an order (known as a "revocation order") revoking the recognition order for a recognised body. The power may be exercised at the request or with the consent of the body concerned. But the FSA also has power to exercise the power unilaterally if it appears to it that a recognised body is failing, or has failed, to satisfy the recognition requirements or to comply with any other obligation imposed on it by or under the Act. Where the power is exercised unilaterally, the revocation order may not come into effect until at least three months from the date on which it is made.

Before giving a direction under s.296 or making a revocation order under s.297, the FSA must normally follow the procedure set out in s.298(1) to (6). It should, however, be noted that there is power under s.298(7) to give a direction (though not to make a revocation order) without following the normal procedure, but only where the FSA considers it "essential" to do so. **5–013**

Where the normal procedure applies, the FSA must:

(a) give written notice of its intention to give the direction or make the revocation order to the recognised body concerned;

(b) take such steps as it considers reasonably practicable to bring the notice to the attention of the body's members (if any); and

(c) publish the notice in such manner as it thinks appropriate for bringing it to the attention of other persons ("affected persons") who are, in its opinion, likely to be affected by the proposed direction or order.

The notice must state why the FSA intends to give the direction or make the revocation order. The recognised body, its members and any affected persons will have a period of not less than two months in which to make representations to the FSA. The FSA is required to have regard to any representations made when deciding whether or not to give the direction or make the order. When the FSA has reached its decision, it must give written notice of the decision to the recognised body and, if the decision is to give the direction or make the order, it must also take such steps as it considers reasonably practicable to bring the decision to the attention of the body's members and any affected persons.

The FSA has given guidance on the exercise of its powers under ss.296 and 297 in the *Handbook*, at REC 4.6 and 4.7. REC 4.6.4G also gives guidance on the circumstances in which the FSA is likely to exercise its power under s.298(7) to give a direction under s.296 without going through the normal consultation procedure set out in the rest of s.298.

The Listing of Securities

The FSA as the United Kingdom Listing Authority

"Listing" refers to the admission of securities to the official list maintained by the "competent authority" (FSMA 2000, s.74(1) and (5)). The competent authority is known as the United Kingdom Listing Authority (UKLA). Its functions were formerly discharged by the London Stock Exchange (LSE). However, when the LSE announced proposals to demutualise, it was felt inappropriate that it should continue to discharge its regulatory role as the UKLA. With effect from May 1, 2000, the functions of the UKLA were accordingly transferred to the FSA (then still operating under the Financial Services Act 1986). The FSA continues to carry out the functions of the UKLA under Pt VI of FSMA 2000. The **5–014** possibility of those functions being transferred to another body in the future is, however, left open by FSMA 2000, Sch.8, which confers power on the Treasury to transfer all or any of the functions of the competent authority to another person if it is satisfied that the transfer would significantly improve the manner in which, or the efficiency with which, the transferred functions are discharged, or that the transfer would otherwise be in the public interest.

In considering the functions of the UKLA, it should be borne in mind that neither the UKLA itself, nor any person who is, or is acting as one of its members, officers or members of staff, is to be liable in damages for anything done or omitted in the discharge, or purported discharge, of the UKLA's functions. This exemption does not, however, apply if the act or omission is shown to have been in bad faith or so as to prevent an award of damages made on the ground that an act or omission was unlawful under s.6(1) of the Human Rights Act 1998 (FSMA 2000, s.102).

5–015 Listing is necessary before securities can be traded on the main market of the LSE. Listing may be attractive to a company as a means of raising additional capital, or of making it easier for its existing investors to find a market for their shares in the company. Listing also serves an important role in the protection of investors, since it ensures that rigorous disclosure requirements are met before securities are listed, and that full and accurate disclosure of relevant information continues to be made on a timely basis so long as the securities remain listed, so facilitating the orderly operation of the market.

5–016 The basic statutory framework for the listing of securities is set out in Pt VI of FSMA 2000, which gives effect in the United Kingdom to the minimum requirements for listing now set out in EC Directive 2001/34 ([2001] O.J. L184/1) (which codifies the three earlier Directives known as the Admissions Directive, 1979/279 ([1979] O.J. L45/55), the Listing Particulars Directive, 1980/390 ([1980] O.J. L100/1) and the Interim Reports Directive, 1982/121 ([1982] O.J. L3/23)). Pt VI also gives effect to the requirements relating to prospectuses in EC Directive 1989/298 ([1989] O.J. L124/8).

5–017 FSMA 2000, s.73(2) defines the UKLA's general functions as being (a) to make rules under Pt VI of the Act; (b) to give general guidance in relation to that Part; and (c) to determine the general policy and principles by reference to which it performs particular functions under that Part. S.73(1) identifies a number of factors to which the UKLA must have regard in discharging its general functions. These include the desirability of facilitating innovation in respect of listed securities, the international character of capital markets and the desirability of maintaining the competitive position of the UK.

The UKLA has the duty to maintain the official list (s.74(1)) and the power to determine the "securities and other things" which may be admitted to the list (s.74(2)). However, nothing may be admitted to the official list except in accordance with Pt VI, and the Treasury is given power to provide by order that anything which falls within a description or category specified in the order may not be admitted to the official list (s.74(3)).

S.74(4) confers on the UKLA its key function of making listing rules for the purposes of Pt VI. The procedure to be followed in exercising the power to make listing rules is set out in s.101.

The importance of the listing rules is emphasised by the fact that admission to the official list may be granted only on an application made to the UKLA in the manner required by the listing rules (s.75(1)) and that the UKLA may not grant an application for listing unless it is satisfied that the requirements of the listing rules are met, along with any other requirements imposed by it in relation to the application (s.75(4)).

The *Listing Rules*

The UKLA's requirements for listing are set out in the *Listing Rules*. The UKLA has given guidance on these requirements in its *Guidance Manual*. Both documents are available on the FSA's website, and will ultimately be included in Block 5 of the *FSA's Handbook*. For the time being, however, they do not form part of the *Handbook*. Many of the more important rules reflect mandatory requirements of the relevant EU Directives, or requirements to be found in Pt VI of FSMA 2000. **5–018**

Applications for Listing

The provisions relevant to applications for listing are to be found in FSMA 2000 and the *Listing Rules*. **5–019**

Two general requirements may be noted at the outset. First, the UKLA may not entertain any application for listing unless it is made by, or with the consent of, the issuer of the securities concerned (s.75(2)). Secondly, r.1.3(a) of the *Listing Rules* imposes an obligation on the issuer to provide the UKLA without delay with all the information and explanations that it reasonably requires for the purpose of deciding whether to grant an application for listing.

The detailed conditions for listing are set out in Ch.3 of the *Listing Rules*. **5–020** An applicant must be duly incorporated or otherwise established according to the law of its place of incorporation or establishment, and must be operating in conformity with its memorandum and articles of association or equivalent constitutional documents. If the applicant is a company incorporated in the UK, it must not be a private company (r.3.2). The applicant (if a company) must have published or filed audited accounts which cover at least three years (r.3.3), though the UKLA may accept accounts relating to a shorter period if it is satisfied that it is desirable to do so in the interests of the applicant or of investors and that investors will have the necessary information available to make an informed judgment about the applicant and the securities to be listed (r.3.4). The company's directors and senior management must collectively have appropriate expertise and experience for the management of the group's business (r.3.8) and the company must normally ensure that each of its directors is free of conflicts between duties to the company and private interests and other duties (r.3.9). The issuer must generally prepare a working capital statement stating that it is satisfied that it and its subsidiary undertakings have sufficient working capital for at least the next 12 months (r.3.10). If the applicant is a company which has a controlling shareholding, it must be capable at all times of carrying on its business independently of the controlling shareholder and any associate of his, and transactions and relationships between the company and the controlling shareholder must be at arm's length and on a normal commercial basis (r.3.12).

5–021 Ch.3 also includes conditions relating to the securities to be listed. They must conform to the law of the applicant's place of incorporation and be duly authorised according to the requirements of its memorandum and articles of association; they must also have any necessary statutory or other consents (r.3.14). To be listed, securities must be admitted to trading on an RIE's market for listed securities (r.3.14A), a requirement which, for the time being at any rate, means in practice that the securities must be admitted to the main market of the LSE.

The securities must be freely transferable (r.3.15). Except where securities of the same class are already listed, the expected aggregate market value of all securities to be listed must normally be at least £700,000 for shares or £200,000 for debentures (r.3.16), though the UKLA has discretion to admit securities of lower value if satisfied that there will be an adequate market for them (r.3.17). Where a class of shares is to be listed, it is normally necessary for at least 25 per cent of the shares to be distributed to the public in one or more Member States, no later than the time of admission; however, a lower percentage may be acceptable where the market will operate properly in view of the large number of shares of that class and the extent of their distribution to the public (rr.3.18–3.20). Where the application for listing relates to shares or a new class of securities, the shares or securities must be eligible for electronic settlement, unless the UKLA otherwise agrees "in exceptional circumstances" (r.3.27).

Methods of bringing Securities to Listing

5–022 Ch.4 of the *Listing Rules* makes provision for the different methods of bringing securities to listing. The following methods are available whether or not the applicant already has listed equity shares:

(a) *An offer for sale.* This is an invitation to the public by or on behalf of a third party to purchase securities of the issuer already in issue or allotted, and may take the form of an invitation to tender at or above a stated minimum price (r.4.4).

(b) *An offer for subscription.* This is an invitation to the public by or on behalf of the issuer to subscribe for securities of the issuer not yet in issue or allotted, and may again take the form of an invitation to tender at or above a stated minimum price (r.4.5).

(c) *A placing.* This is a marketing of securities not yet listed (whether or not already in issue) to specified persons or clients of the sponsor or any securities house assisting with the placing, which does not involve an offer to the public or to existing holders of the issuer's securities generally (r.4.7).

(d) *An intermediaries offer.* This is a marketing of securities (whether or not already in issue) by means of an offer by, or on behalf of, the issuer to intermediaries for them to allocate to their own clients (r.4.10).

In the case of an applicant which already has equity shares listed, a number of additional methods are available for bringing its securities to listing. These include:

(e) *A rights issue.* This is an offer to existing holders of securities to subscribe of purchase further securities in proportion to their holdings made by means of a renounceable letter (or other negotiable instrument) which may be traded (as "nil paid" rights) for a period before payment for the securities is due (r.4.16). When making a rights issue, regard must also be had to the rights of existing shareholders. A company proposing to issue equity securities for cash must offer these securities to existing equity shareholders first, in proportion to their existing holdings (r.9.18). The shareholders may, however, authorise the disapplication of such pre-emption rights under s.95 of the Companies Act 1985, in which case an issue of equity shares for cash (as to which, see (j), below) may proceed in accordance with the authorisation (r.9.20).

(f) *An open offer.* This, too, is an invitation to existing holders of securities to subscribe or purchase securities in proportion to their holdings, but differs from a rights issue in that is not made by means of a renounceable letter or other negotiable instrument (r.4.22).

(g) *An acquisition or merger issue (or vendor consideration issue).* This is an issue of securities in consideration for an acquisition of assets, or an issue of securities on an acquisition of, or merger with, another company as consideration for the securities of that other company (r.4.27).

(h) *A vendor consideration placing.* This is a marketing, by or on behalf of vendors, of securities that have been allotted as consideration for an acquisition (r.4.29).

(i) *A capitalisation issue (or bonus issue) in lieu of dividend or otherwise.* This is an issue to existing holders of securities, in proportion to their holdings, of further shares credited as fully paid out of the issuer's reserves (r.4.31).

(j) *An issue for cash.* This is an issue of securities for cash to persons who are specifically approved by shareholders in general meeting or an issue pursuant to a general disapplication of s.89 of the Companies Act 1985 approved by shareholders in general meeting.

In the case of an applicant without equity shares already listed, the methods described in (e) to (j), above, do not apply. Such an applicant does, however, have the option of bringing its securities to listing by means of an introduction. This method applies where the securities are already widely held by the public and does not involve either the issue of new securities or any marketing of existing securities (r.4.12).

Prospectuses

5–023 In a case where an issuer applies for listing of its securities which are to be offered to the public in the United Kingdom for the first time before admission, it will be necessary for a prospectus to be submitted for approval by the UKLA. The prospectus must be prepared in accordance with the provisions of Ch.5 of the *Listing Rules* and published in accordance with Ch.8. These requirements are imposed (pursuant to the authority conferred by FSMA 2000, s.84) by r.5.1(a) and (c) of the *Listing Rules*.

R.5.1(f) mentions three exceptional cases where the above requirements do not apply. They include cases in which a prospectus issued by an overseas company has been approved by the competent authority in another Member State and a public offer of the same securities is made in another Member State at, or within a short interval of, the public offer in the UK (r.17.72).

By s.103(6), the question whether a person "offers securities to the public in the UK" is to be determined in accordance with Sch.11 to the Act.

Para.1 of that Schedule states the general rule that a person offers securities to the public in the United Kingdom if (a) to the extent that the offer is made to persons in the United Kingdom, it is made to the public and (b) it is not an exempt offer. For this purpose, an offer is treated as made to the public if it is made to any section of the public, whether selected as members or debenture holders of a body corporate, as clients of the person making the offer, or in any other manner.

The various categories of exempt offer (where the requirement to issue a prospectus will not arise) are set out in paras 3 to 24 of Sch.11. They include offers to persons in the context of their trades, professions or occupations; offers to no more than 50 persons; offers to members of a club or association; offers to a restricted circle of persons whom the offeror reasonably believes to be sufficiently knowledgeable to understand the risks involved in accepting the offer; offers to public authorities; offers in connection with a takeover offer or merger; and offers of "free shares" (*viz.* shares which are offered free of charge to any or all of the holders of shares in the offeror).

In those cases where the *Listing Rules* require a prospectus to be published before new securities are listed, it is unlawful to offer any of those securities to the public in the United Kingdom before the required prospectus is published. Breach of this prohibition is a criminal offence, and is actionable at the suit of any person who suffers loss as a result of the contravention (FSMA 2000, s.85).

Listing Particulars

In a case where an issuer applies for listing of its securities *other than* securities which are to be offered to the public in the United Kingdom for the first time before admission, it will be necessary for listing particulars (as opposed to a prospectus) to be submitted for approval by the UKLA. As in the case of a prospectus, the listing particulars must be prepared in accordance with the provisions of Ch.5 of the *Listing Rules* and published in accordance with the provisions of Ch.8. These requirement are imposed (pursuant to the authority conferred by FSMA 2000, s.79) by r.5.1(b) and (c) of the *Listing Rules*. **5–024**

R.5.1(g) mentions four exceptional cases where the above requirements do not apply. They include cases in which listing particulars issued by an overseas company have been approved by the competent authority in another member state and the company has applied for listing of the same securities on a stock exchange in another member state at the same time as, or within a short interval of, its application to the UKLA (r.17.68).

The Contents of Prospectuses and Listing Particulars

Many of the requirements which FSMA 2000 and the *Listing Rules* lay down in relation to listing particulars apply equally to prospectuses (see s.86 and r.5.1(c) to (e)). It is therefore convenient to deal with them together. **5–025**

In each case, a general statutory duty of disclosure arises under FSMA 2000, s.80, which has the effect that, in addition to any information required by the *Listing Rules* or the UKLA, listing particulars or prospectuses submitted for approval by the UKLA must contain all such information as investors and their professional advisers would reasonably require, and reasonably expect to find there, for the purpose of making an informed assessment of the assets and liabilities, financial position, profits and loss and prospects of the issuer of the securities, and the rights attaching to the securities (s.80(1) and (2)). The duty is, however, limited to information which is within the knowledge of any person responsible for the listing particulars or which it would be reasonable for him to obtain by making enquiries (s.80(3)). In determining what information must be included in the listing particulars or prospectus, regard must be had (in particular) to (a) the nature of the securities and their issuer; (b) the nature of the persons likely to consider acquiring them; (c) the fact that certain matters may reasonably be expected to be within the knowledge of professional advisers of a kind which persons likely to acquire the securities may reasonably be expected to consult; and (d) any information available to investors or their professional advisers as a result of requirements imposed on the issuer of the securities by an RIE, by the *Listing Rules* or by or under any enactment (s.80(4)).

FSMA 2000, s.81 will require supplementary listing particulars, or a supplementary prospectus, to be submitted to the UKLA for approval if, between the time the submission of the original document and the **5–026** commencement of dealings in the securities concerned, there is either (a) a significant change affecting any matter contained in the original document whose inclusion was required by the general duty of disclosure under FSMA 2000, s.80, or by the *Listing Rules* or the UKLA; or (b) a significant new matter arises whose inclusion would have been so required if it had arisen when the original document was prepared. In either case, the supplementary listing particulars or prospectus must be prepared in accordance with the *Listing Rules* and, if they are approved by the UKLA, must be published in accordance with those rules (s.81(1)). For these purposes, a change or new matter will be "significant" if it is significant for the purposes of making an informed assessment of the kind mentioned in s.81(2). The UKLA must be advised immediately if supplementary particulars or a supplementary prospectus will be required (the *Listing Rules*, r.5.14).

If the issuer is not aware of the change or new matter in question, it is relieved of the duty to submit supplementary listing particulars or a supplementary prospectus under s.81(1), unless it is notified of the change or new matter by a person responsible for the listing particulars or prospectus (s.81(3)). If, however, any such person is himself aware of the change or new matter, he is under a duty to give notice of it to the issuer (s.81(4)).

5–027 The UKLA has power under FSMA 2000, s.82 to authorise the omission of information which would otherwise need to be disclosed in listing particulars or a prospectus under s.80 (or to be disclosed in supplementary listing particulars or a supplementary prospectus under s.81). The power may be exercised on the ground:

(a) that the disclosure of the information would be contrary to the public interest;

(b) that its disclosure would be seriously detrimental to the issuer; or

(c) in the case of securities of a kind specified in the *Listing Rules*, that its disclosure is unnecessary for persons of the kind who may be expected normally to buy or deal in securities of that kind (s.82(1)).

The UKLA may not, however, rely on ground (b) to authorise the non-disclosure of "essential information" (s.82(2)), which, in this context, means information which a person considering the acquisition of securities of the kind in question would be likely to need in order not to be misled about any facts which it is essential for him to know in order to make an informed assessment (s.82(6)).

As regards ground (a), the Secretary of State or the Treasury has power to issue a certificate that the disclosure of any information would be contrary to the public interest (s.82(3)) and the UKLA will be entitled to act on any such certificate in exercising its power to authorise non-disclosure on that ground (s.82(4)).

5–028 A copy of the listing particulars or prospectus (and of any supplementary particulars or prospectus) must be delivered for registration by the registrar of companies no later than the date on which they are published as required by the *Listing Rules* (s.83(1)). Failure to comply with this requirement will involve the commission of a criminal offence by the issuer and by any person who is a party to the publication and aware of the failure (s.83(3) and (4)).

The *Listing Rules* will require the listing particulars or prospectus to contain a responsibility statement, which (in the case of shares) will declare that the directors of the issuer accept responsibility for the information contained in the document and that to the best of the knowledge and belief of the directors (who have taken all reasonable care to ensure that such is the case) the information contained in the document is in accordance with the facts and does not omit anything likely to affect the import of such information (rr.5.2 and 6.A.3). In addition, the issuer will normally be required to provide the UKLA with a letter signed by every director of the issuer confirming, in effect, that the listing particulars or prospectus include all the information required to be disclosed under the general duty of disclosure under FSMA 2000, s.80 (r.5.5). **5–029**

The listing particulars or prospectus must also contain the information required by Ch.6 of the *Listing Rules*, together with any additional information required by Chs 18 to 26 in relation to specific classes of issuer (*e.g.* property companies) and such additional information as the UKLA may require as appropriate in the particular case (r.5.6). The information required by Ch.6 includes information about (a) the persons responsible for the listing particulars or prospectus; (b) the shares to be listed; (c) the issuer and its capital; (d) the group's activities; (e) the issuer's assets and liabilities, financial position and profits and losses; (f) the management; and (g) the recent development and prospects of the group.

The particulars or prospectus must provide factual information, in as easily analysable and comprehensible a form as possible (r.5.7). Rr.5.9 to 5.10 set out the extensive requirements for the submission of documents to the UKLA prior to the approval and publication of listing particulars or a prospectus. Further documents and other items specified in Ch.7 of the *Listing Rules* must be supplied to the UKLA in the 48 hour period prior to its consideration of the application for listing.

Responsibility for Prospectuses and Listing Particulars

The persons who, for the purposes of Pt VI of FSMA 2000, are responsible for listing particulars (including supplementary listing particulars) are set out in Pt 3 of the Financial Services and Markets Act (Official Listing of Securities) Regulations 2001 (SI 2001/2956). In the normal case, the persons responsible are those set out in reg.6, namely (a) the issuer; (b) its directors at the time when the particulars are submitted to the UKLA; (c) persons named in the particulars as directors, or as having agreed to become a director, either immediately or at a future time; (d) persons who are stated in the particulars as accepting responsibility for them; and (e) any other persons who have authorised the contents of the particulars. It is permissible for a person falling within category (d) or (e) to accept responsibility only in relation to certain specified parts of the particulars or only in certain specified respects (reg.6(3)). A person is not responsible for **5–030** any particulars merely by reason of giving advice as to their contents in a professional capacity (reg.6(4)).

By virtue of reg.10, the same persons will be responsible for a prospectus or supplementary prospectus.

The UKLA's Decision on an Application for Listing

5–031 The UKLA may refuse an application for listing if it considers that the applicant's situation is such that admission of the securities would be detrimental to the interests of investors or if, in the case of securities listed in another member state, the applicant has failed to comply with the obligations to which it is subject by virtue of that listing (FSMA 2000, s.75(5) and (6) and the *Listing Rules*, r.1.4(a) and (b)).

The UKLA's decision on listing must be notified to the applicant within six months of the date when the application was received, or of the date on which the UKLA was provided with any further information which it required in connection with the application (s.76(1)). If no decision is notified within that time, the application will be taken to be refused (s.76(2)).

The UKLA must give the applicant written notice of a decision to grant an application for listing (s.76(3)). If it proposes to refuse an application, it must first give the applicant a warning notice; it must then give a further notice of any decision to refuse the application (s.76(4) and (5)). The applicant has the right to appeal to the Financial Services and Markets Tribunal against a decision to refuse its application for listing (s.76(7)).

Sponsors

5–032 FSMA 2000, s.88 provides that the *Listing Rules* may require an issuer to make arrangements with a sponsor, approved by the UKLA, to provide such services as may be specified in the rules. R.2.6 of the *Listing Rules* will require the appointment of a sponsor whenever an issuer (other than a public sector issuer or an issuer issuing specialist securities or miscellaneous securities) makes any application for listing which requires the production of listing particulars or (by virtue of r.5.1(e)) a prospectus.

The UKLA maintains a list of sponsors approved by it (r.2.2). To be included on the list, a sponsor must (a) be an authorised person or a person regulated by a designated professional body; (b) pay the relevant fees required by the UKLA; (c) be a body corporate or a partnership; (d) have at least four "eligible employees" (*viz.*, employees at an appropriate level of seniority with recent experience of providing advice in connection with a significant transaction); and (e) satisfy the UKLA that it is competent to perform the services required of a sponsor by the *Listing Rules*.

The sponsor will normally be a major investment bank with sufficient expertise to guide the issuer through the complexities of the listing rules, and a reputation which inspires confidence on the part of prospective investors. The sponsor will act as financial adviser to the issuer and will direct the strategy of the issue and co-ordinate the activities of the other professional advisers.

Under the *Listing Rules*, the sponsor will be required to satisfy itself, to the best of its knowledge and belief, having made due and careful enquiry of the issuer and its advisers, that the issuer has satisfied all applicable conditions for listing and other relevant requirements of the rules (r.2.9(a)). Where the sponsor gives guidance or advice on the application or interpretation of the *Listing Rules* (as it almost invariably will), it must ensure that the issuer is given proper guidance and that the service is provided with due care and skill (r.2.10). A sponsor must be independent of any issuer for which it provides services under rr.2.9 and 2.10 (r.2.11) and will be required to complete a prescribed declaration confirming (among other things) that it has satisfied itself having made due and careful enquiry of the issuer and its advisers that all relevant requirements of the *Listing Rules* have been or will be complied with and that all matters known to it which, in its opinion, should be taken into account by the UKLA in considering the application for listing have been disclosed to the UKLA (r.2.12).

The sponsor will also need to be satisfied, before the application for listing is made, that the directors of the issuer have had explained to them by the sponsor or other appropriate professional adviser the nature of their responsibilities and obligations as directors of a listed company under the *Listing Rules* (r.2.13). In the case of a new applicant (*i.e.* an applicant no class of whose securities is already listed), the sponsor must obtain written confirmation from the issuer that the directors have established procedures which provide a reasonable basis for them to make proper judgments as to the financial position and prospects of the issuer and its group, and the sponsor must be satisfied that this confirmation has been given after due and careful enquiry by the issuer (r.2.15). The sponsor must take further steps to ensure that due care has been taken in the provision of any working capital statement (r.2.18), profit forecast (r.2.19) and financial information (r.2.20).

If the UKLA considers that a sponsor has breached any provision of the *Listing Rules* and considers it appropriate to impose a sanction, it will publish a statement censuring the sponsor (r.2.27). The UKLA must give the sponsor a warning notice before publishing any such statement, and must consider any representations made by the sponsor in response (FSMA 2000, s.89(2) and (3)). The sponsor has the right to refer a decision to publish the statement to the Financial Services and Markets Tribunal (s.89(4)).

Advertisements

In a case where listing particulars or a prospectus are to be published in **5–033**
connection with an application for listing, no advertisement may be issued in the United Kingdom unless the UKLA has approved the contents of the advertisement or authorised the issue of the advertisement without such approval (s.98(1)). Breach of this requirement is a criminal offence (s.98(2)), though there is a statutory defence for a person who issues an advertisement if he can show that he believed on reasonable grounds that the advertisement had been approved, or its issue authorised, by the UKLA (s.98(3)).

Continuing obligations under the *Listing Rules*

5–034 The *Listing Rules* set out a number of continuing obligations which a listed company must observe once any of its securities have been admitted to listing. These are set out primarily in Ch.9, but further continuing obligations will be found in Chs 10 to 16.

Two key disclosure obligations are set out in Ch.9. First, r.9.1 requires a company to notify the Companies Announcements Office of the LSE (which is the information dissemination provider approved by the UKLA) of any major new developments in its sphere of activity which are not public knowledge and may, by virtue of the effect of those developments on its assets and liabilities or financial position or on the general course of its business, lead to substantial movement in the price of its listed securities, or (in the case of a company with listed debt securities) significantly affect its ability to meet its commitments. Secondly, r.9.2 requires a company to notify the Company Announcements Office without delay of all relevant information which is not public knowledge concerning a change in the company's financial condition, in the performance of its business, or in the company's expectation as to its performance which, if made public, would be likely to lead to substantial movement in the price of its listed securities.

A recent example of a breach of the obligations imposed by r.9.2 is provided by the failure of Marconi plc to notify the Companies Announcements Office without delay of a change in its expectations as to its performance for the half year ending September 30, 2001 and the full year ending March 31, 2002. The company's expectations changed for the worse on July 2, 2001. The FSA (in its capacity as the UKLA) found that the change, if made public, was likely to lead to a substantial movement in the price of its listed securities and that the notification should have been made by, at the latest, the evening of July 3, 2001. In fact the notification was not made until the evening of July 4, 2001, so placing the company in breach of r.9.2. The price sensitivity of the change in expectations was indicated by the fact that, on July 5, 2001, there was a 25–fold increase in the volume of Marconi's shares traded and a 54 per cent reduction in the share price. In a public statement relating to the contravention published on April 11, 2003, the FSA said:

> "The continuing obligations of a listed company set out in the Listing Rules are designed to promote full disclosure to the market of all relevant information on a timely basis. The FSA regards the continuing obligation requirements of Chapter 9 of the Listing Rules as a fundamental protection for shareholders. Observance of those continuing obligations is essential to the maintenance of an orderly market in securities and of confidence in the financial system. The FSA therefore takes the most serious view of listed companies which fail to comply with these requirements."

Suspension or Cancellation of Listing

5–035 If the UKLA is satisfied that there are special circumstances which preclude normal regular dealings in any listed securities, it has power to discontinue the listing of the securities in accordance with the *Listing Rules* (FSMA 2000, s.77(1)).

It also has power, in accordance with the rules, to suspend the listing of any securities (s.77(2)). R.1.15 of the *Listing Rules* provides for this power to be exercised where the smooth operation of the market is, or may be, temporarily jeopardised or where protection of investors so requires. During a suspension, the issuer must continue to comply with all the listing rules applicable to it, unless the UKLA otherwise agrees.

A discontinuance or suspension may take effect immediately or on a date specified by the UKLA (s.78(1)). In either case, the UKLA must give written notice to the issuer giving details of the discontinuance or suspension and of the reasons for it, and informing the issuer that it may make representations to the UKLA (s.78(2) and (3)). After considering any such representations, the UKLA must give the issuer a further notice of its decision (s.78(5) and (8)). If the decision is that the listing of the securities is (or remains) discontinued or cancelled, the issuer has the right to refer the matter to the Financial Services and Markets Tribunal (s.77(5)).

In a case where the listing has been suspended (rather than discontinued), the issuer may apply for the suspension to be cancelled. If the UKLA proposes to refuse the application, it must give the issuer a warning notice and must consider any representations which the issuer wishes to make in response to that notice. If the UKLA's ultimate decision is not to cancel the suspension, the issuer again has a right to refer the matter to the Tribunal (s.78(10) to (12)).

Compensation

FSMA 2000, s.90(1) provides that a person responsible for a prospectus or listing particulars (including a supplementary prospectus or listing particulars) is liable to pay compensation to any person who has acquired any of the securities to which the document applies and has suffered loss in respect of them as a result of any untrue or misleading statement in the document, or the omission from the document of any information required to be included by virtue of the general duty of disclosure in ss.80 and 81. A number of exemptions from the liability to pay compensation are set out in Sch.10. These include cases where the person responsible ("X") satisfies the court that one of the following applies: **5–036**

(a) when the document was submitted to the UKLA, X reasonably believed (having made such enquiries, if any, as were reasonable) that the statement was true and not misleading and that one or more of the following further conditions apply:

- X continued in that belief until the securities were acquired;
- they were acquired before it was reasonably practicable to bring a correction to the attention of persons likely to acquire them;
- before the securities were acquired, X had taken all reasonable steps to secure that a correction was brought to the attention of those persons; or

- X continued in his belief until the commencement of dealings in the securities and they were acquired after such a lapse of time that he ought in the circumstances reasonably to be excused;

(b) the loss was caused by a statement which purported to made by, or on the authority of, another person as an expert and X reasonably believed that the other person was competent to make or authorise the statement and had consented to its inclusion in the document and that one or more of a set of further conditions (broadly similar to those set out in (a), above) apply;

(c) the person suffering the loss acquired the securities in the knowledge that the statement was false or misleading.

5–037 A person who fails to comply with the duty to submit a supplementary prospectus or listing particulars where one is required under FSMA 2000, s.81 (as to which, see para.5–026, above) is liable to pay compensation to any person who has acquired securities of the kind in question and suffered loss in respect of them as a result of the failure (s.90(4)). The exemptions in Sch.10 apply equally to this liability.

5–038 The statutory right to compensation provided by s.90 does not affect any liability which may be incurred apart from the section (s.90(6)). This clearly leaves the way open for an investor to pursue claims under the general law for damages based on misrepresentation or negligence.

Penalties and Censure

5–039 If the UKLA considers that an issuer of listed securities, or an applicant for listing, has contravened any provision of the *Listing Rules*, it may impose on it such penalty as it considers appropriate (FSMA 2000, s.91(1)). It has a similar power to impose a penalty on any director of the issuer or applicant if it considers that the director was knowingly concerned in the contravention (s.91(2)).

Where the UKLA is entitled to impose a penalty under either of the above powers, it may instead publish a statement censuring that person (s.91(3)).

The UKLA must issue a warning notice before it takes action against a person under these powers (s.92(1)). The warning notice must be given within the period of two years beginning with the date on which the UKLA first knew of the contravention or had information from which the contravention could reasonably be inferred (s.91(6) and (7)). The warning notice must state the amount of the proposed penalty or (as the case may be) the terms of the proposed statement (s.92(2) and (3)). The UKLA must also give notice of a decision to impose a penalty or make a statement, and the person subject to the penalty or censure may then refer the matter to the Financial Services and Markets Tribunal (s.92(4) to (7)).

S.93 provides that the UKLA must prepare and issue a policy statement setting out its policy with respect to the imposition of penalties under s.91, and the amount of those penalties. The current policy is described in Ch.8 of the UKLA's *Guidance Manual*, which sets out the criteria to be applied in deciding whether to take disciplinary action, and in determining the amount of any penalty to be imposed. The UKLA is obliged to have regard to its stated policy when considering the exercise of its powers under s.91 in any particular case (s.93(5)).

Investigations

The UKLA has a further power under FSMA 2000, s.97 to appoint one or more competent persons to carry out an investigation on its behalf if it considers that there are circumstances suggesting that (a) there may have been a breach of the *Listing Rules*; (b) a director of an issuer of listed securities has been knowingly concerned in a breach of the *Listing Rules* by that issuer; (c) a director of an applicant for listing has been knowingly concerned in such a breach by the applicant; or (d) there may have been a contravention of s.83 (registration of listing particulars), 85 (publication of a prospectus) or 98 (advertisements). **5–040**

The Alternative Investment Market

Unlisted Securities

The LSE launched the Alternative Investment Market (AIM) on June 19, 1995 as an alternative market designed to meet the needs of emerging or smaller companies that were unable to meet the requirements for admission to the Official List, or unwilling to incur the very substantial costs of doing so. AIM replaced the earlier Unlisted Securities Market, which was first established in 1980. **5–041**

Securities traded on AIM are "unlisted" in the sense that they will not have been admitted to the UKLA's Official List. They must, however, meet the requirements for admission to AIM, and the issuer will need to comply with the continuing obligations which apply to it under the *AIM Rules for Companies* (the *AIM Rules*).

Given that securities admitted to AIM are not listed, the listing requirements set out in Pt VI of FSMA 2000 and the *Listing Rules* obviously have no application to them. Instead, an issuer seeking admission to AIM will need to comply with the requirements set out in the Public Offers of Securities Regulations 1995 (SI 1995/1537) (the POS Regulations) and the *AIM Rules*.

The Prospectus

The POS Regulations provide that, when unlisted securities are offered to the public in the United Kingdom for the first time, the offeror must publish a prospectus by making it available to the public, free of charge, at **5–042** an address in the United Kingdom, from the time he first offers the securities until the end of the period during which the offer remains open (reg.4(1)). The circumstances in which unlisted securities are treated as offered to the public in the United Kingdom are specified in regs 6 and 7, which are to broadly similar effect as the corresponding provisions for listed securities in FSMA 2000, Sch.11 (see para.5–023, above).

Before publishing the prospectus, the offeror must deliver a copy of it to the registrar of companies for registration (reg.4(2)).

An authorised person who contravenes the requirements for publication and registration of a prospectus in reg.4(1) and (2) is treated as having contravened rules under Pt X of the FSMA 2000, so attracting the FSA's disciplinary powers and laying himself open to an action for breach of statutory duty (under FSMA 2000, s.150) by any private person who suffers loss as a result of the contravention (reg.16(1); and compare reg.16(4)).

5–043 The information to be included in the prospectus is set out the POS Regulations, reg.8 and Sch.1. In addition, reg. 9(1) imposes a general duty of disclosure similar (but not identical) to that in FSMA 2000. Reg.9(1) provides that, as well as the information specifically required by reg.8, the prospectus must contain all such information as investors would reasonably require, and reasonably expect to find there, for the purposes of making an informed assessment of (a) the assets and liabilities, financial position, profits and losses, and prospects of the issuer of the securities; and (b) the rights attaching to those securities.

A supplementary prospectus will have to be published and registered if (a) there is a significant change affecting any matter contained in the prospectus whose inclusion was required by reg.8 or 9; (b) a significant new matter arises whose inclusion would have been so required if it had arisen when the prospectus was prepared; or (b) there is a significant inaccuracy in the prospectus (regulation 10).

5–044 In contrast to the listed securities regime, the POS Regulations do not impose any requirement for the prospectus to be vetted prior to publication.

However, an offeror who wishes to have the prospectus recognised as such in other EU jurisdictions will need to submit the prospectus to the UKLA as a "non-listing prospectus" under FSMA 2000, s.87. The requirements for approval of a non-listing prospectus are set out in the *Rules for approval of prospectuses where no application for listing is made* (printed immediately after Ch.27 of the *Listing Rules*). These rules apply Chs 5 and 6 of the *Listing Rules* to non-listing prospectuses, but with some of the requirements of those Chapters omitted and others modified.

5–045 Reg.13 of the POS Regulations sets out the persons who are responsible for a prospectus (including a supplementary prospectus) relating to unlisted securities. They include the issuer and its directors, and any person who has authorised the contents of the prospectus or any part of it. Any such person will (subject to the exemptions in reg.15) be liable to pay compensation under reg.14 to any person who acquires the securities to which the prospectus relates and suffers loss in respect of them as a result of any untrue or misleading statement in the prospectus, or the omission from it of any matter required to be included by regs 9 or 10.

Requirements under the *AIM Rules*

The requirements which must be met for admission to AIM are set out in the *AIM Rules* and are more relaxed than those which govern admission to the Official List. They include a requirement for the applicant to appoint a nominated adviser and broker, and to provide the LSE, at least ten business days before the expected date of admission to AIM, with the information set out in Sch.1 to the *AIM Rules* (including the applicant's name, country of incorporation, a brief description of its business, the number and type of securities in respect of which it seeks admission and an indication of whether it will be raising capital on admission). The applicant must also produce an admission document disclosing the information set out in Sch.2 to the *AIM Rules*, and this document must be publicly available for at least one month from the admission of the applicant's securities to AIM. The information required by Sch.2 includes a statement by the directors that, in their opinion having made due and careful enquiry, the working capital available to the company and its group will be sufficient for at least twelve months from the date of the admission of its securities. **5–046**

An AIM company is under a continuing obligation to publish annual audited accounts prepared in accordance with United Kingdom or United States generally accepted accounting practice or International Accounting Standards. These accounts must be sent to its shareholders without delay and in any event not later than six months after the end of the financial period to which they relate (r.17). The company must also ensure that any of its securities which have been admitted to AIM are freely transferable except where, in any jurisdiction, statute or regulation places restrictions on transferability or the company is seeking to limit the number of shareholders domiciled in a particular country to ensure that it does not become subject to statute or regulation (r.30). **5–047**

An AIM company must notify the Regulatory Information Service without delay of price-sensitive information, *viz.* information about new developments which are not public knowledge concerning a change in its financial condition, its sphere of activity, the performance of its business or its expectation of its performance and which, if made public, would be likely to lead to a substantial movement in the price of its securities which have been admitted to AIM (r.10).

The LSE has power to suspend the trading of AIM securities where (a) trading in those securities is not being conducted in an orderly manner; (b) it considers that an AIM company has failed to comply with the *AIM Rules*; (c) the protection of investors so requires; or (d) the integrity and reputation of the market has been or may be impaired by dealings in those securities (r.38). **5–048**

The *AIM Rules* also confer various disciplinary powers on the LSE. Where the LSE considers that an AIM company has contravened any of the *AIM Rules*, it may fine or censure the company, publish the fact that it has done so, and/or cancel the admission of the company's AIM securities (r.40). It also has power in certain circumstances to censure a nominated adviser or remove it from the register (r.41).

Chapter 6

Collective Investment Schemes

Background

Collective investment schemes, as a particular class of investment schemes so described, have a short history in English law. They were introduced by the Financial Services Act 1986 as a result of the Directive on Undertakings for Collective Investment in Transferable Securities (the UCITS Directive, Dir.85/611), already mentioned briefly in para.2–068. The particular features of such an undertaking were that it was open-ended and was a means of spreading investment risk. The purpose of the Directive, as might be expected, was to enable a UCITS which complied with the rules of the Member State in which it was established (those rules themselves complying with the Directive) to be sold freely in any other Member State. In practice, the Directive has been of limited effect, not least because Member States retain taxation powers in relation to schemes themselves and in relation to payments to investors and they retain power to determine marketing rules. A further feature of the Directive is that it covers only schemes of a kind which every Member State allows to be marketed to the public. As a result, many schemes which come within the concept of a collective investment scheme for the purposes of English law are not UCITS, as explained further below. **6–001**

The promotion of what are now known as collective investment schemes has been subject to restriction under English law since the Prevention of Fraud (Investments) Act 1944. The central element of those restrictions since the 1986 Act came into force has been that a collective investment scheme cannot be marketed to the public generally unless it is an authorised unit trust, an authorised open-ended investment company or a recognised scheme, all of which types of scheme are defined in or by delegated legislation made under the FSMA 2000. It is understood that the policy rationale is to protect investors, who will be asked to entrust the day-to-day management of the property subject to the scheme to a third party and who may not themselves be expert in the subject matter of the scheme, by ensuring that the types of scheme marketed generally are fairly tightly controlled. As there has been no change of policy in this respect, the position under the 2000 Act is very similar to the position which prevailed under the 1986 Act. **6–002**

Key Definitions

6–003 The definition of primary importance is of course the definition of "collective investment scheme" itself. That is to be found in s.235 of FSMA 2000. Property of any description, including money (*i.e.* not only transferable securities), may form the subject matter of a collective investment scheme. Such a scheme exists where there are arrangements satisfying certain requirements the purpose or effect of which is:

> "to enable persons taking part in the arrangements (whether by becoming owners of the property or any part of it or otherwise) to participate in or receive profits or income arising from the acquisition, holding, management or disposal of the property or sums paid out of such profits or income" (s.235(1)).

The arrangements must be such that the participants in the scheme do not have day-to-day control of the management of the property, although they may have the right to be consulted or to give directions (s.235(2)). In addition, the arrangements must have at least one of the following characteristics (see s.235(3)):

- that the contributions of the participants and the profits or income out of which payments are to be made to them are pooled;
- that the property is managed as a whole by or on behalf of the operator of the scheme.

The Treasury has power by s.235(5) to provide that certain forms of arrangement are not within the scope of the definition, and has exercised that power as discussed at para.6.010 below.

6–004 Of the three forms of collective investment scheme which may be marketed directly to the public, the one with the most straightforward definition is "authorised unit trust scheme". A unit trust scheme is a collective investment scheme under which the property is held on trust for the participants (s.237(1)). It is an authorised unit trust scheme if it is authorised by an authorisation order made under s.243 of the Act (see s.237(3)). The requirements for authorisation are considered at para.6.011 below.

6–005 An open-ended investment company is a collective investment scheme which satisfies two conditions, called in the Act the property condition and the investment condition: s.236(1). The property condition is that the property belongs beneficially to, and is managed by or on behalf of a body corporate which has as its purpose the investment of its funds with the aim of spreading investment risk and giving the members the benefit of the results of the management of those funds by or on behalf of the body (s.236(2)). The investment condition is that a reasonable investor would expect that he would be able to realise, within a period appearing to him to be reasonable, his investment in the scheme (*i.e.* the value of his shares or securities in the body corporate) and would be satisfied that his investment would be realised on a basis calculated wholly or mainly by reference to the value of property in respect of which the scheme makes arrangements (s.236(3)). Certain statutory provisions for the redemption or repurchase of shares or securities are to be ignored in considering whether the investment condition is satisfied (s.236(4)).

The definition of an open-ended investment company may be varied by the Treasury (s.236(5)). It will be appreciated that the effect of the present definition is to introduce a degree of uncertainty, since whether or not the definition is satisfied depends upon the view that the reasonable investor might take of any particular scheme. The FSA has given guidance on how the statutory definition is to be understood in the *FSA Handbook* at AUTH App.2. The general principle is that there should be included any body corporate which, looked at as a whole, functions as an open-ended investment company. Particular points of detail are that the "reasonable investor" is a hypothetical investor, so that whether or not a company is an open-ended investment company does not depend upon the view take by a particular investor, however reasonably; that generally speaking realisation means conversion into cash or money; that an investor's expectation may be determined by reference to a company's practice or its declared policy rather than solely by reference to his contractual rights; and that realisation on a basis calculated wholly or mainly by reference to the value of property means in effect realisation on a net asset value basis. A further effect of the definition is that by, for example, a change of policy, a company which has been open-ended may become one which is closed-ended, or vice versa. **6–006**

An authorised open-ended investment company is one which is incorporated by virtue of regulations made under s.262 of the Act and in respect of which an authorisation order is in force (s.237(3)). These requirements are considered in para.6.023 below.

A "recognised scheme" means a scheme recognised under s.264, 270 or 272 of the Act: s.237(3). All such schemes will in fact be overseas collective investment schemes. A scheme recognised under s.264 is a scheme constituted in another EEA State which satisfies prescribed requirements (considered in para.6.031), provided that the scheme operator has given two months' notice to the FSA of its intention to invite persons in the United Kingdom to participate in the scheme and the FSA has not, within that two month period, notified the operator and the regulatory authorities in the home State that the way in which the invitation is to be made does not comply with the law in force in the United Kingdom. S.265 provides a procedure for challenging any such notice given by the FSA, with a right of appeal to the Financial Services and Markets Tribunal. The scheme must itself be constituted under the law of its home State by contract or under a trust and be managed by a body corporate established under that law, or by an open-ended investment company incorporated under that law (s.264(5)). Rules made by the FSA under FSMA 2000, other than financial promotion rules and rules under s.283(1) (requiring operators of recognised schemes to maintain in the United Kingdom such facilities as the FSA thinks desirable), do not apply to schemes recognised under s.264 (s.266). **6–007**

A scheme recognised under s.270 is a scheme which is not a recognised scheme by virtue of s.264 but is managed in, and authorised under the law of, a country or territory outside the United Kingdom if the country or territory is designated by order made by the Treasury, the scheme is of a **6–008** class specified by the order, the operator has given written notice to the FSA that he wishes the scheme to be recognised and either the FSA has given written approval to the scheme's being recognised or two months have elapsed without the operator's having received a warning notice from the FSA under s.271 (s.270(1)). Before the Treasury may make an order designating a country or territory for the purposes of s.270, it must be satisfied that the applicable law and practice will afford investors in the United Kingdom protection at least equivalent to that provided for them by or under the FSMA 2000 provisions applicable to comparable authorised schemes and that adequate arrangements for co-operation will exist between the supervising authorities of the country or territory in question and the FSA (s.270(2)). Under s.270(5) the Treasury, when considering whether or not to designate a country or territory, must obtain a report from the FSA on the relevant law and practice and existing or proposed arrangements for co-operation.

A warning notice under s.271 is a notice that the FSA proposes to refuse approval of a scheme's being a recognised scheme. If the FSA goes on to decide to do so, it must then serve a decision notice, and the matter may be referred by the operator to the Financial Services and Markets Tribunal (s.271(2)).

6–009 A scheme recognised under s.272 is an overseas scheme which cannot be recognised under s.264 or 270 but which is individually recognised by the FSA on an application made by the scheme operator (s.272(1)). In the absence of any overseas supervisory authorities, such as exist in relation to schemes recognised under the other two sections, a more elaborate application process is required, similar to that which applies to United Kingdom schemes. The requirements which a scheme must satisfy before it can be individually recognised are set out in subsequent provisions of s.272 and are as follows:

- adequate protection must be afforded to participants in the scheme;
- the arrangements for the scheme's constitution and management must be adequate;
- the powers and duties of the operator and, if the scheme has a trustee or depositary, the trustee or depositary, must be adequate;
- the scheme must take the form of an open-ended investment company or, if not, the operator must be a body corporate;
- the operator must, if an authorised person, have permission to act as operator, or, if not an authorised person, be a fit and proper person to act as operator;
- if the scheme has a trustee or depositary, that person must, if an authorised person, have permission to act as such, or, if not an authorised person, be a fit and proper person to act as such;
- the operator and any trustee or depositary must be able and willing to co-operate with the FSA;
- the name of the scheme must not be undesirable or misleading;

- the purposes of the scheme must be reasonably capable of being successfully carried into effect;
- the participants must be entitled to have their units redeemed in accordance with the scheme at a price related to the net value of the property to which the units relate and determined in accordance with the scheme.

In considering the adequacy of the arrangements for the scheme's constitution and management and the powers and duties of the operator and any trustee or depositary, the FSA must have regard to any rule of law and any matters which are or could be the subject of rules applicable in relation to comparable authorised schemes. Generally, there is a considerable similarity in the requirements to the requirements for authorisation of a unit trust scheme as set out in s.243, considered further in para.6.011 below.

The FSA has power to determine the procedure for making applications, except that the application must contain an address in the United Kingdom for the purpose of service of notices or other documents under FSMA 2000 (s.274). Applications are to be determined within six months (s.275), with a long-stop period of twelve months in the case of incomplete applications, and as usual there is a warning and decision notice regime in relation to the proposed refusal of an application, with a right of appeal to the Financial Services and Markets Tribunal (s.276).

Exemptions from Definition

The Treasury's power under s.235(5) to provide that certain arrangements **6–010**
do not amount to a collective investment scheme has been exercised by the Financial Services and Markets Act 2000 (Collective Investment Schemes) Order 2001 (SI 2001/1062). The list of such arrangements, as amended by the Financial Services and Markets Act 2000 (Miscellaneous Provisions) Order 2001 (SI 2001/3650) is as follows:

- individual investment management arrangements;
- enterprise initiative schemes;
- pure deposit based schemes;
- schemes not operated by way of business;
- debt issues;
- common accounts;
- rights or interests in a trust fund within the meaning of s.42(1) of the Landlord and Tenant Act 1987;
- employee share schemes of a specified nature;
- schemes entered into for commercial purposes related to existing business;

- group schemes;
- franchise arrangements;
- trading schemes;
- timeshare schemes;
- other schemes relating to the use or enjoyment of property;
- schemes involving the issue of certificates representing investments;
- clearing services;
- contracts of insurance;
- funeral plan contracts;
- individual pension accounts;
- occupational and personal pension schemes;
- bodies corporate (other than open-ended investment companies).

The Order contains detailed provisions by which these various types of exempted arrangements are defined.

Regulatory Provisions Relating to Authorised Schemes

Unit trusts: FSMA 2000

6–011 Where it is desired to obtain authorisation for a unit trust scheme (as defined in s.237) an application for authorisation must be made by the manager and trustee, or the proposed manager and trustee, of the scheme (s.242(1).) The manager and trustee must be different persons (s.242(2)). As might be expected, the procedure for applying and the contents of the application are matters for the FSA (ss.242(3) to (6)). Under s.243 the FSA has power to make an authorisation order if:

- it is satisfied that the scheme complies with the requirements set out in s.243 itself;
- it is satisfied that the scheme complies with the requirements of the trust scheme rules (that is, rules made under s.247 relating to the constitution, management and operation of authorised unit trust schemes, the powers, duties, rights and liabilities of the manager and trustee of any such scheme, the rights and duties of the participants in any such scheme and the winding up of any such scheme);
- it has been provided with a copy of the trust deed and a certificate signed by a solicitor to the effect that it complies with such of the requirements of s.243 or the trust scheme rules as relate to its contents.

The requirements in s.243 itself are that the manager and the trustee must be independent of each other; that they must each be incorporated in the United Kingdom or another EEA State and have a place of business in the United Kingdom, and the affairs of each must be administered in the country in which it is incorporated; that, if the manager is incorporated in another EEA State, the scheme must not be one which satisfies the requirements for recognition under s.264; that the manager and the trustee must each be an authorised person with permission to act in their respective capacities; that the name of the scheme must not be undesirable or misleading; that the purposes of the scheme must be reasonably capable of being successfully carried into effect; and that the participants must be entitled to have their units redeemed in accordance with the scheme at a price related to the net value of the property to which the units relate and determined in accordance with the scheme.

Under s.244, an application for authorisation must be determined within six months from the date on which the FSA receives the completed application. The FSA has power to determine an incomplete application if it considers it appropriate to do so and must in any case determine such an application within twelve months from the date on which it is received. The applicant may withdraw the application by written notice. If the FSA proposes to refuse an application, it must give a warning notice under s.244 to each applicant, and if it then decides to refuse the application, it must give a decision notice, which gives rise to a right to each applicant to refer the matter to the Financial Services and Markets Tribunal. **6–012**

The FSA also has power, if so requested by the manager or trustee of a unit trust scheme which complies with the conditions necessary for it to enjoy the rights conferred by any Community instrument, to issue a certificate to that effect, either on the making of an authorisation order or at any subsequent time (s.246).

The FSA's power under s.247 to make trust scheme rules has already been noted in para.6.011 above. Such rules may include provision as to the contents of the trust deed (s.247(3)), but are binding on the manager, trustee and participants independently of the contents of the trust deed and, in the case of the participants, have effect as if contained in it (s.247(4)). The rules made are to be found in the *FSA Handbook* in the specialist sourcebook for collective investment schemes at CIS 2.2.5 to 2.2.8. S.247 also confers power on the Treasury, by subs.(5), to modify the FSA's rule-making power if there is a modification of the statutory provisions in force relating to the rights and duties of persons who hold the beneficial title to shares in a company without holding the legal title and it appears to the Treasury expedient to exercise its power in order to assimilate the law relating to companies and the law relating to authorised unit trust schemes. **6–013**

The FSA has a further rule-making power under s.248 by which it may make scheme particulars rules requiring the manager of an authorised unit trust scheme to submit scheme particulars (that is to say, information about the scheme: s.248(2)) to the FSA and to publish them or make them available to the public on request. As well as specifying the particulars initially required, the rules may require managers to submit and publish or **6–014** make available revised or further particulars if there is a significant change in particulars previously given under the rules, or there is a significant new matter which ought to have been included in the particulars if it had arisen when they were prepared (s.248(3) and (4)). It is also to be noted that under s.248(5) the rules may provide for compensation to be paid by the person or persons responsible for the particulars to any "qualifying person" who has suffered loss as a result of an untrue or misleading statement or an omission. A "qualifying person" is one who has become or agreed to become a participant or who, although not a participant, has a beneficial interest in units in the scheme. The rules are to be found in CIS 3.

6–015 By virtue of s.250, the FSA may, as respects both trust scheme rules and scheme particulars rules:

- on the application or with the consent of any person, direct that all or any of the rules are not to apply to him as respects a particular scheme, or are to apply to him with the modifications specified in the direction;
- on the application or with the consent of the manager and trustee of a particular scheme acting jointly, direct that all or any of the rules are not to apply to that scheme, or are to apply to the scheme with the modifications specified in the direction.

The section then brings in by cross-reference the provisions of s.148 relating to the circumstances under which and the procedure by which provisions in other sets of rules may be waived or modified. In particular it is to be noted that the FSA may not give a direction unless it is satisfied that compliance would be unduly burdensome or would not achieve the purpose for which the rules were made, and that the direction would not result in undue risk to persons whose interests the rules are intended to protect (s.148(4)). Generally speaking, although subject to the exceptions specified, the making of such a direction must be published (s.148(6)).

6–016 The manager of an authorised unit trust scheme is obliged by s.251(1) to give written notice to the FSA of any proposal to alter the scheme or to replace its trustee, and similarly the trustee is obliged by s.251(3) to give written notice to the FSA of any proposal to replace the manager. Where notice of a proposal to alter the scheme involving a change in the trust deed is given, it must be accompanied by a certificate signed by a solicitor to the effect that the change will not affect the compliance of the deed with the trust scheme rules (s.251(2)). Effect may not be given to the proposal unless the FSA has given written approval or one month from the date of the notice has expired without the manager or trustee receiving from the FSA a warning notice under s.252 (s.251(4)). The FSA may not approve a proposal to replace the manager or trustee unless it is satisfied that the requirements of s.243 as to the manager or trustee will continue to be met (s.251(5)).

A warning notice under s.252 is a notice warning that the FSA proposes to refuse approval of a replacement of the manager or trustee or of an alteration to the scheme. In the former case, the notice must be given to the person by whom the original notice was given; in the latter case, separate warning notices must be given to the manager and the trustee. As might be expected, if the FSA then decides to refuse approval, it must give a decision notice to the person to whom a warning notice was given, and that person may then refer the matter to the Financial Services and Markets Tribunal (s.252(4)).

The exercise of proper care by managers and trustees is promoted by s.253, under which any provision of the trust deed of an authorised scheme is void in so far as it would have the effect of exempting the manager or trustee from liability for any failure to exercise due care and diligence in the discharge of his functions in respect of the scheme. It may also be noted that, under s.249, if it appears to the FSA that an auditor has failed to comply with a duty imposed on him by trust scheme rules, it may disqualify him from being the auditor for any authorised unit trust scheme or authorised open-ended investment company. A warning and decision notice procedure applies in such a case under s.345 of the 2000 Act (by virtue of s.249(2)) and the auditor has the right to refer the matter to the Financial Services and Markets Tribunal. **6–017**

Under s.254(1), the FSA may revoke an authorisation order if it appears to the FSA that: **6–018**

- one or more of the requirements for the making of the order are no longer satisfied;
- the manager or trustee of the scheme has contravened a requirement imposed on him by or under the Act;
- the manager or trustee of the scheme has, in purported compliance with any such requirement, knowingly or recklessly given the FSA information which is false or misleading in a material particular;
- no regulated activity is being carried on in relation to the scheme and the period of that inaction began at least twelve months earlier;
- although none of the above circumstances exist, it is desirable to revoke the authorisation order in order to protect the interests of participants or potential participants in the scheme.

There is, of course, a warning and decision notice procedure, established by s.255, and either the manager or the trustee (both of whom must be served with notices) may refer the matter to the Financial Services and Markets Tribunal.

The FSA also has power, under s.256, to revoke an authorisation order at the request of the manager or trustee of the scheme. The request may be refused if the FSA considers that the public interest requires that any matter concerning the scheme should be investigated before a decision is taken on revocation, or that revocation would not be in the interests of the participants or would be incompatible with a Community obligation (s.256(3)). There is a warning and decision notice procedure if the FSA proposes to refuse such a request, and either the manager or the trustee (both of whom must again be served with notices) may refer the matter to the Financial Services and Markets Tribunal (s.256(5)). **6–019**

6–020 Revocation of the order authorising a scheme is of course an extreme step. As an alternative, the FSA may give a direction under s.257 if it appears to the FSA that one of the first three circumstances set out in para.6.018 above exists, or that it is desirable to do so in order to protect the interests of participants or potential participants in the scheme. Such a direction may require the manager to cease the issue, or redemption, or both issue and redemption, of units under the scheme or require the manager and trustee of the scheme to wind it up (s.257(2)). Subsequent revocation of the authorisation order does not affect any direction which was then in force, and a new direction may be given after revocation if a direction was in force at the time of revocation (s.257(3) and (4)). The FSA may, on its own initiative or on the application of the manager or trustee of the scheme, revoke or vary a direction if it appears to the FSA that, in the case of revocation, it is no longer necessary for the direction to take effect or continue in force or, in the case of variation, that the direction should take effect or continue in force in a different form (s.257(6)). Under s.260, a warning and decision notice procedure, with a right of reference to the Financial Services and Markets Tribunal, applies to any application for variation made by the manager or trustee which the FSA proposes to refuse. S.261 contains provisions for the giving of notices where the FSA decides to revoke a direction on its own initiative, or to revoke or vary a direction in accordance with an application.

The contravention of a direction is actionable at the suit of a private person who suffers loss as a result in accordance with the provisions of s.150 of FSMA 2000 (s.257(5)).

A direction under s.257 will only take effect immediately if the notice of the direction so specifies (s.259(1)), and the FSA may only make such a direction if it considers, having regard to the ground on which it is exercising its power, that it is necessary for the direction to take immediate effect (s.259(2)). Similarly, a direction will take effect on a specified date only if the notice so specifies, and the FSA may only make such a direction if it considers that necessary. Otherwise, the direction takes effect when the matter is no longer open to review. Under s.391(8), applied by s.259(14), a matter is open to review if it may still be referred to the Financial Services and Markets Tribunal, or if it has been referred but not determined, or if the time for appeal is still running, or if an appeal is pending but has not been determined. S.259 contains detailed requirements as to the contents of notices, including requirements to state the period for making representations and the right to refer the matter to the Tribunal.

6–021 Where the conditions for a direction under s.257 are satisfied, the FSA may also apply to the court under s.258 for an order removing the manager or the trustee or both and replacing him or them with a suitable person nominated by the FSA. The FSA may make such a nomination only if satisfied that the requirements of s.243 as respects the manager and trustee would be complied with. If it appears to the FSA that there is no person it can nominate, it may apply to the court for an order removing the manager or trustee or both and appointing an authorised person to wind up the scheme (s.258(3)). Such an order may later be rescinded by the court and an order appointing a person nominated by the FSA may be made (s.258(5). The court has power to make such order as it thinks fit on an application under the section (s.258(4)). Under s.258(6) any such application must be made on written notice to the manager and trustee.

Open-ended Investment Companies: FSMA 2000 and Regulations

The provisions in FSMA 2000 relating to open-ended investment com- **6–022** panies are very much shorter than the provisions relating authorised unit trusts. Essentially, there is no more than a power for the Treasury to make provision for facilitating the carrying on of collective investment by means of open-ended investment companies and for regulating such companies (s.262(1)). The legislative meat is thus to be found in the regulations themselves, the Open-Ended Investment Companies Regulations 2001 (SI 2001/1228) ("the OEIC Regulations"). A body incorporated under the OEIC Regulations is called in the *FSA Handbook* an "investment company with variable capital".

The OEIC Regulations are divided into five parts: Pt I (general); Pt II **6–023** (formation, supervision and control); Pt III (Corporate Code); Pt IV (the FSA's registration functions); and Pt V (miscellaneous). Pt I is concerned simply with citation, commencement and extent, and with interpretation. Reg.3 goes on to provide that if the FSA makes an authorisation order then immediately upon the coming into effect of the order, the body to which the order relates is to be incorporated as an open-ended investment company, although, at that point, it will not have any shareholders or property. The FSA's power to make such an order is contained in reg.14 and may be exercised if:

- the FSA is satisfied that the company will, on the coming into effect of the authorisation order, comply with the requirements in reg.15 (which are similar to the majority of the requirements applying to an individually recognised overseas scheme, considered in para.6.009 above, but with the addition of a requirement that the head office of the company must be situated in England and Wales or Scotland, and that the depositary must be incorporated in the United Kingdom or another EEA State with a place of business in the United Kingdom. Reg.5 requires the appointment of a depositary to whom all scheme property must be entrusted for safekeeping, and the requirements of Sch.1 apply as respects depositaries);
- the FSA is satisfied that the company will at that time comply with the requirements of FSA rules (meaning rules under reg.6, by which the FSA's power under ss.247 and 248 to make trust scheme rules and scheme particulars rules may be exercised in relation to open-ended investment companies for like purposes and subject to the same conditions). The current rules are to be found in CIS 2.2.2 to 2.2.4 and CIS 3;
- the FSA has been provided with a copy of the proposed company's instrument of incorporation and a certificate signed by a solicitor to the effect that the instrument of incorporation complies with Sch.2

to the OEIC Regulations and such of the requirements of FSA rules as relate to the contents of that instrument;

- the FSA has received a notification under reg.18 (that is, a notification approving the proposed name of the company. Reg.19 contains further detailed provisions about names; in particular, the name may not include "limited", "unlimited" or "public limited company", and may not be the same as any other name appearing in the registrar's index of names).

It will be seen that these requirements bear a close family resemblance to the requirements to be satisfied before the FSA may make an authorisation order in respect of a unit trust scheme, and that is a common feature of the provisions of the OEIC Regulations. The purpose of the requirements is to safeguard investors and the systems are broadly similar, allowing for the differences in the form of vehicles used in the two types of collective investment scheme.

6–024 Again, the procedure for applying for authorisation and the contents of any application are matters for the FSA (reg.12), except that certain particulars in relation to directors are required (reg.13), as under s.242. The substance of s.244 as to time limits and the right to withdraw an application reappears in reg.14. Additionally, however, that regulation introduces Sch.2 to the OEIC Regulations, under which provision is made as to the content of the instrument of incorporation and for the restriction of the right to amend the instrument as respects certain matters required under the OEIC Regulations. As with unit trust schemes, there is a warning and decision notice procedure if the FSA proposes to refuse an application for authorisation, and the applicant may refer the matter to the Financial Services and Markets Tribunal (reg.16). Reg.17 provides an equivalent to the power of the FSA to give a certificate under s.246; if an open-ended investment company complies with the conditions necessary to enable it to enjoy the rights conferred by the UCITS Directive, the FSA may issue a certificate to that effect, either on the making of an authorisation order or at any subsequent time.

The FSA also has power under reg.7 to waive or modify the application of all or any of the FSA rules to any person or company in terms very similar to those of s.250.

6–025 Under reg.21, an open-ended investment company must give written notice to the FSA of:

- any proposed alteration to the company's instrument of incorporation;
- any proposed alteration to the company's prospectus which would be significant;
- any proposed reconstruction or amalgamation involving the company;
- any proposal to wind up the affairs of the company otherwise than by the court;

- any proposal to replace a director of the company, to appoint an additional director or to decrease the number of directors in post;
- any proposal to replace the depositary of the company.

Again, the family resemblance to s.251 can be seen. The restriction there contained on effecting any such alteration or carrying out any such proposal applies equally in this context and there is again a warning and decision notice procedure and a right to refer matters to the Financial Services and Markets Tribunal in reg.22.

Reg.23 sets out the circumstances in which the FSA can revoke an authorisation order on its own initiative in virtually the same terms as those specified in s.254, subject to necessary changes. Additionally, however, before revoking an authorisation order which has come into force, the FSA must ensure that such steps as are necessary and appropriate to secure the winding up of the company, whether by the court or otherwise, have been taken. There is no provision comparable to s.256, under which the company itself might request revocation of the authorisation order. The usual warning and decision notice procedure, with the usual right of reference, is provided by reg.24. **6–026**

The provisions of ss.257 to 261 find their equivalents in regulations 25 to 29, although reg.25(2) envisages a wider range of directions which may be given, to reflect the different methods of operation possible with an open-ended investment company. It is also provided that where a winding-up order has been made by the court, no direction under reg.25 is to have effect. **6–027**

The court's power to wind up an open-ended investment company arises under Pt V of the Insolvency Act 1986, which provides for the winding up of unregistered companies. Provisions relating to the presentation of a winding-up petition are contained in reg.31, and reg.32 provides for dissolution in such a case. The procedure where the winding-up is otherwise than by order of the court is contained in reg.33. **6–028**

The corporate code contained in Pt III of the OEIC Regulations governs the following: the identity of the directors, their obligation to have regard to the interests of employees; availability for inspection of directors' service contracts; general meetings; the capacity of the company; the powers of the directors and the general meeting to bind the company; the exclusion of any duty on a third party to inquire as to the company's powers; the exclusion of deemed notice of a matter by reason of its being in a document available for inspection; the power of shareholders to restrain or ratify acts beyond the company's capacity or powers; the consequences of events affecting the company's status; the invalidity of certain transactions involving directors; the power to issue shares; the obligation to issue share certificates; the power to issue bearer shares; the obligation to keep a register of shareholders, the power to close the register, the power of the court to rectify the register; powers relating to the transfer of shares; a general power to do all such things as are incidental or conducive to the carrying on of the company's business, the obligation for the company's name to appear, the obligations for certain particulars to appear in correspondence and other documents; the formation of contracts; the **6–029** execution and authentication of documents; power to have an official seal for use for sealing issued shares or documents creating or evidencing such shares; personal liability in certain circumstances for contracts and deeds; the avoidance of exemptions from liability, the power of the court to grant relief for certain breaches of duty; the penalty for fraudulent trading; the power to provide for employees on the cessation of business; requirements relating to reports; the auditors; and mergers and divisions. As this list suggests, these are all matters which are commonly dealt with in relation to companies limited by shares either by provisions of the companies legislation or by the memorandum and articles.

6–030 Reg.71, in Pt IV, imposes on the FSA an obligation to keep a register of open-ended investment companies. Each company must have a registered number (reg.72). Pt IV goes on to make further provision for the delivery of documents to the FSA, the keeping of records by the FSA and the inspection of such records. The FSA is also obliged, by reg.78, to cause to be published a notice of changes in certain specified information relating to an open-ended investment company. Reg.4 imposes a general obligation on the FSA to register certain information in relation to such a company forthwith upon making an authorisation order.

Recognised Schemes

6–031 We have already noted, in para.6.007, that a scheme constituted in another EEA State may be a recognised scheme if it satisfies certain prescribed requirements. The relevant requirements are contained in the Financial Services and Markets Act 2000 (Collective Investment Schemes Constituted in Other EEA States) Regulations 2001 (SI 2001/2383) and are short and simple: that the scheme is one which is an undertaking for collective investment in transferable securities within the UCITS Directive. That, however, gives rise to the question what such an undertaking is. To expand to some extent what is said in para.6.001, by Art.1 of the Directive a UCITS is an undertaking:

- the sole object of which is the collective investment in transferable securities or certain other liquid financial assets of capital raised from the public and which operates on the principle of risk-spreading; and
- the units of which are, at the request of holders, repurchased or redeemed, directly or indirectly, out of the assets of the undertaking.

"Transferable securities" are themselves defined as shares in companies and other equivalents to shares in companies, and bonds and other forms of securitised debt.

6–032 The subsequent articles of the Directive contain a number of further requirements. The UCITS must be authorised in the Member State in which it is situated, which requires compliance with a number of further conditions, and the relevant authorities must be satisfied of the reputation and experience of those involved in the depositary. UCITS management companies may not engage in activities other than the management of authorised UCITS, subject to certain limited exceptions. There are conditions to be satisfied by any company which wants to become an authorised management company or an authorised investment company, and again the relevant authorities must be satisfied of the reputation and experience of those involved in the company. There are also restrictions on how the capital raised is to be invested and requirements relating to the information to be made available to participants. The original investment provisions have been amended to give wider investment powers by virtue of the amending UCITS Product Directive (Dir. 01/108 [2002] O.J. L41/35), although not all UCITS in fact operate under the wider powers as yet. Even having regard to those wider powers, the various limitations referred to mean that by no means every body in an EEA State which, if it were based in the United Kingdom, would or could be an authorised unit trust or an authorised open-ended investment company will be a UCITS and thus a recognised scheme which can use its EEA passport rights to carry on business in the United Kingdom.

Although in general the regulation of a scheme constituted in another EEA State is a matter for the home regulators, the FSA does have power under s.267(2) to make a direction which has the effect of suspending the promotion of the scheme if it appears to the FSA that the operator of the scheme has communicated an invitation or inducement to invest in the scheme in a manner contrary to financial promotion rules. The associated procedural requirements are set out in ss.268 and 269 and are similar to those applying in respect of directions given to authorised unit trust schemes under ss.259 to 261, and directions given to open-ended investment companies under regs 25 to 29 of the OEIC Regulations but additionally the FSA is under an obligation to notify the home State authorities of steps taken. **6–033**

The Treasury has exercised its power to designate territories outside the United Kingdom for the purposes of s.270 of the FSMA 2000 by the Financial Services and Markets Act 2000 (Collective Investment Schemes) (Designated Countries and Territories) Order 2003 (SI 2003/1181). The territories so designated are Guernsey, Jersey and the Isle of Man. It is thought that the requirements to be satisfied before the FSA will make an order recognising a scheme individually under s.272 of the 2000 Act are very difficult to satisfy. **6–034**

It will be apparent from the initial discussion that the statutory provisions relating to recognised schemes have as a principal focus the need to ensure for United Kingdom investors protection at least equivalent to that which would apply if the scheme were not an overseas scheme. That policy continues with the remaining provisions of this Chapter of the 2000 Act, which apply to schemes recognised under s.270 or 272. (Presumably the UCITS Directive affords sufficient protection in the case of schemes recognised under s.264). Under s.278, the FSA has power to make rules imposing duties and liabilities on schemes recognised under s.270 or s.272 for purposes corresponding to those for which scheme particulars rules may be made under s.248 in relation to authorised unit trusts. The power has **6–035** been exercised, and the relevant requirements appear in CIS. S.279 confers a power to direct that a scheme should cease to be recognised if it appears to the FSA that:

- the operator, trustee or depositary of the scheme has contravened a requirement imposed on him by or under FSMA 2000;
- the operator, trustee or depositary of the scheme has, in purported compliance with any such requirement, knowingly or recklessly given the FSA information which is false or misleading in a material particular;
- in the case of an order under s.272, one or more of the requirements for the making of an order are no longer satisfied; or
- none of the above paragraphs applies, but it is undesirable in the interests of the participants or potential participants that the scheme should continue to be recognised.

The family resemblance to s.254 and reg.23 of the OEIC Regulations is clear. A warning and decision notice regime applies by virtue of s.280 and the operator, trustee or depositary has a right of reference to the Financial Services and Markets Tribunal.

There is also a directions regime in ss.281 and 282 similar to that which applies to other collective investment schemes which may be marketed direct to the public (see para.6.033 above), but the directions which may be given are simply that the scheme is not to be a recognised scheme for a specified period or until the occurrence of a specified event or until specified conditions are complied with.

6–036 Finally, under s.283 the FSA may make rules requiring operators of recognised schemes to maintain in the United Kingdom, or in such part or parts of it as may be specified, such facilities as the FSA thinks desirable in the interests of participants and as are specified in the rules. The power has been exercised and the requirements are set out in at CIS 17.4. The FSA may also require the operator of any recognised scheme to include explanatory information specified in the notice imposing the requirement in any communication which is an invitation or inducement to engage in investment business and which names the scheme.

Investigations

6–037 The FSA or the Secretary of State, in either case as an "investigating authority", has power under s.284(1) to appoint one or more competent persons to investigate on its behalf: the affairs of, or of the manager or trustee of, any authorised unit trust scheme; the affairs of, or the operator trustee or depositary of, any recognised scheme so far as relating to activities carried on in the United Kingdom; or the affairs of, or of the operator trustee or depositary of, any other collective investment scheme except a body incorporated under the OEIC Regulations. As might be expected, reg.30 gives a similar power in respect of such bodies. The person appointed to conduct the investigation has powers to require information (s.284(3) and reg.30(3)). Many of the general information gathering and investigation provisions of Pt XI of FSMA 2000 (considered further in Ch.15) are incorporated by reference. A limited degree of protection is given in respect of information in respect of which an obligation of confidence arising from the carrying on of banking business exists under s.284(8) and reg.30(8), but the protection does not exist where the obligation is owed by or to a person under investigation.

Restrictions on Financial Promotion

Having now considered the various types of scheme which can be marketed directly to the public, it is appropriate to look at the restrictions which apply generally. S.21 contains an overall prohibition on the communication, in the course of business, of an invitation or inducement to engage in investment activity, unless the communication is made by an authorised person or the content of the communication has been approved for the purposes of s.21 by an authorised person. The section envisages delegated legislation by the Treasury both clarifying the scope of the prohibition and disapplying it in certain circumstances. That power has been exercised in the lengthy Financial Services and Markets Act 2000 (Financial Promotions) Order 2001 (SI 2001/1335), as amended by the Financial Services and Markets Act 2000 (Commencement of Mortgage Regulation) (Amendment) Order 2002 (SI 2002/1777). The general ban, however, is not the particular concern of this chapter. The statutory provision which limits the type of collective investment scheme which may be marketed directly to the public, even by an authorised person, is s.238. Subs.(1) prohibits an authorised person from communicating an invitation or inducement to participate in a collective investment scheme, subject to the remaining provisions of the section and of s.239. **6–038**

The major relaxation of the s.238(1) prohibition is of course the provision, contained in s.238(4), by which authorised unit trust schemes, schemes constituted by an authorised open-ended investment company and recognised schemes may be promoted. In addition, s.238(5) lifts the ban in relation to anything done in accordance with rules made by the FSA for the purpose of exempting the promotion of certain schemes otherwise than to the general public (for which see COB 3 Annex 5), and under s.238(3) the ban applies to communications originating outside the UK only if the communication is capable of having an effect in the UK (although that provision may be repealed by the Treasury). **6–039**

In addition, the Treasury has power, under s.238(6), to specify further circumstances in which the prohibition does not apply. That power has been exercised in the Financial Services and Markets Act 2000 (Promotion of Collective Investment Schemes) (Exemptions) Order 2001 (SI 2001/1060), amended by the Financial Services and Markets Act 2000 (Financial Promotion and Miscellaneous Amendments) Order 2002 (SI 2002/1310) and the Financial Services and Markets Act 2000 (Financial Promotion) (Amendments) (Electronic Commerce Directive) Order 2002 **6–040**

(SI 2002/2157). The Order distinguishes between real time communications (*i.e.* communications in the course of a personal visit, telephone conversation or other interactive dialogue) and non-real time communications (which include letters and emails) (art.4). It also distinguishes between solicited real time communications (where the visit, telephone call or dialogue was initiated by the recipient of the communication or takes place in response to an express request from the recipient) and other real time communications (art.5). The Order then specifies exemptions under the following headings:

- communications to overseas recipients;
- solicited real time communications from overseas;
- communications from overseas to previously overseas customers;
- incoming electronic commerce communications;
- follow-up non-real time communications and solicited real time communications;
- introductions;
- generic promotions;
- investment professionals;
- one-off non-real time communications and solicited real time communications;
- one-off unsolicited real time communications;
- communications required or authorised by enactments;
- persons in the business of placing promotional material;
- existing participants in an unregulated scheme;
- group companies;
- persons in the business of disseminating information;
- certified high net worth individuals;
- high net worth companies, unincorporated associations, etc.;
- sophisticated investors;
- associations of high net worth or sophisticated investors;
- settlors, trustees and personal representatives;
- beneficiaries of trust, will or intestacy;
- remedy following report by the Parliamentary Commissioner for Administration;
- persons placing promotional material in particular publications.

Many of these exemptions are themselves complex and reference should be made to the Order for further details. It may also be noted that many of the exemptions are similar to corresponding exemptions in the Financial Promotions Order referred to above. It is understood that the effect is intended to be to put authorised persons marketing unregulated collective investment schemes in no worse a position than unauthorised persons promoting other types of investment.

The exception envisaged under s.239 is limited to single property schemes. Under s.239(2), such a scheme must have the characteristics specified in subs.(3), namely: **6–041**

- that the property subject to the scheme (apart from cash or other assets held for management purposes) consists of a single building or a single building with ancillary buildings managed by or on behalf of the operator of the scheme, or a group of adjacent or contiguous buildings managed by the operator or on his behalf as a single enterprise, with or without ancillary land and with or without furniture, fittings or other contents; and
- that the units of the participants in the scheme are either dealt in on a recognised investment exchange or offered on terms such that any agreement for their acquisition is conditional on their admission to dealings on such an exchange,

and must also satisfy such other requirements as are contained in regulations made by the Treasury. At the time of writing no such regulations have been made, but in their absence it seems that the Financial Services Act 1986 (Single Property Schemes) (Exemption) Regulations 1989 (SI 1989/28), made under s.76 of the 1986 Act, will continue to apply.

Perhaps not surprisingly, an authorised person may not approve for the purposes of s.21 the content of a communication relating to a collective investment scheme if he would be prohibited by s.238(1) from effecting the communication himself or causing it to be communicated (s.240(1)), and for the purpose of determining whether there has been any contravention of s.21, an approval given in contravention of s.240(1) is to be regarded as not having been given (s.240(2)). S.150, which gives a right to bring an action for damages in certain circumstances, is made applicable to a contravention of s.238(1) or s.240(1) by s.241. **6–042**

The *FSA Handbook*

There are two sourcebooks of particular relevance to collective investment schemes: the general Conduct of Business Sourcebook and the specialist Collective Investment Schemes Sourcebook. Broadly speaking, COB sets standards for the marketing and selling of, among other forms of investment, collective investment schemes, while CIS sets out product regulation requirements for the schemes themselves (CIS 1.1.2). COB has already been considered in Ch.2 (see in particular para.2–096 and the following) and the discussion there is not repeated. The discussion of COB 10, relating specifically to operators of collective investment schemes, however, was postponed to this chapter and now follows. It should be observed that COB **6–043** is concerned both with regulated and with unregulated collective investment schemes, whereas CIS is concerned only with regulated schemes.

6–044 As a general rule, when an operator is involved in activity relating to the management of a scheme, references to the "customer" are to be construed as references to the scheme; in the case of an unregulated collective investment scheme, references to terms of business or a client agreement are to be construed as references to the scheme documents required by COB 10.6.2; and in the case of an unregulated collective investment scheme, when an operator is required to provide information to or to obtain consent from a customer, the operator must ensure that the information is provided to or consent obtained from a participant or potential participant (COB 10.2.3). These modifications reflect that fact that owing to the collective nature of the arrangements, the investor is not the direct customer of the operator; in effect, the scheme intervenes. This of course affects the applicability of many of the other provisions in COB. The provisions which apply, as respects scheme management activity, are the following (COB 10.2.5):

- COB 1 (application and general provisions);
- COB 2.1 (clear, fair and not misleading communication);
- COB 2.2 (inducements and soft commission: subject to modification in relation to a regulated collective investment scheme);
- COB 2.3 (reliance on others);
- COB 2.4 (Chinese walls);
- COB 6.2 (suitability: subject to modification);
- COB 7.1 (conflict of interest and material interest);
- COB 7.2 (churning and switching);
- COB 7.4 (customer order priority);
- COB 7.5 (best execution: subject to modification in the case of an unregulated collective investment scheme);
- COB 7.6 (timely execution);
- COB 7.7 (aggregation and allocation: subject to modification);
- COB 7.12 (customer order and execution records);
- COB 10 itself.

The provisions themselves have already been considered in Ch.2. The details of the modifications may be studied in COB 10.2.5 and 10.3 to 10.6.

6–045 In addition COB 10.6 sets out content requirements for scheme documents in relation to unregulated collective investment schemes. (The requirements for regulated schemes are contained in CIS, as already noted.) COB 10.7, broadly speaking, requires the operator of an unregulated scheme to provide to participants, promptly and at suitable intervals, a written statement containing adequate information on the value and composition of the portfolio of the scheme at the beginning and end of the period of the statement. Again, this is covered by CIS as respects regulated schemes.

We then come to look in some more detail at CIS. As stated in CIS 1.1.8, it performs three main functions: **6–046**

- setting out material relating to the constitution and management of authorised open-ended investment companies ("ICVCs") and authorised unit trusts ("AUTs")
- setting out material relating to the process of authorisation
- setting out material which satisfies the requirements of the UCITS Directive, thereby enabling ICVCs and AUTs which meet those standards to market elsewhere in the EEA.

Since much of the material relates to both ICVCs and AUTs, the term "authorised funds" is used in CIS where both types of investment vehicle are referred to.

The nature of CIS is best indicated by reference to the outline of its contents contained in CIS 1.2. The following matters are covered: **6–047**

- provisions relating to the contents of the documents required to form authorised funds and other matters relating to their constitutional features, such as classes of shares in ICVCs and units in AUTs, and the types of authorised fund which may be established (CIS 2);
- requirements as to the preparation, content, availability of and changes to the prospectus, for ICVCs, or scheme particulars, for AUTs (CIS 3);
- provisions as to the valuation and pricing of authorised funds which are single priced and rules on the sale and redemption of shares or units in such funds (CIS 4);
- requirements for compliance with rules on investment which ensure that the principles of risk spreading are applied (CIS 5 and 5A). The rules in CIS 5 reflect the investment rules in the UCITS Amending Directive, while those in CIS 5A reflect the original UCITS rules. Broadly speaking, transitional arrangements permit a UCITS existing on or before February 13, 2002 to continue to operate under the rules in CIS 5A until February 13, 2007, although they may switch to the CIS 5 rules before that date, while a UCITS authorised after February 13, 2000 but before February 13, 2004 has only until the latter date to begin operating under the CIS 5 rules;
- provisions relating to the register of unit-holders in an AUT and relating to plan registers of both ICVCs and AUTs (CIS 6);
- provisions apportioning responsibilities between the directors and depositary of an ICVC and the manager and trustee of an AUT (CIS 7);

- conditions concerning charges when investors buy or sell shares or units and payments that can be made out of the scheme property (CIS 8);
- the calculation and distribution of income (CIS 9);
- requirements as to the content and publication of annual and half-yearly reports and accounts of authorised funds (CIS 10);
- matters relating to meetings of holders, the conditions under which the instrument constituting the scheme may be changed, how the scheme property of an authorised fund may become the property of another scheme and the use of electronic media for giving notices or sending documents or information (CIS 11);
- special provisions relating to futures and options schemes, geared futures and options schemes, property schemes, feeder funds and funds of funds and umbrella schemes (CIS 12);
- requirements for the suspension of dealings in the shares or units of authorised funds (CIS 13);
- requirements relating to the winding-up of authorised funds and the termination of a sub-fund of an ICVC (CIS 14);
- rules and guidance on the valuation and pricing of units in a dual-priced AUT (that is, an AUT in which units are issued at an offer price and redeemed at a bid price) (CIS 15);
- the application and notification procedures for authorised funds and schemes from other countries or territories which may be recognised by the FSA for marketing in the United Kingdom (CIS 16);
- the information that the FSA requires in order to consider whether schemes under s.264, s.270 or s.272 of the 2000 Act should be permitted to market in the United Kingdom (CIS 17);
- the application and periodic fees payable for the authorisation or recognition of regulated schemes.

The Future

6–048 On May 21, 2003, the FSA published proposals (consultation paper 185) for a substantial revision of CIS. As has already been noted, much of the current regime has been carried over essentially unchanged from the regime in operation under the Financial Services Act 1986 and the time had come to reconsider the system of regulation. The object of the exercise was to construct a system of regulation which delivered appropriate protection to consumers, while removing unnecessarily prescriptive requirements and creating a more flexible regime better suited to meeting varying consumer needs. At the same time, of course, the regime must implement, where necessary, other legislation and be consistent with other regulatory developments. The FSA identifies the main outcome of the proposed changes as a shift of balance in the way authorised collective investment schemes are governed from the regulator's rules to fund documentation. The estimated total cost to firms of updating the documentation is £10 million, but it is proposed that the transitional period should last until February 13, 2007, when firms will be obliged to comply with the rules implementing the UCITS Product Directive, referred to in the preceding paragraph, with the result that many firms will be able to consolidate the cost of complying with the two sets of changes.

The key proposals in the consultation paper are: **6–049**

- a new category of non-retail schemes, restricted to investment by institutional and expert investors only, will be introduced. Such schemes will be subject to lighter product regulation than retail schemes, but the rules will nevertheless be sufficient to distinguish them from unregulated schemes. Investors in such schemes will not enjoy the usual private customer protections
- the various current categories of retail scheme will be rationalised into two broad types: a UCITS type and a non-UCITS type. Schemes of the former type will comply with the UCITS Directive requirements (as amended) and so will be able to enjoy passport rights in respect of marketing in EEA States. Schemes of the latter type will be able to invest in a wider range of assets, including property, which is currently outside the classes of permitted investments under the UCITS Directive
- the charging rules for authorised unit trusts will be aligned with those for open-ended investment companies and performance fees will be allowed for both products. Examples of the operation of such fees will have to be disclosed to investors in advance
- the requirements for giving information to investors will be revised, so that customers receive short-form reports better suited to the needs of non-professional customers, and prospectuses will be in a more user-friendly form
- the requirement that collective investment schemes be open for redemption at all times will be limited in some non-UCITS schemes, in particular those where the investments are relatively illiquid (*e.g.* property). The FSA proposes to permit redemption days to be up to six months apart.

The FSA intends to make final rules, following consultation, in early 2004, at which point the new provisions may be adopted by existing United Kingdom schemes. They will apply to all United Kingdom schemes from February 13, 2007.

The UCITS Directive was amended not only by the UCITS Product Directive, but also by another Directive of the same date, the UCITS Management Directive (Dir.01/107 [2002] O.J. L41/20). As is stated in para.6.032, under the original Directive, the manager of a UCITS scheme cannot in general provide other investment services. The amending **6–050**

Directive introduces a new European passport, which will allow a UCITS management company to carry out cross-border investment services; it imposes new financial resource requirements and conduct of business rules on the UCITS management company; and it provides for a simplified prospectus to be used as a marketing document throughout the EEA. The proposals for implementation were contained in consultation paper 163 and the consultation period ended on April 1, 2003. The new rules are expected to be made by August 13, 2003, the deadline under the Directive. The practical effect will be that AUT managers will no longer be restricted to operating collective investment schemes and connected activities, but that the authorised corporate director of an ICVC will be treated as a management company and some restructuring of operations will be required in some cases. Further, firms will have to comply with new financial resources rules. In that respect, there will be a transitional period until February 13, 2007, provided that a firm relying on that provision does not undertake any of the new activities allowed by the Directive. In other respects, the new rules must be complied with from February 13, 2004.

Chapter 7

The Panel on Takeovers and Mergers

The Panel

Introduction

The Panel on Takeovers and Mergers (the Panel) is a non-statutory, regulatory body, which is responsible for administering the City Code on Takeovers and Mergers (the Code). 7–001

The Panel was set up in 1968, following proposals by the Governor of the Bank of England and the Chairman of the Stock Exchange, in response to concerns that shareholders had been subjected to unfair practices in a number of controversial takeovers. The creation of the Panel also reflected a wider sense that the proper regulation of takeovers and mergers was essential to maintain fairness and investor confidence in the markets.

The first edition of the Code was published in March 1968 and the present (seventh) edition was published in May 2002. The Code now consists of an Introduction, followed by 10 General Principles, a Definitions section and 38 Rules. Guidance notes provide comment on many of the Definitions and Rules. The provisions of the Code are outlined in the second part of this Chapter (paras 7–026 to 7–060). 7–002

The Panel sees its central objective as being to ensure equality of treatment and opportunity for all shareholders in takeover bids. A similar objective can be discerned in the Introduction to the Code itself: 7–003

> "The Code is designed principally to ensure fair and equal treatment of all shareholders in relation to takeovers. The Code also provides an orderly framework within which takeovers are conducted. . . . The Code represents the collective opinion of those professionally involved in the field of takeovers as to business standards and as to how fairness to shareholders can be achieved."

It can be seen, therefore, that the Panel and the Code share the common aim of investor protection—specifically, that of protecting the interests of shareholders in the takeover context.

Between 1968 and 2002, the Panel handled some 7,000 announced offers and about half as many other cases in which no offer was announced.

The Panel is also responsible for the Rules Governing Substantial Acquisition of Shares (the SARs), which counter the problem of "dawn raids". A "dawn raid" occurs when there is a rapid and organised 7–004 acquisition of a substantial shareholding in a company. As we shall see in para.7–062, below, the SARs deal with this problem by restricting the speed with which a person may increase his stake in a company, if the increase will result in his holding between 15 per cent and 30 per cent of the voting rights in the company. The SARs are designed to protect the interest of shareholders, by ensuring that small shareholders have a better opportunity to participate in the premium which a person would expect to pay in order to build up a large stake in the company.

Membership of the Panel

7–005 The full Panel has 17 members, chosen with a view to ensuring that the body is recognised as being authoritative and that it possesses a wide range of experience of takeovers and the securities markets generally. The Governor of the Bank of England appoints five members of the Panel, namely, its Chairman, two deputy chairmen and three independent members, who are industrialists. Each of the following bodies is responsible for nominating one of the remaining eleven members:

- The Association of British Insurers;
- The Association of Investment Trust Companies;
- The Association of Private Client Investment Managers and Stockbrokers;
- The British Bankers' Association;
- The Confederation of British Industry;
- The Institute of Chartered Accountants in England and Wales;
- Investment Management Association;
- The London Investment Banking Association (the LIBA);
- The Corporate Finance Committee of the LIBA;
- The Securities Trading Committee of the LIBA;
- The National Association of Pension Funds Investment Council.

The Role of the Executive

7–006 The day-to-day work of the Panel is carried out through its Executive, which is headed by a Director General who is normally a senior merchant banker on secondment. The other members of the Executive are made up of its permanent staff and a team of professionals (including lawyers, accountants, stockbrokers and bankers) on secondment for periods of two years.

7–007 The Executive's responsibilities include the conduct of investigations and the monitoring of relevant dealings in connection with the Code. The

Executive is also available to give guidance on the interpretation of the Code and the SARs, and to give rulings on points of interpretation, both before and during takeover or merger transactions. The parties to takeover transactions and their advisers are encouraged to seek a ruling from the Executive if there is any room for doubt as to whether a proposed course of action is consistent with the Code: taking legal or other professional advice is not regarded as an adequate substitute for obtaining a ruling from the Executive. Rulings may be given either on a conditional basis (where only one party has been heard) or on an unconditional basis (where all parties have been heard).

Rulings of the Executive are subject to appeal to the Panel. Where a particularly unusual, difficult or important issue involved, the Executive may refer the matter to the Panel for decision without itself giving a ruling on it.

The Executive is also responsible for instituting disciplinary proceedings **7–008** before the Panel when it considers that there has been a breach of the Code or the SARs. In such a case, the Executive will act as "prosecutor" rather than adjudicator. It will invite the person concerned to appear before the Panel and will inform him in writing of the alleged breach and of the material which the Executive will present to the Panel.

In cases where the person concerned agrees the facts and the disciplinary action proposed by the Executive, the Executive may deal with the matter itself.

Hearings before the Panel

The quorum for a Panel hearing is five, including a chairman. The **7–009** proceedings are informal and there are no rules of evidence. The parties (including the Executive) will normally prepare a brief written statement of their case in advance of the hearing, and present their case at the hearing in person or by a non-legal adviser. The parties are free to call such witnesses as they think necessary. Where a party wishes to present evidence of a commercially confidential nature, the Panel may direct that the evidence be heard in the absence of some, or all, of the other parties involved. In most cases, the proceedings will take place in private, but the Panel will normally publish its decision and the reasons for it so that its activities may be explained to the public.

If the Panel finds that there has been a breach of the Code, it may apply one or more of the following sanctions:

(a) private reprimand;

(b) public censure;

(c) reporting the offender's conduct to another regulatory body (*e.g.* the DTI, the Stock Exchange, the FSA or the relevant professional body);

(d) taking action designed to ensure that persons authorised by the FSA, or regulated by certain professional bodies, do not act for the offender in a transaction to which the Code applies.

We consider further in paras 7–12 to 7–19, below, the nature of the Panel's authority to impose sanctions, and the extent to which that authority is underpinned by the disciplinary powers available to the FSA.

The Appeal Committee

7–010 The Appeal Committee of the Panel consists of a chairman and/or deputy chairman (who will normally have held high judicial office), sitting with members of the Panel who were not involved in the decision under appeal. The quorum for the Appeal Committee is three.

There is a right of appeal to the Appeal Committee in three cases, namely: (i) where the Panel has found a breach of the Code and proposes to take disciplinary action; (ii) where it is alleged that the Panel has acted outside its jurisdiction; and (iii) where the Panel has withheld or withdrawn exempt status from a market-maker or fund manager. In other cases, an appeal requires the leave of the Panel. The Panel does not normally give leave against a finding of fact, or against a decision on the interpretation of the Code. Leave may, nonetheless, be granted if the Panel considers that the case is one of general importance or one which, for some other special reason, should be considered by the Appeal Committee.

The Code Committee

7–011 Until recently, the Panel was responsible both for drafting the Code, and for interpreting and enforcing it. To meet concerns that the Human Rights Act 1998 might be infringed by an arrangement under which the same body was responsible for both the drafting and enforcement of the Code, the function of reviewing and amending the Code has now been delegated to a separate committee, known as the Code Committee, whose members are different from the members of the Panel. The Code Committee was established in February 2001, and currently has seven members, drawn from senior practitioners and industry. The Committee will normally consult publicly on proposed changes to the Code.

The Code Committee is also responsible for keeping the SARs under review, and for amending them where necessary.

The Nature of the Panel's Authority

7–012 The Panel is a non-statutory body, and the Code does not have the force of law. Sir John Donaldson M.R. commented on this striking feature of the Panel in *R. v Panel on Take-overs and Mergers, Ex p. Datafin* [1987] Q.B. 815, 824G-H:

> "The Panel on Take-overs and Mergers is a truly remarkable body. Perched on the 20th floor of the Stock Exchange building in the City of London, both literally and metaphorically it oversees and regulates a very important part of the United Kingdom financial market. Yet it performs this function without visible means of legal support."

He went on to point out that, while the Panel had no formal legal powers (whether statutory, contractual or otherwise), it had immense *de facto* power as a result of its role in devising, promulgating, amending and interpreting the Code, in waiving or modifying the application of the Code in particular cases, in investigating and reporting on alleged breaches of the Code and in the application or threat of sanctions.

To a considerable extent, the decisions of the Panel continue to derive their force from the stature of the Panel, which in turn is a reflection of the fact that its members are appointed by bodies representing the interests of virtually all those actively involved in the securities markets: criticism from such a source is therefore likely to be seriously damaging to the reputation of any person found to have contravened the requirements of the Code. **7–013**

The absence of any direct legal support for the Panel is not without its advantages. A statute-based scheme would be likely to be less flexible than the present self-regulatory system. It would therefore have a tendency to impair the Panel's ability to act swiftly and flexibly in the rapidly changing circumstances of a takeover bid, which is one of the perceived strengths of the present regime. A statutory scheme might also be expected to provide the parties to a contested bid with unwelcome opportunities for tactical applications to the courts, so leading to a prolonged period of uncertainty for investors holding, or wishing to trade in, the shares of the parties involved in the bid. **7–014**

Support for the Panel under FSMA 2000

In the *Datafin* case, Sir John Donaldson noted (at pp.834–835) that, while the Panel may be lacking in visible means of legal support, there is abundant invisible or indirect support for its functions. He characterised the position of the Panel as that of a central self-regulatory body which is supported by a periphery of statutory powers and penalties. There is even more force in that observation today than when the *Datafin* case was decided, with the Panel now receiving its principal means of indirect support from the rules set out in Ch.4 of the *Market Conduct* module of the *FSA Handbook*. **7–015**

Ch.4 applies to every authorised person whose permission includes, or ought to include, any designated investment business (MAR 4.1.1R). There are, however, three important exceptions for authorised professional firms (in MAR 4.4.1R), which, in summary, provide that: **7–016**

(a) nothing in Ch.4 requires an authorised professional firm to contravene the professional conduct rules and guidance issued by its designated professional body;

(b) Ch.4 does not prevent an authorised professional firm from providing professional advice which does not constitute the carrying on of a regulated activity and the provision of which is supervised and regulated by a designated professional body;

(c) Ch.4 does not apply to non-mainstream regulated activity (as to which, see para.2A-17, above).

7–017 Turning now to the content of the rules in Ch.4, the first provision to note is MAR 4.2.1R, by which the FSA endorses the Code and the SARs as respects the firms to which Ch.4 applies. The FSA's endorsement has two effects.

First, it means that, at the request of the Panel, the FSA may take enforcement action against any such firm which contravenes any provision of the Code or the SARs (see FSMA 2000, s.143(3) and (4)). Such action may include the cancellation or variation of the firm's Pt IV permission, the publication of a statement censuring the firm, the imposition of an unlimited financial penalty, or an application to the court for an injunction or restitution order.

Secondly, the FSA's endorsement means that, at the request of the Panel, the FSA may take disciplinary action against any approved person who is knowingly concerned in a contravention of the Code or the SARs by the firm which applied for his approval (see s.66(2)(b) and (7), and s.143(3)). This may result in the FSA imposing an unlimited financial penalty on the approved person, or publishing a statement of his misconduct (s.66(3)).

In both of these cases, a failure to comply with a requirement imposed, or ruling given, by the Panel under the Code or the SARs is treated as a failure to comply with the Code or the SARs itself (s.143(6)). Thus, a firm which contravenes a ruling given by the Panel, or an approved person who is knowingly concerned in such a contravention, will be exposed to the same range of enforcement measures as apply to a contravention of the Code itself.

7–018 Further support for the Panel's functions is given by MAR 4.3.1R, which provides that a firm to which Ch.4 applies must not act, or continue to act, for any person in connection with a transaction to which the Code or the SARs apply if the firm has reasonable grounds for believing that the person in question, or his principal, is not complying or is not likely to comply with the Code or the SARs.

The Panel publishes notices regarding compliance with the Code and the SARs. The FSA expects firms to keep themselves informed about notices published by the Panel and to take them into account in seeking to comply with MAR 4.3.1R. If the Panel were to name a person in such a notice as someone who, in the Panel's opinion, is not likely to comply with the Code or the SARs, the FSA would expect a firm to comply with MAR 4.3.1R by not acting, or continuing to act, for that person (MAR 4.3.2G (2)). However, by virtue of the second of the exceptions noted in para.7–016, above, a person who has been named in a notice published by the Panel will not be precluded from obtaining legal or other professional advice.

In addition, MAR 4.3.5R imposes an obligation on firms to provide the Panel, at its request, with any information and documents in their possession or control, and with such assistance as they are reasonably able to provide, to enable the Panel to perform its functions.

7–019 The Introduction to the Code notes the fact that the Panel's ability to invoke the FSA's enforcement powers under MAR 4.2.1R, coupled with the "cold-shouldering" provisions in MAR 4.3.1R, have the effect that those who do not conduct themselves in accordance with the high business standards embodied in the Code may find that, by way of sanction, the facilities of the United Kingdom securities markets are withheld from them.

Relationship with other Bodies

The Panel co-operates with the FSA and other regulatory authorities, including the DTI, the Stock Exchange, other RIE's, professional bodies, the Bank of England and OFEX. This co-operation extends to the sharing of information, and the reporting of breaches of the Code to the relevant authority. The Panel works closely with the Stock Exchange in monitoring share dealings. The Panel has access to the Stock Exchange's computer systems for the surveillance of markets and dealings, and is therefore able to scrutinise share dealings during the course of a bid. **7–020**

The Panel is designated under the Companies Act 1985 and FSMA 2000 to receive restricted regulatory information from the DTI and the FSA (see Sch.1 to the Financial Services and Markets Act 2000 (Disclosure of Confidential Information) Regulations 2001, SI 2001/2188).

Europe

A draft Directive on Takeovers was issued in 1990, with the aim of harmonising the regulation of takeovers throughout the E.C. ([1990] O.J. C240/7). Following publication of the draft, a number of bodies in the United Kingdom, including the Panel and the Law Society's influential Company Law Committee, expressed concern that, if implemented, the Directive would remove the flexibility of the existing system and lead to extensive litigation in the course of takeover bids. **7–021**

Although an amended version of the draft Directive was finally adopted by the Council of Ministers on June 19, 2000, the draft was rejected by the European Parliament in July 2001. The Commission then set up a group of experts under the chairmanship of Professor Winter, which reported in January 2002. A new draft Directive was issued in October 2002, and this has since been the subject of heated debate and revision. The laborious process of agreeing a compromise text is on-going at the time of writing.

The Role of the Courts

The Court of Appeal's decision in *Dunford and Elliott Ltd v Johnson and Firth Brown Ltd* [1977] 1 Lloyd's Rep. 505 shows that the provisions of the Code may have an important influence in determining the outcome of civil litigation between parties to a takeover bid. It also shows that the context of a bid may significantly limit the scope for remedies which would otherwise be available under the general law. In the *Dunford and Elliott* case, the plaintiff was a steel making company which had sustained severe losses over a number of years. It decided to make a rights issue to its shareholders, of whom some 43 per cent were institutional shareholders. The institutional shareholders were invited to form a consortium to underwrite **7–022** the issue and to this end the plaintiff's financial advisers prepared a report on the company's future financial prospects. The report was supplied to the members of the consortium on the basis that it was confidential and was "not to be used in any way to influence investment decisions". Without consulting the plaintiff, the consortium approached two other companies, one of which was a rival steel making company (J.F.B.). J.F.B. was shown the confidential report, but declined to join the consortium. When the underwriting scheme subsequently fell through, J.F.B. launched a takeover bid for the plaintiff company. The plaintiff then applied for an interlocutory injunction preventing J.F.B. from using the confidential information and restraining it from making a bid. The Court of Appeal refused to grant the injunction, holding that it would not be reasonable to prevent the use of the confidential information, because the disclosure of that information to 43 per cent of the plaintiff's shareholders had placed them in a preferential position as compared with the remaining 57 per cent of the shareholders. That was contrary to what is now General Principle 4 of the Code, which required that shareholders (*i.e.* all of them) should be given sufficient information and advice to enable them to reach a properly informed decision and should have sufficient time to do so, and that no relevant information should be withheld from them. In addition, Lord Denning M.R. said that the very act of applying for an injunction seemed to be a breach of what is now General Principle 7 of the Code, which states that, once a bona fide offer has been communicated to the board of the offeree company, the board of that company may not (without the approval of the shareholders in general meeting) take any action which could effectively result in the offer being frustrated. He also pointed out that the context was not one which would permit the ordinary principles governing the grant of an interlocutory injunction to be applied. He said (at p.510):

> "The present is a unique case. It has to be decided today for better or for worse. If an interlocutory injunction is granted against J.F.B., this bid will be frustrated forever. The decision cannot be postponed till a trial, which may be nine or 12 months — or even longer — ahead. The circumstances would be so different that this same bid could never be repeated."

In later proceedings before the Panel, the Panel declined to censure J.F.B. for using the confidential information (which it had received as a potential underwriter) to make a bid for the plaintiff company. The Panel appears to have been influenced in this regard by the fact that the bid was not made until after the underwriting scheme had fallen through (see the Panel Statement in [1977] J.B.L. 161).

Judicial Review of the Panel's Decisions

7–023 While the decisions of the Panel are susceptible to judicial review, three reported cases illustrate the fact that the courts adopt a very light touch in exercising the power to subject the Panel's decisions to review.

The first is the *Datafin* case (cited above, at para.7–012), which arose out of an application by two unsuccessful bidders for leave to apply for judicial review of a decision by the Panel that a rival bidder had not been acting in concert with another party. The Court of Appeal held that, having regard to the Panel's position as a regulatory body performing public law functions, indirectly supported by statutory sanctions, the court must have jurisdiction to entertain applications to review the Panel's decisions. The court was at pains to point out, however, that applications for judicial review should not be allowed to become a mere ploy in takeover battles. To that end, Lord Donaldson observed that the Panel must not be deterred from seeking to enforce one of its decisions which became the subject of such an application. He went on to say (at [1987] Q.B. 815, 842C-E):

> ". . . I wish to make it clear beyond a peradventure that in the light of the special nature of the panel, its functions, the market in which it is operating, the time scales which are inherent in that market and the need to safeguard the position of third parties, who may be numbered in thousands, all of whom are entitled to continue to trade upon an assumption of the validity of the panel's rules and decisions, unless and until they are quashed by the court, I should expect the relationship between the panel and the court to be historic rather than contemporaneous. I should expect the court to allow contemporary decisions to take their course, considering the complaint and intervening, if at all, later and in retrospect by declaratory orders which would enable the panel not to repeat any error and would relieve individuals of the disciplinary consequences of any erroneous finding of breach of the rules."

The later decision of the Court of Appeal in *R. v Panel on Take-overs and Mergers Ex p. Guinness plc* [1990] 1 Q.B. 146 further illustrates the reluctance of the courts to intervene by way of judicial review in the proceedings of the Panel. In the course of Guinness plc's bid for Distillers, the Panel received an assurance that the purchase of a block of Distillers' shares by a Swiss company had not taken place under a concert party agreement between the Swiss company and Guinness (which would have been contrary to the Code). After the conclusion of the bid, the DTI appointed inspectors to investigate the conduct of Guinness during the bid. The Panel initially took the stance that it would await the findings of the inspectors before publishing any findings or judgments of its own. The inspection brought to light a letter from the Swiss company to Guinness which, if genuine, was clear evidence of a concert party agreement between them. The DTI supplied a copy of the letter to the Panel. The Panel Executive then notified Guinness that, contrary to its original stance, the Panel intended shortly to hold a hearing into the apparent breach of the Code. Guinness challenged the authenticity of the letter and requested the Panel to adjourn its hearing into the alleged breach of the Code until after the DTI inspectors had published their report and outstanding criminal proceedings had been concluded. The Panel refused to adjourn the hearing and found that there had been a breach of the Code. Guinness sought judicial review of the Panel's decision, arguing that the company had been prevented from properly presenting its case because the Panel had refused its request for an adjournment. The Court of Appeal held that, having regard to the Panel's non-statutory nature and to the fact that the proceedings in the present case had been essentially inquisitorial rather 7–024 than disciplinary, the court would only intervene by way of judicial review if satisfied that something had gone wrong of a nature and degree which required such intervention. That was not the case here, because the case against Guinness was overwhelming and no further evidence would have been likely to come to light as a result of any adjournment of the hearing. In regard to the position of the Panel, Woolf L.J. said (at p.192G-H):

> "I should . . . make it clear that I regard the unique qualities of the take-over panel as being important in deciding what is the correct outcome of this appeal. I have in mind two particular features of the panel. The first is that its authority is not derived from any statutory power. Instead, it derives its authority from the institutions of the City of London who give it their support and nominate its members. The second is that the scope of its activities is self-determined. Except in so far as the panel itself decides to limit its jurisdiction and to set out its functions, as it has in the [Code], the constraints on its powers are those dictated not by legal but by practical considerations."

7–025 A similar outcome was reached in the subsequent case of *R. v Panel on Take-overs and Mergers Ex p. Fayed* [1992] B.C.L.C. 938, which arose in the wake of the successful bid made by the Fayed brothers for House of Fraser, in which Lonrho had been prevented from bidding because of undertakings it had given to the Secretary of State. Lonrho brought an action against the Fayeds in which it was alleged that the Secretary of State had been induced not to refer the Fayeds' bid to the Monopolies and Mergers Commission by fraudulent representations by the Fayeds. A 1991 report by DTI inspectors concluded that the Fayeds had dishonestly represented their origins, their wealth, their business interests and their resources to the Secretary of State, the shareholders of House of Fraser and others. The Panel Executive sought to bring disciplinary proceedings against the Fayeds on the ground that they had made misleading statements at the time of the bid, contrary to what is now General Principle 5 of the Code. The Panel refused a request by the Fayeds for an adjournment of the disciplinary proceedings until after the conclusion of the Lonrho action. The Fayeds then applied for leave to challenge the refusal by way of judicial review. The Court of Appeal rejected the application on the basis that the Lonrho action would be decided by a judge rather than a jury, and that the judge would be well able to guard against any prejudice which might be caused to the Fayeds by an earlier Panel decision that they had infringed the Code. The Court of Appeal also held that there could be no legitimate expectation that the Panel would adjourn the disciplinary hearing on the basis of a statement in the Panel's 1977 Annual Report which said that the Panel would usually delay the commencement of its own investigation until the outcome of any subsisting litigation was known. Two members of the court were not prepared to hold that this statement had created any legitimate expectation, while the third held that the Panel had had good reason to depart from its normal procedure. Nor, finally, was the court impressed with the argument that the Panel would be acting unfairly by relying on the DTI inspectors' report to establish a breach of the requirements of the Code.

The Code

The Introduction to the Code

As we saw in para.7–001, above, the Introduction to the Code identifies the main aim of the Code as being to ensure fair and equal treatment of all shareholders in relation to takeovers, and to provide an orderly framework within which takeovers are conducted. The Code is not concerned with the financial or commercial merits of a takeover, which are for the company and its shareholders to evaluate. Nor is it concerned with issues, such as competition policy, which are the responsibility of government. **7–026**

The Introduction goes on to state that the responsibilities described in the Code apply to the following groups:

(a) those who are actively engaged in the securities markets;

(b) directors of companies which are subject to the Code;

(c) persons or groups of persons who seek to gain or consolidate effective control of such companies or who otherwise participate in, or are connected with, transactions to which the Code applies; and

(d) all professional advisers, in so far as they advise on the transactions in question.

The responsibilities apply irrespective of whether those involved are directly affiliated to any of the bodies who nominate members of the Panel. The Panel also expects any other persons who issue circulars to shareholders in connection with takeovers to observe the highest standards of care an accuracy.

The key factor in deciding whether the Code applies to a particular transaction is the nature of the company which is the offeree or potential offeree company, or in which control (as defined) may change or be consolidated. For the purposes of the Code, "control" means a holding, or aggregate holdings, of shares carrying 30 per cent or more of the voting rights of a company, irrespective of whether the holding or holdings give *de facto* control. **7–027**

The Code applies to offers for all listed and unlisted public companies (and, where appropriate, statutory and chartered companies) considered by the Panel to be resident in the United Kingdom, the Channel Islands or the Isle of Man. The Panel will not normally treat the residence test as satisfied unless the company is incorporated in the United Kingdom, the Channel Islands or the Isle of Man and has its place of central management in one of those jurisdictions.

The Code does not apply to Open-Ended Investment Companies. The Code will not apply to an offer for a private company unless the company satisfies the residence test and one of the following conditions is satisfied:

(a) the company's equity share capital has been admitted to the Official List maintained by the UKLA at any time during the 10 year period prior to the "relevant date" (that date being, in summary, the date of the announcement of a proposed or possible offer for the company);

(b) dealings and/or prices at which persons were willing to deal in its equity share capital were published on a regular basis for a continuous period of at least six months during the same 10 year period;

(c) its equity share capital has been subject to a marketing arrangement as described in the Companies Act 1985, s.163(2)(b) at any time during the same 10 year period (*e.g.* if its shares have been dealt in on the Unlisted Securities Market); or

(d) it has filed a prospectus for the issue of equity share capital with the registrar of companies at any time during the same 10 year period.

The Code is concerned with takeover and merger transactions, however, effected, of all relevant companies. These include partial offers, offers by a parent company for shares in its subsidiary and certain other transactions where control (in the sense explained above) is to be obtained or consolidated. Thus references in the Code to "takeovers" and "offers" have to be read as including all such transactions.

The Code does not apply to offers for non-voting, non-equity capital except in cases where an offer is made for equity shares and the offeror is required by r.15 to make an offer for convertible securities which the offeree company has outstanding.

The General Principles

7–028 The 10 General Principles are set out at the beginning of the Code. The Panel regards them as expressing the spirit of the Code, which it characterises as being to seek a fair balance between the interests of the offeror and the offeree and its shareholders. The General Principles are intended to establish the framework for takeover activity and to represent statements of high standards of commercial behaviour. Their main objectives are to secure equality of treatment and opportunity for all shareholders in takeover bids, to ensure that shareholders are supplied with adequate information and advice to enable them to assess the merits of the offer, to ensure that no action which might frustrate an offer is made by a target company during the offer period without shareholders being allowed to vote on it, and that fair and orderly markets in the shares of the companies concerned are maintained throughout the period of the offer.

The Introduction to the Code makes it clear that the General Principles are expressed in broad general terms and are applied by the Panel in accordance with their spirit to achieve their underlying purpose. The Panel may modify or relax the effect of their precise wording accordingly.

7–029 The preamble to the General Principles states that each director of an offeror and the offeree company has a responsibility to ensure, so far as he is reasonably able, that the Code is complied with in the conduct of an offer. Financial advisers have a particular responsibility to comply with the

Code and to ensure, so far as they are reasonably able, that an offeror and the offeree company, and their respective directors, are aware of their responsibilities under the Code and will comply with them. Financial advisers should ensure that the Panel is consulted wherever relevant and should co-operate fully with any enquiries made by the Panel. Appendix 3 to the Code gives guidance on directors' responsibilities and on conflicts of interest affecting financial advisers.

The Rules

The Code's 38 Rules are intended to regulate the whole process by which a takeover or merger is conducted, from the first approach to the conclusion of the deal. Many of the Rules are amplified by guidance notes to assist in their application. **7–030**

The Introduction to the Code states that, while most of the Rules are expressed in more detailed language than the General Principles, they are not framed in technical language and, like the General Principles, are to be interpreted according to their underlying purpose. Therefore, their spirit must be observed as well as their letter and the Panel may modify or relax the application of a Rule if it considers that, in the particular circumstances, it would operate unduly harshly or in an unnecessarily restrictive or burdensome, or otherwise inappropriate manner.

Approach, Announcement and Independent Advice

These aspects are covered in rr.1, 2 and 3. As regards the approach, r.1 requires the offer to be put forward to the board of the offeree company or to its advisers and the identity of the offeror to be disclosed at the outset. It also provides that the offeree's board is entitled to be satisfied that the offeror is, or will be, in a position to implement the offer in full. R.2 emphasises the vital importance of maintaining secrecy before the making of an announcement. It goes on to set out the circumstances in which an announcement will be required, which include not only cases in which a firm intention to make an offer is notified to the board, but also cases where, for instance, a potential offeror's actions lead to the offeree becoming the subject of rumour and speculation or to an untoward movement in its share price. R.3 requires the board of the offeree company to obtain competent independent advice on any offer and to make the substance of that advice known to its shareholders. A "success fee", which only becomes payable to the adviser if the offer fails, will normally disqualify the adviser from giving independent advice for this purpose. **7–031**

Restrictions on Dealings and on the Acquisition of Shares and Rights over Shares

The dealing of shares prior to or during an offer can cause significant prejudice to shareholders. The various restrictions on dealings and on the acquisition of shares and of rights over shares are set out in rr.4 to 8. The main restrictions are set out in r.4. By virtue of r.4.1, a person (other than **7–032** the offeror) who is privy to confidential price-sensitive information concerning an offer or contemplated offer is prohibited from dealing in the securities of the offeree company prior to the announcement of a contemplated approach or offer. R.4.2 goes on to provide that, during an offer period, an offeror and those acting in concert with it must not sell any securities in the offeree company except with the prior consent of the Panel and following 24 hours' public notice that such sales may be made.

In addition to the restrictions imposed by r.4, a person may be precluded from dealing or procuring others to deal by the criminal sanctions attached to insider dealing, and by the provisions of FSMA 2000 relating to market abuse. These aspects are covered in more detail in Chs [13] and [14].

7–033 Generally speaking, a person who holds less than 30 per cent of the voting rights of a company may not acquire any voting shares in the company (or rights over such shares) if by doing so he would hold 30 per cent or more of the voting rights (r.5.1(a)), and a person who holds between 30 per cent and 50 per cent of the voting rights in a company, may not acquire any further voting rights (r.5.1(b)). A number of exceptions to these restrictions are set out in r.5.2. These include an acquisition from a single shareholder, if it is the only such acquisition within a period of seven days and if it is notified, not later than midday on the business day following the acquisition, to the company, a regulatory information service and the Panel. The exceptions also include acquisitions by way of acceptance of an offer.

7–034 R.6.1 provides that, if the offeror (or a person acting in concert with it) purchases shares in the offeree company in the period of three months preceding the start of the offer period, then the offeror must ensure that, when the offer is made, the terms offered to other shareholders of the same class are no less favourable. R.6.2 deals with cases in which, after an announcement has been made, the offeror (or a person acting in concert with it) acquires shares for more than the offer price. In such a case, the offeror is obliged to increase its offer to not less than the price paid for the shares so acquired. If the offeror is required to increase its offer, an immediate announcement must be made under r.7.1.

7–035 R.8 requires the disclosure of various dealings in relevant securities (which may be securities of either the offeree company or the offeror) during the offer period.

Where the offeror or the offeree company, or any associates, deal for their own account, the dealings must be publicly disclosed to a regulatory information service (with a copy being sent to the Panel). Public disclosure is also required where the offeror or the offeree company deal in relevant securities for the account of discretionary investment clients. The same requirement applies to dealings by associates for the account of such clients, except that, where the associate is an exempt fund manager connected with the offeror or the offeree company, it is sufficient for the dealing to be disclosed privately to the Panel. Private disclosure to the Panel is also sufficient in cases where the offeror or the offeree company, or an associate, deal for the account of non-discretionary clients.

Public disclosure is normally required for any dealings during the offer period by a person, whether or not an associate, who owns or controls one per cent or more of any class of relevant securities (or who will do so as a result of any transaction).

Remaining Shareholders, the Mandatory Offer and its Terms

A problem arises where an acquirer has obtained control of a company, leaving the remaining shareholders "locked-in". The purpose of r.9 is to prevent this problem arising, by obliging the acquirer, in certain cases, to offer to purchase the shares of the remaining shareholders at the highest price paid by the acquirer. Such an offer is required in two cases. The first is where a person acquires shares which (taken together with shares hold or acquired by persons acting in concert with him) carry 30 per cent or more of the voting rights in the company. The second is where a person, together with persons acting in concert with him, holds between 30 per cent and 50 per cent of the voting rights and that person increases his percentage of the voting rights to any extent. The offer must be in cash or accompanied by a cash alternative. The cash offered must not be less than the highest price paid by the offeror or any person acting in concert with it during the offer period and within 12 months prior to its commencement. The offer must be conditional only upon the offeror having received acceptances which, taking account of the shares acquired or agreed to be acquired before or during the offer, will result in the offeror and any person acting in concert with it holding shares carrying more than 50 per cent of the voting rights. **7–036**

For the purposes of the Code, persons acting in concert are defined as: **7–037**

> "persons who, pursuant to an agreement or understanding (whether formal or informal), actively co-operate, through the acquisition by any of them of shares in a company, to obtain or consolidate control . . . of that company".

Certain persons are presumed to be acting in concert unless the contrary is established. These include:

(1) a company, its parent, subsidiaries and fellow subsidiaries, and their associated companies (*i.e.* companies in which they own or control 20 per cent or more of the equity share capital), all with each other;

(2) a company with any of its directors (together with their close relatives and related trusts);

(3) a company with any of its pension funds;

(4) a fund manager (including an exempt fund manager) with any investment company, unit trust or other person whose investments the fund manager manages on a discretionary basis (but only in respect of the relevant investment accounts);

(5) a financial or other professional adviser with its client;

(6) directors of a company which is subject to an offer or where the directors have reason to believe that a bona fide offer for their company may be imminent.

In addition, investors in a consortium will normally be treated as acting in concert with the offeror.

The Voluntary Offer and its Terms

7–038 Rr.10 to 13 regulate the terms on which voluntary offers may be made.

R.10 provides that it must be a condition of any offer for voting equity share capital which, if accepted in full, would result in the offeror holding over 50 per cent of the voting rights of the offeree company that the offer will not become unconditional as to acceptances unless the offeror has acquired or agreed to acquire shares carrying over 50 per cent of the voting rights attributable to (a) the equity share capital alone and (b) the equity share capital and the non-equity share capital combined.

7–039 R.11.1 requires a cash offer to be made in three cases. The first is where, during the offer period or the preceding 12 month period, the offeror and any person acting in concert with it have made a cash purchase of shares of any class under offer, and the shares so purchased carry 10 per cent or more of the voting rights exercisable at a meeting of that class. In such a case, the offer for that class must be in cash or accompanied by a cash alternative at not less than the highest price which the offeror or any person acting in concert with it has paid for shares of that class during the offer period or the preceding 12 month period. The second case is where, during the offer period (but not during any earlier period), the offeror or any person acting in concert with it have made a cash purchase of shares of any class under offer. Here, the offer for that class must be in cash or accompanied by a cash alternative at not less than the highest price which the offeror or any person acting in concert with it has paid for shares of that class during the offer period. It will be seen that there is a substantial degree of overlap between the first and second cases: thus, if cash purchases have been made which fall within both cases, the obligation which arises in the second case is subject to any more stringent obligation which arises in the first. The third case is where, in the view of the Panel, there are circumstances which mean that a cash offer is necessary to give effect to General Principle 1 (*viz.* that all shareholders of the same class of an offeree company must be treated similarly by an offeror).

R.11.2 requires a securities offer to be made where, during the offer period or the preceding three month period, the offeror and any person acting in concert with it have made purchases of any class of shares in the offeree company carrying 10 per cent or more of the voting rights exercisable at a meeting of that class, and the purchases have been made in exchange for securities. Here, such securities must normally be offered to all other holders of shares of that class.

7–040 Where an offer comes within the statutory provisions for possible reference to the Competition Commission, it must be a term of the offer that it will lapse if there is a reference before the later of the closing date and the date when the offer becomes or is declared unconditional as to acceptances (r.12.1(a)). If the offer falls within the scope of EC merger regulation, it must also be a term of the offer that it will lapse if, before the same date, the European Commission initiates proceedings or (following a referral by the European Commission to a competent authority within the United Kingdom) there is a subsequent reference to the Competition Commission (r.12.1(b)).

R.13 provides that an offer must not normally be subject to conditions which depend solely on subjective judgments by the directors of the offeror or the fulfilment of which is in their hands. The Panel may, however, be prepared to accept an element of subjectivity in special cases where it is not practicable to specify all the factors on which satisfaction of a particular condition may depend. **7–041**

Provisions Applicable to all Offers

Rr.14 to 18 set out further requirements relating to the offer. **7–042**

R.14.1 provides that, where a company has more than one class of equity share capital, a comparable offer must be made for each class, whether or not it carries voting rights. A comparable offer need not necessarily be an identical offer. Where the offer involves two or more classes of listed shares, the ratio of the offer values should normally be equal to the average of the ratios of the middle market quotations taken from the Official List over the previous six months. An offer for non-voting equity share capital should not normally be made conditional on any particular level of acceptances in respect of that class unless the offer for the voting equity share capital is also conditional on the success of the offer for the non-voting equity share capital. R.14.2 provides that, where an offer is made for more than one class of share, separate offers must be made for each class.

R.15 provides that, when an offer is made for equity share capital and the offeree company has convertible securities outstanding, the offeror must make an appropriate offer or proposal to the stockholders to ensure that their interest are safeguarded. Equality of treatment is required. The board of the offeree company must obtain competent independent advice on the offer or proposal to the stockholders, and the substance of the advice must be disclosed to them together with the board's views. **7–043**

R.16 provides that, unless the Panel consents, the offeror and persons acting in concert with it may not deal, or enter into arrangements to deal, in shares of the offeree company, either during the offer or when one is reasonably in contemplation, if there are favourable conditions attached which are not being extended to all shareholders. **7–044**

R.17 makes provision for announcement of acceptance levels. R.17.1 states that there must be an announcement no later than 8.00am on the business day following the day on which an offer is due to expire, or becomes or is declared unconditional as to acceptances, or is revised or extended. The announcement must state the total number of shares and rights over shares for which acceptances have been received (distinguishing between shares held before the offer period and shares acquired or agreed to be acquired during that period) and must also specify the percentages of the relevant classes of share capital represented by these figures. R.17.2 deals with the consequences of a failure to announce. If an offeror fails to make the announcement within the time limit in r.17.1, the UKLA (or the Stock Exchange or OFEX as appropriate) will consider a temporary **7–045** suspension of the listing of the offeree company's shares and, where appropriate, the offeror's shares until the relevant information is given. Furthermore, if an offeror, having announced that the offer is unconditional as to acceptances, fails to comply with any of the other requirements of r.17.1 by 3.30pm on the relevant day, then any acceptor will immediately be entitled to withdraw his acceptance.

Conduct During the Offer

7–046 Rr.19 to 22 regulate the conduct of the offeror and the offeree company during the offer. Their main aim is to ensure that information disseminated during the course of an offer is accurate and equally available to all shareholders.

R.19.1 provides that each document or advertisement issued, or statement made, during the course of an offer must satisfy the highest standards of accuracy and the information given must be adequately and fairly presented. This applies whether it is issued by the company direct or by an adviser on its behalf. The guidance notes state that the Panel regards financial advisers as being responsible for guiding their clients on the release of information during the course of an offer; they also make it clear that, in view of the potential for a misleading impression to be given, comment should be avoided on future profits and prospects, asset values and the likelihood of the offer being revised. Unambiguous language must be used, sources for information must be clearly stated and quotations (*e.g.* from newspapers or stockbroker's circulars) must not be used out of context.

7–047 By virtue of r.19.2, documents issued to shareholders and advertisements published in connection with an offer must state that the directors of the offeror and/or offeree company (as appropriate) accept responsibility for the information contained in the document or advertisement. The parties to an offer and their advisers must also take care not to issue statements which, while not factually inaccurate, may mislead shareholders or the market or may create uncertainty (r.19.3). R.19.4 prohibits the publication of advertisements connected with an offer unless the advertisement falls within one of a number of specific categories (*e.g.* advertisements confined to non-controversial information about an offer, such as a reminder about closing times or the value of an offer). In addition, it is normally necessary for the advertisement to be cleared with the Panel in advance. Further requirements apply to telephone campaigns (r.19.5), interviews and debates (r.19.6), and the distribution and availability of documents and announcements (r.19.7). The requirements of the Code regarding the release of information do not normally apply if the offer period ends on a reference to the Competition Commission or the initiation of proceedings by the European Commission. If, however, the merger is allowed to go ahead, the Panel may require that statements made during the competition reference period be substantiated or, if that is not possible, withdrawn (r.19.8).

7–048 R.20 is concerned with equality of information. It provides that information about companies involved in an offer must be made equally available to all shareholders as nearly as possible at the same time and in the same manner (r.20.1). It is also a requirement that information given to one offeror or potential offeror must, on request, be given equally and promptly to another offeror or bona fide potential offeror, though this requirement normally applies only when the existence of the former party has been publicly announced or authoritatively disclosed to the latter (r.20.2). In a management buy-out or similar transaction, the offeror or potential offeror must, on request, promptly furnish the independent directors of the offeree company or its advisers with all information which has been furnished to external providers of potential providers of finance (r.20.3).

R.21.1 imposes restrictions on the ability of the offeree company's board to take steps to frustrate an offer or expected offer. During the course of an offer, or at any earlier time when the offeree's board has reason to believe that an offer is imminent, the board must not take any of the following steps, except under a contract entered into earlier, without the approval of the shareholders in a general meeting (which must be convened by a notice which includes information about the offer or anticipated offer): **7–049**

(a) issue any authorised but unissued shares;

(b) issue or grant options in respect of any unissued shares;

(c) create or issue, or permit the creation or issue, of any securities carrying rights of conversion into or subscription for shares;

(d) sell, dispose of or acquire assets of a material amount, or agree to do so; or

(e) enter into contracts otherwise than in the ordinary course of business.

R.21.2 regulates the payment of inducement fees (*viz.* an arrangement between the offeror and the offeree company for the latter to make a cash payment on the happening of specified events which have the effect of preventing the offer from proceeding or causing it to fail). Any such fee must be *de minimis* (normally not more than one per cent of the value of the offeree company calculated by reference to the offer price) and the offeree company's board and its financial adviser must confirm to the Panel that they each believe the fee to be in the interests of shareholders. Any inducement fee must be fully disclosed in the announcement of the offeror's intention to make an offer and in the offer document. The Panel must be consulted at the earliest opportunity whenever such an arrangement is proposed.

Documents from the Offeror and the Offeree Board

Rr.23 to 27 impose obligations with regard to the information to be provided to shareholders in the offer document, the first major circular from the offeree company's board, and in subsequent documents to shareholders. **7–050**

R.23 states the general principle that shareholders must be given sufficient information and advice to enable them to reach a properly informed decision as to the merits or demerits of the offer. Such information must be available to shareholders early enough to enable them to make a decision in good time. The offeror's obligations to the shareholders of the offeree company are no less onerous in this respect than its obligations to its own shareholders.

7–051 R.24 sets out in detail the information that must be included in the offer document. This includes information about the offeror's intentions with regard to the offeree company's business and its employees, and information about the financial position of the offeror and the offeree company and the way in which the offer is to be financed.

R.25.1 requires the board of the offeree company to circulate its views on the offer, including any alternative offer, and at the same time to make known to its shareholders the substance of the independent advice obtained by the board under r.3. Rr.25.2 to 25.6 specify in detail the information that must be contained in the first major circular from the offeree company's board.

R.26 lists various documents that must be made available for inspection from the publication of the offer document or offeree board circular, as appropriate, until the end of the offer period. The offer document or offeree board circular must state which documents are so available and the place where inspection can be made (which must be within the City of London unless the Panel otherwise agrees).

Documents subsequently sent to shareholders of the offeree company by either party must contain details of any material changes in information previously published by that party during the offer period.

Profit Forecasts

7–052 R.28 sets out a number of requirements relating to profit forecasts made in the course of an offer. R.28.1 acknowledges the hazards attached to the forecasting of profits, but goes on to state that this in no way detracts from the necessity of maintaining the highest standards of accuracy and fair presentation in all communications to shareholders in an offer. A profit forecast must be compiled with due care and consideration by the directors, whose sole responsibility it is. The financial advisers must satisfy themselves that the forecast has been prepared in this manner by the directors. R.28.2 provides that any document addressed to shareholders in connection with an offer which contains a profit forecast must state the assumptions, including commercial assumptions, on which the directors have based the forecast. The same requirement applies to any press announcement which contains a profit forecast.

Unless the offer is solely for cash, the accounting policies and calculations for the forecast must be examined and reported on by the auditors or consultant accountants, and by any financial adviser mentioned in the document (r.28.3). R.28.6 identifies various classes of statements which will be treated as profit forecasts for these purposes (*e.g.* a general statement that "profits will be somewhat higher than last year's", or an estimate of profits for a period which has already expired). A dividend forecast is not normally treated as a profit forecast unless, for example, it is accompanied by an estimate of dividend cover.

Asset Valuations

R.29 provides that, when a valuation of assets is given in connection with an offer, it should be supported by the opinion of a named independent valuer. This requirement applies not only to land, buildings and process plant and machinery, but also to other assets, including individual parts of a business. The basis of valuation must be clearly stated. There should normally be a statement regarding any potential tax liability which would arise if the assets were to be sold at the amount of the valuation, with a comment about the likelihood of the liability crystallising. The valuation must state the effective date as at which the assets were valued and the professional qualifications and address of the valuer. The document containing the valuation must also state that the valuer has given and not withdrawn his consent to the publication of the valuation report. **7–053**

Timing and Revision

Rr.30 to 34 lay down the timetable for an offer. **7–054**

R.30 provides that the offer document should normally be posted within 28 days of the announcement of a firm intention to make an offer. The Panel must be consulted if the offer document is not to be posted within this period. The board of the offeree company should advise its shareholders of its views on the offer as soon as practicable after publication of the offer document and normally within 14 days.

The offer must initially be open for at least 21 days following the date on which the offer document is posted (r.31.1). If the offer is extended, the announcement of the extension must state the next closing date, except that, if the offer is unconditional as to acceptances, it is permissible instead to state that the offer will remain open until further notice. In the latter case, at least 14 days' written notice must be given, before the offer is closed, to those shareholders who have not accepted (r.31.2). There is no obligation to extend an offer where the conditions of the offer are not met by the first or any subsequent closing date (r.31.3). After an offer has become or is declared unconditional as to acceptances, the offer must remain open for acceptance for not less than 14 days after the date on which it would otherwise have expired (r.31.4).

Unless the Panel consents, an offer may not become or be declared unconditional as to acceptances after midnight on the 60th day after the day on which the initial offer document was posted. In determining whether the acceptance condition has been satisfied, the offeror may only take account of acceptances or purchases of shares for which all relevant electronic instructions or documents have been received by its receiving agent before the last time for acceptance set by the offeror, which must not be later than 1.00pm on the 60th day. An announcement should normally be made by 5.00pm on that day as to whether the offer is unconditional as to acceptances or has lapsed (r.31.6).

If an offer is revised, it must be kept open for at least 14 days following the date on which the revised offer document is posted. Accordingly, no revised offer document may be posted in the 14 days ending on the last day the offer is capable of becoming unconditional as to acceptances (r.32.1). **7–055**

In general, the provisions of rr.31 and 32 apply equally to alternative offers, including cash alternatives (r.33.1).

R.34 provides that, if an offer has not become or been declared unconditional as to acceptances by the 21st day after the first closing date of the initial offer, an acceptor must be entitled to withdraw his acceptance. The right to withdraw must be exercisable until the offer becomes or is declared unconditional as to acceptances of (if earlier) the final time for lodgement of acceptances which can be taken into account under r.31.6.

Restrictions Following Offers and Possible Offers

7–056 R.35.1 applies in cases where an offer (having been announced or posted) is withdrawn or lapses without having become wholly unconditional. In such a case, the offeror and any person acting in concert with it will be debarred for a period of 12 months from the date on which the offer was withdrawn or lapsed from either:

(a) announcing an offer or possible offer for the offeree company (including a partial offer which could result in the offeror holding shares carrying 30 per cent or more of the voting rights in the offeree company); or

(b) acquiring any shares of the offeree company if the offeror or any person acting in concert with it would thereby become obliged to make a mandatory offer under r.9.

The restrictions in r.35.1 may also apply where a person makes an announcement which raises or confirms the possibility that an offer might be made, but fails to announce a firm intention either to make, or not to make, an offer within a reasonable time thereafter (*e.g.* where he announces that he is "considering his options"). However, the restrictions will not normally be applied in such a case unless the potential offeree company persuades the Panel that the damage to its business from the uncertainty outweighs the disadvantage to its shareholders of losing the prospect of an offer.

7–057 R.35.2 provides that the restrictions in r.35.1 will also apply following a partial offer for not less than 30 per cent and not more than 50 per cent of the voting rights of the offeree company, *whether or not* the offer has become or been declared wholly unconditional, and following a partial offer for more than 50 per cent of the voting rights of the offeree company which has *not* become or been declared wholly unconditional.

R.35.3 applies if a person, together with any person acting in concert with him, holds shares carrying more than 50 per cent of the voting rights of a company. It provides that, for a period of six months following the closure of any previous offer made by him, neither that person nor any person acting in concert with him may make a second offer to, or acquire shares from, any shareholder in that company on better terms than those made available under the previous offer.

Finally, r.35.4 provides that, where an offer has been one of two or more competing offers and has lapsed, neither the offeror nor any person acting in concert with it, may acquire shares in the offeree company on terms better than those made available under the lapsed offer until each of the competing offers has either been declared unconditional in all respects or has itself lapsed.

Partial Offers

R.36 makes provision for partial offers. Such offers are unusual. Tender offers are more common in cases where the acquirer wishes to increase its holding to less than 30 per cent of the voting rights of a company; tender offers, however, fall within the scope of the SARs rather than r.36. **7–058**

The Panel's consent is required for any partial offer, but will normally be granted where the offer could not result in the offeror holding shares carrying 30 per cent or more of the voting rights of a company (r.36.1). Where, however, the offer could result in the offeror holding shares carrying 30 per cent or more (but less than 100 per cent) of the voting rights of the company, consent will not normally be granted if the offeror or persons acting in concert with it have acquired, selectively or in significant numbers, shares in the offeree company during the 12 months preceding the application for consent or if shares have been purchased at any time after the partial offer was reasonably in contemplation (r.36.2).

The offeror and persons acting in concert with it are debarred from purchasing shares in the offeree company during the offer period. Where a partial offer is successful, neither the offeror nor any persons acting in concert with it may purchase shares during a period of 12 months after the end of the offer period, unless the Panel consents (r.36.3).

Any offer which could result in the offeror holding shares carrying 30 per cent or more of the voting rights of a company must normally be conditional, not only on the specified number of acceptances being received, but also on approval of the offer (normally signified by a separate box on the acceptance form) being given by shareholders holding over 50 per cent of the voting rights not held by the offeror and persons acting in concert with it (r.36.5).

If a partial offer could result in the offeror holding shares carrying over 50 per cent of the voting rights in the offeree company, the offer document must contain specific and prominent reference to this and to the fact that, if the offer succeeds, the offeror will be free (subject to r.36.3) to acquire further shares without incurring any obligation under r.9 to make a mandatory general offer.

Redemption or Purchase by Company of its Own Shares

R.37.1 provides that, where a company redeems or purchases its own voting shares, any resulting increase in the percentage of voting rights held by a shareholder or group of shareholders acting in concert will be treated as an acquisition for the purposes of r.9 (mandatory offers). **7–059**

During the course of an offer, or during any earlier period when the board of the offeree company has reason to believe that a bona fide offer might be imminent, the offeree company may not redeem or purchase its own shares (except pursuant to an earlier contract) without the approval of the shareholders in a general meeting (r.37.3).

Dealings by Connected Exempt Market Makers

7–060 R.38 prohibits an exempt market-maker connected with an offeror or the offeree company from carrying out any dealings for the purpose of assisting the offeror or (as the case may be) the offeree company.

Rules Governing Substantial Acquisition of Shares

7–061 As noted in para.7–004, above, the purpose of the SARs is to counter "dawn raids", which occur when there is a rapid and organised acquisition of a substantial shareholding in a company.

7–062 The SARs are designed to slow down the rate at which a person (or persons acting together) can increase a shareholding to between 15 per cent and 30 per cent of the shares holding voting rights in a company. The SARs apply if the company is resident in the United Kingdom, the Channel Islands or the Isle of Man and its shares are listed on the Stock Exchange, dealt in on AIM or traded on OFEX. The SARs do not apply to a person who has announced a firm intention to make an offer for the Company (which will be governed by the Code). Nor do they apply to an acquisition which results in the acquirer holding 30 per cent or more of the voting rights of a company. R.5 of the Code will, however, apply in such a case and r.9 of the Code may require a mandatory offer to be made.

There are five SARs, which are accompanied by guidance notes as to their interpretation and application.

7–063 A person may not, in any period of seven days, acquire shares carrying voting rights in a company or rights over such shares representing 10 per cent of the voting rights, if such an acquisition, when aggregated with any shares which he already holds, would carry 15 per cent or more, but less than 30 per cent of the voting rights of that company (r.1). This rule does not apply to the acquisition of new shares or the rights to subscribe for new shares or to the exercise of options over existing shares (r.1, n.4). The rule applies to market makers and other dealers in the same way as to any other person except where there is a block trade or when a market maker or other dealer purchase a portfolio without knowledge of its contents (r.1, n.6).

7–064 R.2 provides certain exemptions, where the 10 per cent ceiling imposed by r.1 will not apply. These include cases where the acquisition of shares is from a single shareholder and is the only acquisition within any seven day period; where the acquisition takes place pursuant to a tender offer; or where the offer will be publicly recommended by, or the acquisition is made with the agreement of the board of, the offeree company and the acquisition is conditional on the announcement of the offer.

7–065 Following the acquisition of shares carrying voting rights in a company which increases a person's holding to more than 15 per cent of the total or, if he already holds 15 per cent, where the acquisition is of more than one per cent of the total voting shares, the person acquiring the shares must notify the acquisition and his total holding to the company and the Panel (r.3).

R.4 applies to tender offers and sets out the procedure and clearance which is required when such an offer is made. A tender offer must be advertised in two national newspapers and must be notified to the company concerned. A tender offer must be for cash, but may be at a fixed price or a maximum price. The offer must treat all shareholders equally. R.4.2 regulates the contents of tender offer advertisements. A buyer may circulate copies of the tender announcement to shareholders of the company whose shares are sought (r.4.3). The result of the tender offer must be announced by 8.00am on the business day following the close of tender (r.4.4). The buyer in a tender offer may not acquire or dispose of voting shares in the company between the time of the publication of the tender offer and the announcement of the result of the offer (r.4.5). **7–066**

Where two or more persons act together, their holdings and acquisitions are aggregated and treated as a single holding or acquisition for the purpose of the SARs (r.5).

Chapter 8

Insurance

Lloyd's

Introduction

Lloyd's is not an insurance company but is a formally constituted society of underwriters ("the Society") which comprises traditional "Names"—private individuals who have historically traded with unlimited liability—and corporate members who trade with limited liability. The capital they provide supported 108 syndicates (that is, groups of members) in 2001. Syndicates are managed by an underwriting agent who appoints a professional underwriter for each main class of business the syndicate deals with. The structure of Lloyd's is considered further below. **8–001**

As Lord Cromer set out in the Cromer Report, a Lloyd's working party report in December 1969:

> "The Name does not invest in Lloyd's, as does a shareholder in a company, but he does put his capital at risk in the anticipation of profit being earned thereon by the skill of the underwriter. Against these considerations, the Name is liable, without any control over the conduct of the business and can only withdraw from participation (profitable or unprofitable) after a protracted period."

Since a Name puts his capital at risk in anticipation of the making of profit, though not in a technical sense, he is to be regarded for all practical purposes as an investor of funds whose interests need to be protected and regulated, just as if he were making an investment in a more conventional way. Notwithstanding the problems faced in the 1990s by Lloyd's it continues to be the world's leading insurance market and a significant contributor to the economy of the City of London. In 2001, for example, Lloyd's had the capacity to accept insurance premiums of some £11 billion with business from 64 countries worldwide.

Lloyd's of London: History

Lloyd's of London began its long and eventful history in the coffee houses of Edward Lloyd in Tower Street in the City of London. Lloyd's coffee house was well established by the end of the 1680s as a place where those willing to issue insurance gathered and it soon became the centre for **8–002** marine underwriting in London. It was also a centre where information about shipping could be exchanged; Edward Lloyd founded a short-lived newspaper, "Lloyd's News" which contained shipping information. This was the forerunner of the "Lloyd's List" which was first published in 1734 and continues to this day.

Following the collapse of the South Sea Company in 1720, Parliament restricted the issuing of marine insurance by bodies corporate to two charter companies, The Royal Exchange and London Assurance, but did not restrict individuals from issuing marine insurance. These "merchant underwriters" were to be found at Lloyd's coffee house and it is from their activities that today's Lloyd's has developed. By 1771, a group of 79 merchants and brokers paid £100 each to set up a formal organisation. The Napoleonic Wars were a time of expansion for Lloyd's when there were huge profits to be made. By 1814 Lloyd's had grown to some 2,150 underwriters. In 1811, Lloyd's first formal constitution was introduced, in the form of a Trust Deed which established the authority of the Lloyd's Committee.

8–003 In 1871 Lloyd's was incorporated as a society of private underwriters by Act of Parliament. Even so, true to its early roots, Lloyd's has always been a collection of individuals rather than a single entity. The workings of Lloyd's have historically been based on trust; its motto is *Fidentia*, meaning confidence, and its traditional trading standard has been *Uberrima Fides*, meaning utmost good faith. Until the crisis of the 1980s, considered in the following paragraphs, Lloyd's had had a virtually unassailable reputation for probity and profitability.

The History of Regulation at Lloyd's

8–004 Historically the operation of Lloyd's has been governed by the Lloyd's Acts 1871 to 1982 and by numerous byelaws. In the past, the management and regulation of Lloyd's has traditionally relied upon Lloyd's being essentially a "club" and the governing Committee was traditionally enormously secretive. For example, in the wake of Hurricane Betsy in 1965 and three years of losses, Lord Cromer was appointed by the Committee of Lloyd's to chair a committee to examine whether the existing capital structure of Lloyd's was adequate for the needs of the market. The Committee made a number of criticisms and recommendations but its report was circulated in confidence only to the professionals in the market. Not even the external Names whose interests the committee was seeking to safeguard were permitted to see the report.

One of the few recommendations of the Cromer Committee that was implemented was a relaxation in the qualifying requirement for becoming a Name. This led to a rapid expansion in Lloyd's membership in the 1970s and 1980s. Membership grew from 8,565 in 1976 to 19,137 by 1981 and to 33,532 by 1987 (a rise of some 436 per cent between 1976 and 1987). The rise in the numbers of members was accompanied by a number of good years between 1977 to 1987 when Lloyd's made a pre-tax profit to Names of £3,084 million. At this time, few took seriously the formal warning given to new names that they could lose everything "down to their last shirt button" and the large profits being made often masked the levels of incompetence and malpractice amongst underwriters.

The Fisher Report

In 1979, Sir Henry Fisher was appointed to chair an inquiry into self-regulation at Lloyd's. There was never any question at this time that anything other than a system of self-regulation should persist. Sir Henry Fisher's recommendations led to the Lloyd's Act 1982, the principal plank of which was that the old Lloyd's Committee should be replaced by a broadly based Council in which working members would be balanced by external Names. The Council would have powers of inquiry and discipline over brokers, agents and underwriters. The Fisher Committee also recommended that brokers should no longer be allowed to own managing agencies because of the obvious conflict of interests that such ownership engendered. This recommendation found its way into the 1982 Lloyd's Act in ss.10 to 12. (Self-Regulation at Lloyd's—Report of the Fisher working party May 1980.) **8–005**

The Neill Report

Following a number of scandals in the 1980s, including the disciplining of Sir Peter Green, a former Chairman of Lloyd's (disciplined by a Lloyd's Tribunal for discreditable conduct. He was fined a total of £50,000 and a notice of censure was posted in the underwriting room.), Sir Patrick Neill Q.C. was appointed to look into regulation at Lloyd's. His report was published in February 1987 and drew attention to the conflicts of interest that continued to exist at Lloyd's. An example of this was the existence of "baby syndicates" in which market insiders creamed off profits from the main syndicates. Sir Patrick Neill recommended that the composition of the Lloyd's Council should be changed to increase the number of independent members so that working members were no longer in the majority. (Regulatory Arrangements at Lloyd's—Sir Patrick Neill Q.C. January 1987). **8–006**

The Losses of the 1980s

The problems faced by Lloyd's in the 1980s and 1990s flowed in large part from the enormous losses incurred on its 1987 to 1992 underwriting years. These losses arose out of a series of disasters in both the marine and non-marine insurance and reinsurance markets between 1987 and 1993. In addition to losses arising from these natural disasters were the problems arising out of "long-tail" US liability, in which insured risks take a long time for the claims to emerge and even longer to settle. The effects of these losses were compounded by incompetence and, in some cases, malpractice on the part of some underwriters which came to light in a series of scandals involving underwriters in the 1980s. Questions were inevitably asked about how such a series of scandals could have been allowed to come about. One **8–007** of the effects of the disastrous results of the late 1980s and early 1990s was that individual membership of Lloyd's fell dramatically from 32,433 in 1988 to 2,852 in 2001. This has in turn dramatically reduced the "capacity" provided by individual members. In response to this corporate members with limited liability were introduced at Lloyd's for the first time in 1994 and there were also significant changes for individual names. By 2001, the underwriting capacity of Lloyd's was in excess of £11 billion of which more than 80 per cent comes from its corporate members.

Under the Financial Services Act 1986, the Society of Lloyd's and underwriters who came under the control of the Council of Lloyd's were exempted persons in respect of investment business. The question whether Lloyd's Names required authorisation under the Financial Services Act 1986 was considered by the SIB in 1989, but the argument in favour of authorisation was rejected (see SIB Guidance Release 2/89 Lloyd's Names). The only external regulation of Lloyd's before the introduction of the FSMA regime was that the Department of Trade and Industry acted as the external regulator to monitor Lloyd's global solvency and to agree standards for the valuation of liabilities.

Lloyd's and FSMA 2000

8–008 For the first time in its long history, Lloyd's of London is now the subject of prudential supervision by an external body. The FSMA 2000 includes provisions in Pt XIX to bring Lloyd's under the umbrella of the FSA after N2. David Gittings, the Director of Lloyd's, recognised that proper regulation is essential in today's marketplace:

> "An effective regulatory system is fundamental in maintaining confidence that the Lloyd's market is a fair and orderly place in which to do business. Insurance purchasers, capital providers and market businesses trading under the Lloyd's name all benefit from a framework of rules maintaining financial security along with high standards of business conduct and professional competence." (David Gittings, Director of Lloyd's)

8–009 As already explained, before the FSMA 2000 came into force, Lloyd's was regulated by the Lloyd's Acts 1871 to 1982 and by numerous byelaws, but there was no independent external body which had the power to oversee the proper and effective regulation of Lloyd's. The role of the FSA under the new regime is to ensure that Lloyd's is appropriately and effectively regulated by the Society of Lloyd's and the Council of Lloyd's. In other words, the FSA has taken on the function of overseeing the regulation of Lloyd's whilst leaving the day to day regulation of Lloyd's very much as it was before the enactment of the FSMA. Such regulation of Lloyd's continues to be conducted by the Society of Lloyd's and its various subsidiary bodies utilising the provisions of the various Lloyd's Acts and the byelaws, which can be found in "Lloyd's Acts, Byelaws and Regulations" published by Lloyd's of London Press Ltd. These have also been supplemented by the incorporation of the core principles which apply to Lloyd's members.

It is intended that the introduction of the new structure will promote confidence in the market at Lloyd's by ensuring its proper regulation and by protecting both policyholders and members of Lloyd's. In carrying out its regulatory functions it is intended that the Society of Lloyd's should establish and maintain clear, appropriate and effective delegation of responsibilities for the carrying out of its regulatory functions in a way which allows the Council of Lloyd's to monitor and control such functions. Committees set up by the Society of Lloyd's to which regulatory functions are delegated should now have formal terms of reference, make and retain proper records including minutes of meetings and be composed of an appropriate number of individuals who are collectively and individually fit and proper. Further, a person to whom the Society of Lloyd's delegates a regulatory function should have a written statement of the scope of his delegated authority and the purpose for which is to be exercised; he should make and retain proper records of the exercise of his delegated authority and be fit and proper. (See the *FSA Handbook*, LLD 1.2.1–5) **8–010**

The Society of Lloyd's is required to be open and co-operative with the FSA in respect of its regulatory functions and should give the FSA prompt notice of anything which has a bearing on the FSA's regulatory functions. In this spirit, the Society of Lloyd's should ensure that the FSA can interview or otherwise obtain information directly from committees, individuals or other persons to whom the Council of Lloyd's has delegated its regulatory functions.

The Prudential Requirements for the Society of Lloyd's

The purpose of applying high level prudential requirements to the Society of Lloyd's is to protect policyholders against the risk that the Society and members may not have adequate financial resources to meet claims as they fall due; to promote confidence in the market of Lloyd's by requiring the Society and its members to maintain resources which are adequate to meet their liabilities; to promote confidence in the market at Lloyd's and enhance public awareness by improving the transparency of financial reporting by the Society; and to protect the interests of consumers of insurance business at Lloyd's (LLD 9.1.4). **8–011**

The general prudential requirements of the Society of Lloyd's are set out in the Handbook at LLD 9.2 and include:

- the Society must manage its affairs, including the exercise of its byelaw-making powers, with due regard to the interests of policy holders and potential policyholders (LLD 9.2.1 R);
- the Society must ensure that its affairs are soundly and prudently managed and take reasonable steps to ensure that the Lloyd's market is soundly and prudently managed (LLD 9.2.2 R);
- the Society must adopt the standards of due care and diligence set out in the custody rules (see Handbook COB 9) in relation to the custody of assets that constitute members' funds (LLD 9.2.3 R);

- the Society may not permit any syndicate to carry on both long-term insurance business and general insurance business (LLD 9.2.4 R);
- the Society must, having regard to the availability and value of the central assets of the Society, ensure that its assets and its members' assets are adequate to meet the liabilities which members assume in their insurance business at Lloyd's (LLD 9.2.5 R).

The Society is also required to ensure that its admissible assets and those of its members are investments which are diversified and adequately spread and are of appropriate safety, yield, maturity and marketability. (LLD 9.2.6 R).

8–012 Under the new regulatory structure the Society of Lloyd's will make an annual report to the FSA within six months of the end of the financial year which will cover its financial situation and solvency and the insurance business carried out by its members. The report will also include copies of accounts for each syndicate required to prepare accounts by byelaw. (LLD 15.2) The purpose of the annual report by Lloyd's is to allow for a minimum level of disclosure of financial information and of transparency.

The Structure of Lloyd's

8–013 The Corporation of Lloyd's is a collection of individuals who trade under the Lloyd's banner and are subject to its rules but the Corporation itself has no statutory or legal persona. In effect, the Corporation of Lloyd's does not carry any responsibility for individual underwriters but provides a market place for them to work. Lloyd's writes world-wide business; in 2001 Lloyd's business came from some 64 countries.

The Membership of Lloyd's: the Names

8–014 Underwriters undertake liability on contracts of insurance and associate together to form syndicates, in which one of the members is given the authority to underwrite policies in the names of the other members of the syndicate (the "Names"). The management of underwriting syndicates is undertaken by a managing agency which charges Names an annual fee for participation in a syndicate.

Names provide the risk capital. Historically there were two types of Name, the working Name and the external Name. Working Names were professionals who worked in the market as underwriters, brokers and agents. External Names were passive investors with no control over the underwriter who writes insurance business. Unlike every other type of investor, the Names took on unlimited liability, each Name typically spreading his risk by joining several syndicates. The number of external Names peaked in the mid 1980s at more than 34,000. They took the brunt of the losses incurred in the period 1988–1992 and when re-insurance and stop-loss cover proved inadequate the old maxim of being liable down to their last shirt button became an uncomfortable reality for many. Change became inevitable and corporate Names were introduced in 1994 with limited liability. There are now some 900 corporate Names, which account for more than 80 per cent of Lloyd's capacity. In addition, an effective firebreak had to be constructed between the losses up to 1992 and business after this period. This was achieved by the implementation of the Lloyd's Reconstruction and Renewal Plan and the diversion of pre-1992 reinsurance and risk to Equitas, a limited liability reinsurance run-off company subject to regulation by the Department of Trade and Industry.

The Solvency Test

Names have always had to show a minimum amount of capital, often in the form of a bank guarantee, and to deposit a proportion of their "shown" capital with Lloyd's for safekeeping in a form of liquid assets such as shares. Names continue to be subject to a solvency test designed to ensure that the Name has sufficient assets to meet his underwriting liabilities and Names must now submit their underwriting accounts to an independent auditor annually. If it is found that a Name has insufficient funds to meet his underwriting liabilities he may be asked to lodge additional assets to make up the shortfall or else be asked to stop underwriting. Where these measures prove insufficient, the Central Fund (considered in para.8.21 below) may have to cover the liabilities. Lloyd's keeps a register, revised annually on July 1, of the Names of the Society — Sch.1 Lloyd's Act 1982 and Byelaw 100; The Register of Members Byelaw No.22 of 1983. **8–015**

Syndicates

As already mentioned, Names, both individual and corporate, conduct business at Lloyd's through syndicates. Syndicates are run by Managing Agents. The Managing Agent appoints and supervises the Active Underwriter for the syndicate. The Lloyd's Byelaws set out the standard format of the Managing Agent's agreement and allow the Managing Agent absolute discretion as to the risks which may be underwritten. The Name thus has no right to interfere or participate in any way in the underwriting decisions made on his behalf and on which he takes the risk. In addition to managing agents who manage Names' underwriting activities, the affairs of the Names are looked after by Member's agents who advise the Name on such matters as which syndicates to join. The role of a Member's agent has been examined by the Court of Appeal in *Brown v KMR Services Ltd* [1995] 4 All E.R. 598. However, the importance of Member's Agents has diminished in recent years, their numbers having fallen from 110 in 1984 to just 5 in 2001. **8–016**

The practice of Lloyd's is that underwriters do not do business directly with the public, but deal with brokers who act as intermediaries between underwriters and those wishing to effect insurance with them. The relationship between the underwriter and the broker is that of principals, although once the contract has been made, privity of contract is established between the underwriter and the assured. The underwriter looks to the broker for his premium who in turn looks to the assured, and it is usually through the broker that the underwriter receives notice of a claim.

The Council of Lloyd's

8–017 The Council of Lloyd's is established by s.3 of the Lloyd's Act 1982. Members of the Council include working members and external members (elected by working and external members), members nominated by the Bank of England and a chief executive officer. Under s.4, the Council is required to elect from the working members of the council a Chairman of Lloyd's and Deputy Chairmen.

The powers of the Council are set out in s.6 of the Lloyd's Act 1982 which provides that:

> "the Council shall have the management and superintendence of the affairs of the Society and the power to regulate and direct the business of insurance at Lloyd's".

This is achieved through the various Lloyd's byelaws. Sch.2 sets out the purposes for which byelaws may be made and it is through the byelaws that Lloyd's is regulated. The Council comprises a balance of all its members together with the chief executive officer. The Lloyd's Acts 1871 to 1982 require the Council to prepare accounts giving a view of the state of affairs of the Corporation and/or the surplus or deficit for each financial year. This is in addition to the annual report required from the Society of Lloyd's under the new regulatory structure.

Lloyd's Regulatory Board

8–018 Since 1993, many of the functions of the Council of Lloyd's have been delegated to the Lloyd's Regulatory Board and the Lloyd's Market Board. The Regulatory Board was created by the Council of Lloyd's in 1993 to act as an independent-minded and objective source of authority for Lloyd's regulation. It is responsible for supervisory and regulatory matters and is the body through which the Council exercises most of its regulatory responsibilities and powers. The Board comprises five nominated members (four working members) including its Chairman, five external members representing non-working Names and a director of regulatory services.

Broadly, the Regulatory Board's responsibilities are:

- to ensure that all those who work in the market are appropriately qualified and that all businesses in the market are properly resourced and managed. This is to be achieved by authorising only those individuals and entities that are fit and proper, that meet standards of sound and prudent management and that meet high standards of market behaviour and practice;
- to ensure sufficient resources in the market to support the underwriting;
- to safeguard policyholders' rights and to look after the best interests of all categories of members;
- to work for transparency in the market and to ensure all relevant information, including accounts, is properly disseminated;

- to provide the necessary written rules and guidelines to enable all the principles of fair and proper commercial conduct to be observed.

In addition, the Regulatory Board oversees the disciplinary functions of the Council of Lloyd's.

The Lloyd's Market Board

The Lloyd's Market Board is responsible for all other market services: for example, it sets the standards of conduct for those trading at Lloyd's. It also has responsibility for advancing the interests of Members, media relations and dialogue with government. **8–019**

Other Bodies

In addition, there are six market associations representing marine, non-marine and aviation underwriters, underwriting agents and brokers. Further, Lloyd's members are served by the Association of Lloyd's Members. **8–020**

The Central Fund

The Central Fund is held and administered by the Council of Lloyd's. It is primarily a fund available for the protection of policyholders. Members contribute to the Fund annually on a percentage basis of their allocated premium limit. The Fund may be used to cover underwriting deficiencies of Names and the assets of the fund are also available to discharge the underwriting liabilities of Names should they become due in the event of default (see The Central Fund Byelaw No.4 of 1986). Because of the significance of the Central Fund in the protection of policyholders the Society of Lloyd's is required to report quarterly to the FSA on the state of the fund. (Handbook LLD 3.3.1 R). **8–021**

The Disciplinary Committee and the Appeal Tribunal

The *FSA Handbook* (LLD 1.2.6) sets out that the Society of Lloyd's should ensure a prompt, fair and independent hearing for any person accused of breaching a byelaw, and that this complies with the requirements of the Human Rights Act 1998. This is achieved through the Disciplinary Committee established under the Disciplinary Committees Byelaw (No.31 of 1996) which also creates a summary disciplinary procedure to be administered by Summary Disciplinary Committees. The Appeals Tribunal is established under the Appeal Tribunal Byelaw (No.32 of 1996). Reports on disciplinary proceedings are published. In *The Society of Lloyd's v Clementson* [1995] C.L.C. 117, Lloyd's brought an action to recover payments made from the Central Fund in respect of unpaid underwriting losses made by Mr Clementson, who was a Lloyd's Name. In his defence, it **8–022** was argued for Mr Clementson that some Lloyd's byelaws caused a restriction or distortion of competition affecting trade between EU Member States in violation of Art.85 of the Treaty of Rome. The court found that it was arguable that the Central Fund Byelaw affected competition in the insurance company market in Member States.

8–023 Members of Lloyd's may be disciplined for acts of misconduct which fall within the Misconduct and Penalties Byelaw (No.30 of 1996). Misconduct broadly includes any contravention or failure to observe any provision of the Lloyd's Acts 1871 to 1982 or any byelaw made by virtue of them, a contravention or failure to observe any regulation or direction imposed under the Lloyd's Acts 1871 to 1982, a contravention or failure to observe any order, condition or requirement imposed, or undertaking given or decision made, under the Lloyd's Acts 1871 to 1982, a contravention of or failure to observe any of the Core Principles, a failure to take reasonable steps in connection with insurance business to avoid risk of harm to Lloyd's policyholders, the Society, its members or those doing business at Lloyd's, and engaging in or being associated with any discreditable conduct whether or not it is connected with the insurance business.

Sanctions include exclusion or suspension from membership of Lloyd's, a requirement to cease underwriting (which may be either permanent or temporary), revocation or suspension of the permission to act as a Lloyd's adviser, revocation of permission to act as a broker of insurance business, revocation or suspension of permission to act as a members' agent or managing agent, revocation or suspension of permission to act as an approved run-off company, revocation or suspension of permission to act as an underwriting agent, revocation or suspension of the right to act at Lloyd's as an annual subscriber, termination of or suspension of the registration of a registered individual, suspension of rights of admission to the Room and revocation (either permanent or temporary) of the right to transact the business of insurance at Lloyd's, a fine or the posting of notice of censure in the Room.

Summary offences are punishable by the imposition of a fine up to a maximum of £15,000 in the case of an individual or £30,000 in the case of a company or partnership or a censure. (Misconduct and Penalties Byelaw No.30 of 1996).

8–024 The Misconduct (Reporting) Byelaw imposes a duty on members of Lloyd's, underwriters, their agents and employees to report instances of misconduct (where the misconduct is of more than a minor nature) to the Director of Regulatory Services. The duty to report applies to a person who knows of any actual or proposed misconduct or believes or has reason to believe that such misconduct is likely to occur or is likely to have occurred. (Misconduct (Reporting) Byelaw No.11 of 1989).

The Regulatory Board has a system of on-site investigative reviews which is combined with office based analysis of regular returns.

Complaints and Disputes

8–025 As in other areas of the financial services industry, the Ombudsman principle has been adopted by Lloyd's. The role of the Lloyd's members' Ombudsman is to investigate complaints by members of the Society or resigned members with open years of account who believe that they have suffered injustice in consequence of maladministration in relation to action taken by the Society. The jurisdiction of the Ombudsman does not extend to complaints made by Names against underwriting agents—see The Members' Ombudsman Byelaw No.13 of 1987, Members Ombudsman (Amendment) Byelaw No.3 of 1989, and Members Ombudsman (Amendment No.2) Byelaw No.3 of 1994.

Complaints from policyholders now fall to be dealt with by the Financial Ombudsman Service. This is achieved by s.316(1) of FSMA 2000, which enables the FSA to direct that the general prohibition on carrying on regulated activities and the "core provisions" of the Act apply to members of Lloyd's. The core provisions are Pts V, XI, XII, XIV, XV, XVI, XXII and XXIV, ss.384 to 386 and Pt XXVI (s.317). A direction that a core provision should apply is called an "insurance market direction", and is intended to protect the interest of policyholders and potential policyholders by making Lloyd's members subject to the compulsory jurisdiction of the Financial Ombudsman Service with respect to the carrying on of insurance business, so that the complaints of policyholders who are eligible complainants may be dealt with under the rules of the Financial Ombudsman Service (as to which, see Ch.16 below) like the complaints of other policyholders. Guidance on the Financial Ombudsman Service is given in DISP 2.5.3G and the handling of a policyholder complaint against a member is covered in DISP 1.7.1R and DISP 1.7.2G. **8–026**

The Society of Lloyd's must also establish appropriate and effective arrangements for the handling of any complaint from a member or former member about regulated activities carried out by the Society, the Society's regulatory functions, advice given by an underwriting agent to a person to become, continue or cease to be, a member of a particular syndicate and the management by a managing agent of the underwriting capacity of a syndicate on which the complainant participates or has participated. (LLD 7.2.1 R) **8–027**

Further, the Society must maintain by byelaw an effective scheme for the resolution of disputes between an individual member or a former member and his underwriting agent or the Society itself. (LLD 7.5.1 R). **8–028**

Compensation Arrangements for Individual Members

The Society is required to maintain byelaws establishing a compensation scheme to compensate individual members and former members if underwriting agents are unable or are likely to be unable to satisfy claims by those members in relation to regulated activities carried on in connection with their participation in Lloyd's syndicates (LLD 8.2.1 R). **8–029**

Judicial Review

Lloyd's has historically enjoyed statutory immunity by virtue of s.14 of the Lloyd's Act 1982 from liability in damages at the suit of members of the Lloyd's community both past and present, including Names, brokers **8–030** and underwriting agents. The issue of whether Lloyd's was subject to judicial review was considered by the Divisional Court in the case of *R. v Lloyd's of London Ex p. Briggs and others* [1993] 1 Ll. R. 176, which arose out of the losses made by syndicates managed by Gooda Walker. Those syndicates had made substantial losses in run-off reinsurance of asbestosis and pollution claims from the USA and from London Excess of Loss Market (LMX) business. Gooda Walker went into liquidation in October 1991 and Lloyd's appointed G.W. Run-off Ltd. as substitute agents. G.W. Run-off Ltd. made cash calls on a number of Names. There had previously been actions brought by a number of Names seeking injunctions for the purpose of putting off until the hearing of the actions the procedure laid down by Lloyd's to obtain money to meet claims by the draw down procedure. The application for the injunction was refused and Saville J. held in those proceedings that under the contracts between the Names and their agents they were obliged to pay cash calls made by the managing agents in good faith.

A number of the Names sought judicial review against Lloyd's, the Committee of Lloyd's, the Chairman and Deputy Chairman of Lloyd's and against G.W. Run-off Ltd. One of the issues which was considered by the Divisional Court (Leggatt J. and Popplewell J.) was whether Lloyd's was subject to judicial review. The court came to the view that Lloyd's was not a public law body. It operated within one section of the insurance market and its powers were derived from a private Act of Parliament which did not extend to any person in the insurance business other than those who wished to operate in the section of the market governed by Lloyd's. There could not, therefore, be any public law element about the relationship between Lloyd's and its Names which would place it within the public domain and for this reason Lloyd's was not susceptible to judicial review.

Reform at Lloyd's

8–031 In January 2002, Lloyd's of London issued for consultation proposals for a package of radical reforms designed to modernise the Lloyd's insurance market. (Press Release LL03/02 dated 17/01/02). The proposed reforms, drawn up by the Lloyd's Chairman's Strategy Group, include:

- the modernisation of the structure of Lloyd's, replacing the existing Lloyd's regulatory and market boards with a single franchise board (the proposal being that Lloyd's would act as a franchisor in the management of the marketplace and that the managing agents would be franchisees);
- changing the way the market reports its results by replacing the Lloyd's three year accounting system with a more conventional one year system;
- a new vehicle for Names to participate in the market after January 2005. This would require the implementation of a transitional mechanism possibly including a scheme to buy out all third party security;

- an end to unlimited liability and the annual venture (*i.e.* the requirement that syndicates reform their capital bases every year). To this end, no new unlimited liability Names will be accepted and existing Names will have to convert to limited liability by January 2005.

At the time of writing, it seems that these proposals are unlikely to go through unopposed. In particular opposition is expected from the Association of Lloyd's Members representing the Lloyd's Names.

Insurance Companies

Introduction

The Insurance Companies Act 1982

The Insurance Companies Act 1982 was a consolidating measure which can be traced back in part as far as the Insurance Companies Act 1958. It is an area of law in which the European Economic Community (as it was) has been active for some 30 years, a solvency requirement having been imposed for direct insurance business (other than life insurance) by the First Non-Life Insurance Directive (Dir.73/239 [1973] O.J. L228/3). Direct life business was covered by the First Life Insurance Directive (Dir.79/267 [1979] O.J. L63/1). This reflects the importance to many investors of the appropriate regulation of insurance companies. "Direct" business excludes reinsurance. **8–032**

The basic scheme under the 1982 Act, which of course reflected the two Directives, was that insurance business could only be carried on by a person authorised by the Secretary of State to carry it on, subject to certain exemptions (including business carried on by members of Lloyd's). Insurance business was divided into long-term and general insurance business and there were different classes of business within those two broad divisions, which in effect corresponded to the division between life and non-life business. A person might be authorised to carry on business in certain classes or parts of classes. Long-term business included life assurance, annuities and permanent health insurance, and did in fact extend to long-term reinsurance business (*Re NRG Victory Reinsurance Ltd* [1995] 1 W.L.R. 239). General insurance business included accident, sickness, vehicles (including motor vehicles, ships, aircraft and railway rolling-stock), goods in transit, fire and natural forces, damage to property and credit.

Precisely what was meant by carrying on insurance business came under some judicial scrutiny. In *Re Sentinel Securities Plc* [1996] 1 W.L.R. 316 it was held that a guarantee protection scheme in respect of improvements to domestic premises constituted insurance business, although if the guarantee was called upon the benefit received was in kind rather than in cash. In *Re Great Western Assurance Co.*, July 31, 1996, unreported, it was held that it **8–033** was only business which provided the cover or which amounted to effecting and carrying out the relevant insurance contracts which was required to be authorised. In the criminal case of *R. v Wilson* [1997] 1 W.L.R. 1247, it was held that a person issuing a document in which he sought insurance business and holding himself out as having authority to make insurance contracts and to receive premiums on behalf of an insurer was carrying on insurance business. The business carried out had to involve a policy of insurance (*Fuji Finance Inc. v Aetna Life Insurance Ltd* [1995] Ch. 122) and had to be carried out within the jurisdiction (*Re Eagle Star Insurance Co. Ltd. and Eagle Star Life Assurance Co. Ltd*, unreported, *The Times*, December 7, 1990).

8–034 Together with authorisation requirements, there came, of course, further regulatory and supervisory provisions. Assets relating to long-term business had to constitute a separate fund from assets relating to general business and there were further requirements as to the keeping of accounts, the making of statements and, in relation to long-term business, actuarial appointments and investigations. As already mentioned, there was a solvency requirement. The Secretary of State had powers of intervention and powers to investigate and there were conduct of business rules.

In addition to the foregoing, the Financial Services Act 1986 contained provisions relating to the promotion and advertisement of contracts of insurance and the consequences of contravention of those requirements or of the restrictions in the 1982 Act on carrying on insurance business at all. It also dealt with misleading statements as to insurance contracts. Redress for complaints was offered on a voluntary basis through the Insurance Ombudsman Bureau, set up in 1981 by a group of insurance companies with powers given by contract.

The European Dimension

8–035 The First Non-Life Insurance Directive, referred to above, has been followed by two further Non-Life Directives (the second Directive being Dir.88/357 [1988] O.J. L172/1 and the third Dir.92/49 [1992] O.J. 228/1), and the first Life Insurance Directive has similarly been followed by two further Life Insurance Directives (Dirs 90/619 [1999] O.J. 330/50 and 92/96 [1992] O.J. 360/1). The two Third Directives completed the single market for direct insurance in the European Economic Area. The Directives taken together deal with solvency requirements (including assets which may be counted and principles of valuation), systems of supervision and regulation, management and conduct of business (including polarisation requirements such as are discussed in Ch.2), and the entitlement of duly authorised bodies to exercise their EEA passport rights (also considered in Ch.2). Following various amendments, they were reflected in the Insurance Companies Act and regulations made thereunder by the time FSMA 2000 came into force. Inevitably, the Directives also underpin much of the regulatory material in the *FSA Handbook*, and in this respect the situation of insurance companies is of course similar to that of banks and building societies, considered in Ch.3. It follows that there is a substantial degree of continuity between the final position under the Insurance Companies Act 1982 and that under the FSMA 2000 regime.

In addition, the FSA has had the task of giving effect to the Insurance Groups Directive (Dir.98/78). Under the principal Directives, the common standards imposed relate only to what is known as "solo supervision" and do not deal fully with the position of an insurance undertaking within a group. The supplemental provisions of the Insurance Groups Directive require Member States to introduce:

- an adjustment to the solo supervision solvency-margin test in relation to interests in other insurance undertakings;
- a parent-undertaking solvency-margin calculation;
- new supervisory requirements including rules as to internal controls regarding the production of information relevant to supplementary supervision, the exchange of information within the group and the supervision of intra-group transactions;
- co-operation between competent regulatory authorities in Member States;
- information-gathering and investigation powers relevant to groups for the regulatory authority.

With the exception of the last requirement, these matters are covered by rules made by the FSA and included in the *FSA Handbook* at IPRU (INS). To this extent, where the necessary provisions are new to United Kingdom regulation (which is not always the case), IPRU (INS) departs from the general principle applied to the Interim Prudential Sourcebooks that they will restate existing material, pending the production of the final Integrated Prudential Sourcebook.

Finally, it is to be noted that the regime under the Insurance Groups Directive also affects Lloyd's, although in general the Lloyd's regulatory regime is distinct. Lloyd's members are entitled to the benefit of the European passport rights under provisions in the other Directives and must equally comply with relevant requirements of the Insurance Groups Directive.

Insurance Companies and FSMA 2000

As has been seen in Ch.2, effecting and carrying out contracts of insurance **8–036** is a specified activity (strictly, two separate activities, one of effecting and one of carrying out) under the Financial Services and Markets Act 2000 (Regulated Activities) Order 2001 (SI 2001/544). This is subject to limited exceptions for EEA firms in relation to Community co-insurance operations (as defined in the Community Co-insurance Directive (Dir.78/473 [1978] O.J. L151/25)) and in relation to information society services (defined in the Electronic Commerce Directive (Dir.00/31 [2000] O.J. L178/1)). There is also an exception for vehicle breakdown services. Moreover, rights under a contract of insurance are specified investments. A contract of insurance is a contract within either of the two broad categories previously discussed, namely, long-term (life) insurance and general (non-life) insurance. It follows that the carrying on of either kind of insurance business is a regulated activity and as such is subject to the general prohibition in s.19 of FSMA of the carrying on of a regulated activity by a person who is not an authorised person or an exempt person. By this means, a result comparable to the position under the Insurance Companies Act 1982 is achieved.

8–037 It follows, of course, that the various elements of regulation considered in Ch.2 apply to the carrying on of the vast majority of insurance business in the United Kingdom. As noted in para.2.45, permission to carry on insurance business will be given only to a body corporate, a registered friendly society or a member of Lloyd's (COND 2.1.1). The remainder of the threshold conditions, discussed in the following paragraphs, must also be satisfied. Assuming that a potential insurer is able to satisfy those conditions and proceeds to apply for permission, there are further specific obligations, as outlined in AUTH 3.12. It should be observed that IPRU (INS) contains restrictions as to the other regulated activities which may be carried on by an insurer and that will be reflected in any permission granted (AUTH 3.12.3); further, a single body corporate will only be given permission to carry on a limited class of general insurance business in addition to long-term business (AUTH 3.12.4). AUTH 3.12.6 to 3.12.12 contains provisions relating to the ancillary and supplementary business which may be carried on pursuant to various types of permission. Particular reporting requirements apply during the first three years of carrying on insurance business (SUP App. 2).

8–038 The approved persons regime applies to authorised insurance companies as to other authorised bodies, and it is to be noted that the appointed actuary function is one of the controlled functions falling within the category of significant influence functions (SUP 10.4.5). The underlying requirement, carried over from the previous regime, that an actuary must be appointed by a company carrying on long-term insurance business, is now to be found in SUP 4.3.1. This is supplemented by SUP 4.3.8 and 4.3.9 as to the qualifications required for an appointed actuary and SUP 4.3.13 to 4.3.21 as to the duties and responsibilities of the actuary and of the company in relation to the actuary. A further aspect of the supervision regime which applies only in respect of insurance business is the regime governing the transfer of an insurance business within the meaning of s.105. Under s.104 of the FSMA 2000, no scheme for such a transfer is to have effect unless it has been sanctioned by an order of the court under s.111. Broadly speaking, the schemes covered are schemes under which a United Kingdom authorised person is to transfer business in circumstances in which the transferred business will be carried on from an EEA Member State. (An approval regime applies in respect of transfer of banking business schemes, but in somewhat different circumstances.) The Treasury has made the Financial Services and Markets Act 2000 (Control of Business Transfers) (Requirements on Applicants) Regulations 2001 (SI 2001/3625 under the relevant sections of the Act and substantial guidance in relation to such schemes is given in SUP 18. The machinery was successfully operated in *WASA International (UK) Insurance Co. Ltd v WASA International Insurance Co Ltd* [2002] EWHC 2698, December 10, 2002.

The distinction between general and long-term insurance business reappears in various contexts. The Principles for Businesses apply generally, but as respects accepting deposits, general insurance business and long-term insurance business involving pure protection contracts (*i.e.* certain policies offering payment on death or incapacity due to injury, sickness or infirmity), the FSA "will proceed only in a prudential context" (PRIN 1.1.3). That is explained as meaning that the FSA would not expect to exercise the powers brought into play by a contravention of a Principle unless it amounted to a serious and persistent violation which had implications for confidence in the financial system, or for the fitness and propriety of the company, or for the adequacy of its financial resources. COB also has limited application to such activities (COB 1.3.2, and see further COB 3.2.3 as respects financial promotions and much of COB 6 as respects product disclosure and the right to withdraw). The rationale for the distinction in this context is that there is likely to be a much greater investment element in long-term insurance arrangements, other than pure protection arrangements, than in general insurance (again essentially a protective form of contract) or in accepting deposits (in relation to which the concern is to get the deposit back and to receive interest). 8–039

Interim Prudential Sourcebook for Insurers

IPRU (INS) applies to every insurer except a friendly society or a member of Lloyd's (IPRU (INS) 1.1 and 1.2). (Both friendly societies and Lloyd's of course have their own regime.) It is in three volumes: the Rules; the Appendices to the Rules; and Guidance. It also begins with a section of guidance which draws attention to the particular relevance of the Principles for Businesses to an insurer's internal systems and controls, pointing out that one of the features of a contract of insurance is the long period of risk which the contract may cover. Risk limitation and solvency requirements are therefore principal features of the Sourcebook. The contents of Volume 1 are as follows: 8–040

- Ch.1: deals with the application of the Sourcebook (already noted) and requires that the business of an insurer is limited to insurance business and activities arising directly from that business (IPRU (INS) 1.3). (That will include management of pension fund assets for its own officers or employees or officers or employees of the group.)
- Ch.2: contains the basic provisions as to margins of solvency. An insurer with its head office in the United Kingdom has to maintain a margin of solvency; one with its head office elsewhere has usually to maintain a margin of solvency and a United Kingdom margin. If the insurer carries on both general and long-term business, the margin or margins must be satisfied separately as respects each category. The general requirement is that an insurer must ensure that its liabilities are covered by assets of appropriate safety, yield and marketability, having regard to the classes of business carried

on, are appropriately diversified and adequately spread and that excessive reliance is not placed on investments of any particular category or description. Different approaches to the calculation are specified in relation to different types of insurance business.

- Ch.3: deals with long-term insurance business. This includes provisions designed to ensure that distinct funds and assets are used for distinct purposes where appropriate, subject to exceptions in cases where the funds or assets exceed a specified level, or are exchanged for others of equivalent value. It also deals with the allocation of assets to policyholders where the terms of the insurance contract enable policyholders to participate in surplus. The insurer must satisfy itself that the premiums to be received in respect of a long-term contract and the income likely to be generated are adequate, on reasonable actuarial assumptions, to meet the expected liability. In addition, the chapter contains requirements relating to linked long-term policies (*i.e.* broadly speaking, policies associated with an entitlement to receive benefits related to the value of or income from some property (IPRU (INS) 2.3.(4)).
- Ch.4: makes provision for the valuation of assets, in connection with prudential requirements, of different kinds, namely: shares in a group undertaking; debts due or to become due from a group undertaking; assets sold to or purchased from an approved credit institution or an approved investment firm subject to an agreement for resale or repurchase; debts and other rights; land; equipment; securities and beneficial interests in limited partnerships; beneficial interests in collective investment schemes; deferred acquisition costs; reversionary interests; derivative contracts; contracts and assets having the effect of derivative contracts; and assets only to be taken into account to a specified extent. Assets other than cash which are not specified in the Valuation Rules are to be left out of account in determining an insurer's assets (IPRU (INV) 4.1.(3)), and if the actual value is less than the value determined in accordance with the Rules, the actual value is to be taken (4.1.(4)).
- Ch.5: deals with the converse situation, that is, the determination of liabilities. In principle, generally accepted accountancy methods must be adopted and all contingent or prospective liabilities must be included, although liabilities in respect of share capital, other than cumulative preference shares, are excluded (IPRU (INV) 5.2). The amount of the liabilities is to be determined differently for general and for long-term business.
- Ch.6: provides for equalisation reserves in relation to general insurance business. Such reserves are required in respect of certain classes of business in order to maintain solvency during a period of abnormal claims.
- Ch.7: requires liabilities in one currency to be substantially matched with assets in that currency and provides for assets to be held in appropriate locations.

- Ch.8: relates to non-United Kingdom insurers. It covers deposits, the location of accounts and records and rules applicable to branches. The deposit requirements affect non-EEA insurers, as do the accounts and records requirements, but the rules applicable to branches are liable to affect EEA insurers as well as others.
- Ch.9: contains reporting provisions relating to accounts and statements. Again, there are differences between the obligations which apply to an insurer carrying on general insurance business and those which apply to an insurer carrying on long-term insurance business. Additionally, an insurer in the latter category has to obtain an investigation of its affairs from its appointed actuary at least once in every 12 months, and has to make the report of the investigation available (IPRU (INS) 9.4). There are rules as to the form and content of the accounts and documents to be deposited with the FSA. Policyholders have the right to see copies of deposited documents. Insurers who carry on general insurance business must classify the business into risk groups (IPRU (INS) 9.18). The reporting requirements are extensive and detailed.
- Ch.10: contains the provisions relating to the parent undertaking solvency calculation required by the Insurance Groups Directive. The purpose of these requirements has already been discusssed.
- Ch.11: contains the definitions used throughout IPRU(INS). It also provides (IPRU(INS) 11.4) that s.150(1) of FSMA 2000 does not apply to contraventions of IPRU(INS), so such a contravention does not give rise to an action for damages for breach of statutory duty.
- Ch.12: is intended to deal with transitional provisions, but in fact contains no such provisions applicable specifically to insurance companies.

The Appendices in Volume 2 are lengthy and detailed, and cross-refer back to particular provisions of the rules. Volume 3 consists of guidance notes from the FSA, "Dear Director" letters from the FSA, addressed to the directors of insurance companies, and "Dear Appointed Actuary" letters from the Government Actuary's Department, which were in fact written under the previous regime, before FSMA 2000 came into force. **8–041**

Complaints

As has already been mentioned, under the old system, there was no statutory ombudsman to deal with complaints against insurance companies. Redress was available only through the Insurance Ombudsman Bureau. If the relevant insurer had joined the scheme, a complainant could use its mechanisms, but if the insurer was not a member, the complainant was stymied. As a consequence, the Insurance Ombudsman Bureau was not amenable to judicial review: see *R. v Insurance Ombudsman Bureau, Ex p. Aegon Life Assurance Ltd, The Times*, January 7, 1994. **8–042**

Now, of course, the Financial Ombudsman Service has jurisdiction to consider complaints made against an insurance company and the position is as described in Ch.16.

Chapter 9

Mortgages

Introduction

A mortgage is not in itself an investment, but rather a debt secured on land. It may not be immediately obvious, therefore, why a discussion of mortgages should be included in a book on the law of investor protection. There are, however, three reasons why such a discussion is called for here. The first is that, where a mortgage is being used to finance the purchase of land, the purchase and mortgage will have many of the hallmarks, from the mortgagor's point of view, of a composite investment transaction, in which the performance of the "investment" depends on the potential for the value of the land to increase over the term of the mortgage at a rate which exceeds the rate at which interest is charged under the mortgage on the money borrowed to finance the purchase. Many homeowners will look on the purchase of their home on mortgage as the biggest investment they will ever make. Secondly, any interest-only mortgage (that is to say, a mortgage which provides for the borrower to make payments consisting solely of interest during the mortgage term, and to repay the loan in a lump sum at the end of the term) is likely to require the borrower to put in place and maintain an investment product, such as an endowment policy or pension plan, to provide the source from which the loan is to be repaid. In such a case, the mortgage transaction will include an investment element in the conventional sense. Thirdly, we shall see that, with effect from October 31, 2004, most first mortgages of residential land are to be regulated under FSMA 2000. They will then fall within the same regulatory framework as currently applies to true investment products, and rights under a regulated mortgage contract will themselves become an "investment" for the purposes of s.22(1) of the 2000 Act. **9–001**

Endowment Mis-selling Cases

The endowment mortgage is the classic example of an interest-only mortgage packaged with an investment product. Under this type of mortgage, the borrower is required to maintain an endowment policy on his own life for a term of years equal to the term of the mortgage. The mortgage will provide for the proceeds of the policy to be applied in or towards repayment of the loan at the end of the term. It used to be the **9–002** invariable practice of mortgage lenders to take a charge over the policy (either by formal assignment by way of security or, more commonly, by taking a deposit of the policy by way of equitable charge). Nowadays, however, it is increasingly common for the lender to forgo a charge over the policy, and to rely instead on a covenant from the borrower to maintain the policy and to use its proceeds to repay the mortgage debt.

9–003 Endowment policies were formerly the first choice of the majority of mortgage borrowers. However, their reputation has been tarnished in recent years by the failure of many policies to produce a sufficient sum on maturity to repay the full amount owing under the mortgage. One consequence of the resulting disillusionment with endowment mortgages has been a renewal of interest on the part of borrowers in the traditional repayment mortgage, under which the loan is repaid over the mortgage term by instalments consisting of both capital and interest.

9–004 In 1999, the FSA and the ABI jointly set up a programme under which providers of mortgage endowment policies were required to send their policyholders information about their policy and the prospects of its producing the target amount at maturity. As part of this programme, endowment providers began sending out re-projection letters to policyholders in April 2000. These letters were coded as green, amber or red, according to the perceived likelihood of the policy yielding the target sum on maturity. A "green" letter advised the customer that the provider believed the policy to be on track to reach its target; an "amber" letter stated that the provider considered it possible that that the policy might not pay out enough; and a "red" letter stated that the provider considered that there was now a high risk that the policy would pay out enough and strongly suggested that the customer consider taking action.

9–005 This exercise prompted large numbers of borrowers who received "red" letters to seek compensation from their lender or endowment provider (or both) and, in a substantial number of cases, to take their complaints to the FOS. While the fact that the policy is likely to produce a shortfall will not be enough in itself to entitle the borrower to compensation, the FOS may well award compensation if it finds that the policy was missold, *e.g.* because a representative of the lender or the insurer wrongly represented to the borrower prior to completion of the mortgage that the policy was guaranteed to produce a sufficient sum to repay the loan, or because such a representative failed to take adequate steps to ensure that the borrower was prepared to take the risk that the maturity value of the policy (being dependent on the performance of the underlying stock market investments) would fall short of the target figure.

9–006 The FSA has given detailed guidance in its *Handbook*, at DISP App.2, about the way in which compensation should be assessed in cases where an endowment policy has been missold. The guidance will be followed by the FOS in decide any complaints made to it, and should also be followed by firms seeking to resolve complaints without the need for a decision by the FOS. The basic approach is set out at DISP App.2.2.1G:

> "If there has been a failure to give compliant and proper advice, or some other breach of the duty of care, the basic objective of redress is to put the

> complainant, so far as is possible, in the position he would have been in if the inappropriate advice, or the other breach had not occurred. In many cases, although it must be a matter for inquiry and assessment in each individual case, this position is likely to have resulted in the complainant taking a repayment mortgage with accompanying life cover, and this is the assumption which underpins the standard approach to redress."

Typically, therefore, it will be necessary to compare the borrower's actual capital position under the endowment mortgage, as measured by the current surrender value of the endowment policy, with the capital position he would have been if he had opted for a repayment mortgage instead. The latter will be measured by reference to the amount of capital that the borrower would have repaid, at the time when the comparison is made, by making the monthly instalments that would have fallen due under the mortgage. If the surrender value of the policy falls short of the capital that would have been repaid under a repayment mortgage, then, *prima facie*, the borrower will be entitled to compensation. The compensation will then require adjustment, however, to reflect the fact that the payments actually made under the endowment mortgage (*viz.* the interest-only payments made to the lender, plus the endowment policy premiums paid to the insurer) will almost certainly have been different from the payments that would have been made under a repayment mortgage (*viz.* the combined instalments of capital and interest that would have been payable to the lender). **9–007**

Mortgage Regulation

Although the necessary power to regulate mortgages was included in the Financial Services and Markets Bill, the Government announced in April 1998 that the decision whether or not to activate the power would depend on the outcome of a review to be conducted in 1999. The review consisted in part of a consultation exercise by the Treasury launched in July 1999 and in part by a cost benefit analysis carried out by the FSA. **9–008**

The results of the Treasury consultation (published in January 2000) disclosed that consumers were suffering detriment in four distinct areas: **9–009**

(1) *Poor or misleading information and lack of transparency.* The Treasury found that the main examples of detriment under this heading concerned:

- misleading payment illustrations and APR (annual percentage rate) calculations in advertising literature;
- a lack of transparency in fees (*e.g.* valuation and arrangement fees);
- a lack of transparency in costs and commissions associated with related products (*e.g.* linked insurance policies);
- advertising literature and contract documents, where product restrictions, complex redemption charge calculations and other

aspects of the mortgage were included in the small print and not explained to borrowers;
- advisers who provided information only on a limited range of products and pushed higher commission products; and
- the general difficulty in making like for like price comparisons between products.

9–010 (2) *Product features, requirements and lenders' systems*. The Treasury gave a number of examples of consumer damage in this area, including:

- the compulsory purchase of associated insurance products, which were more expensive for the consumers than if they were to be allowed to shop around;
- prohibitive early repayment charges;
- ties and lock-in periods, particularly after the end of a fixed term;
- mortgage indemnity guarantees for high loan-to-value customers;
- the annual calculation of interest, where borrowers pay interest on capital they have already repaid;
- punitive interest rates for minor repayment breaches; and
- delays in passing on movements in bank base rates and (in some areas of the non-status lending market) not reducing interest rates at all on some supposedly variable rate mortgages.

9–011 (3) *Regulatory gaps*. Under this heading, the Treasury drew attention to the partial, and overlapping, regulatory regimes currently applicable to mortgages. These include the OFT's power under the Consumer Credit Act 1974 to regulate all lenders in relation to advertisements and extortionate credit bargains, and licence those lenders who make regulated loans under the 1974 Act (which, in summary, are "consumer" loans, whether secured or unsecured, for an amount not exceeding £25,000). In addition to this, a different part of the OFT has power under the Unfair Terms in Consumer Contracts Regulations 1999 to control unfair terms generally, including those in mortgages securing loans to consumer. As already noted, the regulation of investment vehicles for the repayment of interest-only mortgages falls within the remit of the FSA, and many lenders require authorisation from the FSA because they are involved in selling other investment products.

In addition to the patchwork of statutory regulation, mortgage lenders may also need to have regard to the OFT's guidelines on non-status lending, the ABI's code of practice on the sale of life insurance products, the Mortgage Code (as to which, see Ch.4–081), and decisions and guidance from the FOS on mortgage cases.

9–012 (4) *Treatment of arrears*. The Treasury gave a number of examples of questionable practices relating to arrears. These included:

- a failure to provide borrowers and the courts with clear and accurate breakdowns of the total amount owed;

- the imposition of additional (and sometimes disproportionate) administration charges on top of the arrears;
- an unnecessary resort to court action;
- an insistence on arrears being paid off within an unreasonably short time, rather than over the full term of the mortgage, as required by the Court of Appeal's decision in *Cheltenham & Gloucester Building Society v Norgan* [1996] 1 W.L.R. 343;
- an unreasonable refusal to allow the borrower to sell the mortgaged property himself; and
- unacceptable delays, sometimes of years, in notifying borrowers of the amount owing after possession.

The cost benefit analysis undertaken by the FSA also produced evidence **9–013** of consumer detriment arising from limited competition and product unsuitability (due to an imbalance of information between the lender and borrower). Research showed that products from some new entrants to the market, and some products offered by mainstream lenders to new borrowers, were cheaper than those offered to long-standing borrowers. The FSA inferred from this that the rates on some products did not reflect the efficient cost of providing the loan, and that some consumers were paying more than they would be in an effectively competitive market. In addition, the range and complexity of mortgage products available, and the problems of poor information, made it hard for consumers to compare value. Finally, the FSA observed that the size of the mortgage market meant that the total amount of consumer detriment might be very large. The FSA stated that, at the end of 1998, about 11 million households (or 40 per cent of all households) had a mortgage; and two thirds of households were owner occupiers who could be expected to have or have had a mortgage. In 1999, there were 2.1 million mortgage advances with a total value of £115 billion (with around a quarter of those transactions involving re-mortgaging). The outstanding stock of mortgage loans was over £500 billion at the beginning of 2000. Furthermore, on average, housing represented the largest single item of expenditure for those with a mortgage, amounting to around 18 per cent of all weekly expenditure. (See the FSA's Consultation Paper 70: *Mortgage Regulation: the FSA's high level approach*, November 2000, paras 2.4–2.5.)

Having considered the findings of the Treasury and the FSA, the **9–014** Government decided that there was a case for statutory regulation of mortgages and that, given that a chief cause of consumer detriment was limited product transparency, the regulatory approach should focus on improving information for consumers. Accordingly, on January 26, 2000, the Economic Secretary to the Treasury announced that the FSA would be given responsibility for regulating key aspects of mortgage selling.

The Treasury's original proposals envisaged that the regulation of **9–015** mortgages would focus exclusively on mortgage lenders. The intention was that the FSA would authorise lenders to carry on mortgage business (covering both mortgage lending and mortgage administration), but would not regulate the provision of advice in relation to mortgages. In December 2001, however, the Treasury announced that it had changed its mind and that the scope of regulation was to be extended to include advising on and arranging mortgages. When the system of regulation finally comes into effect (currently projected to for October 31, 2004), the regulatory net will therefore catch not only mortgage lenders, but also brokers and other intermediaries involved in the sale of mortgage products.

9–016 At present, the Financial Services and Markets Act 2000 (Regulated Activities) Order 2001 (SI 2001/544) (the RAO) only makes provision for the activities originally intended to be covered by mortgage regulation, that is to say, mortgage lending and mortgage administration. Amendments to the RAO will be required to extend its scope to advising on and arranging mortgages, and the text of a draft Order making the necessary amendments has been published by the Treasury as an Annex to its Consultation on Regulating Mortgages, published on February 28, 2002.

9–017 As regards mortgage lending and mortgage administration, art.61(1) and (2) of the RAO provide that entering into a mortgage contract as lender and administering a regulated mortgage contract are both specified kinds of activities for the purposes of FSMA 2000. When in force, the effect of these provisions will be that both kinds of activity will be regulated by the Act when they are carried on by way of business in relation to an investment of a specified kind (see s.22 of the Act). Rights under a regulated mortgage contract will then be included among the investments specified in Pt III of the RAO: see art.88.

By art.61(3)(a) of the RAO, a contract will be a "regulated mortgage contract" if, at the time it is entered into, the following conditions are met:

> "(i) the contract is one under which a person ("the lender") provides credit to an individual or to trustees ("the borrower");
> (ii) the contract provides for the obligation of the borrower to repay to be secured by a first legal mortgage on land (other than timeshare accommodation) in the United Kingdom;
> (iii) at least 40 per cent of the land is used, or is intended to be used as, or in connection with a dwelling by the borrower or (in the case of credit provided to trustees) by an individual who is a beneficiary of the trust, or by a related person"

For the purposes of condition (iii), above, the area of any land which comprises a building or other structure containing two or more storeys is to be taken to be the aggregate of the floor area of each of those storeys (art.61(4)(b)), and the expression "related person" includes, in addition, to a person's spouse, parent, brother, sister, child, grandparent or grandchild "a person (whether or not of the opposite sex) whose relationship with that person has the characteristics of the relationship between a husband and wife" (art.61(4)(c)).

It will be seen that the effect of the above definition is to exclude from the category of "regulated mortgage contracts" (and hence from the scope of mortgage regulation) all of the following types of mortgages:

- mortgages which secure loans to bodies corporate (except where the body corporate is a trustee for individual beneficiaries);

- second or subsequent mortgages; and
- mortgages of land which is used (or more than 60 per cent of which is used) for non-residential purposes.

Regulated mortgage contracts will therefore consist primarily of the traditional bank or building society loan to an individual borrower, secured by a first mortgage of land for the borrower's residential use. It should, however, be borne in mind that many secured loans to individual borrowers which fail to qualify as regulated mortgage contracts will be likely to constitute agreements regulated by the Consumer Credit Act 1974, especially if, as the DTI has proposed, the £25,000 limit which currently applies to agreements regulated by the Act is increased or removed altogether.

The activity of entering into a regulated mortgage contract is self-explanatory and is not elaborated in the RAO. The activity of administering a regulated mortgage contract is defined in art.61(3)(b) as meaning either or both of the following: **9–018**

> "(i) notifying the borrower of changes in interest rates or payments due under the contract, or of other matters of which the contract requires him to be notified; and
> (ii) taking any necessary steps for the purposes of collecting or recovering payments due under the contract from the borrower."

It is, however, provided that a person is not to be treated as administering a regulated mortgage contract merely because he has, or exercises, a right to take action for the purposes of enforcing the contract (or to require that such action is or is not taken). In addition, arts 62 and 63 have the effect that a person who is not an authorised person will not be treated as administering an regulated mortgage contract where he:

(a) arranges for the contract to be administered by someone who is an authorised person with the necessary permission to carry on the administration;

(b) administers the contract himself for not more than one month after the ending of any arrangement mentioned in (a), above; or

(c) administers the contract under an agreement with a person who has permission to carry on the administration.

These exclusions should normally make it possible for special purpose vehicles under mortgage securitisations to avoid carrying on a regulated activity themselves.

It is currently proposed that the activities of arranging regulated mortgage contracts and advising on such contracts will become regulated activities under a new art.25A and a new art.53A, to be inserted by amendment into the RAO. Art.25A is expected to cover the making of: **9–019**

(a) arrangements for another person to enter into a regulated mortgage contract as borrower;

(b) arrangements for another person to vary the terms of such a contract entered into by him as borrower after October 31, 2004; and

(c) arrangements with a view to a person who participates in the arrangements entering into a regulated mortgage contract as borrower.

Art.53A is expected to cover giving advice to person in his capacity as a borrower or potential borrower on the merits of his entering into a particular regulated mortgage contract or of his varying the terms of any such contract which he entered into after October 31, 2004. Art.53A will, however, be subject to exclusions for advice given in print, electronic or broadcast media, advice given in the course of the administration of the contract by an authorised person, advice given by a person carrying on a profession or business, and advice given by a person in the capacity of trustee or personal representative.

The draft Mortgages: Conduct of Business Sourcebook

9–020 The content of the obligations imposed on a person who carries on any of the regulated activities discussed in paras 9–017 to 9–019, above, has yet to be finalised. However, volume 2 of the FSA's Consultation Paper 186, *Mortgage regulation: draft conduct of business rules and feedback on CP146* contains the draft of the FSA's proposed *Mortgages: Conduct of Business Sourcebook* (MCOB) which, when finalised, will be included in the *Handbook* and will set out the main body of rules and guidance relevant to mortgage regulation. When in force, the sourcebook is likely to have a profound impact on the way in which mortgage lenders, administrators and intermediaries carry on their businesses.

The draft sourcebook is a lengthy and detailed document, and it would be impracticable to attempt more than a very brief outline of its provisions here. The following summary may, however, be helpful as an indication of the scope and content of the draft. In considering the summary, it should be borne in mind that, whereas the rules contained in Chs 3, 10, 12 and 13 of the draft sourcebook are in near-final form, those in the remaining Chs (1, 2, 4–9, 11 and 14) are still subject to consultation and may change significantly when the consultation process is complete.

9–021 As is apparent from Ch.1 of the draft sourcebook, the rules, evidential provisions and guidance contained in it will apply to every firm which carries on "regulated mortgage activities" or communicates or approves a "qualifying credit promotion". In summary, "regulated mortgage activities" cover arranging, advising on, entering into and administering regulated mortgage contracts whereas a "qualifying credit promotion" is a promotion relating the provision by a mortgage lender or administrator of credit secured on land (which, it will be noted, is a wider concept than the provision of credit under a regulated mortgage contract). For the most part, the provisions of the sourcebook will not apply to authorised professional firms with respect to their non-mainstream regulated activities (as to which, see Ch.3–017, above).

As regards the territorial scope of the sourcebook, the general principle is that its provisions will apply if the customer of a firm carrying on regulated mortgage activities is resident in the United Kingdom at the time when the activity is carried on. The sourcebook may also apply where the customer is resident in another EEA State, but only if the activity is carried on from an establishment maintained by the firm (or its appointed representative) in the United Kingdom. The territorial scope of the provisions relating to qualifying credit promotions will be subject to the special rules set out in MCOB 3.3.

Ch.2 of the sourcebook will impose a general obligation on firms to communicate information to the customer in a way that is clear, fair and not misleading (though, in the case of a qualifying credit promotion, this general obligation is displaced by the more detailed requirements set out in MCOB 3.6 and 3.8). Ch.2 will also impose restrictions on the use of inducements in connection with regulated mortgage contracts. Thus, a firm will be under a duty to take reasonable care to ensure (among other things) that neither it nor any person acting for it offers or accepts an inducement where this is likely to conflict to any material extent with any duty which the firm owes to its customers in relation to a regulated mortgage contract. Firms will also be banned from operating a system of giving or offering inducements to intermediaries where the value of the inducement increases after a customer has entered into a regulated mortgage contract, or after the intermediary has exceeded a target set for the volume of business referred. **9–022**

As already mentioned, Ch.3 of the sourcebook will regulate the form and content of qualifying credit promotions. Many of the provisions to be included in Ch.3 will be substantively identical to those already contained in COB3, dealing with financial promotions generally (as to which, see para.2–099, above). As is the case with COB3, different requirements will apply to "real time qualifying credit promotions" (*viz.* promotions communicated in the course of an interactive dialogue, such as a meeting or telephone conversation) and "non-real time qualifying credit promotions" (*viz.* promotions communicated in any other way, such as by letter or in a newspaper or television programme). **9–023**

Under Ch.4, a firm providing information or advice to customers seeking to enter into or vary a regulated mortgage contract will have to make it clear to the customer whether its service is based on the whole market, a limited number of mortgage lenders, or a single mortgage lender. In each case, any recommendation given must be suitable for the customer (*i.e.* the contract recommended must be affordable, appropriate to the customer's needs and the most suitable of those available within the scope of the service provided to the customer). **9–024**

Ch.5 will require that, before the customer submits an application for a particular regulated mortgage contract, he is supplied with a detailed illustration explaining the main features of the contract and the costs which would be incurred under it and under any tied product which the customer must take out with it. The content and format of the illustration will be prescribed in considerable detail by Ch.5. **9–025**

Ch.6 provides that, if a firm makes an offer to enter into a regulated mortgage contract with a customer, the offer document must include a **9–026** further, updated illustration enabling the customer to check the features and cost of the contract being offered. The updated illustration will have to comply with the requirements prescribed in Ch.5 (suitably modified to reflect the fact that the updated illustration is being supplied at the offer stage rather than the pre-application stage). The offer document itself will be required to contain a prominent statement of a number of other matters, including an explanation of when interest rate changes will take effect.

9–027 Ch.7 will provide that, if a firm enters into or varies a regulated mortgage contract, it must supply the customer with further information before the first payment becomes due. The purpose of this requirement is to enable the customer to check that the mortgage has been set up or varied in accordance with his wishes. The required information will include such matters as the amount of the first payment and (if different) the subsequent payments, and confirmation of whether the mortgage is a repayment mortgage or interest-only mortgage. Ch.7 will also require the firm to provide the customer, at least once a year, with a statement covering the mortgage and setting out certain prescribed information (*e.g.* the current cost of redeeming the mortgage). In addition, the firm will be required to give the customer reasonable advance notice of any change in the payments that the customer is required to make resulting from changes in the interest rate, and of any material change by the firm in the terms and conditions of the contract. Moreover, the firm will be obliged to supply the customer with a further illustration if he applies for a further advance, or for a change in the type of interest rate which applies to the mortgage (*e.g.* a switch from a variable to a fixed rate).

9–028 Chs 8 and 9 will prescribe additional requirements for "lifetime mortgages". These mortgages (often known as equity release mortgages) are targeted at elderly borrowers, and normally provide that the capital will not become repayable until the borrower dies or moves into long-term care, and that the interest which is charged in the meantime will be rolled-up (*i.e.* it will be allowed to remain unpaid but will be capitalised at periodic intervals). Lifetime mortgages are complex products designed for potentially vulnerable section of the mortgage market. Accordingly, Ch.8 will require firms giving advice about a lifetime mortgage to consider a wide range of additional factors which are relevant to the suitability of this type of mortgage for the particular customer, *e.g.* whether the benefits to the customer will outweigh any adverse effect on the customer's entitlement (if any) to means-tested benefits and on his tax position. The firm will also be required to consider the customer's preferences for his estate and his health and life expectancy. Similarly, Ch.9 will modify the requirements of Ch.5 relating to illustrations to ensure that any illustration relating to a lifetime mortgage reflects the specific features of this type of product.

9–029 Ch.10 sets out the formula and assumptions to be used in calculating the APR (which will need to be stated on any illustration supplied to the customer to provide him with a basis for comparing the cost of the credit described in the illustration with that available elsewhere). The methodology is largely the same as that prescribed for agreements regulated by the Consumer Credit Act 1974 by the Consumer Credit (Total Charge for Credit) Regulations 1980 (SI 1980/51), as amended.

Ch.11 will impose a duty on any mortgage lender who enters into a regulated mortgage contract with a customer, or makes a further advance under such a contract, to take account of the customer's ability to repay the loan. Lenders will be required to put in place a written policy setting out the factors they will take into account in assessing the customer's ability to repay. **9–030**

Ch.12 of the sourcebook will deal with the question of charges imposed under a regulated mortgage contract. It will require any early repayment charge to be expressed in cash and to be a reasonable pre-estimate of the cost to the firm of the premature termination of the contract. Similarly, it will require any arrears charges to be a reasonable estimate of the administrative costs caused by the customer being in arrears. In addition, firms will be subject to a general obligation not to impose charges which are "excessive", and a particular obligation not to subject customers to excessive charges in connection with the making of further advances and the variation of the contract. **9–031**

Ch.13 deals with arrears and repossessions under regulated mortgage contracts. It will require firms to deal fairly with any customer who is in arrears under such a contract or who, following the sale of the mortgaged property, continues to owe part of the debt formerly secured by the mortgage (referred to as a "mortgage shortfall debt"). Firms will be required to put in place a written policy and procedures which include provision for making reasonable efforts to reach agreement on the method of repayment and the time over which repayment is to be made. There will also be an obligation to provide any customer who falls into arrears with a range of information, including a list of the payments which have been missed or not paid in full. Before commencing action to recover possession, the firm will have to update this information, and inform the customer of the need to contact the local authority to determine whether he will be eligible for local authority housing if the property is repossessed. The firm will also have to state clearly what action will be taken with regard to repossession. Firms will be placed under a duty not to put pressure on the customer through excessive telephone calls or correspondence, or by contact at an unreasonable hour. There will also be an obligation to ensure that, where a property is repossessed, it is marketed as soon as possible and is sold for the best price that might reasonably be paid. The customer must be informed of any mortgage shortfall debt as soon as possible after the property is sold. **9–032**

Finally, Ch.14 makes provision for the terms on which mortgage intermediaries will hold any client money in the course of arranging or advising on regulated mortgage contracts. **9–033**

Chapter 10

Pensions

Introduction

When the first edition of this work was written, it was possible to draw a straightforward distinction between personal pensions and occupational pensions. The interests of investors in personal pension arrangements were protected under the Financial Services Act 1986, while members of occupational pension schemes were protected primarily by the provisions of the Pensions Act 1995. The 1995 Act continues to be the principal source of protection as respects occupational pension schemes, and the framework established under FSMA 2000 now replaces the 1986 Act. In addition, however, a new form of pension arrangement has appeared on the scene, in the shape of the stakeholder pension introduced by s.1 of the Welfare Reform and Pensions Act 1999. The purpose of the new arrangement was to widen public access to pension savings, by ensuring that those who did not have access to an occupational pension scheme did have access to pension arrangements which were flexible and which avoided the relatively heavy charges often associated with personal pension schemes. The original intention was in particular to encourage pension saving by those in low to middle income groups and to ensure by appropriate statutory regulation that there was general confidence in stakeholder pensions, after the damage done to the personal pension market by the pension mis-selling scandal of the late 1980s and early 1990s (as to which see further para.10.47 below). In the event, the applicable tax regime does not limit the attractions of stakeholder pensions to those in the original target groups. **10–001**

A significant new feature of the stakeholder pension arrangements is that under s.3 of the 1999 Act an employer (other than one exempted by regulations) must ensure that at all times there is at least one designated stakeholder scheme which offers membership to all his relevant employees. That obligation carries with it obligations to consult on designation, to supply information to relevant employees, to permit representatives of a designated scheme to have reasonable access to relevant employees, to provide for payroll deduction of contributions and to withdraw designation from any scheme which ceases to be registered under s.2 of the Act.

Generally speaking, a stakeholder pension is likely to be provided under personal pension arrangements and it is often to be found described as a type of personal pension. In fact, however, it is possible for a stakeholder pension scheme to be either an occupational pension scheme or a personal **10–002** pension scheme (see the definition of "pension scheme" in s.8(1) of the 1999 Act), although by virtue of s.1(4) the benefits to be provided must be money purchase benefits (*i.e.* the benefits which the contributions will buy) rather than benefits defined by reference to final salary, as has traditionally usually been the case with the principal benefits under occupational pension schemes. Moreover, under s.8(2) of the Welfare Reform and Pensions Act, the Secretary of State may by regulations make provision for a stakeholder pension scheme of a prescribed description which, apart from the regulations, would be an occupational pension scheme to be treated for all purposes or such purposes as may be prescribed as a personal pension scheme, while by virtue of s.6(3) and Sch.1, a large number of provisions in the Pensions Schemes Act 1993 and the Pensions Act 1995 which apply to occupational pension schemes are made applicable to trust-based stakeholder pension schemes also. The overall effect is that stakeholder pensions have some of the features of each of the other two types of pension arrangement. In outline, the FSA regulates the marketing of stakeholder pension schemes and the provision of advice on whether to join such a scheme, and authorises and supervises those responsible for managing the funds invested in such schemes. In those respects, the arrangements correspond with those applicable to personal pension scheme. Under s.2 of the 1999 Act, however, stakeholder pension schemes must be registered with the Occupational Pensions Regulatory Authority ("OPRA"), which will regulate the governance of such schemes, as it does the governance of occupational pension schemes (and now, employers who make employer or employee payments into personal pension schemes).

10–003 The primary conditions which a pension scheme must satisfy before it can be registered as a stakeholder pension scheme are set out in s.1 of the 1999 Act as follows:

- the scheme is established under a trust or in such other form as may be prescribed;
- the documents establishing the scheme comply with prescribed requirements;
- (as already noted) the benefits provided are money purchase benefits;
- the scheme complies with requirements limiting the charges which may be defrayed out of scheme funds (currently 1 per cent of the value of the member's fund each year);
- the scheme complies with disclosure requirements;
- members may make such contributions as they think fit, provided that they make the prescribed minimum contribution (currently £20);
- the scheme is obliged to accept transfer payments in respect of rights under other pension schemes, except where the scheme's tax position would be affected;
- the scheme is a tax-approved or tax-exempt scheme.

The necessary regulations are the Stakeholder Pension Schemes Regulations 2000 (SI 2000/1403), as amended (see SIs 2001/104, 2001/934, 2002/1480 and 2002/2098), which do in fact permit stakeholder pension schemes to be established otherwise than under a trust. Under reg.2 of the 2000 Regulations, such a scheme must be established by means of one or more instruments in writing which provide for one or more contracts to be entered into between the manager of the scheme and each member of the scheme, or a person acting on his behalf, and the manager of the scheme must be a person who is either mentioned in s.632(1) of the Income and Corporation Taxes Act 1980 as authorised to establish a personal pension scheme, or the authorised corporate director of an open-ended investment company (for which see Ch.6), in order to ensure that an appropriate regulatory regime applies. The attraction for regulatory purposes of schemes established under a trust, the almost invariable basis for an occupational pension scheme, is the well-developed system of regulation relating to trustees' duties and responsibilities which already exists, partly as a matter of general trust law and partly under the Pensions Act 1995, and which covers, for example, the trustees' duties to act in the best interests of the beneficiaries, to develop an investment policy, to obtain and act on proper advice, to keep proper accounts and to maintain a minimum funding level. The regulations contain additional provisions relating to schemes not established under a trust to provide something of an equivalent framework for such schemes. The current exemptions from the obligations on employers, set out in the regulations, are limited to cases in which the employer already offers certain occupational or personal pension arrangements, or in which there are fewer than five employees or all the employees earn below the national insurance lower earnings limit.

A helpful summary of what a stakeholder pension is may be found in the explanatory notes in COB 6 Annex 1.

Regulation under FSMA 2000

We have already observed in Ch.2 the general ban under s.22 of the Act **10–004**
which prevents any person from carrying on a regulated activity in the United Kingdom unless he is an authorised person or an exempt person. As mentioned at para.2–024, the following are (among others) specified activities under the Financial Services and Markets Act 2000 (Regulated Activities) Order 2001 (SI 2001/544):

- dealing in investments as principal;
- dealing in investments as agent;
- arranging deals in investments;
- managing investments;
- safeguarding and administering investments;
- advising on investments.

"Investments" includes, under art.75, rights under a contract of insurance (itself defined by art.3 to include certain pension fund management contracts), securities (defined by art.3 to include shares, instruments acknowledging indebtedness or giving entitlement to investments, government and public securities and certificates representing certain securities) and, under art.89, rights or interests in such investments (with the exception of rights under the trusts of an occupational pension scheme and certain excepted funeral plan contracts).

10–005 It may be noted that the full description of "managing investments" involves managing assets belonging to another person in circumstances involving the exercise of discretion (art.37). This may be contrasted with "safeguarding and administering investments", which appears to be a non-discretionary activity (art.40).

The full description of "advising on investments", contained in art.53, merits some consideration. The advice must be given to a person in his capacity as an investor or potential investor or in his capacity as agent for an investor or potential investor. The advice must be advice on the merits of buying, selling, subscribing for or underwriting a particular investment or exercising a right to buy, sell, subscribe for or underwrite a particular investment. A distinction is to be drawn between the provision of information and the giving of advice, and the FSA gives some guidance on the distinction in the *FSA Handbook* at AUTH App. 1.28. Essentially, the provision of information may constitute the giving of advice if the circumstances in which the information is provided carry with it a recommendation for action. An example of such circumstances appears from *Re Market Wizard Systems (U.K.) Ltd* [1998] 2 B.C.L.C. 282, in which Carnwath J. decided that a computer package which provided signals to users to buy, sell or hold options in traded stocks, depending upon the user's current position, involved the giving of advice.

10–006 An activity, even if specified in the Order, is only a regulated activity if it is carried on by way of business. This element is clarified by the Financial Services and Markets Act 2000 (Carrying on Regulated Activities by Way of Business) Order 2001 (SI 2001/1177). Under art.3, a person is not to be regarded as carrying on by way of business any of the activities listed above unless he carries on the business of engaging in that activity. That, of course, can be expected to be the case with the providers of personal pension arrangements, and it can therefore be seen that activities relating to personal pension schemes will be regulated activities falling to be carried out by authorised persons. This was equally the position under the Financial Services Act 1986.

10–007 The position as respects occupational pension schemes is slightly more complicated. Although rights in investments under the trusts of such a scheme are not themselves "investments", the assets held by the trustees clearly will largely consist of investments and at first sight the trustees are therefore likely to be engaged in the regulated activity of managing investments. That immediate impression is displaced by the Business Order just mentioned, since many trustees will not carry on the business of engaging in the management of investments. Art.3, however, is subject to art.4, under which a person who manages investments where the assets in question are held on trust for an occupational pension scheme is to be regarded as carrying on that activity by way of business unless:

- he is a trustee of a "relevant scheme" who is a beneficiary or potential beneficiary under the scheme or who takes no routine or day-to-day decisions relating to the management of any relevant assets; or
- all routine or day-to-day decisions (other than certain decisions taken in accordance with specified advice) are taken on his behalf by an authorised person who has permission to carry on the activity of managing investments, or a person who is an exempt person in relation to that activity or an overseas person (*i.e.* one who carries on that activity, but not from a permanent place in the United Kingdom).

A "relevant scheme" is a small self-administered scheme (an "SSAS" for the purposes of the *FSA Handbook*) under which, broadly speaking, either the scheme is a trust-based scheme with no more than twelve members, all of whom are trustees and involved in management decisions, or the scheme is one under which all the contributions are used to purchase insurance contracts, there are no more than fifty members, the only management decision to be taken is the selection of the contracts and each member has the opportunity to select his own contract or contracts. In effect, then, the management of the assets of an occupational pension scheme, other than an SSAS, will usually be carried on by an authorised person, either because the trustees themselves are required to be authorised or because the relevant management decisions are taken on behalf of the trustees by such a person. Again, this was broadly the position under the Financial Services Act 1986.

It might have been thought that stakeholder pensions established under personal pension arrangements would be adequately covered by the foregoing and that stakeholder pensions forming part of an occupational pension scheme could, where necessary, either be brought within the regime by delegated legislation under the power given by s.8(2) of the 1999 Act, referred to in para.10–002 above, or could be left to the protection afforded by the general occupational pensions scheme provisions. Instead, establishing, operating or winding up a stakeholder pension scheme is a regulated activity under art.52 of the Regulated Activities Order and rights under a stakeholder pension scheme are "investments" under art.82 and so are brought within the various activities already considered by that route. These provisions do not distinguish between the two possible regimes by which a stakeholder pension may be governed. The exclusion of rights and interests in relation to occupational pension schemes under art.89 applies only where the right or interest would be an investment by virtue of that article and not in cases in which the right or interest is independently made an investment. **10–008**

The question when exactly a person involved in some way with pension management and administration may require authorisation is not a straightforward one, as the above shows. The FSA therefore proposes to add further guidance in the form of an Appendix 6 to AUTH. As this text is written, the draft is out for consultation in Consultation Paper 179 and the FSA's intention is to issue the final text in September 2003. The topics **10–009** covered will include guidance as to the meaning of "routine or day-to-day decisions" (see para.10–007 above) and the circumstances in which pension scheme administration service providers may need authorisation.

Conduct of Business Rules

10–010 Under para.20 of Sch.1 to the Financial Services and Markets Act 2000 (Collective Investment Schemes) Order 2001 (SI 2001/1062), occupational and personal pension schemes do not amount to collective investment schemes, with the exception of a personal pension unit trust which is a feeder fund (*i.e.* an authorised unit trust scheme the sole object of which is investment in units of a single authorised unit trust or shares in a single open-ended investment company: art.2). The special provisions relating to promotion of such schemes, considered in Ch.6, therefore do not apply and the promotion of pension scheme arrangements, as part of carrying on a regulated activity, is covered by the general promotion provisions in COB 3, considered in Ch.2. A person carrying on a regulated activity in relation to a pension scheme will in fact generally be conducting designated investment business, and the provisions of COB will apply accordingly.

10–011 In addition, there are certain provision in COB which have particular application to pension schemes, or to stakeholder pension schemes. Reference has been made in para.2–102 to the provisions of COB 5.1 relating to the application of the policy of polarisation as respects adopted packaged products. The facility to advise on an adopted packaged product (a stakeholder pension scheme not produced by the advising firm or a member of its marketing group, but one in relation to which the firm has decided that it will provide advice) is a relaxation of the strict policy of polarisation in respect of stakeholder pension schemes, since the strict policy would not extend to advice on adopted packaged products. COB 5 again makes special provision in relation to stakeholder pension schemes in COB 5.9. That section reflects the Government's hope that stakeholder pensions will be promoted in a variety of ways, including promotions at meetings arranged by employers. It therefore requires that where information is provided by a firm at a meeting of five or more employees sponsored by one or more employers, the information must be given by an adviser appointed by the firm to give advice to private customers on packaged products (COB 5.9.2).

10–012 A general feature of COB is the product disclosure requirements contained in COB 6. As discussed in para.2–107, those requirements oblige firms to produce "key features" for each packaged product offered, and the particular requirements vary according to the nature of the product. Special provision is made within those requirements for stakeholder pension schemes. A feature applicable only to such schemes is the requirement, under COB 6.5.5 to 6.5.10, to provide decision trees in the form contained in COB 6 Annex 1, unless the product is being bought as a result of a personal recommendation. The decision trees are intended to assist potential purchasers of stakeholder pensions to decide whether or not to make such an acquisition and appear in three versions, one for employed persons, one for the self-employed and one for those without employment. The *FSA*

Handbook states that it is the intention to review the decision trees every year, as soon as possible after the end of the tax year, and the current requirements of the *Handbook* show traces of the revisions which have already taken place. There is only a very limited range of variation permitted in the format of the decision trees.

Further product disclosure requirements contained in COB 6.6 relate to projections for pension schemes more generally. The rights of withdrawal and cancellation set out in COB 6.7 also apply beyond the limited context of stakeholder pension schemes.

Training and Competence Sourcebook

In addition to the COB requirements, TC contains material relating to the **10–013** training and competence requirements applying in connection with pension scheme arrangements. TC2 Annex 9 deals specifically with requirements for those who oversee on a day-to-day basis taking private customers through decision trees in relation to stakeholder pension schemes.

Regulation under the Pensions Act 1995

The principal stimulus to the passing of the Pensions Act 1995 was the **10–014** disappearance of Robert Maxwell and the subsequent discovery of the funds, amounting to more than £400 million, missing from the Mirror Group pension schemes. This gave rise to widespread and understandable concern, reflecting the considerable importance of a satisfactory occupational pension scheme for a large number of people. As a result, a committee was appointed in July 1992 under the chairmanship of Professor Goode to conduct a comprehensive review of the law relating to occupational pensions. Its key recommendations were as follows (see *Pension Law Reform*, 1993 Cmnd. 2342, paras 1.1.13 to 1.1.15):

- trust law should continue to provide the foundation for occupational pension schemes, but it should be supplemented by a Pensions Act administered by a pensions regulator;
- the freedom of trusts should be limited to ensure the reality of the pension promise and to protect accrued rights;
- there should be greater provision of information to scheme members;
- the security of members' entitlements should be strengthened by a minimum solvency requirement, monitored by a pensions regulator and by scheme auditors and actuaries;
- there should be restrictions on the withdrawal of surpluses by employers;
- a compensation scheme should be introduced;
- there should be a general reduction in the administrative burden imposed on employers and scheme administrators through the

simplification of the law by the replacement of detailed investment rules with a general prudent person standard and statutory investment criteria.

Many, but not all, of these recommendations were put into effect by the Pensions Act 1995. In the discussion which follows, we shall give a general outline of the way in which that process was carried out. This is not, however, a fully comprehensive statement of this very detailed area of law.

Occupational Pensions Regulatory Authority (OPRA)

10–015 The proposed pensions regulator was given substance by the 1995 Act in the form of OPRA, established as a body corporate by s.1. As already mentioned in para.10.002 above, although OPRA began as a regulator of occupational pension schemes, it now also regulates personal schemes into which employers pay contributions. It consists of not less than seven members, one of whom is to be the chair, one is to be representative of employers and one of employees, one is to be knowledgeable about life assurance business, one is to have experience and to have shown capacity in the management or administration of occupational pension schemes and two are to be knowledgeable about such schemes (s.1(2)). Appointments are made by the Secretary of State, to whom OPRA is obliged by s.2 to make annual reports. (There are currently nine members in addition to the chair, all of whom are part-time.) Further provision for the constitution and procedure of OPRA is contained in Sch.1. It is to be noted, however, that OPRA does not have a general monitoring function in respect of pension schemes; it acts responsively, when the fact that a scheme is in difficulty is brought to its attention. In that connection, it is further to be noted that s.48 imposes obligations on the auditors and actuaries of occupational pension schemes to give a written report to OPRA if they have reasonable cause to believe that there has been a breach of a duty relevant to the administration of the scheme which is likely to be of material significance in the exercise by OPRA of its functions. Other persons connected with such a scheme may also make a report in similar circumstances, but are not obliged to do so. These provisions, commonly called "whistle-blowing" provisions, may go some way to ensuring that schemes in difficulties do come to the attention of OPRA, but clearly, even assuming a general willingness to report matters which ought to be reported, there will be cases in which there can be a legitimate difference of opinion on the question whether the criteria are satisfied. (Whistle-blowing obligations also apply in respect of personal pension schemes under the provisions of s.33A of the Pension Schemes Act 1993, introduced by the 1995 Act.) OPRA publishes guidance on the whistle-blowing provisions. The limitation to a responsive role is a purely practical one, arising from the fact that the monitoring of all occupational pension schemes was perceived as an impossible task.

OPRA is financed by levies made on pension schemes under s.175 of the Pension Schemes Act 1993, in accordance with the Occupational and Personal Pension Schemes (Levy) Regulations 1997, SI 1997/666), as amended.

The Act gives OPRA the following powers: **10–016**

- power to make a prohibition order prohibiting a person from being a trustee of a particular trust scheme in specified circumstances, including the serious or persistent breach of duties (s.3). (Many provisions of the Act itself include a statement that s.3 applies to a trustee who behaves in a certain way);
- power to make a suspension order suspending a trustee of a trust scheme in specified circumstances, essentially as a holding operation (s.4);
- power to disqualify a person from being the trustee of any occupational pension scheme in specified circumstances, including the making of an order under s.3, removal from office by the court or incapacity (s.29);
- power to appoint a trustee to replace one who is prohibited from acting or disqualified or as an additional trustee to secure the proper administration of the scheme or in other prescribed circumstances (s.7);
- power to impose a civil penalty, not exceeding £5,000 in the case of an individual or £50,000 in any other case, in respect of specified acts or omissions (s.10). (Again, many provisions of the Act itself include a statement that s.10 applies.);
- power to wind up schemes, if OPRA is satisfied that the scheme or any part of it ought to be replaced by a different scheme, that the scheme is no longer required or that it is necessary in order to protect the interests of the generality of the members that the scheme be wound up (s.11);
- power to give certain directions to trustees (s.15).

The Act contains associated procedural provisions in ss.5 and 15(3), and consequential provisions in ss.6, 8, 9 and 30. In addition, OPRA may apply to the court for an order restraining a threatened misuse or misappropriation of assets of an occupational pension scheme (s.13) or for an order requiring restitution by an employer who has received a payment or distribution of scheme assets in contravention of certain provisions and by any other person who appears to the court knowingly to have been involved in the contravention (s.14).

In support of the powers listed above, OPRA has a range of information-gathering powers under ss.98 to 103 of the Pensions Act. S.98 contains a power to require the production of any document (defined to include information recorded in any form). S.99 permits an inspector appointed as such by OPRA to enter premises liable to inspection (*i.e.* premises at which it is reasonably believed that members of the scheme are employed or documents are kept or administration is carried out), to make such examination and inquiry as may be necessary, to require the production of documents and to examine any person. S.100 enables OPRA to obtain a **10–017** warrant from a justice of the peace to allow inspection of premises and removal of documents if satisfied there are reasonable grounds for believing that there are documents at the premises which should have, but have not, been produced. Failures in compliance constitute criminal offences under s.101, although the privilege against self-incrimination and legal professional privilege are preserved by s.102. OPRA may, if it considers it appropriate, publish a report of any investigation under the above provisions.

Ss.104 to 108 then go on to make provision for dealings with "restricted information" in relation to OPRA. Such information is essentially information obtained by OPRA or a corresponding overseas authority in exercise of its functions which relates to the business or affairs of any person, unless the information is already available to the public from other sources or is in the form of a summary so framed as to prevent identification. Broadly speaking, restricted information may only disclosed to facilitate the discharge of its functions by OPRA or another supervisory authority, or to the Secretary of State (originally the Secretary of State of Health and Social Services, but now the Secretary of State for Work and Pensions). There are special provisions in s.109 for the disclosure of tax information held by the Inland Revenue.

10–018 In general, any determination by OPRA of a question which it is within its functions to determine is final (s.96(1)). OPRA must, however, review its determination on the application of a person who is the subject of a prohibition order, or who has been required to pay a civil penalty, or who has been disqualified (s.96(2)) and it may review any other determination on the application of a person appearing to OPRA to be interested on any ground within a period of six months or such longer period as OPRA may allow or at any time if satisfied that there has been a relevant change of circumstances or that the determination was made in ignorance of a material fact or based on a mistake as to a material fact or was erroneous in point of law (s.96(3)). OPRA may then vary or revoke its determination, substitute a different determination and generally deal with matters arising (including any need for savings and transitional provisions). Under s.97(1) OPRA may refer a question of law to the High Court and under s.97(3) a person aggrieved by the determination of OPRA on a review or its refusal to review a determination may appeal to the court on a point of law.

Trustees and Possible Conflicts

10–019 The security of an occupational pension scheme inevitably depends significantly on the quality of the trustees and the Goode Committee report contained recommendations directed towards ensuring sufficient independence from employers, auditors and actuaries and the removal of unsatisfactory trustees. Reference has already been made to OPRA's power to prohibit a person from acting as a trustee of a particular scheme, to suspend him, or to disqualify him, and its power to appoint a new trustee (para.10.016 above). In addition, a person is automatically disqualified from being a trustee of a trust scheme if he has been convicted of any offence involving dishonesty or deception, he is an undischarged bankrupt, if (in the case of a company), any director has been so convicted or is such a bankrupt, he has made a composition or arrangement with his creditors and remains undischarged in respect of it, or he is subject to a disqualification order under the Company Directors Disqualification Act 1986 or to an order made under s.429(2)(b) of the Insolvency Act 1986 (s.29(1)). A person automatically disqualified may ask OPRA to waive the disqualification (s.29(5)).

The principal route to the independence of trustees provided by the Act is via the provisions for member-nominated trustees and directors. The statutory provisions are contained in ss.16 to 21 of the Act and are supplemented by delegated legislation. The essential point is that, subject to limited exceptions in ss.17 and 19, arrangements must be made to ensure that at least one-third of the trustees (s.16(6)) or the directors of a corporate trustee (s.18(6)) are nominated by the members. There must be at least two such trustees or directors if the scheme has 100 or more members, although the number of member-nominated trustees or directors is not to be greater than that required to satisfy the minimum requirement without the consent of the employer. Such trustees are likely to be relatively independent of the wishes of the employer not least because the membership of the scheme will of course include pensioner and deferred members, as well as active members still employed by the employer, and such members will have significantly less interest in what the wishes of the employer might be. This reasoning does, however, illustrate the possibility of conflicts of interest within the body of members, which may assume significance if a system of nomination is adopted which is based on classes of membership. **10–020**

Ss.42 to 46 of the Act contain provisions for the protection of employee trustees, requiring the employer to permit such an employee to take time off during working hours to act as trustee or to undergo training relevant to the performance of trustee duties, to pay him for time off which is taken and not to subject the employee to any detriment on the ground of his performance or proposed performance of functions as a trustee.

In addition to the foregoing, there are specific provisions to tackle the case in which an insolvency practitioner begins to act in relation to an employer company or the official receiver becomes involved in relation to such a company or an individual employer. Under s.23, the practitioner or official receiver must satisfy himself that at all times at least one of the trustees of the scheme is an independent person, and if he is not so satisfied, he must appoint, or secure the appointment of, such a person. A person is "independent" for this purpose if he has no interest in the assets of the employer or of the scheme, otherwise than as trustee, and he is not connected with or an associate of the employer, the insolvency practitioner or official receiver, or any other prescribed person. Under s.123, "connected" and "associated" have the meanings given by ss.249 and 435 of the Insolvency Act 1986. Any member of the scheme may apply to the court under s.24 for an order requiring the insolvency practitioner or official receiver to discharge his duties under s.23, if he does not do so. This requirement provides a safeguard in particular against the risk that the exercise of trustees' powers and discretions will be affected by the financial position of the employer. The point is reinforced by s.25, which provides **10–021** for the exercise of discretionary powers only by the independent trustee or trustees, although they may act by a majority, and for the removal of the employer as trustee upon the appointment of an independent trustee, if the employer was previously the sole trustee. By amendment, the Act now contains in ss.26A to 26C provisions requiring trustees and those involved in the administration of schemes to give information to OPRA about the absence of an independent trustee in certain circumstances. The provision discussed in this paragraph are, however, subject to disapplication under the Occupational Pension Schemes (Independent Trustee) Regulations 1997 (SI 1997/252).

10–022 Further, the trustee of a trust scheme and any person connected with or an associate of such a trustee is ineligible under s.27 to act as auditor or actuary of the scheme. Although "connected" and "associated" again have their Insolvency Act meanings, a person who is a director, partner or employee of a firm of actuaries is not ineligible to act as an actuary of a trust scheme merely because another director, partner or employee is a trustee (s.27(2)). There is also power for certain other persons to be exempted from the general prohibition by regulations. A person who acts as auditor or actuary of a scheme when he is ineligible to do so by virtue of s.27 commits an offence (s.28(1)). The acts done as auditor or actuary, however, are not invalid merely because he is ineligible (s.28(3)).

These provisions are to be read in the light of the fact that s.47 now requires the trustees or managers of every occupational pension to appoint an auditor and an actuary. The section contains further provisions requiring the appointment of a fund manager if the assets include investments for the purposes of FSMA 2000 and preventing the trustees and managers from placing reliance on any auditor, actuary, fund manager or legal adviser appointed otherwise than by the trustees or managers. The section also makes provision for regulations requiring the disclosure of information to professional advisers.

Functions of Trustees

10–023 The next group of sections in the Act is concerned with how the trustees perform their functions. The general requirement of trust law is that trustees should act unanimously in the absence of a special provision in the trust deed. S.32 reverses the effect of that rule by providing that in the absence of contrary provision in the scheme documents, trustees may act by a majority, although it also envisages that the trustees may themselves determine a minimum number of trustees who are to be present when a decision is to be taken by majority vote. S.33 prohibits the exclusion (as defined) by the scheme of liability on the part of trustees or their delegate in investment decisions for breach of a duty of care relating to the performance of investment functions. S.34 gives the trustees the same investment powers as if they were absolutely entitled to the assets of the scheme and permits the delegation of investment decisions only in carefully limited circumstances, including that the delegation should be to a fund manager who is an authorised person under FSMA 2000 (or who does not require authorisation). The fact that the trustees have the investment powers of a person absolutely entitled does not absolve them of the duty to act prudently (see *Learoyd v Whiteley* (1887) 12 App. Cas. 727; *Bartlett v Barclays Bank Trust Co. Ltd (No. 1)* [1980] Ch. 515). S.35 requires the trustees to adopt a statement of investment principles and s.36 sets out the approach to be taken to investment decisions. S.37 deals with the repayment of surplus to an employer by a continuing scheme in order to reduce the surplus, and provides that the power to make such a repayment must be exercised by the trustees and only upon satisfaction of certain conditions. S.38 permits the trustees of a scheme which, under the scheme rules, would have to be wound up, to resolve that the scheme should continue, but as a scheme closed to new members, and with power to determine that no further contributions are to be paid or no new benefits to accrue. S.39 excludes any rule of general trust law (exemplified by *Boardman v Phipps* [1967] 2 A.C. 46) which might have the effect that a trustee cannot exercise powers vested in him because of a conflict between his personal interest and his duties to the scheme, if the source of the conflict is merely that the exercise of the powers in the manner proposed benefits, or may benefit, him in his capacity as a member of the scheme. This final provision results from the decision in *Manning v Drexel Burnham Lambert Holdings Ltd* [1995] 1 W.L.R. 32, which identified the general rule as a source of considerable potential difficulty in relation to the exercise of trustee powers and discretions. It may be noted, however, that a trustee is not to be indemnified out of the trust fund in respect of any fines or civil penalties he may have incurred (s.31).

The effect of all the provisions referred to above is to change what would have been, or potentially would have been, the position either under the general law or under the rules of a particular scheme. By virtue of s.117, those provisions override any contrary provisions in a scheme.

Further positive duties are placed on trustees and managers by s.40, **10–024** which requires compliance with regulations governing the proportion of the scheme's resources which may be invested in employer-related investments (*i.e.* shares or other securities issued by the employer or a connected person or associate, land occupied or used by or subject to a lease in favour of the employer or such a person, other property used for the purposes of any business carried on by the employer or any such person, loans to the employer or any such person, and other prescribed investments). Under the Occupational Pension Schemes (Investment) Regulations 1996 (SI 1996/3127) investments in a collective investment scheme which invests in employer-related resources are prescribed, as are guarantees of, or securities to secure, the liabilities of the employer or any connected person or associate, loan arrangements where repayment depends on the employer's actions or situation (unless it was not the trustees' or managers' purpose to provide financial assistance to the employer) and certain insurance policies. The general limitation, although subject to the detailed provisions of the regulations, is that not more than five per cent of the current market value of the resources of the scheme may at any time be invested in employer-related securities. The question arises what is the position if the limit is exceeded by changes in market values rather than a deliberate new investment. In *Wright v Ginn* [1994] O.P.L.R. 83, decided in relation to the similar limit under the previous regulations, it was held that when the prescribed limit is reached and an investment becomes unauthorised, it can continue to be held provided that the trustees can justify doing so, but if they cannot, they might be liable for a breach of trust. Clearly there may be circumstances in which it would be imprudent in a broad sense for trustees to attempt to realise an investment immediately upon exceeding the limit. It is an offence to make an investment in breach of the limit.

The Minimum Funding Requirement

10–025 The requirement is contained in s.56 of the 1995 Act and is simply that the value of the assets of the scheme must not be less than the amount of its liabilities. It is significantly less stringent than the minimum solvency requirement proposed by the Goode Committee. The requirement applies to all occupational pension schemes other than money purchase schemes (where there are no defined benefits to be funded) and schemes within a prescribed description. In order to assess whether or not the minimum funding requirement is being met, the trustees or managers must obtain valuations at prescribed intervals (in practice, every three years) and a certificate from the scheme actuary stating whether or not in his opinion the contributions payable towards the scheme are adequate for the purpose of securing that the minimum funding requirement will continue to be met during the period until the next valuation, or (if it is not being met), will be met by the end of the period, and indicating any relevant changes which have occurred since the last actuarial valuation was prepared. Remedial steps are to be taken where there are difficulties in meeting the minimum funding requirement. As a tool for assessing the likelihood of doing so, the trustees or managers must prepare a schedule of contributions satisfying prescribed requirements, and it must be certified by the scheme actuary (s.58). The trustees or managers must report to OPRA any failure to pay contributions in accordance with the schedule and any case in which it seems that the minimum funding requirement is not met. It is to be borne in mind that pension benefits under occupational pension schemes are generally subject to indexation in accordance with the provisions of ss.51 to 54. Although the position is different with money purchase schemes, the Act makes provision for a schedule of contributions in such cases also under ss.87 to 90.

10–026 If an actuarial valuation shows that on the effective date of the valuation, the value of the scheme assets is less than 90 per cent of the amount of the scheme liabilities, there is serious underprovision within the meaning of s.60. In such a case, the employer must take steps to eliminate the shortfall either by making an appropriate payment to the scheme or by another prescribed method, within a prescribed period. Again, if the shortfall is not made up within the prescribed period, the trustees or managers must make an appropriate report to OPRA.

Other Miscellaneous Statutory Provisions

10–027 Traditionally, if an occupational pension scheme has contained a power of modification in the scheme documents, the power has usually been in very wide terms. This was perceived by the Goode Committee as potentially prejudicial to members' interests, in that it frequently allowed too much power to employers and did not adequately safeguard the position of the members. S.67(2) now provides that a power of modification cannot be exercised in a manner which would or might affect any entitlement, accrued right or pension credit right (*i.e.* a right under pension sharing arrangements in consequence of divorce) of any member of the scheme acquired before the power is exercised, unless specified requirements are satisfied. The effect is that usually a certificate from the scheme actuary will be required that the exercise will not adversely affect any member in respect of his entitlement or accrued rights without his consent. S.68 enables the trustees to modify the scheme by resolution in order to extend the class of persons who may receive benefits on the death of a member (in which case the consent of the employer is required), to enable the scheme to comply with the requirements in s.16 for member-nominated trustees, to enable the scheme to comply with requirements of the Compensation Board (as to which see para.10–031 below), to enable the scheme to comply with provisions of the Act relating to repayment of surplus, the inalienability of pensions and their forfeiture, to enable the scheme to accommodate persons with pension credits or pension credit rights and for other prescribed purposes. OPRA also has power under s.69 to make an order authorising the modification of a scheme, or in fact modifying it, with a view to achieving any of the purposes set out in the section.

Where a salary-related scheme to which the minimum funding requirement applies is being wound up, s.73 makes provision for the order of priority in which the assets of the scheme are to be applied. S.74 provides for the discharge of the liabilities of the scheme by transfer to another occupational pension scheme, by transfer to a personal pension scheme, by the purchase of annuities or by subscribing to other pension arrangements which satisfy prescribed requirements. If there is a deficiency in the value of the assets, the amount of the deficiency becomes a debt due from the employer to the trustees or managers in accordance with s.75. S.76 governs the making of repayments of surplus to an employer when a scheme is wound up.

The Act makes provision for the adequate supply of documentary material to members by s.41. It also contains administrative provisions relating to the maintenance of a separate bank account and record-keeping generally (s.49).

In the remaining part of this section, we shall consider the disputes and compensation provisions of the 1995 Act. For the remaining provisions of the Act and for any additional detail, the reader is referred to more specialist works

Disputes and Compensation

The starting point for dispute resolution in the 1995 Act is s.50, under **10–028**
which the trustees or managers of an occupational pension scheme must secure that the scheme makes arrangements which provide for a person, on application, to give a decision on a disagreement between prescribed persons and require the trustees or managers, on application following such

a decision, to reconsider the matter in question and confirm the decision or give a new one. The principal regulations prescribing the details of the obligation are the Occupational Pension Schemes (Internal Dispute Resolution Procedures) Regulations 1996 (SI 1996/1270), as amended. If disputes are not settled by the internal scheme, they may be referred to the Pensions Advisory Service (OPAS).

10–029 OPAS is a free service available to members of the public which provides information and guidance and assists those who have a problem, complaint or dispute in relation to their occupational or personal pension arrangements. It is funded by grants from the Department of Work and Pensions through OPRA (pursuant to s.174 of the Pension Schemes Act 1993) and the work is largely carried out by volunteers. The help offered can only be of a general nature, because OPAS does not hold any scheme records or personal information. Frequently asked questions relate to part-time working, divorce, improving pension provision, choice of pension arrangements, early retirement on health grounds, calculation queries and sources of help for disputes. If help is sought to resolve a dispute or complaint, OPAS will require that the complainant should already have attempted to resolve the matter in writing with the parties concerned and will require copies of the documentation. The approach then is to try to seek a resolution through conciliation and mediation; OPAS has no powers to determine a matter. In the year ending March 31 2003, OPAS dealt with 61,271 inquiries and complaints. The next point of recourse after OPAS may be the Pensions Ombudsman, considered further in conjunction with the Financial Ombudsman Service in para.10–034 and following, below.

10–030 The final principal recommendation of the Goode Committee noted above was the establishment of a compensation scheme, and this recommendation also was adopted. The statutory framework begins with s.78 of the Act, which provides for the establishment of a Pensions Compensation Board, consisting of not less than three members, appointed by the Secretary of State, one of whom is to be appointed chair. Of the others, one is to be appointed following consultation with employers' organisations, and the other following consultation with employees' organisations. Further provisions are contained in Sch.2 to the Act. The meat of this part of the Act is contained in s.81, under which the Board may pay compensation in respect of an occupational scheme if:

- the scheme is a trust scheme;
- the employer is insolvent;
- the value of the assets of the scheme has been reduced and there are reasonable grounds for believing that the reduction was attributable to an act or omission constituting a prescribed offence;
- in the case of a salary-related scheme, immediately before the date of the application the value of the assets of the scheme was less than the protection level; and
- it is reasonable in all the circumstances that the members of the scheme should be assisted by the Board paying to the trustees of the

scheme, out of finds for the time being held by them, an amount determined in accordance with the compensation provisions.

The protection level is defined in s.81(2A) to mean, broadly, the amount of the total liabilities of the scheme after reducing the liabilities in respect of other than pensioner members (unless otherwise prescribed) by 10 per cent. The prescribed offences are offences of a fraudulent nature.

An application must be made, as required by the Board, within the **10–031** period of twelve months from the later of the date when the employer became insolvent and the date when the auditor, actuary or trustees knew or ought reasonably to have known that a relevant reduction in value had occurred (s.82). The Board has discretion to extend the period. The amount of the compensation must not exceed the shortfall at the application date, together with interest, or, in the case of a salary-related scheme a figure amounting in substance to the protection level. Under s.80, the Board may review its determination of any question which it is within its function to determine, on any ground within three months of the determination or at any time if it is satisfied that there has been a relevant change of circumstances, or that the determination was made in ignorance of a material fact or based on a mistake as to a material fact, or was erroneous in point of law.

S.110 of the Pensions Act empowers the Board to require a trustee, professional adviser or employer and any other person who appears to hold, or to be likely to hold, relevant information to produce documents (defined to mean information in any form) and s.111 sets out penalties for refusal to do so. As with OPRA, there is a saving for the privilege against self-incrimination and legal professional privilege (s.112) and there are provisions in s.114 governing the disclosure of information.

Again like OPRA, the Board is financed by levies made on pension schemes under s.175 of the Pension Schemes Act 1993, in accordance with the Occupational and Personal Pension Schemes (Levy) Regulations 1997 (SI 1997/666), as amended. Its operation generally is governed by a number of statutory instruments initially made in 1997, several of which have since been amended.

It will be appreciated that by requiring not only the insolvency of the employer but also a reduction in the value of assets believed to be attributable to a prescribed offence, the Act imposes fairly stringent requirements before compensation is likely to be payable under this scheme.

Stakeholder Pensions

Many of the provisions considered above have been made applicable to **10–032** stakeholder pensions which are personal pensions. Those which have not are principally the requirement for member-nominated trustees, the provisions for the appointment of an independent trustee, the protective provisions for employee trustees, the surplus provisions, the restriction on employer-related investments and the minimum funding requirement. These exclusions are largely to be explained simply on the basis that there will be no employer in connection with a personal pension in the way that there is in connection with an occupational pension.

Complaints

10–033 As has been seen, a primary purpose of the 1995 Act was to improve the protection offered to members of pension schemes. The Pension Schemes Act 1993 had a different genesis and was substantially a consolidating Act bringing together statutory provisions bearing upon the social security aspects of pensions law. It was the 1993 Act, however, which introduced the Pensions Ombudsman and the principal provisions are still to be found in Pt X (ss.145 to 152) of that Act, although the provisions have undergone amendment.

10–034 The office of Pensions Ombudsman is established by s.145, which provides for the appointment of the Ombudsman by the Secretary of State. By virtue of amendments made by the Pensions Act 1995 and the Child Support, Pensions and Social Security Act 2000, s.146(1) gives him power to investigate and determine the following matters:

- a complaint by or on behalf of an actual or potential beneficiary of an occupational or personal pension scheme who alleges that he has sustained injustice in consequence of maladministration in connection with any act or omission of a person responsible for the management of the scheme;
- a complaint by or on behalf of a person responsible for the management of an occupational pension scheme who alleges maladministration in connection with any act or omission of another person responsible for the management of the scheme;
- a complaint by or on behalf of the trustees or managers of an occupational pension scheme who allege maladministration in connection with any act or omission of any trustee or manager of another such scheme;
- a complaint by or on behalf of an independent trustee who alleges maladministration in connection with any act or omission of trustees who are not independent or former trustees who were not independent;
- any dispute of fact or law in relation to an occupational or personal pension scheme between a person responsible for the management of the scheme and an actual or potential beneficiary;
- any dispute of fact or law between the trustees or managers of an occupational pension scheme and another person responsible for the management of the scheme or any trustee or manager of another scheme;
- any dispute between trustees of the same occupational pension scheme;

- any question relating, in the case of an occupational pension scheme with a sole trustee, to the carrying out of the functions of that trustee.

This provision is then supplemented by the remaining provisions of s.146 and by the Personal and Occupational Pensions Schemes (Pensions Ombudsman) Regulations 1996 (SI 1996/2475), as amended.

It is to be noted that although an allegation of maladministration is required in many cases, the Ombudsman also has power to deal with disputes of fact and law where there is no such allegation. "Maladministration" is the classic basis for a complaint to the Ombudsman and is traceable back to the Parliamentary Commissioner Act 1967. Its meaning in that context was illustrated by what has become known as "the Crossman catalogue" from the examples given in the debate: "bias, neglect, inattention, delay, incompetence, ineptitude, perversity, turpitude, arbitrariness and so on". The catalogue was cited by way of assistance in *R. v Local Commissioner for Administration, Ex p. Bradford Metropolitan Borough Council* [1979] Q.B. 287. What constitutes maladministration may, however, depend upon the tasks that the body concerned is required to perform: see *Halifax Building Society v Edell* [1992] Ch. 436, a case relating to the Building Societies Ombudsman. **10–035**

Once a complaint has been made or a dispute has been referred to the Pensions Ombudsman, any subsequent court proceedings by any party to the investigation against another party to the investigation may be stayed if the court is satisfied that there is no sufficient reason why the matter should not be investigated by the Ombudsman and that the applicant for a stay was and remains ready and willing to do all things necessary to the proper conduct of the investigation (s.148). S.149 contains some brief procedural provisions and authorises the making of procedural regulations, made in the form of the Personal and Occupational Pension Schemes (Pensions Ombudsman) (Procedure) Rules 1995 (SI 1995/1053), as amended. S.150 gives the Ombudsman power to require any person responsible for the management of the relevant scheme and any person who, in the opinion of the Ombudsman, is able to furnish information or produce documents relevant to the investigation to furnish any such information or produce any such documents. The Ombudsman has the same powers as the court in respect of the attendance and examination of witnesses and the production of documents. Obstruction of the Ombudsman in the performance of his duties or an act or omission which, if the investigation were proceeding in the court, would constitute a contempt, may be certified to the court and the court may then deal with the person concerned as if he had been guilty of a contempt of court. The Ombudsman is also expressly empowered to obtain, and pay for, advice, and may refer a question of law to the court for determination. **10–036**

The Ombudsman's own determinations are dealt with by s.150. A written statement of the determination, with reasons, must be sent to the person by whom or on whose behalf the complaint was made and to any person (if different) responsible for the management of the scheme to which the complaint or reference related. The Ombudsman may direct any **10–037** person responsible for the management of the scheme to take, or refrain from taking, such steps as the Ombudsman specifies in his statement. The determination will be final and binding on the persons to whom the statement is sent and any person claiming under such a person. There is an appeal to the court on a point of law.

A determination is enforceable in a county court as if it were a judgment or order of the county court. S.152 gives the Secretary of State power to make rules in that connection, and the County Courts (Pensions Ombudsman) (Enforcement of Directions and Determinations) Rules 1993 (SI 1993/1978) have been made accordingly.

10–038 The first Pensions Ombudsman made a relatively gentle start to the exercise of the jurisdiction, but his successor, Professor Julian Farrand, took a more adventurous line. As a result there is now a body of law relating to the Pensions Ombudsman, and at times there has been an appearance of conflict between the Ombudsman and the judges of the Chancery Division, who have dealt with pensions cases. It is clear that different perceptions of what is fair have been at work at times. The debate cannot be traced in detail here and readers are referred to appropriate pensions works. It is interesting, however, to note the following passage from the present Ombudsman's evidence to the Select Committee on Work and Pensions:

> "The key points I would wish to emphasise to the Committee are:
>
> 10.1. The need for less detailed Regulation applying both to occupational pension schemes generally and my own office.
>
> 10.2. The need for those administering Pension Schemes to be accountable both to their membership and to the Pensions Ombudsman.
>
> 10.3. I would be helped by an indication from Parliament that it does indeed intend the Pensions Ombudsman (like other Ombudsmen) to investigate and provide remedies for maladministration even though the acts of maladministration might not be regarded as unlawful by the Courts or the same remedy may not be available by way of legal action.
>
> 10.4. The present legislative arrangements may not provide sufficient protection against acts of dishonesty or incompetence by those charged with safeguarding, managing or otherwise doing acts connected with the administration of pensions funds. Unless people perceive that their funds are going to be properly safeguarded they are likely to be reluctant to use a pension mechanism as a means of making adequate provision for their later years."

10–039 It is clear from the outline of the Pensions Ombudsman's jurisdiction given in para.10–034 above that there is a potential overlap between that jurisdiction and the jurisdiction of the Financial Ombudsman Service, considered in Ch.16. This was previously the case as between the Pensions Ombudsman and the Personal Investment Authority Ombudsman and the position was resolved by a Memorandum of Understanding, which in effect allowed the PIA Ombudsman to deal with all complaints relating to personal pension schemes. A new memorandum was required as a result of changes to the original ombudsman provisions of the 1993 Act, the coming into force of FSMA and the introduction of stakeholder pensions. The new

Memorandum of Understanding was made on October 7, 2002 and covers complaints relating to occupational and personal pensions (including stakeholder pensions) after April 1, 2002. It provides that the Financial Ombudsman Service will deal with "complaints and disputes which predominantly concern the sale and/or marketing" of both personal and occupational pension schemes and their related investments, while the Pensions Ombudsman deals with "complaints and disputes predominantly concerning the management (after sale or marketing)" of both types of scheme. Where it is not clear into which category a complaint falls, or where the relevant Ombudsman "is unable to deal with the complaint as categorised", the two organisations are to take immediate steps to agree how each case will be handled subject to the relevant rules of investigation and the complainant's wishes. Any complaints which appear to have been wrongly directed will be passed on.

The Future: the Myners Review and the Green Paper

The Myners review was a review of institutional investment undertaken by Paul Myners in response to a request from the Chancellor of the Exchequer in March 2000. The conclusions reached were published in March 2001 and included recommendations for: **10–040**

- a set of principles for institutional decision-making;
- the replacement of the minimum funding requirement discussed in paras 10–025 and 10–026 above;
- the incorporation into United Kingdom law of principles on shareholder activism, obliging fund managers to intervene where it is in shareholders' and beneficiaries' interests;
- clarification of the legal ownership of surplus pension fund assets;
- provisions relating to the duty of care of trustees, requiring them to be familiar with investment matters when they take investment decisions.

The Government announced its acceptance of the Myners recommendations in order to promote long-term investment and to protect investors.

The most immediate result of the review has been the introduction of two sets of principles for investment, one for defined benefit schemes (in which the member knows in advance the benefit intended to be produced by the scheme) and the other for defined contribution schemes (in which the pension provision depends upon the investment performance of the contributions). Such sets of principles were put forward in the review itself, but were revised by the Government following consultation. **10–041**

The principles applicable to defined benefit schemes cover the following:

- steps to ensure effective decision-making (including the principle that those taking decisions should have the necessary skills, information and resources, that trustees should look at the skills they possess, individually and collectively, that they should ensure they have sufficient in-house staff and that it is good practice to have an investment sub-committee);

- clear objectives (representing the trustees' best judgment of what is necessary to meet the fund's liabilities, taking account their attitude to risk);
- focus on asset allocation (not excluding any major asset class and reflecting the fund's own characteristics);
- expert advice (contracts for actuarial services and investment advice being opened to separate competition, with a willingness to pay realistic fees);
- explicit mandates agreed with investment managers (covering an objective, benchmarks, risk parameters, the manager's approach and timescales of measurement and evaluation);
- incorporation in the mandates of appropriate principles for shareholder activism;
- explicit consideration of the appropriateness of the benchmarks adopted;
- performance measurement arrangements;
- transparency (involving a strengthened statement of investment principles covering decision makers, objectives, the asset allocation strategy, the mandates given and the fee structure);
- regular reporting.

The principles applicable to defined contributions schemes are, not surprisingly, similar, but include:

- giving sufficient information to members to enable them to make an appropriate choice, where a choice is given;
- objectives in fund selection rather than meeting the particular fund's expected liabilities;
- making sure that objectives are set for any default fund;
- basing contracts for investment advice on fees rather than commission.

10–042 These principles are at present voluntary and surveys suggest that many schemes are taking steps to comply. The review proposed a public assessment of compliance after two years and the Government has announced that the assessment process is expected to run from March 2003 until the end of that year. There will be a first stage of qualitative research, the results of which will be published, and then a second stage of quantitative research.

Progress on the question of the abolition of the minimum funding requirement has been rather less speedy. The objective is to introduce a scheme-specific, long-term approach to ensuring solvency and consultation has taken place, but to implement the Government's proposals will require primary legislation and so depends upon the availability of Parliamentary time. In principle, schemes currently affected by the minimum funding requirement will have to publish a new funding standard and a schedule of contributions designed so that the scheme can meet its on-going liabilities in full in the long term. There will be a relatively short period in which corrections must be made if the scheme drifts away from the funding standard. Proposals were contained in the Green Paper on pensions reform (dealing also with many other pensions issues), published on December 17, 2002. **10–043**

In addition to commissioning the Myners review, the Chancellor of the Exchequer also commissioned from Ron Sandler a review of medium and long-term retail savings in the United Kingdom. The report was published in July 2002 and contains proposals for the introduction of some simpler regulated products, in respect of which clear information will be provided to consumers, and as a result of which investors may be able to make investments with some confidence but without obtaining detailed investment advice on a whole complex range of products. It is hoped that such products would encourage greater saving in particular by those who are less well-off. Proposals to give effect to these recommendations are also contained in the Green Paper. **10–044**

The Green Paper as a whole is a lengthy document covering a wide range of matters which are not all directly relevant to investor protection. There should be noted in addition, however, the proposal for a new pensions regulator separate from, but operating side by side with, the FSA. Its objectives would be directly related to the protection of members' benefits, and it would continue to be funded by a levy on schemes. Unlike OPRA in its present form, it would be proactive rather than reactive and would focus its investigative efforts on schemes in which there is a higher risk of fraud, bad governance or maladministration. Further detail is contained in the *Quinquennial Review of the Occupational Pensions Regulatory Authority*, also published on December 17, 2002. The essential point of the review was that OPRA had performed its task well, but that a price had been paid in that whistle-blowing requirements had applied to minor matters and had produced a heavy degree of regulation. A more risk-based approach to regulation, and a more proactive one, is now required, building on the success of OPRA to date. There should also be further consideration of what is appropriate for small and very small schemes. The latter point picks up a concern to be found in some of the commentary on the Myners report, that it does not sufficiently distinguish between very large schemes and much smaller ones. **10–045**

On June 11, 2003, the Department of Work and Pensions published a part of the fruits of the consultation exercise on the Green Paper, entitled "Action on occupational pensions". It contains the following proposals: **10–046**

- the creation of a Pensions Protection Fund, by means of a levy, to guarantee members a specified minimum level of pension when the sponsoring employer becomes insolvent;

- a requirement on solvent employers who choose to wind up a pension scheme to meet their pension promise in full;
- a revision of the priority order which applies on winding-up to ensure what is described as the fairest possible sharing of assets (a response to recent cases in which the present rules have secured pensions in full for existing pensioners but have left those on the point of retirement with no pension at all, or a greatly reduced pension);
- an increase of the protection given when firms are bought out by an amendment of the regime governing the transfer of undertakings to cover pension schemes of workers in the private sector;
- some protection for employees who have been members of an occupational scheme for at least three months but who leave their jobs before completing two years' employment;
- a requirement on employers to consult before making changes to pension schemes;
- the replacement of the minimum funding requirement with scheme-specific arrangements, as already discussed;
- a reduction in the cap on mandatory indexation of pensions;
- increased flexibility for schemes to rationalise the structure of their benefits;
- simplification of the legislation to make it easier to administer a pension scheme.

Of these various proposals, the one which seems to have provoked the greatest volume of immediate comment is the proposal for a Pension Protection Fund. Concern has been expressed that the costs have been substantially underestimated and that well-run schemes will end up subsidising schemes which are badly run. Time will tell how far such fears are to be realised.

Pension Mis-selling

10–047 In April 1988 it became possible for the first time for employees to transfer out of, or to opt out of, an employer's occupational pension scheme. Many people decided to do so and to enter into personal pension arrangements. Before long, there began to develop considerable concern over the quality of the advice which had been given in many instances. In October 1994 the Securities and Investment Board initiated a review of the way in which personal pension policies had been sold from April 29, 1988 up to June 30, 1994, with a view to identifying investors who had been wrongly sold personal pension schemes and to the provision of a mechanism for redress. The extensive operation which followed is only just coming to its conclusion. Firms were required to contact customers who had made personal pension arrangements and who might be affected and to ask them whether they wanted their case checked. The process had two phases, older customers approaching retirement being reviewed first. Standard provisions for calculating the appropriate redress were in place, intended so far as possible to put customers back into the position in which they would have been had they not received bad advice, and the actuarial assumptions involved were revised from time to time to reflect changing circumstances.

By June 27, 2002, the FSA was able to announce that the review was over 98 per cent complete and that it was expected that by the end of the month 1.6 million cases would have been reviewed. The final estimated costs were £11.5 billion in redress and £2 billion in administration. It was originally hoped that the review would have been complete by June 30, 2002, but completion was delayed by the "windfall" cases, in which it was contended on the part of the firm liable to pay compensation that an investor should give credit for any windfall received in the form of shares or cash on demutualisation of a previously mutual personal pension provider. It was held in *Needler Financial Services Ltd. v Tabor* [2002] 3 All E.R. 501, a test case, that the negligent advice had not caused the benefit in question and that accordingly credit was not required to be given. The target date for completing those cases was extended to March 2003.

In addition, the financial services industry has also faced a much smaller review in connection with advice to make additional voluntary contributions under free-standing arrangements (FSAVCs) rather than through an additional voluntary contributions facility in an employer's scheme. This review was set up in February 2000 and related to sales between April 29, 1998 and August 15, 1999. It was expected that the various cases would be dealt with by December 31, 2002, leading to payment of £330 million in redress and costs of £80 million. More than 87,500 cases had been dealt with by June 30, 2002. **10–048**

Not least in view of the lapse of time since some of the mis-selling, there is inevitably a possibility that a firm under regulatory obligations by virtue of the reviews is no longer in existence to complete the review and to pay any necessary compensation. In such a case, the FSA Pensions Unit will complete the review work and the Financial Services Compensation Scheme will pay the compensation. **10–049**

Those who did not respond to the invitation to ask for a check under the special procedures are not precluded from making a complaint in accordance with the usual complaints procedure considered in Ch.16, but may of course increasingly find that they face difficulties with time limits.

Finally, it may be noted that at the time of the press release on June 27, 2002, disciplinary action had been taken against 346 firms, resulting in fines totalling £9,627,250.

It will be realised that both the above reviews were established before December 1, 2001, when FSMA came fully into force, and so were set up under previous regulatory powers. Pt XXVIII of FSMA contains provisions for enabling the Treasury to authorise the FSA, in cases in which the Treasury is satisfied that there is evidence suggesting that there has been a widespread or regular failure on the part of authorised persons to comply with the rules relating to a particular kind of activity and that as a result private persons have suffered or will suffer loss in respect of which **10–050** authorised persons are or will be liable to make compensation payments, to establish and to operate a scheme for determining the nature and extent of the failure, the liability of authorised persons to make compensation payments and the amounts payable by way of such payments (s.404). This provision is not, of course, limited to pension mis-selling, but would plainly be available for use if circumstances similar to those which existed between 1988 and 1994 were to arise again. Under the Financial Services and Markets Act 2000 (Transitional Provisions) (Reviews of Pensions Business) Order 2001 (SI 2001/2512) the Treasury exercised a power given by ss.426 to 428 of the Act to enable the FSA to designate any current pension review provision as a scheme to be treated as made under s.404. A designation order was duly made so that the reviews could continue under the provisions of the 2000 Act after it came into force.

Chapter 11

Distance and E-Selling

Distance Selling

Introduction

The EC Directive on Distance Selling (Dir.97/7 [1997] O.J. L144/19) requires Member States to implement a number of measures for the protection of consumers in relation to "distance contracts". Although, as we shall see, the Directive does not apply to contracts relating to financial services, a brief survey of its provisions may be helpful, since in many respects the Directive served as the model for the later Distance Marketing of Financial Services (Dir.2002/65 [2002] O.J. L271/16), which is specifically targeted at the distance selling of financial services products. 11–001

In the Distance Selling Directive, the expression "distance contracts" covers most contracts for the supply of goods or non-financial services to a consumer, where (under an organised distance sales or service-provision scheme run by the supplier) the contract is concluded by the exclusive use of one or more means of distance communication up to and including the time of contracting. For this purpose, a means of distance communication is defined as any means which, without the simultaneous physical presence of the supplier and the consumer, may be used for the conclusion of a contract between them. The indicative list set out in Annex I to the Directive gives the following examples of means of distance communication: printed matter (addressed or unaddressed), letter, press advertising with order form, catalogue, telephone (with or without human intervention), radio, videophone, videotext, e-mail, fax and television (teleshopping).

Where a contract is concluded in this way, there is an obvious risk that the consumer will be prejudiced by the lack of proper information about the goods or services being supplied, and by the lack of an opportunity to see the product or ascertain the nature of the service before entering into the contract. To combat these risks, the Directive requires the consumer to be provided with specified information in good time before the conclusion of the contract, followed up in most cases by written confirmation of that information, and to be given a period of at least seven working days from the provision of that confirmation in which to withdraw from the contract. The Directive also includes a number of additional consumer-protection provisions, including a prohibition on the inertia selling of goods and services, a requirement to enable the consumer to request cancellation of any payment where fraudulent use has been made of his credit card or other payment card 11–002 in connection with a distance selling contract, and a requirement to ensure that the supplier is prevented from using an automatic calling machine or fax machine without the consumer's prior consent.

11–003 The Distance Selling Directive was implemented in the United Kingdom by the Consumer Protection (Distance Selling) Regulations 2000 (SI 2000/2334), which came into force on October 31, 2000.

While important in its own field, the Distance Selling Directive has had a very limited impact on the law relating to investor protection, because, as already noted, contracts relating to financial services are expressly excluded from the scope of the Directive (Art.3(1) and Annex II). A similar exclusion applies to the 2000 Regulations (see reg.5(1)(c) and Sch.2). In both cases, an indicative list of financial services contracts includes contracts relating to investment services, insurance and reinsurance operations, banking services and services relating to dealings in futures and options.

The exclusion of contracts for financial services from the scope of the Directive resulted from an amendment introduced by the Council in its common position and accepted by the European Parliament. The Commission was, however, concerned by the exclusion of such contracts from the Directive, particularly by the absence of any right of withdrawal from non-life insurance contracts concluded at a distance. The Commission accordingly formulated proposals for a Directive dealing specifically with the distance selling of financial services. Those proposals led to the adoption on September 23, 2002 of the EC Directive on the Distance Marketing of Financial Services, which is discussed in the following paragraphs.

The Distance Marketing of Financial Services Directive

11–004 The recitals to the Distance Marketing of Financial Services Directive (the DMD) recognise that, because of their intangible nature, financial services are particularly suited to distance selling. They also recognise, however, that a high degree of consumer protection is required to enable consumers to exercise a free choice between the wide range of different products on offer, including those offered by suppliers established in another Member State. The purpose of the DMD is to set out the framework for that protection.

11–005 Member States must implement the requirements of the DMD by October 9, 2004. While the Treasury has overall responsibility for implementing the DMD in the United Kingdom, the FSA will be responsible for its implementation in the areas which it already regulates or, in the case of general insurance and regulated mortgage contracts, which it will regulate in the future. The DTI will be responsible for implementing the DMD for consumer credit, mortgages which fall outside the scope of regulation by the FSA (*e.g.* second charges), and related activities.

The FSA issued a Discussion Paper in March 2003 on *Implementation of the Distance Marketing Directive* (DP 21), setting out its current view on the interpretation of a number of provisions in the DMD and inviting comments and information. The FSA aims to publish a Consultation Paper with draft rules in the summer of 2003.

A Treasury Consultation Paper on the DMD is expected shortly.

The Definition of "Distance Contract"

The DMD applies where a supplier and a consumer enter into a "distance contract". This definition of this expression is closely modelled on that contained in the Distance Selling Directive and is crucial to an understanding of the scope of the DMD. The definition (in Art.2(a)) reads as follows: 11–006

> "any contract concerning financial services concluded between a supplier and a consumer under an organised distance sales or service-provision scheme run by the supplier, who, for the purposes of that contract, makes exclusive use of one or more means of distance communication up to and including the time at which the contract is concluded."

For this purpose, "financial services" are defined as meaning any service of a banking, credit, insurance, personal pension, investment or payment nature (Art.2(b)). 11–007

A "supplier" means any natural or legal person, public or private, who, acting in his commercial or professional capacity, is the contractual provider of services subject to distance contracts (Art.2(c)). A "consumer" means any natural person who, in distance contracts covered by the DMD, is acting for purposes which are outside his trade, business or profession (ar.2(d)).

The reference to an organised distance sales or service-provision scheme is not defined, but recital (18) states that the intention is to exclude services provided on a strictly occasional basis and outside a commercial structure dedicated to the conclusion of distance contracts. The FSA has stated that, in its view, few firms will be able to take advantage of this exclusion, since the provision of even the most basic facilities for consumers to deal with the firm by post or telephone will mean that there is a sufficient commercial structure for the DMD to apply (see DP 21, para.3.12).

The expression "means of distance communication" refers to any means which, without the simultaneous physical presence of the supplier and the consumer, may be used for the distance marketing of a service between those parties. In contrast to the Distance Selling Directive, there is no indicative list of means of distance communication. Recital (15) to the DMD, however, recognises that the constant development of these means of communication requires the principles to be formulated in a way that will be valid for means that are not yet in widespread use. The recital therefore states simply that distance contracts "are those the offer, negotiation and conclusion of which are carried out at a distance". There is no doubt, however, that any of the means of communication itemised in Annex 1 to the Distance Selling Directive would qualify as a means of distance communication for the purposes of the DMD. 11–008

It is important to note that the definition of "distance contract" only requires the exclusive use of a means of distance communication "for the purposes of [the] contract". The fact that, prior to the time of contracting, there is some face to face contact between the supplier and the consumer for a purpose other than the offer, negotiation and conclusion of the contract will not of itself prevent the contract from qualifying as a distance contract.

11–009 Before considering the substantive requirements of the DMD, it should be noted that Art.1(2) provides that, where a contract for financial services comprises "an initial service agreement followed by successive operations or a series of separate operations of the same nature performed over time", then the provisions of the DMD will apply only to the initial agreement. As examples of an initial service agreement followed (apparently) by "successive operations", recital (17) to the DMD instances: (i) the opening of a bank account, followed by the deposit or withdrawal of funds to or from the account; (ii) the acquisition of a credit card followed by the use of the card to make payments; and (iii) the conclusion of a portfolio management agreement followed by transactions made within the framework of the agreement. Recital (17) also instances the subscription to new units of the same collective investment fund as an example of "successive operations of the same nature" (which suggests that, in Art.1(2) the words "of the same nature" have to be read as qualifying both "successive operations" and a "series of separate operations"). In each of these cases, the DMD must be complied with if the initial service agreement is concluded by the use of distance communications. But there is no need to comply with it again whenever an operation of the relevant kind is carried out by the use of such communications.

Where, however, new elements are added to the initial service agreement (such as the possibility of using an electronic payment instrument together with an existing bank account), recital (17) states that this will not constitute an "operation", but rather an additional contract to which the DMD will apply.

11–010 It should also be noted that recital (19) states that, where an intermediary is involved in the marketing stages of a distance contract, the relevant provisions of the DMD should apply to the intermediary, whatever his legal status. The FSA has indicated that intermediaries will therefore need to comply with the DMD when acting on behalf of a supplier (DP 21, para.3.5).

The Right to Information

11–011 The first of the substantive requirements of the DMD is set out in Art.3. Art.3(1) provides that, in good time before the consumer is bound by any distance contract or offer, he must be provided with specified information concerning the following:

(1) the supplier, including his identity, main business and geographical address, and details of any professional the consumer deals with instead of the supplier;

(2) the financial service, including a description of the main characteristics of the service, the total price to be paid or (where an exact price cannot be indicated) the basis for calculating it, and an appropriate risk notice;

(3) the distance contract, including the existence or absence of a right of withdrawal and, where such a right exists, its duration and the

conditions for exercising it, together with information about any rights the parties may have to terminate the contract early or unilaterally, including any penalties payable in such cases; and

(4) redress, including information about any out-of-court complaints and redress mechanisms and compensation arrangements.

Art.3(2) provides that the commercial purpose of the above information must be made clear, and that the information must be provided in a clear and comprehensible manner and in a way which is appropriate to the means of distance communication used. Due regard must be had to the principles of good faith in commercial transactions, and to the principles governing the protection of those (such as minors) who are unable to give their consent under the legislation in force in the Member States.

In the case of communications by telephone, Art.3(3) requires the **11–012** identity of the supplier and the commercial purpose of any call initiated by the supplier to be made explicitly clear at the beginning of the conversation. If the consumer gives his explicit consent, the supplier may provide the consumer with a more limited range of information than that summarised in para.11–011, above. The supplier must, however, inform the consumer of the availability and nature of the further information summarised in that paragraph.

Art.4(1) of the DMD provides that, where there are provisions in **11–013** Community legislation governing financial services which contain prior information requirements additional to those listed in Art.3(1), those requirements will continue to apply (see, too, recitals (14) and (22)). So, for instance, if a life assurance contract is concluded at a distance, the requirement to supply the consumer with information under the DMD will not displace the insurer's obligation to provide the more detailed information required by Annex II to the Third Life Directive. Similarly, where a financial services contract is concluded by the use of the internet, it will be necessary for the supplier to comply not only with the requirements of the DMD, but also with the requirements of the Electronic Commerce Directive (as to which, see paras 11–026 to 11–052, below).

Art.4(2) states that the requirements imposed by Art.3(1) for the provision of information at the pre-contract stage are minimum requirements, so that Member States are free, pending further harmonisation, to impose more stringent requirements, so long as they are in conformity with Community law.

Art.5(1) requires the supplier to communicate to the consumer: **11–014**

- all the contractual terms and conditions;
- the information referred to in Art.3(1); and
- any further information which falls within Art.4.

The above material must be communicated to the consumer on paper or on another "durable medium" so as to be available and accessible to the consumer in good time before he is bound by any distance contract or offer.

The expression "durable medium" is defined in Art.2(f) as meaning any instrument which enables the consumer to store information addressed personally to him in a way accessible for future reference for a period of time adequate for the purposes of the information and which allows the unchanged reproduction of the information stored. As is apparent from recital (20), durable mediums include floppy discs, CD-ROMs, DVDs and the hard drive of the consumer's computer on which any email is stored. A website would not normally qualify as a durable medium, though it would be capable of doing so if it managed to meet all the requirements of the definition.

11–015 As noted in the preceding paragraph, the obligation to provide the material mentioned in Art.5(1) must normally be satisfied in good time before the consumer is bound by the contract. This obligation is, however, relaxed by Art.5(2) in cases where the contract is concluded at the consumer's request using a means of distance communication which does not enable the required material to be provided on a durable medium prior to the time of contracting (*e.g.* where the contract has been concluded by telephone). In such a case, the supplier is required to communicate the required material to the consumer on a durable medium immediately after the conclusion of the contract.

Art.5(3) provides that the consumer is entitled, at his request, to receive the contractual terms on conditions on paper at any time during the contractual relationship. He is also entitled to change the means of distance communication used, unless this is incompatible with the contract concluded or the nature of the financial service provided (*e.g.* where he has entered into a contract for the supply of internet banking services).

The Right of Withdrawal

11–016 Art.6(1) sets out the general rule that the consumer must be given a period of 14 days to withdraw from a distance contract without penalty and without giving any reason. The period is extended to 30 days in the case of a life insurance contract covered by the second life insurance directive or personal pensions contract. The withdrawal period starts on the later of:

- the day on which the contract is concluded (or, in the case of a life insurance contract, the time when the consumer is informed of the conclusion of the contract); and
- the day on which the consumer receives the material which the supplier is obliged to provide under Art.5(1) or (2).

11–017 The practical importance of right of withdrawal under Art.6(1) is, however, considerably reduced by the exclusions in Art.6(2), and the further exclusions which Member States have the option of adopting under Art.6(3).

Art.6(2) provides that the right of withdrawal will not apply to distance contracts in any of the following categories:

(a) financial services whose price depends on fluctuations in the financial market outside the supplier's control which may occur during the withdrawal period; Art.6(2) gives a number of examples of these, which include services relating to foreign exchange, transferable securities, units in collective investment undertakings and financial futures contracts;

(b) travel and baggage insurance policies or similar short-term insurance policies of less than one month's duration;

(c) contracts whose performance has been fully completed by both parties at the consumer's express request before the consumer exercises what Art.6(2) calls "his right of withdrawal" (which must be a reference to the right of withdrawal that he would have had but for the present exclusion).

Art.6(3) allows Member States to provide that the right of withdrawal will not apply to a further three categories of distance contract, namely: **11–018**

(a) any credit intended primarily for the acquisition or retention of property rights in land or a building, or for the renovation or improvement of a building;

(b) any credit secured either by a mortgage on immovable property or by a right related to immovable property;

(c) declarations by consumers using the services of an official, provided that the official confirms that the consumer is guaranteed the rights under Art.5(1).

The FSA has indicated that its initial view is that it will not require firms to give a right of withdrawal in mortgages concluded by means of a distance contract (DP 21, para.6.15).

Despite the exclusions mentioned in paras 11–017 and 11–018, above, the right of withdrawal will still apply to a significant number of distance contracts for the provision of financial services, *e.g.* contracts for a deposit or savings account, unsecured loans (not related to land or buildings), general insurance (other than short-term travel insurance, etc.), life insurance and personal pensions. Where the right arises, a consumer wishing to exercise the right must notify the supplier before the expiry of the deadline. If the notification is given on paper or another durable medium, it is sufficient if the notification is dispatched before the deadline expires (Art.6(6)). **11–019**

If the consumer withdraws from the contract, the withdrawal will have the effect of cancelling, without penalty, any connected distance contract which concerns services provided by the supplier or by a third party on the basis of an agreement between the third party and the supplier (Art.6(7)). An example would be a case in which the consumer enters into a distance contract with the supplier for an unsecured loan and also takes out a payment protection policy with a third party (under arrangements agreed between the supplier and the third party); in such a case, the exercise of the consumer's right to withdraw from the loan contract will cancel the payment protection policy automatically and without penalty. **11–020**

11–021 Art.7(1) provides that, where the consumer exercises his right of withdrawal, he may only be required to pay for the service actually provided by the supplier. The supplier's entitlement to payment is, however, qualified in a number of ways. First, the performance of the contract may only begin after the consumer has given his approval. Secondly, the supplier is debarred from claiming any payment if he starts to perform before the expiry of the withdrawal period without the consumer's prior request (Art.7(3), second sentence). Thirdly, the supplier's right to payment is conditional on his proving that the consumer was informed about the amount payable in conformity with Art.3(1) (Art.7(3), first sentence). Fourthly, Member States have the option of providing that the consumer cannot be required to pay any amount when withdrawing from an insurance contract (Art.7(2)).

11–022 Where the supplier is entitled to payment, the amount payable must not exceed an amount which is proportionate to the service provided in comparison to the full coverage of the contract; nor must it be capable of being construed as a penalty (Art.7(1)). If the supplier has received an amount from the consumer which exceeds the payment to which he is entitled, then he must return the excess without delay and in any event within 30 days from the date on which he received notification of the withdrawal (Art.7(4)).

For his part, the consumer is obliged to return to the supplier any money or property received from the supplier without undue delay and within 30 days from the date on which he dispatched his notification of withdrawal (Art.7(5)).

Further Provisions

11–023 The DMD also contains provisions which:

- require Member States to put in place appropriate measures to request cancellation of a payment where fraudulent use has been made of a consumer's payment card in connection with a distance contract (Art.8);
- require those Member States which have laws permitting the tacit renewal of distance contracts to prohibit the supply of financial services on terms which include a request for payment (whether immediate or deferred), otherwise than at the consumer's prior request (Art.9);
- prohibit the use of automated calling machines or fax machines without the consumer's prior consent (Art.10(1)); and
- require Member States to ensure that other means of distance communication may only be used if either the consumer's consent has been obtained or the consumer has not expressed his manifest objection (Art.10(2)).

Limited Scope for More Stringent Provisions

11–024 In general, Member States do not have the right to enact more stringent provisions than those required by the DMD, since the liberty to do so could impede the operation of the internal market in financial services. The

DMD has therefore aimed at a high level of consumer protection on the basis that the standards it lays down will set both the maximum and minimum requirements for Member States (recital (13)). As we have seen, however, there are a number of specific areas in which the DMD gives Member States the option of imposing more stringent standards (*e.g.* the option in Art.4(2) to impose more stringent requirements for the provision of pre-contractual information). Member States do not, however, have the option to extend the right of withdrawal more widely than is required by Art.6. One consequence of this is that a number of rights of withdrawal which currently apply to certain types of financial services contracts under the *FSA's Handbook*, COB 6.7 will need to be removed in cases where those contracts are concluded at a distance (see DP 21, paras 6.3 and 6.14).

E-selling

Introduction

As we have seen in the first part of this Chapter, the use of electronic means to supply financial services to investors will be subject to the requirements of the DMD. It also, however, constitutes a form of electronic commerce, which falls within the scope of the E.C. Directive on electronic commerce (2000/31) and the Regulations implementing the Directive in the United Kingdom. This part of the Chapter gives an outline of these measures, so far as they are relevant to the protection of the interests of investors. **11–025**

The Electronic Commerce Directive

The Electronic Commerce Directive (the ECD) establishes a general framework for the provision of "information society services" within and between Member States. The expression "information society services" (IS services) is defined by reference to other E.C. legislation, but is conveniently summarised in recital (17) to the ECD as covering: **11–026**

> "any service normally provided for remuneration, at a distance, by means of electronic equipment for the processing (including digital compression) and storage of data, and at the individual request of a recipient of a service."

The general principle established by the ECD is that IS services are subject to the law of the Member State in which the provider of the service is established (the country of origin principle). So, for example, a provider established in the United Kingdom will generally be subject to UK law when providing IS services to recipients in other Member States, whereas a provider established in another Member State will generally be subject to the law of that Member State when providing IS services to recipients in the United Kingdom. The first limb of the principle is expressed in

Art.3(1), which requires each Member State to ensure that the IS services provided by a service provider established on its territory comply with the national provisions applicable in that Member State which fall within the "coordinated field" (the latter expression being defined in Art.2(h) to mean, in summary, the Member State's legal requirements relating to the taking up and pursuit of the activity of an IS service provider). The second limb of the principle is expressed in Art.3(2), which provides that Member States may not, for reasons falling within the coordinated field, restrict the freedom to provide IS services from another Member State. By virtue of Art.3(3), however, Art.3(1) and (2) do not apply to the fields described in the Annex to the ECD. These include:

- the advertising of units by collective investment undertakings falling within the Directive on undertakings for collective investment in transferable securities (85/611) (the UCITS Directive);
- effecting or carrying a contract of insurance as principal, where that activity falls within the scope of any of the insurance directives;
- contractual obligations concerning consumer contracts; and
- the permissibility of unsolicited commercial communications by e-mail.

In these areas, therefore, the country of origin principle will be excluded, and the provider will need to observe whatever local requirements apply in the Member State in which the service is supplied.

11–027 In addition, Art.3(4) of the ECD allows Member States to take specific measures derogating from Art.3(2) (the freedom to provide IS services from another Member State) in cases where a given IS service prejudices, or presents a serious and grave risk of prejudicing, public policy (such as the prevention of crime), public health, public security, or the protection of consumers, including investors. Any such measures must be proportionate and (except in cases of urgency) must not be taken until:

- the Member State proposing to introduce the measures (the receiving state) has asked the Member State from which the IS service originates (the originating state) to take measures itself and either the latter did not take such measures or they were inadequate; and
- the receiving state has notified the Commission and the originating state of its intention to introduce such measures.

If the Commission concludes that the measures are incompatible with Community law, it must ask the receiving state to refrain from taking the measures or (if it has already introduced them) to put an end to them as a matter of urgency (Art.3(6)).

Implementation of the Electronic Commerce Directive in the United Kingdom

11–028 Outside the area of financial services, the ECD is implemented in the United Kingdom by the Electronic Commerce (EC Directive) Regulations 2002 (SI 2002/2013), which were the responsibility of the DTI. For our purposes, however, it is more relevant to consider three statutory instruments made by the Treasury to implement the ECD in areas which are within the scope of regulation by the FSA. These are:

- The Electronic Commerce Directive (Financial Services and Markets) Regulations 2002 (SI 2002/1775);
- The Financial Services and Markets Act 2000 (Regulated Activities) (Amendment) (No. 2) Order 2002 (SI 2002/1776); and
- The Financial Services and Markets Act 2000 (Financial Promotion) (Amendment) (Electronic Commerce Directive) Order 2002 (SI 2002/2157).

It will also be necessary to say something about the FSA rules relating to the ECD, including rules made by the FSA in exercise of the powers conferred on it by the first of the above statutory instruments.

The Financial Services and Markets Act 2000 (Regulated Activities) (Amendment) (No. 2) Order 2002

It is convenient to begin by considering the second of the statutory **11–029** instruments listed in the preceding paragraph, which amends the Financial Services and Markets Act 2000 (Regulated Activities) Order 2001 (the RAO). The principal amendment made by the Order is the addition of a new Art.72A to the RAO. Art.72A(1) gives effect to the country of origin principle by excluding from the list of regulated activities in Pt II of the RAO any activity consisting of the provision of an IS service from an EEA State other than the United Kingdom. By Art.72A(2), however, the exclusion does not apply to the activity of effecting or carrying out a contract of insurance as principal, where the activity is carried on by an undertaking which has received official authorisation in accordance with the first life directive, or the first non-life directive, and the insurance falls within the scope of any of the insurance directives. This limitation on the exclusion takes advantage of the fact that these activities fall within one of the fields referred to in the Annex to the ECD, so that Member States are not debarred from restricting the freedom to provide IS services in this field from another Member State: see para.11–026, above.

The Electronic Commerce Directive (Financial Services and Markets) Regulations 2002

These Regulations are referred to in the *FSA Handbook* as "the ECD **11–030** Regulations", and (despite the potential for confusion with the DTI Regulations mentioned at the beginning of para.11–028, above) the same abbreviation is adopted here.

(1) Outgoing Providers

As noted in para.11–026, above, Art.3(1) of the ECD requires each Member **11–031** State to ensure that IS services provided by a service provider "established" on its territory comply with that Member State's national provisions relating to the taking up and pursuit of the activity of an IS service provider. This requirement is implemented by reg.13 of the ECD Regulations, which amends FSMA 2000, ss.417 and 418.

11–032 The amendment to s.417 consists of the addition of a new s.417(4). S.417(a) provides that an IS service is provided from an EEA State if it is provided from an "establishment" in that State. The term "establishment" is then elaborated (in line with recital (19) to the ECD) by s.417(b) to (d), as follows:

- in connection with an IS service, an establishment is the place where the provider of the service effectively pursues an economic activity for an indefinite period;
- the presence in one place of a particular piece of equipment or other technical means of providing an IS service (*e.g.* the technology supporting the provider's website) does not, of itself, constitute that place an establishment;
- where it cannot be determined from which of a number of establishments a given IS service is provided, the service is to be regarded as provided from the establishment where the provider has the centre of his activities relating to the service.

The amendment to s.418 has the effect a person carrying on a regulated activity will now be regarded as carrying it on within the United Kingdom in any case where the activity consists of the provision of an IS service to person or persons in one or more EEA States and the activity is carried on from an establishment in the United Kingdom.

The effect of these amendments is that a firm will be subject to regulation by the FSA when it is acting as an outgoing provider, *i.e.* when it is carrying on a regulated activity by the provision of an IS service from an establishment in the United Kingdom to a recipient in another EEA State.

As we shall see, the *FSA Handbook* includes a number of further provisions relevant to outgoing providers. These are considered at paras 11–046 and 11–047, below.

(2) Incoming Providers

11–033 We saw in para.11–026, above, that Art.3(2) of the ECD prohibits Member States from relying on national requirements relating to IS service providers to restrict the freedom to provide IS services from another Member State. A number of provisions in the ECD Regulations are relevant to the implementation of this prohibition.

11–034 First, reg.3 modifies the FSA's power to make rules under FSMA 2000, s.138 in its application to persons (called "incoming providers") who provide an "incoming electronic commerce activity". The latter expression is defined (in reg.2(1)) as an activity:

- which consists of the provision of an IS service from an establishment in an EEA State other than the United Kingdom to a person or persons in the United Kingdom; and

- which would be a regulated activity but for Art.72A of the RAO (considered in para.11–029, above).

Reg.3 has both a widening and a narrowing effect on the FSA's rule-making power under s.138. It widens the power (which normally only permits the making of rules which apply to authorised persons) so as to enable the FSA to make rules with respect to incoming providers who are not authorised persons. It narrows the power by providing that rules made by the FSA under s.138 will not apply to incoming providers (whether authorised or not) in relation to the carrying on of incoming electronic activities, unless the rules:

(a) impose consumer credit requirements;

(b) apply with respect to communications that constitute an advertisement by the operator of a UCITS Directive scheme of units in that scheme; or

(c) relate to the permissibility of unsolicited commercial communications by email.

It will be noted that these three categories of rules fall within fields referred to in the Annex to the ECD, where Member States are permitted to derogate from the requirements of Art.3.

For the purposes of category (a), above, a "consumer credit requirement" is defined (in reg.3(6)) as a requirement that information be provided to a consumer before he enters into a contract for the provision of an IS service, or a requirement as to the manner in which such information is to be provided. Reg.4 of the ECD Regulations sets out the information which may be the subject of a consumer credit requirement.

As we shall see, the FSA has made use of its power to make rules applying to incoming providers within the categories mentioned in this paragraph. The rules are considered in paras 11–045 and 11–046, below.

Finally, reg.6 of the ECD Regulations take advantage of Art.3(4) of the **11–035** ECD (discussed in para.11–027, above) by providing that, where certain conditions are satisfied, the FSA may direct that an incoming provider may no longer carry on a specified incoming electronic commerce activity, or may only carry it on subject to specified conditions. This is a potentially important power, which enables the FSA to act against particular providers where necessary to combat crime or protect consumers. The conditions for making such a direction are set out in regs 7 and 8.

Reg.7 sets out three conditions (referred to as policy conditions). The **11–036** first is that the FSA must consider the making of the direction to be necessary for any of the following objectives, namely: the prevention, investigation, detection or prosecution of criminal conduct, the protection of consumers or any other reasons of public policy relevant to the regulatory objectives set out in Pt I of FSMA 2000. Secondly, the FSA must consider that the carrying on of the incoming electronic commerce activity by the person to whom the direction is to apply prejudices, or presents a serious risk and grave risk of prejudice to, any of the above objectives. Thirdly, the direction must appear to the FSA to be a proportionate means of achieving, or addressing the prejudice or risk of prejudice to, any of those objectives.

11–037 Reg.8 sets out a further four conditions (referred to as procedural conditions). The first is that the FSA must have requested the relevant EEA regulator to take measures to remedy the situation giving rise to the request. The second condition is that either the relevant EEA regulator has not taken such measures within what the FSA considers to be a reasonable time, or it has taken such measures but they appear to the FSA to be inadequate in the circumstances. Thirdly, the FSA must have notified the Commission and the relevant EEA regulator of its intention to make the direction. Fourthly, the FSA must have notified the person to whom the direction is to apply of its proposal to make the direct, and afforded that person the opportunity to make representations.

11–038 If the case appears to the FSA to be one of urgency, reg.9 permits it to make a direction regardless of whether the procedural conditions are met. In such a case, however, the Commission and the relevant EEA regulator must be notified as soon as possible, and must be supplied with a statement of the FSA's reasons for considering the case to be one of urgency. Reg.10 confers power on the FSA to vary or revoke a direction, and reg.11 makes provision for the person to whom a direction applies to refer to the matter to the Financial Services and Markets Tribunal.

The Financial Services and Markets Act 2000 (Financial Promotion) (Amendment) (Electronic Commerce Directive) Order 2002

11–039 This Order (the Financial Promotion Amendment Order) amends the Financial Services and Markets Act 2000 (Financial Promotion) Order 2001 (SI 2001/1335) (the Financial Promotion Order) and the Financial Services and Markets Act 2000 (Promotion of Collective Investment Schemes) (Exemptions) Order 2001 (SI 2001/1060) (the Scheme Promotion Order) to take account of the ECD.

11–040 The amendments to the Financial Promotion Order are designed, broadly speaking, to permit outgoing electronic promotions to be regulated by the FSA, but to ensure that incoming electronic promotions are exempt, unless they fall within areas in which Art.3(3) of the ECD allows Member States to derogate from Art.3(2) of the ECD. Shortly stated, these two objectives are achieved as follows:

- Under FSMA 2000, s.21, the general rule (the financial promotion restriction) is that a financial promotion must be made or approved by an authorised person. By virtue of the exemption contained in Art.12(1) of the Financial Promotion Order, the financial promotion restriction is generally inapplicable to communications which are made to a person who receives it outside the United Kingdom, or are directed only at persons outside the United Kingdom. The Financial Promotion Amendment Order narrows the scope of this exemption so that it no longer applies to an "outgoing electronic commerce communication" (*viz.* a communication which is made from an establishment in the United Kingdom to a person in another EEA state, and which constitutes the provision of an IS service): see the new Art.12(7) of the Financial Promotion Order. Outgoing electronic communications may, however, still qualify for the specific exemptions set out elsewhere in the Financial Promotions Order.

- The Financial Promotions Amendment Order also provides a new exemption from the financial promotion restriction to cover incoming electronic commerce communications (*viz.* communications made from an establishment in another EEA State, and which constitute the provision of an IS service): see the new Art.20B of the Financial Promotions Order. However, this new exemption does not apply to communications falling within three of the fields mentioned in the Annex to the ECD. These are, first, advertisements by the operator of a UCITS Directive scheme for units in that scheme; secondly, invitations or inducements made by an insurer which has received official authorisation in accordance with the First Life Directive, or the First Non-Life Directive, to enter into a contract of insurance falling within the scope of any of the insurance directives; and, thirdly, unsolicited communications made by email.

The amendments to the Scheme Promotion Order generally follow the **11–041** same pattern as those to the Financial Promotions Order. Accordingly, a new Art.8(7) brings outgoing electronic commerce communications within the restriction imposed by FSMA 2000, s.238(1) on the promotion of collective investment schemes, and a new Art.10A provides a new exemption for incoming electronic commerce communications (other than advertisements by the operator of a UCITS Directive scheme for units in that scheme, and unsolicited communications made by email).

The FSA Handbook

The remaining pieces of the intricate legislative mosaic implementing the **11–042** ECD are to be found in the *FSA Handbook*, and in particular in the Electronic Commerce Directive Sourcebook (ECO). To make sense of ECO, it is necessary to bear in mind that the *Handbook* makes use of the following defined expressions (which are not the same as the defined expressions used in the ECD Regulations):

- "Electronic commerce activity": this refers to an activity which consists of the provision of an IS service from an establishment in an EEA State and is a regulated activity, or would be such an activity but for reg.72A of the RAO (considered in para.11–029, above).
- "Incoming ECA provider": this refers to a person who provides an electronic commerce activity from an establishment in another EEA State with or for a recipient in the United Kingdom.
- "Outgoing ECA provider": this refers to a firm which provides an electronic commerce activity from an establishment in the United Kingdom with or for a recipient in another EEA State.

- "Domestic ECA provider": this refers to a firm which provides an electronic commerce activity from an establishment in the United Kingdom to a recipient in the United Kingdom or in a non-EEA State.

Broadly speaking, the scheme of ECO is that Ch.1 deals with incoming ECA providers, Ch.2 deals with outgoing ECA providers and Ch.3 deals with domestic ECA providers. Annex 1 to Ch.3 then sets out a number of important information requirements which apply both to outgoing and domestic ECA providers.

(1) Incoming ECA Providers

11–043 ECO 1 starts by recognising that the *FSA Handbook* generally has no application to an incoming ECA provider acting as such (see ECO 1.1.6R, but note the qualifications in ECO 1.1.10R). That, of course, is consistent with country of origin principle reflected in Art.3(2) of the ECD. However, ECO 1 then goes on to make rules which apply to incoming ECA providers in two of the areas in which Art.3.3 of the ECD allows Member States to derogate from Art.3.2, namely, contracts with consumers (covered by ECO 1.2) and the conduct of insurance business falling with the insurance directives (covered by ECO 1.3).

11–044 As regards contracts with consumers, ECO 1.2.1R provides that, before entering into a contract with a UK recipient who is a consumer (*i.e.* an individual who is acting for purposes other than those of his trade, business or profession), an incoming ECA provider must supply the recipient with certain essential information relevant to the contract. The provider may discharge this obligation either by complying with the detailed UK requirements referred to in ECO 1.2.6E, or by complying with any corresponding requirements which apply in the provider's country of origin (ECO 1.2.7E). More limited information requirements (set out in ECO 1.2.4R (2)) apply where the electronic commerce activity relates to a deposit (other than a cash deposit ISA), or where it relates to certain types of insurance contract (namely, a general insurance contract, a pure protection contract or a reinsurance contract), though these contracts may instead be caught by the insurance regime in ECO 1.3, mentioned in the next paragraph.

11–045 As regards insurance business, ECO 1.3 makes provision for certain cases in which insurance business carried out by an incoming ECA provider. ECO 1.3 will only apply where the provider is an insurer which has received official authorisation in accordance with the first life directive, or the first non-life directive, and the insurance falls within the scope of any of the insurance directives. In such a case, the requirements in ECO 1.2 will not apply, and the insurer must instead comply with those requirements of the COB rules which are referred to in ECO 1.3.3R.

(2) Outgoing ECA Providers

11–046 Outgoing ECA providers must generally comply with all the relevant requirements of the *FSA Handbook*. It will, however, be appreciated that the EEA State in which the recipient is present will be free to apply its own requirements to the provider in those areas in which derogations from the country of origin principle are allowed by Art.3.3 of the ECD. That is reflected in ECO 2.2 which dispenses outgoing ECA providers from complying with those UK requirements which, in the consumer and insurance areas, incoming ECA providers are obliged to meet under ECO 1.2 and 1.3.

By virtue of ECO 2.3.1R, outgoing ECA providers are also required to comply with the applicable information requirements set out in ECO 3 Ann 1R. These are important requirements, which derive directly from the ECD and are intended to promote confidence and transparency in e-commerce. As they apply also to domestic providers, they are summarised separately, at paras 11–049 to 11–052, below. **11–047**

(3) Domestic ECA Providers

A domestic ECA provider will be fully subject to the requirements of the *FSA Handbook*, even in the consumer and insurance areas. **11–048**

In addition to meeting the normal *Handbook* requirements, a domestic ECA provider is also obliged by ECO 3.2.1R to comply with the applicable information requirements in ECO 3 Ann 1R (summarised below).

Information Requirements Common to Outgoing and Domestic ECA Providers

As already indicated, ECO 3 Ann 1R sets out various information requirements which apply both to outgoing ECA providers and domestic ECA providers. **11–049**

The initial set of requirements derives from Arts 5 and 6 of the ECD and focuses on the provider and its products or services. First, the provider must make the following information easily, directly and permanently available to the recipient: the name of the provider; the address in the United Kingdom at which it is established; its email address (if any); a statement of its statutory status with a link to the FSA's register; a statement that it is entered in the FSA's register and its register number; and, if the service is subject to VAT, the relevant identification number. Secondly, if the provider refers to the price of its services or products, it must do so clearly and unambiguously and, where relevant, indicate whether the price is inclusive of tax and delivery costs. Thirdly, the provider must ensure that commercial communications which are comprised in an electronic commerce activity are clearly identifiable as such, that the person on whose behalf the communication is sent is clearly identifiable as such, and that promotional offers, competitions or games are clearly identifiable as such and any qualifying conditions are set out clearly and unambiguously. Finally, the provider must ensure that any unsolicited commercial communication sent by email is clearly and unambiguously identifiable as such as soon as it is received.

The next set of requirements implements Art.10 of the ECD and concerns the technical steps required to place an order. First, the provider must make the following information clearly, comprehensively and unambiguously available to the recipient before he places an order: the technical **11–050** steps the recipient should follow in order to conclude the contract; an indication of whether the provider will keep a record of the contract and whether it will be accessible to the recipient; the technical means of identifying and correcting errors before the recipient submits the order; and the language or languages in which the contract may be concluded. Secondly, the provider must mention any relevant code of conduct to which it subscribes and provide information on how to access the code electronically. Thirdly, the provider must ensure that the terms and conditions of the contract are made available in a way which allows the recipient to store and reproduce them. In cases where the recipient is not a consumer, the three requirements mentioned in this paragraph may be wholly or partly excluded by agreement between the parties. Furthermore, the second and third requirements have no application to contracts concluded exclusively by exchange of email or equivalent individual communications.

11–051 The next set of requirements implements Art.11 of the ECD and relates to the receipt of orders. First, when the recipient places an order by electronic means, the provider must ensure that receipt of the order is acknowledged without delay. For this purpose, the order and acknowledgement are deemed to be received when the parties to whom they are addressed are able to access them. Secondly, the provider must ensure that it makes available to the recipient appropriate, effective, and accessible technical means allowing him to identify and correct technical errors before placing an order. These two requirements have no application to contracts concluded exclusively by exchange of email or equivalent individual communications, and they may be wholly or partly excluded by agreement in cases where the recipient is not a consumer.

11–052 The final set of requirements (which implements Art.5(1)(f) of the ECD) applies only to providers who are a professional firm or a person that is regulated by the equivalent of a designated professional body in another EEA State. In such a case, the provider must make the following information easily, directly and permanently available to the recipient: the name of the professional body or similar institution with which the provider is registered; the provider's professional title and the EEA State where it was granted; and details of the professional rules to which the provider is subject in the EEA State where it has its establishment.

Electronic Signatures

Introduction

11–053 The availability of secure and reliable electronic signatures to authenticate contracts concluded over the internet is of great importance for the development of e-commerce generally. In the investment context, the use of electronic signatures clearly has the potential to facilitate the conclusion of investment contracts over the internet. In view of the substantial sums of money that may be at stake, and the long-term nature of some investment contracts, there is a particular need for each party to the contract to be confident that the other party is who they claim to be and that the communications passing between them have not been tampered with.

The Electronic Signatures Directive

The Electronic Signatures Directive (1999/93) (the ESD) established a Community framework for the use of electronic signatures. For the purposes of the ESD, the expression "electronic signature" is defined (in Art.2(1)) as meaning: **11–054**

> "data in electronic form which are attached to or logically associated with other electronic data and which serve as a method of authentication".

The ESD also employs the concept of an "advanced electronic signature", which is defined (in Art.2(2)) as an electronic signature which is:

- uniquely linked to the signatory and capable of identifying him;
- created using means that the signatory can maintain under his sole control; and
- linked to the data to which it relates in such a manner that any subsequent change of the data is detectable.

The ESD has two main strands. The first relates to the certification of electronic signatures. While the ESD debars Member States from making the provision of certification services subject to prior authorisation, it requires them to establish an appropriate system for supervising providers of certain types of certificate, and also to ensure that providers of such certificates are liable for damage caused to those who rely on them. The second strand relates to the legal effects of electronic signatures. Here, Member States are required to ensure that electronic signatures are not denied legal effectiveness and admissibility in evidence, and that certain advanced electronic signatures will have the same legal status for electronic documents as handwritten signatures have for paper documents. **11–055**

These two aspects are considered in the following paragraphs.

Certification

The ESD defines a "certificate" (in Art.2(9)) as "an electronic attestation which links signature-verification data to a person and confirms the identity of that person". The expression "signature-verification data" is in turn defined (in Art.2(8)) as "data, such as codes or public cryptographic keys, which are used for the purpose of verifying an electronic signature". The ESD also uses the expression "signature-creation data" to refer to unique data, such as codes or private cryptographic keys, which are used by the signatory to create an electronic signature (Art.2(4)). **11–056**

As is indicated by the reference in the above definitions to the use of public and private cryptographic keys, dual key cryptography is a widespread means of providing electronic signatures, and plays an important role in the provision of certification services. The operation of the relevant technology is helpfully summarised in the DTI's explanatory notes on the Electronic Communications Act 2000 (which is considered further, below):

> "Public key cryptography can be used to provide an electronic signature: the *private key* (which is known only to its owner) is used as the 'lock' to transform the data, by scrambling the information contained in it. The transformed data is the electronic signature, which can be verified by 'unlocking' it with the *public key* of the person who signed it. Anyone with access to the public key can check the signature, so verifying that it was signed by someone with access to the private key and also verifying that the content of the document has not been changed."

11–057 Thus, the certification of an electronic signature will frequently involve the provider of the certificate using the signatory's public key to authenticate the signature created by the use of his private key. Authentication by a trusted third party is needed to assure the person relying on the signature that the public key actually belongs to the purported signatory. This aspect is explained by Steffen Hindenlang in *No Remedy for Disappointed Trust*, *Journal of Information Law and Technology*, 2002, Issue 1, para.2.1.3, in which the author considers a hypothetical case in which Bob receives a document purporting bear Alice's electronic signature:

> ". . . the utility of an electronic signature as an authenticating tool is limited by the ability of the recipient to ensure the authenticity of the key used to verify the message digest. In other words, it proves only that private key and public key belong together. If the evil Dr. No is forging a message from Alice he will send his own public key as well, claiming that it actually belongs to Alice. In order to rely on the authenticity of that public key, however, Bob needs to get it from some source other than Alice. If Bob has access to Alice's public key from some outside source, and uses it to verify the message signed with Dr. No's private key, purporting to be Alice, the verification will fail, revealing the forgery.
>
> In a nutshell, if Alice and Bob had no previous dealings, are strangers, then no electronic signature will reliably identify them to each other without assistance of some outside source to provide a link between their identities and their public keys. Any outside source that reasonably inspires trust will suffice. Here certification authorities come in."

The Certification Requirements of the Directive

11–058 Turning now to the certification provisions in the ESD, Art.3(1) begins by stating that Member States must not make the provision of certification services subject to prior authorisation. They may, however, introduce or maintain voluntary accreditation schemes aimed at enhanced levels of certification-service provision (Art.3(2)).

11–059 Art.3(3) then goes on to provide that each Member State must ensure the establishment of an appropriate system that allows for the supervision of "certification-service-providers", which are established on its territory and issue "qualified certificates" to the public. A certification-service-provider (CSP) is an entity or person who issues certificates or provides other services related to electronic signatures (Art.2(11)). A qualified certificate is a certificate which meets the requirements of Annex 1 to the ESD and is provided by a CSP who fulfils the requirements of Annex 2. The requirements in Annex 1 include the need for the certificate to contain an indication that it is issued as a qualified certificate, the name (or pseudonym) of the signatory, and the advanced electronic signature of the CSP who issues the certificate. The requirements in Annex 2 are extensive. They include the need for the CSP to demonstrate the reliability necessary for providing certification certificates, to ensure that the date and time when a certificate is issued or revoked can be determined precisely, to verify the identity of the person to whom a qualified certificate is issued, to employ personnel possessing the requisite technical expertise, and to maintain sufficient financial resources to operate in accordance with the requirements of the ESD (including the resources needed to meet any liability to damages under the provisions mentioned in the next paragraph).

Art.6(1) of the ESD requires Members States to ensure that by issuing or guaranteeing a qualified certificate to the public, a CSP will be liable (unless he proves that he has not acted negligently) for damage caused to any entity or person who reasonably relies on the certificate: **11–060**

(a) as regards the accuracy at the time of issuance of all information contained in the certificate and as regards the fact that the certificate contains all the details required for a qualified certificate (*i.e.* the details set out in Annex 1 to the ESD);

(b) for assurance that at the time of issuance the signatory identified in the certificate held the signature-creation data (*e.g.* the private key) corresponding to the signature-verification data (*e.g.* the public key) given or identified in the certificate;

(c) for assurance that the signature-creation data and the signature-verification data can be used in a complementary manner in cases where the CSP generates them both.

Member States must also ensure that a CSP placed under a similar liability (again with a reversed burden of proof) for damage caused by a failure to register revocation of a qualified certificate which it has issued to the public (Art.6(2)).

Member States must also ensure, however, that CSPs are free to issue qualified certificates which include limitations on the use of the certificate or a limit on the value of the transactions for which the certificate can be used (Art.6(3) and (4)).

The tScheme Voluntary Accreditation Scheme

As we have seen, Art.3(2) of the ESD permits Members States to introduce voluntary accreditation schemes aimed at enhancing levels of certification-service provision. In the United Kingdom, Pt I of the Electronic Com- **11–061** munications Act 2000 made provision for the DTI to establish a register of approved providers of cryptography services. The Government, however, announced in July 1999 that the power to set up a statutory registration scheme would be held in reserve, to be used only if industry failed to work out a suitable model for self-regulation. Such a model has now been established by industry and is known as *tScheme*. As the Government currently regards *tScheme* as meeting the need for a voluntary accreditation scheme within the United Kingdom, Pt I of the Electronic Communications Act 2000 has not yet been brought into force.

11–062 *tScheme* was incorporated in May 2000 as a not-for-profit company limited by guarantee. It operates an independent, industry-led, self-regulatory scheme, and it was set up to create strict assessment criteria (known as "approval profiles") against which it will consider applications for the approval of providers of cryptographic services (generally known as "trust services"). The approval process involves the following steps:

(1) *tScheme* develops, authorises and publishes an appropriate range of approval profiles.

(2) An independent organisation (UKAS in the United Kingdom), working with *tScheme*, accredits suitably qualified assessors to undertake audits against the approval profiles. These assessors are recognised by *tScheme*.

(3) A trust service provider engages a recognised assessor to audit its defined services against the appropriate profiles and receives an assessment report.

(4) The trust service provider applies to *tScheme* for formal grant of approval, citing the assessor's report certifying compliance.

(5) *tScheme* considers the assessment report and, if satisfied, invites the trust service provider to sign a contract covering the provider's use of the *tScheme* mark and the attendant conditions, and to pay the approval fee.

(6) *tScheme* adds the trust service provider to its web-based directory of approved services. The provider displays the approved service mark for the period of its contract with *tScheme*, thereby indicating to its service users that the service conforms to standards which are deserving of trust.

The Electronic Signatures Regulations 2002

11–063 The requirements of the ESD summarised in paras 11–059 and 11–060, above, are implemented in the United Kingdom by the Electronic Signatures Regulations 2002 (SI 2002/318). The Regulations employ the same terminology as the ESD.

Reg.3(1) implements Art.3(3) of the ESD by placing the Secretary of State for Trade and Industry under a duty to keep under review the carrying on of activities of CSPs who are established in the United

Kingdom and who issue qualified certificates to the public, and the persons by whom they are carried on, with a view to her becoming aware of the identity of those persons and the circumstances relating to the carrying on of those activities.

Reg.3(2) provides that it is also the duty of the Secretary of State to establish and maintain a register of CSPs who are established in the United Kingdom and who issue qualified certificates to the public. No such register has yet been established.

Reg.4 places CSPs under a liability to pay damages in the circumstances **11–064** envisaged by Art.6(1) and (2) of the ESD (as to which, see para.11–060, above). In order to achieve the required reversal of the burden of proof, reg.4 provides that, if the CSP would be liable in damages if a duty of care had existed between him and the person relying on the qualified certificate (or, as the case may be, on the certificate's not having been revoked) and the CSP had been negligent, then the CSP will be so liable to the same extent notwithstanding that there is no proof that the CSP was negligent, unless the CSP proves that he was not negligent. Given that liability is made to depend on an assumed duty of care, it is presumably open to the CSP to limit his liability in the ways permitted by Art.6(3) and (4) of the ESD by incorporating appropriate terms in the certificate.

The Legal Effect of Electronic Signatures

Art.5 of the ESD is substantially implemented in the United Kingdom by **11–065** s.7 of the Electronic Communications Act 2000 (although s.7 differs from Art.5 in that it makes no separate provision for what the ESD refers to as advanced electronic signatures).

S.7(1) provides:

> "In any legal proceedings—
>
> (a) an electronic signature incorporated into or logically associated with a particular electronic communication or particular electronic data, and
> (b) the certification by any person of such a signature,
>
> shall each be admissible in evidence in relation to any question as to the authenticity of the communication or data or as to the integrity of the communication or data."

In s.7(1) (as in the Act generally) the reference to the "authenticity" of the communication or data is a reference to whether it comes from a particular person or source, whether it is accurately timed and dated, or whether it is intended to have legal effect (s.15(2)(a)). The reference to the "integrity" of the communication or data is a reference to whether there has been any tampering with it, or other modification of it (s.15(2)(b)).

It will be noted that s.7(1) provides for the effect of both electronic **11–066** signatures and the certification of such signatures.

The concept of an electronic signature is elaborated in s.7(2), which states (in summary) that, for something to qualify as an electronic signature, it must purport to be incorporated into, or associated with, the relevant communication or data for the purpose of being used in establishing its authenticity or integrity, or both.

The function of certification is explained in s.7(3), which provides that an electronic signature is certified by any person:

> ". . . if that person (whether before or after the making of the communication) has made a statement confirming that—
>
> (a) the signature,
> (b) the means of producing, communicating or verifying the signature, or
> (c) a procedure applied to the signature,
>
> is (either alone or in combination with other factors) a valid means of establishing the authenticity of the communication or data, the integrity of the communication, or both."

11–067 While anything which qualifies an electronic signature, or the certification of such a signature, will be admissible in any legal proceedings under s.7(1), the weight to be placed on the signature or certificate will depend on the particular facts of the case. It is to be expected, however, that, where an electronic signature has been certified by a *tScheme*-recognised trust service provider, the certified signature would normally be treated as cogent evidence of the authenticity and integrity of the communication or data to which the signature relates.

The Use of Electronic Communications for Statutory Purposes

11–068 Finally, it should be noted that many statutes contain references to steps being taken in a way which presupposes the use of paper-based means of communication. Obvious examples are statutory references to notices and other documents being "in writing" or being sent "by post". S.8 of the Electronic Communications Act 2000 confers power on the appropriate Minister to modify existing legislation by statutory instrument so as to authorise the use of electronic communications instead of paper-based communications. One example of the use of this power is the Companies Act 1985 (Electronic Communications) Order 2000 (SI 2000/3373), which enables companies to use electronic means to send out various documents to their members, including the summary financial statement and notices of general meetings. Another is the Building Societies Act 1986 (Electronic Communications) Order 2003 (SI 2003/404), which makes similar provision with respect to building societies.

Part 3

Market Manipulation and Market Abuse

Chapter 12

Marketing and Financial Promotion

Introduction

Background

The new provisions that govern the law on financial promotions are set out in s.21 of the Financial Services & Marketing Act 2000 (FSMA) and are supplemented by the FSA Conduct of Business Rules, which puts flesh onto the provision. The Conduct of Business Rules (COBR) are a product of Art.11 of the EC Investment Services Directive which directs Member States, to draw up business rules which promote the principles of: a) honesty and fairness, b) skill care and diligence and c) disclosure. These principles help to create a climate for a stronger market and protection for the investor. **12–001**

Although the new provisions are, very much in line with the old law on promotions (ss.56–58 Financial Services Act 1986), there are some differences which should be considered at the out set. The FSMA now splits responsibility of exemption orders with regards to financial promotions to two bodies, where the Treasury has jurisdiction over unauthorised persons and the FSA over authorised persons. The FSMA has also amalgamated the different heads of promotion into one, thus instead of distinguishing between advertisements and unsolicited calls, we need now only consider "financial promotion", which benefits the investor as it increases the scope of what can be covered by this provision of the Act. Finally it must also be noted that there are now criminal sanctions for breaches of this section for unauthorised persons, which is another step to protect the investor better.

Additionally, a criminal offence of making misleading statements as contained in s.397 of the FSMA should be considered in relation to this Chapter and read with reference to Chs 13 (Insider Dealing and Market Manipulation) & 14 (Market Abuse).

General Promotional Restrictions

Other than the promotional restrictions administered by the FSMA, it may be useful to consider in brief other general advertising restrictions as they apply to financial promotions in a more general way. **12–002**

The largest advertising regulatory authority in the United Kingdom is the Advertising Standards Authority (ASA), which is a self regulatory body and covers mediums such as the press, cinemas, videos, the internet and direct mail. It administers some of its regulatory functions via the Radio Authority and the Independent Television Commission.

One of its primary roles it to ensure that the industry observe the British Code of Advertising and Sales Promotion (October 1, 1999), which contains a number of general principles as well as some specific rules on products including financial services. The ASA has the power, when it upholds complaints by consumers, to ask the advertisers to either withdraw or amend their advertisements and, as the ASA Annual Report 1998 indicated (p.17), the ASA received 12,217 complaints in 1998. Of these it upheld 623, which would suggest that this is not a very effective way to seek redress for investors.

12–003 There is also an EC Directive on Misleading Advertising (Dir. 84/450 [1984] O.J. L250/17), which asserts in Art.4(1) that Member States are to ensure that adequate and effective means exist for the control of misleading advertisements in the interest of consumers as well as competitors and the general public. The UK response to this has been the Misleading Advertisements Regulation 1988 (SI 1988/915), which defines what is to be considered to be misleading and provides powers for the Director of Fair Trading to bring actions against offenders.

These are just some of the main bodies governing advertisements and although not very effective in protecting the investor against questionable financial promotions, they are useful to know about in general terms.

Financial Promotion

12–004 As mentioned above the restriction on financial promotion is laid out in s.21(1) of the FSMA, which provides that a person must not in the course of business, communicate an invitation or inducement to engage in investment activity. This restriction does not however apply in the instance where the person making the communication is an authorised person pursuant to the FSMA or if an authorised person, approves the communication in question.

Scope

12–005 As one can see there are four components to satisfy this provision of the FSMA which shall be dealt with in turn:

(1) The promotion must have been carried out "in the course of business". This suggests that for a person to fall under s.21, they must be communicating not at a personal level but at a level that could be considered as a business transaction. Thus communicating to a family member or a friend would not fall in the scope of the FSMA. However, it is unclear at this stage whether this would cover one off activities, but it is more conceivable than not. (It should also be noted that the Treasury have been given the power to define what is to be considered as acting or not acting in the course of business).

(2) There must also be a communication for the promotion to fall under this section, which is a wide concept as illustrated by COBR para.3.3.2 where it states that there is no restriction on the type of media s.21 applies to. Thus communication for the purposes of this section includes all forms of written, oral, technological and interactive sources. Further, by virtue of s.21(13), communication also includes to cause to communicate.

(3) In a change from the old Act, there is now a requirement that the promotion in question be an "invitation or inducement", thus protecting those who are promoting but not inducing anyone to their investments.

(4) Finally for the promotion to fall under the prohibition under s.21, it has to be in relation to "engaging in an investment activity", which s.21(8) describes as entering or offering to enter into an agreement, the making or performance of which by either party, constitutes a controlled activity, or exercising any rights conferred be a controlled investment to acquire, dispose of, underwrite or convert a controlled investment.

In simple terms this means that the promotion must be in relation to one of the investment activities as specified by the FSMA or the Financial Promotions Order, as drafted by the Treasury and includes, company shares and stocks, government and public securities, etc. (For a more exhaustive list please consult s.22 and Sch.2 to the FSMA). **12–006**

New Concepts

The COBR paras 3.3.3–3.3.4 introduce two forms of promotion that the FSMA covers, that is "real time promotions" and "non real time promotions". The former in this case relates to financial promotions which are communicated in a personal and interactive form, *i.e.* personal visit, telephone conversation or electronic dialogue, where as the latter in concerned about non personal and non-direct communication, *i.e.* letters or TV broadcasts. Thus it relates to cases where the promotion is communicated to more than one person in identical terms and where the communication can often be referred back to as a record. The relevance of these concepts will be made clear below. **12–007**

Direct Offer Financial Promotions (Non-Real Promotions)

The COBR ch.3.9 discusses the scope of the FSMA further by reference to direct offer financial promotions. This provision relates to what it states, financial promotions offering investments directly to the investor in cases such as direct mail, which form part of non-real time financial promotions. **12–008**

The COBR para 3.9.5 states that a firm must not communicate or approve a communication directly promoting broker funds, unregulated collective investment schemes, derivatives or warrants. However after the general prohibition on this type of financial promotion, in line with the rest of the FSMA, the COBR qualifies the prohibition by stating that it is allowed in circumstances where the firm has adequate evidence to suggest that the investment may be suitable for the customer to whom it is directed. It would also be appropriate at this stage to mention that, deposits (except ISA's), general insurance contracts and pure protection contracts are exempt by virtue of para 3.9.3.

12–009 Once a firm has taken the step to accept that the direct financial promotion is suitable, it must make sure that amongst other things the promotion in question contains the following:

(1) A prominent statement that the firm communicating or approving the communication is authorised or regulated by the FSA.

(2) A prominent statement to the extent that if the investor queries the suitability of the investment communicated, that he seek advise from the firm who has communicated the promotion or that he seek independent advice.

(3) Sufficient information so that the investor can make an informed judgment of the investment.

(4) Full information as to the expenses that the investor will or may bear and commission or remuneration payable by the firm to another party.

(5) Statement indicating that the investment may fluctuate in value, which must not be smaller than the text of the main body of the promotion and where the firm decides that it is best communicated on a separate paper, it should satisfy themselves on reasonable grounds that this is the best prospect of being seen by the customer.

12–010 There are also additional requirements which relate to execution only firms, where they deal with the administration alone. In such cases the firm must indicate the charges the investor is likely to bear, the procedures if there is likely to be a delay in the execution of the investors order including the normal time taken and reasons for and extent of any such delays.

The direct offer promotions must also contain information with regards to cancellation rights if they are subject to them. Theses right must describe and explain the length of the cancellation period or withdrawal and when it will begin, whether the cancellation is a legal right or voluntarily conferred and finally if there may be a shortfall on cancellation.

Unsolicited Real Time Financial Promotions

12–011 As discussed above, this type of promotion was what the previous Act described as cold calling and covers financial promotions which are made without an express request from the recipient. Without express request pursuant to this area includes omissions to indicate that the recipient does not wish to receive such material and agreeing to standards terms that state that such communication will be made unless stated otherwise.

COBR 3.10.2 also asserts that firms should not communicate unsolicited real-time financial promotions to a private client unless it is exempt from such restriction or if the customer being communicated to has an existing business relationship with the firm and envisages receiving such calls. It is important to highlight at this point that other than just being an existing customer, the customer should also have envisaged being called, which is an extra hurdle to cross as far as the promoters are concerned. Finally real time communications are allowed as far as the communication is in relation to takeovers or related to issues in the Take Over Code in the United Kingdom or other EEA States and the scope of these rules do not extend to direct offer financial promotions, which are dealt with by COBR 3.9.

Electronic Media

Moving with technology, the COBR recognises that it must make specific **12–012** reference to the electronic media of communication with regards to financial promotion. COBR 3.14 gives guidance to firms on the use of electronic media in relation to financial promotion, which are also dealt with in COBR 1.8.

The scope of electronic media covered include any video or moving image material and or any web site containing financial promotion information, which for the purposes of these rules could fall in the category of either non real or real financial promotions.

The rules contained in COBR 3.14 state that financial promotions communicated in this format must comply with the rules as contained in COBR 3.8 (see above) and 3.9 (see below). In addition to these requirements the COBR also indicates that such promotions should include full text on relevant terms and key features, which can be via a hypertext link but as long as it is easily located and a full hard copy should be available on request. It must also be noted that where the site is unable to provide a copy of the application form electronically, it is to be treated as a direct offer financial promotion.

The COBR contains some specific rules with regards some areas of promotion too, namely that if promoting an unregulated collective investment scheme, the website should be designed so as to reduce, as far as possible, the risk of people not being targeted when using the site. It also states in COBR 3.14.5 (5), directing customers to the FSA website specific to customers does not constitute a replacement of the rules in this area and that banner adverts and hyperlinks are subject to the rules contained in the FSMA and COBR.

Exceptions to the rules above include situations where the promotion can be regarded as not being directed at persons in the United Kingdom.

Unregulated Collective Investment Schemes

Over and above the general prohibition on financial promotion, the **12–013** promotion of collective investment schemes has further restrictions as contained in s.238 of the FSMA. Collective investment schemes are discussed in greater detail in Parts 2 and 4. A collective investment scheme is an investment which reduces the risks, as it is worked by pooling investors money, which is invested as a portfolio thus spreading the risk to investors. In the United Kingdom there are three types of collective investment schemes, i) investment companies; ii) unit trusts; and iii) open-ended investment companies.

12–014 These further restrictions as mentioned above are contained in s.238 of the FSMA and in COBR 3.11. The FSMA in this regard takes the approach taken in s.9, as it places a general prohibition on authorised persons in this instance from communicating an inducement(s) to participate in collective investment schemes. Thus unlike s.21, restrictions in this section prohibit even authorised persons from financially promoting or approving communication for unregulated collective investment schemes.

However this prohibition is then qualified further down in the section as allowing an authorised person to communicate or approve such a promotion if the unit trust or open-ended investment company is itself authorised, if the collective investment schemes are recognised, if the promotion is for persons otherwise than the general public, or the scheme is exempt by the Financial Promotions Order. (See s.238 subss.(4) (a)-(c), (5) and (6) respectively.)

12–015 In looking at this section of the FSMA it must be noted that only invitations and inducements are covered. Territorial scope is also an important issue for investor protection and in this instance focuses on communications originating from the United Kingdom and can only be extended outside of this jurisdiction if the inducement or invitation for a collective investment scheme, is capable of having effect in the United Kingdom.

S.241 also introduces the right for an investor to bring civil actions against the authorised person who has contravened s.238. This shall be discussed further below in the Enforcement section.

Territorial Scope

General

12–016 With the ever-increasing modes of communication and the globalisation of the financial markets especially within the European Union, there are legitimate concerns as to how the investor should be protected from overseas financial promoters. This concern has been met by s.21(3) and COBR 3.4.

S.21(3) states that the restriction on financial promotion extends to and includes communications originating from outside the United Kingdom. However this is qualified by the assertion in subs.(1) of the same provision, which states that it only applies to communications which have effect in the United Kingdom and is further diminished by Art.15 of the Financial Promotions Order. Art.15 states that to fall within the remit of s.21, the communication must be directed at a class of persons in the United Kingdom. This concept is further discussed in COBR 3.3.8 and may be established if the recipients of the promotion can show on reasonable grounds that they fall in a class of persons, or that the promotion was directed at them, being a member of a class.

Having discussed the general concept of the territorial scope of s.21, it would be useful to have an overview of the cases in which the financial promotion rules would apply. This is discussed further in COBR 3.4. and is summarised below. In the following circumstances s.21 applies where, i) a financial promotion is communicated by a firm in the UK and directed at persons in the same; ii) the financial promotion is communicated by others, directed to persons in the UK and is approved by an authorised person; and iii) the financial promotion is communicated by a firm outside the UK, but is directed to persons within the UK. **12–017**

There is also a situation where not all the restriction imposed by the COBR apply but only COBR 3.8.4, 3.8.11 and 3.8.12, which imposes rules on form and content of the promotions. For example r.3.8.4 directs firms acting within the scope of this remit to ensure that the non-real time promotions, which the firm communicates or approves have been reasonably checked by the firm to ensure that the promotion is clear, fair and not misleading. The situation where this exists is where a financial promotion is not directed to persons in the United Kingdom and communicated by others, but has been approved by an authorised firm. **12–018**

Overseas Communication

Where the firm or person is communicating from overseas as seen above and the material is not approved or the firm is not authorised, the communication is prohibited (COBR 3.12). However if the communication has been approved, the overseas firm may communicate the financial promotion, so long as it makes clear in the communication the firm which has approved their material; that the rules which protect the investor under the FSMA do not apply here; and the level at which they are entitled to compensation. It must also be noted that the above rules do not apply to overseas persons when dealing with takeovers or where the person has a related operation in another EEA State. **12–019**

The person who has got approval from an authorised firm is also limited in the activities that he can do with approval, as the approval only relates to what material is covered and breach of this could lead the unauthorised person to face sanctions under s.21(1) of the FSMA.

Overseas Promotion of Life Policies

There are additional requirements from those discussed above (COBR 3.13), for overseas financial promotions relating to life policies. Communication cannot be made from overseas unless it is done so by an authorised or exempt person with regards to the insurance business to which the promotion relates, also the company must have its head office or branch in an EEA State and be entitled to carry insurance business under the domestic state law). **12–020**

12–021 Other than compliance with authorisation there are also content requirements that need to be fulfilled if the firm does not have establishment in the United Kingdom. These requirements include ensuring that the firm promoting the life policy includes in its communication, the country which it is registered and where its head office is if different. There must also be a prominent statement indicating that investors are in such cases not protected by the compensation scheme of the United Kingdom under the Financial Services Compensation Scheme and a further prominent statement with regards to the non-independent agents named in the communication. For the purposes of these rules a prominent statement is one which is made immediately after the company's full name, alongside the full name or where the name is stated more than once, the most prominent or the first if equally prominent (COBR 3.13.5).

Exemption Orders

12–022 The COBR 3.5.1 states that financial promotions rules do not apply to a firm in relation to a financial promotion of the kind listed below, except that if such a financial promotion relates to an unregulated collective investment scheme, where COBR 3.11 applies or if the firm approves the financial promotion, where COBR 3.12.4 applies.

12–023 For the purposes of this chapter, the full non exhaustive list of exemptions as found in the Financial Promotions Order is not going to be dealt with in full, save to say that the focus here is on COBR 3.5.2 and some exemption as found in the Financial Promotions Order, which highlight some of the more relevant exemptions with regards investors.

The COBR 3.5.2 states that financial promotions made by a firm who is an unauthorised person is exempt from the rules governing financial promotions, as is "one off" real and non-real financial promotions. By virtue of the COBR a "one off" promotion is such if the following three conditions are satisfied: i) that the communication is only communicated to one recipient or a group of recipients who are to engage in an investment activity jointly; ii) the product to be promoted has been determined having regard to the recipients particular circumstances; and iii) the promotion is not a part of a co-ordinated promotional strategy.

It must be noted that in these circumstances mass mail shots, even if *prima facie* it appears to be individualised is not exempt under these rules without regard to its content. As, if the material is the same and not tailored to the recipient's individual needs, it cannot be considered to be a "one off" promotion.

12–024 The exemptions also apply to communications which only carry one or more of the following in its promotion. That is the firms name, the name of the investment, a contact point, *i.e.* telephone number, a logo, a brief factual description of the firms activities, fees and investment products and price yields and charges of its products.

12–025 A brief outline of what the above exemptions cover are communications such as list prices contained in a newspaper or a Company's Annual Report pursuant to the requirements of the Companies Act 1985.

Other exemptions mentioned in COBR 3.5.2 are personal quotations or illustration forms on the investment or takeover promotions and the Financial Promotions Order states that generic communications which do not relate to a particular investment provided by a particular person either directly or indirectly is exempt by virtue of Art.14 as are communication documents between investment professionals and Annual Company accounts and directors reports as found in Art.60. **12–026**

On a final note in this area, it must also be observed that even where exemptions apply, the firm communicating material should still have regard to Principle 7 and the COBR 2.1.3, *i.e.* that communications are clear, fair, not misleading to mention but a few. **12–027**

Compliance Requirements

(i) Approval

Before a firm communicates or authorises promotional materials to be distributed, it must by virtue of COBR 3.6.1 ensure that the material conforms to the requirements set out in COBR 3.7 and 3.8. This form of prior approval is directed to non-real time financial promotions. **12–028**

Approval is by confirming that the promotion is compliant with the regulations by a suitable person of relevant expertise and where a firm becomes aware that a promotion is no longer in compliance, they should withdraw the promotion as soon as is reasonably practicable and withdraw with it its approval. A review process to monitor promotions is also recommended to firms.

The COBR 3.6.4 also addresses situations where the investor may have been misled and states that in such circumstances the firm should decide whether it would be appropriate to contact the customer with a view to clarifying the promotion, or in situations where the customer has sustained financial losses, offer appropriate redress. **12–029**

COBR 3.6.5 goes on to state that the rules governing this area will not be contravened where a firm communicates promotional material which it has not approved, if it can establish with reasonable care that such material has already been approved by another firm, which when communicated to the recipients, was not misleading in the time that the approval was given. **12–030**

(ii) Records

Once a firm has made an approval, it must comply with the requirement as set out in COBR 3.7, to keep adequate records of each of the financial promotions it has confirmed pursuant to the above rules. The records should be kept for an indefinite period if it relates to a pension transfer, opt-out or FSAVC, for six years if it is a life policy, pension contract or stakeholder pension scheme and for three years in all other cases. Such records must then be "readily accessible" for inspection in any format. Thus it must be available within 48 hours of such a request. **12–031**

(iii) Form and Content

12–032 COBR 3.8 splits its content requirements into two sub-headings, one which has application to non real time financial promotions and the other which applies to real time financial promotions.

Non Real Time Financial Promotion

12–033 Where a firm approves or communicates a non real time financial promotion, it must ensure that it contains its name and either a contact point or address, which can include a location address or email.

There is a requirement that direct offer promotions name the FSA as regulator, which does not apply to non real time financial promotions. However if the firm in this instance chooses to name the FSA as its regulator and it has non-regulated material in the promotion, it should state so.

12–034 As a general content requirement, the COBR 3.8.4 asserts that the firm communicating or approving the material must be able to show that it has taken reasonable steps to ensure that the communication in question is clear, fair and not misleading.

There are also rules which govern communications which include comparisons and in general these rules are there to prevent unfair practices such as discrediting the competitor and to stop misleading. Looking at the rules governing stopping unfair practices, COBR 3.8.4 states that a firm should ensure that it does not discredit or denigrate the trademark, name or other distinguishing marks of a competitor, that they do not take advantage of the reputation of a competitor by use of its distinguishing traits or imitate or produce a replica of a service or investment of a competitor which is protected by trademark.

12–035 In relation to preventing misleading the investor, the rules then go on to say that the comparisons made must be done so objectively, in a way which is verifiable, and with a service or product which has the same needs or purposes. There are also rules preventing confusion in the market place with the firms competitors, *i.e.* by the use of similar names. There are also further rules on potentially misleading statements in COBR 3.8.5.

12–036 Other than describing practices which should be followed to meet the content requirement of the rules governing this area, the COBR at para 3.8.7 (3) indicates situations where a financial promotion may be considered as not having met the general requirements in COBR 3.8. These include situations where the promotions have not included any statement with regards to pricing where there is a difference between the offer price and the bidding price. The phrase frozen pensions should also be avoided as well as making statements relating to the amount of share capital issued without mentioning the issued share capital or mentioning the company's total assets without mentioning the company's liabilities. The COBR also go on to say that quotations given should be fair and if there is a connection between the holder of the opinion in the quotation and the firm, this should be disclosed.

12–037 COBR 3.8.10–11 then goes on to look at the promotional requirements regarding communications which compare past performance of a particular investment. Staying with the usage of disclosure, the rules state that when such comparisons are made there must be statements to the effect that this trend may not be repeated. The rules also take the step of describing circumstances where the communication may be in breach of requirements if it makes unfair comparisons with other types of investments, selects an irrelevant investment period which may include unreasonably short period comparisons.

Real Time Financial Promotions

Now we turn to the second head of requirements as contained in the COBR 3.8.18–22, which deals with real time financial promotions. The rules governing this area only apply to solicited and non-solicited communications which are not exempt. Emphasis is put on the firm procedure in this instance ensuring amongst other things that its representative makes representations which are clear, fair and not misleading. There are also rules which relate to the timing of the calls and the right to respect the customer's wishes. **12–038**

In relation to promotions which use past performances, the communication should include information that compares yearly performance for at least five years ending on the date of approval or confirmation. If the performance cannot be checked for a period of five years due to the age of the investment, then the communication should date back as far as it can.

Enforcement

When looking at the provisions for the enforcement of the restrictions to the financial promotions, the starting point should be s.25 of the FSMA as it deals directly with contravention of s.21. **12–039**

S.25 asserts that a person found guilty of contravening s.21(1) is liable for either summary conviction with a maximum sentence of six months or a fine not exceeding the statutory maximum or both. In more serious cases there is also scope under s.25 (1)(b) to be convicted on indictment, where the maximum sentence cannot exceed two years, however the fine that can be imposed does not have a limit. In such cases, there is also scope to impose both a custodial sentence and a fine.

The provisions under s.25(2) also provide a defence for the accused, if he could show that either he believed on reasonable grounds that the content of the communication was prepared, or approved for the purposes of s.21, by an authorised person or that he took all reasonable precautions and exercised all due diligence to avoid committing the offence.

In connection to this offence one can also find a person can be found liable for claiming to be authorised or exempt for the purposes of financial promotion. S.21(2)(a) states that a person who is authorised can make financial promotions, thus if someone claims to be authorised or exempt, they may find themselves subject to s.24. **12–040**

S.24 asserts that someone who is neither authorised or exempt is guilty of an offence under the FSMA if, he describes himself to be authorised or exempt in whatever terms, or by conduct behaves as though he is authorised or exempt. If found guilty under this section, the accused may be liable on summary conviction for no more than six months imprisonment, a fine not exceeding level 5 or both. However, where the offence included a public display of material, the fine is the standard level 5 fine, but multiplied for every day the display continued.

12–041 As discussed above the promotion of unregulated collective investment schemes have additional requirements to that expressed in s.21 of the FSMA, thus its enforcement needs to be considered separately to the mechanisms in place above.

12–042 S.241 asserts that private actions may be brought by an aggrieved investor against the authorised person who contravened the requirements as imposed by s.238 or s.240, which is dealt with under s.150 of the FSMA.

S.150 states that contravention by an authorised person of a rule is actionable by a private suit by the person who suffers loss as a result of the contravention. This action however is subject to defences and other incidents applying to actions for breach of statutory duty. There are also limitations placed on the actions which can be brought in that s.151 states that a person is not guilty of an offence by reason of a contravention of a rule made by the Authority and in no circumstances does a contravention make any transaction void or unenforceable.

Misleading Statements and Practices

12–043 S.397 of the FSMA creates two offences concerning misleading statements and practices and as such s.397 replaces s. 47 of the Financial Services Act 1986. S.397(1) and (2) makes it an offence for an investor to be induced dishonestly or recklessly into making an investment on the basis of a misleading, false or deceptive statement or where material facts have been dishonestly concealed. It is likely that most cases falling within the ambit of s.397 will arise in circumstances where the investment is transferable on a recognised securities market, but the section is not confined to this situation. S.397(3) is couched in the same terms as s.47(2) of the Financial Services Act 1986 and is aimed at an act or a course of conduct which creates a false or misleading impression as to the market in or the price or value of any investments.

Section 397

12–044 S.397(1) and (2) of the Financial Services and Markets Act 2000 provides that:

> "(1) This section applies to a person who—
>
> (a) makes a statement, promise or forecast which he knows to be misleading, false or deceptive in a material particular;
> (b) dishonestly conceals any material facts whether in connection with a statement, promise or forecast made by him or otherwise; or
> (c) recklessly makes (dishonestly or otherwise) a statement, promise or forecast which is misleading, false or deceptive in a material particular.

(2) A person to whom subsection (1) applies is guilty of an offence if he makes the statement, promise or forecast or conceals the facts for the purpose of inducing, or is reckless as to whether it may induce, another person (whether or not the person to whom the statement, promise or forecast is made)-

(a) to enter or offer to enter into, or refrain from entering or offering to enter into, am relevant agreement; or
(b) to exercise, or refrain from exercising, any rights conferred by a relevant investment."

Defences: By virtue of s.397(4), it is a defence for a person who makes a statement, promise or forecast which he knows to be misleading, false or deceptive in a material particular (see s.397(1)(a)), if he can show that the statement, or promise or forecast was made in conformity with price stabilising rules or with the control of information rules. **12–045**

Jurisdiction: S.397(6) places territorial limits on where the offences created in s.397(1) and (2) may be committed. In short, a person will only commit an offence under s.397(1) and (2) if the statement, promise or forecast is made in or from the United Kingdom; or the concealment of facts is accomplished in or from the United Kingdom; or where the arrangements to make a statement, promise or forecast or to conceal facts are made in the United Kingdom or from the United Kingdom; or where the person on whom the inducement is intended to have effect on whom such inducement may have effect is in the United Kingdom; or where the agreement is or would be entered into in the United Kingdom or the rights are or would be exercised in the United Kingdom. **12–046**

Several statements: Where several statements are made together, it is the effect of the statements taken together which has to be considered. Several statements taken together could be misleading even if individually, each was true—see *Aaron's Reefs Ltd v Twiss* [1896] A.C. 273. **12–047**

Recklessness: A statement will be reckless in the context of s.397(1) and (2) if it is a rash statement to make and the person who made the statement had no real basis of facts on which he could support the statement. This was established in *R v Grunwald* [1963] 1 Q.B. 935 which concerned the making of reckless statements within the meaning of s.13 of the Prevention of Fraud (Investments) Act 1958. **12–048**

Dishonesty: The meaning of dishonesty is considered in Ch.18, Theft Act Offences. The same meaning applies here. **12–049**

The terms "relevant agreement" and "relevant investment" are defined in s.397 (9) and (10) respectively.

Section 397(3)

S.397(3) of the FSMA which repeats s.47(2) of the Financial Services Act 1986, contains the second offence namely that of creating a false or misleading impression. The sub-section reads as follows: **12–050**

"(3) Any person who does any act or engages in any course of conduct which creates a false or misleading impression as to the market in or the price or value of any investments is guilty of an offence if he does it for the purpose of creating that impression and of thereby inducing another person to acquire, dispose of, subscribe for or underwrite those investments or to refrain from doing so or to exercise, or refrain from exercising, any rights conferred by those investments".

12–051 **A false or misleading impression**: An impression is to be regarded as the perception received by the investor. A false impression is one which is objectively incorrect. It will be necessary to assess the effect of the impression on the particular class of person at whom the impression was aimed and not on an average investor. In *North v Marra Developments Ltd* [1982] 56 A.L.J.R. 106 the New South Wales Court of Appeal suggested that the following questions could be asked when seeking to determine whether a false or misleading impression had been created:

- what is the apparent state of affairs, with respect to the market or the price for the securities in question, conveyed by the transactions or the conduct impugned?
- was that the true state of affairs?
- if it was not, was the apparent state of affairs false or misleading?
- if it was, were the transactions or the conduct impugned calculated to create that false or misleading appearance?

12–052 Examples of artificial devices by which a false impression as to the market in a security may be created and which would be prohibited by s.397(3) are:

- Wash sales. These are transactions effected through the market which involve no change in beneficial ownership of the shares. The transaction is a fiction and the buyer incurs no real financial obligation to the seller. It does however, create a false appearance of active trading in those shares. An example of a wash sale can be seen in the Canadian case of *R v Lampard* [1969] SCR 373.
- Matched orders. A matched order occurs where a transaction (purchase or sale) is entered in the knowledge that a mirror transaction is to be entered into by another of substantially the same size, price and type again creating the impression of active trading.

12–053 **Engaging in conduct**: This will include acts and omissions to act. The concept that an omission to act may lead to a criminal sanction is unusual since the criminal law has been traditionally reluctant to impute criminal liability for omissions except in cases where there is a recognised duty to act. It may be said that a market maker has a duty to act in accordance with the rules of the market. In the case of *Adams v R*, *The Times*, November 4, 1994, the Privy Council held that a person could be guilty of fraud when he dishonestly concealed information from another which he was under a duty to disclose to that other or which that other was entitled to require him to disclose.

False price or value: In the case of a security listed on an exchange the correct value is the market price which is arrived at by a consensus of the bona fide purchasers and sellers. A false price or value will be created when there is a shift in the equilibrium of the market. One of the most obvious situations where there is a tampering with the correct market price is in a takeover where a share support operation is mounted or where tactics are employed to resist a drawn raid. The implementation of s.397(3) by the FSA has the potential therefore, to overlap with the work of the Panel on Takeovers and Mergers. To this end the FSA and the Panel on Takeovers and Mergers have issued joint operating guidelines on how they propose to implement their overlapping functions. **12–054**

Intent: S.397(3) requires proof of an intention to create an impression as to the market in or the price or value of a security. The intent required by s.397(3) is subjective. If no reasonable person in the position of the defendant would have held the belief, this is powerful evidence that he did not honestly hold that belief—see *R. v MacKinnon* [1959] 1 Q.B. 150 which concerned the now repealed Prevention of Fraud (Investment) Act 1939. **12–055**

Inducing another to act: It must be shown that the defendant's act was for the purpose of inducing another to deal in the securities. It would not be an offence under s.397(3) if the defendant could show that he was merely shuffling his own investments. The Court will be obliged to look at the primary motive of the defendant. It is probably enough to show that the defendant intended to affect investors generally or a class of investors and not that he had some specific person in mind. **12–056**

Defences: S.397(5) provides that it is a defence for a person accused of an offence under s.397(3) to show that he reasonably believed that his act or conduct would not create an impression that was false or misleading as to the matters set out in subs.(3): that he acted or engaged in the conduct for the purpose of stabilising the price of investments and in conformity with price stabilising rules; or that he acted or engaged in the conduct in conformity with control of information rules. **12–057**

Jurisdiction

S.397(7) requires that the act is done or the course of conduct is engaged in the United Kingdom and that the false or misleading impression is created in the United Kingdom. **12–058**

Penalties: A person convicted of an offence under s.397(1) and (2) or s.397 (3) is liable to a maximum of six months imprisonment and/or a fine of up to the statutory maximum if convicted in the magistrates court or to a maximum of seven years imprisonment and/or a fine if convicted in the Crown Court. Some guidance as to the approach likely to be taken by a court faced with the prospect of sentencing an offender for an offence of making misleading statements is to be gained from the case of *R. v Robert Philip Feld* (unreported) April 6, 1998, Case No. 97/3093/X5, in which the Court of Appeal upheld sentences of six years imprisonment to run concurrently for a number of offences of making misleading statements contrary to s.47 of the Financial Services Act 1986. In the course of the judgment, Smedley J. also set out a list of ten factors which, though not **12–059**

exhaustive, were likely to be borne in mind by the sentencing Judge when approaching cases of this kind and which were additional to the usual factors which are set out in the case of *R. v Barrick* (1985) 81 Cr. App. R. 78 (Sentencing). These were:

(1) The amount involved and the manner in which the fraud is carried out.

(2) The period over which the fraud is carried out and the degree of persistence with which is carried out.

(3) The position of the accused within the company and his measure of control over it.

(4) Any abuse of trust which is revealed.

(5) The consequences of the fraud.

(6) The effect on public confidence in the City and the integrity of commercial life.

(7) The loss to small investors, which will aggravate the fraud.

(8) The personal benefit derived by a defendant.

(9) The plea.

(10) The age and character of the defendant.

In considering the gravity of the offences, Smedley J. said: "we emphasise that it is vitally important if confidence in the City and its financial institutions is to be maintained, that when Circulars and similar documents are issued to the public in support of Rights Issues and the like, those documents are honest and complete."

Chapter 13

Insider Dealing and Market Manipulation

In this chapter we consider the two principal criminal sanctions which seek to offer investors some protection against manipulation of the financial markets. Theses are the legislation against insider dealing, and the making of false statements to induce investment contrary to s.397 of the FSMA. The application of conspiracy to defraud to cases where the victim is an investor and the crime involves market manipulation or some other improper practice such as the deception of a regulatory body has been considered in Ch.20. **13–001**

Introduction

The history of legal intervention in cases of market manipulation dates back to the Napoleonic Wars in *De Berenger* 3 M. & S. 66; 105 E.R. 536. In this case a man called De Berenger who was dressed as a soldier, arrived at Winchester and spread a false rumour that Napoleon had been killed. The news caused a rise in the price of government securities. De Berenger and his associates were convicted of conspiring by false rumours to raise the price of government funds, in contemporary terms a conspiracy to defraud. **13–002**

Over 100 years later, by virtue of s.13 of the Prevention of Fraud (Investments) Act 1958 Parliament made it an offence to make false and misleading statements for the purpose of inducing investment although this offence was not directed specifically at market manipulation.

It was not until 1980 that legislation was introduced that focused directly on market manipulation when insider dealing was made a criminal offence by ss.68 to 73 of the Companies Act 1980. By comparison, there has been anti-manipulation legislation in the United States since the Depression in the form of the American Securities Exchange Act 1934 which was enacted in the wake of the Wall Street crash. In the United Kingdom, the position was that although certain share dealings had been subject to regulation under the City Code on Takeovers and Mergers, it was not until 1973 that the Stock Exchange and Takeover Panel issued a joint statement calling for criminal sanctions against insider dealers. Regulation against market manipulation was perceived to be necessary in order to protect investors against unfair practices and to safeguard the public interest in maintaining open and fair markets because it is only when markets are open and fair that the will be confidence in them. As Mason J said in the Australian case **13–003** of *North v Marra Developments Ltd* [1982] 56 A.L.J.R. 106, regulation is necessary:

> "to ensure that the market reflects the forces of genuine supply and demand. By genuine supply and demand I exclude buyers and sellers whose transactions are undertaken for the sole or primary purpose of setting or maintaining the market price. It is in the interests of the community that the market for the securities should be real and genuine, free from manipulation."

Insider Dealing

Nature of Insider Dealing

13–004 In essence insider dealing involves the use of restricted information about a company by a buyer or seller of its securities to gain an advantage.

> "Insider dealing is understood broadly to cover situations where a person buys or sells securities when he, but not the other party to the transaction, is in possession of confidential information which affects the value to be placed on those securities. Furthermore, the confidential information will generally be in his possession because of some connection which he has with the company whose securities are to be dealt in (e.g. he may be a director, employee or professional advisor of that company) or because someone in such a position has provided him, directly or indirectly, with the information" (Conduct of Company Directors (1977) (Cmnd. 7037)).

13–005 It is sometimes said that insider dealing is a "victimless" crime. Whilst no individual "victim" can be identified in any particular insider dealing transaction, the general perception of the probity of those involved in the market is undermined. This point has been underlined in the recitals to the European Communities Council Directive 89/592 ([1989] O.J. L334/30) on Insider Dealing where the importance of the smooth operation of the market is emphasised. The smooth operation of the market is said to be dependant to a large extent on the confidence it inspires in investors:

> "The factors on which such confidence depends include the assurance afforded to investors that they are placed on an equal footing and that they will be protected against the improper use of inside information".

13–006 The provisions of the Companies Act 1980 concerning the regulation of insider dealing were replaced by the provisions of the Company Securities (Insider Dealing) Act 1985. Today the offence is contained in Pt V of the Criminal Justice Act 1993. This last legislative change was made in order to ensure that the law complied with the requirements of the 1989 European Communities Council Directive. The Criminal Justice Act 1993 came into force on the March 1, 1994.

The FSA has the power to institute criminal proceedings for insider dealing by virtue of s.402 of the FSMA.

A Criminal Sanction

The Criminal Justice Act 1993 imposes criminal liability but it does not include provision for any civil remedy for the company or an unwitting outsider. Although the inside information comes from the company, the victims of insider dealing are usually outsiders who bought or sold shares in ignorance of the information which, if made public, would affect their price. 13–007

There is some discussion in the leading texts about the availability of civil remedies on the basis of constructive trusteeship, fiduciary accountability or breach of confidence, but the position is far from clear. Directors are entitled under existing civil law to buy shares without disclosing an intended takeover offer or to sell shares knowing that the company is in difficulties (*Percival v Wright* [1902] 2 Ch. 421). Readers are referred to Chs 26 and 27 for a more detailed discussion of these principles. The situation is significantly different in the USA where comprehensive civil and criminal sanctions have existed since the 1930s.

The Offence

S.52 of the Criminal Justice Act 1993 sets out three forms of the offence: acquiring and disposing of securities, encouraging another person to do so, and disclosing inside information to someone else. Proof of an offence has retained the two step approach of the Company Securities (Insider Dealing) Act 1985, whereby commission of the offence rests on the status of the person charged as an insider and on the type of information in his possession being inside information. 13–008

S.52 provides as follows: 13–009

> "(1) An individual who has information as an insider is guilty of insider dealing if, in the circumstances mentioned in subsection (3), he deals in securities that are price-affected securities in relation to the information.
>
> (2) An individual who has information as an insider is also guilty of insider dealing if—
>
> (a) he encourages another person to deal in securities that are (whether or not that other knows it) price-affected securities in relation to the information, knowing or having reasonable cause to believe that the dealing would take place in the circumstances mentioned in subsection(3); or
>
> (b) he discloses the information, otherwise than in proper performance of the functions of his employment, office or profession, to another person.
>
> (3) The circumstances referred to above are that the acquisition or disposal in question occurs on a regulated market, or that the person dealing relies on a professional intermediary or is himself acting as a professional intermediary.
>
> (4) This section has effect subject to section 53".

An Individual

The prohibition in s.52 applies to "an individual". The use of the word "individual" excludes limited companies and other institutions like local authorities. However, an unincorporated partnership or firm could commit 13–010 insider dealing since it is no more than a collection of individuals. This is not to say that a company can escape liability completely. A company may be liable for the secondary offence of encouraging another person to deal.

An Insider

13–011 Under s.52 an individual must have information "as an insider", the meaning of which is defined by s.57 as follows:

> "(1) . . . a person has information as an insider if and only if
>
> (a) it is, and he knows that it is, inside information, and
> (b) he has it, and knows that he has it, from an inside source.
>
> (2) For the purposes of subsection (1), a person has information from an inside source if and only if—
>
> (a) he has it through—
>
> (i) being a director, employee or shareholder of an issuer of securities; or
> (ii) having access to the information by virtue of his employment, office or profession; or
>
> (b) the direct or indirect source of his information is a person within paragraph (a)."

13–012 It follows that s.57 has established a distinction between a primary insider (subs.(2)(a)) being a person who comes by inside information by virtue of his direct connection with a company and a secondary insider (subs.(2)(b)) who is a person who comes by the information from an inside source. A primary insider is a person who has information through being a director, employee or shareholder of an issuer of securities or any person who has information because of his employment, office of profession. A secondary insider is someone whose source of information is directly or indirectly a primary insider. Brokers and analysts who rely on market intelligence could be caught by the provisions of s.57 if they know that the intelligence comes from a primary insider as could financial journalists. However, in practice it is likely that it will be easier to prove that a person is a primary insider than it will to be prove that he is a secondary insider. An example of the difficulties which may arise is to be found in the Scottish case of *Mackie v H.M. Advocate* [1994] T.L.R. (30.3.94), in which the High Court of Justiciary overturned the conviction of the accused for offences charged under ss.1(7) and (8) of the Company Securities (Insider Dealing) Act 1985 where it was alleged that the defendant, who was an investment analyst, had been guilty of insider dealing by way of counselling or procuring the salesman who worked for the same company as himself, to deal with the securities of a company about which the accused had obtained unpublished price-sensitive information from one of its directors that a profits warning and new share issue were imminent.

Inside Information

13–013 S.56 defines the meaning of inside information:

"(1) . . . inside information means information which—

(a) relates to particular securities or to a particular issuer of securities or to particular issuers of securities and not to securities generally or to issuers of securities generally;
(b) is specific or precise;
(c) has not been made public; and
(d) if it were made public would be likely to have a significant effect on the price of any securities.

(2) . . . securities are 'price-affected securities' in relation to inside information, and inside information is 'price-sensitive information' in relation to securities, if and only if the information would, if made public, be likely to have a significant effect on the price of the securities.
(3) For the purposes of this section 'price' includes value."

For information to be "inside information" it must be price sensitive information. It is interesting to note that s.56 has been drafted more widely than the EC Directive 89/592 in respect of the requirement that the inside information has to be specific or precise. Art.1 of the Directive requires the inside information to be "of a precise nature" which is a narrower than information which is "specific". As s.56 passed through the House of Commons, the Economic Secretary to the Treasury explained the variation in the following way: **13–014**

". . . if somebody were to say during . . . lunch . . . 'Our results will be much better than the market expects or knows' that person would not be precise. That person would not have disclosed what the results of the company were to be. However, it would certainly be specific because he would be saying something about the company's results, and making it pretty obvious that the information had not been made public . . . It would be insider information because it would be specific" (Standing Committee B, col.175, June 10, 1993).

In *R. v Staines and Morrissey* [1997] 2 Cr. App. R. 426, information which did not include naming a particular company, but which nevertheless was sufficient that it was possible without expending much additional effort to identify the company, was found to be sufficiently specific and precise to fall within the definition of inside information. **13–015**

Whether information is "price sensitive" information is ultimately a question for a jury to decide although they may be assisted by the calling of expert evidence—see *R. v Gray* [1995] 2 Cr. App. R. 100 at 118–9.

Public Information

Information loses its confidential quality for the purposes of s.56 if it is made public or is to be treated as made public. Ss.58(2) and (3) provide examples of information which has entered the public domain but, as the language of subs.(3) demonstrates, the list is by no means exhaustive: **13–016**

"(2) Information is made public if—

(a) it is published in accordance with the rules of a regulated market for the purpose of informing investors and their professional advisers;

(b) it is contained in records which by virtue of any enactment are open to inspection by the public;
(c) it can be readily acquired by those likely to deal in any securities—

(i) to which the information relates, or
(ii) of an issuer to which the information relates; or

(d) it is derived from information which has been made public.

(3) Information may be treated as made public even though

(a) it can be acquired only by persons exercising diligence or expertise;
(b) it is communicated to a section of the public and not to the public at large;
(c) it can be acquired only by observation;
(d) it is communicated only on payment of a fee; or
(e) it is published only outside the United Kingdom".

13–017 It is important to note that information may be treated as public even though steps have to be taken in order to obtain the information. In due course the Courts will be asked to adjudicate on the parameters of s.58(3). Whilst each case will turn on its particular facts, it is unfortunate that the statutory language should be ambiguous with regard to a provision which goes to the heart of mischief which the legislation has been enacted to prevent. The penultimate recital in EC Directive 89/592 makes it clear that estimates developed from *publicly available data* cannot be regarded as inside information and any transaction carried out on the basis of such estimates does not constitute insider dealing within the meaning of the Directive. The domestic Courts will be compelled to construe s.58(3) widely in the light of this recital and at some stage a "coach and horses" can be expected to be driven through this legislation.

Price-Affected Securities

13–018 Price-affected securities are defined in Sch.2 to the Criminal Justice Act 1993. The range of securities to which the insider dealing provisions apply has been extended and now covers shares, bonds, gilts, warrants, depositary receipts, options, futures and contracts for differences.

It is worth noting that dealings in derivatives by directors is proscribed by s.323 of the 1985 Companies Act discussed in Ch.21.

Deals On and Off Market

13–019 To be caught by the legislation, dealings must take place on a regulated market or off-market but involving a professional intermediary. As to the term "regulated markets" see the Insider Dealing (Securities and Regulated Markets) Order 1994 (SI 1994/187) as amended by the Insider Dealing (Securities and Regulated Markets) Amendment Order 1996 (SI 1996/1561) and the Insider Dealing (Securities and Regulated Markets) Amendment Order 2000 (SI 2000/1923).

13–020 S.55 defines "dealing" in securities:

"(1) For the purposes of this Part, a person deals in securities if—

(a) he acquires or disposes of the securities (whether as principal or agent); or
(b) he procures, directly or indirectly, an acquisition or disposal of the securities by any other person."

There is no need to establish any causal link between the information and the dealing—see Lord Lane C.J. (at pp.979–980) in *Attorney General's Reference (No. 1 of 1988)* [1989] 1 A.C. 971: 13–021

"[T]he offence is not one of using information but of dealing in the securities whilst being in possession of the relevant information."

Professional Intermediaries

S.59 puts forward a definition of a professional intermediary in the following terms: 13–022

"(1) For the purposes of this Part a "professional intermediary" is a person—

(a) who carries on a business consisting of an activity mentioned in subsection (2) and who holds himself out to the public or any section of the public (including a section of the public constituted by persons such as himself) as willing to engage in any such business; or
(b) who is employed by a person falling within paragraph (a) to carry out any such activity.

(2) The activities referred to in subsection (1) are—

(a) acquiring or disposing of securities (whether as principal or agent); or
(b) acting as an intermediary between persons taking part in any dealing in securities".

Takeovers

Extending the statutory prohibition to off-market deals can cause difficulty when there is a takeover bid. The involvement of a professional intermediary taints the transaction so that if the bidder and its financial advisor have inside information about the target, being itself a listed company, the dealing restriction could potentially apply. The value of the bidder's own securities is price-affected by the approach to the target. A bidder may seek to adopt the solution of making the bid in their own name rather than through the financial institution. 13–023

Defences

S.53 repeats a number of defences available under the old legislation. Broadly these are that there was no intention in that the accused did not expect the deal to result in a profit attributable to the fact that the 13–024 information in question was price-sensitive. Profit in this context may be taken to include the avoidance of a loss. It is also a defence to show that the defendant reasonably believed that the information had been disclosed. Lastly, it is a defence if it can be shown that the defendant would have acted as he did irrespective of whether he was in possession of the price sensitive information.

The burden of proving a defence under s.53 rests on the defendant and is to the civil standard on the balance of probabilities.

13–025 S.53 provides:

> "(1) An individual is not guilty of insider dealing by virtue of dealing in securities if he shows—
>
> (a) that he did not at the time expect the dealing to result in a profit attributable to the fact that the information in question was price sensitive information in relation to the securities; or
> (b) that at the time he believed on reasonable grounds that the information had been disclosed widely enough to ensure that none of those taking part in the dealing would be prejudiced by not having the information; or
> (c) that he would have done what he did even if he had not had the information.
>
> (2) An individual is not guilty of insider dealing by virtue of encouraging another person to deal in securities if he shows—
>
> (a) attributable to the fact that the information in question was price sensitive information in relation to the securities; or
> (b) that at the time he believed on reasonable grounds that the information had been disclosed widely enough to ensure that none of those taking part in the dealing would be prejudiced by not having the information; or
> (c) that he would have done what he did even if he had not had the information.
>
> (3) An individual is not guilty of insider dealing by virtue of a disclosure of information if he shows—
>
> (a) that he did not at the time expect any person, because of the disclosure, to deal in securities in the circumstances mentioned in subsection (3) of s.52; or
> (b) that, although he had such an expectation at the time, he did not expect the dealing to result in a profit attributable to the fact that the information was price sensitive in relation to the securities".

Special Defences

13–026 Sch.1 to the Criminal Justice Act 1993 sets out a number of specific defences to an allegation of insider dealing. It is a defence for an individual dealing in securities or encouraging another person to deal if he acted in good faith in his capacity as a market maker. To come within the provisions of the special defence it is necessary for the market maker to be regulated by an "approved organisation" meaning a self-regulating organisation approved under para.25B of Sch.1 to the Financial Services Act 1986.

It is a defence to insider dealing for an individual to show that the information he had as an insider was market information. In deciding whether the information was market information, regard must be had to the content of the information, the circumstances in which the information was first obtained and the capacity in which the insider now acts. **13–027**

It is a defence for an individual to show that his actions were in conformity with the price stabilisation rules made under s.48 of the Financial Services Act 1986.

Penalties

An individual guilty of insider dealing is liable to a maximum of seven years imprisonment and/or an unlimited fine if tried on indictment or to a maximum of six months imprisonment and/or a fine not exceeding the statutory maximum if tried summarily—see s.61(1). **13–028**

Jurisdiction

Provisions relating to jurisdiction are contained in s.62 of the Criminal Justice Act 1993. For the UK Courts to have jurisdiction, some element of the offence under s.52(1) or (2) must have taken place within the United Kingdom, *i.e.* the tippee was located in the United Kingdom or the dealing was on a UK regulated market, or the broker or market maker was carrying on business in the United Kingdom. **13–029**

Where an individual in the United Kingdom seeks to avoid the territorial scope of the legislation by causing a company which he controls outside Europe to effect the trade, he cannot be a primary insider but could be an encourager or discloser of the inside information. An example occurred in the case involving Geoffrey Collier, former head of securities at Morgan Grenfell, who was convicted in 1987 on the basis of counselling and procuring a Cayman Island company which he controlled to deal in shares on the London Stock Exchange. He was fined £25,000 and received a 12 month suspended prison sentence, having admitted using confidential information to buy shares before a bid in which he actually lost £10,000.

Chapter 14

Market Abuse

Introduction

Pt VIII of the FSMA 2000 (ss.118–131) sets out a new framework for tackling market abuse. In addition, the Financial Services Authority has issued a Code to give guidance as to whether "behaviour" amounts to market abuse. The Code is relevant to all persons seeking guidance as to whether or not behaviour amounts to market abuse and is not confined only to persons who are authorised. This is a significant innovation brought in under the new regime. (MAR 1.1.1). The Code is intended to give guidance for the purpose of determining whether or not behaviour amounts to market abuse, accordingly it must be noted that the Code is not, and is not intended to be, an exhaustive list of all types of behaviour which may, or may not, amount to market abuse (MAR 1.1.8, MAR 1.1.13) (The Code of Market Abuse is included as Ch.1 of the Market Conduct sourcebook of the FSA Handbook. The Code is also published as a separate document which is available to persons who are not authorised). **14–001**

Market abuse arises in circumstances where market users have been unreasonably disadvantaged by others in the market who have used information which is not generally available, created a false or misleading impression or distorted the market to their own advantage. The new framework introduces a regime which is intended to complement the existing criminal offence of insider dealing (s.52 of the Criminal Justice Act 1993) and the prohibitions on misleading statements and practices contained in s.397 of the FSMA 2000. Indeed the Code makes it clear that in addition to compliance with the requirements of the Code, market users and others to whom the Code applies also have a duty to ensure that their behaviour does not breach any applicable criminal law (*e.g.* the insider dealing provisions of the Criminal Justice Act 1993), rules (*e.g.* Principle 5 of the Principles for Businesses (PRIN), the Conduct of Business sourcebook (COB), and the Statements of Principle and Code of Practice for Approved Persons (APER)) or any other legal or regulatory requirements (*e.g.* the rules and regulations of RIEs, the Takeover Code, the SARs, the provisions of the Companies Acts, and relevant overseas rules). (MAR 1.9) **14–002**

One of the most important features of the new market abuse regime is that for the first time, under the FSMA 2000, all market participants whether authorised or unauthorised will be subject to the same regime for dealing with market abuse. The measures intended to prevent market abuse have been described as "one of the most important and innovative aspects of the new regulatory regime. It is not without its controversial elements, **14–003** but the key message is that market abuse will not be tolerated in the U.K. That is not only the position of the regulator, it is also the desire of market participants themselves, as clean markets benefit all market users." (Gay Wisbey, Director of Markets and Exchanges, FSA Press Release — FSA/PN/098/2000.)

14–004 There are three main types of behaviour which, if left unchecked, may give rise to market abuse and which the new market abuse regime seeks to address. These are:

(i) the misuse of relevant information that is not generally available to other market users

(ii) the giving of false or misleading impressions;

(iii) market distortion.

In order to amount to market abuse, behaviour must correspond to one of these three elements and be likely to be regarded by a regular user of the market as a failure on the part of the person concerned to observe the standard of conduct reasonably expected of someone in his position in relation to the market. The regular user is the financial services equivalent of the reasonable man on the Clapham omnibus or the man on the Docklands Light railway, perhaps.

What is Market Abuse?

14–005 Market abuse is defined in s.118(1) of the FSMA 2000:

> "For the purposes of the Act, market abuse is behaviour (whether by one person alone or by two or more persons jointly or in concert)-
>
> (a) which occurs in relation to qualifying investments traded on a market to which this section applies;
> (b) which satisfies any one or more of the conditions set out in section 118(2); and
> (c) which is likely to be regarded by a regular user of that market who is aware of the behaviour as a failure on the part of the person or persons concerned to observe the standard of behaviour reasonably expected of a person in his or their position in relation to the market."

14–006 In order to establish that behaviour (whether by one person alone, or two or more acting together) amounts to market abuse, these tests must be satisfied and it should be noted that behaviour will only amount to market abuse if all three of these tests are satisfied. These are that:

(1) the behaviour must occur in relation to a qualifying investment traded on a prescribed market (see MAR 1.11)

(2) the behaviour must satisfy one or more of the three conditions set out in s.118(2), these are:

(a) the behaviour is based on information which is not generally available to those using the market but which, if available to a regular user of the market, would or would be likely to be regarded by him as relevant when deciding the terms on which transactions in investments of the kind in question should be effected;

(b) the behaviour is likely to give a regular user of the market a false or misleading impression as to the supply of, or demand for, or as to the price or value of, investment of the kind in question;

(c) a regular user of the market would, or would be likely to, regard the behaviour which would, or would be likely to distort the market in investments of the kind in question.

(3) the behaviour must fall below the standard of behaviour that a regular user of the market would reasonably expect of a person in the position of the person in question.

Penalties and Enforcement

S.123 of the Act provides the FSA with the power to impose a penalty if it **14–007** is satisfied that a person has engaged in market abuse or, by taking or refraining from taking any action has required or encouraged others to engage in market abuse. Where the FSA is satisfied that a person (A) has engaged in market abuse or has required or encouraged another person to engage in behaviour that would amount to market abuse had it been done by A himself, then under s.123(1) of the Act, the FSA has the power to impose a penalty or make a statement to the effect that the person has engaged in market abuse (MAR 1.1.4). No penalty may be imposed if there are reasonable grounds to satisfy the FSA that the person (i) believed on reasonable grounds that his behaviour did not amount to market abuse; or (ii) had taken all reasonable precautions and exercised all due diligence to avoid engaging in market abuse (s.123(2) and MAR 1.1.15). Similarly, no penalty may be imposed if there are reasonable grounds to satisfy the FSA that a person (i) believed on reasonable grounds that his behaviour had not required or encouraged another person to engage in behaviour which, if engaged in by the first person, would have amounted to market abuse; or (ii) had taken all reasonable precautions and exercised all due diligence to avoid requiring or encouraging another person to engage in behaviour, which if engaged in by the first person would have amounted to market abuse (s.123(2) and MAR 1.1.6).

The FSA is required by virtue of s.124 of the Act to publish a statement **14–008** of its policy as to when penalties will be imposed and the quantum of such penalties. The statement includes an indication of when a person will be regarded as having a reasonable belief that his behaviour did not amount to market abuse or having taken reasonable precautions and exercised due diligence to avoid engaging in market abuse. The FSA's statement is contained in the Enforcement manual.

The enforcement of the requirements contained in the Code or Market Abuse falls upon the the FSA's Regulatory Decisions Committee. The Committee has the power to impose financial penalties, order public censure of miscreants or direct the restitution of money to those who have been the victims of market abuse where such abuse has been found to have taken place. This last is obviously of considerable interest to wronged investors. There is a right of appeal from the decision of the Regulatory Decisions Committee to an independent statutory tribunal. Only after an appeal has been completed may any penalty be enforced or there be any publication of the decision of the original Committee. The operation of this committee is covered in detail in Part 4 of this book.

In addition, the FSA can also enforce the market abuse regime through civil remedies including court injunctions where these are appropriate, or through its own administrative processes.

The Scope of the Market Abuse Regime

14–009 S.118(1) of the Act defines market abuse as behaviour which amongst other things "occurs in relation to qualifying investments traded on a market to which this section applies." The Treasury is permitted to prescribe markets and qualifying investments by virtue of s.118(3). This has been achieved in the FSMA 2000 (Prescribed Markets and Qualifying Investments) Order (SI 2001/996). All markets established under the rules of one of the following have been designated as prescribed markets:

- COREDEAL Limited;
- The International Petroleum Exchange of London Limited;
- Jiway Limited;
- LIFFE Administration and Management;
- The London Metal Exchange Limited;
- London Stock Exchange plc;
- OM London Exchange Limited;
- Virt-x plc.

Qualifying Investments

14–010 A qualifying investment is any investment of a kind which is admitted to trading under the rules of any market prescribed by Art.2. (Art.3(2) of the Prescribed Markets and Qualifying Investments Order SI 2001/996). In the majority of cases it will be obvious whether an investment is traded on a prescribed market. To avoid doubt the Code sets out at MAR 1.11.3, what types of investments would be traded on a prescribed market. These are:

(i) investments which have not yet traded subject to the rules of a prescribed market from the point they start trading subject to the rules of a prescribed market (including first trade);

(ii) investments which are currently trading subject to the rules of a prescribed market; and

(iii) investments which have traded in the past and can still be traded subject to the rules of a prescribed market.

The Regular User Test (MAR 1.2)

The concept of the "regular user" is central to the market abuse regime as **14–011** market abuse is defined by reference to the standards of behaviour that a regular user would expect of a person in the position of the person in question. A "regular user" is defined in s.118(1) as "in relation to a particular market means a reasonable person who regularly deals on that market in investments of the kind in question." For behaviour to amount to market abuse it must fall short of the standards of behaviour which a user of the market could reasonably expect from a person in the position of the person in question. The regular user test is analogous to the ubiquitous "reasonable man on the Clapham omnibus" as it is clear that the regular user is simply a hypothetical user of the market rather than a particular or actual user. Behaviour amounting to market abuse will be determined by considering objectively whether a hypothetical reasonable person familiar with the market in question would regard the behaviour as acceptable in the light of all the relevant circumstances (MAR 1.2.2).

In practice a distinction may well be drawn between the standard of **14–012** behaviour that may be tolerated by actual users of the market (normal market practice) and the standard of behaviour which is consistent with an objectively acceptable standard when the regular user test is applied. Where historically, behaviour has been accepted by actual market users this will be a relevant consideration in determining whether such behaviour falls within the standard expected but it will not be determinative. In circumstances where there is a range of practices which are generally accepted by users of the market, each practice will have to be judged objectively on its own merit (MAR 1.2.10). However, it is clear from the Code that the concept of the hypothetical regular user should not operate in a vacuum entirely divorced from the standards that actually prevail in the market. The balancing of the objective test of behaviour acceptable to the hypothetical regular user and the subjective elements introduced by taking into account the actual accepted behaviour of users in a market may well create tensions in practice. There may of course be obvious examples of where actual tolerated behaviour is clearly unacceptable to the objective regular user such as the widespread misuse of information A further factor which may well assist in determining how the regular user test will be applied is that firms which are authorised have been obliged to comply with the requirements of the FSA's Principles for Businesses including the requirement that a firm must observe proper standards of market conduct. (The

FSA Principle for Business 5: Market Conduct (previously Principle 3)). It seems highly probable that where a "normal market practice" has been or is acceptable for the purposes of the FSA Principles for Businesses then it is unlikely to fall foul of the regular user test. The Code gives detailed guidance as to the types of behaviour that would not be regarded as acceptable (see MAR 1.4 to MAR 1.6). However, it should be noted that the Code is not intended to be exhaustive in its descriptions of behaviour that does or does not amount to market abuse. It is open to a person to seek guidance from the FSA about his proposed behaviour if he is in any doubt as to whether it would be acceptable or otherwise (MAR 1.2.13).

The Standard of Behaviour Expected

14–013 Whether behaviour falls below the standards expected will require the regular user to consider all the circumstances of the behaviour including:

(i) the characteristics of the market in question, the investments traded on that market, and the users of the market;

(ii) the rules and regulations of the market in question and any applicable laws;

(iii) prevailing market mechanisms, practices and codes of conduct applicable to the market in question;

(iv) the position of the person in question and the standards reasonably expected at the time of the behaviour in the light of that person's experience, level of skill and standard of knowledge. The standard expected of a retail investor will be different from that expected of a market professional;

(v) the need for market users to conduct their affairs in a manner that does not compromise the fair and efficient operation of the market as a whole or unfairly damage the interests of investors.

14–014 The Code anticipates that the regular user will recognise that it is in the interests of all market users that the market functions properly. The standard of behaviour which is to be reasonably expected of persons using a market will be one that takes into account the need for the market as a whole to operate fairly and efficiently. The objective standard applied to assess behaviour will also be influenced by the type of person engaged in that behaviour. Different standards may well be expected in relation to retail investors, professional market participants or public sector bodies. The factors which must be considered in this context are the experience, levels of skill and the standard of knowledge that a regular user would expect from a person in that position. Further, where a public sector body is involved, account will have to be taken of their statutory and other official functions.

It may be that with the benefit of hindsight, certain behaviour which has historically been viewed as normal market practice may no longer pass the regular user test. However, when making such an assessment, the FSA will assess the behaviour in the light of the circumstances which applied at the time. So if behaviour would have been viewed as acceptable at the time when it was carried out then there would be no finding that that person has engaged in market abuse.

Applying the regular user test, it is unlikely that a mistake would amount to market abuse in circumstances where it could be shown that the person or firm in question had taken reasonable care to prevent such mistakes and to detect them once they had occurred (MAR 1.2.6).

Variations in Conduct Across Different Markets

The FSA recognises that practices vary across different markets (MAR 1.2.7). The standard against which the behaviour is to be assessed will partially depend on the market in which in takes place and on the type of investments concerned. **14–015**

The growing internationalisation of markets also means that attention will be paid to the local rules, practices and conventions prevailing on non-UK markets where the behaviour which occurs abroad has an impact on a prescribed market in the United Kingdom when determining what standards are reasonably to be expected of the person trading the non-UK market (MAR 1.2.9). However, just because behaviour complies with the requirements of an overseas market it does not mean that it will automatically fulfill the requirements of the UK market abuse regime. It seems probable that the FSA will adopt an approach similar to that adopted in the Price Stabilising Rules where the FSA recognises the stabilisation rules of another authority only when they deliver broadly equivalent protection to the FSA's own rules.

It has already been seen that the focus of the market abuse regime is on the effects of behaviour on the market and does not focus on the intent behind such behaviour (MAR 1.2.5). The statutory definition does not require the person engaging in the behaviour to have intended to abuse the market. An intention to abuse the market need not be present in order that it can be shown that there has been actual market abuse. The Code recgonises, however, that in reality there will be situations when it will be necessary to look at the intention which lies behind the behaviour which resulted in Market abuse to see what the purpose was of the person in question. Abuse of the market may not be the only purpose behind particular behaviour but it will be the actuating purpose. The actuating purpose is defined as "a purpose which motivates or incites a person to act". **14–016**

Compliance with Other Applicable Rules

Behaviour which has taken place in compliance with other applicable rules including the rules of a prescribed market, the Takeover Code or FSA rules, may still be such that it amounts to market abuse. This is so because other applicable rules may not be specifically directed at the types of **14–017** behaviour prohibited by the Act. However, the FSA is likely to give greater weight to a rule that expressly requires or permits particular behaviour. On the other side, a failure to comply with other applicable rules does not automatically mean that such behaviour would amount to market abuse. If the prescribed market or Takeover Panel has granted dispensation from or given guidance in advance on its rules this is likely to be a relevant factor in considering whether the particular behaviour amounts to market abuse. It is expected that the FSA will attach considerable weight to the views of the Takeover Panel in interpreting and applying the Takeover Code and SARs (MAR1.2.8).

Behaviour

14–018 Behaviour is defined in the Annex C to the draft Code as "any kind of conduct, including action or inaction" (MAR1.3). An example of where inaction may amount to market abuse would be where a person is under a legal or regulatory obligation to make a particular disclosure and does not do so (MAR 1.3.2). The Code at MAR 1.3.1 sets out the types of behaviour which fall within the scope of the market abuse regime, however it should be noted that these types of behaviour are not intended to be exhaustive. Behaviour that falls within the market abuse regime includes

- dealing in qualifying investments;
- dealing in commodities or investments which are the subject matter or whose price is determined by reference to a qualifying investment (in this case, the commodity will be a "relevant product" in relation to the qualifying investment);
- acting as an arranger in respect of qualifying investment;
- causing or procuring or advising others to deal in qualifying investments;
- making statements or representations or otherwise disseminating information which is likely to be regarded by the regular user as relevant to determining the terms on which transaction in qualifying investments should be effected;
- providing corporate finance advice and conducting corporate finance activities in qualifying investments; and
- managing qualifying investments belonging to another.

14–019 Behaviour which is capable of amounting to market abuse must take place within the United Kingdom or must be in relation to qualifying investments traded on a market to which this s.118 applies which is situated in the United Kingdom or which is accessible electronically in the United Kingdom (see s.118 (5)).

Behaviour Occurring in Relation to Qualifying Investments

14–20 Behaviour amounting to market abuse must occur in relation to qualifying investments by virtue of s.118(1)(a) of the Act (MAR 1.11.6–9). The type of behaviour which is to be regarded as occurring in relation to qualifying investments is set out in s.118(6) of the Act as including behaviour which:

"(a) occurs in relation to anything which is the subject matter, or whose price or value is expressed by reference to the price or value, of those qualifying investments; or

(b) occurs in relation to investments (whether qualifying or not) whose subject matter is those qualifying investment."

Clearly this definition of what is behaviour in relation to a qualifying investment is not exhaustive. What is plain is that there must be a clear relationship between the behaviour and a qualifying investment for the behaviour to be regarded as occurring in relation to a qualifying investment. Subs.6(a) brings behaviour which takes place in relation to other investments which are not themselves qualifying investments as such behaviour can have a damaging effect on the confidence of prescribed markets. Such related investments are referred to in the Code as relevant products (MAR 1.11.8). MAR 1.11.9 lists relevant products which may come within this section. **14–021**

Subs.6(b) brings investments which are derivatives of qualifying investments (*e.g.* options on options) within the scope of s.118. Further, investments which are not themselves qualifying investments may fall within the scope of s.118 if their price is expressed by reference to the price or value of qualifying investments, *e.g.* spread betting. Examples are given in the code of where something will be the subject matter of an investment or qualifying investment where there is a clear (contractual or documented) relationship between the two (see MAR 1.11.10). The Code also sets out examples of the price or value relationship between qualifying investment and a relevant product (MAR 1.11.11). **14–022**

Misuse of Information (MAR 1.4)

The market abuse regime introduced by the Act significantly extends the scope of the measures available to prevent the misuse of information to markets beyond those encompassed by the provisions relating to insider dealing found in Pt V of the Criminal Justice Act 1993 which are limited to offences in relation to the securities markets. The regime under s.118 and the Code will also apply to markets in commodity derivatives and financial futures. S.118(2) of the Act defines behaviour based on the misuse of information as: **14–023**

> "behaviour which is based on information which is not generally available to those using the market but which, if available to a regular user of the market, would or would be likely to be regarded by him as relevant when deciding the terms on which transaction in investments of the kind in question should be effected."

Like the insider dealing legislation, this aspect of the regime is designed to maintain investors' confidence in the market by ensuring that all market users have the same access to information. In practice, the extent to which market users may reasonably expect to have access to information will **14–024** differ between different markets and this is recognised by the Code (MAR 1.4.3).

14–025 It will be a misuse of information where a person deals or arranges deals in any qualifying investment or relevant product where all four of the following conditions are present (MAR 1.4.4):

"(1) the dealing or arranging is based on information. The person must be in possession of information and the information must have a material influence on the decision to engage in the dealing or arranging. The information must be one of the reasons for the dealing or arranging, but need not be the only reason;
(2) the information must be information which is not generally available. (See MAR 1.4.5E).
(3) the information must be likely to be regarded by a regular user as relevant when deciding the terms on which transaction in the investments of thekind in question should be effected. Such information is referred to in the Code as 'relevant information'. The factors to be taken into account are set out in MAR 1.4.9 to 1.4.11.
(4) the information must relate to matters which the regular user would reasonably expect to be disclosed to users of the particular prescribed market. This includes matters which give rise to such an expectation of disclosure or are likely to do so either at the time in question, or in the future". (See MAR 1.4.12 and 1.4.13).

Generally Available (MAR 1.4.5–1.4.8)

14–026 By virtue of s.118 (7) of the Act, "Information which can be obtained by research or analysis conducted by, or on behalf of, users of a market is to be regarded for the purposes of this section as being generally available to them". The Code of Market Conduct sets out a number of pointers, the presence of one or more of which will indicate whether particular information is generally available (MAR 1.4.5). These are

(1) whether the information has been disclosed through an accepted channel for dissemination of information or otherwise under the rules of a prescribed market;

(2) whether the information is contained in records which by virtue of any enactment are open to inspection by the public;

(3) whether the information has otherwise been made public or is derived from information which has been made public;

(4) whether the information can be obtained by observation.

14–027 Information which has been obtained through diligent research, analysis or other legitimate means including the observation of a public event is information which is generally available even if others do not have access to it because of lack of resources, expertise or competence (MAR 1.4.6). Examples of information which might be obtainable through legitimate research will include information which is only available overseas and has not been published or otherwise made available to the public in the United Kingdom or where the information is only available on payment of a fee (MAR 1.4.7).

An accepted channel for dissemination of information is defined as "an approved channel of communication whereby information concerning investments traded on the market is formally disseminated to other market users on a structured and equitable basis". In practice it will be necessary to look at the rules of the particular prescribed market to see what rules apply to the dissemination of information concerning trading on that market (see Annex C of the Code).

Relevant Information (MAR 1.4.9–1.4.11)

Whether information is likely to be regarded as relevant information by a regular user will depend on the circumstances of the case. The factors which will may taken into account by a regular user when deciding whether or not information is relevant include (MAR 1.4.9): **14–028**

(1) how specific and precise the information is;

(2) how material the information is;

(3) how current the information is;

(4) how reliable the information is, including how near the person providing the information is, or appears to be to the original source of that information;

(5) other material information which is already generally available to inform a regular user of the market; and

(6) the extent to which the information differs from information which is generally available and can therefore be said to new or fresh information.

Where the information relates to possible future developments, the Code suggests two further factors which are to be taken into account when determining whether that information is relevant information, these are (MAR 1.4.10): **14–029**

(1) whether the information provides, with reasonable certainty, grounds to conclude that the possible future developments will, in fact, occur; and

(2) the significance those developments would assume for a regular user given their occurrence.

The Code gives examples of relevant information at MAR 1.4.11.

Disclosure of Information on an Equal Basis (MAR 1.4.12–18)

During the consultation process it became clear that the reality of markets was such that it is impossible for every piece of information to be made known on an equal and simultaneous basis all market participants. The **14–030**

Code does not therefore require all information to be disclosed in such a way but requires instead that the information in question must relate to matters which a regular user would reasonably expect to be disclosed to other market participants on a equal basis. Such information will be either "disclosable information" or "announceable information" (MAR 1.4.12). In respect of information relating to possible future developments, whether the information provides, with reasonable certainty, grounds to conclude that the possible future developments will occur and that a disclosure announcement will be made must also be taken into consideration (MAR 1.4.13).

14–031 Disclosable information includes information which is required to be disseminated under the Takeover Code or SAR's on, or in relation to, qualifying investments traded on a prescribed market; information relating to officially listed securities which is required to be disclosed under the Listing Rules; and information which is required to be disclosed to a prescribed market under the rules of an RIE. (MAR 1.4.14)

14–032 Announceable information includes information which is to be the subject of an official announcement by government, central monetary or fiscal authorities or regulatory authorities; changes to published credit ratings of companies whose securities are qualifying investments or relevant products; and changes to the constituents of a securities index where the securities are qualifying investments or relevant products (MAR 1.4.15). Information which is not announceable information includes surveys or research based on information generally available *e.g.* CBI surveys or MORI polls (MAR 1.4.16)

Safe Harbours

14–033 The Code sets out a number of examples of behaviour that would not amount to market abuse in that such behaviour would not constitute a misuse of information (MAR 1.4.19). These include where the dealing or arranging deals was required in order to comply with a legal (including contractual) or regulatory obligation where such an obligation existed before the relevant information came into the person's possession (MAR 1.4.20). Dealing or arranging deals would not amount to a misuse of information where the possession of relevant information that was not generally available did not influence the decision to engage in the dealing or arranging to deal. This obviously begs the question of how to demonstrate that possession of relevant information did not influence a person, some guidance is given by the Code in that it will be presumed that the person's possession of information did not influence his decision to deal or arrange to deal if the person had taken a firm decision to deal or arrange to deal before he got the relevant information and the receipt of such information did not change the terms on which the person proposed to enter into the transaction (MAR 1.4.21, 1.4.22).

14–034 Where it is an organisation that is dealing and individuals within the organisation are in possession of relevant information it will be presumed that this had no influence on the organisation's decision to deal or arrange to deal if none of those in possession of the information had any involvement in the decision to deal or behaved in such a way to influence, directly or indirectly, the decision to deal or had any contact with those who made the decision to deal by which the information could be transmitted (MAR 1.4.23). Relevant information does not influence the decision to deal if it has been held behind an effective Chinese wall. (MAR 1.4.24).

Trading Information

Dealing or arranging deals will not amount to a misuse of information solely because it is based on information as to the person's or another person's intention to deal or arrange a deal in a qualifying investment. This safe harbour excludes dealing or arranging deals based on information as to a possible takeover bid or deals based on information relating to new offers, issue, placements or other primary market activity (MAR 1.4.26). **14–035**

Dealing or arranging deals do not amount to a misuse of information if it is engaged in by a person (or someone acting for him or his associate) in circumstances where the dealing or arranging of deals was in connection with the acquisition or disposal of an equity or non-equity stake in a company and was engaged in for the sole purpose of making such an acquisition or disposal and was for the sole benefit of the person making the acquisition or disposal. Furthermore the information in question must relate to one or more of the following facts: that investments of a particular kind have been or are to be acquired or disposed of, or that their acquisition or disposal is under consideration or the subject of negotiation; that investments of a particular kind have not been or are not to be acquired or disposed of; the number of investments acquired or disposed of, or to be acquired or disposed of, or whose acquisition or disposal is under consideration or the subject of negotiations; the price (or range of prices) at which investments have been, or are to be acquired or disposed of, or the price (or range of prices) at which the investments whose acquisition or disposal is under consideration or the subject of negotiation may be acquired or disposed or; the identity of the persons involved, or likely to be involved, in any capacity in an acquisition or disposal (MAR 1.4.28).

False or Misleading Impressions

The market forces of supply and demand should determine the price or value of investments traded on prescribed markets and there is an expectation that the price or value of investments and the volume of trading will reflect such market forces. Any activity which gives market users a false or misleading impression of the price, value or volume of trading will undermine confidence in the market and ultimately be to the detriment of all market users including investors. The Code of Market Abuse seeks to regulate behaviour so that the creation of false or misleading impressions is avoided. Behaviour giving rise to a false or misleading **14–036** impression is defined by s.118(2)(b) of the Act as "behaviour [which] is likely to give a regular user of the market a false or misleading impression as to the supply of, or demand for, or as to the price or value of, investments of the kind in question."

False or Misleading Impression: the Test

14–037 The Code sets out a two fold test of what will fall within the scope of false or misleading impressions. MAR 1.5.4 says that in order to fall within the false or misleading impressions test:

> "(1) the behaviour must be likely to give the regular user a false or misleading impression. Behaviour will amount to market abuse if the behaviour engaged in is likely to give rise to, or give an impression of, a price or value or volume of trading which is materially false or misleading; and
>
> (2) in order to be likely, there must be a real and not a fanciful likelihood that the behaviour will have such an effect, although the effect need not be more likely than not. The behaviour may, or may be likely to, give rise to more than one effect, including the effect in question."

14–038 The Code goes on to set out the factors which will be taken into account when determining whether or not behaviour is likely to give the regular user of the market a false or misleading impression as to the levels of supply, demand, price or value of a qualifying investment or relevant product. The Code sets out five general factors but does not exclude the possibility there may be other additional factors which may have a bearing. The Code also recognises that there may be some overlap between behaviour which amounts to creating a false or misleading impression and bahviour which gives rise to market distortion (MAR 1.6). The general facts to be taken into account are set out in MAR 1.5.5:

(1) the experience and knowledge of the users of the market in question;

(2) the structure of the market, including its reporting, notification and transparency requirements;

(3) the legal and regulatory requirements of the market concerned and accepted market practices;

(4) the identity and position of the person responsible for the behaviour which has been observed (if known); and

(5) the extent and nature of the visibility or disclosure or the person's activity.

Artificial Transactions (MAR 1.5.8)

14–039 "Behaviour will constitute market abuse where

> (1) a person enters into a transaction or series of transactions in a qualifying investment or relevant product; and

(2) the principal effect of the transaction or transactions on the market will be, or will be likely to be, to inflate, maintain or depress the apparent supply of, or the apparent demand for, or the apparent price or value of a qualifying investment or relevant product so that a false or misleading impression is likely to be given to the regular user; and
(3) the person knows, or could reasonably be expected to know, that the principal effect of the transaction or transactions on the market will be, or will likely to be, as set out in MAR 1.5.8E(2);
unless the regular user would regard:
(4) the principal rationale for the transaction in question as a legitimate commercial rationale; and
(5) the way in which the transaction is to be executed is proper."

The making of a profit or the avoidance of a loss is not of itself sufficient to establish a legitimate commercial rationale for a transaction. It is necessary to look at the purpose behind a transaction. The purpose need not be the only purpose but it must be the actuating purpose. (An "actuating purpose" is defined as a purpose which motivates or incites a person to act.) If the purpose behind a transaction was to induce others to trade or to move the price of the relevant investment or product this is unlikely to be considered as a transaction having a legitimate commercial rationale (MAR 1.5.9). **14–040**

The fair and efficient operation of the market as a whole requires that transactions be executed in a proper way. Where a transaction was executed in such a way that a false or misleading impression was created this would be to the detriment of the market as a whole (MAR 1.5.10). **14–041**

The factors which may be taken into account when determining whether a person's behaviour amounts to market abuse by creating an artificial market includes those set out below. It should be noted however, that the presence of one or more of these factors does not automatically mean that there has been market abuse by the creation of an artificial market. The factors are: **14–042**

"(1) whether the transaction causes or contributes to an increase (or decrease) in the supply of, or demand for, or the price or value of a qualifying investment or relevant product and the person has an interest in the level of the supply of, or the demand for, or the price or value of the qualifying investment or relevant product;
(2) whether the transaction involves the placing of buy and sell orders at prices higher or lower than the market price, or the placing of buy and sell orders which increase the volume of trading;
(3) whether the transaction coincides with a time at or around which the supply of, or the demand for, or the price or value of a qualifying investment or relevant product is relevant to the calculation of reference prices, settlement prices, and valuations;
(4) whether those involved in the transaction are connected parties;
(5) whether the transaction causes the market price of the investment in question to increase or decrease, following the market price immediately returns to its previous level;
(6) whether a person places a bid (or offer) which is higher (or lower) than the previous bid (or offer) only to remove the bid (or offer) from the market before it is executed."

14–043 In addition, the extent to which the transaction generally either opens a new position, so creating exposure to market risk, or closes out a position so removing market risk will tend to suggest that the transaction is likely to have a legitimate commercial rationale. Examples of transactions which typically have a legitimate commercial rationale include "permitted transactions" (see MAR 1.5.24C below)(MAR 1.5.12).

14–044 Examples of behaviour which might give rise to a false or misleading impression in respect of which there may not be a legitimate commercial rationale include arrangements for the sale or purchase of a qualifying investment or relevant product where there is no change in beneficial interest or market risk or, if there is such a transfer it is between persons acting in concert or collusion and where a transaction is designed to conceal the ownership of a qualifying investment or relevant product so as to avoid disclosure requirements, such transactions are often structured so that risk remains with the seller. Fictitious transactions would also obviously not have a legitimate commercial rationale (MAR 1.5.14).

Dissemination of Information (MAR 1.5.15)

14–045 Behaviour will amount to market abuse where a person disseminates information which would be relevant information if it were true and the person know, or could reasonably be expected to know, that the information is false or misleading and the information is disseminated for the purpose of creating a false or misleading impression. Although the creation of a false or misleading impression need not be the only purpose for the dissemination of the information, it must be the actuating purpose. In other words the purpose for which the information is disseminated must be the purpose which motivates or incites the person to act. Whether or not a person has an interest in a qualifying investment or relevant product (MAR 1.5.13E) is one factor to be taken into consideration when determining what the purpose is of the person disseminating the information. (MAR 1.5.16) However, just because a person has no interest in the qualifying investment or relevant product does not automatically mean that the behaviour does not amount to market abuse. An example of disseminating false or misleading information would be if information purporting to be about a potential takeover bid that was not true was posted on an internet bulletin board (MAR 1.5.17).

Dissemination of Information Through Accepted Channels

14–046 An accepted channel for the dissemination of information is an approved channel of communication whereby information concerning investments traded on the market is formally disseminated to other market users on a structured and equitable basis. Users of such information should be able to rely on the accuracy and integrity of information coming through such accepted channels. Those who disseminate information through accepted channels such as companies themselves, companies' financial advisors or their public relations advisors are required under the Code to take reasonable care to ensure that the information is neither inaccurate nor misleading. Failure to do so may constitute behaviour amounting to market abuse. Behaviour will amount to market abuse in this context, where a person who is responsible for the submission of information to an accepted channel for dissemination, submits information which would be relevant information if it were true and which is likely to give a false or misleading impression to a regular user as to the supply of, demand for, the price or value of a qualifying investment or relevant product and the person responsible for submitting such information has not taken reasonable care to ensure that the information is not false or misleading.

Course of Conduct (MAR 1.5.21)

It would be a market abuse where a person engages in a course of conduct, the principal effect of which is to create a false or misleading impression to the regular user of the supply of, demand for, price of value of a qualifying investment or relevant product and the person engaging in such a course of conduct either knew or could reasonably have been expected to know that the main effect of such conduct would be the creation of such a false or misleading impression. Such behaviour would not amount to market abuse if there was a legitimate commercial rationale for the conduct (MAR 1.5.9), and the way in which the conduct was engaged in was proper (MAR 1.5.10). **14–047**

Safe Harbours (MAR 1.5.24, 1.5.25, 1.5.27 and 1.5.28)

The Code gives examples of behaviour which would not amount to market abuse. **14–048**

Permitted Transactions (MAR 1.5.24)

(i) Certain types of transactions will be viewed as permitted transactions and thus will not constitute behaviour amounting to market abuse even though the conditions set out in MAR 1.5.8E(1)-(5) are fulfilled. Permitted transactions are transactions "which effect the taking of a position, or the unwinding of a position taken, so as to take legitimate advantage of: (a) differences in the taxation of income or capital returns generated by investments or commodities (whether such differences arise solely because of the identity of the person entitled to receive such income or capital or otherwise); or (b) differences in the prices of investments or commodities as traded in different locations; or

(ii) transactions which effect the lending or borrowing of qualifying investments or commodities so as to meet an underlying commercial demand for the investment or commodity."

Required Reporting or Disclosure of Transactions (MAR 1.5.25)

The creation of a false or misleading impression will not arise by way of the making of a report or disclosure, if that report or disclosure is made in accordance with applicable legal or regulatory requirements and such a **14–049** report or disclosure is expressly required or permitted by the rules made by the FSA under the Act in accordance with s.417(1) of the Act including (a) a Principle (see the FSA Handbook "Principles for Businesses) and (b) an evidential provision, by the rules of a prescribed market (*e.g.* rule 9.10(j) of the Listing Rules), the rules of the Takeover Code or the SARs or by any other applicable statute (*e.g.* s.198 of the Companies Act 1985) or regulation or the rules of any competent statutory governmental or regulatory authority.

Chinese Walls (MAR 1.5.27)

14–050 Where a "person" who disseminates information is in reality an individual within an organisation (whether that organisation is a company, a partnership, a trust or an unincorporated association), the individual who disseminates information which he would know or could reasonably be expected to know, was false or misleading if he was aware of information held by other individuals within the organisation, he will not be behaving in a way which would amount to market abuse if the other information is held behind an effective Chinese wall or some similar arrangement. (A Chinese wall is defined as "an arrangement that requires information held by a person (organisation) in the course of carrying on one part of its business to be withheld from or not to be used for, persons with or for whom it acts in the course of carrying on another part of its business".) Further, there must be nothing known or which ought to have been known to the individual who disseminated the information which should have led him to conclude that the information was false or misleading. The fact that a person did not know or could not have reasonably been expected to know that information was false or misleading can be demonstrated by showing that the requirements in MAR 1.4.22 (dealing or arranging not based on information) have been satisfied.

Journalists

14–051 An example of how the Code has a wider application than the old financial services regime which was largely restricted to authorised persons is that financial journalists dealing as an "insider" on information that is not generally available or publishing misleading information with a view to influencing the prices of shares will be covered by the regime and could be fined or publically censured by the FSA.

Distortion of the Market (MAR 1.6)

14–052 Distortion of the market undermines general confidence in the market and can have a damaging effect on efficiency generally which is bad for all market users including investors. The FSA recognises that this section of the Code is viewed by many commentators and market users as controversial. In particular, there has been a widespread concern that the scope of "distortion" is such that in addition to covering behaviour which, left unchecked, would have a detrimental effect on the confidence of the markets and investors interests, "distortion" as described in the Code also potentially covers legitimate behaviour. S.118(2)(c) of the Act defines behaviour amounting to distortion of the market as : "a regular user of the market would, or would be likely to, regard the behaviour as behaviour which would, or would be likely to, distort the market in investments of the kind in question".

The definition of distortion then depends on what is acceptable behaviour pertaining to a particular market. There is no universal definition of distortion which covers the broad range of markets, instead the Code seeks to establish benchmarks against which behaviour may be judged when trying to determine whether or not a market has been the subject of distortion. Furthermore, it should be borne in mind that there may well be situations in which behaviour which amounts to market abuse by distortion the market will also fall within the scope of behaviour that gives rise to a false or misleading impression and thus is an abuse of the market (see MAR 1.5).

Market Distortion: the Test (MAR 1.6.4)

MAR 1.6.4 sets out the test of what is necessary for behaviour to amount distortion of the market. MAR 1.6.4 states that: **14–053**

> "In order to fall within the distortion test:
>
> (1) the behaviour must be such that a regular user would, or would be likely to, regard it as behaviour which would, or would be likely to, distort the market in the investment in question. Behaviour will amount to market abuse if the behaviour engaged in interferes with the proper operation of market forces with the purpose of positioning prices at a distorted level. This need not be the sole purpose of entering into the transaction or transactions, but it must be an actuating purpose; and
> (2) in order to be likely, there must be a real and not fanciful likelihood that the behaviour will have such an effect, although the effect need not be more likely than not. The behaviour may, or may be likely to, give rise to more than one effect, including the effect in question."

Behaviour which gives rise to market distortion falls under two main headings, these are price positioning and abusive squeezes.

Price Positioning (MAR 1.6.9–12)

Price positioning is where a person enters into a transaction or series of transactions for the main purpose of positioning the price of a qualifying investment or relevant product at a distorted level either above or below that price which would normally be dictated by the operation of the market. Transactions entered into for the purpose of distorting the price of **14–054** an investment cannot have a legitimate commercial rationale behind them. The factors which will be taken into account when considering whether or not a person has engaged in behaviour designed to distort the price of an investment will include the extent to which the person's timing of the transaction(s) coincided with the calculation of reference prices, settlement prices and valuations, *e.g.* at close of trading or the end of a quarter; the extent to which the person had an interest whether directly or indirectly in the price or value of the qualifying investment or relevant product; the size of the person's trading in comparison to the reasonable expectations of the depth and liquidity of the market at the time; the extent to which the volatility of the price, rate or option movements are outside the normal range for a period whether that be intra-day, day, weekly or monthly; whether the market returned to its previous level following the change in price caused by the person's transaction(s); and whether a person has successively and consistently increased or decreased his bid, offer or the price he has paid for a qualifying investment or relevant product.

Abusive Squeezes (MAR 1.6.13–18)

14–055 Abusive squeezes occur when there is a positioning of a price at a level which is materially different from the level had it been left to the proper market forces of supply and demand. Left unchecked, abusive squeezes damage both liquidity in the market and confidence in the market as a whole. An abusive squeeze is where a person engages in behaviour for the main purpose of positioning at a distorted level the price at which others have to deliver or take delivery of or defer delivery to satisfy their obligations. The person engaging in the behaviour must have a significant influence over the supply of demand for, or delivery mechanisms for a qualifying investment or relevant product and that person has a position either directly or indirectly in an investment under which quantities of the qualifying investment or relevant product in question are deliverable.

In determining whether or not a person has been involved in an abusive squeeze the following factors must be considered: the price and the extent to which a person is willing to relax his control or other influence in order to maintain an orderly market; the extent to which a person's activity causes, or risks causing, settlement default by other market users; the extent to which prices under the delivery mechanisms of the market diverge from the prices for delivery of the investment outside those mechanisms; the extent to which the spot or immediate market compared to the forward market is unusually expensive or cheap or the extent to which borrowing rates are unusually high or low.

Safe Harbours (MAR 1.6.19)

14–056 The behaviour expected of long position holders will not amount to distortion of the market and market abuse if the behaviour complies with the London Metal Exchange rules: "Market Aberrations: The Way Forward" (October 1998)

Statutory Exceptions

Behaviour Which is Not Market Abuse (MAR 1.7)

S.118(8) of the Act states that "Behaviour does not amount to market abuse if it conforms with a rule which includes a provision to the effect that behaviour conforming with the rule does not amount to market abuse.". The Code describes behaviour that in the opinion of the FSA does not amount to market abuse. Behaviour which falls within one of the relevant sections of the Code is to be taken conclusively as not amounting to market abuse for the purpose of the Act, these are called safe harbours and are identified within the Code by the letter C. (MAR 1.1.10). The relevant sections of the Code which contain "safe harbours" are MAR 1.4.20C, MAR 1.4.21C, MAR 1.4.24C, MAR 1.4.26C, MAR 1.4.28C, MAR 1.5.24C, MAR 1.5.25C, MAR 1.5.27C, MAR 1.5.27C, MAR1.5.28C and MAR 1.6.19C. **14–057**

In addition, behaviour which conforms to an FSA rule which includes a provision that compliance with that rule would not amount to market abuse must expressly permit or require the person to engage in the behaviour in question (MAR 1.7.2). The FSA rules which contain a provision to the effect that behaviour conforming to that rule does not amount to market abuse are: **14–058**

(i) the Price Stabilising rules made under ss.144(1) and 144(3) of the Act (MAR 2);

(ii) the rules relating to Chinese walls (COB 2.4) and (MAR 1.4.23C and MAR 1.5.27C);

(iii) those parts of the Listing Rules which relate to the timing, dissemination or availability, content and standard of care applicable to a disclosure, announcement, communication or release of information. See MAR 1 Annex G;

(iv) rule 15.1(b) of the Listing Rules (relating to share buy-backs).

Also in this context, the FSA has made it clear that it is satisfied that the Takeover Code and SARs do not permit or require behaviour which amounts to market abuse (MAR 1.7.6).

Interaction between FSA Code and Takeover Code

S.120 of the Act permits the Financial Services Authority to include provision in the Code for Market Abuse to the effect that behaviour which conforms to the City Code on Takeovers and Mergers issued by the Panel on Takeovers and Mergers does not amount the market abuse per se (s.120(1)(a)); does not amount to market abuse in specified circumstances **14–059** (s.120(1)(b)); or does not amount to market abuse if engaged in by a specified type of person (s.120(1)(c)).

The Code: A Civil or Criminal Regime?

14–060 There is considerable debate as to whether the new regime is to be viewed as civil or criminal. The Governments intention was to create a civil regime applicable to all market users where the standard to be applied to suspected breaches was the civil test of the balance of probabilities. A number of leading commentators, most notably Lord Lester of Herne Hill Q.C. and Javan Herberg (Counsel's Opinions on the "Impact of the ECHR on the Draft Financial Services and Markets Bill" in *The Human Rights Act and the Criminal and Regulatory Process* (Oxford: Hart Publishing)) have concluded that the ambit of the market abuse regime was such that Art.6 of the European Convention on Human Rights required that the criminal standard of beyond reasonable doubt should apply. Further, the arguable uncertainty evident in some of the market abuse provisions in the Act and Code are such that it seems likely that these will prove fertile ground for challenges brought under Art.7 of the European Convention.

Restrictions on the Use of Compelled Statements

14–061 S.174(1) of the Act permits the admission into evidence of statements made to investigators in compliance with an information requirement subject to the usual rules governing the admissibility of evidence. However, by virtue of s.174(2) such compelled statements are not admissible in criminal proceedings (save for prosecutions for offences of making false statements) or in proceedings in relation to action to be taken against a person under s.123 of the Act.

Market Abuse: the European Directive

The Need for a European Directive

14–062 The pre-existing situation in Europe was that there were no common provisions in respect of the prevention of market manipulation. Each individual Member State has its own regulatory regime to deal with market manipulation, each with its own set of rules and legal requirements. Indeed in some Member States no legislation exists to address market manipulation nor is it always clear which body is responsible for dealing with such practices. These differences have a number of consequences leading to competitive distortions in the financial markets and generally hindering the establishment of a European financial market place based on a level playing field. Developments in the financial market place including the introduction of new products and technology and the increasing internationalisation of the markets leading to the establishment of cross-border trading means that interconnected markets are emerging which require a common legal framework to protect market integrity by setting across Europe standards for the prevention, detection, investigation and punishment of market abuse.

The Lisbon European Council made a commitment to integrate the **14–063**
European Financial markets by 2005 at the latest whilst the Stockholm European Council considered that every effort should be made towards integration by 2003 with priority being given to securities markets legislation. The aim of the Directive is to ensure the integrity of the European financial markets by implementing common standards across Europe in response to market abuse which in turn is intended to enhance investor confidence in the European markets. The stated objective of the Financial Services Action Plan is to "enhance market integrity by reducing the possibility for institutional investors and intermediaries to rig markets and to set common disciplines . . . to enhance investor confidence."

When the Commission put forward its proposal for a single market abuse **14–064**
directive in 2001, the Internal Market Commissioner, Frits Bolkestein set out the goals of the directive by saying:

> "This proposal represents a fundamental pillar of building an integrated European capital market by 2003. I want to enhance the integrity of European financial markets by establishing and implementing common standards against market abuse throughout Europe. This will boost investor confidence in our markets and help them to develop and grow. We must have common rules on what is allowable practice and what is not. Let me be clear: the European Union has no truck with greedy financial cheats. This proposal is an important step towards ensuring stable, transparent, integrated and efficient European markets for the benefit of every consumer and investor."

A Single Directive Against Market Abuse

To this end the European Commission has come to the view that there **14–065**
should be a single Market Abuse Directive which covers both insider dealing and market manipulation. The goal of a single directive is to introduce a single framework for the allocation of responsibilities, enforcement and co-operation thereby avoiding, it is hoped, potential inconsistencies and confusion. The theory being that a single directive will prove to be administratively simpler and have the effect of reducing the number of different rules and standards which apply across the member states of the European Union.

The Approach of the Directive

The Commission recognises that the Directive has to be sufficiently flexible **14–066**
to meet the needs of a rapidly changing market. Further, the provisions of the Directive are intended to extend beyond "regulated" markets so as to

ensure that other types of markets, Alternative Trading Systems and others are not being used for abusive purposes. However, the Directive is not intended to replace national provisions but rather it is envisaged that set a Community wide standard through which national regulatory regimes will converge so setting an across Europe standard of regulation.

The Directive

14–067 Article 1 of the Directive sets out a number of definitions including a definition of what is meant by "inside information" and by "market manipulation". Art.2 enjoins member states to "prohibit any natural or legal person who possesses inside information from taking advantage of that information by acquiring or disposing of for his account or for the account of a third party, either directly or indirectly, financial instruments to which that information relates." Art.5 prohibits "any natural or legal person from engaging in market manipulation." Annex B to the Directive sets out a list of methods commonly used for the purposes of manipulating the market although it is not intended to be exhaustive. Art.11 requires each member state to designate a single administrative authority as being competent to ensure that the provisions of the Directive are implemented. The necessary powers of such an authority are set out in Art.12 and include at least the right to:

(a) have access to any document and to receive a copy of it;

(b) demand information from any person, and if needed, to require the testimony of a person;

(c) carry out on-site inspections;

(d) require telephone and data traffic records;

(e) request the freezing and/or the sequestration of assets;

(f) request temporary prohibition of professional activity.

14–068 The Directive recognises that the sanctions necessary to ensure its implementation may cover the spectrum of both civil and criminal sanctions (Art.14) but that decision taken by the competent authority *may* (note not "*must*") be subject to the right to apply to the courts (Art.15). There is a requirement that the various competent authorities will co-operate with one another (Art.16) in particular in facilitating the exchange of information and co-operation in investigation activities.

Implementation in the UK

14–069 At the time of writing, the CESR Expert Group was analysing the responses from various member states to the draft Directive published in the Spring of 2003 before making recommendations to the Commission during the summer of 2003. Implementation of the finalised Directive is expected to take place in the UK no later than October 12, 2004 and again at the time of writing, the FSA was in the process of consulting with the Treasury on the UK's implementation strategy including consultations on any necessary changes to the existing legislation and to the Handbook. It is expected that the FSA will publish formal consultation papers in due course.

Part 4

Enforcing the New Regime

Chapter 15

Enforcement

Introduction

One of the principal ways in which the FSA seeks to pursue its regulatory objectives is through the use of its enforcement powers. These are contained in the FSMA and in the Enforcement Manual (ENF). The various enforcement powers and disciplinary measures available to the FSA are designed to deter future violations of the rules and to ensure that high standards of regulatory conduct are maintained. Consumer protection depends on the effective implementation of such measures, for example, the use of the power to require a firm to take immediate remedial action it intended to protect the interests of consumers which is preferable in many respects that the more traditional approach of punishment after the damage has been done. Furthermore, the FSA hopes through the use of its varied enforcement powers, to advance its objective of increasing public awareness it is expected that this will be achieved through the use of measures such as public censure and public statements of misconduct. In addition, the regulatory objective of market confidence is supported by the use by the FSA of its powers to bring criminal prosecutions for offences ranging from insider dealing to market abuse and for breaches of the proscribed regulations (*e.g.* the Money Laundering Regulations) which, if left unchecked would seriously undermine confidence in the financial markets. The use of criminal sanctions by the FSA is discussed in Ch.15 together with the use of certain civil penalties, in particular the power to impose a civil fine for a wide range of impropriety in the financial market place. **15–001**

The underlying principles governing the exercise of the powers of enforcement given to the FSA are that: **15–002**

(i) the effectiveness of the regulatory regime depends on the maintenance of an open and co-operative relationship between the FSA and those whom it regulates;

(ii) the FSA will seek to exercise its enforcement powers in a manner that is transparent, proportionate and consistent with publicly stated policies; and

(iii) the FSA will seek to ensure fair treatment when exercising its enforcement powers (ENF1.3.1)

In addition to its powers of enforcement, the FSA also has a range of regulatory tools at its disposal to help in the drive to meet its regulatory objectives. These include the power to conduct investigations which may lead to formal disciplinary action, the power of intervention and the power to obtain restitution. These powers are in addition to the other regulatory tools available to the FSA in the context of authorisation and the approval of persons in controlled functions which aim to ensure that the necessary criteria for engaging in regulated activities are fulfilled. Such criteria include honesty, competence and integrity. In addition, the FSA may decide that informal action may be the most appropriate approach in circumstances where the interests of the wider financial community would be better served by the maintenance of an established open and co-operative relationship between the regulator and those being supervised. Prompt remedial action by a firm is more likely to lead to the FSA taking informal action (ENF 1.3.4).

Information Gathering and Investigation Powers (ENF. 2)

15–003 The FSA has power to gather information from firms and conduct investigations of firms, approved persons, individuals involved in firms, and appointed representatives and may issue preliminary findings letters. The FSA's power to gather information and to appoint investigators is contained in ss.165 to 169 and s.284 of the FSMA. The FSA will not normally make public the fact that an investigation into a particular person or firm is underway unless publicity is desirable to maintain public confidence in the financial system, to protect consumers or prevent widespread malpractice, or to assist in the investigation itself by bringing forward witnesses. (ENF 2.13) Under it powers of investigation the FSA may:

15–004 (i) require firms to provide information and documents. This includes specified information or information of a specified description or the production of specific documents or documents of a specific description which the FSA reasonably requires in connection with the exercise of its functions under the FSMA (s.165). This power may be exercised on a person who is connected with a firm, an operator, trustee or depositary of certain types of recognised collective investment schemes who is not an authorised person or a recognised investment exchange or a recognised clearing house (ENF. 2.3.2–7);

15–005 (ii) require a firm to provide a report by a skilled person (s.166 FSMA). The person appointed to make the report must be nominated or approved by the FSA and appear to the FSA to have the necessary skill to report on the matter in question. There is a duty to provide the skilled person appointed to compile the report by the FSA with the information he might reasonably require. This duty may be enforced by way of an application by the FSA for an injunction (in Scotland, by an order for specific performance) (ENF. 2.3.8–11);

15–006 (iii) appoint general investigators to conduct investigations of firms and appointed representatives (s.167). An investigator will be appointed under s.167 if there appears to the FSA (or the Secretary of State) that there is a good reason to do so. The scope of the investigation will encompass the nature, conduct or state or business of a firm or of an appointed representative or a particular aspect of that business or the ownership or control of a firm (ENF 2.3.12–13);

(iv) investigate specific contraventions, offences and other matters; under s.168 FSMA the FSA may appoint investigators to carry out an investigation where it appears that a person has breached regulations made under s.142 FSMA; or a person may be guilty of an offence under ss.177, 191, 346 or 398(1) of and under Sch.4 of the FSMA (see s.168(1) and (3). Additionally, an investigator may be appointed under s.168(2) and (3) FSMA if there are circumstances suggesting that an offence under s.24(1) of the Criminal Justice Act 1993 may have been committed or where there may have been a breach of the general prohibition or a contravention of the restrictions on financial promotion contained in ss.21 and 238 of the FSMA or where market abuse may have taken place. Under s.168(4) and (5) the FSA may appoint an investigator if circumstances suggest that a firm may have breached the requirement for permissions in s.20 of the FSMA; a person may be guilty of an offence under the Money Laundering Regulations; a firm may have breached a rule made by the FSA; an individual may not be a fit and proper person; a person may have performed or agreed to perform a function in breach of a prohibition order; a firm or an exempt person may have failed to comply with s.56(6) of the FSMA; a firm may have failed to comply with s.59(1) or (2) FSMA; a person to whom the FSA has given approval under s.59 may not be a fit and proper person to perform the functions for which approval has been granted; a person may be guilty of misconduct for the purposes of s.66 of the FSMA (ENF. 2.3.14); **15–007**

(v) under s.169 of the FSMA, use its powers to require information or documents or to appoint an investigator in response to a request for assistance from an overseas regulator (ENF 2.3.17 and ENF 2.8 and see ENF 2 Annex 2G); and **15–008**

(vi) make investigations into collective investment schemes: The FSA has powers under s.284 FSMA to appoint investigators where it appears that it would be in the interests of the participants or potential participants or that the matter is of public concern (ENF 2.3.19 and 2.3.20). **15–009**

The Powers of Investigators Appointed by the FSA (ENF 2.4)

The scope of the powers of an FSA appointed investigator is derived from the provision of the FSMA under which he was appointed. The powers of a s.167 investigator are contained in ss.171 and 175 of FSMA and are described in ENF. 2.4.5G and ENF 2.4.10G to 2.4.12G. Broadly, a s.167 investigator may require a person who is the subject of an investigation or **15–010** is connected with such a person to attend before the investigator at a specified time and place or otherwise to provide such information as the investigator may require or produce any specified documents or documents of a specified description where the provision of such information or documents is reasonably considered by the investigator to be relevant to the investigation. Under s.175, an investigator has the power to require a third party to produce a document if it is potentially relevant to the investigation if the investigator would have had the power to require production of such a document from the person under investigation or from a connected person. If a third party fails to produce a document when required to do so by an investigator, he may be required to state to the best of his knowledge and belief where the document is. If documents or information is not provided, the FSA and its investigators may apply to a magistrate for a search warrant to search for and seize documents or information (s.176 FSMA, ENF 2.15).

There is no requirement to produce documents which attract legal professional privilege (s.413 FSMA, ENF. 2.10.2). By virtue of s.175(5) no person may be required to give information or produce documents in respect of which he owes an obligation of banking confidentiality unless the circumstances are such that the person to whom the obligation is owed is the person under investigation or a related company or the person to whom the duty is owed consents to its disclosure or the requirement to disclose has been specifically authorised by the FSA.

The Powers of an FSA Investigator

15–011 The powers of a s.168 investigator appointed to investigate matters listed in s.168(1) and (4) are contained in ss.172 and 175 of the FSMA and are described in ENF 2.4.8G to 2.4.7G and 2.4.10G to 2.4.12G. The powers of a s.168 investigator appointed to investigate matters under s.168(2) are contained in ss.173 and 175 of the FSMA and are described in ENF 2.4.8G and 2.4.10G to 2.4.12G. The powers of an investigator appointed under s.168 replicate those of a s.167 investigator but go further in the sense that a s.168 investigator may require the attendance before him of any person who is or may be able to give potentially relevant information.

The powers of s.169 investigators are contained in ss.172 and 175 and are described in ENF 2.4.8G and 2.4.10G to 2.4.12G. The powers of a s.169 investigator appointed in support of an overseas regulator has the same powers as an investigator appointed under s.168(1).

The powers of s.284 investigators are contained in s.284(3) FSMA and described at ENF 2.4.13G. Under s.284(3) an investigator may require a person whom he considers is able to or may be able to give information which is relevant to the investigation to produce any documents in his possession or under his control which may be relevant; the investigator may require a person to attend before him and that person must give the investigator all assistance which he is reasonably able to give.

Compulsory Interviews

Where the FSA exercises through an investigator the power to compel a person to answer questions, that person must be allowed to be accompanied by a legal advisor, be given the appropriate warning and explanation of the limited use to which compelled statements may be put and be given a record of the interview (ENF 2.14.3). **15–012**

Admissibility of Statements: s.174 of the FSMA

Statements required to be made by FSA appointed investigators may be used as evidence in any proceedings if they compel with the normal rules governing admissibility of evidence. The major exception to this is that under s.174(2) such statements cannot generally be used in criminal proceedings in which the person who made the statement is the defendant in the case or in relation to action against the maker for market abuse under s.123 FSMA. Statements by the defendant made as pursuant to the powers of an FSA appointed investigator may only be used against him if the defendant himself adduces evidence about the statement or asks questions relating to it. Of course, the restriction imposed by s.174 as to the use to which statements may be put in criminal proceedings do not apply if the statement was made voluntarily rather than in compliance with an investigators requirement to make it. Furthermore, no restriction applies to the use of a compelled statement in the course of proceedings for offences under s.174(3) which include making false statements or providing the investigator with false or misleading evidence. When conducting interviews, the FSA should ensure that the normal safeguards are available to the interviewee, *i.e.* access to legal advice, warning about the use to which the interview may be put, giving the interviewee a copy of the record of interview. Such safeguards should apply whether or not the interview is voluntary or under caution pursuant to the FSA's role as a prosecuting authority by virtue of ss.401 and 402 FSMA (see ENF 2.14). Furthermore, when the FSA is acting as a prosecuting authority and is conducting an interview with someone who is suspected of a criminal offence then the FSA investigators are subject to the requirement of the Police and Criminal Evidence Act 1984 and its Codes and to the provisions of the Criminal Procedure and Investigations Act 1996. If a person has already been interviewed under one of the FSA's compulsory powers of interview, then he must be given a transcript of that interview before being interviewed under caution and an explanation of the differences between the two types of interview must be given to him. Similarly, if a person has already been interviewed under caution and the FSA investigators then seek to interview him under one of their compulsory powers, the interviewee must be told of the different uses to which the interviews may be put. **15–013**

Search Warrants (ENF 2.15)

S.176 FSMA deals with the entry of premises under a warrant. A justice of the peace may issue a warrant under s.176 if he is satisfied on the basis of information given on oath by the FSA or its investigators that there are reasonable grounds for believing that: **15–014**

(i) a person has failed to comply with a requirement to provide information or produce documents or information, and that the documents or information are on the premises (s.176(2)); or

(ii) the premises specified in the warrant are those of a firm or an appointed representative and there are documents or information on the premises which could be the object of an information requirement and the requirement would not be complied with or the documents or information would be removed, tampered with or destroyed if such a requirement was made (s.176(3); or

(iii) a serious offence (*i.e.* offences mentioned in s.168 for which the maximum sentence on indictment is two years or more) has been or is being committed and that documents or information relevant to that offence are on the premises and that an information requirement could be imposed on those documents or information and that the requirement would not be complied with or the documents or information would be removed, tampered with or destroyed (s.176(4)).

15–015 A search warrant issued under s.176 will authorise a constable to:

(i) enter the premises specified in the warrant;

(ii) search the premises and take possession of documents or information relevant to the warrant, or to take any other necessary steps to preserve or prevent interference with the documents/information;

(iii) take copies or extracts of any documents/information;

(iv) require any person on the premises to explain any documents/information or to say where they may be found;

The FSA has said that as a matter of policy it will usually seek to ensure that the FSA investigator is also named on the warrant and will be entitled to accompany the constable to execute the warrant.(ENF 2.15.4 G)

Non-Co-operation with the FSA

15–016 A failure to co-operate with an FSA investigator may be treated as a contempt of court where the investigator certifies in writing to a court that the person has failed to comply with a requirement under Pt XI of FSMA and the court is satisfied that the person has no reasonable excuse for his failure to comply. The court, in those circumstances, may deal with him as if he were in contempt (s.177(1)). Where the person who fails to comply is a body corporate the court may hold a director or officer of the company in contempt (s.177(2)). In addition, s.177 (3)-(6) creates three criminal offences of non-co-operation with the FSA in its exercise of its information gathering and investigation roles. These are broadly, failing to co-operate with, or giving false information to FSA appointed investigators (under s.177(3) and (4)). These offences are triable either way. On summary conviction the penalty is imprisonment up to a maximum of six months and/or a fine not exceeding the statutory maximum and on conviction on indictment to imprisonment for a maximum of two years and/or a fine. Further, it is a summary offence(s.177(6)) to obstruct intentionally the exercise of any rights conferred by warrant under s.176 which is punishable by a maximum of three months imprisonment and/or a fine not exceeding level five on the standard scale.

Preliminary Findings Letters

The person or firm under investigation will generally be sent a preliminary findings letter setting out the facts which the investigator considers relevant to the matter under investigation before the investigator considers what enforcement action should be taken. The person under investigation is then invited to confirm the accuracy of the facts contained in the letter within 28 days and the investigator must take the response into account before reaching his final conclusions. The only exception to this is in cases of urgency where the sending of a preliminary findings letter would be impractical. **15–017**

Publicity Following an Investigation

The FSA must publish under s.391 FSMA a final notice containing such information about an investigation and its conclusions which the FSA considers appropriate (s.391(4)). Similarly, where a supervisory notice takes effect, the FSA must publish appropriate information about the matter. Only if the FSA considers that publication would be unfair to the person who has been investigated or in some way prejudicial to the interests of consumers will there be no publicity at the end of an investigation (ENF 2.13.8). **15–018**

Variation of Pt IV Permission on the FSA's Own Initiative (ENF 3.5)

Ss.45 to 47 FSMA contain the powers of the FSA to vary a firm's Pt IV permission on its own initiative. In exercising these powers the FSA will have regard to its regulatory objectives and also to the responsibilities of a firm's management to deal with concerns about the firm or the way in which its business is being or has been run and the principle that a restriction imposed on a firm should be proportionate to the objectives of the FSA. The FSA will only intervene when it considers that a firm together with its directors and senior management are failing to conduct their business in compliance with the Act, the Principles and the rules. The various cases in which the FSA may vary or cancel a firm's Pt IV permission are contained in s.45, for example where it appears that a firm may not comply with the threshold conditions or where the firm has not carried on the regulated activity for a period of 12 months or more for **15–019** which permission had been granted or where the variation permission is desirable in order to protect the interests of consumers or potential consumers. S.46, gives the FSA power to vary a firm's Pt IV permission when a person has acquired control of a firm (see SUP 11.7.18) and s.47 gives the FSA power to vary or cancel a firm's Pt IV permission in support of an overseas regulator. The exercise of the FSA's own initiative powers to vary Pt IV permission may be published under s.391(5) FSMA unless publication would be unfair against the person against whom the decision has been made or would be prejudicial to the interests of consumers (ENF 3.7).

15–020 The exercise of its own initiative power to vary Pt IV permission may take effect immediately (s.53(2)(a) or on a specified day (s.53(2)(b)) or when the matter is no longer open to review (s.53 (2)(c)). In urgent cases the factors which will influence the FSA in deciding whether it needs to exercise its own initiative power include where:

(i) there is a risk of significant loss, loss or other adverse effects for consumers, where it is necessary to protect their interests;

(ii) there is a risk of financial crime;

(iii) the firm has submitted inaccurate or misleading information giving rise to concerns that the firm cannot meet its regulatory obligations;

(iv) where it is questionable whether the firm continues to meet the threshold conditions.

Own Initiative Power to Cancel Pt IV Permissions

15–021 The FSA also has power to cancel Pt IV permissions under its own initiative under ss.45 and 47 of the FSMA and the FSA has a duty to withdraw authorisation under s.33 where Pt IV permission is cancelled and as a result there is no regulated activity for which the person has permission. The FSA must give a direction withdrawing the person's status as an authorised person. The procedure to be adopted when the FSA seeks to exercise its own initiative powers are set out in the Handbook at ENF 5. The FSA's own initiative powers to cancel Pt IV permission do not apply to unauthorised persons. Where actual or threatened breaches or market abuse occurs perpetrated by an unauthorised person the only power the FSA has is to apply for an injunction.

Injunctions (ENF 6)

15–022 The use of injunction (interdict in Scotland) by the FSA is seen as a major tool in the armoury to ensure that it meets its regulatory objectives or protects the consumer, maintaining confidence in the financial system and reducing financial crime.

The FSA may apply to the High Court (in Scotland to the Court of Session) for an injunction in relation to the following:

(i) In relation to the contravention of a relevant requirement (s.380); the relief applied for may be preventative, *i.e.* an injunction to restrain behaviour before it takes place; remedial, an injunction to put right behaviour once it has occurred; or to prevent a person from disposing of or otherwise dealing with any assets, a power similar to a Mareva injunction. It should be noted that the exercise of the powers under s.380(3) does not preclude the possibility of a separate application under the court's inherent jurisdiction for an asset freezing injunction (the old Mareva injunction) in appropriate circumstances. A relevant requirement for the purposes of s.380, is a requirement which is imposed by or under the FSMA or is a requirement which is imposed by or under any other Act the contravention of which constitutes an offence which the FSA has the power to prosecute. (s.381(6)). Where the contravention of a requirement for which injunctive relief is sought may also constitute a criminal offence it would be open to the FSA to institute prosecution proceedings in appropriate circumstances in addition to seeking an injunction. **15–023**

The factors which the FSA will take into account when deciding whether or not to apply for an injunction will include the nature and seriousness of the contravention; whether the losses suffered are substantial; whether the numbers of consumers who have suffered loss are significant; whether the assets at risk are substantial; whether the numbers of consumers at risk is significant.

(ii) In cases of market abuse (s.381) the FSA may apply to the court for an injunction to restrain behaviour which in its opinion will amount to market abuse; to remedy or mitigate the effects of the market abuse once it has occurred; or to prevent a person from disposing of or otherwise dealing with any assets. The factors which the FSA will take into consideration when applying for an injunction include the impact or potential impact on the financial system and the extent of any losses or other costs which might be imposed as a result of the misconduct on other market users. **15–024**

(iii) At the request of the Home State regulator of an incoming EEA firm (s.198) in respect of certain overseas insurance companies. **15–025**

(iv) The FSA may also apply to a court for an injunction under Reg.12 of the Unfair Terms in Consumer Contracts Regulations 1999 which permits a qualifying body with the consent of the Director General of Fair Trading to apply for an injunction (or an interim injunction) against any person appearing to them to be using or recommending the use of an unfair term drawn up for general use in contracts concluded with consumers. The FSA will only consider using this power where the firm and the contract complained about relates to regulated activities carried out by the firm. **15–026**

A person who does not comply with an injunction may be in contempt of court and would be liable to imprisonment, to a fine and/or to having his assets seized.

Withdrawal of Approval (ENF 7)

15–027 The FSA has the power under s.63 FSMA to remove approval which has been granted under s.59, from an approved person. The power to withdraw approval is a regulatory tool employed by the FSA to help it to achieve its regulatory objectives. It is intended that the use of this power will ensure high standards of regulatory conduct by preventing an approved person from continuing to perform a controlled function if he is not a fit and proper person to perform such a function. The matters to which the FSA will have regard when considering whether or not someone is a fit and proper person for the purposes of approval are set out in s.61 and are broadly whether a person has obtained a qualification, has undergone or is undergoing training and whether or not such a person possesses a level of competence required by general rules relating to a person performing functions of the kind to which the approval relates, also see in this context Handbook FIT Annex C. Withdrawal of approval will also demonstrate to other approved persons the consequences of failing to comply with the necessary standards of conduct. If the FSA proposes to withdraw approval it must give each of the interested parties a warning notice (s.63(3)). The interested parties are the person on whose application approval was given (A), the person in respect of whom the approval was given (B) and the person who retains the services of the approved person if that person is not A. Once a decision has been made to withdraw approval, the FSA must issue a decision notice (s.63(4)). Once the decision has been made by the FSA to withdraw approval, any of the interested parties may refer the matter to the Tribunal (s.63(5)).

When considering whether or not it should withdraw approval from an approved person the FSA may also employ its investigation powers under s.168(4)(d), (h) or (i), consider taking disciplinary action under s.66 or it may consider making a prohibition order.

Prohibition Orders (ENF 8)

15–028 The FSA's power to make a prohibition order is contained in s.56 of the FSMA. The power has a wide ambit and is intended to ensure that individuals are fit and proper persons to carry out regulated activities. The power is considered to be a more serious penalty than the withdrawal of approval as a prohibition order is likely to have a much wider impact and as such it is likely to be employed by the FSA only in the most serious cases of lack of fitness and propriety. Prohibition orders may apply to all individuals whether or not they are approved by the FSA and are intended to prohibit individuals from carrying out functions in relation to regulated activities. Where the individual concerned is not an approved person, then the imposition of a prohibition order may be the only option available as the FSA could not withdraw approval or utilise its disciplinary powers.

The prohibition order may relate to a specified regulated activity, any regulated activity falling within a specified description or all regulated activities and to firms generally or to any specified firm within a specified class of firm. The FSA will use its power to impose a prohibition order where is considers that an individual presents such a risk to consumers or to the confidence in the market generally that it is necessary to prevent him from carrying out any function in relation to regulated activities or from being employed by any firm or to restrict the functions which he may carry out or the type of firm by which he may be employed. An authorised person must take reasonable care to ensure that no function of his in relation to the carrying on of a regulated activity is performed by a person who is the subject of a prohibition order prohibiting him from performing that function.

A person who performs or agrees to perform a function in breach of a prohibition order commits an offence and is liable on summary conviction to a fine not exceeding £5,000 (s.56(4)). It is defence for a person to show that he took all reasonable precautions and exercised all due diligence to avoid committing the offence (s.56(5)). **15–029**

If the FSA intends to impose a prohibition order it must give the individual a written warning notice which sets out the terms of the prohibition. Once a decision has been made to impose a prohibition order, the individual must be given a written notice setting out the name of the individual to whom the order applies, the terms of the order and the notice must be given to the person named in the order. The person against whom a prohibition order is made may refer the matter to the Tribunal (see ss.57 and 58). In addition, an individual against whom an order has been imposed, may apply at any time to the FSA to have the order varied or revoked.

The FSA must keep a public record of individuals against whom it has made a prohibition order (s.347(1)). The FSA must balance the interests of consumer protection against the possible prejudice to the individual against whom the order has been made when deciding what information to include on the register.

Restitution (ENF 9)

The FSA may apply to the court under s.382 of the FSMA for a restitution order against a person (whether authorised or not) who has contravened a relevant requirement under Pt XXV. This is an important power in that it allows the FSA to seek redress for consumers where there has been a breach of a relevant requirement of the Act. Before making a restitution order, the court must be satisfied that the person in contravention has accrued profits as a result of the contravention or that one or more persons have suffered loss or been otherwise adversely affected as a result of the contravention. Applications for a restitution order may be combined with injunctions made under s.380. The court may order that the person concerned must make payment to the FSA, the amount of such payment will be determined having regard to the amount of profits which appear to the court to have accrued and/or the extent of the loss or other adverse effect (s.382(2)). The FSA must make sure that the restitution ordered is distributed to those who suffered loss or were adversely affected by the contravention of a requirement (s.382(3)). The court may require the **15–030** person concerned to supply information or accounts for the purposes of establishing whether any profits have accrued to him and if such profits have accrued the extent of such profits. The information may also be used to establish whether any person(s) have suffered any loss or adverse effect and the extent of the loss or adverse effect. The court may require verification of any information or accounts with which it is supplied. Restitution orders made under Pt XXV do not prevent a private action for restitution (s.382(7)).

Similar provisions are provided by s.383 for cases of market abuse. Under this section the FSA may apply to a court for a restitution order in cases of market abuse where it can be shown that profits have accrued to a person as a result of market abuse or that one or more persons have suffered loss or been otherwise adversely affected. The only difference between s.382 and s.383 is that under s.383(3) a court may not make an order for restitution if it is satisfied that the person concerned believed on reasonable grounds that his behaviour did not amount to market abuse or that he took all reasonable precautions and exercised all due diligence to avoid behaving in a way which amounted to market abuse.

The Administrative Power of the FSA to Require Restitution

15–031 In addition to the ability to apply to a court to order restitution, the FSA, by virtue of s.384 of the FSMA, has the administrative power to require an authorised person to pay restitution for contravening a Pt XXV requirement or for engaging in market abuse. The FSA envisages that it will consider using its own administrative powers under s.384 before it considers taking court action under s.382 and 383 (see ENF 9.7.2 G). If the FSA utilises its powers under s.384, the authorised person against whom restitution is ordered may refer the matter to the Tribunal. The FSA may not use its administrative powers to obtain restitution from unauthorised persons except in cases of market abuse, most cases where redress is obtained from unauthorised persons are thus likely to be dealt with by an application to the court. The FSA must be satisfied that the person has accrued profits as a result of the contravention or market abuse or that one or more persons have suffered loss as a result of the contravention or the market abuse. Before such a power may be exercised, the FSA must issue a warning notice (s.385). Once a warning notice has been issued, the FSA must not exercise its powers if it is satisfied that the approved person believed on reasonable grounds that his behaviour did not contravene a Pt XXV requirement or amounted to market abuse or that he took all reasonable precautions and exercised all due diligence to avoid behaving in such a way. Where the FSA concludes that there should be a restitution order then it must issue a decision notice to the person in relation to whom the power is exercised (s.386) which must state the amount that the person has to pay or distribute, identify the person(s) to whom payment is to be made or amongst whom distribution is to be made and state the arrangements in accordance with which payment or distribution is to be made.

15–032 There are a number of factors which the FSA will take into account when considering whether or not to seek restitution under ss.382–384.

These include the availability of redress through any other route, *i.e.* through the Financial Ombudsman Service or the compensation scheme. This will be relevant in cases where the loss is as a result of the conduct of a firm but will not be relevant where the loss is as a result of the conduct of unauthorised persons operating in breach of the general prohibition. In addition, the FSA will not take action where it would be more appropriate for action to be taken by another regulatory authority, *e.g.* the Takeover Panel where matters have arisen in the context of a takeover bid.

There may also be circumstances where it would be more appropriate for a person who has suffered loss to bring their own civil action, *e.g.* where the person who has suffered loss is a market counterparty. The FSA may also consider obtaining a compulsory insolvency order against a firm or an unauthorised person rather than a restitution order where to do so might place the solvency of the firm or unauthorised person at risk. The conduct of the persons who have suffered loss is another factor which may have a bearing on whether the FSA seeks a restitution order. The FSA may consider whether the persons who have suffered loss may have contributed to their own loss or failed to take reasonable steps to protect their own interests.

Insolvency Proceedings (ENF 10)

The FSA has numerous powers and rights in insolvency proceedings which it will utilise to stop firms and unauthorised persons from carrying on insolvent or unlawful business and to ensure the orderly realisation and distribution of their assets. These powers and rights are derived from Pt XXIV of the FSMA and the underlying insolvency legislation including the Insolvency Act 1986 as amended by the Insolvency Act 2000, the Bankruptcy (Scotland) Act 1985 and the Insolvency (Northern Ireland) Order 1989. The FSA has powers to seek administration (s.359), compulsory winding up (s.367) and bankruptcy orders (s.372 and s.264 of the Insolvency Act 1986), and in Scotland, sequestration awards. It also has powers to apply to the court to challenge acts and omissions in company moratoria and to challenge an approved voluntary arrangement in respect of a corporate or individual authorised person (ss.356 and 357) (in Scotland, a trust deed for creditors granted by an authorised person (s.358)). The FSA also has power to apply to the court for orders against debt avoidance (s.375). **15–033**

The FSA has rights in certain cases in respect of firms or former firms or others who are or have been carrying on a regulated activity while unauthorised: **15–034**

(a) to be informed of third party petitions for administration, compulsory winding up and bankruptcy orders and, in Scotland, sequestration orders (see s.362);

(b) to receive information and to attend and be heard at meetings of creditors and creditors' committees in the following regimes:

 (i) voluntary and compulsory winding up (ss.365–371);

(ii) administrations (s.359);
(iii) receiverships and administrative receiverships (ss.363 and 364);
(iv) bankruptcies and sequestrations (s.373);
(v) company moratoria and voluntary arrangements (Sch.A1 to the Insolvency Act 1986);
(vi) individual voluntary arrangements (s.357);
(vii) trust deeds for creditors in Scotland.

Discipline of Authorised Firms and Approved Persons—ENF 11–13

15–035 The FSA has a number of disciplinary measures available to it including the issuing of public statements and public censures and the imposition of financial penalties. The disciplinary measures available to the FSA are important in that they allow the FSA to enforce the requirements of the FSMA, the rules and the Statements of Principle. The imposition of disciplinary measures in particular the use of public statements and public censure also shows publicly that regulatory standards are being enforced and upheld which should have the effect of enhancing confidence in the market, promoting awareness of regulatory standards and deterring financial crime. The focus of disciplinary measures will usually be on the firm since the primary responsibility for ensuring compliance with a firm's regulatory obligations lies with a firm. The FSA will however, look directly at disciplinary measures against approved persons when for example a firm is able to show that it took all reasonable steps to prevent a breach occurring and there is evidence of personal culpability on the part of the approved person. There may of course be occasions when disciplinary action is necessary against both the firm and an approved person. S.66 FSMA sets out the disciplinary powers of the FSA in respect of approved persons (see ENF 11.5). The FSA may consider it appropriate to discipline a firm on the basis of a breach of the Principles for Businesses set out in PRIN 2.1.1R. which are a statement of the fundamental obligations of a firm under the regulatory system.

15–036 The factors which the FSA will take into account when determining whether to take disciplinary action will include (ENF 11.5):

(1) the nature and seriousness of the suspected breach including whether the breach was deliberate or reckless, the duration and frequency of the breach, the amount of any benefit gained or loss avoided as a result of the breach, whether the breach reveals serious or systematic weaknesses of management systems or internal controls, the impact of the breach on the financial markets and public confidence in the markets, the loss or risk of loss to consumers or other market users, and the nature and extent of any financial crime facilitated;

(2) the conduct of the approved firm after the breach has occurred including the speed with which the firm or approved person notified

an appropriate regulatory body of the breach, the level of co-operation during investigation of the breach, the remedial steps taken by the firm or approved person and the likelihood of the breach being repeated;

(3) the previous regulatory record of the firm or approved person;

(4) whether the FSA handbook gives any guidance in respect of the behaviour that gives rise to the breach;

(5) what action the FSA has taken in similar cases in the past; and

(6) what action has been taken in similar case by other regulatory bodies.

When considering whether disciplinary action is appropriate, there are many instances where the FSA must take into account whether a firm or an approved person has taken reasonable care in relation to particular behaviour. In so doing, the FSA should have regard to the information that was known to the firm at the time of the breach and the level of information that should have been known to the firm in such circumstances. The FSA will also look at what steps the firm took to comply with the relevant rule and what steps should have been taken in compliance. Lastly, the FSA should consider the standards of the regulatory system that applied at the time of the behaviour (ENF 11.7 G). **15–037**

Financial Penalties for Late Submission of Reports (ENF 13.5)

The FSA requires various types of reports and other documents to be submitted to it within set timeframes, for example annual controller's reports, annual close link reports, compliance reports, financial reports, accounts and balance sheets, actuaries' and auditors' reports and certificates and statements (see SUP 16, IPRU(INS) 9.37(4)R and 9.6(1)R, IPRU(FSOC) 3.1(8)R, 3.2(5)R, 5.1(2)R and 5.2(2)R, DISP 1.1.8R, 1.5.4 to 1.5.7R, 5.1.7R and 5.5.1R and LLD 3.3.2R, 4.3.2R, 15.2.1R and 15.10.2R.). Failure to comply with the time limits for the submission of such reports may lead to the imposition of financial penalties the level of which will relate to the number of working days which have elapsed between the date when a report was due and the date it was actually submitted. This scale of penalties is set out in ENF 13 Annex 1G. **15–038**

Private Warnings (ENF 11.3)

The FSA may decide that, rather than bringing formal disciplinary action, the circumstances of the case are such that it would be more appropriate to make the firm or the approved person aware that they have come close to formal disciplinary action. Examples of when a private warning may be the appropriate course of action is when the matter giving cause for concern is minor in nature or where the firm or approved person has already taken full and immediate action to put the matter right. It is also open to the FSA **15–039** to issue private warnings to persons who are not authorised, it is envisaged that such a course might be taken in cases of potential market abuse or where the FSA is considering making a prohibition order or a disapplication order.

Public Censure and Public Statements

15–040 The FSA may issue a public censure on a firm where it considers that the firm has contravened a requirement imposed on it under the FSMA (s.205). The FSA has power to issue a public statement of misconduct on an approved person whom the FSA considers to be guilty of misconduct (s.66). Misconduct is defined as failure to comply with a Statement of Principle (s.64) or being knowingly concerned in a contravention by a firm of a requirement imposed on that firm by the FSMA (s.66). The FSA may also issue a public statement (s.123) where a person has engaged in market abuse (see ENF 14) and where there has been a contravention of the listing rules (s.91 and UKLA sourcebook).

Where the FSA intends to issue a public statement or a public censure, the firm or approved person concerned will be given a warning notice setting out the terms of the statement or the censure (see ss.207, 67, 126, 92).

Collective Investment Schemes (ENF 16)

15–041 Ss.242 to 261 of the FSMA set out the provisions relating to authorised unit trust schemes. The FSA has a number of enforcement powers in respect of authorised unit trust schemes. These include a power to revoke authorisation of an authorised unit trust scheme otherwise than by consent (s.254); a power for the FSA to give directions (s.257); and a power for the FSA to apply to court for the removal of a manager or trustee or the winding up of an authorised unit trust scheme (s.258). The FSA may use these powers individually or in combination. The FSA also has a similar set of powers in respect of open-ended investment companies (See The Open-ended Investment Companies Regulations 2001 SI 2001/1228 and ENF 16.3). In respect of recognised schemes, ss.264 to 283 of the FSMA are applicable and the FSA has enforcement powers under s.267 to suspend promotion of a scheme constituted in another EEA State and recognised under s.264; the FSA also has the power to revoke recognition of a scheme recognised under s.270 and a scheme individually recognised under s.272. The FSA may also give directions in respect of recognised schemes under s.281 and ENF 16.4.1G(2).

In addition, the FSA has the power to disqualify auditors and actuaries who fail to comply with the provisions imposed under unit trust schemes under s.249.

Disqualification of Auditors and Actuaries (ENF 17)

15–042 Where an auditor or an actuary has failed to comply with any provisions of the FSMA (see in particular Pt XXII (Auditors and Actuaries) of the FSMA) the FSA has the power by virtue of s.345 to disqualify auditors and actuaries from acting for particular authorised persons or from acting for particular classes of person. The FSA must issue warning notices and decision notices in much the same way as it must to others whom it seeks to discipline and an auditor or actuary may have the matter referred to the Tribunal.

Disapplication Orders Against Members of the Professions (ENF 18)

The FSA has the power by virtue of s.329 FSMA to make an order disapplying s.327(1) of the Act. In other words the FSA may ban a professional whom it deems is not a fit and proper person from carrying on regulated activities. A disapplication order may be made against an individual or a partnership. Professionals such as solicitors, accountants and actuaries may carry out certain regulated activities although, being exempted persons, they are exempt from the requirement to obtain permissions form the FSA to do so. The FSA continues to have a general duty to keep itself informed about the way in which the various professional bodies supervise and regulate their members who carry out regulated activities (see Pt XX of the FSMA). The Treasury has the power to designate the professional bodies to which such exemption applies. For a professional to qualify for a general exemption he must pass the tests set out in s.327 which are, in general terms, that the person must belong to a professional body which is recognised by the Treasury, he must not be in receipt of commission for the activity from a third party unless he accounts to his client for the commission, and the activity must be ancillary to his main professional practice and not relate to the provision of life or other sensitive products. In many cases where the FSA is concerned about the fitness and propriety of an individual involved in exempt regulated activities it will more appropriate for the FSA to consider utilising its general power to issue a prohibition order under s.56 of the FSMA. The FSA may also consider issuing a private warning as an alternative to making a prohibition order or a disapplication order. **15–043**

The Financial Services and Markets Appeal Tribunal

The tribunal is established by virtue of s.132 FSMA and replaces the tribunals of the previous financial regulators namely the Personal Investment Authority, the Investments Management Regulatory Organisation, the Securities and Futures Authority and the tribunals responsible for banks, buildings societies and friendly societies. The Tribunal consists of a Chairman and two lay members who are selected for their experience and credibility in the financial services industry. The Tribunal will normally hold its hearings in public although it has a discretion to hold them in private if in all the circumstances such a private hearing would be appropriate. Firms and certain individuals who are employed in regulated businesses may refer a matter to the Tribunal. The timetable for making a reference is set out in s.133 of the FSMA which requires that a reference to **15–044** the Tribunal must be made within 28 days from the date on which the decision notice or supervisory notice was given although it should be noted that this period may be altered by virtue of rules made under s.132 of the FSMA. A referral may be made after 28 days if the Tribunal agrees subject only to any rules made under s.132. Once a matter has been referred, the Tribunal may consider any evidence relating to the subject matter of the reference including evidence which may not have been available to the FSA at time of the original decision (s.133(3)).

15–045 When a matter has been referred to it, the Tribunal must determine what appropriate action should be taken by the FSA (if any) in respect of the matter referred to the Tribunal (s.133 (4)) and the Tribunal must remit the matter to the FSA with appropriate directions to give effect to the determination of the Tribunal (s.133(5)). The FSA is required to act in accordance with the determination of the Tribunal and any directions given by it (s.133(10)) and an order of the Tribunal may be enforced as if it is an order of the county court (or the Court of Session in Scotland) (s.133(11)).

Legal Assistance Scheme

15–046 By virtue of ss.134 and 135, the Lord Chancellor has the power to make regulations to establish a scheme providing legal assistance in connection with proceedings before the Tribunal. It is intended that the legal assistance scheme is to be funded by the FSA which in turn will raise the funds necessary by way of a levy on those it authorises (s.136).

Appeals from the Tribunal

15–047 An appeal against the decision of the Tribunal is only available on a point of law. The Appeal is to the Court of Appeal if leave is granted or the Court of Session in Scotland. Leave to appeal may be granted by the Tribunal itself or by the appellate court.

Complaints against the Financial Services Authority

15–048 The FSA is required to make arrangements for the investigation of complaints arising in connection with the exercise of, or failure to exercise, any of its functions other than legislative functions. Sch.1, para.7 FSMA requires the FSA to appoint an investigator (the Complaints Commissioner) who is an independent person to be responsible for the conduct of investigations under the complaints scheme. (Sch.1 of the FSMA, paras 7 and 8). It is intended that the arrangements will be such that the investigator is able to act independently of the FSA and that complaints will be investigated under the complaints scheme without favouring the FSA. The complaints procedure is concerned simply with complaints about the way in which the FSA has discharged is functions and it does not cover complaints about the actions of the Financial Ombudsman Service or the Financial Services Compensation Scheme.

The complaints procedure envisages a two stage process; initially, the FSA will investigate any complaint and take such action as it deems appropriate (COAF 1.5.2–1.5.6). Only if a complainant remains dissatisfied with the FSA's own investigation will the second stage of the procedure come into play whereby an investigation is conducted by the Complaints Commissioner. (COAF 1.5.10–1.5.18) Where the Complaints Commissioner concludes that a complaint is well founded he may recommend that the FSA remedies the matters of complaint and/or that the FSA makes a compensatory payment to the complainant. The Complaints Commissioner must report his findings and his report may be made published if it contains matters which ought to be brought to the attention of the public (COAF 1.5.19–24). Complainants using the complaints procedure will not be charged for using the scheme (COAF 1.4.7)

Anyone including firms and issuers of listed securities and any customer or prospective customer whether as an individual or a body corporate or a market counterparty who is directly affected by the way in which the FSA carried out its functions may bring a complaint under the complaints scheme (COAF 1.2.1) The scheme also applies in relation to complaints about the way in which the FSA, PIA, IMRO or SFA exercised their functions under the Financial Services Act 1986. (The arrangements for such complaints are set out in COAF 2: Transitional Complaints Scheme). **15–049**

The Scope of the Scheme

The complaints scheme covers complaints about the way in the FSA has acted or omitted to act including complaints alleging: **15–050**

- mistakes and lack of care;
- unreasonable delay;
- unprofessional behaviour;
- bias; and
- lack of integrity (COAF 1.4.1).

To come within the scope of the scheme, a complainant must be seeking a remedy, including an apology, in respect of some inconvenience, distress or loss which has arisen as a result of being directly affected by an act or omission of the FSA (COAF 1.4.3).

The scheme does not apply to complaints about the FSA's relationship with its own employees, complaints connected with contractual or commercial disputes involving the FSA and not connected to its functions under the FSMA or to complaints in relation to the FSA's legislative functions (*e.g.* the making of rules and the issuing of codes and general guidance. (COAF 1.4.2). Complaints should be made within 12 months of the complainant becoming aware of the circumstances giving rise to the complaint. The onus is on the complainant to show reasonable grounds for any delay beyond the 12 month period. (COAF 1.4.6). **15–051**

The complaints scheme does not apply where the complaint could be dealt with in another more appropriate way, for example by reference to the Tribunal or other legal proceedings or where the complaint is nothing more than dissatisfaction with the FSA's general policies or the exercise of discretion by the FSA where there is no suggestion of unreasonable, unprofessional or other misconduct. Furthermore, a complainant must exhaust all other relevant procedures and remedies available under the Act unless there are exceptional circumstances which would make it unreasonable for the complainant to wait for the conclusion of all other available remedies (COAF 1.4.4).

Chapter 16

Compensation and Complaints

The Financial Services Compensation Scheme

Introduction

16–001 The collapse of a financial institution holding substantial sums of investors' money is an event which can have major repercussions, including, of course, serious hardship for individual investors and a damaging loss of confidence in the financial services industry generally. In the last decades of the twentieth century, this was increasingly recognised and some degree of protection for investors was introduced through various investor protection schemes. In the insurance field, protection was introduced by the Policyholders Protection Act 1975 (eventually extended to cover insurance activities of friendly societies). There followed the deposit protection scheme relating to banks, introduced by the Banking Act 1979, and that in turn was followed in 1986 both by the investor protection scheme for building societies, under the Building Societies Act 1986, and the investor compensation scheme brought in by the Financial Services Act 1986, which offered protection where investment business was carried out by authorised persons or firms which were unable, or likely to be unable, to satisfy claims in respect of civil liability incurred by them in connection with carrying on investment business.

16–002 The attitude of different sectors of the financial services industry to compensation schemes has varied considerably, perhaps as a result of experience. Generally speaking, building societies in the twentieth century made voluntary arrangements for the protection of investors in the rare event of the collapse of a society and a formal voluntary scheme was established in 1982 under the auspices of the Building Societies Association. The statutory scheme, which has now been replaced by the Financial Services Compensation Scheme under the FSMA 2000 (in this chapter referred to as "the Scheme"), was never called into operation. Nor were the protection provisions relating to friendly societies. The banking scheme was tested in relation to the collapse of Bank of Commerce and Credit International (see *Deposit Protection Board v Barclays Bank plc* [1994] 2 A.C. 367), but again has not been widely operated. The policyholders' protection scheme was active, and received judicial consideration in *Policyholders Protection Board v Official Receiver* [1976] 1 W.L.R. 447 (in effect a friendly case concerning the Board's powers); *Re Capital Annuities Ltd* [1979] 1 W.L.R. 170 (also such a case); and *Scher v Policyholders Protection Board*

[1994] 2 A.C. 57 (concerning the liability of the Board to indemnify overseas plaintiffs in respect of claims made against them in the United States and Canada). The investor compensation scheme has been invoked in many more cases, no doubt because an authorised firm may be a very much smaller organisation than a deposit-taking institution or an insurer and may be significantly more vulnerable. In this area, there has been much greater resistance to the scheme and correspondingly more litigation. Its funding arrangements were considered in *R. v SIB, Ex p. Sun Life Assurance*, unreported, August 31, 1995; the liabilities covered were considered in *SIB v FIMBRA* [1992] Ch. 268; *R. v Investors Compensation Scheme Ltd, Ex p. Bowden* [1996] A.C. 261; and *R. v Investors Compensation Scheme Ltd, Ex p. Taylor* [1998] Q.B. 963; and the range of potential applicants was considered in *R. v Investor Compensation Scheme Ltd, Ex p. Weyell* [1994] Q.B. 749. These various cases on the previous schemes have now been superseded by the provisions of the Scheme.

16–003 Although, as the previous paragraph indicates, the former schemes have now been brought together into the one Scheme, that is not to say that the provisions which apply to each sector of the financial services industry are now identical. Some distinctions remain, not least because different sectors are affected by different European Directives. The general structure of the Scheme, however, applies universally. It now offers protection in respect of protected deposits, in relation to which the Deposit Guarantee Schemes Directive (Dir.94/19 [1994] O.J. l135/5) applies, protected contracts of insurance and protected investment business, in relation to which the Investor Compensation Directive (Dir.97/9 [1997] O.J. L84/22) applies. The meaning of "protected deposit" is fairly straightforward; the term means funds deposited with banks or building societies in the United Kingdom or in an EEA branch of a United Kingdom bank or building society, other than funds forming part of the institution's capital or a deposit made without disclosing the depositor's identity (*FSA Handbook*, COMP 5.3.1). (For this purpose, share accounts with building societies are treated as deposited funds.) "Protected investment business" also has a fairly straightforward meaning (*FSA Handbook*, COMP 5.5.1); subject to the territorial limitations set out in COMP 5.5.2, it refers to:

- designated investment business carried on by the relevant person (see para.16–006 below) with the claimant or as agent on his behalf;
- the activities of the manager or trustee of an authorised unit trust, provided that the claim is made by a holder; and
- the activities of the authorised corporate director or depositary of an investment company with variable capital (see Ch.6 above), provided that the claim is made by a holder.

16–004 The definition of protected contracts of insurance is rather more complicated. Such a contract is:

- a contract made on or after December 1, 2001, which relates to a protected risk or commitment, is issued by the relevant person through an establishment in the United Kingdom or another EEA State or in the Channel Islands or Isle of Man and is a long-term insurance contract or a relevant general insurance contract (COMP 5.4.2)

- a contact made before December 1, 2001, which is a relevant general insurance contract, a contract of insurance within the credit class or a long-term insurance contract, provided that it is one of a specified class of employers' liability insurance contracts or was a United Kingdom policy at the beginning of the liquidation for the purposes of the Policyholders Protection Act 1975 (COMP 5.4.5).

A risk or commitment is a protected risk or commitment for the purposes of this definition if it complies with the territorial conditions set out in COMP 5.4.3 and 5.4.4. "Long-term insurance contracts" and "relevant general insurance contracts" are defined in art.3(1) of the Financial Services and Markets Act 2000 (Regulated Activities) Order 2001 (SI 2001/544) and "contracts of insurance within the credit class" are defined in para.14 of Sch.1 to the Order. Long-term contracts include life and annuity policies, permanent health insurance, capital redemption policies and pension fund management policies; general insurance contracts include sickness and accident policies, fire insurance, cover for damage to property and motor insurance; contracts within the credit class are contracts to cover the risk of non-payment by a debtor, whether through insolvency or otherwise.

Structure of the Scheme

Under s.212(1) of FSMA, the FSA is required to establish a body corporate (to be known as "the scheme manager") to exercise the functions which the Act gives to the scheme manager. There must be a chairman and board of directors, appointed and liable to removal by the FSA, although the chairman may be removed only with the approval of the Treasury (s.212(4)). The independence of the chairman and board is intended to be safeguarded by the further provision in s.212(5) that the terms of appointment, and in particular the terms governing removal, must be such as to secure their independence from the FSA in the operation of the Scheme. The scheme manager does not exercise functions on behalf of the Crown and its board members, officers and staff are not Crown servants (s.212(6) and (7)), so they may be sued in the ordinary way. They are, however, protected by an exemption from liability in damages in respect of anything done or omitted in the discharge or purported discharge of the scheme manager's functions, except in cases in which the act or omission is shown to have been in bad faith or where the exclusion would prevent an award of damages in respect of any act or omission on the ground that the act or omission was unlawful as a result of s.6(1) of the Human Rights Act 1998 (which provides that it is unlawful for a public authority to act in a way which is incompatible with a right under the European Convention on Human Rights). 16–005

16–006 The Scheme itself appears in s.213(1), which requires the FSA to establish a compensation scheme "for compensating persons in cases where relevant persons are unable, or likely to be unable, to satisfy claims against them". A "relevant person" is a person who was an authorised person at the time the act or omission giving rise to the claim against him took place, or an appointed representative (s.213(9)). The essentials of the Scheme are set out in s.213(3), which requires that the Scheme must provide for the scheme manager:

(1) to assess and pay compensation, in accordance with the Scheme, to claimants in respect of claims made in connection with regulated activities carried on (whether or not with permission) by relevant persons; and

(2) to have power to impose levies on authorised persons, or any class of authorised person, for the purpose of meeting the expenses (including in particular expenses incurred, or expected to be incurred, in paying compensation, borrowing or insuring risks).

Funding

16–007 As already noted, the experience of different sectors of the financial services industry under the previous schemes varied considerably. This is reflected in the fact that in making provision for levies, the FSA must take account of the desirability of ensuring that the amount of the levies imposed on a particular class of authorised persons reflects, so far as practicable, the amount of the claims made, or likely to be made, in respect of that class of person (s.213(5)). Cross-subsidy is thus to be avoided. The Scheme may also provide for the Scheme manager to impose levies on authorised persons for the purpose of recovering the cost of establishing the Scheme (s.213(4)). An amount payable to the scheme manager by virtue of any provision of the Scheme may be recovered as a debt due to the scheme manager. The present arrangements are set out in the *FSA Handbook* at COMP 13, which permits the imposition of two distinct types of levy: a management expenses levy and a compensation costs levy (COMP 13.2.2). Recoverable management expenses are limited by s.223 of the 2000 Act. The compensation costs levy may include anticipated compensation costs for the next 12 months (COMP 13.2.3).

16–008 In accordance with the policy of avoiding cross-subsidy, the funding arrangements are split into three sub-schemes: the accepting deposits sub-scheme; the insurance business sub-scheme; and the designated investment business sub-scheme (COMP 13.2.4). COMP 13.2.5 provides that the business carried on by a participant determines into which sub-scheme, or sub-schemes, the participant falls, thus making clear that a participant may fall within more than one sub-scheme. Each sub-scheme is divided into contribution groups, determined by reference to the business activities of the authorised person under consideration, again to avoid cross-subsidy. The management costs levy may consist of a base costs levy, in respect of costs which are not dependent on the level of activity in the Scheme, a specific costs levy, in respect of costs associated with a particular default, and, during the first three years of the Scheme only, an establishment costs levy (COMP 13.2.7 to 13.2.9). The base costs and establishment costs levy applies to all participants, but the specific costs levy is allocated to the contribution group or groups of which the relevant person in default was a member, as is the compensation costs levy.

The effect of these provisions is that both levies relate to actual costs incurred or costs anticipated to be incurred during the next financial year, and accordingly there is no substantial standing fund. The scheme manager may, however, impose a levy at any time if it has reasonable grounds to believe that the funds available to meet relevant expenses are, or will be, insufficient (COMP 13.4.1). There are limits to the amount of compensation costs which participants in each sub-scheme may be required to pay, as follows: **16–009**

- a participant in the accepting deposits sub-scheme may not be asked to pay a share amounting, when taken together with all previous net sums paid pursuant to levies under that sub-scheme or under the deposit protection scheme (affecting banks), to more than 0.3 per cent of its protected deposits (COMP 13.4.5)
- a participant in the insurance business sub-scheme may not be asked to pay a share amounting, together with all previous amounts paid in that financial year, to more than 0.8 per cent of its relevant net premium income (COMP 13.4.6)
- the maximum amount of a compensation costs levy on the designated investment business sub-scheme in any one financial year is £400 million (COMP 13.4.7).

Any amount collected from a specific costs or compensation costs levy must be held to the credit of the sub-schemes and relevant contribution groups (COMP 13.4.9). If the scheme manager has more funds to the credit of a contribution group than it believes will be required to meet levies over the next 12 months, it may refund the surplus to member or former members of the group on any reasonable basis (COMP 13.4.18).

Terms of the Scheme

The provisions as to levies discussed above are envisaged in general terms by s.214(1) of the 2000 Act, which gives further details of matters which may be covered by the Scheme. In addition to provisions concerning levies, the subsection authorises in particular provision: **16–010**

- as to the circumstances in which a relevant person is to be taken to be unable, or likely to be unable to satisfy claims against him;
- for a claim to be entertained only if it is made by a specified kind of claimant;
- for a claim to be entertained only if it falls within a specified kind of claim

- as to the procedure to be followed in making a claim;
- for the making of interim payments before a claim is finally determined;
- limiting the amount payable on a claim to a specified maximum amount or a maximum amount calculated in a specified manner;
- for payment to be made, in specified circumstances, to a person other than the claimant.

The section goes on specifically to authorise different provisions for different kinds of claims, provision for the determination and regulation of matters relating to the Scheme by the scheme manager, territorial limitations, provisions relating to EEA participants and a power for the scheme manager to make a full payment of compensation to a claimant who has a claim under a comparable scheme and then to recover from that scheme.

16–011 It is helpful to look at the Scheme terms in relation to the above matters from the viewpoint of an investor wishing to make a claim. In the *FSA Handbook*, at COMP 1.3.3, a hypothetical claimant asks what he needs to do to in order to receive compensation and is answered as follows:

> "In order to receive compensation (1) you must be an eligible claimant (2) you must have a protected claim (3) you must be claiming against a relevant person (4) the relevant person must be in default. In addition, if the [scheme manager] requires you to do so, you must assign your legal rights in the claim to the [scheme manager]. And you must bring your claim to the [scheme manager] within a set time (normally within six years of the date on which your claim against the relevant person occurred). It is possible, in certain circumstances, for someone else to make a claim on your behalf."

16–012 The question who is an eligible claimant is answered in COMP 4.2. Generally speaking, as COMP 4.2.1 provides, any person is an eligible claimant. In fact, however, there is a substantial list of exceptions in COMP 4.3.2, which broadly excludes financial services institutions, collective investment and pension schemes, supranational, central and local administrative authorities, persons with a connection with the relevant person in default or who in the opinion of the scheme manager are responsible for or have contributed to the default, large companies, mutual associations or partnerships and persons whose claim arises from transactions in connection with which they have been convicted of an offence of money-laundering. (These exceptions are themselves subject to exceptions in COMP 4.2.3.) A person may make a claim on behalf of another person if the latter is or would have been an eligible claimant and would have been paid compensation if he had been able to make or pursue the claim himself (COMP 3.2.2). COMP 3.2.3 indicates that such circumstances may arise when the claim is made by a personal representative, a trustee, a donee of a power of attorney or the Master of the Court of Protection, or following the death of an eligible claimant who has already made a claim which has not yet been determined.

16–013 We have already looked in paras 16–003 and 16–004 above at the types of investment which are protected under the Scheme, and in para.16–006 at who is a relevant person. The next question, then, is whether the relevant person is in default. This is to be determined by the scheme manager (or by the FSA if the claim falls within the scope of the Deposit Guarantee Schemes Directive or the Investor Compensation Directive) (COMP 6.3.2). Such a determination may be made when the relevant person is, in the opinion of the scheme manager or the FSA, unable to satisfy protected claims against it, or likely to be unable to do so (COMP 6.3.3). A relevant person is also in default if a judicial authority has made a ruling that had the effect of suspending the ability of eligible claimants to bring claims, if the ruling is made before any such determination (COMP 6.3.1). In relation to claims concerning protected investments covered by the Investment Compensation Directive, the scheme manager, if it is satisfied that a protected claim exists, has an additional power to determine that a relevant person is in default if it is further satisfied that the relevant person cannot be contacted at its last place of business and that reasonable steps have been taken to establish a forwarding or current address, but without success, and that there appears to the scheme manager to be no evidence that the relevant person will be able to meet claims against it (COMP 6.3.4). The scheme manager may also determine a relevant person to be in default if it is satisfied that a protected claim exists and that the relevant person is the subject of any of a number of types of proceedings (whether in the United Kingdom or another jurisdiction) which tend to show, either by judicial act or otherwise, that the relevant person is unlikely to be able to meet claims against it (COMP 6.3.3). In relation to insurance claims, the scheme manager must treat any term in an insurance undertaking's constitution or contracts limiting its liabilities under a long-term insurance contract to the amount of its assets as limiting its liability to any claimant to an amount which is not less than its gross assets (COMP 6.3.5). Where an insurance undertaking is in default, the scheme manager must treat liabilities in respect of premiums paid (if the contract has not commenced), the proceeds of a long-term insurance contract which has matured or been surrendered but which have not been paid to the claimant, the unexpired portion of any premium in relation to relevant general insurance contracts and claims by persons entitled to the benefit of a judgment under the Road Traffic Act 1988 (or the Northern Ireland equivalent) as giving rise to claims (COMP 5.4.7).

It may be thought that it will not be easy for an investor wondering whether he has a claim to find his way through the above provisions. Possibly in recognition of that fact, the scheme manager is expressly required to take appropriate steps to ensure that potential claimants are informed of how they can make a claim for compensation as soon as possible after a determination has been made that a relevant person is in default (COMP 2.2.7). The scheme manager is also obliged, by COMP 2.2.3, to publish information for claimants and potential claimants on the operation of the Scheme. An application for compensation should be in writing and may be rejected if it contains any material inaccuracy or omission, unless the scheme manager considers that to be wholly unintentional (COMP 8.2.1). In such a case the application may be resubmitted, with the appropriate amendments (COMP 8.2.2). It must be rejected if the **16–014** liability of the relevant person to the claimant has been extinguished by operation of law, or if the scheme manager considers that a civil claim in respect of the liability would have been defeated by a defence of limitation at the earlier date the relevant person is determined to be in default or the date at which the claimant first indicates in writing that he may have a claim against the relevant person (COMP 8.2.3). It is this provision which is the basis for the general requirement that the claim should be brought within six years, since that is the standard period of limitation for claims in contract under s.5 of the Limitation Act 1980. Where the claim is made in connection with protected investment business, however, the scheme manager may disregard a defence of limitation if it considers that it would be reasonable to do so.

16–015 If the scheme manager accepts the claim, it will make an offer of compensation to the claimant. The claimant has 90 days from the date on which the offer is made to accept it or to dispute it; if he does not do so, the scheme manager may withdraw the offer (COMP 8.3.1). If the claimant disputes the offer, again the scheme manager may withdraw the offer, but must consider exercising its powers, considered in para.16.018 below, to make a reduced or interim payment before doing so. An offer which has been withdrawn under these provisions may be repeated (COMP 8.3.3). An offer must be withdrawn if it appears to the scheme manager that no such offer should have been made (COMP 8.3.4), and the scheme manager must seek to recover any compensation actually paid if it appears to the scheme manager that no such payment should have been made, unless it believes on reasonable grounds that it would be unreasonable to do so, or that the costs of doing so would exceed any amount which could be recovered (COMP 8.3.5). Questions of unreasonableness would presumably arise if the claimant appeared likely to have a change of position defence as a matter of law.

16–016 By virtue of COMP 7.2.1, the offer may be conditional upon the claimant's assigning the whole or any part of his rights against the relevant person, or against any third party, or both, to the scheme manager on such terms as it thinks fit, and in such a case the scheme manager comes under an obligation to make such recoveries as it reasonably can through the rights so assigned (COMP 7.2.3). Any recoveries so made must be paid to the claimant to the extent that the amount recovered exceeds the amount of the compensation (excluding interest) received by the claimant in respect of the protected claim, or, if there is no such excess, to the extent that a failure to pay any sums recovered would leave a claimant who had promptly accepted an offer of compensation at a disadvantage relative to a claimant who had delayed in accepting such an offer (COMP 7.2.4). An example in the *FSA Handbook* at COMP 7.2.6 explains how such a disadvantage may arise. The facts are that A accepts an offer before the liquidator pays any dividend, assigns his rights and receives the maximum sum payable from the scheme manager. When the liquidator pays the dividend, it is less than the compensation paid and A recovers nothing further. B, however, accepts an offer after receiving a dividend from the liquidator. His claim is only for the balance of his loss, but the total of the compensation for the balance and the dividend exceeds the amount received by A as compensation alone. In the absence of the provision in COMP 7.2.4, A would be penalised by his prompt acceptance.

As a general rule, the scheme manager is obliged to pay compensation as soon as is reasonably possible after (a) it is satisfied that the claimant is an eligible claimant who has made an application for compensation and that the claim is in respect of a protected claim and is made against a relevant person who is in default, and the claimant has assigned the whole or any part of his rights against the relevant person if so required and (b) the scheme manager has calculated the compensation due (COMP 9.2.1). Compensation must be paid within three months of that date unless the FSA has granted an extension, which itself may not exceed a further three months. There are, however, exceptions to the general principle in COMP 9.2.2. In relation to protected deposits, the exception is that the claimant has been charged with an offence arising out of or in relation to money-laundering and those proceedings have not yet concluded. In respect of protected contracts of insurance and protected investment business, the exceptions principally relate to cases where the claimant may have other rights by virtue of which he can make recovery or where the claim falls within special review provisions (*i.e.* the pensions mis-selling review in connection with sales of personal pension schemes and retirement annuity schemes to those who were, or were likely to be, members of occupational pension schemes, and the FSAVC review relating to additional voluntary contributions policies). Detailed provisions relating to the quantification date and for calculating the amount of the compensation are contained in the *FSA Handbook* at COMP 12.2 to 12.4. **16–017**

Payment is to be made to the claimant or as the claimant directs (COMP 11.2.1). An interim payment on account may be made if the scheme manager is satisfied that compensation is in principle payable, but that immediate payment in full would not be prudent because of uncertainty as to the amount, or because the claimant has a reasonable prospect of recovery from another source (COMP 11.2.4 and 11.2.5). A reduced final payment may be made if neither the Deposit Guarantee Scheme Directive nor the Investor Compensation Directive applies. Where an interim or reduced payment is made, interest is payable as the scheme manager considers appropriate and is not to be taken into account when applying the limits on the compensation payable (COMP 11.2.7 and 11.2.8). Special provision is made by COMP 11.2.2 for the case where the claim arises in the context of pension mis-selling; then any compensation must be paid not to the claimant, but to the trustee of an occupational pension scheme or to a suitable pension provider, unless exceptional circumstances apply. **16–018**

The maximum amount of compensation payable is set out in COMP 10.2.3. In respect of protected deposits held by a relevant person in default, it is 100 per cent of the first £20,000 and 90 per cent of the next £33,000, which produces a total maximum payment of £48,700. The maximum amount payable in respect of protected contracts for designated investment business is 100 per cent of the first £30,000 and 90 per cent of the next £20,000, producing a maximum payment of £48,000. The limits applicable to protected contracts of insurance are as follows: **16–019**

- where the contract is a relevant general insurance contract and the claim is in respect of a liability subject to compulsory insurance, the full amount of the claim;
- where the contract is a relevant general insurance contract and the claim arises under the Third Party (Rights Against Insurers) Act 1930, is an employers' liability contract and is in connection with an art.9 default (for which see art.2(2) of the Financial Services and Markets Act 2000 (Transitional Provisions, Repeals and Savings) (Financial Services Compensation Scheme) Order 2001 (SI 2001/2967)), 90 per cent of the claim;
- in all other general insurance cases, 100 per cent of the first £2,000 and 90 per cent of the remainder
- where the contract is a long-term insurance contract, 100 per cent of the first £2,000 and 90 per cent of the remainder.

The limit applies to the aggregate amount of claims which the claimant has in respect of each category of protected claim against the relevant person in default, so that, for example, a bank depositor who has two different accounts in each of which he has deposited £2,000 will receive £3,800 (£2,000 plus 90 per cent of £2,000), rather than £4,000 (COMP 10.2.2).

16–020 Special provision is made for cases involving trustees, personal representatives and agents, and for joint claims. The following principles apply in relation to trustees:

(1) if a person has a claim both as a trustee and on his own behalf, the scheme manager must treat him as if his claim as trustee were a claim of a different person (COMP 12.6.1). The compensation limits will therefore apply separately to the claim in each capacity.

(2) if a claimant has a claim as a bare trustee for one or more beneficiaries, the scheme manager must treat the beneficiary or beneficiaries as having the claim (COMP 12.6.2).

(3) if a group of persons has a claim as trustees, the scheme manager must treat them as a single and continuing person distinct from the persons who may from time to time be the trustees (COMP 12.6.3).

(4) where the same person has a claim as trustee for different trusts, the scheme rules apply as if the claims relating to each trust were the claims of different persons (COMP 12.6.4).

(5) where the claimant is a trustee and some of the beneficiaries are persons who would not be eligible claimants if they had a claim themselves, the scheme manager must adjust the amount of the overall net claim to eliminate the part of the claim which, in its view, is a claim for those beneficiaries (COMP 12.6.5).

(6) in all these cases, the scheme manager must try to ensure that any compensation paid to the trustee is for the benefit of beneficiaries who would be eligible claimants if they had a claim themselves and

does not exceed the amount of loss suffered by those beneficiaries (COMP 12.6.6).

Where a person is entitled to a deposit made out of a clients' or other similar account containing money to which one person or more is or are entitled, the scheme manager must treat each of those other persons, and not the first person, as entitled to the part of the deposit which corresponds to the proportion of the money in the account to which the other person was entitled (COMP 12.6.7). If a person has a claim as personal representative, he is to be treated as standing in the shoes of the dead investor in respect of the claim (COMP 12.6.8). If a claimant has a claim as agent for one or more principals, the scheme manager must treat the principal or principals as having the claim and not the agent (COMP 12.6.9).

If two or more persons are carrying on business together in partnership **16–021** and have a joint beneficial claim, the claim is to be treated as a claim of the partnership. There is thus a single limit on the amount of compensation recoverable. In other cases of a joint beneficial claim, each person has a claim for his share, and in the absence of satisfactory evidence as to their respective shares, the scheme manager must regard each person as entitled to an equal share (COMP 12.6.10). There will then be a separate limit on the share of each joint owner.

Where the claim arises out of business done with a branch or establish- **16–022** ment of the relevant person outside the United Kingdom, the scheme manager must interpret references to persons entitled as personal representatives, trustees, bare trustees or agents, or references to persons having a joint beneficial claim or carrying on business in partnership, as references to persons entitled under the law of the relevant country in a capacity appearing to the scheme manager to correspond as nearly as may be to that capacity (COMP 12.6.11).

Having regard to the particular requirements of investors involved in **16–023** insurance business, s.216 of the 2000 Act itself specifically authorises the inclusion in the Scheme of provisions intended to secure continuity of insurance cover for policyholders under long-term insurance contracts, and s.217 specifically authorises the inclusion of provisions dealing more generally with insurers in financial difficulties. The Scheme accordingly requires the scheme manager, broadly speaking, to make arrangements to secure continuity of cover in long-term insurance cases if it is reasonably practicable to do so (COMP 3.3.1). Before it does so, the scheme manager must reduce the eligible claimant's interest in the protected contract to 90 per cent of the amount which would otherwise have been payable, and reduce all premiums which have not fallen due before the time when the reduction is to take effect to 90 per cent of the amount which would otherwise have been payable (COMP 3.3.5). Where an insurer is in financial difficulties (defined in COMP 3.3.6), the scheme manager must take such measures for the purpose of safeguarding eligible claimants on such terms as the scheme manager considers appropriate if, in its opinion at the time it proposes to take the measures, the cost is likely to be less than the cost of paying compensation (COMP 3.3.3). Where the relevant person is in provisional liquidation or liquidation, then, unless such arrangements or measures have been or are being made, the scheme manager may make payments to or on behalf of eligible claimants on such terms as it thinks fit, or may encourage the liquidator to make payments to the claimant by giving him an indemnity (COMP 11.2.3).

16–024 The 2000 Act also envisages that there may be circumstances in which the scheme manager requires to obtain documents or information from a person whose act or omission might give rise to a liability on the scheme manager to make a compensation payment. Such a power is given to the scheme manager by s.219, subject to modification in ss.220 and 224 in cases in which the relevant person is insolvent. Failure to comply with a requirement under s.219 or 220 may lead to the defaulter's being dealt with as if he (and, in the case of a body corporate, any director or officer) were in contempt of court.

16–025 The Scheme expressly obliges the scheme manager to administer the Scheme in a way which is procedurally fair and is in accordance with the European Convention on Human Rights (COMP 2.2.1). Under COMP 2.2.8, it must also put in place and publish procedures satisfying such requirements for the handling of any complaint of maladministration relating to any aspect of the operation of the Scheme. The scheme manager may agree to pay the reasonable costs of an eligible claimant in bringing or continuing insolvency proceedings against a relevant person if it is satisfied that those proceedings would help it discharge its functions under the rules (COMP 2.2.4). Generally, the scheme manager must have regard to the need to use its resources in the most efficient and economic way in carrying out its functions (COMP 2.2.6).

Other EEA States

16–026 Credit institutions (*i.e.* bodies subject to the Deposit Guarantee Schemes Directive) and bodies subject to the Investor Compensation Directive whose home state is in another EEA State will necessarily be participants in a deposit protection or investor compensation scheme in their home state, but the level of protection offered by such a scheme will not necessarily be the same level of protection as that offered under the Scheme. The Scheme therefore makes provision for such institutions or bodies to elect to participate in the Scheme on terms which mean in effect that the participant can top up the cover available under the home state scheme to the level available under the Scheme itself (COMP 16.1.6). When the scheme manager accepts an application to participate, it must allocate the participant to the contribution group or groups which seem most appropriate, taking into account the nature of the business for which cover is sought (COMP 16.2.4). The scheme manager must have in place procedures to enable an appeal to be brought against the rejection of an election or the allocation to a particular contribution group, and those procedures must satisfy the minimum requirements of procedural fairness and comply with the European Convention on Human Rights (COMP 16.2.5). Where such top-up arrangements exist, the scheme manager must seek to establish with the relevant home state scheme appropriate procedures for the payment of compensation to claimants (COMP 16.3.1). Provision is also made for the termination of such cover (COMP 16.4).

The effect of making such top-up arrangements is, of course, that the EEA institution or body concerned is able to offer investors protection equal to that which they would enjoy if investing in a United Kingdom body or institution. It follows that it may be important for investors to know if the cover is terminated, and the termination arrangements include an obligation on the scheme manager to bring the ending of the cover to the attention of clients by means of a public notice.

Transitional Provisions

Although there is a considerable degree of continuity between the previous schemes and the present Scheme, not least because of the influence of the relevant European Directives, transitional arrangements were necessary. They are contained in the Financial Services and Markets Act 2000 (Transitional Provisions, Repeals and Savings) (Financial Services Compensation Scheme) Order 2001 (SI 2001/2967). Very briefly, applications for compensation, whether made before or after December 1, 2001, where there was a relevant default before that date, are to be determined by the scheme manager in accordance with the relevant former scheme, and the making of the necessary modifications of such schemes is provided for. Provision is also made for the case in which there was no relevant default before that date but the circumstances could have given rise to an obligation on the Board of certain former schemes to pay compensation. If the claimant would have had a claim under a former scheme and does not under the new scheme, the scheme manager may nevertheless deal with the claim. **16–027**

The funds, assets, rights and liabilities of the former Boards have been transferred to the scheme manager.

The Financial Ombudsman Service

Introduction

By the time the Bill which became FSMA 2000 was published, there were eight dispute resolution schemes in the financial services world, some of which were statutory and some of which were voluntary. This was unsatisfactory from the point of view of an investor, for whom the number of schemes, the fact that some were compulsory and some were not and the fact that some firms had a degree of choice over which scheme to join, if any, was clearly liable to lead to confusion. The policy adopted was therefore to establish a single ombudsman scheme under the auspices of the FSA. Although the scheme is referred to in the Act as "the ombudsman scheme", it operates under the name "the Financial Ombudsman Service" (in this chapter called "the FOS"). It became effective on December 1, 2001. **16–028**

16–029 The purpose of the FOS is, as stated in s.225(2) of the FSMA 2000, to provide a scheme "under which certain disputes may be resolved quickly and with minimum formality by an independent person". It has both a compulsory and a voluntary jurisdiction, as envisaged by ss.226 and 227, and is administered by a body corporate called "the scheme operator", established by the FSA in accordance with the provisions of Sch.17 of the 2000 Act. Those provisions are very similar to the provisions relating to the scheme manager considered in para.16.005 above; the same principles apply in respect of the structure of the board, appointment to and removal from the board and whether or not functions are exercised on behalf of the Crown or as Crown servants. The ombudsmen who make determinations under the FOS are not themselves board members, officers or staff, however, and it is separately provided that they also are not Crown servants. Again, there is an exemption from liability for damages for the scheme operator and the ombudsmen in the same terms as that which applies to the scheme manager, but only in relation to the compulsory jurisdiction. For the purposes of the law of defamation, proceedings in relation to a complaint which is subject to the compulsory jurisdiction are to be treated as if they were proceedings before a court.

16–030 The detailed funding arrangements for the FOS are set out in the *FSA Handbook* at DISP 5. The principle adopted is that there is an annual fee in the form of a general levy charged on all those whose activities are subject to the FOS's jurisdiction and there are case fees in respect of individual complaints. As with the Scheme, during the first three years of the FOS's operation, there is a supplementary levy to cover the costs of establishment.

Functions, Duties and Powers of Scheme Operator

16–031 Under Sch.17 of the 2000 Act, the scheme operator must:

- appoint and maintain a panel of persons to act as ombudsmen, one of whom must be the Chief Ombudsman;
- report annually to the FSA and publish its report;
- adopt a budget, approved by the FSA, for each of its financial years;
- in relation to the compulsory jurisdiction, make scheme rules setting out the procedure for the reference of complaints and for their reference, consideration and determination by an ombudsman; and
- in relation to the voluntary jurisdiction, make rules governing that jurisdiction and fix the standard terms on which complaints under that jurisdiction are to be dealt with and determined.

The scheme operator may additionally:

- publish guidance consisting of such information and advice as it considers appropriate and may charge for it or distribute it free of charge

- make arrangements with other similar bodies to delegate to another such body the exercise of any part of the voluntary jurisdiction or to exercise on behalf of another such body any function of that body.

Detailed provisions relating to the exercise of the duty to appoint the panel of ombudsmen are contained in paras 4 and 5 of Sch.17. The size of the panel is not specified. Those appointed must appear to the scheme operator to have appropriate qualifications and experience. The terms of the appointment are at the discretion of the scheme operator, but must be consistent with the independence of the person appointed. This latter requirement is clearly important, given the involvement of the FSA in the constitutional and budget arrangements of the scheme operator. The Chief Ombudsman also reports to the FSA annually (para.7 of Sch.17), and again the report is to be published. In practice, his report is published with the scheme operator's report. **16–032**

Although, as already mentioned, the scheme operator has various rule-making powers and duties, the FSA also has a rule-making responsibility. The FSA must make rules specifying a time limit within which complaints must be referred (although the ombudsman may be given power to extend it in specified circumstances; requiring the complainant first to communicate the substance of the complaint to the person complained about ("the respondent") and to give him a reasonable opportunity to deal with it; and requiring potential respondents to establish appropriate internal complaints procedures. The provisions made appear in DISP 1 and 2, and are considered further in para.16.041 below. **16–033**

The rules made by the scheme operator in relation to the compulsory jurisdiction govern the procedure to be followed in the case of a complaint properly referred. They are made in the context of s.228(1) of FSMA 2000, which requires that a complaint is to be determined by reference to what is, in the opinion of the ombudsman, fair and reasonable in all the circumstances of the case. Again they are considered further below. The standard terms established by the scheme operator in relation to the voluntary jurisdiction as a matter of policy mirror the terms applying to the compulsory jurisdiction as far as possible: see further para.16–039. **16–034**

Jurisdiction

Under s.226, a complaint is to be dealt with by the FOS under the compulsory jurisdiction if: **16–035**

- the activity in the course of carrying on which the act or omission complained of occurred is one to which compulsory jurisdiction rules apply;
- the complainant is eligible and wishes to have the complaint dealt with by the FOS;
- the respondent was an authorised person at the time of the act or omission to which the complaint relates; and

- the act or omission occurred at a time when compulsory jurisdiction rules were in force in relation to the activity in question.

"Compulsory jurisdiction rules" are made by the FSA and the rules presently in force are contained in the *FSA Handbook* at DISP 2.6. The activities in question are: regulated activities; lending money (other than restricted credit); paying money by a plastic card (other than a store card); the provision of ancillary banking services; and activities ancillary to those activities (which includes the giving of advice in connection with those activities). An authorised person is responsible for the activities of its appointed representatives (DISP 2.6.5). The FSA does not have power to specify as an activity to which compulsory jurisdiction rules apply an activity which is not a regulated activity and which could not be made a regulated activity (see s.266(3)). The concept of carrying on an activity is a wide one (see the examples in DISP 2.6.4), and it is thought that a complainant need only show that the authorised person or representative offers the service in question and that there has been an act or omission affecting the complainant in relation to the provision or intended provision of the service. It is not necessary to show that the service was ultimately provided or that the complainant was the person to whom the service was or might have been provided.

16–036 It is again the responsibility of the FSA to make rules governing the question who is an eligible complainant, subject to the provisions of s.226(7) that persons other than individuals may be eligible, but authorised persons may not be eligible except in specified circumstances or in relation to complaints of a specified kind. The rules made are to be found in DISP 2.4. Broadly speaking, a person is an eligible complainant if he is a private individual, a business with a group annual turnover of less than £1 million at the time of the reference to the respondent, a charity with an annual income of less than £1 million at that time or a trustee of a trust which has a net asset value of less than £1 million at that time. The complainant must be a customer, a potential customer or a person with an indirect complaint (*i.e.* the complaint arises out of one of a number of specified relationships or is derived from another person and arises from one of a number of specified circumstances: see DISP 2.4.10). The complainant must not be an intermediate customer or market counterparty of the respondent at the time of the act or omission and in relation to the activity which is the subject of the complaint, nor a firm or participant in the voluntary jurisdiction whose complaint relates to an activity which that firm itself has permission to carry on or that participant conducts and which is subject to the compulsory or the voluntary jurisdiction. The effect of the exception is thus to exclude complainants who might be regarded as "professionals" in the relevant financial services field.

16–037 Express provision is made for a complaint to be brought by a representative on behalf of an eligible complainant or a deceased person who would have been an eligible complainant (DISP 2.4.16 and 2.4.17). The representative must be authorised by the eligible complainant or by law, but if so authorised, it is immaterial whether or not he can satisfy the criteria for eligibility or has a claim of his own.

Under s.227, a complaint is to be dealt with by the FOS under the voluntary jurisdiction if: **16–038**

- the activity in the course of carrying on which the act or omission complained of occurred is one to which voluntary jurisdiction rules apply;
- the complainant is eligible and wishes to have the complaint dealt with by the FOS;
- at the time of the act or omission to which the complaint relates, the respondent was a participant;
- at the time when the complaint is referred, the respondent has not withdrawn in accordance with the scheme provisions to that effect;
- the act or omission to which the complaint relates occurred at a time when voluntary jurisdiction rules were in force in relation to the activity in question; and
- the complaint cannot be dealt with under the compulsory jurisdiction.

"Voluntary jurisdiction rules" are made by the scheme operator, but the scheme operator must obtain the approval of the FSA to the rules (s.227(6)) and may only specify activities which could be specified in compulsory jurisdiction rules (s.227(4)). The rules made are at DISP 2.6 and specify: general insurance business; accepting deposits; lending money secured by a charge on land; lending money (other than restricted credit); paying money by a plastic card (other than a store card); the provision of ancillary banking services; acting as an intermediary for a loan secured by charge over land; acting as an intermediary for general insurance business or long-term insurance business; a financial services activity carried out after December 1, 2001 which had been covered by a former scheme in so far as the respondent was a member of the former scheme, in respect of that activity, immediately before that date; and activities ancillary to those activities (which again includes the giving of advice in connection with those activities).

The definition of "eligible complainant" discussed in relation to the compulsory jurisdiction applies equally in relation to the voluntary jurisdiction.

Participants for the purposes of the voluntary jurisdiction are referred to in DISP as "VJ participants" and may or may not be authorised persons (s.227(10)).

Under the standard terms in respect of the voluntary jurisdiction, set out in DISP 4: **16–039**

- the specified complaints handling procedures for authorised persons apply also to VJ participants, with the exception of the record-keeping and reporting requirements;
- the jurisdiction provisions applicable in respect of the compulsory jurisdiction apply also to the voluntary jurisdiction, with the

exception of the provisions which define the activities within the voluntary jurisdiction;

- the complaints handling procedures apply equally whether the jurisdiction being exercised is compulsory or voluntary, except where their application to VJ participants is specifically excluded or necessarily inapplicable;
- liability in damages is excluded, subject to the exceptions which apply in relation to the compulsory jurisdiction;
- the ombudsman has power to make a money award against a VJ participant of such amount as he considers fair compensation for financial loss, pain and suffering, damage to reputation or distress and inconvenience, and power to make a direction that the VJ participant take such steps in relation to the complainant as the ombudsman considers just and appropriate;
- if the ombudsman's determination is accepted by the complainant within the time limit specified by the ombudsman, it will be binding on the VJ participant and final, and may be enforced in court by the complainant;
- once a person has become a VJ participant, he may not withdraw from the voluntary jurisdiction until the scheme operator has approved a plan for notifying customers of the participant's intention and handling complaints prior to withdrawal and agreed the date for withdrawal, and until the VJ participant has paid the general levy for the year of withdrawal and any other fees payable.

16–040 Territorially, the FOS is concerned primarily with activities in the United Kingdom and so the principal territorial provision defines the scope of the jurisdiction as covering complaints about activities carried on from an establishment in the United Kingdom (DISP 2.7.1). The voluntary jurisdiction, however, extends also to complaints about activities within the scope of that jurisdiction which are carried on from elsewhere in the European Economic Area if the activity is directed wholly or partly at the United Kingdom, or part of it, contracts governing the activity are or (in the case of a potential customer) would have been made under the law of one of the constituent parts of the United Kingdom and the VJ participant has notified appropriate regulators in its home state of its intention to participate in the voluntary jurisdiction (DISP 2.7.2).

The residence or base of the complainant is irrelevant (DISP 2.7.6).

Internal Complaint Handling

16–041 Reference has been made in para.16–033 to the obligation for potential respondents to establish internal complaint handling procedures. The basic requirement is that an authorised person must have in place and operate appropriate and effective internal complaint handling procedures (which must be written down) for handling any expression of dissatisfaction, whether oral or written, and whether justified or not, from or on behalf of an eligible complainant about its provision of, or failure to provide, a financial service (DISP 1.2.1). An "appropriate" procedure will take account of the type of business the authorised person undertakes, its size and organisational structure, the nature and complexity of the complaints it is likely to receive and the likely number of complaints (DISP 1.2.5). A third party administrator may be used to handle complaints (DISP 1.2.6) and a complainant should be able to make a complaint by any reasonable means (*e.g.* by letter, telephone, email or in person) (DISP 1.2.8). As recognised in DISP 1.2.3, the authorised person does not, of course, need to restrict use of its internal procedure to complainants who are eligible complainants for the purposes of FOS.

However effective the internal procedure may be, it will be of little benefit to investors if they are unaware of its existence. DISP 1.2.9 contains various publicity requirements designed to ensure that the availability of the procedure comes to the attention of investors at the point of sale and whenever a complaint is made (unless the complaint is resolved by close of business on the next business day). Details of the procedure must be published and copies must be available on request.

Further general requirements to be found in DISP 1.2 are that: **16–042**

- the procedure must provide for complaints to be investigated by an employee of sufficient competence who, where appropriate, was not directly involved in the matter which is the subject matter of the complaint; for the person with the task of responding to the complaint either to have authority to settle complaints (including authority to offer redress where appropriate) or to have ready access to someone with such authority; and for responses to complaints to address adequately the subject matter of the complaint and, where a complaint is upheld, to offer appropriate redress;
- if the authorised person decides that redress is appropriate, the procedure must provide the complainant with fair compensation for any acts or omissions for which the authorised person was responsible and comply with any offer of redress which the complainant accepts;
- the authorised person must take reasonable steps to ensure that all relevant employees, including employees of appointed representatives, are aware of the internal complaint handling procedure and must endeavour to ensure that employees act in accordance with it, and must also put in place appropriate management controls and take reasonable steps to ensure that complaints are handled fairly, consistently and promptly and that any recurring or systemic problems are identified and remedied.

Speed of response is in fact a matter which attracts detailed coverage in **16–043**
DISP 1.4. Time limits are specified for the provision of an acknowledgment, a final or holding response and, if a holding response has been given, a final response or a further holding response indicating when the

authorised person expects to be able to give a final response. The requirements of DISP 1.4 include requirements as to the information to be given at each stage. Slightly different requirements apply if there are two stages to the internal procedure. A final response must inform the complainant that he may refer the matter to the FOS within six months, and must enclose a copy of the FOS explanatory leaflet unless a copy has already been sent. There is an exception to these requirements where the complaint is subject to the FSAVC review relating to additional voluntary contribution schemes, in which case the complaint will be dealt with under the terms of a policy statement issued by the FSA on February 18, 2000.

In relation to the compulsory jurisdiction, there are record-keeping and reporting requirements which will enable the FSA to keep informed of the way in which internal complaint procedures are operating (DISP 1.5). Authorised persons are expressly required to co-operate fully with the ombudsman in the handling of complaints against them (DISP 1.6.1).

Determinations by the FOS

16–044 The bare bones of how the ombudsman is to approach his task and what is to happen when a determination has been made are contained in s.228 of FSMA 2000. The basis of the determination, as has already been noted, is what, in the opinion of the ombudsman, is fair and reasonable in all the circumstances of the case. When a determination has been made, it is to be notified to both complainant and respondent by a written statement which will give reasons, be signed, and require the complainant to notify the ombudsman whether or not the determination is accepted (s.228(4)). If the complainant does accept the determination, it becomes binding on the respondent and is final (s.228(5)). Once it has become binding, a direction in a determination that the respondent take certain steps is enforceable by injunction (s.229(9)) and a money award may be enforced in accordance with provisions contained in Sch.17 (s.229(8)(b)). Under the Schedule, if a money award has been registered in accordance with the scheme rules, it may be recovered by execution issued from the county court (or otherwise), if a county court so orders, as if it were payable under an order of that court. (Special provision is made for execution in Scotland and Northern Ireland.)

16–045 As the foregoing suggests, under s.229(2) there are two forms of award which may be made if the ombudsman determines a complaint in favour of the complainant, namely, a money award and a direction that the respondent take steps in relation to the complainant. The money award is to be of such amount as the ombudsman considers fair compensation for loss or damage suffered by the complainant, and the steps directed are to be such steps as the ombudsman considers just and appropriate, whether or not a court could order such steps to be taken. A money award may compensate for financial loss or for loss or damage of any other kind specified in compulsory jurisdiction rules. As with the voluntary jurisdiction, the loss or damage specified, in addition to financial loss, consists of pain and suffering, damage to reputation and distress and inconvenience (DISP 3.9.2). The maximum money award (specified by the FSA under s.229(4)) which may be made is £100,000, although if interest is awarded under the power given by s.229(8)(a), it does not form part of the award for the purposes of calculating the monetary limit (DISP 3.9.5). If in the view of the ombudsman fair compensation would require a payment greater than the amount of the maximum money award, he may recommend that the respondent pays the complainant the difference (s.229(5)).

In addition to the power to make awards of the kind discussed above, the ombudsman has a distinct power to award costs. This power arises under DISP 3.9.10, made by the scheme operator in exercise of the power to that effect given by s.230, but it is not envisaged that the power will be used frequently (DISP 3.9.11). The section does not authorise rules which provide for an award against the complainant in respect of the respondent's costs, but does permit rules which provide for an award against the complainant in favour of the scheme operator, for the purpose of providing a contribution to resources deployed in dealing with the complaint, if in the opinion of the ombudsman the complainant's conduct was improper or unreasonable, or the complainant was responsible for an unreasonable delay. No such rules have yet been made. An amount due under an award in favour of the scheme operator is recoverable as a debt due to the scheme operator (s.230(6)) and any other award is to be treated as a money award for the purposes of the enforcement provisions already discussed (s.230(7)). **16–046**

Like the scheme manager under the Scheme, the ombudsman may need to obtain information or documents to carry out his responsibilities effectively. S.231 therefore gives him a power to do so very similar to that referred to in para.16.024 above, again with the sanction that failure to comply with a requirement under s.31 may lead to the defaulter's being dealt with as if he (and in the case of a body corporate, any director or officer) were in contempt of court. **16–047**

That, then, is the background against which the ombudsman is to work. On receiving a complaint, the ombudsman's first task, as set out in DISP 3.2.1, is to consider: **16–048**

- whether or not the complaint is one which can be dealt with by the FOS;
- whether or not the complaint is within the time limits for referral;
- whether or not the complainant is an eligible complainant;
- whether or not the complaint is one which should be dismissed without consideration of its merits.

Nothing further needs to be said about whether the complaint is within the jurisdiction of the FOS and whether the complainant is an eligible complainant.

There are three time limits to be noted: first, that the ombudsman cannot consider a complaint which has been referred less than eight weeks after receipt of the complaint by the respondent, unless the respondent has already sent its final response; second, that the ombudsman cannot consider a complaint referred more than six months after the complainant is advised by the respondent in its final response that the complaint may be referred; third, that the ombudsman cannot consider a complaint referred more than six years after the event complained of or (if later) more than three years from the date on which the complainant became aware, or ought reasonably to have become aware, that he had cause for complaint (DISP 2.3.1). The latter two time limits may be extended by the ombudsman if, in his view, the failure to comply was as a result of exceptional circumstances, suggested examples of which are that the complainant is or has been incapacitated, or that the respondent failed in its final response to inform the complainant of the possibility of reference to the FOS or of the time limit for making the reference (DISP 2.3.3). The third time limit is also subject to specific exceptions in relation to complaints relating to particular areas of activity. Its general effect is presumably intended to be analogous to the effect of the Limitation Act 1980 as respects claims in contract and tort, although more generous as respects contractual claims involving latent damage.

Failure to satisfy the ombudsman on the first three points set out above will not necessarily be fatal. If the complaint is premature, it will simply be referred back to the respondent (DISP 3.2.3). If the ombudsman considers that the complaint or the complainant may be ineligible, he must give the complainant an opportunity to make representations and must give reasons for a decision of ineligibility (DISP 3.2.5). A similar procedure applies if the respondent disputes the eligibility of the complaint or the complainant, although both sides must have the opportunity to make representations and must be given the reasoned decision (DISP 3.2.7).

16–049 DISP 3.3.1 lists 17 circumstances in which a complaint may be dismissed without consideration of its merits. Broadly speaking, they may be divided into the following groups: cases in which the complainant is unlikely to receive any, or any further, redress; cases in which the complaint has already been, or still is, or ought to be, the subject of consideration by some other appropriate body (including the court); cases in which the complaint is about matters not appropriate for the ombudsman to review (namely, the legitimate exercise of the respondent's commercial judgment, employment matters, investment performance or a discretionary decision under a will or trust); cases in which the complaint involves, or may involve, others who have not consented to the referral; and any other case in which the ombudsman is satisfied that there are other compelling reasons why it is inappropriate for the complaint to be dealt with under the scheme.

Where the ombudsman proposes to dismiss the complaint without consideration on one of the above grounds, he must again give the complainant the opportunity to make representations and if he decides to dismiss the complaint he must give reasons for his decision.

16–050 Once the ombudsman has decided to entertain the complaint, the next step is for him to consider whether there is a reasonable prospect of resolving the complaint by mediation, in which case he may attempt to negotiate a settlement between the parties (DISP 3.2.9). Alternatively, he may refer a complaint to another complaints scheme where he considers that it would be more suitable for the matter to be determined by that scheme and the complainant consents (DISP 3.4.1). If he decides that an investigation is necessary, he will give each party the opportunity of making representations and will send them a provisional assessment, setting out his reasons and stating a time limit within which they must respond. If either party disagrees with the provisional assessment, they have a right (of which they must be informed) to make representations and the ombudsman will then proceed to a determination (DISP 3.2.11 and 3.2.12). A hearing will not be held automatically, but if the ombudsman considers that the complaint cannot fairly be determined without a hearing, he will convene one and either party may in writing request a hearing, setting out the issues he wishes to raise and any reasons why he considers it should be in private (DISP 3.2.12 and 3.2.13). In deciding whether or not to hold a hearing and if so, whether it should be in public or in private, the ombudsman must have regard to the European Convention on Human Rights. Art.6 of the Convention entitles everyone to a fair and public hearing in the determination of his civil rights and obligations, and the effect of making a determination of the ombudsman binding is that civil rights and obligations are affected.

The ombudsman has various procedural powers in relation to the **16–051**
investigation and determination of complaints. He may, under DISP 3.5.2:

- give directions as to the issues on which evidence is required, the extent to which the necessary evidence should be oral or written and the way in which evidence should be presented (these powers follow Pt 32.1 of the Civil Procedure Rules);
- exclude or admit evidence, whether or not the evidence would be admissible in a court of law;
- accept information in confidence, so that only an edited version or summary is disclosed;
- reach a decision on the basis of the information supplied and take account of the failure of either party to supply information;
- dismiss a complaint if the complainant fails to supply requested information.

He may also fix and extend time limits for any aspect of the consideration of a complaint (DISP 3.6.1). If the respondent fails to comply with a time limit, the ombudsman may proceed to the next stage of the consideration of the complaint and may, if appropriate, make provision for any material distress or inconvenience caused by that failure in any award he decides to make (DISP 3.6.2). If the complainant fails to comply with a time limit, the ombudsman may either proceed to the next stage or dismiss the complaint (DISP 3.6.3). Only an ombudsman may determine a complaint or decide the circumstances in which information may be disclosed to a regulatory body, but he may designate members of the FOS staff to exercise any of his other powers relating to the reference, investigation or consideration of a complaint (DISP 3.7).

In considering what is fair and reasonable, the ombudsman will take into **16–052**
account the relevant law, regulations, regulators' rules and guidance and standards, relevant codes of practice and, where appropriate, what he

considers to have been good industry practice at the relevant time (DISP 3.8.1). It should be noted that the ombudsman is not bound by the provisions of the contract entered into. It is not thought, however, that contractual provisions are generally to be ignored. It is suggested that the circumstances in which the ombudsman might depart from the contract are circumstances in which it would be unfair to rely on the particular provision in question.

The ombudsman must maintain a register of each money award and direction made (DISP 3.9.15).

Practical Operation of the FOS

16–053 At the time of writing, the FOS has been in operation for only a short period and it is too early to draw wide-ranging conclusions. Two points about its operation may, however, be noted. First, there has been some concern about the accountability of the FOS, apparently because it is not under an obligation to consult and because there is no appeals process. The first point is not easy to follow; it is not normally expected of an adjudicator that he should consult about his decisions, which are in any event made on an individual basis. While it is true that material has been published indicating the likely response of the ombudsman in certain circumstances, the FOS does not thereby become a regulatory body publishing requirements, in which case an obligation to consult might be reasonable and indeed desirable. The FOS is not enthusiastic about an appeals process because of the perceived risk that the process of dispute resolution would be slowed and an appeal system might be seen as undermining the speedy and informal complaints mechanism which is regarded as the essence of an ombudsman scheme. It is thought likely that some of the early concerns may arise from the need to unify the different approaches previously adopted under the different predecessor schemes.

16–054 One feature of the FOS arrangements is that the way in which the FOS deals with complaints may itself be the subject matter of a complaint to be considered by an independent assessor, appointed by the board, who may recommend payment of compensation in appropriate cases. On the limited material so far available, the independent assessor has commented, first, that delay or insufficient explanation were the two most frequent reasons for his upholding a complaint in whole or in part, and, second, that none of the cases investigated gave any evidence of bias on the part of the FOS either for or against consumers.

Transitional Arrangements

16–055 Clearly there was a need for transitional provisions to govern the switch from the eight former schemes to the FOS. The statutory framework is to be found in the Financial Services and Markets Act 2000 (Transitional Provisions) (Ombudsman Scheme and Complaints Scheme) Order 2001 (SI 2001/2326). There were two categories of complaint to be covered: complaints which were partly completed under a former scheme when the FOS arrangements came into force, and complaints made after that date about acts and omissions which occurred before that date.

Complaints in the first category, if properly referred to the former scheme and not determined before December 1, 2001 (referred to as "commencement" in the Order), are to be dealt with under the new scheme (art.2(1)). A complaint is to be treated as determined if, before commencement, it had been rejected, withdrawn, settled or determined, whether by a substantive decision or by the closure of the case without a substantive decision. A case is not, however, to be treated as determined if, pursuant to the terms of the former scheme, it was at commencement subject to or capable of being subject to an appeal, a reference to arbitration or a similar procedure. A complaint falling to be dealt with by the FOS under these provisions is called a "relevant existing complaint" (art.2(5)).

Complaints in the second category fall within the compulsory jurisdiction of the FOS by virtue of art.3(1) and (2) if:

- the act or omission is that of a person who was, immediately before commencement, subject to a former scheme;
- the act or omission occurred in the carrying on by that person of an activity to which that former scheme applied;
- the complainant is eligible and wishes to have the complaint dealt with under the new scheme.

If the complainant is not an eligible complainant, the ombudsman may nevertheless, if he thinks it appropriate, treat him as eligible if the complainant would have been entitled to refer an equivalent complaint to the former scheme immediately before commencement. A complaint falling to be dealt with by the FOS under these provisions is called a "relevant new complaint" (art.3(5)).

A relevant existing complaint is to be determined, so far as practicable, **16–056** by reference to such criteria as would have applied to the determination of the complaint under the former scheme immediately before commencement and may include such remedy as could then have been awarded (art.6). The provisions of the new scheme as to the enforcement of money awards and directions will apply to any award made or direction given, and the ombudsman may award costs in accordance with any provision of the former scheme which permitted such an award.

A relevant new complaint is to be determined in accordance with the general compulsory jurisdiction provisions, except that in determining what is fair and reasonable in all the circumstances of the case and what amount, if any, constitutes fair compensation, the ombudsman must take into account what determination the former ombudsman might have been expected to reach and what amount, if any, might have been expected to be awarded, in relation to an equivalent complaint dealt with under the former scheme immediately before commencement (art.7).

Further detailed provisions may be found in the Order itself and in the *FSA Handbook* at DISP TP 1 and Appendix 1.

Chapter 17

Criminal or Civil Penalty

Introduction

In this chapter we shall consider the scope and interrelationship of the criminal and civil penalties available to the FSA in its enforcement role. As Howard Davies, the Chairman of the Financial Services Authority, said in the annual lecture to the Worshipful Company of Chartered Secretaries & Administrators delivered on March 5, 2002: **17–001**

> "One of the government's principal aims in reforming financial regulation was to improve our ability to police our financial markets, and to cope with the threats to market integrity from insider dealing and other forms of market manipulation. It is widely accepted that markets in which investors suspect that inside information is used against them are less efficient, thus raising the cost of capital, and damaging investment and economic growth. It is also widely accepted, I think, that our previous arrangements for policing market abuse, with their emphasis on criminal prosecutions, were ineffective and inadequate. Successful prosecutions were remarkably rare, in spite of the number of well publicised episodes of, shall we say, doubtful market behaviour.
>
> So the new regime incorporates a new civil offence of market abuse, backed by a code of market conduct published by the FSA.
>
> In simple terms, this means that, rather than chasing every small insignificant case, we will use our resources to tackle cases of market abuse that pose a threat to confidence in the UK's financial markets. So we are simply not interested in pursuing technical or inadvertent infringements of the rules. Nor are we out to take scalps in order to make a point. That would be the surest way of damaging the credibility of the regime and, indeed, of London's markets.
>
> This approach should certainly not give comfort to those who seek to manipulate our markets for personal or corporate gain. Market manipulation is not a victimless crime. Other investors have bought or sold at false prices, and the credibility of the market is damaged for all its users. So where we see activity which poses a threat to our market confidence or consumer protection objectives, then we will draw on the full range of powers available to us.
>
> In deciding whether to pursue a case, we will ask ourselves three main questions:
>
> - has there been an impact on market confidence or have consumers actually or potentially lost money?
> - will prompt action by the FSA prevent further damage?
> - will action by the FSA have the effect of deterring future such behaviour?
>
> If, based on these criteria, we judge that there is a case for us to pursue, then we shall do so."

Criminal Sanctions: the Power to Prosecute

17–002 The Financial Services Authority has the power to prosecute in England, Wales and Northern Ireland. However, the Financial Services Authority has no power to prosecute offences committed in Scotland. Offences occurring in Scotland which would fall within the remit of the Financial Services Authority if they occurred south of the border will be prosecuted by the Crown Office.

When deciding whether or not to bring a criminal prosecution the FSA will apply the principles set out in the Code for Crown Prosecutors. Under the Code, the FSA will consider:

(1) whether there is sufficient evidence to provide a realistic prospect of conviction against the defendant on each charge; and

(2) whether, having regard to the seriousness of the offence and all the circumstances, a criminal prosecution is in the public interest.

When the FSA is acting as a prosecuting authority in England and Wales in accordance with ss.401 and 402 of the FSMA, investigations conducted by the FSA are subject (with certain appropriate adaptations) to the provisions of the Police and Criminal Evidence Act 1984 together with the Codes of Practice and to the provisions of the Criminal Procedure and Investigations Act 1996 (ENF 2.14.4).

Criminal Offences

17–003 Many of the offences created by the FSMA are discussed in detail elsewhere in this book. In this chapter we seek to highlight the types of offences that fall within the remit of the FSA as a prosecuting body and to set out, in summary, the types of offences for which the FSA has the power to prosecute. The Financial Services Authority has the power to prosecute the following offences (see FSMA 2000, s.401):

17–004 (1) **Carrying on or purporting to carry on a regulated activity without authorisation or exemption in contravention of the general prohibition imposed by s.19 of the Act (under s.23(1)).** This is an either way offence. On summary conviction the penalty is up to a maximum of 6 months imprisonment and/or a fine not exceeding the statutory maximum. The penalty on conviction in the Crown Court is a maximum of 2 years imprisonment and/or a fine. S.23(3) provides a defence where the accused took all reasonable precautions and exercised due diligence to avoid committing the offence.

17–005 (2) **Making false claims to be authorised or exempt (under s.24(1)).** This is a summary only offence. The penalty on conviction in the Magistrates Court being up to a maximum of six months imprisonment and/or a fine not exceeding the statutory maximum. In addition, if the conduct constituting the offence involved or included the public display of any material the maximum fine for the offence is level 5 on the standard scale multiplied by the number of days for which the display continued. S.23(3) provides a defence where the accused took all reasonable precautions and exercised due diligence to avoid committing the offence (s.24(2)).

(3) **Communicating an invitation or inducement to engage in investment activity in breach of the restriction on financial promotion imposed by s.21 of the Act (under s.25).** This is an either way offence. On summary conviction the penalty is up to a maximum of 6 months imprisonment and/or a fine not exceeding the statutory maximum. The penalty on conviction in the Crown Court is a maximum of 2 years imprisonment and/or a fine. S.25(2) provides a defence if the accused can show that he believed on reasonable grounds that the content of the communication was prepared, or approved for the purposes of s.21 of the Act, by an authorised person; or that he took all reasonable precautions and exercised all due diligence to avoid committing the offence. **17–006**

(4) **Providing information which is false of misleading.** Sch.4 para.5(2) requires a Treaty firm to give the FSA notice of its intention to carry on a regulated activity in writing seven days before it wishes to carry out the activity. A person is guilty of an offence if he provides information which he knows to be false or misleading in a material particular; or he recklessly provides information which is false or misleading in a material particular (para.6 (3) of Sch.4). The offence is triable either way and punishable on summary conviction by a fine not exceeding the statutory maximum. On conviction in the Crown Court, the offence is punishable by an unlimited fine. It is a defence to show that the accused took all reasonable precautions and exercised all due diligence to avoid committing the offence (para.6 (2) of Sch.4). **17–007**

(5) **Performing a function in breach of a prohibition order.** It is an offence to perform or agree to perform a function in breach of a prohibition order (under s.56(4)). This is a summary only offence and carries the penalty of a fine not exceeding that level 5 on the standard scale. It is a defence to show that the accused took all reasonable precautions and exercised all due diligence to avoid committing the offence (s.56(5)). **17–008**

(6) **Failure to register listing particulars.** S.83(1) requires that on or before the date on which listing particulars are published as required by the listing rules, a copy of the particulars must be delivered for registration to the registrar of companies. Failing to register a copy of listing particulars on or before publication by either the issuer of the securities in question or any person who is party to the publication and aware of the failure to register is an offence (under s.83(3)). The offence is triable either way and is punishable by a fine not exceeding the statutory maximum if convicted in the Magistrates Court or by an unlimited fine if convicted in the Crown Court (s.83(4)). **17–009**

17–010 (7) **Offering new securities before issuing a prospectus.** It is an offence to offer new securities to the public before publishing a prospectus as required by the listing rules made under s.84 of the Act (s.85(1) and (2)). This offence is triable either way and is punishable on summary conviction to imprisonment not exceeding three months or a fine not exceeding level five on the standard scale and on conviction on indictment, to imprisonment for a term not exceeding two years and/or a fine.

17–011 (8) **Issuing an advertisement, or other information specified in the listing rules, without prior approval or authorisation from the competent authority (under s.98(2)).** This is an either way offence. On summary conviction the penalty is a fine not exceeding the statutory maximum and on conviction on indictment to imprisonment for a maximum of two years and/or a fine.

17–012 (9) **Failing to co-operate with, or giving false information to, FSA appointed investigators (under s.177(3) and (4)).** These offences are triable either way. On summary conviction the penalty is imprisonment up to a maximum of six months and/or a fine not exceeding the statutory maximum and on conviction on indictment to imprisonment for a maximum of two years and/or a fine. Further, it is a summary offence to obstruct intentionally the exercise of any rights conferred by warrant under s.176 (s.177(6)) which is punishable by a maximum of three months imprisonment and/or a fine not exceeding level five on the standard scale.

17–013 (10) **Failing to comply with the provisions about control over authorised persons.** There are a number of offences of failing to comply with the provisions about control over authorised persons (see s.191);

(i) Failing to comply with the duty to notify the Authority imposed by s.178(1) or 190(1) (under s.191(1));
(ii) Failing to comply with the duty to notify the Authority imposed by s.178(2) or 190(2) (under s.191(2));
(iii) Carrying out a proposal to which a notice of control given to the Authority relates if the period of three months beginning with the date on which the Authority received the notice is still running and the Authority has not responded to the notice by either giving its approval or giving him a warning notice under s.183(3) or 185(3) (under s.191(3));
(iv) Carrying out a proposal to which a warning notice issued by the Authority relates before the Authority has decided whether to give the persona notice of objection (under s.191(4));
(v) Acquiring the control to which a notice of objection given by the Authority applies at a time when the notice is still in force (under s.191(5));
(vi) Failing to comply with the duty to notify the Authority imposed by s.178(1) or 190(1) where the person had no knowledge of the act or circumstances by virtue of which the

duty to notify the Authority arose, but subsequently became aware of that act or circumstances, yet failed to notify the Authority within 14 days of becoming aware (under s.191(11)).

Offences under subss.(1), (2), (3) and (4) and (11) are summary only offences and carry the penalty of a fine not exceeding level 5 on the standard scale. An offence under s.191(5) is an either way offence and punishable on summary conviction by a fine not exceeding the statutory maximum, plus a fine not exceeding one tenth of the statutory maximum for each day on which the offence has continued. On conviction by a Crown Court, the penalty is a maximum of 2 years imprisonment and/or a fine. It is a defence for a person charged under s.191(1) to show that he had, at the time of the alleged offence, no knowledge of the act or circumstances by virtue of which the duty to notify the Authority arose (s.191(9)). 17–014

(11) **Carrying on, or purporting to carry on, business in contravention of a consumer credit prohibition (under s.203(9)).** This offence may only be committed by a firm and is triable either way. The penalty on summary conviction is a fine not exceeding the statutory maximum and on conviction on indictment, the penalty is an unlimited fine. 17–015

(12) **Making false claims to be a person to whom the general prohibition does not apply as a result of Pt XX (under s.333).** This is a summary only offence and carries a penalty of imprisonment of a maximum of six months and/or a fine not exceeding level five on the standard scale. Where the commission of the offence involved or included the public display of any material, the maximum fine for the offence is level five on the standard scale multiplied by the number of days for which the display continued. It is a defence for the accused to show that he took all reasonable precautions and exercised all due diligence to avoid committing the offence. 17–016

(13) **Providing knowingly or recklessly false or misleading information to an auditor or actuary (under s.346).** This offence is an either way offence and is punishable on summary conviction by a term of imprisonment not exceeding six months and/or a fine not exceeding the statutory maximum. On conviction by the Crown court the penalty is imprisonment for up to two year and/or a fine; 17–017

(14) **Disclosing confidential information in contravention of the statutory restrictions under ss.348 and 350(5) (under s.352).** This is an either way offence and is punishable on summary conviction by imprisonment not exceeding three months and/or a fine not exceeding the statutory maximum. On conviction on indictment the penalty is imprisonment for up to two years and/or a fine. It is a defence for the accused to prove that he did not know and had no reason to suspect that the information was confidential information or that it had been disclosed in accordance with s.350 or to prove that he took all reasonable precautions and exercised all due diligence to avoid committing the offence (s.352(6)); 17–018

17–019 (15) **Making use of information which has been disclosed to a person under the regulations made under s.349 or 350 in contravention of those regulations or s.350(4) (under s.352 (3) and (4)).** These offences are summary only offences and punishable by a term of imprisonment not exceeding three months and/ or a fine not exceeding level five on the standard scale. It is a defence for the accused to prove that he did not know and had no reason to suspect that the information was confidential information or that it had been disclosed in accordance with s.350 or to prove that he took all reasonable precautions and exercised all due diligence to avoid committing the offence (s.352(6));

17–020 (16) **Failure by a director of an insurer carrying on long-term insurance business to notify the FSA of a general meeting to propose a resolution for voluntary winding up (under s.366(3)).** This is a summary only offence punishable by a fine not exceeding level five on the standard scale;

17–021 (17) **Misleading statements and practices offences (under s.397).** A person guilty of such an offence is liable on summary conviction to imprisonment for up to six months and/or a fine not exceeding the statutory maximum and on conviction on indictment to imprisonment for up to seven years and/or a fine. Certain defences do exist for some of the offences listed under this section, subject to certain conditions (see subss.(4), (5) and (7));

17–022 (18) **Misleading the FSA (under s.398).** An offence under this section is either way. On summary conviction a person is liable to a fine not exceeding the statutory maximum and on conviction on indictment, is liable to an unlimited fine (s.398(3)).

Insider Dealing and Money Laundering

17–023 In addition to the offences summarised above, the Financial Services Authority has the power to prosecute offences of insider dealing under Pt V of the Criminal Justice Act 1993 and for breaches of the prescribed regulations relating to money laundering (s.402). These two topics are covered in detail elsewhere in this book.

Cautions and the Financial Services Authority

17–024 In addition to bringing a criminal prosecution, it is open to the FSA to issue formal cautions rather than to bring a prosecution against an offender. If the FSA takes this route, then the Authority will follow the Home Office Guidance (see Home Office Circular 18/1994). A caution will only be appropriate where the FSA is satisfied that:

(1) there is sufficient evidence of the offender's guilt to give a realistic prospect of conviction;

(2) the offender admits the offence; and

(3) the offender understands the significance of a caution and gives informed consent to being cautioned.

A record of the caution will be kept by the FSA, and will form part of a firm's or approved person's regulatory record for the purposes of ENF 11.4.1G(3). The FSA may take a caution into account when considering whether or not disciplinary action is appropriate for subsequent regulatory misconduct. An earlier caution may also be taken into account by the FSA when considering a person's honesty, integrity and reputation and his fitness or propriety to perform controlled or other functions in relation to regulated activities. (ENF 15.6).

Information Gathering and Investigation Powers: Investigations of Specific Contraventions, Offences and Other Matters (ENF. 2)

The powers of the FSA to gather information from firms and conduct investigations of firms, approved persons, individuals involved in firms, and appointed representatives is discussed generally in Ch.15, Enforcement and Sanctions. Generally, the powers vested in the FSA to gather information and to appoint investigators is contained in ss.165 to 169 and s.284 of the FSMA. **17–025**

The FSA has been provided with specific powers to enable it to carry out its function to investigate and prosecute criminal offences (see list above). For example, under s.168 of the FSMA the FSA may appoint investigators to carry out an investigation where it appears that a person has breached regulations made under s.142 FSMA; or a person may be guilty of an offence under ss.177, 191, 346 or 398(1) under Sch.4 of the FSMA (see s.168(1) and (3)). Additionally, an investigator may be appointed under s.168(2) and (3) of the FSMA if there are circumstances suggesting that an offence under s.24(1) of the Criminal Justice Act 1993 may have been committed or where there may have been a breach of the general prohibition or a contravention of the restrictions on financial promotion contained in ss.21 and 238 of the FSMA or where market abuse may have taken place. Under s.168(4) and (5) the FSA may appoint an investigator if circumstances suggest that: **17–026**

- a firm may have breached the requirement for permissions in s.20 FSMA;
- a person may be guilty of an offence under the Money Laundering Regulations;
- a firm may have breached a rule made by the FSA;
- an individual may not be a fit and proper person;
- a person may have performed or agreed to perform a function in breach of a prohibition order;
- a firm or an exempt person may have failed to comply with s.56(6) FSMA; a firm may have failed to comply with s.59(1) or (2) FSMA;

- a person to whom the FSA has given approval under s.59 may not be a fit and proper person to perform the functions for which approval has been granted;
- a person may be guilty of misconduct for the purposes of s.66 FSMA (ENF. 2.3.14).

The Powers of Investigators Appointed by the FSA (ENF 2.4)

17–027 The scope of the powers of an FSA appointed investigator is discussed in Ch.15. Broadly speaking, an FSA investigator has wide powers to require the production of information both by the person under investigation and from third parties. Exceptions to the requirement to supply information arise in the context of legal professional privilege or banking confidentiality. It is worth noting however, that non-cooperation with the FSA appointed investigators may be treated as a contempt of court or as a criminal offence in itself. S.177 (3) —(6) creates three criminal offences of non-cooperation with the FSA in its exercise of its information gathering and investigation roles. These are broadly, failing to co-operate with, or giving false information to FSA appointed investigators, (under s.177(3) and (4)). These offences are triable either way. On summary conviction the penalty is imprisonment up to a maximum of six months and/or a fine not exceeding the statutory maximum and on conviction on indictment to imprisonment for a maximum of two years and/or a fine. Further, it is a summary offence (s.177(6)) to obstruct intentionally the exercise of any rights conferred by warrant under s.176 which is punishable by a maximum of three months' imprisonment and/or a fine not exceeding level five on the standard scale.

Admissibility of Statements Made by the Defendant: (s.174 FSMA)

17–028 As has been discussed in Ch.15, statements which have been required to be made by an FSA appointed investigator may be used as evidence in any proceedings if they comply with the normal rules governing admissibility of evidence. The major exception to this is that under s.174(2) such statements cannot generally be used in criminal proceedings in which the person who made the statement is the defendant in the case or in relation to action against the maker for market abuse under s.123 FSMA. Statements by the defendant made pursuant to the powers of an FSA appointed investigator may only be used against him if the defendant himself adduces evidence about the statement or asks questions relating to it. Of course, the restriction imposed by s.174 as to the use to which statements may be put in criminal proceeding do not apply if the statement was made voluntarily rather than in compliance with an investigators requirement to make it.

The obvious exception to the general rule that compelled statements by a defendant cannot be used against him is where a prosecution is brought for offences of making false statements or providing the investigator with false or misleading evidence under s.174(3).

Interview Safeguards

When conducting interviews, the FSA should ensure that the normal safeguards are available to the interviewee, *i.e.* access to legal advice, warning about the use to which the interview may be put, giving the interviewee a copy of the record of interview. Such safeguards should apply whether or not the interview is voluntary or under caution pursuant to the FSA's role as a prosecuting authority by virtue of ss.401 and 402 of the FSMA. (See ENF 2.14). Furthermore, when the FSA is acting as a prosecuting authority and is conducting an interview with someone who is suspected of a criminal offence then the FSA investigators are subject to the requirements of the Police and Criminal Evidence Act 1984 and its Codes of Practice and to the provisions of the Criminal Procedure and Investigations Act 1996. **17–029**

If a person has already been interviewed under one of the FSA's compulsory powers of interview, then he must be given a transcript of that interview before being interviewed under caution and an explanation of the differences between the two types of interview must be given to him. Similarly, if a person has already been interviewed under caution and the FSA investigators then seek to interview him under one of their compulsory powers, the interviewee must be told of the different uses to which the interviews may be put.

Search Warrants (ENF 2.15)

S.176 FSMA deals with the entry of premises under a warrant. A justice of the peace may issue a warrant under s.176 if he is satisfied on the basis of information given on oath by the FSA or its investigators that there are reasonable grounds for believing that: **17–030**

(i) a person has failed to comply with a requirement to provide information or produce documents or information, and that the documents or information are on the premises (s.176(2)); or

(ii) the premises specified in the warrant are those of a firm or an appointed representative and there are documents or information on the premises which could be the object of an information requirement and the requirement would not be complied with or the documents or information would be removed, tampered with or destroyed if such a requirement was made. (s.176(3); or

(iii) a serious offence (*i.e.* offences mentioned in s.168 for which the maximum sentence on indictment is two years or more) has been or is being committed and that documents or information relevant to that offence are on the premises and that an information requirement could be imposed on those documents or information and that the requirement would not be complied with or the documents or information would be removed, tampered with or destroyed. (s.176(4)).

17–031 A search warrant issued under s.176 will authorise a constable to:

(i) enter the premises specified in the warrant;

(ii) search the premises and take possession of documents or information relevant to the warrant, or to take any other necessary steps to preserve or prevent interference with the documents/information;

(iii) take copies or extracts of any documents/information;

(iv) require any person on the premises to explain any documents/ information or to say where they may be found;

The FSA has said that as a matter of policy it will usually seek to ensure that the FSA investigator is also named on the warrant and will be entitled to accompany the constable to execute the warrant (ENF 2.15.4 G).

Criminal or Civil Action

17–032 Even where the FSA has decided to pursue criminal proceedings, the Authority may also consider whether it may additionally take civil or regulatory action. Such action may include injunctions, restitution, own initiative action, withdrawal of approval or cancellation of permission and withdrawal of authorisation and the prohibition of individuals from carrying out functions in connection with regulated activities all of which are discussed in more detail in Ch.13.

In coming to a decision as to whether it should take any of the civil or regulatory actions available to it in addition to pursing its powers to prosecute in the criminal courts, the Authority will have regard to whether or not the taking of civil or regulatory action might unfairly prejudice the prosecution or proposed prosecution of criminal offences; whether the taking of civil or regulatory action might unfairly prejudice the defendants in criminal proceedings in the conduct of their defence; and whether it is appropriate to take civil or regulatory action having regard to the scope of the criminal proceedings and the powers available to the criminal courts. (ENF 15.4) An example of how the FSA will approach the decision whether to pursue the criminal or civil route can be seen in ENF 15.7 which sets out the factors which the FSA will take into consideration (but to which it is not limited) when deciding whether or not it should commence a criminal prosecution for market misconduct rather than impose a sanction for market abuse. The factors include:

(1) the seriousness of the misconduct;

(2) whether there are victims who have suffered loss as a result of the misconduct;

(3) the extent and nature of the loss suffered;

(4) the effect of misconduct on the market;

(5) the extent of any profits accrued or loss avoided as a result of the misconduct;

(6) whether there are grounds for believing that the misconduct is likely to be continued or repeated;

(7) whether the person has previously been cautioned or convicted in relation to market misconduct or has been subject to civil or regulatory action in respect of market misconduct;

(8) the extent to which redress has been provided to those who have suffered loss as a result of misconduct and/or whether steps have been taken to remedy any failures in systems or controls which gave rise to the misconduct;

(9) the effect that a criminal prosecution may have on the prospects of securing redress for those who have suffered loss; in particular where the losers are consumers, the FSA may decide that a criminal prosecution is not the most effective remedy where a prosecution would have an adverse effect on the solvency of the firm or individual so affecting their ability to repay any loss suffered;

(10) whether the person has been voluntarily co-operative with the FSA in taking corrective measure; merely fulfilling a statutory duty to co-operate will not affect the decision to prosecute;

(11) a criminal prosecution is more likely where the individual's misconduct involves dishonesty or an abuse of a position of authority or trust;

(12) a criminal prosecution is more likely against an individual who has played a leading role in the commission of misconduct carried out by a group;

(13) the personal circumstances of an individual may also be relevant to a decision to prosecute.

As a matter of policy the FSA will not impose a sanction for market abuse in addition to instituting criminal proceedings for market misconduct (ENF 15.7.4) however, where the FSA decides to commence criminal proceedings for market misconduct or imposes a sanction for market abuse, it may also consider taking civil or regulatory action which may include applying for an injunction (ENF 6.4), applying to a court for restitution (ENF 9.4), or exercising its administrative power to require restitution in relation to profits accrued by the person or loss suffered by others as a result of the abuse (ENF 9.5). The FSA may also decide to withdraw approval (ENF 7) or cancel permission and withdraw authorisation (ENF5) or prohibit individuals from carrying out functions in connection with regulated activities (ENF 8). **17–033**

Civil Fines

The FSA has the power to impose a financial penalty on: **17–034**

- a firm which has contravened a requirement imposed on it under the FSMA (s.206),

- an approved person who is guilty of misconduct (ss.64 and 66),
- any person whether approved or not who is found to have engaged in market abuse or who has required or encouraged another person to engage in market abuse (s.123);
- an issuer of listed securities or an applicant for listing where there has been a contravention of the listing rules (s.91).

The FSA is required to issue statements of policy as to the imposition of financial penalties on firms and approved persons by virtue of ss.69 and 210 of the FSMA. This has been achieved in the Enforcement Handbook at ENF 13.3. Broadly the FSA will consider all the relevant circumstances of a case when determining the appropriate level of financial penalty which must also be in proportion to the seriousness of the contravention for which it is being imposed but the FSA has not and does not intend to issue a tariff for financial penalties the reasoning being that each case should be considered individually and the issuing of a tariff would limit flexibility. When considering the level of financial penalty to impose on a firm or an approved person the FSA will take into account a number of relevant factors which will include:

- the seriousness of the misconduct or contravention; the duration and frequency of the misconduct or contravention; whether the misconduct or contravention revealed serious or systematic weaknesses of management systems or internal controls; the impact of the misconduct or contravention on the financial markets including the impact on public confidence; and the loss or risk of loss to consumers or other market users.
- The extent to which the misconduct or contravention was deliberate or reckless.
- Whether the person on whom it is intended to impose the financial penalty is an individual or a firm and the financial resources of that person.
- The amount of profits accrued or loss avoided.
- The conduct following the contravention.
- The disciplinary record and compliance history.
- Previous action taken by the FSA
- Action taken by other regulatory bodies.

17–035 The power to impose financial penalties for various types of misconduct has already been demonstrated to be a powerful tool in the armoury of the FSA. In the first quarter of 2003, the FSA announced fines amounting to hundreds of thousands of pounds against a number of well known financial institutions including ABN Amro Equities £900,000 for market misconduct in April 2003, Lincoln £485,000 for mis-selling savings plans in April 2003,

Royal Sun Alliance £950,000 for mortgage endowment failings in March 2003 , Scottish Amicable £750,000 also for mortgage endowment failings in March 2003, MPL Private Finance plc £100,000 for regulatory failings in February 2003, Bank of Scotland £750,000 for mal-administration of PEPs and ISAs in February 2003. The highest ever fine imposed by a UK Regulator was imposed in December 2002 when the FSA fined Credit Suisse First Boston £4 million for attempting to mislead a Japanese regulator and tax authority. That this fine was the highest ever imposed by a UK financial regulator garnering massive publicity, was obviously intended to send out the message that the FSA meant business to those involved in the financial community. The size fine was described by Carol Sergeant, FSA Managing Director responsible for Enforcement as making "it clear that we consider any attempt to mislead regulators and other authorities whether in the UK or in other countries to be an extremely serious issue. Ensuring that firms have organisational cultures that prevent this type of behaviour is essential to maintaining the confidence we all expect to have in our financial markets." (FSA Press Release, December 19, 2002.)

Chapter 18

Public Interest Disclosure Act

Background

When scandals such as Robert Maxwell's pension fund abuses and Nick Leeson's rogue trading break, the common cry is that "someone must have known". The presumption being that if that someone had blown the whistle then some action could have been taken to prevent harm being done. It has been a constant theme of recent major accidents, financial scandals and episodes of abuse that someone inside the organisation realised early on that something was wrong but was afraid to speak out. **18–001**

It is not surprising that before the introduction of the Public Interest Disclosure Act in July 1998 this was the case. In the past an employee who discovered some great misconduct on the part of his employer or colleague was placed in a difficult position. As a citizen his duty may have been to reveal all in the public interest, as an employee, however, his duty of loyalty to his employer included the duty not to betray confidences. The dilemma presenting itself was that although disclosing in the public interest may have been seen as the morally right course of action, at common law the employee's duty of loyalty to the employer was a legally binding obligation. The disclosure of information was likely to be seen as a deliberate betrayal of the employer and thus a repudiatory breach of contract. Consequently, an employee tempted to blow the whistle having discovered foul play on the part of the employer might render himself liable to discipline and dismissal.

In fact, this has often been the case. A survey conducted in 1999 of more than 230 whistleblowers in the United Kingdom and the USA (cited in the *Independent*, January 28, 1999) found that 84 per cent consequently lost their jobs. This was the case when Harry Templeton, printer at the Daily Record, the Scottish newspaper, and a trustee of the Mirror Group Pension Scheme spoke out against Robert Maxwell. When he warned fellow trustees, colleagues and union members that Maxwell intended to steal the pension money he was fired (*The Financial Times*, February 9, 2002). Furthermore, a study of 161 whistleblowers by Jos, Tompkins and Hayes (*In Praise of Difficult People: A Portrait of the Committed Whistleblower* (1989) 49 *Public Administration Review* 552) found that dismissal was not the only thing whistleblowers had to fear. Of those who were not dismissed it was found that 11 per cent had their salaries reduced, others were re-deployed in less high profile departments, passed over for promotion or sidelined from the partnership track. **18–002**

At common law there has always been a defence to an allegation of breach of the duty of confidentiality by an employee where it can be said that disclosure of the information in question was in some sense in the public interest. However, this defence has always been ill defined and was originally limited to the disclosure of criminal acts or danger to the state (*Weld-Blundell v Stephens* [1920] A.C. 956, HL). The later approach tended to be wider, however in *British Steel Corporation v Granada Television Limited* [1981] A.C. 1096 at 1168 Lord Wilberforce gave a pertinent warning that not everything that is interesting to the public may be disclosed in the public interest.

18–003 In *Lion Laboratories Ltd v Evans* [1984] 2 All E.R. 417, CA, it was held that in deciding whether the defence could be raised, the court had to take into account four factors. Firstly, as noted in *British Steel Corporation v Granada Television Limited,* the court should recognise the wide difference between what was interesting to the public and what was in the public interest to make known. The second factor to be borne in mind was that the media had a private interest in publishing what appealed to the public in order to increase circulation. Thirdly the court should consider that the public interest may be best served by the information being given to the police or some other responsible body rather than to the press. Finally as a development of the existing rule, the court decided that a defendant ought not to be restrained solely because the matter to be published did not show misconduct.

Lion Laboratories Ltd were the only manufacturers licensed to produce the Intoximeter 3000, approved by the Home Office as the device for testing the breath of drivers suspected of drink driving contrary to the Road Traffic Act 1972. The defendants, two former technicians of the company, contacted national newspapers with internal correspondence showing that the intoximeters were prone to serious error. At first instance Lion Laboratories Ltd were granted an injunction to restrain the employees and a national newspaper from disclosing or making use of any confidential material and were allowed to claim damages for breach of confidence and copyright. On appeal the injunction was upheld. On a second appeal, the court accepted that a public interest defence could be raised. They then went on to weigh the public interest in maintaining the confidentiality of the claimant's documents against the public interest in the accuracy of an approved device on which depended the liability of a person for a drink driving offence. The court held that it was unquestionably in the public interest and that the information could be published.

18–004 What is significant about this, and other such cases, is that the question of whether the defence can be raised and, if so, how the competing interests should be decided, often travels to the higher courts before it is decided. This is because the law in this area has been inconsistent and sometimes contradictory in its approach. Whistleblowing may, in some contexts, be a criminal offence governed by statute, in others a breach of trust governed by the common law. In addition to this, before the introduction of the Public Interest Disclosure Act, the widespread use by employers of confidentiality or "gagging" clauses in contracts of employment also served to prevent employees making bona fide disclosures in the public interest.

On the other hand, however, in some instances employees may conversely find themselves in a position where their contractual duty or implied duty of fidelity required them to report wrongdoing to their employer. This was the case in *Sybron Corp v Rochem Ltd* [1983] 2 All E.R.707 where the Court of Appeal held that an employee placed within the hierachy of an organisation had a duty in the circumstances to report the misconduct of his supervisors or subordinates when their conduct amounted to theft. **18–005**

Furthermore, it was held in *Re A Company's Application* [1989] 2 All E.R. 248 (Ch D) that where a regulatory body had been set up to monitor an industry, though an injunction may be granted to prevent general disclosure of confidential information, the court would not prevent disclosure to that body. The claimant company was subject to regulation by FIMBRA (the predecessor of the FSA) and sought an injunction to recover its documents from the defendant, a former employee, who alleged they revealed various breaches of FIMBRA regulations as well as tax irregularities. The claimant also sought to restrain the disclosure of any such documents. The court held that the defendant's undoubted duty of confidentiality to his former employers did not prevent him from disclosing to those regulatory authorities matters which it was their province to investigate. Indeed, the court ruled that it would be contrary to the public interest if employees of such companies were inhibited in reporting possible breaches of the regulatory system or fiscal irregularities. **18–006**

Despite the fact that it may have been the employee's duty to report misconduct either internally or to the appropriate regulatory body, the absence of procedures for reporting concerns often left an employee isolated and unsure to whom such concerns should be addressed. Before the Public Interest Disclosure Act very few employees within the financial services industry reported such irregularities to either their employers or to FIMBRA. A culture of keeping a discreet silence and of keeping misconduct hidden from the outside world prevailed.

In an address to the House of Lords (at the third reading of the Public Interest Disclosure Bill), Lord Borrie the former Director-General of the Office of Fair Trading, voiced the growing concern about the lack of protection and guidance for those making necessary public interest disclosures (whistleblowers): **18–007**

> "The Zeebrugge ferry disaster, the rail crash at Clapham Junction, the explosion at Piper Alpha and the scandals at BCCI, Maxwell, Barlow Clowes and Barings have all revealed that staff were well aware of the risk of serious physical and financial harm. But they were either too scared to raise their concern or they did so in the wrong way or with the wrong person."

The passing of the Public Interest Disclosure Act was the result of many years campaigning, in particular by the charity Public Concern at Work, an independent consultancy and legal advice centre launched in 1993. Four earlier attempts at reform had failed to pass through parliament before Tony Blair, then Leader of the Opposition, committed the next labour government to legislation to protect whistleblowers. Labour won the election in 1997 and the Public Interest Disclosure Bill received Royal Assent on July 2, 1998.

18–008 The Act, as its name suggests, is designed to encourage workers to make disclosures about matters relating to their employer or employment which are deemed to be in the public interest. Under the Act they can do so without the fear of victimisation or dismissal. There are three strands to the statutory protection. First, any confidentiality term in a worker's contract of employment or other agreement that seeks to gag the worker from making a public interest disclosure is now void. Secondly, it is automatically unfair to dismiss a worker for making a protected disclosure. Thirdly, it is unlawful to victimise a worker for making a protected disclosure.

According to Public Concern at Work there have been over 200 claims under the Act so far, the first successful case for unfair dismissal being brought in July 2000 by Antonio Fernandes (*Fernandes v Netcom Consultants UK* ET (May 2000)). Mr Fernandes was dismissed from his position as finance director of Netcoms Consultants after reporting that his managing director had claimed over £300,000 in unauthorised expenses. The employment tribunal awarded him the sum of £293,000 in compensation.

How the Act Works

18–009 The Public Interest Disclosure Act inserts a new Pt IVA in to the Employment Rights Act 1996. It makes provisions about the kinds of disclosures that may be protected, the circumstances in which such disclosures are protected and the persons who may be protected.

Persons Who May Be Protected

18–010 The standard definition of "worker" in s.230(3) of the Employment Rights Act is "a servant or apprentice or any other person who contracts personally to work for another, save for professional/client or business/customer relationships". However, for the purposes of the new Pt IVA, a person who is not a worker by that definition may become a worker within the extended definition of the Public Interest Disclosure Act if he falls within any of the following four categories in s.43K:

(a) agency and other such workers

— where the individual works or worked in circumstances where he was introduced or supplied to do that work by a third person and where the terms of employment were substantially determined by the person for whom he works or worked, the third person or both of them;

(b) home workers and suchlike

— where the workplace is not under the control or management of the employer and the worker would fall within the ambit of s.230(3) but for the requirement that he *personally* must do the requisite work;

(c) certain National Health Service Practitioners

— doctors, dentists, ophthalmologists and pharmacists providing their services under certain specified enactments;

(d) trainees

– those not under a contract of employment but enjoying work experience provided pursuant to a training course or those training for employment except where they are on a course run by an educational establishment.

Under the Public Interest Disclosure Act no qualifying period of continuous employment is required for the right to exist and it is no bar to protection that the worker is above normal retirement age. Only two classes of employment are wholly excluded from the right against victimisation, foreign merchant seamen and those working in the police service. The right extends to all Crown employees except those excluded by ministerial certificate in the interests of national security and those working for the Security Service, the SIS and GCHQ. Similarly the right does not extend to parliamentary staffs. **18–011**

The Employer

S.43K(2) defines "employer" for Pt IVA of the Employment Rights Act. In relation to a worker falling within s.43K(1)(a), the employer is the person who substantially determined the terms upon which the worker was engaged. In relation to a worker falling within s.43(1)(c), the employer is the authority or board referred to in that section. Finally, in relation to s.43(1)(d) the employer is the person providing the work experience or training. **18–012**

What Can Be Disclosed

S.43B(1) of the Act sets out those kinds of disclosures which qualify for protection (qualifying disclosures). A qualifying disclosure means any disclosure of information which, in the reasonable belief of the worker making the disclosure, tends to show one or more of the following matters is either happening now, has happened or is likely to happen in the future: **18–013**

(a) a criminal offence;

(b) the breach of any legal obligation including negligence, breach of contract or breach of administrative law;

(c) a miscarriage of justice;

(d) a danger to the health or safety of any individual;

(e) damage to the environment; or

(f) deliberate concealment of any information tending to show any matter falling within one of the preceding paragraphs.

18–014 The offences or breaches listed above are known for the purposes of Pt IVA as "relevant failures". It is immaterial whether the relevant failure takes place within the United Kingdom or abroad and it does not matter whether the relevant failure is subject to UK law or that of some other jurisdiction.

There are a number of exceptions to the above and where such an exception applies the disclosure does not qualify for protection. A disclosure of information will not be a qualifying disclosure if the person making the disclosure commits an offence by making it, for example breaches the Official Secrets Act 1989. Secondly, a disclosure of information, which would be protected from disclosure because of legal professional privilege, cannot be a qualifying disclosure if made by the legal adviser to whom the information was disclosed in the course of obtaining legal advice.

Circumstances in Which Qualifying Disclosures Become Protected

18–015 S.43A sets out the meaning of a protected disclosure. In the Act a "protected disclosure" means a qualifying disclosure which is made by a worker in accordance with any of the procedures for disclosure set out in ss.43C to 43H of the Act.

There are thus six ways in which a worker can make a protected disclosure. The Act encourages workers to disclose the information first to those who have some form of direct responsibility for the failure, in other words their employer or other responsible person. If this is not possible a worker may report the matter through other appropriate (prescribed) channels. Only if neither of the above routes is not possible or if the worker has tried that route already without success will it become appropriate to bring the matter to the attention of a wider audience. Where disclosures are made to those outside the work place the Act imposes extra conditions that must be met if the qualifying disclosure is to become protected. The only exception to this general principle is contained in s.43H. If the worker uncovers some serious scandal (a failure "of an exceptionally serious nature") then it may be appropriate to publish the facts immediately.

18–016 In s.43C a worker who makes a qualifying disclosure to his employer or by procedures authorised by the employer for that purpose or to another person whom the worker reasonably believes to be solely or mainly responsible for the relevant failure will be protected. The only additional requirement is that the worker should act in good faith.

18–017 Ss.43D and 43E cover protected disclosures in narrowly defined circumstances. S.43D states that a disclosure will be protected if it is made to a legal adviser in the course of obtaining legal advice. There are no further conditions attached to this method of disclosure since, due to the rules of legal professional privilege, it is not a disclosure that risks becoming public knowledge. S.43E states that a disclosure to a Minister of the Crown will be protected where the worker is employed in a Government-appointed organisation such as a non-departmental body. Again the only condition is that the disclosure must be made in good faith.

Under s.43F workers who are concerned about relevant failures can also make a disclosure to a person or body prescribed by the Secretary of State for the purpose of receiving disclosures about the matters concerned. These persons and bodies are listed in the Public Interest Disclosure (Prescribed Persons) Order 1999, SI 1999/1549 and include such bodies as the Health and Safety Executive, the Environment Agency and the Financial Services Authority. A full list of those persons and bodies and the matters which can be reported to them are set out below. **18–018**

Persons and descriptions of persons	*Descriptions of matters*
Accounts Commission for Scotland and auditors appointed by the Commission to audit the accounts of local government, and health service, bodies.	The proper conduct of public business, value for money, fraud and corruption in local government, and health service, bodies.
Audit Commission for England and Wales and auditors appointed by the Commission to audit the accounts of local government, and health service, bodies.	The proper conduct of public business, value for money, fraud and corruption in local government, and health service, bodies.
Building Societies Commission.	The operation of building societies.
Certification Officer.	Fraud, and other irregularities, relating to the financial affairs of trade unions and employers' associations.
Charity Commissioners for England and Wales.	The proper administration of charities and of funds given or held for charitable purposes.
Lord Advocate, Scotland.	The proper administration of charities and of funds given or held for charitable purposes. Serious or complex fraud.
Chief Executive of the Criminal Cases Review Commission.	Actual or potential miscarriages of justice.
Chief Executive of the Scottish Criminal Cases Review Commission.	Actual or potential miscarriages of justice.
Chief Registrar of Friendly Societies.	The operation of credit unions, clubs, housing associations, co-operatives and other industrial and provident societies, benevolent societies, working men's clubs and specially authorised societies.
Assistant Registrar of Friendly Societies for Scotland.	The operation of clubs, housing associations, co-operatives and other industrial and provident societies, benevolent societies, working men's clubs and specially authorised societies.

Persons and descriptions of persons	*Descriptions of matters*
Civil Aviation Authority.	Compliance with the requirements of civil aviation legislation, including aviation safety.
The competent authority under Pt IV of the Financial Services Act 1986	The listing of securities on a stock exchange; prospectuses on offers of transferable securities to the public.
Commissioners of Customs and Excise.	Value added tax, insurance premium tax, excise duties and landfill tax. The import and export of prohibited or restricted goods.
Commissioners of the Inland Revenue.	Income tax, corporation tax, capital gains tax, petroleum revenue tax, inheritance tax, stamp duties, national insurance contributions, statutory maternity pay and statutory sick pay.
Comptroller and Auditor General of the National Audit Office.	The proper conduct of public business, value for money, fraud and corruption in relation to the provision of centrally-funded public services.
Auditor General for Wales.	The proper conduct of public business, value for money, fraud and corruption in relation to the provision of public services.
Data Protection Registrar.	Compliance with the requirements of legislation relating to data protection.
Director General of Electricity Supply.	The generation, transmission, distribution and supply of electricity, and activities ancillary to these matters.
Director General of Fair Trading.	Matters concerning the sale of goods or the supply of services which adversely affect the interests of consumers. Matters relating to consumer credit and hire, estate agency, unfair terms in consumer contracts and misleading advertising. The abuse of a dominant position in a market and the prevention, restriction or distortion of competition.
Director General of Gas Supply.	The transportation, shipping and supply of gas through pipes, and activities ancillary to these matters.
Director General of Telecommunications.	The provision and use of telecommunication systems, services and apparatus.

Persons and descriptions of persons	*Descriptions of matters*
Director General of Water Services.	The supply of water and the provision of sewerage services.
Director of the Serious Fraud Office.	Serious or complex fraud.
Environment Agency.	Acts or omissions which have an actual or potential effect on the environment or the management or regulation of the environment, including those relating to pollution, abstraction of water, flooding, the flow in rivers, inland fisheries and migratory salmon or trout.
Scottish Environment Protection Agency.	Acts or omissions which have an actual or potential effect on the environment or the management or regulation of the environment, including those relating to flood warning systems and pollution.
Financial Services Authority.	The carrying on of investment business or of insurance business; the operation of banks, deposit-taking businesses and wholesale money market regimes; the functioning of financial markets, investment exchanges and clearing houses; the functioning of other financial regulators; money laundering, financial crime, and other serious financial misconduct, in connection with activities regulated by the Financial Services Authority.
Friendly Societies Commission.	The operation of friendly societies and industrial assurance companies.
Health and Safety Executive.	Matters which may affect the health or safety of any individual at work; matters which may affect the health or safety of any member of the public, arising out of or in connection with the activities of persons at work.
Local authorities which are responsible for the enforcement of health and safety legislation.	Matters which may affect the health or safety of any individual at work; matters which may affect the health or safety of any member of the public, arising out of or in connection with the activities of persons at work.
Investment Management Regulatory Organisation.	The activities of persons regulated by the Investment Management Regulatory Organisation.

Persons and descriptions of persons	*Descriptions of matters*
Occupational Pensions Regulatory Authority.	Matters relating to occupational pension schemes and other private pension arrangements.
Personal Investment Authority.	The activities of persons regulated by the Personal Investment Authority.
Rail Regulator.	The provision and supply of railway services.
Securities and Futures Authority.	The activities of persons regulated by the Securities and Futures Authority.
Treasury.	The carrying on of insurance business.
Secretary of State for Trade and Industry.	Fraud, and other misconduct, in relation to companies, investment business, insurance business, or multi-level marketing schemes (and similar trading schemes); insider dealing. Consumer safety.
Local authorities which are responsible for the enforcement of consumer protection legislation.	Compliance with the requirements of consumer protection legislation.
A person ("person A") carrying out functions, by virtue of legislation, relating to relevant failures falling within one or more matters within a description of matters in respect of which another person ("person B") is prescribed by this Order, where person B was previously responsible for carrying out the same or substantially similar functions and has ceased to be so responsible.	Matters falling within the description of matters in respect of which person B is prescribed by this Order, to the extent that those matters relate to functions currently carried out by person A.

18–019 A qualifying disclosure to a prescribed person or body will only be a protected disclosure if certain conditions are fulfilled. The disclosure must be made in good faith, the worker must reasonably believe that the information, and any allegation it contains, is substantially true and must reasonably believe that the matter falls within the description of matters for which the person or body has been prescribed.

18–020 S.43G covers disclosures made to a wider audience, in other words real public disclosures such as may be made to the press. This fifth means of disclosure is a somewhat "catch-all" provision that allows for a qualifying disclosure to be protected only if stringent conditions are met. First the worker must be acting in good faith and believe that the information, and any allegation contained in it, is substantially true. Furthermore, the worker must not be acting for personal gain. In addition one or more of the conditions set out in subs.2 must be met. The worker must reasonably believe either:

(a) that he will be subjected to a detriment by his employer if he makes the disclosure to his employer or to a prescribed person under s.43F, or

(b) that in a case where there is no such prescribed person under s.43F the evidence relating to the relevant failure will be concealed or destroyed if he makes a disclosure to his employer, or

(c) the worker must have previously disclosed substantially the same information to his employer or to a prescribed person

It seems clear that the intention behind the Act was to discourage disclosure to a very public audience, except where other routes had already failed or would prove unsatisfactory. Finally therefore, in addition to the other requirements, it must also be "reasonable" under "all the circumstances of the case" for the worker to make the disclosure. This implies something quite different from a reasonable belief in the truth of the allegations as is required under other sections. An allegation may be true but it may still be unreasonable to take the information to a wide public audience. **18–021**

The Act states that in determining "reasonableness" an employment tribunal will give regard to the identity of the person to whom the disclosure was made, the seriousness of the relevant failure and whether the failure is continuing or likely to recur. In *Bladon v ALM Medical Services* ET (April 2000) the fact that there was no internal channel for communicating concerns was a point the Tribunal considered in determining that it was reasonable for the applicant to make a wider disclosure.

If such a channel had existed, in assessing the reasonableness of the disclosure, regard would then have been given to any action which the employer or relevant person to whom the previous disclosure was made took or might reasonably have been expected to take. The distinction thus appears to lie in determining whose fault it is that the disclosure has had to be made publicly.

S.43H covers those disclosures where the subject matter of the disclosure is serious enough to merit by passing the above procedures. Such a disclosure will be protected if the worker makes the disclosure in good faith, reasonably believes the information is substantially true and does not make the disclosure for the purposes of personal gain. **18–022**

The Protection Against Victimisation, Dismissal and Redundancy

After s.47A of the Employment Rights Act 1996 there is inserted by the Public Interest Disclosures Act s.47B. In this section a worker is guaranteed the right not to be subjected to any detriment by any act or any deliberate failure to act, by his employer done on the grounds that the worker has made a protected disclosure. A detriment may include action such as demotion, withholding a pay rise or failing to promote. In the case of workers who are not employees, detriment will also cover termination of their contract. **18–023**

In cases where the worker has suffered a detriment short of dismissal (victimisation) then the worker may bring a claim in an employment tribunal. There is a time limit of three months for making a complaint but there is no limit to the amount of compensation that may be awarded.

18–024 If a worker who is an employee is dismissed because they made a protected disclosure that dismissal is regarded as automatically unfair. The same is true if the reason, or principal reason, an employee was selected for redundancy is that he has made a protected disclosure. An employee may bring an application for interim relief within seven days of dismissal. If he does so and shows that he is likely to win the case then the employment tribunal will normally order reinstatement. The Public Interest Disclosure (Compensation) Regulations 1999 (SI 1999/1548) remove the ceiling on the compensatory award in cases where dismissal is the result of the worker making a protected disclosure. The regulations also provide for a higher level of additional award where there is a failure to reinstate or re-engage the employee.

Workers who are not employees cannot apply for reinstatement or re-engagement. They will be awarded compensation on the same basis as victimisation short of dismissal but subject to the maximum they would have received had they been an employee.

Practical Implications for the Financial Services Industry

18–025 Persons working within the financial services industry are protected from suffering any detriment as a result of making a protected disclosure in the same way as are persons working within any other industry. It is clear, therefore, that the Act has and will have practical implications for the industry. Enquiries into some of the worst frauds and disasters affecting the industry in recent years have highlighted the importance of acting early on concerns raised by employees. In 1991 the Bank of Credit and Commerce International closed, the victim of a 19 year-old fraud causing estimated losses of over £2 billion worldwide. The inquiry found that BCCI had an "autocratic environment" in which no one dared to speak up. Rumours about the bank's probity had circulated throughout the City and abroad however the only employee, an internal auditor, known to have reported concerns about irregularities was subsequently made redundant (*Inquiry into the supervision of the Bank of Credit and Commerce International*, London: HMSO, 1992).

18–026 It is for reasons such as this that the Financial Services Authority has welcomed the Public Interest Disclosure Act. Carol Sergeant, Managing Director for Regulatory Processes and Risk rightly noted that "establishing effective whistleblowing arrangements is enlightened self-interest for firms, and in the best interests of consumers" (*FSA Press Release*, July 3, 2001). The reason for this is obvious. A whistleblowing policy will help the financial services industry avoid crises, minimise bad press and reassure customers and regulator alike. Not only may the introduction of internal whistleblowing procedures help guard against fraud being committed and allow for irregularities to be reported before such harm as described above is done, they will also help ensure that concerns can be dealt with privately instead of in the public arena. Another persuasive reason for adopting an internal procedure is that if employers have effective procedures which are known to and used by workers, it is less likely that a situation will arise which will lead to a claim against the firm under the Public Interest Disclosure Act.

The Financial Services Authority has seen its designation as a prescribed body under s.43F as a natural extension of its existing role as a public regulator. In July 2001 it launched a consultation paper entitled *Whistleblowing, the FSA and the financial services industry* (Consultation Paper 101 can be found at *www.fsa.gov.uk/pubs*). The purpose of the paper was to draw the attention of firms to the provisions of the Public Interest Disclosure Act and to explain how they can be applied in the context of financial services. The aim of issuing such guidance was to encourage firms to adopt their own internal procedures for processing whistleblowers' concerns, draw attention to model whistleblowing arrangements and to inform the industry of the Authority's own revised arrangements, as a prescribed body, for handling disclosures. **18–027**

The consultation paper proposes that an effective internal system for raising concerns should include:

(a) a clear statement that malpractice is taken seriously in the organisation and an indication of the sorts of matters regarded as malpractice;

(b) respect for the confidentiality of staff raising concerns, if they wish, and the opportunity to raise concerns outside the line management structure;

(c) penalties for making false and malicious allegations;

(d) an indication of the proper way in which concerns may be raised outside the organisation if necessary.

This guidance is in line with that given by the charity Public Concern at Work and was accepted as sufficient by the 2nd Report of Lord Nolan's Committee on Standards in Public Life (Cm 3270–1 (1996)). **18–028**

The consultation paper goes on to highlight the fact that a policy and procedures in themselves will not produce the desired effect. The FSA advises firms to ensure that all workers are aware of the system, whether in isolation or as part of a package including the firm's grievance procedure, any staff consultation arrangements and/or trade union arrangements. The paper continues with a list of practical points for smaller firms who, though they may not need a full whistleblowing procedure, still need to address the issue of public interest disclosures.

In terms of its role as a prescribed body under the Act the FSA uses the consultation paper to outline its own arrangements. These have now been centralised so that all disclosures are dealt with appropriately. The FSA has also set up a dedicated telephone line and email address for the purpose of receiving qualifying disclosures. An information sheet with the number **18–029** and address of the FSA and information on whistleblowing is planned and will be sent to all firms in the financial services industry.

Finally the paper informs the industry that the FSA will continue to monitor and review the effectiveness or otherwise of the industry's whistleblowing arrangements. The FSA does not rule out making more stringent rules under the Financial Services and Markets Act 2000 should it prove necessary. In addition, the FSA make it clear that it would regard as a serious matter any evidence that a firm had acted to the detriment of a worker who had made a protected disclosure. Such evidence, it warns, could call into question the fitness and propriety of the firm concerned and/ or relevant members of the firm's staff.

18–030 There are other provisions made by the FSA under the Financial Services and Markets Act 2000 which seek to encourage an air of openness in the industry. The FSA Handbook (*www.fsa.gov.uk*) sets out in *The Statements of Principle for Approved Persons* that such persons must act with integrity, skill, care and diligence. In particular, an approved person must deal with the FSA and other regulators in an open and co-operative way and must disclose appropriately any information of which the FSA would reasonably expect notice (Statement of Principle 4). Such information may include evidence of misconduct or fraud or any other such matters as would qualify for protection under the Public Interest Disclosure Act.

18–031 *The Code of Practice for Approved Persons* gives some indication of the type of conduct that would not comply with Statement of Principle 4. For example, it would be a failure to abide by the FSA rules if an approved person did not report promptly in accordance with his firm's internal procedures (or if none existed direct to the FSA), information which it would be reasonable to assume would be of material significance. It would also be a breach of the FSA rules if an approved person responsible within the firm for reporting such matters to the FSA failed to do so promptly.

The significance of the Statement of Principle 4, in conjunction with the protection offered under the Public Interest Disclosure Act is twofold. First, whilst any employee *may* make a qualifying public interest disclosure in the correct manner and be protected from detriment, the approved person *must* make such a disclosure or he may suffer a detriment. This is because any failure by an approved person to abide by FSA rules is actionable in damages, this being a remedy an aggrieved investor may wish to pursue. Secondly, on a disclosure being made by an employee and investigated by the FSA, an approved person must openly co-operate. It would be a failure on their part to fail to supply the FSA or other regulator with appropriate documents or information when requested or required to do so and within the time limits prescribed.

18–032 It seems clear that the FSA's position in relation to disclosures of information is compatible with their broad regulatory objectives under the Financial Services and Markets Act 2000. In particular the effect of the Statement of Principle 4 and their proposed guidelines on whistleblowing procedures should be encourage greater public confidence in the financial system. They should also lead to greater protection for customers by promoting strong, safe, internal and external reporting mechanisms. It is also obvious that such provisions will also be constructive in reducing financial misconduct and crime.

Chapter 19

International Mutual Assistance

Introduction

It is appropriate to consider the means available at an international level for the investigation of financial fraud at a time when fraud can be carried out at the press of a computer key or mouse button, affecting financial markets on the other side of the world. Authorities encounter serious difficulties in investigating financial fraud when no one state has complete jurisdiction. For this reason, mutual assistance between states is becoming of increasing importance in a wide variety of cases. **19–001**

The oldest method of international co-operation in investigations is the procedure for the international exchange of evidence in civil matters via the use of letters rogatory and the taking of evidence abroad, established since the Hague Convention on Civil Procedure of 1896. Development of international exchange of evidence in criminal matters came later when states began entering into bilateral treaties on the matter. One such bilateral treaty is the 1959 European Convention on Mutual Assistance in Criminal Matters, enacted in this jurisdiction in the form of the Criminal Justice (International Co-operation) Act 1990. Also, at the investigation stage, a framework exists for the transmission of information between regulatory authorities in the form of Memoranda of Understanding with regulatory authorities abroad and most recently Pt XI of the FSMA 2001.

It is the distinct and separate nature of these various methods of obtaining evidence that can justify the use of information obtained via one method being used for a purpose different to that for which it was originally requested. Following the recent decision in *Barlow v BOC Ltd* [2001] EWCA Civ 854, evidence from abroad obtained under the Criminal Justice (International Cooperation) Act 1993 for the purposes of a criminal trial, can now be made available to a civil litigant. Interestingly, the same information could not be used in a subsequent criminal trial but simply on the basis that civil proceedings are entirely separate can be used in subsequent civil proceedings. **19–002**

This is just one example of how the courts have interpreted and developed the options available to UK investigators when seeking to obtain and use evidence from abroad. While there is no lack of will to investigate, the principle difficulties as this chapter will illustrate, remain difficult to surmount.

Mutual Assistance in Civil Proceedings

19–003 In Civil Proceedings which are either pending or contemplated, the Evidence (Proceedings in Other Jurisdictions) Act 1975, together with RSC, Ord.70, enable a foreign court to invoke the assistance of the High Court to obtain evidence in the United Kingdom.

Procedure

19–004 On receiving a request for assistance from a foreign court, the jurisdiction to make an order giving effect to the request of the foreign court. It is a matter of discretion as to whether to make or refuse such an order. In accordance with the principle of judicial and international comity, the approach of the English Courts is, in general, to assist a foreign court wherever it is possible. This was recently confirmed in *State of Minnesota v Philip Morris Inc* [1998] I.L.Pr. 170. In doing so, the Court may, in its order make such provision for obtaining the requested evidence "as may appear to the Court appropriate for the purposed of giving effect to the request in pursuance of which the application is made" (s.2(1)). Despite this broad power of the court there are a number of limitations on the extent to which the English Court may assist a foreign court.

Rule Against Fishing Expeditions

19–005 English Courts will only grant an order giving effect to a request for assistance where the documents are properly specified and not where there is an attempt to obtain discovery. "Something in the nature of a roving enquiry in which a party was seeking to 'fish out' some material which might lead to obtaining admissible evidence at the trial", will be denied by the English Courts. This principle is derived from RSC, Order 70 and from the case law (See *Rio Zinc Corporation and Others v Westinghouse Electric Corporation* [1978] A.C. 547 and *State of Norway's Application, Re* [1987] Q.B. 433).

19–006 The fact that letters rogatory may have been issued for the purposes of obtaining discovery or pre-trial information which fall foul of the above principle does not mean that the English Court has no jurisdiction to give effect to that Request. In *Refco Capital Markets Ltd v Credit Suisse First Boston Ltd* [2001] EWCA Civ 1733, it was held that the request went far beyond anything that could properly be ordered in accordance with the English rules of civil procedure. Nevertheless the court was able to give effect to the letters rogatory by restricting the number of documents ordered for production and by disallowing certain witnesses from being examined.

19–007 A note of caution was sounded in *(1) Genira Trade & Finance Inc (2) Binzer Enterprises Corporation v (1) Refco Captial Markets Ltd (2) Refco Group Limited* [2002] C.P. Rep.15, CA. Here it was stated that is not the function of the English court to give effect to the letters of request by redrafting them especially where there are serious doubts about the admissibility of the evidence requested. This was particularly so in the instant case where it did not appear that the foreign court had considered precisely what evidence was being sought for trial, or its likely weight if obtained. The Court held that if further Letters Rogatory were to be made, they should only be made following further consideration by the foreign court.

Privilege Against Self Incrimination

In addition to limitations on the scope of the investigation, the English courts are limited by s.3 of the 1975 Act which deals with privilege. CPR, Ord.70, r.6, gives teeth to this provision. It establishes that a witness is entitled to claim privilege from giving any evidence which he could not be compelled to give on any ground recognised under the law of England or under the law of the requesting Court. The claim to privilege against giving evidence extends not only to giving answers to any questions, whether oral or in writing but to producing any documents. **19–008**

The Court will give effect to the claim for privilege on any ground recognised by English law. Thus in *RTZ v Westinghouse* [1978] A.C. 547 it was held that persons were entitled to claim privilege against self-incrimination because the evidence required was likely to render them liable to financial sanctions under the Treaty of Rome. Where the ground of privilege claimed is not one recognised by English law, but is recognised by the law of the requesting State, the claim to privilege must either be supported by a statement contained in the request or be conceded by the applicant for the order. If it is not, and the witness claims privilege, the relevant questions and answers are recorded in a separate transcript and the matter is referred to the requesting court to determine whether or not to uphold the privilege

Civil Proceedings Only

The Court in *Westinghouse* also dealt with a further limitation on the court's power, namely that the Court must be satisfied that the evidence sought relates to civil and not criminal proceedings. This is provided for in s1 of the 1975 Act. In *Re State of Norway's Application No 1* [1987] 1 Q.B. 433, it was held that "civil proceedings" had to be interpreted in an international sense and not simply by reference to English law notions. In the next section we will examine the appropriate mechanisms for the taking of evidence in relation to a criminal trial. **19–009**

Mutual Assistance in Criminal Proceedings

The 1975 Act does not provide for the taking of evidence of a person for the assistance of foreign courts and tribunals in relation to a criminal trial. When evidence for criminal trials is sought for use in the United Kingdom or sought in the United Kingdom for use overseas the appropriate mechanism is the Criminal Justice (International Co-operation) Act 1990. **19–010**

This Act enabled the United Kingdom to comply with its obligations under the European Convention on Mutual Assistance of 1959, which provides, *inter alia,* for the mutual provision of evidence. The Act provides the United Kingdom with the Central Authority required by the Convention to process incoming and outgoing requests for information.

Obtaining Evidence for Use in the UK

Procedure

19–011 Evidence can be obtained from abroad through what is known as the "Letter of Request" procedure. Designated Authorities such as the DTI, SFO and CPS may send requests directly to the foreign Central Authority. Others—defence or prosecution who are not designated authorities, for example local authority prosecutors—must apply to a magistrate or Judge for a letter of Request. It must be shown that there are grounds for suspecting that an offence has been committed and that proceedings have been issued or than an investigation of an offence is under way.

Admissibility of Evidence

19–012 The procedure outlined in the 1990 Act allows evidence to be taken in a form that is likely to be admitted in any criminal proceedings that follow. The European Convention of May 29, 2000 on Mutual Assistance in Criminal Matters reinforces this approach. The new Convention, which was introduced to improve judicial co-operation between States, lays down the principle that a Member State which is executing a request must comply with the "formalities and procedures" expressly indicated by the requesting Member State. In this way, the UK when requesting assistance can ensure in advance that appropriate methods are used in the foreign jurisdiction so that the evidence gathered is admissible in any subsequent litigation and is not rendered inadmissible as a result of the methods used to obtain it.

Use of Evidence in Subsequent Civil Proceedings

19–013 Particular care must be taken when describing in the letter of request the purpose for which the evidence is required. This limitation is attributed to s.3(7) of the Act which provides that evidence obtained by virtue of a letter of request shall not by used for any purpose other than that specified in the letter without the consent of the foreign authority.

The case of *R v Gooch* [1999] I Cr. App. R. (*S.*) 283 is a case in point. Here the prosecutors sought to confiscate the proceedings of drug importation. However, the Court of Appeal refused to allow the information obtained as a result of the letters of request to be used in the confiscation proceedings since such purpose had not been mentioned in the letters and the prosecutors had failed to obtain the consent of the foreign authority.

This limitation has been somewhat eroded by the recent decision In *(1) Frederick Edward Barlow (2) David William Barlow v (1) BOC Ltd (2) Edwards High Vacuum International Ltd* (2001), [2001] EWCA Civ 854. This case concerned an order freezing the individual assets of the defendants granted pursuant to civil proceedings. The defendants appealed against the order freezing their Swiss bank accounts. It was submitted that the order was based on evidence the use of which was prohibited by s.3(7) of the Act. (Evidence of the Swiss accounts had been obtained by means of a letter of request to the Swiss authorities in relation to prior criminal proceedings, and the consent of the Swiss authorities to use the evidence in the later civil proceedings had not been sought). **19–014**

The Court of Appeal held, dismissing the appeal, that the restriction in s.3(7) applied only to the use of information by the prosecuting authority or defendant in criminal investigations and proceedings. Such prohibition, it was held, did not extend to the use of such information in civil proceedings by someone other than the person who made the letter of request in the context of the prosecution of the crime. In the instant case, BOC had been entitled to rely on the evidence indicating the existence of the Swiss bank accounts since there was no prohibition under s.3(7) to the tendering of such evidence in the context of civil proceedings.

Obtaining Evidence for Use Overseas

Procedure

On receipt of a letter of request from a foreign court, the Central Authority must be satisfied that the request is certified by the requesting authority as being in connection with a criminal investigation or with criminal proceedings which have been instituted in the requesting State. If so, the Central Authority will nominate a court in writing to give effect to the request. **19–015**

There are two ways in which the nominated court can comply with the terms of the letter requesting documents. First, it is provided in Sch.1 of the Act that a court can summon a person before them to produce documents and give evidence on oath. Proceedings before the nominated court are regulated by the Magistrates Courts (Criminal Justice (International Co-operation) Rules 1991 and also by the corresponding Crown Court Rules. Secondly, if the investigations relate to a serious arrestable offence the Court may issue a warrant relating to entry, search and seizure (as provided for in Pt II of the PACE Act 1984). Any application for a search warrant must necessarily be carefully scrutinised.

(It is worth noting that in some instances it may not be necessary for the courts to be involved and the police may undertake to carry out the necessary enquiries on behalf of the foreign requesting authority. Also, the central authority can forward the request directly to the appropriate regulatory body. The 1990 Act provides the framework for this, enabling the Secretary of State to accept requests and order UK evidence gathering by the police or magistrates court.) **19–016**

19–017 Under the 1990 scheme, the Secretary of State need only be satisfied that an investigation into a particular offence was being carried out and that there were reasonable grounds for suspecting that it had been committed. The rule against fishing expeditions applies equally to requests for assistance under the 1990 Act. However because it is necessary, when dealing with a request under this Act, to examine more material than would constitute evidence at any trial, the permissible area of search has to be wider than when once the investigation has been completed. This distinction was drawn by the High Court in *R. v Secretary of State for the Home Department, Ex p. Finninvest SpA* [1997] 1 All E.R. 942. Here it was accepted that since the 1990 Act had created a wholly new scheme for mutual assistance with regard to criminal investigations, the term "evidence" had to have a different and wider meaning than in the legislation under consideration in *Westinghouse*.

Compulsion

19–018 Para.4 of Sch.1 of the 1990 Act provides that a person shall not be compelled to give any evidence which he would not be compelled to give in criminal proceedings in the United Kingdom or in criminal proceedings in the state from which the request for evidence has come.

The privilege against self-incrimination is paramount in English law. In order for the witness to be entitled to remain silent

> "the court must see from the circumstance of the case and the nature of the evidence which the witness is called to give, that there is reasonable ground to apprehend danger to the witness from being called to answer. The danger. . .must be real and appreciable with reference to the ordinary operation of law in the ordinary course of things; not a danger of an imaginary and insubstantial character." (*R. v Boyes* [1861] 1 B.&S. 3.11 *Per* Cockburn, C.J.; Cited in Harris and Murray; *Mutual Assistance in Criminal Matters* (London, Sweet and Maxwell, 2000)).

Neither will a witness be compelled to give evidence where the material sought is protected by legal professional privilege.

Investigation by Regulatory Bodies

19–019 The procedure for Mutual Assistance is limited when it comes to the rapid investigation of international financial practices. It can frequently be slow, complicated and might not always lead to a trial. Given the speed with which a transborder offence can be carried out and the much slower pace of the formal procedures for investigation, direct co-operation between regulatory agencies has played an increasingly important role.

International Co-operation

19–020 The Committee of European Securities Regulators facilitates this co-operation at the European level. The CESR, (formerly known as FESCO) has established a Multilateral Memorandum of Understanding on the

Exchange of Information between Member States of the EEA. A number of international organisations have also been established for example, the Basle Committee on Banking Supervision and the International Organisation of Securities Commissions (IOSCO). The latter organisation recognises the difficulties encountered by regulatory bodies when necessary information or evidence is located in another jurisdiction and promotes the importance of international co-operation in investigations and inquiries. (See IOSCO Public Documents, Objectives and Principles of Securities Regulation, in particular ss.8 and 9). In early 1996, the Basle Committee and the IOSCO in association with the International Association of Insurance Supervisors formed the Joint Forum on Financial Conglomerates. The United Kingdom is represented at this forum which reviews various means to facilitate the exchange of information between supervisors within their own sectors and has investigated legal or other barriers which could impede the exchange of information between supervisors within their own sectors and between supervisors in different sectors.

Memorandums of Understanding

UK regulators have initiated a number of bilateral agreements on the exchange of confidential information with their foreign counterparts. These agreements, known as Memorandums of Understanding establish a framework for the facilitation for speedy communication between regulatory bodies involved in investigations and have been concluded with the securities regulators of France (*Commission des Operations de Bourse*), Italy (*Commissione nazionale per la Societa e la Borsa*), Spain (*Commission del Mercado de Valores*) as well as other foreign regulator bodies. These MOUs complement the more formal procedures already in place, allowing a faster simpler, method of exchanging information and ensuring that regulatory authorities play a role in fighting financial crime alongside the criminal prosecution agencies. **19–021**

Under the FSMA 2000, the Financial Services Authority has inherited these memoranda and created several more. For example, the FSA has signed a Memorandum of Understanding with the US Securities and Exchange Commission and the US Commodities and Futures Trading Commission providing for co-operation and information sharing.

Financial Services and Markets Act 2000

The Financial Services and Markets Act equips the FSA with powers to investigate and to obtain evidence on behalf of its overseas equivalents and to exercise its statutory powers to acquire documents, witness testimony and to conduct interviews in support of overseas regulatory investigations. This complements the powers of the DTI to assist international regulatory authorities under the Companies Act 1989 as well as those of the SFO under the Criminal Justice Act 1987 (as amended by the Criminal Justice and Public Order Act 1994). **19–022**

The FSA, under s.169, has a general power to demand information or documents in order to investigate matters on behalf of an overseas regulator. The authority may appoint investigators to conduct an investigation in certain circumstances into any relevant matter. The exercise of its powers is *discretionary*, s.169(4) lists four factors that may be taken into account by the Authority in deciding whether to exercise its discretion. These include consideration of the likelihood that the country from which the request emanates could or would reciprocate if it received a similar request from the United Kingdom. Also relevant, is the nature of the crime being investigated and whether it has a close parallel in UK law and whether the case is serious and relevant to UK law. (ENF 2.8.4 to ENF 2.8.6G).

19–023 If the Authority considers the powers are appropriate and that the necessary criteria exist he may still feel that he has only limited resources to carry out the investigation requested. The FSA may decide not to use its investigative powers unless the overseas regulator agrees to make such contribution to the costs as appears appropriate. (ENF 2.8.6G). The use made of a similar provision contained in the 1989 Companies Act has been criticised on the grounds that the Secretary of State—rather than simply asking the requesting States to pay a contribution—often allows the request to lie unprocessed for want of resources. "It seems a pity that important international co-operation in this field should fail for want of resources when the more practical approach of asking the requesting States to pay a contribution would mean quicker results". (Chase, B. "Mutual Assistance to Overseas Business Regulatory Bodies" (1992) 18 C.L.B. 4, 1430–1434).

Admissibility of Evidence Obtained under Part XI of the FSMA

19–024 The limitations on the usefulness of these provisions are clear in that any evidence obtained under the above provisions are not admissible in criminal or market abuse proceedings (FSMA, s.174(2)). Since the evidence is compelled it cannot be used or referred to other than by the person who gave the evidence.

This follows from the rule of the European Court of Human Rights in the case of *Saunders v UK* (1977) 23 EHRR 313. In that case it was held that evidence compulsorily obtained from Mr Saunders under an earlier version of the investigation provisions of the Companies Act 1985, should not have been adduced against him in criminal proceedings. Thus, his right to a fair trial under Art.6 of the European Convention on Human Rights, in particular, the privilege against self-incrimination had been infringed. It is for the foreign court intending to use the evidence obtained to decide what evidence to admit in each individual case.

19–025 The categorisation of a case as criminal or civil therefore will be a crucial element in deciding the admissibility of compelled evidence. The wrong decision may lead to a breach of the HRA. (See Coffey, J., Pinto, T, "The Compatibility of the Financial Services and Markets Act 2000 with the Human Rights Act 1998" (2001) 12 I.C.C.L.R. 2, 50–56). The fact that the authority has the ability to impose fines for market abuse creates difficulties in making this decision. However, in *R.(Fleurose) v Securities and Futures*

Authority [2001] E.W.H.C. 292, judgment April 26, 2001, Morrison J. took the view that in Convention jurisprudence, disciplinary proceedings are to be classified as civil rather than criminal since they are categorised under domestic law as civil. The nature of the proceedings leads to the same conclusion in Convention Law: "While the Human Rights Act 1998 also applies to civil proceedings and will afford substantial procedural protection to those charged with an offence, it is unlikely that these express rights will add anything to the disciplinary regime which is now in place for financial services". (Clayton, R. "Article 6 of the ECHR and Financial Services" [2001] 3 J.I.F.M. 4, 143–148).

Confidentiality

19–026 The English Court can also decline to make an order assisting in a foreign investigation on the grounds of confidentiality. In *Pharaon v BCCISA*, *The Times*, July 22, 1998, the English court held that the public interest in making confidential information available to parties to private foreign litigation outweighed the public interest in preserving confidentiality in those documents.

In the earlier case of *Securities and Exchange Commission v Stockholders of Santa Fe International Corp* [1985] ECC 187 it was held that considerations involving the confidential relationship of banker and client could not be invoked to prevent disclosure of information by the oral examination of the applicants. The court acknowledged that there could be cases where a court could decide, in the public interest and/or in the interests of justice, that a witness should not be compelled to answer questions involving a breach of the confidential relationship between client and banker. However, the public interest in the instant case heavily favoured the information being given.

It would appear therefore that a balancing exercise has to be carried out, on the one hand considering the policy of assisting the foreign court and on the other the desirability of upholding a duty of confidentiality where possible to do so. (See Band and Christa, "Trustees and Insider Dealing" (2000) P.C.B. 6, 361–370).

Which Route to Use?

19–027 The overriding question for an investigator is which procedure will be the most appropriate. It is clear that procedure under the FSMA Act puts in place a mechanism for the swift investigation of commercial and financial practices, even where those practices extend across national boundaries. The speed with which an investigation is carried out is paramount given the changing nature in the way money is transferred. In this respect, mutual assistance between regulatory bodies can be more or at least as effective as the criminal process. However, where there is evidence of serious fraud, the SFO, together with the police, the DTI and the CPS, will continue to take effective action through the criminal courts, using their powers to investigate charges which cover a wider field than those available to the FSA. (Wright, R. "Fighting Fraud in the UK — The Interaction of the Criminal and the Regulatory process" (2000) F.I. 29 (Jul/Aug), 7–12).

Conclusion

19–028 There are difficulties inherent in each of the options available to UK investigators. While on the one-hand trademark delays in judicial assistance can be offset against the benefit of the likely admissibility of any evidence obtained at trial, investigations by regulatory authorities can be much speedier and even more effective and yet the usefulness of evidence obtained in this manner can be limited. The decision as to which method to chose therefore will depend on the level that the investigation is being carried out i.e. at the investigation stage it is most likely that letters of request between regulatory authorities will be used. If proceedings follow, it is apposite that mutual assistance between judicial authorities will be relied upon.

The severe criticisms of recent years directed towards the slowness and inefficiency of the various mechanisms for international mutual assistance have not gone unheard. Important efforts have been made, for example, the establishment of the European Judicial Network to ensure better co-operation between investigators at judicial and law enforcement level. Recent evaluations carried out in the EU context have confirmed that the last few years has seen a speeding up in the execution of mutual legal assistance requests and better co-operation between investigators both at judicial and law enforcement level. (Final Report on the First Evaluation Exercise — Mutual Legal Assistance in Criminal Matters [2001] O.J. C216/14).

This and other examples of similar developments outside the EU context, along with the general willingness to co-operate illustrated by all relevant institutions, indicates positive prospects for the continuing improvement of cross border assistance in legal matters.

Part 5

Investor Protection in Criminal Law

Chapter 20

Theft Act Offences

Until 1968 the law of stealing had developed in an arcane and random manner. The old law of larceny was abolished in that year and replaced by a new generic offence of theft created by the Theft Act 1968 which Parliament intended to embrace all manner of dishonest conduct. Twenty seven years in the development of English criminal law is perhaps a handbreadth, but against the sophistication of contemporary investor fraud the inadequacies of the existing law are regrettably as great today as those which the 1968 Act set out to remedy. **20–001**

The practical application of the Theft Act 1968 has not proved to be as simple and effective as the legislators had hoped or intended, and as Beldam L.J. remarked recently in *Hallam and Blackburn* [1995] Crim. L.R. 323, CA:

> "Once again the law of theft is in urgent need of simplification and modernisation, so that a jury of twelve ordinary citizens do not have to grapple with concepts couched in the antiquated *franglais* of *choses in action*, and scarce public resources in time and money are not devoted to hours of semantic argument divorced from the true merits of the case."

Not before time the Law Commission has embarked upon a review of the workings of the legislation in this field and its recommendations are awaited with some alacrity. In a letter to *The Times*, February 1, 1996, Mr Stephen Silber Q.C. acknowledged on behalf of the Law Commission that the review was needed because "there had been radical and multifarious technological advances" and that "it was likely that some acts of dishonesty might not be effectively covered by present legislation". The Law Commission hopes to produce a series of Consultation Papers and then a report. The urgency of the task cannot be under-stated. In *Preddy* [1996] 3 All E.R. 481, a case involving the obtaining of a mortgage advance by deception, Lord Jauncey acknowledged (at p.496j) that: **20–002**

> "it is singularly unfortunate that Parliament has achieved . . . the result of legalising fraudulent conduct of the type involved in these appeals—conduct which was almost certainly criminal prior to the 1968 Act. Building Societies may . . . derive small comfort from the fact that in Scotland common law and common sense rather than Parliamentary wisdom still prevail. It is almost certain that conduct such as that of the appellants would constitute the common law offence of fraud in that country".

20–003 A broad examination of Theft Acts 1968 and 1978 is beyond the scope of this work. Instead this chapter focuses on the ways in which prosecutors have sought to utilise the provisions of the Theft Acts 1968 and 1978 and the Forgery and Counterfeiting Act 1981 against those who have perpetrated investor fraud. A review of the cases demonstrates that the existing law is a blunt weapon in the armoury of investor protection.

Theft Act 1968

Theft

20–004 Theft is defined in s.1(1) of the Theft Act 1968 in the following terms: a person is guilty of theft if he dishonestly appropriates property belonging to another with the intention of permanently depriving the other of it. Megaw L.J. spelt out the ingredients of the offence in *Lawrence* [1971] 55 Cr. App. R. 73 at p.76:

> "Theft . . . involves four elements: (i) a dishonest (ii) appropriation (iii) of property belonging to another (iv) with the intention of depriving the other of it".

Dishonesty

20–005 Dishonesty is an essential ingredient of the offence of theft. It is also an ingredient of a number of other offences which are covered in this chapter, these offences being: under the 1968 Theft Act; obtaining property by deception contrary to s.15, obtaining a pecuniary advantage by deception contrary to s.16, false accounting contrary to s.17, suppression of documents contrary to s.20(1), procuring the execution of a valuable security by deception contrary to s.20(2) and handling stolen goods contrary to s.22; and under the 1978 Theft Act, obtaining services by deception contrary to s.1 and evasion of a liability by deception contrary to s.2. The test to be applied when determining the issue of dishonesty was set out by Lord Lane C.J. in the leading case of *R. v Ghosh* [1982] Q.B. 1053, 75 Cr. App. R. 154 as follows:

> "In determining whether the prosecution has proved that the defendant was acting dishonestly, a jury must first of all decide whether according to the standards of reasonable and honest people what was done was dishonest. If it was not dishonest by those standards, that is the end of the matter and the prosecution fails. If it was dishonest by those standards, then the jury must consider whether the defendant himself must have realised that what he was doing was by those standards dishonest."

20–006 Subject to this test, however, there are a number of circumstances in which Parliament has declared that a person's actions will not be regarded as dishonest. If property is taken in the belief that the taker has in law the right to deprive the owner of it or if property is taken in the belief that the taker would have the owner's consent if the owner knew of the appropriation and the circumstances of it, the person's appropriation of the property will not be regarded as dishonest. Also, if a person takes property in the belief that a person to whom the property belongs cannot be discovered by taking reasonable steps, the appropriation is not be regarded as dishonest.

In the context of investor fraud, issues concerning dishonesty have **20–007**
tended to arise where a director takes money from his own company. In *Attorney General's Reference (No 2 of 1982)* [1984] 78 Cr. App. R. 131 the Court of Appeal rightly rejected an argument that where a defendant was the sole directing mind of the company he could not be guilty of theft from the company because the company must have necessarily consented to his actions. Such knowledge should not be imputed to the company for the essence of such an arrangement was to deprive the company improperly of a large part of its assets. The company was a victim, and it would be irrational to treat the directors notionally as having transmitted this knowledge to the company.

In a later decision, *Mazo* [1996] Crim. L.R. 435, it was held that where **20–008**
valid consent is given, it would be unacceptable to hold that the transaction amounted to theft since the defendant had acquired an absolute, indefeasible right to the property in question. (After all, where a person has been given the item in question how can he or she be said to be acting dishonestly?). But in *R. v Hopkins, Kendrick* [1997] Crim. L.R. 359 the donees were convicted notwithstanding that they had been the recipients of a valid gift *inter vivos*. The donees could be convicted notwithstanding the fact that they had on the face of it acted honestly. It is clear that this creates a conflict between the civil and criminal law.

Appropriation

Parliament sought to encapsulate the notion of an appropriation in s.3. **20–009**
However the statutory definition of the term has not proved to be comprehensive, not because of any drafting difficulties but rather because of the diversity of circumstances in which property can be appropriated. The statutory provision defines appropriation as any assumption by a person of the rights of an owner and includes circumstances where a person keeps or deals with property which has come into his possession (innocently or not) without stealing it. The keeping or dealing with property will amount to an assumption of the rights of an owner in those circumstances. Again, as with the issue of dishonesty, problems in the commercial context have focused on the position where a person (often a corporate person) might be said to have consented to the appropriation. Where consent is relevant, it is relevant only to the question of dishonesty and not to that of appropriation.

This thorny issue was considered by the House of Lords in *Gomez* [1992] 3 W.L.R. 1067 in a case where an owner was induced to authorise the taking of property by a fraudulent deception. Deciding between conflicting Court of Appeal cases on the point the House of Lords held that it was the actual taking of property in circumstances where it was intended to assume the rights of the owner which amounted to an appropriation. The question of whether the owner had consented or not was irrelevant to whether there had been an appropriation. There were obvious policy considerations which led the House of Lords to this conclusion. As Lord Browne-Wilkinson said in a passage at the end of his judgment which resonates in the investor context:

> "The pillaging of companies by those who control them is now all too common. It would offend both common sense and justice to hold that the very control which enables such people to extract the company's assets constitutes a defence to a charge of theft from the company. The question in each case must be whether the extraction of the property from the company was dishonest, not whether the alleged thief has consented to his own wrongdoing".

20–010 That there is no requirement that appropriation be without the consent of the owner was again made clear by the Court in *R. v Snaresbrook Crown Court* L.T.L. June 18, 2001. Here it was stated that the fact that the Claimant either acting on his own or in concert with a co defendant could ensure that the company, as a matter of law, is to be regarded as consenting to the actions of the Claimant does not provide the Claimant with a defence if he would otherwise be guilty of theft. The salient point is that s.3 does not require misappropriation but only appropriation. Thus in this case, the motivation behind the appropriation of the money and the "consent" of the company were irrelevant for the purposes of establishing appropriation.

Acute difficulties concerning appropriation may arise in a case where an investor has paid money to an investment adviser who is supposed to invest the money on the investor's behalf. If the investment adviser does not invest the money or invests it in some way other than that intended by the investor, is he guilty of theft? Has the investment adviser appropriated the money within the meaning of s.3 of the Theft Act 1968?

20–011 This question was raised directly in the case of *Hallam and Blackburn* [1995] Crim. L.R. 323, which concerned the sale of investment products by financial advisors through the medium of a company. In some cases the investor's money was not invested on the investor's behalf but was paid into the defendants' or the company's business account. In other cases policy surrender cheques from insurance companies were not paid to investors. The defendants appealed with the leave of the trial judge who certified a question of law for the Court of Appeal to decide whether a payment into a defendant's bank account of a cheque with the consent or approval of the drawer of the cheque amounted to an appropriation of those funds by reason of the fact that it is made with a dishonest intent and as a preliminary step to the misuse of those funds.

20–012 By the time the case came to be heard by the Court of Appeal the answer to the certified question had been given by the House of Lords in *Gomez*. However, this was not the end of the matter. It remained to be determined exactly when the appropriation took place. The prosecution alleged that the appropriation took place on the date when the cheques from the clients or the insurers were paid into the personal or company bank accounts. If this allegation was correct, so the defendants argued, the funds were not the investor's property of the client and therefore the investor did not have any rights to appropriate at the time when the fund were paid into the personal or company bank accounts. Instead of charging the defendants with theft of monies, the appellants submitted that they should have been charged with theft of the cheque or chose in action it represented.

The Court of Appeal circumvented the point by relying on s.5(2) of the Theft Act 1968, this being a special provision enacted to deal with such technical points. This section is considered later in this Chapter. Suffice it to note here that the Court held that the defendants had been entrusted with funds to invest on behalf of their clients. After the investors had passed the cheques to the defendants the investors retained an equitable interest in the funds which attached not only to the cheque but to its proceeds and any balance in the accounts operated by the defendants or the company to which payment could be traced. It was this equitable interest which was appropriated at the time when the funds were paid into the personal or company bank accounts as a preliminary step to the dishonest misuse of those funds.

Whilst the Court of Appeal's decision is to be welcomed, it by no means **20–013** eradicates the myriad of technical problems in this area. Suppose an investment adviser intends to invest funds on the investor's behalf at the time when he pays the investor's cheque into the company account but due to commercial pressures he subsequently decides to use the funds to discharge the company's business liabilities. The dishonest intention will not coincide with the appropriation. Nor will the investment adviser be guilty of obtaining property by deception, because at the time when the property was obtained there was no deception. This is the situation that arose in *R. v Breaks and Huggan* [1998] Crim. L.R. 349. Here the reason that the premiums were not paid on behalf of the clients was that debtors to whom credit had been advanced had not honoured their obligations so the account was exhausted. This meant that there had been no dishonest intention at the time of "appropriation" of the premiums, nor could the defendant be accused of obtaining property by deception. In those circumstances the prosecution had failed to prove that any appropriation of funds had occurred that fell within section.

Appropriation of a Chose in Action

A "chose in action" is a legal phrase which is used to describe all personal **20–014** rights over property which can be claimed or enforced by an action in law. Typically in this context, a debt is a chose in action. In respect of monies held by a deposit-taking institution (such as a bank or building society), although the monies paid into the account belong to the deposit-taking institution, the latter owes a debt to the depositing customer which it undertakes (subject to special terms) to repay on demand. It is this debt which is capable of appropriation and act of appropriation is the usurpation of the account holder's rights. The leading cases on appropriation of a chose in action are *Wille* [1988] 86 Cr. App. R 296 and *Kohn* [1979] 69 Cr. App. R. 395. While *R. v Duru* [1973] 3 All E.R. 715 treated the obtaining of a cheque as the obtaining of a thing in action, this was stated not to be the case in *Preddy*.

The development of new types of financial instrument in the commercial sector has resulted in a wide range of methods by which money may be transferred. Other types of choses in action are rights which belong to a shareholder as a result of his holding of shares in a company or the rights of an owner in copyright. The problems associated with reconciling the concept of property within the Theft Act 1968 with these new methods of money transfer is considered later in this chapter.

Appropriation by Innocent Agent

20–015 A defendant is guilty of theft if he uses an innocent agent to carry out the appropriation for him. In *Stinger* [1991] 94 Cr. App. R. 13 a dishonest company employee signed bogus invoices which initiated company procedures and caused innocent employees to authorise payment. The company's bank account was debited in consequence. Whilst the defendant did not authorise payment, he was guilty of theft from the company bank accounts under the ordinary principles of criminal law.

Multiple Assumptions of the Rights of an Owner

20–016 The need to identify the precise time of appropriation is important when drafting charges. A mistake cannot be saved by resorting to a second appropriation where the circumstances of an earlier appropriation by the same defendant can be substantiated. In *Atakpu*, *The Times*, March 22, 1993 the defendants hired cars abroad and brought them to England where they were sold. The Court of Appeal held that once the cars had been stolen abroad they could not be appropriated again in England by the same thief. Difficulties were encountered in this case because the initial assumption of the rights of the owner occurred outside the jurisdiction. This same problem has often been met in the commercial context where instructions to transfer funds are given in one jurisdiction and the funds are held in another. Pt I of the Criminal Justice Act 1993 was enacted to resolve these problems. This is discussed at the end of this chapter.

Property

20–017 Property is given an inclusive and not an exhaustive definition by s.4(1) of the Theft Act 1968. It is defined to include "money and all other property, real or personal, including things in action and other intangible property". Before 1968 the property that could be stolen was property which was capable of being carried away, in other words tangible property which had a physical existence. Intangible property could not be stolen because it had no physical existence. S.4(1) of the Theft Act 1968 changed the position by including intangible property in the definition of property which was capable of being stolen. This change had major significance in the commercial context since it embraced the amorphous chose in action as a species of intangible property which was capable of being stolen. In consequence the focus of attention has shifted away from concentration on the physical attributes of the nature of property to an examination of the legal incidents of relationships which arise when commercial arrangements of this nature are made.

Cheques

The degree of scrutiny to which commercial arrangements have been subject under the present law is well demonstrated by a consideration of the leading case involving theft of cheques. In *Kohn* [1979] 69 Cr. App. R. 395 a defendant drew cheques on various company bank accounts, the proceeds of which were intended for the defendant's personal benefit. The thefts fell into three categories. First, there was the situation where the company bank account was in credit. In this instance the drawing of a cheque on the company bank account amounted to theft of a chose in action which was identified as the debt owed by the bank to the company. Secondly, there were occasions where the balance of the company bank account was in overdraft but the amount dishonestly drawn did not exceed the agreed limit. Again, the drawing of a cheque was held to amount to theft of a chose in action which was identified as an obligation owed by the bank to the company to meet the cheque if the balance on the account did not exceed the overdraft limit. Thirdly, there were occasions where the overdraft limit was exceeded. Here, however, there could not be any theft of a chose in action because there was no relationship of debtor and creditor between the bank and the company. The bank had no obligation to meet the cheque in excess of the overdraft limit. Even though the bank met the cheque as a matter of grace it made no difference to the legal incidents of the arrangement. The meeting of the cheque could not retrospectively create any personal right of property in the customer nor any retrospective duty on the duty holder. **20–018**

As mentioned earlier, the perception that a defendant obtains a thing in action belonging to the plaintiff when he induces him to draw a cheque in his favour was rejected in *Preddy*. It was held that he does not do so because the thing in action belonged from the instant of its creation to D. It never belonged nor could belong to, P.

While the Court in *Preddy* was not called upon to consider whether D might be guilty of obtaining the cheque itself, the physical thing, it stated obiter that a cheque was not a chose in action.

Credit Balances

Following the decision in *Kohn*, there was some concern that the breadth of its effect had been restricted by the Court of Appeal in *Thompson (Michael)* [1984] 79 Cr. App. R. 191, [1984] 3 All E.R. 565 where a bank operator in Kuwait programmed the bank computer to credit accounts opened by him in Kuwait with amounts dishonestly debited from the accounts of customers with corresponding amounts. On his return to England the bank operator instructed the Kuwaiti bank to transfer the funds from his accounts in Kuwait to his English bank accounts. The bank operator was charged with obtaining property by deception from the Kuwaiti bank. In a **20–019** cleverly worded indictment the particulars of the charges alleged that he had obtained the transferred sum by falsely representing that the amount credited to his account was a genuine and accurate credit and that he was entitled to receive payment of the sum. On appeal the bank operator argued that the Court lacked jurisdiction to try him because he had not committed any offences in England. He said that he had obtained the property abroad when he obtained control of the credit balances in Kuwait. No offence had been committed in England.

In an effort to defeat this argument the Court of Appeal held that the bank operator had not obtained a chose in action against the bank when the funds were transferred from the customer accounts to his personal accounts in Kuwait because an apparent credit balance on a customer's bank account could not be properly be described as a chose in action in English law. May L.J. said that it was not possible to describe as a chose in action a liability which had been brought into existence by fraud where the action to enforce that liability is capable of immediate defeasance as soon as the fraud is pleaded.

20–020 Whilst the decision in *Thompson* was unimpeachable in its application of civil law, there were concerns about its consequences in criminal law, lest fraudsters sought to apply the same reasoning in cases where there was no extra-jurisdictional aspect. Suppose the events in Kuwait had happened in England? If the first part of the fraudulent scheme was to be the reflected in a criminal charge the charge would have to be directed towards the dishonest programming of the bank computer (*i.e.* false accounting) rather than the transfer of funds from the customer accounts. Yet the real vice of the fraud was the theft of the credit balances from the customer accounts. Some astute drafting on the part of prosecutors would be needed to avoid the pitfalls.

20–021 Following the Privy Council decision in *Chan Man-sin v AG of Hong Kong* [1988] 1 W.L.R. 196, [1988] 1 All E.R. 1 it no longer seems open to a defendant to raise such an unmeritorious point in his defence. In *Chan Man-sin* a company accountant drew forged cheques on a company's bank account. He was charged with theft of choses in action, namely debts owed by the company's bank to the company. In his defence the accountant argued that a forged cheque was a nullity so far as the customer was concerned and the bank was not entitled to debit the customer's account with the amount of the forged cheque. Accordingly, so he submitted, there was no intangible property which was capable of appropriation. The leading civil banking case of *Tai Hing Cotton Mill Ltd v Lui Chong Hing Bank (No.1)* [1985] 2 All E.R. 947 [1986] A.C. 80 was cited in support. The Privy Council robustly rejected this argument, saying that it was entirely immaterial whether the end result of the transaction may be a legal nullity. It is not possible to read into the definition of appropriation any requirement that the assumption of rights there envisaged should have a legally efficacious result. It has to be said that this decision sits uneasily with established principles of banking law. The theft in *Chan Man-sin* was artificial in the sense that, applying these principles of civil law, the customer did not suffer any loss. If loss is suffered in this type of case, it is borne by the deposit-taking institution. (The interaction between principles of civil law and criminal law are considered at the end of this chapter).

However in *R. v Hilton* [1997] Crim. L.R. 761, the Court did not see this approach as artificial. Instead the focus was placed on the act of "appropriation", *i.e.* assuming the rights of the owner by causing the transfer to be made out of the account. The fact of the transfer is enough to complete the offence regardless of the continuing obligation on the bank to replenish the account.

Electronic transfers

The bank credit created by a CHAPS order (clearing house automated payment system order) is recognised as a chose in action. As Lord Lane C.J. said in *King* [1991] Crim. L.R. 906, [1991] 3 All E.R. 705, if the payee's right to the bank credit were to be called into question, the CHAPS order could be relied upon as his document of title to the credit. To similar effect, the reduction of a sum standing in one customer's bank account and the corresponding increase in the sum standing to the credit of another customer's bank account will constitute the obtaining of property even though the transfer between the bank accounts was effected by electronic means—*Crick*, *The Times*, August 18, 1993. In *Hilton*, the Court rejected the suggestion that there was a difference between cases where the appropriation was by means of a cheque and where it was by means of electronic transfer. The ultimate transfer of funds, it was stated, would be made by an electronic method even where a cheque is used. It follows that intangible property will include a sum of money represented by a figure in an account maintained by a deposit-taking institution. **20–022**

Documents

In the age of electronic banking it will be the exception rather than the norm for charges to be based on theft of documents rather than a chose of action in cases which involve the loss of an investor's funds. Nevertheless, where a person dishonestly obtains a document which gives rise to certain legal rights on the part of the holder of the document, it is open to the prosecutor to allege theft of the document in question. A person entrusted with shares in his capacity as trustee or stockbroker will commit theft of tangible property (*i.e.* the shares and not just a piece of paper) if he wrongfully pledges the shares as security or sells them when not authorised to do so—*Smith* [1963] 36 D.L.R. (2d) 613; [1963] 1 C.C.C. 68. **20–023**

Precise Identification of Property Stolen

Another problem which frequently occurs in investor fraud cases concerns the precise identification of the stolen property where the case involves the repeated taking of small amounts of money over a long period of time. Where there is an appropriation of a number of sums but no evidence as to when the individual appropriations took place the prosecution is entitled to **20–024** charge the appropriation of the aggregate amount on a day within the period during which the appropriations took place—*D.P.P. v McCabe* [1992] Crim. L.R. 885.

Sometimes a different problem arises where there is doubt as to whether a defendant stole the property or the proceeds arising from sale of the stolen property. In this situation a prosecutor may properly allege that the defendant has stolen the property or its proceeds. It is immaterial that it cannot be shown whether the defendant stole the original property or its proceeds as long as the jury is sure that he stole one or the other. In *Hallam and Blackburn*, above, the defendants argued that they should have been charged with theft of a cheque or chose in action represented by the cheque rather than theft of a specified sum of money. The Court of Appeal said that although it was not possible to prove whether the defendants had stolen a chose in action or the proceeds of a chose in action, it would nevertheless be sufficient to show that the defendants had failed to account for the sums with which they had been entrusted.

Belonging to Another

20–025 The prosecution must establish that the appropriated property belongs to another person before an offence of theft is committed. At first blush this additional statutory requirement may seem unnecessary since the essence of appropriation is an assumption of another's rights. In fact, this additional requirement is vital because of the various categories of ownership which exist in English law. A person may own the legal and/or equitable interest in personal property in the same way as ownership of land is classified. Also, a person may have property in his possession not because he owns any legal or equitable interest over it but because he has been entrusted with possession of it as bailee. It would be absurd if the law of theft were to apply only to cases where property had been taken from the custody and control of its legal owner. S.5 of the Theft Act 1968 was enacted to deal with these points and it provides as follows:

> "(1) Property shall be regarded as belonging to any person having possession or control of it, or having any proprietary right or interest (not being an equitable interest arising from an agreement to transfer or grant an interest).
>
> (2) Where property is subject to a trust, the persons to whom it belongs shall be regarded as including any person having a right to enforce the trust, and an intention to defeat the trust shall be regarded accordingly as an intention to deprive of the property any person having that right.
>
> (3) Where a person receives property from or on account of another, and is under an obligation to the other to retain and deal with that property or its proceeds in a particular way, the property or proceeds shall be regarded (as against him) as belonging to the other.
>
> (4) Where a person gets property by another's mistake, and is under an obligation to make restoration (in whole or in part) of the property or its proceeds or of the value thereof, then to the extent of that obligation in the property or proceeds shall be regarded (as against him) as belonging to the person entitled to restoration, and an intention not to make restoration

shall be regarded accordingly as an intention to deprive that person of the property or proceeds.

(5) Property of a corporation sole shall be regarded as belonging to the corporation notwithstanding a vacancy in the corporation."

Subss.(2) and (3) have proved to be a fertile breeding ground for fraudsters seeking to escape liability in criminal law in cases of investor loss. **20–026**

Naylor and Clowes—Investors Funds Held on Trust

In a case following the well publicised collapse of the Barlow Clowes group of companies, the Court of Appeal had to consider the application of s.5 in the context of England's largest investor swindle. The case is reported as *R. v Clowes (Peter) (No.2)*, [1994] 2 All E.R. 316. Barlow Clowes had advertised for funds to be deposited in investment schemes which were said to be based on investment in British Government stocks. The monies were not invested and Clowes was charged with theft of investor funds which he had used for his own purposes. The principal issue argued in the Court of Appeal turned on whether Clowes was a trustee of the invested funds or a beneficial owner of the funds. If a trustee of the funds, Clowes would have been taken property deemed to belong to investors by virtue of s.5(2), thereby rendering him guilty of theft as charged. If on the other hand Clowes was not a trustee of the funds but beneficially entitled to them, and subject only to a contractual obligation to pay back on demand equivalent sums to those who invested, Clowes would not have appropriated property belonging to another. In this event he would not have been guilty of the charges of theft which had been brought against him. **20–027**

Clowes argued that on a proper construction of the investment brochures and application forms the relationship between Barlow Clowes and each investor was not that of a trustee and beneficiary but simply that of a creditor and debtor. The investment clause in the application form attached to each brochure did not limit Barlow Clowes to investing in British Government stock but also authorised it to invest the funds in, amongst other things, the purchase of shares of any public or private company or by lending it to anybody or person in the discretion of Barlow Clowes. In support of his argument Clowes relied upon a well established line of civil cases in which the Courts had demonstrated a reluctance to construe a relationship of trust in commercial transactions, particularly where the terms of the transaction did not require segregation of funds.

It required some deft judicial footwork to uphold the convictions for theft. Notwithstanding the fact that an investors' funds were not to be held in a segregated account but mixed with other investors' funds, the Court held that there were clear indicators which showed that Barlow Clowes had received the investment funds on trust to invest them in British Government stocks. In the Court's view the authority to place the monies elsewhere was limited to a temporary placement pending investment, re-investment or return of the money to the investor.

20–028 In *Breaks and Huggan*, referred to earlier, the defendants were charged with theft in relation to premiums received from clients which were never invested. The prosecution case was that the premiums received by the company remained the property of the clients, being destined for the onward transmission to the brokers, and the company owed an obligation to the clients to use the payment for that purpose but did not do so, spending them in some other way. The court cited Lord Taylor C.J.'s statement that "section 5(3) would only apply if (the jury) were sure that the appellant and his client both clearly understood that the (monies) were to be kept separate from the appellant's own money and that of his business." It was held that whether there is an obligation to maintain a separate fund must generally be answered by applying an *objective* test.

The problem however is that in a criminal case, where the prosecution rely on s.5 (3) or s.5 (4) they must prove that the defendant was aware at least of the facts giving rise to the obligation to maintain separate funds and probably that he was aware that it was an obligation. If he was not so aware, he may have thought he was entitled to do what he liked with the money and in that case he would not be dishonest.

Preddy

20–029 The House of Lords in *Preddy* [1996] A.C. 815 decided that credit is new property, *i.e.* that where D procures a transaction whereby P's bank account is debited by £x and consequently D's bank account is credited by £x, D has created a new thing in action that never belonged to P and therefore D cannot be guilty of obtaining property belonging to P.

The effect of *Preddy* can be seen in the case of *R. v Nathan* [1997] Crim L.R. 835 where a loan had been obtained by deception. It was argued on behalf of the Crown that the new chose in action belonged to the bank and the appellant had obtained it in the sense of securing legal ownership and control. However, the court rejected this argument and held that since the loan had been transferred into the borrower's account telegraphically, the credit balance in the borrower's account was a new chose in action that had never been the property of the lender.

20–030 The lacuna in the law created by *Preddy* can be overcome insofar as s.5(3) offences are concerned where it can be established that the defendant was obliged to retain or deal with property in a certain way and that this obligation had been breached. Thus in *R. v Dyke and Munro* [2001] EWCA Crim 2184 where the defendants trustees of a charity had misappropriated funds belonging to the charity and the particulars of the offence were that the appellants had stolen money belonging to "person or persons unknown", the Court held that the Charity's property was stolen by whoever acted inconsistently with the Charity's ownership of that property. The Court made it clear that not being able to identify the victims would not be fatal to a conviction since both at common law and by statute when a person was subject to account for money, that imposed a trust and to misappropriate that money was to take property that belonged to the beneficiaries of that trust.

20–031 The court in *R. v Klineberg and Marsden* (1998) L.T.L. November 6, went a step further and relied on the decision of *R. v Smith* (1997) L.T.L. May

14, as authority for the proposition that s.5(3) was essentially a deeming provision by which property or its proceeds "shall be regarded" as belonging to another. In other words even thought the investors in that case did not have a legal or equitable interest in the credit balance under consideration, under s.5(3) it nevertheless belonged to them. In this way the *Preddy* problem can be overcome once the prosecution can show that the defendants were obliged to retain and deal with the property and its proceeds in a particular way and that that obligation had been breached.

Intention to Permanently Deprive

The final ingredient of theft identified by Megaw L.J. in *Lawrence* [1971] **20–032**
55 Cr. App. R. 73 is the intention of permanently depriving the other of the property in question. The defendant's intention is a question of fact to be determined in each case and no particular problems have been encountered in the investor fraud context. Defendants are commonly heard to assert that they took monies with the intention of repaying the investor in the fullness of time. Whilst this assertion goes to the issue of their dishonesty in taking the monies in the first place, s.6 of the Theft Act 1968 effectively precludes a defendant from raising the matter in connection with his intention to permanently deprive. The section reads as follows:

"(1) A person appropriating property belonging to another without meaning the other permanently to lose the thing itself is nevertheless to be regarded as having the intention of permanently depriving the other of it if his intention is to treat the thing as his own to dispose of regardless of the other's rights; and a borrowing or lending of it may amount to so treating it if, but only if, the borrowing or lending is for a period and in circumstances making it equivalent to an outright taking or disposal.

(2) Without prejudice to the generality of subsection (1) above, where a person, having possession or control (lawfully or not) of property belonging to another, parts with the property under a condition as to its return which he may not be able to perform, this (if done for purposes of his own and without the other's authority) amounts to treating the property as his own to dispose of regardless of the other's rights."

Property by Deception

Obtaining Property by Deception

The offence of obtaining property by deception contrary to s.15 is the next **20–033**
offence which is often utilised in cases of investor fraud. By this section:

"(1) A person who by any deception dishonestly obtains property belonging to another, with the intention of permanently depriving the other of it, shall on conviction on indictment be liable to imprisonment for a term not exceeding ten years.

(2) For the purposes of this section a person is to be treated as obtaining property if he obtains ownership, possession or control of it, and "obtain" includes obtaining for another or enabling another to obtain or retain."

20–034 A deception is defined in s.15(4) as "any deception (whether deliberate or reckless) by words or conduct as to fact or as to law, including a deception as to the present intentions of the person using the deception or any other person". Dishonesty and property mean the same as they do in the case of theft, and s.6 is expressly stated to apply when considering whether there was any intention to permanently deprive. It follows that the same considerations apply to the use of s.15 in the investor fraud context. Practical problems have been encountered when seeking to prove that property was obtained by deception. The dishonest deception must precede the obtaining of the property and operate on the mind of the person deceived. Unfortunately, with the sophistication of some investor frauds, this causative aspect is not always easy to prove. In cases involving a company, a company was fixed with the knowledge acquired by one of its employees only if the employee had its authority to act in relation to the particular transaction in question. Where the company had been the victim of fraud, an employee who was party to the fraud would not be acting with its authority. Knowledge acquired by such an employee which was relevant to the fraud was not therefore to be attributed to the company—*Rozeik* [1996] Crim. L.R. 271.

20–035 In any case where the reasoning in *Preddy* would be fatal to a conviction for theft, it would be likely to be fatal to a conviction for obtaining by deception under s.15 also. Thus in *R. v Horsman* [1998] Crim. L.R. 128, where the appellant was charged with obtaining a cheque by deception, it was held to be "common ground" that, following *Preddy*, the conviction must be quashed "since all that happened was the payer's account was reduced by the amounts of the cheques and a new chose in action was created in favour of the recipient, no property of either of the payers was obtained by the appellant". Similarly in *R. v Graham* [1997] Crim. L.R. 340 the Court of Appeal heard a number of cases where the property in question was a CHAPS payment, a telegraphic transfer or a cheque. The Court held that all of the convictions must be quashed on the basis of *Preddy*.

This situation was remedied by the 1996 Theft (Amendment) Act which provided for a new offence of obtaining a money transfer by deception.

20–036 S.2 of the 1996 Act, which became s.24A of the 1968 Act, filled another gap in the law after *Preddy* overcoming situations such as that which arose in *R. v Forsyth* [1997] Crim. L.R. 589. Here it had not been possible to procure a conviction for handling of stolen goods where the Defendant had dishonestly procured a transfer of stolen funds into her own account.

Multiple Share Applications

20–037 Some years ago, during the heyday of share privatisation, a number of successful prosecutions were brought under s.15 for multiple share applications. One case involved a barrister and former MP, Keith Best, *The Times*, October 6, 1987. Best was convicted of three specimen offences of attempting to obtain property by deception after he had made six applications in the British Telecom flotation for a total of 39,000 shares. The applications were made in variations of Best's name and address. Initially

Best had been charged with the full offence under s.15 but the charge was altered to an attempt after the prosecution failed to call the scrutineer who considered the Best applications to testify that he or she was deceived. Best contested the case on the basis that he was not acting dishonestly but he was convicted by a majority verdict. The trial judge sentenced him to four months imprisonment and a fine but on appeal the sentence was reduced to a fine of £4,500. Lord Lane C.J. commented that all types of stock market dishonesty were easy to commit, difficult to detect, and potentially very lucrative for the perpetrator:

> "Let it be clearly understood that from now on those who indulged in such or any other sort of cheating connected with the stock market were on notice that it was not only their assets which were at risk but also their liberty."

In an earlier case, *Greenstein* [1976] 1 All E.R. 1, the Court of Appeal had upheld convictions for obtaining property by deception where multiple share applications had been made and the cheques accompanying the share applications were at risk of bouncing. The jury had been asked in that case to decide whether it was merely irregular or a breach of contract to make applications for shares in this way, or whether a dishonest deception was involved. **20–038**

False Accounting

False accounting is an extremely useful offence in the prosecution of investor fraud. Whether details of the fraud are recorded in the business records, it is axiomatic that the business records will not provide a true and genuine picture of the business activity in question. It is not uncommon for fabricated invoices to be recorded in business records in a manner which artificially inflates expenses and enables funds to be extracted by dishonest directors or employees in an irregular fashion. It is equally not uncommon for income to be omitted from business records in an effort to reduce the declared income and conceal the appropriation of business funds by a dishonest director or employee for his private use. In both cases the business records will conceal the fraudulent activity which has been perpetrated to the prejudice of the shareholders or business creditors. S.17 of the Theft Act 1968 exposes the falsifiers of business records to a maximum punishment of seven years imprisonment and unlimited fine. **20–039**

S.17 provides as follows: **20–040**

> "(1) Where a person dishonestly, with a view to gain for himself or another or with intent to cause loss to another,-
>
> (a) destroys, defaces, conceals or falsifies any account or any records or document made or required for an accounting purpose; or
>
> (b) in furnishing information for any purpose produces or makes use of any account, or any such record or document as aforesaid, which to his knowledge is or may be misleading, false or deceptive in a material particular;

he shall, on conviction on indictment, be liable to imprisonment for a term not exceeding seven years.

(2) For the purposes of this section a person who makes or concurs in making an account or other document an entry which is or may be misleading, false or deceptive in a material particular, or who omits or concurs in omitting a material particular from an account or other document, is to be treated as falsifying the account or document."

20–041 The word "record" is wide enough to cover a mechanical account such as a meter—*Edwards v Toombs* [1983] Crim. L.R. 43. It follows that business accounts and records kept on computer will constitute a record within the meaning of this section. This was confirmed in *Re Levin*, March 1, 1996, unreported, when the Divisional Court held where a person made an entry made into a continuous record stored on computer disc which was false or misleading, he was to be treated as having falsified an account for the purposes of s.17. In *Scot-Simmonds* [1994] Crim. L.R. 933 the Court of Appeal confirmed that the word "account" has its meaning in ordinary usage and that the words "made or required for an accounting purpose" do not qualify the word "account". An entirely bogus set of accounts will constitute a false account within the meaning of this section.

20–042 Documents which are made or required for some purpose other than an accounting purpose fall within s.17 if the documents are required for an accounting purpose as a subsidiary purpose. It will not be difficult therefore for the prosecution to prove that the document was "required" for an accounting purpose. Thus in *Osinuga v DDP* [1998] Crim. L.R. 216, it was held that even where there is no direct evidence that a particular document had been required for an accounting purpose, the court is entitled to draw such an inference looking at all the circumstances of the case. For example, in *R. v John Lawrence Manning* [1999] Crim. L.R. 151, a dishonest insurance business man was convicted of false accounting on the basis of cover notes issued to clients falsely stating that certain brokers with whom their money had been placed were acceptable. (No direct evidence was adduced that the notes had been required for an accounting purpose. However the Court stated that in future, prosecutors should call evidence (of a brief and if possible, unchallenged nature) as to how documents on which they relied under s.17(1)(a) of the Act were actually used to save court time). The fact that the falsified information is contained in a different part of the document from that required for an accounting purpose is irrelevant since the document must be examined as a whole—*Attorney General's Reference (No 1 of 1980)* [1980] 72 Cr. App. R. 60.

With a View to Gain or With Intent to Cause Loss

20–043 S.34(2)(a) of the Theft Act 1968 provides that:

"'gain' and 'loss' are to be construed as extending only to gain or loss in money or other property, but as extending to any such gain or loss whether temporary or permanent; and -

(i) 'gain' includes a gain by keeping what one has, as well as a gain by getting what one has not; and

(ii) 'loss' includes a loss by not getting what one might get, as well as a loss by parting with what one has."

Although generally not problematic this statutory definition is unduly restrictive in a case where a financial services consultant falsifies an accounting document, for example an investment portfolio valuation, with the intention of inducing the investor to forbear from starting legal proceedings against him.

In *Goleccha and Choraria* [1989] 90 Cr. App. R. 241 the Court of Appeal held that where a debtor dishonestly falsifies documents required for an accounting purpose, intending to induce his creditor to forbear from suing on the debt, he does not have " a view to gain" or an "intent to cause loss" within the meaning of s.34(2). Therefore in this type of case the financial services consultant (the debtor) will not be possessed of any proprietary rights. He will not have money and the chose in action represented by the debt will be owned by the investor (the creditor). **20–044**

The essential ingredients of the offence as per *R. v Graham* [1997] Crim. L.R. 340 are the existence of an account or record or document made or required for an accounting purpose. In that case the court was not persuaded that knowledge of the purpose for which the record or document was made formed part of the *mens rea* of the offence, *i.e.* D may be convicted of false accounting although he has not the slightest idea that what he is doing is going to result in a false account.

Valuable Securities

There are two offences contained in s.20 of the Theft Act 1968 which concern dealing with a valuable security. It is an offence contrary to s.20(1) to dishonestly destroy or deface a valuable security, and contrary to s.20(2) it is an offence to dishonestly procure the execution of a valuation security by deception. In both cases the offence has to be committed with a view to gain or with intent to cause loss. Commonly the offence has been used to prosecute cases of traveller's cheque fraud, banking fraud and mortgage fraud. **20–045**

A valuable security is defined in s.20(3) as: **20–046**

"any document creating, transferring, surrendering or releasing any right to, in or over property, or authorising the payment of money or delivery of any property, or evidencing the creation, transfer, surrender or release of any such right, or the payment of money or delivery of any property, or the satisfaction of any obligation".

An irrevocable letter of credit is a valuable security—*Benstead and Taylor* [1982] 75 Cr. App. R. 276. Likewise, a CHAPS (Clearing House Automated Payment System) order—*King* [1992] 1 Q.B. 20, 93 Cr. App. R. 259 ; and all forms of electronic transfer—*Bolton* [1991] 94 Cr. App. R. 74, and *Crick*, *The Times*, August 18, 1993. The prosecution must be able to specify the valuable security which was procured. It was insufficient to allege that the **20–047** valuable security was "a cheque or telegraphic transfer authority", without bringing evidence to prove that it was one or the other—*Mensah Lartey and Relevy* [1996] Crim. L.R. 203. In *Preddy*, Lord Goff (at p.492h) declined to speculate on whether the defendants could have been charged with dishonestly procuring the execution of a valuable security by deception since the issue did not arise for consideration in the appeal. The court in *Preddy* did however clarify one thing and that is that a cheque is not a chose in action (as it was held to be in *Duru* [1973] 3 All E.R. 715) but a tangible thing. A cheque is therefore a valuable security. This means that the difficulties posed for the prosecution in establishing theft of a cheque under s.15 may be avoided by using s.20(2) of the Act instead.

20–048 The Court in *R. v Horsman* [1998] Crim. L.R. 128, however failed to recognise the opportunity. It was held to be "common ground" following *Preddy*, that the conviction for obtaining cheques by deception must be quashed "since all that happened was the payer's account was reduced by the amounts of the cheques and a new chose in action was created in favour of the recipient, no property of either of the payers was obtained by the appellant". If the appellant had been charged with obtaining a thing in action, then this conclusion would have been right. But he was not charged with obtaining a thing in action but with obtaining a cheque, *i.e.* a valuable security and therefore a conviction would have been possible under s.20(2).

20–049 As with an offence of obtaining property by deception, the element of causation has to be established. Under s.20(2) the execution of the valuable security must be procured by the dishonest deception. This means that the *mens rea* is essentially the same for a s.20(2) as for a s.15(1). Thus in *R. v N'Wandou, Ashton* (1998) L.T.L. January 19, it was held that a s.20(2) conviction could be substituted for a s.15(1) conviction because the mens rea was essentially the same. The Court of Appeal held in *Beck* [1984] 80 Cr. App. R. 355 that the word "procure" has no special meaning for the purpose of s.20(2). It means simply to cause or bring about. "Execution" means doing something to the face of the document, such as signing it, or the due performance of all formalities to give it validity—*Kassim* [1992] 1 A.C. 9. The offences under ss.20(1) and (2) are each punishable by a maximum sentence of seven years imprisonment and unlimited fine on indictment and six months imprisonment and a fine of up to £5,000 if convicted summarily.

Theft Act 1978

20–050 There are two offences contained in the Theft Act 1978 which have marginal relevance in the investor context.

A person who by deception dishonestly obtains services from another contravenes s.1(1) of the Act. Deception has the same meaning as for s.15(1) of the Theft Act 1968 and once again the deception must be operative in relation to the services which are obtained. By s.1(2) a person is deemed to obtain services where the other is induced to confer a benefit by doing some act, or causing or permitting some act to be done, on the understanding that the benefit has been or will be paid for.

In *Shortland* [1995] Crim. L.R. 893 the Court of Appeal held that a benefit could include the provision of banking facilities but it had to be established evidentially that the defendant would have been required to pay for the banking services. Otherwise, no benefit had been established. A hire purchase agreement was held to be capable of amounting to a service in *Widdowson* (1986) 82 Cr. App. R. 314 but, according to the decision in *Halai* [1983] Crim. L.R. 624 a mortgage advance is not. There is some doubt as to whether *Halai* was correctly decided. In *Preddy* the House of Lords was invited to hear argument on the correctness of the decision in *Halai* but it declined to do so because the question did not arise for decision in the appeal. Lord Goff said (at p.495j) that he recognised that this left prosecuting authorities in a difficult position, and that the problem would best be solved by the enactment of a short Act of Parliament which declared that dishonestly inducing another to make a loan could constitute the offence of dishonestly obtaining services by deception. **20–051**

This is the effect of the s.15A(3) of the Theft (Amendment) Act 1996 which overrules *Halai* so far as events occurring after December 18, 1996 are concerned. In *R. v Cooke* [1997] Crim. L.R. 436, the Court appeared to have decided that the decision in *Halai* had been wrongly decided. However, in *R. v Naviede* [1997] Crim. L.R. 662, the Court merely distinguished *Halai* implying that it remained good law for events before December 18, 1996. **20–052**

The second relevant offence is created by s.2(1) of the Theft Act 1978 which provides that a person commits a criminal offence where, by deception, he: **20–053**

> "(a) dishonestly secures the remission of the whole or any part of any existing liability to make a payment, whether his own or another's; or
> (b) with intent to make permanent default in whole or in part on any existing liability to make a payment, or with intent to let another do so, dishonestly induces the creditor or any person claiming on behalf of he creditor to wait for payment (whether or not the due date for payment is deferred) or to forgo payment; or
> (c) dishonestly obtains any exemption from or abatement of liability to make a payment."

For purposes of this section "liability" means any legally enforceable liability. The Law Commission intended that s.2(1) should create three distinct offences but in practice there is considerable overlap. The decided cases emphasise that the defendant must intend to gain a permanent remission of liability before any one of three offences is committed. If convicted on indictment a person is liable to a maximum of five years imprisonment and/or an unlimited fine if convicted of an offence under s.1 or 2 of the Theft Act 1978. The maximum penalty on summary conviction is 6 months imprisonment and/or a fine of up to £2,000.

Forgery and Counterfeiting Act 1981

Like the offence of false accounting contrary to s.17 of the Theft Act 1968, offences of forgery are often committed during the course of an investor fraud. "The essence of forgery . . . is the making of a false document **20–054** intending that it be used to induce a person to accept and act upon the message contained in it, as if it were contained in a genuine document" (Law Commission Report on Forgery and Counterfeit Currency (Law Comm. No. 55), para.22). The Forgery and Counterfeiting Act 1981 covers this area of the law. The purpose of the Act is to preserve confidence in the authenticity of documents on which reliance might be placed.

By s.1 a person is guilty of forgery if he makes a false instrument, with the intention that he or another shall use it to induce somebody to accept it as genuine, and by reason of so accepting it to do or not to do some act to his own or any other person's prejudice. The meaning of an "instrument" is defined by s.8 (1) as any document, whether of a formal or informal character but the definition is artificially extended to include "electronic" documents which appear in or on a disc, tape, sound track or other device on or in which information is recorded or stored by mechanical, electronic or other means. It was held in *Re Levin*, March 1, 1996 (unreported), that a magnetic disc fell within the term of "instrument" within the meaning of s.8(1)(d) and embraced the information stored as well as the medium on which it was stored. A disc could be falsified by entering false instructions on to the disc.

20–055 The House of Lords placed a gloss on the wording of s.8(1) in *Gold and Schifreen* [1988] A.C. 1063 when their Lordships held that the information must be preserved for an appreciable time with the object of subsequent retrieval or recovery. *Gold and Schifreen* was a case in which the defendants gained access to a Prestel computer data bank by a dishonest trick. They were charged with an offence under s.1 of the Forgery and Counterfeiting Act 1981 but it was held on appeal that the language of the Forgery and Counterfeiting Act 1981 did not cover the facts of the case. The facts of the case would now fall within the Computer Misuse Act 1990.

The meaning of "false" is defined in s.9 and follows the recommendations of the Law Commission. Essentially an instrument will be false if it tells a lie about itself—*Jeraj* [1994] Crim. L.R. 595. "Prejudice" is defined in s.10. The prejudice must be directed at someone other than the deceiver—*Utting* [1987] 86 Cr. App. R 164. There is no direct authority on whether a person might be guilty of forgery by omission. The issue was left unresolved in *Hopkins and Collins* [1957] 41 Cr. App. R. 231.

20–056 There are four other offences created by the Forgery and Counterfeiting Act 1981.

Copying a false instrument is an offence under s.2 where the person makes a copy of an instrument which is, and which he knows or believes to be, a false instrument with the intention that he or another shall use it to induce somebody to accept it as a copy of a genuine instrument, and by reason of so accepting it to do or not to do some act to his own or any other person's prejudice.

Using a false instrument is an offence contrary to s.3 of the Act. Under the terms of this section it is an offence for a person to use an instrument which is, or which he knows or believes to be false, with the intention that he or another shall use it to induce somebody to accept it as genuine, and by reason of so accepting it to do or not to do some act to his own or any other person's prejudice.

Using a copy of a false instrument is an offence under s.4, and by s.5 it is an offence to have custody or control of certain false instruments and manufacture, custody or control of equipment or materials with which such instruments may be made.

S.5(5) sets out the instruments to which the offences created in ss.1 to 4 apply. These include money orders, postal orders, share certificates, cheques, traveller's cheques, cheque cards and credit cards. Custody means physical custody, control imports some notion of the power to direct what shall be done with the things in question. **20–057**

A person convicted on indictment of an offence contrary to s.5 of the Act will be liable to a maximum sentence of 10 years imprisonment and an unlimited fine. A maximum sentence of six months imprisonment and a fine of up to £5,000 can be imposed if convicted summarily.

Jurisdiction

There have been a number of problems concerning the jurisdiction of the Court to try cases of theft and obtaining property by deception where either the subject-matter of the offence was located abroad or the conduct giving rise to the offence was committed abroad. A significant change in the law was made by ss.1 to 6 of the Criminal Justice Act 1993 which were enacted by Parliament to overcome the technical problems which had arisen. Under these sections Theft Act offences (theft, obtaining property by deception, false accounting, procuring execution of a valuable security, etc.) and offences under the Forgery and Counterfeiting Act 1981 can be tried in the United Kingdom where any one of the constituent elements of the offence occurs in England and Wales. S.3(1) states that a person may be guilty of an offence, whether or not he was in England and Wales at any material time, and whether or not he was a British citizen at any such time. **20–058**

For an instructive consideration of the law as it applied before Pt 1 of the Criminal Justice Act 1993, see the decision of the Court of Appeal in *Smith* [1996] Crim. L.R. 326. The old law will remain relevant until the new provisions are brought into effect. Surprisingly, this has yet to occur.

Conclusion

It is axiomatic that the interests sought to be protected by the Theft Act 1968 and associated legislation are essentially property rights. The nature and scope of these property rights have been refined over many years by the civil courts and in some cases they are complex indeed. Traditionally the criminal courts have tried to shy away from introducing concepts of civil law into criminal cases in an effort, no doubt, to spare the jury from having to decide complex legal issues. With reference to the Theft Act 1968 this sentiment was powerfully expressed by Sachs L.J. in *Baxter* [1971] 2 All E.R. 359 in the following terms: **20–059**

> ". . . the Theft Act 1968 was designed to simplify the law—it uses words in their natural meaning and is to be construed thus to produce sensible results; when that Act is under examination this Court deprecates attempts to bring into too close consideration the finer distinctions in civil law as to the precise moment when contractual communications take effect or when property passes".

20–060 Similar sentiments were echoed in *Morris* [1984] A.C. 320, when Lord Roskill expressed concern that it was:

> "on any view wrong to introduce into this branch of the law [the meaning of appropriation] questions of whether particular contracts are void or voidable on the grounds of mistake or fraud or whether any mistake is sufficiently fundamental to vitiate a contract."

20–061 Yet notwithstanding these judicial protestations some interaction between the civil and criminal law is inevitable. When the question whether property belongs to another is raised in the course of a criminal prosecution for theft, how else are the nature of relationships to be determined if not by reference to civil law? Consider, for example, the position in *Tillings and Tillings* [1985] Crim. L.R. 393. In that case the defendants were held to be not guilty of theft where they induced a patient in a residential home to alter her will in their favour because those disinherited had no interest in the property covered by the will until after the testator's death. The identification of a property right capable of appropriation was an essential ingredient which the prosecution had to prove before the defendants could be found guilty of theft. Clearly it is absurd that the criminal law should be impotent to embrace this dishonest behaviour, but it is wrong to blame the application of established civil law principles for this outcome. Parliamentary draughtsman should ensure that the provisions of the criminal law are sufficiently broad to ensure that crooks and swindlers do not escape from the consequences of dishonest behaviour by reliance on well established principles of civil law. Experience since the enactment of the Theft Act 1968 has demonstrated that the enactment of a general fraud offence is needed to obviate these problems. It is unacceptable that prosecutions for fraudulent conduct should founder on an application of the niceties of civil law.

Chapter 21

Fraudulent Trading

Increasingly, the offence of fraudulent trading is being used to prosecute the perpetrators of investor fraud. Prosecution of offenders under other provisions of the criminal law is bedevilled with pitfalls in the context of investor fraud, and in recent years, in the absence of a generic "catch all" offence of fraud, prosecutors have striven to expand the width of fraudulent trading to encompass a multitude of investor sins. A typical case of fraudulent trading in this context might involve a financial intermediary who has supported his failing business by the retention of investor funds. It is difficult to convict the financial intermediary under the law of theft because the investor deposits his funds with the intermediary to be used in the course of his investment business. An offence of obtaining property by deception is also problematic because the financial intermediary invariably asserts that he intended to invest the funds at the time when they were paid to him by the investor. **21–001**

With the benign approval of Parliament, fraudulent trading has been utilised by prosecutors to circumvent these difficulties, the offence having started life as a technical insolvency offence under earlier legislation. The principal restriction with the offence is that it can be committed only by a defendant who uses a company as a vehicle for his fraudulent activities. This restriction was considered by the Cork Committee which recommended the creation of a parallel offence of fraudulent trading by an individual. (Cork Committee, Cmnd 8558, at para.1890).

The Legislative History

Fraudulent trading was introduced into company law by s.75 of the Companies Act 1928, only to be replaced by s.275 of the Companies Act in 1929. The provision survived the post-war reforms and during this period of its history it was to be found in s.332 of the Companies Act 1948. The 1948 legislation created a civil and criminal liability with the same constituent elements and some of the cases decided under s.332 continue to be relevant to an understanding of the contemporary law. Until 1981 the scope of the fraudulent trading was artificially restricted by the requirement that the fraudulent conduct had to occur in the course of winding up a limited liability company. This requirement was abolished by s.96 of the Companies Act 1981 and from this time onwards fraudulent trading has been detached from its roots as an insolvency offence. **21–002**

The Companies Act 1985 recast the provision by separating civil and criminal liability for fraudulent trading. Today the civil provisions are contained in the Insolvency Act 1986 under which civil liability can accrue under two heads of fraudulent trading, either as fraudulent trading contrary to s.213 or wrongful trading contrary to s.214. These civil provisions are discussed in chapters 26 and 30 respectively. The criminal offence is contained in s.458 of the Companies Act 1985 which forms a separate part of the Act, Pt XVI, under the rubric "fraudulent trading by a company". Following conviction on indictment the offence is punishable by a maximum period of seven years imprisonment plus an unlimited fine. On summary conviction the maximum period of imprisonment is six months imprisonment and a fine of the statutory maximum, presently £5,000.

The Criminal Offence

21–003 S.458 of the Companies Act 1985 provides as follows:

> "If any business of a company is carried on with intent to defraud creditors of the company or creditors of any other person, or for any fraudulent purpose, every person who was knowingly a party to the carrying on of the business in that manner is liable to imprisonment or a fine or both.
>
> This applies whether or not the company has been, or is in the course of being, wound up."

To establish an offence of fraudulent trading it must be proved that: (1) there was conduct which formed part of the carrying on of the business of the company, (2) the defendant played an active role in this conduct, (3) the defendant intended to defraud the creditors of the company or the creditors of some other person, or alternatively intended some fraudulent purpose, and (4) the defendant acted dishonestly. In this context an intention to defraud may be inferred from circumstances which are considered to be dishonest. In *R. v Grantham* [1984] 79 Cr. App. R. 86; [1984] 1 Q.B. 647 the Court of Appeal approved the terms of the trial judge's direction to the jury that if a trader obtained or helped to obtain credit when he knew there was no good reason for thinking funds would become available to repay the debt when it became due or shortly thereafter, a jury could properly conclude that this conduct was dishonest and the defendant intended to defraud.

If any Business of a Company is Carried on

21–004 The Courts have tended to give a generous construction to the statutory requirement that the conduct must form part of the carrying on of the business of the company. In *Re Gerald Cooper Chemical Limited* [1978] 2 All E.R. 49; [1978] Ch. 262, a Court held that a single transaction was capable of amounting to the carrying on of a business with intent to defraud creditors. What is more, the conduct need not relate to the carrying on of the company's trade. In *Re Sarflax* [1979] 1 All E.R. 529 a company had gone into liquidation and its assets were used to discharge its business liabilities. Oliver J. held that the use of proceeds from sale of the company's assets to discharge business liabilities could constitute the carrying on of a business. In the context of investor fraud, however, the liberality of this approach may be misleading since in practical terms proof of an isolated dishonest act will be unlikely to satisfy the threshold requirement that the business of the company has been carried on with intent to defraud.

As Oliver J. said in *Re Murray Watson* (unreported) April 6, 1977, the **21–005**
section was:

> "aimed at the carrying on of a business . . . and not at the execution of individual transactions in the course of carrying on the business".

The director of a financial services company may make false representations about the security of an investment or its rate of return. This, to use Oliver J.'s language, may make him a "fraudulent rascal". But whilst it is true that the director carries on a particular business transaction in a fraudulent manner, it does not necessarily follow that the director carries on the company's business for a fraudulent purpose.

In this type of case a Judge must give a clear direction to the jury on the **21–006**
meaning of "carrying on the business of the company" and counsel should be invited to address him on the legal issues before he sums up—*Miles* [1992] Crim. L.R. 657; [1992] T.L.R. 195. What amounts to "carrying on the business of the company" will vary depending on the circumstances of each case. To take but one example, a distinction can be drawn between an enterprise conceived in fraud and the bona fide trading company which runs into difficulties. The financial intermediary who sells bogus shares on behalf of a company acquired for the purpose of selling bogus shares is much more obviously carrying on the business of the company with intent to defraud than the registered market maker who sells stock which he does not hold on an isolated occasion.

A Party to the Carrying on of a Business

In order to be guilty of an offence of fraudulent trading the prosecution has **21–007**
to prove not just that a person has taken an active step in furthering the activity of the business but also that he was a party to the carrying on of the business in a managerial or supervisory sense. In *Re Maidstone Building Provisions Ltd* [1971] 1 W.L.R. 1085, in the context of a civil case for fraudulent trading, Pennycuick V.C. rejected an attempt to attach liability to the company secretary on the grounds that, knowing the company was insolvent, he failed to advise the directors that the company should cease trading. Participation involves taking some step of a positive nature. Inertia or omission is not enough. What is more, the participating step must be taken by a person who exercised a controlling or managerial function. A salesman employed by a company who sells worthless shares in a non-existent enterprise participates in the business of the company but he is not guilty of fraudulent trading if he does not exercise a controlling or managerial function over the business.

21–008 A person will not be a party to the carrying on of a business if he is participating in the business on the instructions of others and a judge should direct a jury to this effect—*Miles* (cited above, para.21–006). Of course this is not to say that the ordinary principles of secondary liability will not apply in a fraudulent trading case. If a salesman of bogus shares knows that the controllers of the business are defrauding its creditors, the salesman will assist and encourage the fraudulent trading and his position is no different to the accomplice who keeps a look out whilst the burglar uses a jemmy to open the door. Just as the look out is guilty of burglary as an aider and abetter, so the salesman is guilty of fraudulent trading. The salesman is guilty of fraudulent trading not as a principal offender but as an aider and abetter, a secondary party. Support for this view may be derived from a consideration of the decision in *Re Gerald Cooper Chemicals Limited* [1978] 1 All E.R. 49; [1978] Ch. 262 where in a civil case the Court held that a creditor was a party to the carrying on of a business where he accepted money in fraudulent preference to other creditors. There was no suggestion that the creditor was involved in the running or management of the company. Certainly, the Chancery Division in *Re Augustus Barnett & Sons Ltd* [1986] B.C.L.C.170, and latterly in *Morris v Banque Arabe et Internationale d'Investissment SA (No.2)* [2001] 1 B.C.L.C. 263, contemplated that a person could be knowingly a party to the carrying on of business for a fraudulent purpose where he was an outsider, provided he participated in the fraudulent acts.

With Intent to Defraud Creditors . . . or for any Fraudulent Purpose

21–009 In *R. v Inman* [1967] 1 Q.B. 140 the Court of Appeal held that s.332 of the Companies Act 1948 encompassed two different offences, namely fraudulent trading with intent to defraud creditors (either the company's or those of some other person) and fraudulent trading for the purpose of achieving certain objectives.

Intent to Defraud

21–010 The phrase "with intent to defraud" is used to denote a state of mind whereby a person dishonestly prejudices or takes the risk of prejudicing another's right, knowing that he has no right to do so. In the context of fraudulent trading, a good working definition of the phrase was put forward by Maugham J. in *Re William C Leitch Bros Ltd* [1932] 2 Ch. 71 which forms the basis of its meaning in contemporary times:

> "With regard to the meaning of the phrase "carrying on business with intent to defraud creditors", if a company continues to carry on business and to incur debts at a time when there is to the knowledge of the directors no reasonable prospect of the creditors ever receiving payment of those debts it is, in general, a proper inference that the company is carrying on business with intent to defraud."

21–011 In the leading House of Lords case of *Welham v DPP* [1961] A.C. 103 it was held that "to defraud" was "to act to the prejudice of another's right", which would include carrying on business (to the potential prejudice of creditors) when the defendant knew there was a risk that the company would not be able to meet its debts as they fell due. The following passage approved by the Court of Appeal in *Grantham* [1984] 79 Cr. App. R. 86, reflects the standard direction which is given to a jury in a case involving fraudulent trading with intent to defraud creditors:

> "Some fraudulent traders intend from the outset never to pay or never to pay more than a fraction of the debt. If that is true in your view in this case then the intent to defraud would be made out but a trader can intend to defraud if he obtains credit when there is a substantial risk of the creditor not getting his money or not getting the whole of his money and the defendant knows that is the position and knows he is stepping beyond the bounds of what ordinary decent people engaged in business would regard as honest".

The potential liability for company receivers where they continue to operate parts of the business is relieved in the normal case by the requirement to prove an intention to defraud creditors. For example, in *Brown v City of London Corporation* [1996] 22 E.G. 118, the Court held that there was no fraudulent trading by receivers when they decided to postpone sale of various properties during the course of business. **21–012**

That said, investors should always subject a "hive down" or transfer of assets arrangement with great care. Plainly, there are circumstances where an "hive down" arrangement will not infringe the law against fraudulent trading, particularly where counsel has advised on the efficacy of a transfer of assets scheme, but the line is a thin one and any false representation made to creditors that payments would be met could amount to dishonest conduct in all the circumstances. An example of this situation occurred in *Morphites v Bernasconi, Monti, Nicholas Bennet & Co* (unreported) March 9, 2001, where the directors of an insolvent company made a misrepresentation to the company landlords about the date when the next instalment of rent would be paid, in a manner which went well beyond the implementation of a transfer of assets scheme which counsel had advised. The Chancery Division held that directors had made the misrepresentation dishonestly, and to this extent civil liability for fraudulent trading had been attracted.

Creditors

S.458 envisages that fraudulent trading will be directed to the prejudice of the company's creditors or creditors of any other person. Who are creditors for the purposes of this section? Notwithstanding the use of the plural, the term includes the defrauding of a single creditor—*Re Gerald Cooper Chemicals Limited* [1978] 2 All E.R. 49; [1978] Ch. 262. It appears that the term includes a potential creditor where the liability will come into existence in the future. **21–013**

In *Seillon* [1982] Crim. L.R. 676 the Court of Appeal held that a reference to creditors in an indictment alleging conspiracy to defraud would include potential creditors because:

> "if the law were otherwise it would mean that nobody could be found guilty of conspiracy to defraud his creditors until the creditor had obtained judgment against him".

21–014 It was thought that the same reasoning would apply to s.458, particularly after the legislative change in 1981 when the criminal offence was detached from the insolvency section of the Companies Act. This has recently been confirmed by the Court of Appeal in *Smith*, [1996] Crim. L.R. 329. The word "creditor" in its ordinary meaning denoted one to whom money was owed; whether that debt could found an action in debt was immaterial. The Court observed that s.458 was a continuing offence and future as well as present creditors might be prejudiced by fraudulent trading.

For any Fraudulent Purpose

21–015 If a prosecution is brought for fraudulent trading in a case where investors have suffered losses, the allegation is likely to be laid under the second limb of fraudulent trading, namely fraudulent trading for the purpose of achieving certain objectives. Customers of financial services companies are rarely creditors of the company, and for this reason an allegation of fraudulent trading has to be couched in different terms.

Kemp [1988] 87 Cr. App. R. 95 is the seminal case on point, where the Court of Appeal upheld a conviction for fraudulent trading after the appellant had dishonestly supplied between 20 and 30 customers with carbon paper which the customers had not ordered but paid for. The allegation of fraudulent trading did not contain any reference to creditors but instead asserted that the appellant had been a party to carrying on the business of a named company trading for a fraudulent purpose, namely the obtaining of property by deception. The Court concluded that the mischief of s.438 was directed at fraudulent trading and not fraudulent trading just in so far as it affects creditors. The Court of Appeal certified that a point of general public importance had arisen but leave to appeal to the House of Lords was refused. A similar conclusion was reached in *Phillipou* [1989] 89 Cr. App. R. 290.

Chapter 22

Conspiracy

Introduction

S.1 of the Criminal Law Act 1977 replaced most offences of common law conspiracy with a statutory offence. Only conspiracy to defraud, conspiracy to cheat and conspiracy to do acts tending to corrupt public morals or outrage public decency survived as common law offences. Where serious cases of investor fraud are discovered, prosecuting authorities often bring charges of conspiracy, and therefore to this extent the use of these offences is relevant to any consideration of investor protection. The general principles concerning conspiracy are set out fully in all the standard criminal textbooks and it is beyond the scope of this chapter to offer more than a cursory summary of the essential principles. **22–001**

Statutory Conspiracy

S.1 (1) of the Criminal Law Act 1977 sets out the statutory offence of conspiracy: **22–002**

> "Subject to the following provisions of this Part of this Act, if a person agrees with any other person or persons that a course of conduct shall be pursued which, if the agreement is carried out in accordance with their intentions, either—
>
> (a) will necessarily amount to or involve the commission of any offence or offences by one or more of the parties to the agreement, or
> (b) would do so but for the existence of facts which render the commission of the offence or any of the offences impossible,
>
> he is guilty of conspiracy to commit the offence of offences in question."

The maximum penalty on conviction for conspiracy to commit an indictable offence is the same as the maximum sentence that could be imposed for the indictable offence itself.

A conspiracy requires that two or more persons enter into an agreement which will necessarily amount to or involve the commission of a criminal offence or would do so but for the existence of facts which render the commission of the offence impossible. It is what is agreed to be done not what is actually done which is important in a charge of conspiracy. In *R. v Aspinall* (1876) 2 Q.B.D. 731, Brett J. said: **22–003**

> "The crime of conspiracy is completely committed the moment two or more have agreed that they will do, at once or at some future time, certain things. It

> is not necessary in order to complete the offence that any other thing should be done beyond the agreement. The conspirators may repent and stop, or may have no opportunity, or may be prevented, or may fail. Nevertheless the crime is complete: it was completed when they agreed."

22–004 A husband and wife cannot conspire together, neither can the sole director of a company conspire with his company although a company is capable of entering into a conspiracy. It is not necessary that a conspirator be a party throughout the duration of the agreement. It must be shown, however, that all the conspirators joined together in a single agreement. In *R. v Griffiths* 49 Cr. App. R. 279 Paull J. said:

> ". . . in law all must join in the one agreement, each with the others, in order to constitute one conspiracy. They may join at various times, each attaching himself to that agreement; any one of them may not know all the other parties, but only that there are other parties; any one of them may not know the full extent of the scheme to which he attaches himself; but what each must know is that there is coming into existence, or is in existence, a scheme which goes beyond the illegal act which he agrees to do."

22–005 The mental element of conspiracy requires proof of an intention to be a party to an agreement to do an unlawful act. The leading case is *R. v Anderson* [1986] 1 A.C. 27, HL. There are situations where the mental element to commit the substantive offence would not be sufficient to prove a conspiracy to commit that offence. The usual text book example is the offence of murder where an intent to cause grievous bodily harm would be sufficient to prove the substantive offence but would not be sufficient to prove a charge of conspiracy to murder.

The advantage of charging conspiracy is that it often allows the prosecution to place before a Court a course of criminal conduct whereas substantive offences may show only a small aspect of the behaviour complained of.

Where the course of conduct complained of reveals more than one conspiracy these must not be charged as one "rolled-up" count.

Conspiracy to Defraud

22–006 When the Criminal Law Act 1977 replaced offences of common law conspiracy with a statutory offence, conspiracy to defraud was retained as a common law offence. The law was considerably complicated by the decision of the House of Lords in *R. v Ayres* [1984] A.C. 447 where it was held that a charge of conspiracy to defraud contrary to common law was inappropriate if the evidence also supported the commission of a conspiracy to commit a substantive criminal offence. This decision severely dented the range of offences available to the prosecuting authorities. Prosecutors did not like to prosecute for statutory conspiracy because the penalties which could be imposed for conspiracy were no greater than those which could be imposed for the substantive offence. The decision in *Ayres* was overturned by Parliament in s.12 of the Criminal Justice Act 1987 and today, once again, prosecutions for conspiracy to defraud are commonly brought in investor fraud cases.

S.12(1) Criminal Justice Act 1987 provides that: 22–007

> " If
>
> (a) a person agrees with any other person or persons that a course of conduct shall be pursued; and
> (b) that course of conduct will necessarily amount to or involve the commission of any offence or offences by one or more of the parties to the agreement if the agreement is carried out in accordance with their intentions,
>
> the fact that it will do so shall not preclude a charge of conspiracy to defraud being brought against any of them in respect of the agreement."

S.12(3) limits the penalty for a person guilty of conspiracy to defraud to 10 years imprisonment and/or a fine. 22–008

Conspiracy to defraud is indictable only. Guidance on the drafting of an indictment alleging conspiracy to defraud was given by the Court of Appeal in the case of *R. v Landy* [1981] 72 Cr. App. R. 237, CA. The need to particularise the indictment to enable the defence and the Court to know the nature of the prosecution's case was emphasised. The Court of Appeal referred to *Landy* in *R. v Cohen* (unreported) July 28, 1992, when it was said that the particulars "must not be more than is necessary having regard to the limitations imposed by a jury trial".

The usual starting point when considering what amounts to a conspiracy to defraud is the case of *Scott v Metropolitan Police Commissioner* [1975] A.C. 819; [1974] 3 All E.R. 1032: 22–009

> "An agreement by two or more dishonesty to deprive a person of something which is his or to which he is or would be or might be entitled and an agreement by two or more dishonesty to injure some proprietary right of his, suffices to constitute the offence of conspiracy to defraud".

This definition cannot be treated as exhaustive but it is undoubtedly authoritative, having been accepted by the Law Commission in its recent consideration of conspiracy to defraud (Law Com. 228).

The meaning of defraud was considered by the Court of Appeal in *R. v Sinclair* 52 Cr. App. R. 618 at 621, where it was said that to prove fraud it had to be established that the conduct was deliberately dishonest. It is fraud if it is proved that there was the taking of a risk which there was no right to take which would cause detriment or prejudice to another. 22–010

An interesting example of a case in which the offence of conspiracy to defraud was utilised by the prosecution occurred in what became known as "the Butte Mining Case". Two of the defendants were directors of a company which was formed to exploit certain mining rights in Butte, Montana, USA. The third defendant was an expert in mining matters and he was the technical adviser to the company. The company was floated on the London Stock Exchange on the October 1, 1987. The listing particulars contained a mining report in short form. Around £60 million was raised on the floatation from investors in the City. Subsequent share issues were made and further listing particulars were published. The prosecution alleged against the defendants that the mining reports were false and misleading, and that they had agreed to defraud investors who purchased shares in the company. Also, the prosecution alleged as further evidence of dishonesty that the defendants had failed to disclose that they stood to receive substantial benefits from the floatation and the shares issues. The jury convicted the defendants, who appealed to the Court of Appeal contending that the prosecution ought not to have linked the concealment of benefits with the assertion that the mining reports were false and misleading. The Court of Appeal rejected the argument, holding that there had been no prejudice to the defendants in the way in which the case against them had been advanced. Moreover, the Court held that the sentences of imprisonment of three years for one of the directors and eighteen months for the technical advisor were not excessive—*R. v Clarke, Smith, Clews* (unreported) July 16, 1999.

22–011 The Court of Appeal's ruling on sentence was entirely consistent with a previous ruling given in 1997, after the Attorney General had petitioned the Court in a case where defendants had been sentence to community service after convictions for conspiracy to defraud and theft in a case where they had created a false market in shares in order to influence a takeover bid. The Court of Appeal said that the creation of a false market in shares to influence the fate of a takeover bid was a very serious matter. Such conduct might lead not only to a fraud on the shareholders but it also caused considerable damage to the reputation of the City of London and its institutions, which had consequences for the whole country. What is more, an important element in the sentencing process in such cases must be deterrence. Rigging the share market was quite easy to do without outsiders realising what had happened. It was important that those contemplating committing such activities should know that it they are caught it is highly likely that they will go to prison, and the payment of compensation and a plea of guilty might not save them from such a sentence—*R. v Ward* (unreported) March 21, 1997.

Conspiracy to Defraud a Regulatory Body

22–012 In most cases of investor fraud there will be an obvious and identifiable economic loss but this does not always follow. Situations can be envisaged where there is no economic loss but there is an obvious intention to defraud. One such example is where the allegation relates to the activities of a financial advisor or company offering financial advice and the fraudulent behaviour complained of amounts to the deception of a regulatory body in order to ensure that the regulatory body allows the financial advisor to continue trading.

The leading case on the need to prove economic loss is *Welham v D.P.P* [1961] A.C. 103 where the House of Lords was concerned with the meaning of "intent to defraud" in the Forgery Act 1913. The question arose whether an intent to defraud was confined to an intent to cause or take the risk of causing pecuniary loss to another. The House of Lords found that an intent to cause pecuniary loss was not necessary to prove an intent to defraud. The fraud consisted of taking a risk of injuring another's right which the accused knows he has no right to take. Lord Radcliffe set out the position in his speech at p.124:

> "There is nothing in any of this that suggests that to defraud is in ordinary speech confined to the idea of depriving a man by deceit of some economic advantage or inflicting upon him some economic loss. Has the law ever so confined it? In my opinion, there is no warrant for saying that it has. What it has looked for in considering the effect of cheating upon another and in so defining the criminal intent is the prejudice of that person: what Blackstone (4 Comm. 245) called 'to the prejudice of another's right'."

In *Scott v Metropolitan Police Commissioner* [1975] A.C. 819 the House of Lords considered the question of whether fraud necessarily required deceit, and found unanimously that it did not. Lord Diplock suggested (erroneously, it is thought) that if the victim of the fraud was an individual then it was necessary that the fraudster intended to cause that person economic loss. Lord Diplock's view was not accepted by the other judges in *Scott* nor has it been followed in subsequent cases. Lord Denning, giving his judgment in *Scott*, explained his approach in the following terms: **22–013**

> "'To defraud', they say 'involves economic loss'. I cannot agree with them on this. If a drug addict forges a doctor's prescription so as to enable him to get drugs from a chemist, he has, I should have thought, an intent to defraud, even though he intends to pay the chemist the full price and no one is a penny the worse off."

Lord Denning's approach was supported by the Court of Appeal in *R. v Allsop* [1976] 64 Cr. App. R. 29 which was approved by the Privy Council in *Wai Yu-Tsang v R.* [1992] 1 A.C. 269, PC, and more recently in *Adams v R.* [1995] 1 W.L.R. 52, PC. In *Adams* the Privy Council confirmed that cases of conspiracy to defraud are not confined to cases of intention to cause economic loss. The prosecution must prove that the victim had a right which was capable of being prejudiced either by actual loss or by being put at risk. The Privy Council went on to say that if a person was entitled to have information disclosed to him or that a person was under a duty to disclose information and that information was withheld, then the person who should have disclosed the information could be guilty of fraud. In practice this would apply in the situation where a person was under a duty to disclose information to a regulatory body—for example to demonstrate compliance with solvency requirements to be allowed to continue trading —and the information disclosed was false or misleading. **22–014**

The deception of a public body was also considered in *R. v Moses and Ansbro* [1991] Crim. L.R. 617, CA, where the defendants had been charged with conspiracy to defraud by facilitating applications by immigrants to get work permits. It was held that where the intended victim of a conspiracy to defraud was a person performing public duties, it was sufficient if the purpose was to cause him to contravene that duty, and the intended means of achieving it was dishonest. It was not necessary that the purpose involved causing economic loss to anyone.

"Fraudulently" or "Dishonestly"

22–015 It is clear from the line of authorities from *Welham* onwards that the appellate courts have not considered that the addition of the word "dishonesty" adds anything to the meaning of intention to defraud. It is, however, conventional for judges when summing up to add the word "dishonesty" to their definition of "with intent to defraud" and "fraudulently". See in this context the direction given by Henry J. to the jury in *R. v Saunders*, *Independent*, May 17, 1991.

Jurisdiction

22–016 In these days of electronic communication and global markets, conspiracy to defraud like other commercial crimes, is increasingly likely to have a significant foreign element. The position at common law was that conspiracies formulated abroad but intended to result in the commission of a criminal offence in England or Wales were triable by the English courts. The increasingly international face of crime has been recognised by Parliament in Pt I of the Criminal Justice Act 1993 which widens the jurisdiction of the English courts, by giving them jurisdiction to try certain cases of fraud and related offences where there is a significant foreign element. This has been effected by designating conspiracy to defraud as a Group B offence by virtue of s.1(3) of the Act. The Act has extended the jurisdiction of the English courts to cases where there is an agreement made abroad amounting to a conspiracy to defraud where the substantive fraud is intended to be effected in England. Jurisdiction has also been extended over conspiracy to defraud where the fraud is intended to take place in a foreign jurisdiction—see s.5(3). S.6 requires that a person may only be convicted in this country by virtue of the provisions of s.5 if the objective of the offence represents an offence in the territory where it is intended to take place.

Reform of the law of Conspiracy to Defraud

22–017 The Law Commission report on Conspiracy to Defraud (Law Com. No. 228) recommends that conspiracy to defraud should be retained for the time being. The Law Commission's recommendation to retain conspiracy to defraud appears to be based on the need for an offence which enables the prosecution to present the "overall criminality" and the recognition that its abolition might leave large areas of criminal activity which may not be covered by any other existing substantive offence. The Commission also sees the retention of conspiracy to defraud as "a means of simplifying and shortening fraud trials and enabling individual defendants to be convicted of an offence appropriate to their conduct". The subject will, no doubt, be reviewed again during the course of the Law Commission's study of offences involving dishonesty.

Chapter 23

Companies Act Offences

The directors control the company and its dealings with third parties, and they are responsible for proper management of the company's assets. Investor confidence depends on the effective regulation of directors' conduct in the management of companies, particularly with regard to their personal interests *vis-à-vis* the company. As is discussed in Ch.33, the Courts recognise that breach of a director's fiduciary duty to deal with the company in good faith gives rise to a cause of action against the director in civil law. Parliament has sought to set additional standards of good conduct and breach of these standards will expose a director to criminal as well as civil sanctions. Many requirements, however, are rather technical and there is considerable scope to undermine the Parliamentary intention by paying lip-service to the statutory provisions. **23–001**

Directors

Restrictions on directors taking financial advantage

In the interests of investor protection it is critical to ensure that the directors of the company do not take an unfair financial advantage of their position within the company. Ss.311 to 322 of the Companies Act 1985 contain various provisions designed to prevent directors of a company from taking financial advantage of their position within the company which include provisions relating to directors' remuneration and the duty to disclose any interest, direct or indirect, in a contract with his company. Penalties for non-compliance are financial. **23–002**

Interest in contracts

By s.317(1) of the Companies Act 1985 a duty is imposed on a director of a company who is in any way, whether directly or indirectly, interested in a contract or a proposed contract to declare the nature of his interest at a meeting of the directors of the company. By s.317(7) a director who fails to comply with this section is liable to a fine. The requirement to make disclosure to a meeting of the directors has been construed strictly by the Courts. In *Guinness plc v Saunders* [1988] 2 All E.R. 940, the Court of Appeal held that the requirement could not be satisfied by a disclosure to a **23–003** sub-committee of the directors. Although the reasoning of the Court of Appeal was rejected by the House of Lords on appeal, the Court of Appeal determination on this point continues to be accepted as good law (also see *Guinness plc v Saunders* [1990] 2 A.C. 663).

23–004 In *Runciman v Walter Runciman plc* [1992] B.C.L.C. 1084, Brown J. held that the obligation to make disclosure applied to a director's contract of service although the Judge did express some doubt in that case as to whether s.317 extended to a variation concerning salary or some other term of employment. Certainly the stringency, and perhaps the absurdity, of the requirement was demonstrated more recently in *Re Neptune (Vehicle Washing Equipment) Ltd* [1995] T.L.R. 132 where a Court held that it was the duty of a sole director no less than a co-director to comply with the obligations imposed by the statutory provision. Lightman J. said that when holding the meeting on his own, the director had still to make the declaration to himself and have the statutory pause for thought. Although the declaration need not be read out loud, the Judge advised that it should be recorded in the minutes because a Court might find it hard to accept that the declaration had been made if it was not so recorded. Who said the payment of lip-service was not enough!

Share Dealings by Directors and Their Families

23–005 Share dealings by directors and those connected with them in companies in which the director may be thought to have some inside knowledge or unfair advantage over the investor are strictly regulated by the Companies Act. The regulation in the Companies Act is supplemented and strengthened by legislation specifically designed to counteract market manipulation by those who may be thought to be "in the know" and thus have an unfair advantage. These provisions are discussed in Ch.29. The obligations of a company director and the obligations of a board of directors are discussed in Ch.33.

Prohibition on Directors Dealing in Share Options

23–006 S.323(1) renders it an offence for the director (including a shadow director) of a company to deal in share options in the company of which he is a director, any subsidiary company, its holding company or any subsidiary company of its holding company where the shares are listed (whether in Great Britain or abroad). This prohibition is absolute, the prosecution do not have to prove that the defendant had any inside knowledge of any likely future price movements. The prohibition does not apply to the purchase of a right to subscribe in shares or debentures of the company (s.323 (5)).

This prohibition extends to the spouse and children (including step children) aged under 18 of directors who are not themselves directors of the relevant companies (s.327). It is a defence for a person charged under s.327 to prove that he had no reason to know of their spouse's or parent's status as directors of the company in question.

The maximum sentence for contravention of s.323(1) is two years imprisonment and/or an unlimited fine if convicted on indictment and six months imprisonment and/or a fine of the statutory maximum (£5,000) if convicted summarily.

Director failing to notify interest in company's shares or making false statement in purported notification

S.324 imposes a duty on a director (including a shadow director) to disclose shareholding but is rendered an offence by s.324(7)(a). It is also an offence for a director to make what he purports to be disclosure to the company knowing the disclosure to be false or recklessly making a statement which is false (s.324(7)(b)). **23–007**

S.328 extends the obligations imposed under s.324 to the spouse and children under the age of 18 of the director who are not themselves directors of the company. Failure to notify the company of any interests held by the family of a director is an offence with the same punishment as for contravention of s.324 (s.328(6)).

Register of directors' interests

A company is under an obligation to keep a register of directors' interests for the purposes of s.324 which may be inspected by anyone on payment of a fee. The company is also under a duty to provide a copy of the register if requested to do so, again on payment of a fee (s.325 and Pt IV of Sch.13.) If default is made in complying with the requirements of s.325 and Pt IV of Sch.13 those in default may be punished by the imposition of a fine. Continued contravention may lead to the imposition of a daily default fine (ss.326 (2), (3), (4) and (5)). **23–008**

Loans to Directors

Ss.330 to 347 of the Companies Act 1985 set out restrictions on a company's power to make loans (including quasi-loans, guarantees and other forms of credit transactions) to directors and persons connected with them. **23–009**

The prohibitions on the making of loans to directors and persons connected with them are set out in s.330 of the Companies Act 1985. The prohibitions apply to certain identified transactions, viz: loans (s.330(2)(a)), quasi-loans (s.330(3)(a) and (b)), credit transactions (s.330 (4)(a)), guarantees for the provision of security in connection with loans, quasi-loans and credit transactions (ss.330 (2)(b), 330 (3)(c), 330(4)(b)), arrangements for the assignment to the company or the assumption by the company of any rights, obligations or liabilities under a prohibited transaction (s.330 (6)) and back to back arrangements where a person enters into an arrangement which would have been prohibited by s.330 if it had been entered into by the company, and that person obtains some benefit from the company or from another company in the same group (s.330 (7) (a) and (b)). Breaches of the s.330 prohibitions are rendered offences by s.342.

23–010 Those who may commit a criminal offence in breach of s.330 are:

(1) a director of a relevant company who authorises or permits the company to enter into a prohibited transaction knowing or with reasonable cause to believe that the company was thereby contravening the provisions set out in s.330;

(2) the relevant company, though the company has a defence if it's directors did not know the relevant circumstances at the time it entered into the transaction; and

(3) a person who procures the relevant company to enter into a prohibited transaction knowing or having reasonable cause to believe that the transaction is prohibited.

The offence is punishable by a maximum sentence of two years' imprisonment and/or an unlimited fine if convicted on indictment and six months' imprisonment and/or a fine of the statutory maximum (£5,000) if convicted summarily. The offence may also be committed by a "shadow director" who is deemed to be treated as a director by s.330 (5).

Connected persons are defined by s.346 and include a director's spouse, a director's child under the age of 18 (including a step child) but not a child over the age of 18, a body corporate with which the director is associated, a person acting in his capacity as trustee of any trust the beneficiaries of which include the director or persons connected to him, a person acting in his capacity as partner of the director or of any person connected with the director and any Scottish firm with which the director is connected.

23–011 Ss.332 to 338 create eight exceptions to the s.330 prohibition. Broadly these exceptions are transactions within a group of companies (ss.333 and 336), transactions in the ordinary course of business (ss.335(2), 337 and 338), and other transactions permitted up to certain specified limits (ss.332, 334 and 335(1) as amended by s.138 of the Companies Act 1989 and the Companies (Fair Dealing by Directors) (Increase in Financial Limits) Order 1990 (S.I. 1990/1393) and see Sch.10 Pt I, para.10 of the Companies Act 1989 and Sch.6, para.18(6) of the Banking Act 1987).

Allotment of Shares

23–012 The rules governing the allotment of shares and debentures are set out in Pt IV of the Companies Act 1985. Pt IV of the 1985 Act has created a number of criminal offences in support of these regulatory provisions.

Prohibition on Shares Being Allocated at a Discount

23–013 Ss.99 to 107 of the Companies Act 1985 regulate the amount to be paid for shares and the means of payment. Contravention of any of the provisions of ss.99 to 104 and 106 renders the company or any defaulting officer liable to a fine. In this context also see The Companies (Acquisition of Own Shares) (Treasury Shares) Regulations 2003 SI 2003/1116 Sch.1, para.7.

S.104 relates to the transfer to a public company of non-cash assets in the initial period after its formation. A new public company is prohibited from making certain agreements with certain persons unless a stipulated procedure is followed. One of the requirements of the stipulated procedure is that of an independent valuer making a report to the company. It is an offence contrary to s.110(2) to knowingly or recklessly make to the valuer an oral or written statement which is misleading false or deceptive in a material particular and which conveys (or purports to convey) any information or explanation which he requires or is entitled to require.

Other Offences in Pt IV of the Companies Act 1985

There are over 60 offences contained in the Companies Act 1985 which are directed towards the protection of the investor. The list of offences with maximum punishments and mode of trial is set out in Sch.24 of the Act as amended. Sch.24 is reproduced at Part 8. **23–014**

Who may Commit Criminal Offences Under the Companies Act

Offences in the Companies Acts may be committed by the company, a company officer and on occasions by other persons such as the company auditors. It is necessary to look at the wording of each offence to see who may be liable. S.733(2) of the Companies Act specifies certain offences (ss.210, 216(3), 394A(1) and ss.447–451) for which the company and the director, manager, secretary or other similar officer of the body corporate or any other person who was purporting to act in such a capacity may incur criminal liability. In addition to these specifically mentioned sections, joint liability of the company and individuals is imposed under the Act by the inclusion in specific offences of the words "and every officer in default". Criminal proceedings may be brought against unincorporated bodies (s.734) in respect of offences alleged under ss.389A, 394A(1) and ss.447–451. **23–015**

The Company

It is well established in criminal law that a company may be directly liable for the commission of a criminal offence, liability being attached by the imputation of wrongdoing on the part of the senior officers of the company. The leading case is *Tesco v Nattrass* [1971] 2 W.L.R. 1166; [1972] A.C. 153 where the House of Lords held that corporate liability was derived from a concept of the company in which there existed a nerve-centre of command represented by the board of directors, the company secretary and perhaps the managing director. Only the wrongdoing of those who belonged to the nerve centre can be imputed to the company. **23–016**

The Company Officers

23–017 The liability of company officers was considered in the case of *Boal* [1992] 95 Cr. App. R. 272 where the statutory phrase "any director, manager, secretary or other similar officer of the body corporate" fell to be construed. Brown J. said that the expression was intended to fix with criminal liability "only those who are in a position of real authority, the decision makers within the company who have both the power and responsibility to decide corporate policy and strategy."

Consent to Prosecute

23–018 Certain offences under the Companies Act 1985 (ss.210, 324, 329, 447–451 and 455) may be prosecuted only with the consent of the Secretary of State, the Director of Public Prosecutions or the Industrial Insurance Commissioner (s.732).

Accounting Records

23–019 The content, accuracy and availability of company accounting records are of paramount importance to investors and are regulated by the provisions of the Companies Act. Failure to meet these requirements gives rise to criminal sanctions. Indeed, by far the greatest number of prosecutions brought by the DTI under their Companies Acts powers concerned offences relating to company accounts and annual returns. In 2001–2002 the DTI launched 2,544 prosecutions for failure to deliver company accounts to Companies House and 1,023 prosecutions for failure to deliver annual returns. Failure to keep or preserve accounting records was the next most frequently charged offence, 157 prosecutions having been brought in 2001–2002. To put these figures into some context, during the same period the DTI brought 32 charges of fraudulent trading and 21 further charges under other provisions of the Companies Act 1985. These figures are taken from Tables D2 and D3 of the DTI's report on Companies for 2001–2002 published in July 2002.

In addition the DTI brought 117 prosecutions under the Insolvency Act 1986 (ss.206, 207, 208, 210, 216 and 235), 174 prosecutions under the Company Directors Disqualification Act 1986 and 5 prosecutions for insider dealing under s.52 Criminal Justice Act 1993.

Duty to Keep Accounting Records

23–020 Pursuant to s.221 of the Companies Act 1985 (as amended by s.2 of the Companies Act 1989) every company, whatever its size, is required to keep accounting records which are sufficiently detailed to disclose with reasonable accuracy the financial position of the company and to enable the directors to ensure that any balance sheet or profit and loss accounts are correctly prepared. Failure to keep such accounting records in accordance with s.221 is rendered an offence by s.221(5) and the offence will be committed by every officer of the company who is in default. The penalty following conviction on indictment is two years imprisonment and/or an unlimited fine. If convicted summarily the penalty is six months imprisonment and/or a fine of the statutory maximum (£5,000). It is a defence to this offence to show that the officer of the company acted honestly and that the default was excusable in the circumstances. The burden of proving the statutory defence rests on the company officer and it must be established on the balance of probabilities.

S.222 of the Companies Act 1985 provides that the accounting records **23–021** must be kept at the registered office of the company or such other place as the directors think fit. The accounting records must be open to inspection at all times by the company's officers. Again it is a defence to show on the balance of probabilities that the company officer acted honestly and that the default was excusable in the circumstances. By s.222(5) company accounts must be preserved for at least three years for a private company and six years for a public limited company. An officer of the company is guilty of an offence if he fails to take all reasonable steps to secure compliance by the company or if he intentionally causes any default by the company. Contravention is visited by the same penalties which may be imposed for an offence contrary to s.221.

Failure to Deliver Annual Accounts

Under s.242(1) of the Companies Act 1985 company accounts, a copy of the **23–022** director's report and a copy of the auditor's report must be delivered annually to Companies House. Failure to deliver company documents amounts to a criminal offence under s.242 (2) which is committed by every person who was a director of the company immediately before the end of the period allowed for the delivery of the accounts. The penalty is a fine and if the contravention continues a daily default fine can be imposed. Under s.242(4) it is a defence for the director to prove that he took all reasonable steps for securing that the requirements would be satisfied. It is not a defence to show that company accounts had not been prepared.

Failure to Deliver an Annual Return

By s.363(1) every company is under a duty to deliver an annual return to **23–023** the Registrar of Companies at Companies House. Failure to deliver the annual return within the specified period (28 days from the company's return date as statutorily defined) renders the company guilty of an offence and liable to a fine and in the case of continuing contravention a daily default fine. Where a company is guilty of the offence, under s.363(4) every director or company secretary is also guilty unless he can show that he took all reasonable steps to avoid the commission or continuation of the offence.

Rights of Auditors

23–024 Every company is under a duty to appoint an auditor or auditors in accordance with s.384(1) of the Companies Act 1985. As from the April 1, 1990 the company auditors have a right of access at all times to the company's accounting records and they are entitled to require from the company's officers such information and explanations as they think necessary for the performance of their duties as auditors. These provisions, brought into law by s.389A of the Companies Act 1985, are important in the context of investor protection because they confer on the company auditor an opportunity to act in a pro-active way if fraudulent conduct is suspected.

Company auditors need not be confined to the information with which they have been supplied by dishonest directors. It is an offence under s.389A(2) for a company officer to make false, misleading or deceptive statements to company auditors. Contravention of this section exposes a company officer to the same penalties as commission of an offence under s.221 or 222. Similar provisions apply to the supply of information concerning subsidiaries or parent companies of the company being audited.

Company Investigations

23–025 Under the Companies Acts, the Secretary of State for Trade and Industry has the power to appoint investigators to investigate the affairs of a company—see ss.431, 432, 442, 444, 446 and 447 of the Companies Act 1985. The objective of these investigations is to increase confidence in corporate integrity through effective enforcement action. The conduct of a DTI investigation is covered in Ch.29. To assist in the effective conduct of investigations the DTI is empowered by the Companies Act 1985 to require documents (however recorded, including computer records) to be produced to it by companies and company officers. Failure to assist in the course of an investigation may give rise to a number of criminal offences (ss.444(3), 447(6), 448(7), 449(2), 451). In addition, the DTI has the power to appoint investigators to assist an overseas regulator under s.82 of the Companies Act 1989. The DTI also has the power to investigate investment business under s.167 of the FSMA which is a similar power to that under s.447 of the Companies Act 1985. The DTI may also investigate possible market abuse under s.168 of the FSMA to determine whether offences have occurred.

Destroying or Mutilating Company Documents

23–026 It is an offence under s.450(1) of the Companies Act 1985 for a company officer to destroy, mutilate, falsify or be privy to the destruction, mutilation or falsification of a document relating to the company's property or affairs or to make or be privy to the making of a false entry in such a document. It is a defence to show that there was no intention to conceal the state of the company's affairs or to defeat the law. By s.450(2) it is also an offence for an officer of the company to fraudulently part with, alter or make an omission to a company document or be privy to the fraudulent parting with, alteration or making of omission from such a document.

There can be little doubt that Parliament intended the commission of these offences to be taken seriously since the maximum penalty if convicted on indictment is seven years imprisonment and/or an unlimited fine. If convicted summarily the maximum penalty is 6 months imprisonment and/ or a fine of the statutory maximum (£5,000). These penalties are the same as the maximum penalties which can be imposed for fraudulent trading contrary to s.458 of the Act. The introduction of this offence has been used surprisingly rarely, notwithstanding the fact that a person will be vulnerable to conviction for an offence under s.450(1) unless, reversing the usual rule on the burden of proof in a criminal case, he can establish an absence of dishonest intent. The dearth of prosecutions under this section is probably explained by the fact that a prosecution can be brought only with the consent of the Secretary of State, the Director of Public Prosecutions or the Industrial Assurance Commissioner. Consideration should be given to the abolition of this restriction.

The Efficacy of Companies Act Regulation

As already noted the Companies Acts bring together a large number of disparate criminal offences. The majority of these offences are of a largely technical nature and apart from failure to file company documents and fraudulent trading these offences are rarely, if ever, prosecuted in practice. The figures available from the Department of Trade and Industry for prosecutions brought by them reveal the extremely narrow range of offences for which prosecutions are brought. Of course there is always going to be a tension between the concerns of investor protection and the ability of company officers to function commercially in their field of activity, but instead of creating a myriad of technical criminal offences which are satisfied by lip-service and little else, perhaps it is time to give some consideration to the introduction of some alternative coercive mechanisms which might encourage errant companies to obey the rules. **23–027**

That company law as an area is ripe for review has been recognised by the Government. In July 2002, the Competition Minister Melanie Johnson described the state of company law as "creaking with age" and in need of modernisation. To this end, in July 2002 the Government published a White paper following the final report of the independent Company Law Review which recognised that the Company Law framework in the UK had become cumbersome over the passage of time. The main proposals of the White Paper are aimed at simplifying the ways in which companies take decisions and at creating greater transparency in the way in which companies are set up and run. In particular, the White Paper proposes that directors' general duties should be codified and that company reporting should provide accurate, accessible information at reasonable cost. In addition to simplifying the law, the draft bill is **23–028** intended to give auditors the statutory right to ask for company information from employees and certain contractors and directors will be obliged to volunteer information to auditors. Failure to provide honest information or any attempt to deliberately conceal the true state of company accounts to auditors are expected to incur penalties of up to two years imprisonment and/or unlimited fines.

The Government included a draft bill in the White Paper. Consultation on the proposals set out in the White Paper were invited by November 29, 2002. At the time of writing, the DTI was still in the process of considering the responses to the draft bill and it was not possible to predict when the draft bill might become law.

Chapter 24

A Company's Purchase of its own Shares

This chapter examines the provisions contained in the Companies Acts which prohibit the purchase by a company of its own shares, the prohibition on a company from giving financial assistance to purchase its own shares, and the exemptions to the general prohibitions set out in the legislation. In particular this chapter will look at the way in which these provisions regulate corporate conduct so as to protect the interests of an investor, in this context a shareholder, who has bought shares in a limited liability company. The provisions regulate corporate behaviour through a combination of civil and criminal sanctions. The way in which the provisions have been applied by the Courts will be considered in the context of investor protection. **24–001**

The Fundamental Prohibition on the Acquisition by a Company of its own Shares

It is a fundamental principle of English company law that a limited liability company shall not reduce its capital or purchase its own shares save in accordance with some specific statutory provisions which permit this course. **24–002**

This fundamental principle is set out in s.143(1) of the Companies Act 1985 which provides that: **24–003**

> ". . . a company limited by shares or limited by guarantee and having a share capital shall not acquire its own shares whether by purchase, subscription or otherwise."

The rationale underlying this fundamental principle was explained by Lord Watson in the House of Lords case of *Trevor v Whitworth* (1887) 12 App. Cas. 409 in the following terms: **24–004**

> "Paid up capital may be diminished or lost in the course of the company's trading; that is a result which no legislation can prevent; but persons who deal with and give credit to the limited company naturally rely upon the fact that the company is trading with a certain amount of capital already paid, as well as upon the responsibilities of its members for the capital remaining at call; and they are entitled to assume that no part of the capital which has been paid into the coffers of the company has been subsequently paid out except in the

legitimate course of its business. When a share is forfeited or surrendered the amount which has been paid upon it remains with the company, the shareholding having been relieved of liability for future calls, the share itself reverts to the company, bears no dividend, and may be reissued. When shares are purchased at par and transferred to the company the result is very different. The amount paid up on the shares is returned to the shareholder; and in the event of the company continuing to hold the shares (the amount) is permanently withdrawn from its trading capital."

24–005 Breach of the prohibition in s.143(1) of the Companies Act 1985 gives rise to an actionable cause of action in the civil courts. In addition, enforcement of this prohibition is bolstered by the criminal law. S.143 (2) of the Companies Act 1985 makes it a criminal offence to contravene s.143(1).

The offence may be committed by the company or any of its officers. The term "company officers" is defined by s.744 of the Companies Act 1985 as being a director, manager or secretary of a body corporate. Although the point has yet to be confirmed judicially, it appears that the criminal offence can also be committed by a shadow director of the company. A "shadow director" is defined by s.741(2) of the Companies Act 1985 as "a person in accordance with whose directions or instructions the directors of the company are accustomed to act".

24–006 The offence created by s.143 (2) is triable either on indictment (in the Crown Court) or summarily (in the Magistrates Court). If tried on indictment the penalty is, where the company is convicted, an unlimited fine. If an officer of the company is convicted, the maximum sentence is two years imprisonment and/or an unlimited fine. When tried summarily the penalty is, where the company is convicted, a fine of the statutory maximum (presently £5,000) and where an officer of the company is convicted, six months imprisonment and/or a fine of the statutory maximum.

Exceptions to the Fundamental Principle

24–007 S.143 (3) provides that the general prohibition on the acquisition by a company of its own shares does not apply in a number of limited circumstances. There are express provisions to permit the redemption or purchase of shares in circumstances sanctioned in ss.159 to 181 of the Act. The general prohibition will not apply where the purchase of shares is made pursuant to an order of the court (*i.e.*: relief to members unfairly prejudiced, authorised reduction of share capital, etc), or where there is a permitted forfeiture or surrender of shares. The prohibition will not apply to the redemption of redeemable shares—s.143(3)(a) and s.160(4).

24–008 In addition to the statutory exceptions, it was recently established by the High Court in *Acatos & Hutcheson plc v Watson* (unreported) December 13, 1994, that the prohibition in s.143(1) of the Companies Act 1985 may not prevent a company from acquiring shares in a target company where the target company's sole asset is shares in the acquiring company. In that case the acquiring company, Acatos & Hutcheson plc, sought to purchase the entire issued share capital of Acatos Ltd. The problem arose because the sole asset of Acatos Ltd was a holding of 29.4 per cent of the voting share capital in Acatos & Hutcheson plc. The Court was asked to decide whether the corporate veil should be lifted so as to expose the commercial reality underlying the transaction. In the particular circumstances of this case the Court was satisfied that the corporate veil did not need to be lifted but in other cases the position might be different. However, the decision in *Acatos and Hutcheson plc* is limited in its effect. The Judge was aware of the ramifications of this decision in the context of investor protection, and at the end of his judgment he added this warning:

> ". . . whilst such a purchase by one company of a shareholder in it is not absolutely prohibited, in view of the potential for abuse and for adverse consequences for shareholders and creditors, the Court will look carefully at such transactions to see that the directors of the acquiring company have acted with an eye solely to the interests of the acquiring company (and not e.g. to the interests of the directors) and have fulfilled their fiduciary duties to safeguard the interests of shareholders and creditors alike".

Suppose, for example, the intended subsidiary company was set up as the first of two stages in a single scheme. The first stage could involve the acquisition by the intended subsidiary of shares in the holding company. The second stage could involve the subsequent acquisition by the holding company of the intended subsidiary. In such a case the corporate veil would almost certainly be lifted, because the arrangement would be a façade or sham—see Mitchell J. in *August Investments Pty Ltd v Poseidon Ltd and Samin Ltd* [1971] 2 S.A.S.R. 71 at p.90. **24–009**

Financial Assistance

Provision by a Company of Financial Assistance for the Acquisition of its own Shares

History of the Rule

Prior to the passing of the Companies Act 1981 it was unlawful for a company to give financial assistance for the purchase of, or subscription for, its own shares. S.54 of the Companies Act 1948 made the giving of financial assistance a criminal offence. The prohibition was expressed in wide terms and included financial assistance whether given "directly or indirectly and whether by means of a loan, guarantee, the provision of security or otherwise". The giving of assistance by a subsidiary company to anyone wanting to acquire shares or subscribing in shares in the holding company was also prohibited. **24–010**

The purpose of this prohibition was considered by the Jenkins Committee (Report of the Company Law Committee Cmnd 1749) and expressed in the following terms: **24–011**

> "If people who cannot provide the funds necessary to acquire control of a company from their own resources, or by borrowing on their own credit, gain

> control of a company with large assets on the understanding that they will use the funds of the company to pay for their shares it seems to us all to likely that in many cases the company will be made to part with its funds either on inadequate security or for an illusory consideration. If the speculation succeeds, the company and therefore its creditors and minority shareholders may suffer no loss, although their interests will have been subjected to an illegitimate risk; if it fails, it may be little consolation for creditors and minority shareholders to know that the directors are liable for misfeasance" (at para.171).

The Jenkins Report recognised that there may be legitimate commercial reasons why a company might wish to offer financial assistance in the purchase its own shares and it recommended that there should be limited provision to allow such transactions. The Companies Act 1981 repealed s.54 of the Companies Act 1948 and replaced it with provisions which are now contained in Ch.VI (ss.151 to 158) of the Companies Act 1985.

The Prohibition

24–012 The provision of financial assistance by a company in the purchase of its own shares continues to be generally prohibited. Ss.151(1) and (2) of the Companies Act 1985 repeat the prohibition by rendering it unlawful for a company or any of its subsidiaries to give financial assistance directly or indirectly to a person acquiring or proposing to acquire shares in that company prior to, or at the time of, the acquisition. The prohibitions are as follows:

24–013 S.151(1)—

> ". . . where a person is acquiring or is proposing to acquire shares in a company, it is not lawful for the company or any of its subsidiaries to give financial assistance directly or indirectly for the purpose of that acquisition before or at the same time as the acquisition takes place."

24–014 S.151(2)—

> ". . . where a person has acquired shares in a company and any liability has been incurred (by that or any other person), for the purpose of that acquisition, it is not lawful for the company or any of its subsidiaries to give financial assistance directly or indirectly for the purpose of reducing or discharging the liability so incurred".

24–015 S.151(3) provides that breach of the prohibitions in ss.151(1) and (2) will constitute a criminal offence which may be tried on indictment or summarily. The offence may be committed by the company and by an officer of the company who is in default. The definition of an officer of the company and the potential liability of shadow directors has already been set out in this chapter. If tried on indictment the penalty is, where the company is convicted, an unlimited fine and where an officer of the company is convicted two years imprisonment and/or an unlimited fine. When tried summarily the penalty is, where the company is convicted, a fine of the statutory maximum (presently £5,000) and where an officer of the company is convicted six months imprisonment and/or a fine of the statutory maximum.

Breach of the prohibitions has consequences in civil law also. Breach will render the transaction void (in whole or in part) and unenforceable in civil law. The Courts may enforce a contract of sale where there has been provision of financial assistance if the financial assistance is severable in some way. Financial assistance will be severable if it is ancillary to the overall transaction and its elimination would leave the subject matter of the transaction unchanged. The directors involved in an unlawful transaction could be sued for breach of trust to compensate the company for any loss suffered (see Ch.27). Also, a director who is party to a breach of the prohibitions in s.151(1) and (2) could be vulnerable to an action for breach of fiduciary duty (see Ch.26), or where the company has been wound up, an action for misfeasance to recover the loss (see Ch.30).

Meaning of Financial Assistance

"Financial assistance" is defined by s.152(1)(a) as follows: **24–016**

> "(i) financial assistance given by way of gift,
> (ii) financial assistance given by way of guarantee, security or indemnity, other than an indemnity in respect of the indemnifier's own neglect or default, or by way of release or waiver,
> (iii) financial assistance given by way of a loan or any other agreement under which any of the obligations of the person giving the assistance are to be fulfilled at a time when in accordance with the agreement any obligation of another party to the agreement remains unfulfilled, or by way of the novation of, or the assignment of rights arising under, a loan or such other agreement, or
> (iv) any other financial assistance given by a company the net assets of which are thereby reduced to a material extent or which has no net assets."

The definition is widely drawn and is inclusive rather than exhaustive. The definition includes direct financing by a company and, what is more common in practice, indirect financing.

Examples of the types of transaction prohibited by s.151 can be found in cases decided under the old legislation. The Court of Appeal held in the leading case of *Belmont Finance Corporation v Williams Furniture Ltd (No 2)* [1980] 1 All E.R. 393 that financial assistance was afforded where a company, without regard to its own commercial interests, bought something from a third party with the sole purpose of putting the third party in funds to acquire shares in the company. Financial assistance was given irrespective of whether the company received a fair price for its assets if the transaction was not in the ordinary course of the company's business and did not enable the company to acquire anything which it genuinely needed for its own purposes. **24–017**

A loan was made by a company to finance the borrower's purchase of shares in the *Craddock (No 3)* [1968] 1 W.L.R. 1555. In *Wallersteiner v Moir (No 1)*[1974] 1 W.L.R. 991 the Court of Appeal considered unlawful an arrangement under which a purchaser of shares undertook a liability as **24–018** part of the consideration which he would never discharge or cause the company to discharge. (See also *Armour Hick Northern Limited v Whitehouse* [1980] 1 W.L.R. 1520 where it was held to be sufficient that assistance was given "in connection with" an acquisition).

In *Parlett v Guppys (Bridport) Ltd, The Times*, February 8, 1996 the Court of Appeal held that the s.151 prohibition did not apply to an agreement whereby four private companies together assumed liability for making future payments of salary, bonus and pension to one of their shareholders in return for that shareholder transferring shares in one of the companies. The critical aspect in this case was the fact that there was no reduction in the net assets of the company in respect of which the shareholder transferred his shares.

24–019 In order for a company to be liable under s.152(1)(a)(ii) for giving assistance by way of indemnity, the Court of Appeal has recently held that the indemnity in question must give assistance of a financial nature for the purpose of the acquisition of the shares. The fact that there was a contract under which a party might recover the same amount by way of damages as he would have recovered under an indemnity was not sufficient to convert that contract into an indemnity—*British and Commonwealth Holdings v Barclays Bank* [1996] 1 All E.R. 381.

More recently, in *MT Realisations Ltd (In Liquidation) v Digital Equipment Co Ltd* [2003] EWCA Civ 494, the Court of Appeal upheld a decision of the Chancery Division that no unlawful assistance was given where companies within the same group had entered into agreements for the assignment of a loan and the rescheduling of repayments concurrently with an agreement for the sale of shares. The Court of Appeal agreed with the trial Judge's determination that the transaction was financially neutral.

24–020 In the context of a company takeover, the payment by a target company of the fees of accountants retained by the purchaser company to prepare a "long form" report has been held to amount to unlawful financial assistance — *Chaston v SWP Group Ltd* (unreported) December 20, 2002. Giving judgment in the Court of Appeal, Lady Justice Arden noted that s.151 had been enacted to confront the mischief of the previously common practice of purchasing the shares of a company having a substantial cash balance or easily realisable assets and so arranging matters that the purchase money was lent by the company to the purchaser. "It is clear from the way in which s.151 and s.152 are drafted that it covers financial assistance in many forms apart from loans (see for example the wide wording of s.152(3)). The general mischief, however, remains the same, namely that the resources of the target company and its subsidiaries should not be used directly or indirectly to assist the purchaser financially to make the acquisition. This may prejudice the interests of the creditors of the target or its group, and the interests of any shareholders who do not accept the offer to acquire their shares or to whom the offer is not made".

Ultimately, each case will depend on its particular facts, and unless declaratory of some point of principle, the influence of past decisions will be limited. As Hoffman J. said in *Charterhouse Investment Trust Ltd v Tempest Diesels Ltd* [1985] 1 B.C.C. 99544, the question of financial assistance has to be considered against the commercial realities of the particular transaction.

On the facts of that case, where a letter surrendering tax losses of one company to other companies within the group formed a collateral contract which was part of a composite transaction, the Court determined that the surrender could not in any acceptable commercial sense be regarded as a giving of financial assistance when the transaction was considered as a whole.

Financial Assistance from Foreign Subsidiaries

In the case of *Arab Bank PLC v Mercantile Holdings Ltd* [1994] 2 All E.R. 7 **24–021**
the Court held that s.151 did not have extra-territorial effect and that a foreign subsidiary was not prohibited from giving financial assistance for the purpose of an acquisition of shares in its parent company. Nonetheless, the Court was concerned to safeguard the interests of investors in this context. Towards the end of his judgment Millett J. noted that the hiving down of the assets by an English company to a foreign subsidiary in order that they may be available for the purpose of assisting in the financing of a contemplated purchase of the parent company's own shares would constitute the indirect provision of financial assistance by the parent company.

Exceptions

S.153(1) and (2) exempt certain transactions from the prohibitions in s.151 **24–022**
against the giving of financial assistance directly or indirectly for the acquisition of shares by a company in itself or in its holding company. A company is not prohibited from giving financial assistance for the purpose of acquiring shares in itself or its holding company if:

(i) the company's principal purpose in giving the assistance is:

(a) where the assistance is caught by section 151(1), not to give that assistance for the purpose of any such acquisition of shares; or
(b) where the assistance is caught by section 151(2), not to reduce or discharge any liability incurred by a person for the purpose of the acquisition of shares in the company or its holding company; or

(ii) where the assistance is caught by either section 151(1) or (2), where the assistance is but an incidental part of some larger purpose of the company, and
(iii) the assistance is given in good faith and in the interests of the company.

The alternative exceptions are referred to as "the principal purpose" exception and "the larger purpose" exception. In each case it must be shown that the assistance was given in good faith and in the interests of the company.

The Company's Principal Purpose

24–023 The principal purpose of the transaction must be a bona fide commercial purpose which can be divided from the share acquisition. The transaction must be capable of being justified commercially in the company's own interests. A transaction under which a company purchases from another goods in the ordinary course of its business but also with the intention of putting the seller in a position to acquire shares in the purchasing company will not prohibited if the latter purpose is not the principal purpose of the transaction—*Belmont Finance Corporation v Williams Furniture Ltd (No 2)* [1980] 1 All E.R. 393.

Some Larger Purpose

24–024 The House of Lords has given the phrase "some larger purpose" a narrow interpretation by drawing a distinction between a "purpose" and the "reason" why a purpose is formed. In order to establish some larger purpose, it is necessary to show some overall larger corporate purpose in which the resultant financial assistance to purchase shares is merely incidental. The purpose must be a corporate purpose and it must be immediate or proximate and well defined. A non-specific or long term business strategy may not be enough.

24–025 The meaning of the phrase "some larger purpose" was considered at some length in the leading case of *Brady v Brady* [1988] B.C.L.C. 579; [1989] A.C. 755. The case concerned the corporate reorganisation of a family company following a quarrel between directors. To prevent winding up of the company it was agreed that the business should be divided equally between the directors with a cash adjustment being made to bring about equality between the two sides. The scheme involved merger of the family company with its wholly owned subsidiary company. The assets of the merged companies would then be divided and transferred to two new companies. Transfer of assets was to be achieved by the issuing of fully paid up shares in the new companies, to be paid for by the issue of loan stock. In the course of the merger the family company had to provide financial assistance to the subsidiary company in order to reduce the subsidiary company's liabilities. It was this aspect of the transaction which fell foul of the prohibition in s.151(2) and the question arose as to whether the transaction could be saved by the larger purpose exception. It was in this context that the House of Lords came to construe the phrase "some larger purpose" in comparatively narrow terms:

> "In applying sub-section 1(a) one has . . . to look for some larger purpose in the giving of financial assistance than the mere purpose of the acquisition of the shares and to ask whether the giving of assistance is a mere incident of that purpose. . . . The ultimate reason for forming the purpose of financing an acquisition may, and in most cases probably will, be more important to those making the decision than the immediate transaction itself. But "larger" is not the same thing as "more important" nor is "reason" the same as "purpose". If one postulates the case of a bidder for control of a public company financing

his bid from the company's own funds, the obvious mischief at which this section is aimed, the immediate purpose which it is sought to achieve is that of completing the purchase and vesting control of the company in the bidder. The reasons why that course is considered desirable may be many and varied. . . . These may be excellent reasons but they cannot, in my judgment, constitute a "larger purpose" of which the provision of assistance is merely an incident" (*per* Lord Oliver).

Lord Oliver explained that the purpose of financial assistance in this case was to enable the shares to be acquired. Whilst the commercial advantages flowing from the acquisition were laudable, they remained a by-product of the financial assistance rather than an independent purpose for which the financial assistance had been provided. The principles set out in *Brady v Brady* were applied by Morritt J. in *Plaut v Steiner* (1989) 5 B.C.C. 352, which was also concerned the division of a business in order to resolve management deadlock. **24–026**

Other Statutory Exceptions to the s.151 Prohibitions

Additional express exemptions from the s.151 prohibitions are set out in ss.153(3) and (4). These include: **24–027**

(1) the payment of a lawful dividend—s.153(3)(a);

(2) the allotment of bonus shares—s.153(3)(b);

(3) loans in the ordinary course of business by money lending institutions —s.153(4)(a). Both the lending of money and the particular loan must be within the ordinary course of the company's business. Loans made with the purpose of an acquisition in mind are unlikely to be regarded as loans made in the usual course of business—see *Steen v Law* [1964] A.C. 287;

(4) arrangements in connection with employee share schemes—s.153(4)(b) as amended by s.196 of the Financial Services Act 1986 and s.132, Sch.18, para.33 of the Companies Act 1989. The provision of financial assistance for the purpose of an employee share scheme must be given in good faith and in the interests of the company. The section covers provision of financial assistance as distinct from money;

(5) loans to employees to permit them to acquire fully paid shares—s.153(4)(c). This does not apply to directors. There are restrictions on loans to directors and persons connected with them—see Ch.19.

Special Restrictions for Public Companies

There are special restrictions for public limited liability companies. S.154 authorises the giving of financial assistance only if the company has net assets which are not thereby reduced or, to the extent that net assets are reduced, if the assistance rendered is provided out of distributable profits. **24–028**

"Net assets" are defined as the amount by which the aggregate of the company's assets exceeds the aggregate of its liabilities. "Liabilities" are defined to include any amount retained as reasonably necessary for the purpose of providing for any liability or loss which is either likely to be incurred or certain to be incurred but uncertain as to amount or as to the date on which it will arise.

Private Companies

24–029 Ss.155 to 158 contain a general exemption for private companies from the prohibition on giving financial assistance for the acquisition of its own shares. The exemption is obtained by compliance with a prescribed procedure and timetable set out in ss.155 to 158. The Act makes specific provision for the protection of creditors in s.155(2) and minority shareholders in s.157. Private companies may rely on the exceptions in s.153 as well as the specific exemption in ss.155 to 158. In *Brady v Brady*, where the transaction was not saved by the larger purpose exception in s.153(2), the House of Lords concluded that the conditions of s.155(2) had been fulfilled, and on this basis the transaction was not prohibited. The private company exemption applies for the purposes of the acquisition of shares by a company in itself or in its holding company provided that the holding company is also a private company. Under s.155(2), the burden rests with the party challenging the legality of the arrangement to demonstrate that financial assistance had not been provided out of distributable profits—*In the Matter of In a Flap Envelope Company Ltd (In Liquidation)* (unreported) April 11, 2003.

24–030 Financial assistance can only be given if:

(1) there is no reduction of net asset—s.155(2);

(2) there is a statutory declaration by the directors of the company as to its solvency prior to giving assistance—s.155(6);

(3) a special resolution is passed approving the giving of financial assistance by the company—s.155(4);

(4) the timetable for compliance with the requirements of ss.156 to 158 is adhered to.

24–031 The statutory declaration must be in the prescribed form—see the Companies (Forms) Regulations 1985 (SI 1985/854) reg.4(1), Sch.3 and Pt II of Sch.4. The declaration must include details of the assistance to be given, the business of the company giving assistance, and it must identify the recipient of the assistance— s.156(1). The Courts have considered the question of how detailed the particulars contained in such a statutory declaration must be to comply with the prescribed form. The principal purpose of the statutory declaration is to ensure that the company providing financial assistance meets with the solvency requirements. The statutory declaration must therefore, contain information which gives "particulars" of the form of assistance to be provided and of the principal terms on which the assistance will be given—*Re S.H. & Co. (Realisations) 1990 Ltd* [1993] B.C.L.C. 1309; [1993] B.C.C. 60.

Although the statutory declaration must be in the prescribed form, it is not a requirement that the declaration made be on a prescribed form but, if it is not, it must contain all the statutory requirements—*Re NL Electrical* [1994] 1 B.C.L.C. 22. Directors must state that in their opinion the company will be able to pay its debts both immediately after the rendering of assistance and as the debts fall due within the year following the rendering of assistance. If the company is to be wound up, the directors must state that the company is in a position to pay its debts in full. S.156(5) requires the statutory declaration to be registered at Companies House. Failure to register the statutory declaration is a criminal offence which is triable summarily and for which a director if found guilty may be fined—s.156(6).

The declaration must have annexed to it an auditor's report to the effect **24–032** that the auditors have made enquiry into the affairs of the company and are not aware of anything to contradict the opinion of the directors as to its solvency position—s.156(4). It is a criminal offence for the directors of a company to make a statutory declaration if they do not have reasonable grounds for giving the opinion expressed— s.156(7). The penalty is, on indictment, a maximum of two years imprisonment and/or an unlimited fine. On summary conviction the maximum penalty is six months imprisonment and/or a fine of the statutory maximum (presently £5,000). The auditors of a company are not subject to any criminal sanction in respect of any report they may provide.

A special resolution must approve the giving of financial assistance by the company. If the financial assistance is for the purpose of the acquisition of shares in a holding company there must be a special resolution passed by both the holding company and the assisting company and any intermediate company between them in the group— s.155(5). Wholly owned subsidiaries are, by their very nature, exempt from the requirement to pass a special resolution.

The various requirements are subject to a strict timetable which is **24–033** contained in the respective provisions. Non-compliance with the statutory requirements is not a mere procedural irregularity capable of waiver and it cannot be validated by unanimous agreement of all members entitled to vote at meetings of the company—*Precision Dippings Ltd v Precision Dippings Marketing Ltd* (1985) 1 B.C.C. 539 at p.543 *per* Dillon L.J.

The legislation has made specific provision for the protection of minority shareholder interests. After the passing of any of the requisite special resolutions, a dissenting minority may apply to the Court to have the resolution set aside. A dissenting minority must hold at least 10 per cent of the issued share capital or if the company is not limited by shares by at least 10 per cent of its members. The application must be made within 28 days of the passing of the special resolution. The Court has wide powers in the event of such an application, including ordering that the minority be bought out or ordering that the resolution be cancelled —s.157(2). Reference may also be made in this context to the power of the Court to protect minority shareholders more generally (see Ch.10).

S.151 in Practice and Calls for Reform

24–034 Although the Courts have endeavoured to uphold the width of the prohibitions in s.143 and s.151, the prohibitions have proved a blunt tool in the context of investor protection. The statutory language is technical and difficult to apply, and the exceptions to both sets of prohibitions are sufficiently wide to deprive shareholders of any effective protection.

In so far as the criminal sanctions are concerned, these are rarely utilised, and the Courts have proceeded on the assumption that in order to establish an offence under s.151(3) the prosecution must show that a defendant has contravened one of the s.151 prohibitions dishonestly and that none of the s.153 exemptions apply in the case. The point is well demonstrated by a consideration of the Court of Appeal decision in *R. v Saunders*, *Independent*, May 17, 1991. The Court held that it was necessary to explain that proof of a substantive offence depended in part on the ability of the prosecution to show the absence of any s.153 exemption. Since the s.153 exemption brings the issue of a defendant's good faith into question, it follows that the prosecution has to prove a defendant's dishonesty before the defendant can be convicted of the criminal offence. This is difficult to establish in practice, since directors will quite sensibly take detailed legal advice before entering into any arrangement of this nature. In practical terms, unless the arrangement takes place under the cloak of false documentation, dishonesty will be impossible to prove. Where more than one person is a party to a dishonest transaction it is possible for the prosecution to charge a conspiracy to defraud (see Ch.18), but again the prosecution has to prove an intention by the defendant to be party to an agreement to commit an unlawful act—*Churchill v Walton* [1967] 2 A.C. 224, HL; *R. v Anderson* [1986] 1 A.C. 27, HL. It follows that a prosecution under s.151(3) will not enhance the prospects of conviction.

24–035 There have been calls for reform of this area of the law, and suggestions have included the decriminalisation of s.151 and its replacement by a more effective civil sanction. There is much to support this line of thought. The origin of the current provisions on maintenance of capital came from the Second EEC Directive (Dir. 77/91 [1977] O.J. L26/1), and it is from Europe that further initiatives in the reform of company law are likely to come.

Chapter 25

Directors Disqualification

Introduction

S.1 of the Company Directors Disqualification Act 1986 empowers a Court to make an order for a specified period against a person that he shall not be a director of a company or an administrator or liquidator of a company, a receiver or manager of a company's assets or in any way whether directly or indirectly be concerned in or take part in the promotion, formation or management of a company. As Sir Donald Nicholls V.C. said in *Secretary of State for Trade and Industry v Ettinger* [1993] B.C.L.C. 896: **25–001**

> "The procedure for disqualifying directors was an important sanction . . . Those who took advantage of limited liability had to conduct their companies with due regard to the ordinary standards of commercial reality."

Directors disqualification is a sanction which is exercised in the investor context and the circumstances in which an order for disqualification may be made is considered in this chapter.

The definition of a director is set out in Ch.29. Suffice it to note that a director will include any person occupying the position of a director and for the purposes of ss.6 to 9 of the Company Directors Disqualification Act 1986 it will include a shadow director. In *Re Lo-Line Electric Motors Ltd* [1988] Ch. 477 it was held that a person acting as a de facto director was a director for the purposes of this Act.

Disqualification on Conviction for an Indictable Offence

S.2(1) of the Act allows a Court to make a disqualification order against a person where he is convicted of an indictable offence (whether on indictment or summarily) in connection with the promotion, formation, management or liquidation of a company, or with the receivership or management of a company's property. **25–002**

The Court

For the purposes of s.2, a Court includes (a) any Court having jurisdiction to wind up the company in relation to which the offence was committed, (b) the Court by or before which the person is convicted of the offence and (c) in the case of a summary conviction in England and Wales, any other Magistrates Court acting for the same petty sessional area. **25–003**

Discretion

25–004 The extent of the Court's discretion to make a disqualification order was considered in *R. v Young* (1990) 12 Cr. App. R. (S). The appellant pleaded guilty to managing a company as an undischarged bankrupt and was disqualified from being a director for two years and conditionally discharged. The Judge accepted that there had been no fraud or dishonesty on the part of the defendant. The disqualification was appealed on the basis that there had been no finding that the appellant was unfit to be a company director. The Court of Appeal held that under s.2 of the Company Directors Disqualification Act 1986 there was an unfettered discretion to make a disqualification order against a person convicted of an indictable offence committed in connection with the promotion, formation, management or liquidation of a company.

In Connection with the Management of a Company

25–005 The meaning of "in connection with the management of a company" has been considered in a number of cases. A good statement of the principles to be applied was set out by Mann J. in *R. v Austen* [1985] 7 Cr. App. R. (S.) 214, where fraudulent hire purchase transactions had been carried out by the appellant through a number of limited companies. The Court of Appeal considered whether the phrase "in connection with the management of a company" was restricted to the internal management of the company. In giving judgment Mann J. said at p. 216:

> "In our judgment the words of the section when they refer to "the management of the company" refer to the management of the company's affairs and there is no reason in language for differentiating between internal affairs and external affairs. Indeed as a matter of policy it may be thought appropriate that management should extend to both internal and external affairs. The section should cover activity in relation to the birth, life and death of a company."

25–006 There are a number of cases which demonstrate the application of these principles. In *R. v Corbin* [1984] 6 Cr. App. R. (S) 17, an earlier decision, the appellant was convicted on six counts of obtaining property by deception. He and his father operated a business dealing in yachts using three limited companies. Through deception they obtained money and boats. On appeal it was argued that "in connection with the management of a company" related only to the internal management of a company. The Court of Appeal held that the management of a company was not restricted to the management of a company's affairs internally.

25–007 Similarly, in *R. v Georgiou* [1988] 87 Cr. App. R. 207, the appellant pleaded guilty to an offence of carrying on insurance business without the authorisation of the Secretary of State contrary to ss.2 and 14 of the Insurance Companies Act 1982 He was sentenced to six months imprisonment, a fine of £1,000 and disqualified from being a director for a period of five years. In the course of his appeal against sentence the Court of Appeal considered what was meant by "in connection with the management of a company". The court held that carrying on an insurance business through a limited company is a function of management and if that function is performed unlawfully in any way which makes the person guilty of an indictable offence it can properly be said that is in connection with the management of a company.

What amounted to the management of a company was again considered **25–008** in *R. v Goodman* [1993] 2 All E.R. 789; [1994] 1 B.C.L.C. 349, where the defendant was a director and chairman of a public company who was convicted in relation to insider dealing offences. The court included in sentence a disqualification from being a director under s.2(1) of the Act. The defendant appealed on the basis that his conviction was not relevant to his involvement in the management of a company. The Court of Appeal held that the conviction was indeed relevant to involvement with the management of a company.

Period of Disqualification

Under s.2(3) of the Act, the maximum period of disqualification is five **25–009** years where the disqualification order is made by a Magistrates' Court and 15 years in any other case.

The appropriate length of disqualification was considered in *Re Seven Oaks Stationery (Retail) Ltd* [1991] Ch. 164 where (at p.174) Dillon L.J. gave the following guidelines:

> "I . . . endorse the division of the potential 15 year disqualification period into three brackets . . . viz: (i) the top bracket of disqualification for periods over 10 years should be reserved for particularly serious cases. These may include cases where a director who has already had one period of disqualification imposed on him falls to be disqualified again. (ii) The minimum bracket of two to five years disqualification should be applied where, though disqualification is mandatory, the case is relatively not very serious. (iii) The middle bracket of disqualification for six to 10 years should apply for serious cases which do not merit the top bracket."

Although set out in a "civil" case, these guidelines have been applied by the criminal courts. In the case of *R. v Millard* (1994) 15 Cr. App. R. (S.), for example, the original sentence of 15 years disqualification in respect of nine counts of fraudulent trading was reduced to eight years on appeal.

A significant period of disqualification may be imposed in a case where **25–010** there is no dishonesty on the part of the defendant. In *Secretary of State for Trade and Industry v Ettinger* [1993] B.C.L.C. 896, *The Times*, February 18, 1993, the Court of Appeal increased a period of disqualification from 3 to 5 years and stressed that persistent failure to file accounts was to be viewed seriously even where there was no dishonest intent.

Imposition of Disqualification when Coupled with Compensation Orders

In *R. v Holmes* (1992) 13 Cr. App. R. (S) the Court of Appeal considered **25–011** whether it was appropriate to impose a compensation order at the same time as imposing disqualification from being a director. The Court held that when a compensation order is made it is generally wrong in principle to inhibit a defendant from freely engaging in business activities which must have been contemplated as necessary for the purposes of fulfilling the obligations of the compensation order.

Disqualification for Persistent Breach of Companies Legislation

25–012 Under s.3 of the Act a disqualification order may be made against a person who has been persistently in default of any requirements under the companies legislation. This includes a persistent failure to file audited accounts for the company—*Secretary of State of Trade and Industry v Ettinger* [1993] B.C.L.C. 896; *The Times*, February 18, 1993, and failure to maintain proper accounting records for a company—*Re New Generation Engineers Ltd* [1993] B.C.L.C. 435 and *Re Firedart Ltd, Official Receiver v Fairall* [1994] 2 B.C.L.C. 340.

The maximum period of disqualification under section 3 is five years.

Disqualification for Unfitness

25–013 S.6 of the Act imposes a duty on a court to disqualify a director who is or has been a director of a company which has at any time become insolvent (whether while he was a director or subsequently) and where his conduct as director of that company (either taken alone or taken together with his conduct as a director of any other company or companies) makes him unfit to be concerned in the management of a company.

Applications for disqualification under s.6 may be made by the Secretary of State, by the official receiver or the liquidator. The application must normally be made within two years of the date on which the company became insolvent.

25–014 There is a growing body of decided cases dealing with the circumstances in which a court must make a disqualification order under s.6. The standard to be applied on the question of whether a person is unfit to be concerned in the management of the company was considered in the case of *Secretary of State of Trade and Industry v Lewinsohn* (unreported) March 19, 1996. It was held that the Court must ask whether the standard of conduct fell below the standard which is today expected of a director who enjoys the privilege of limited liability. The standard of proof is the balance of probabilities rather than the criminal standard but regard has to be had to the seriousness of the issues raised. This is particularly so in the case of professional men where the complaints are as to lack of probity rather than negligence.

25–015 In *Re Continental Assurance Company of London plc* (unreported) June 14, 1996, Chadwick J. held that incompetence may justify the making of an order under s.6. A failure to read and understand statutory accounts amounted to sufficient incompetence and neglect to justify the making of an order. The Court referred to *Re Lo-Line Electric Motors Ltd* and *Re Grayan Ltd* [1995] Ch. 241 in this context.

25–016 It is not open to a director to avoid disqualification by contending that at the material time he did not know that the company was insolvent. Where it can be demonstrated that a company has continued trading for a substantial period of time while it was insolvent and as a result has put the claims of existing and new creditors at unwarrantable risk of not being repaid, it is not open to a director to avoid responsibility by arguing that he was not aware of the company's financial position. It is the duty of all directors to ensure that they have a reasonably clear picture of the financial state and trading profitability of their companies. It they are unable to ascertain the state of the company it is incumbent on them to procure that immediate steps are taken to put the books and records in a reasonable state or to bring trading to an end—*Secretary of State for Trade and Industry v Harry Laing* (unreported) June 20, 1996.

Under s.6(4) the minimum period of disqualification is two years and the maximum is fifteen years. The principles concerning the length of disqualification as set out in *Re Seven Oaks Stationery Retail Ltd* (see above, para.25–009) will apply.

Procedure

By analogy with other situations such as a plea of guilty in criminal cases, 25–017
the court has jurisdiction to deal with an application under s.6 summarily without requiring a full trial and without requiring the parties to contest every point provided some evidence, and not merely an assertion of no evidential value or an admission which was unsupported by evidence, was presented to the court which established unfitness—*Re Carecraft Construction Co Ltd* [1993] 4 All E.R. 499. It must be remembered in this context that it was a condition precedent to the making of a disqualification order under s.6 that the court was satisfied that the conduct of a director in relation to a particular company or companies made him unfit to be concerned in the management of a company.

In *Secretary of State for Trade and Industry v Rogers* (unreported) July 30, 1996, a case came before the court on agreed facts in which no allegation of dishonesty had been made. In his written judgment the Judge include a finding of dishonesty which the Court of Appeal held it was not open for him to make. However, the Court of Appeal was concerned to note that by using the *Carecraft Construction Co Ltd* procedure parties cannot oblige the Judge to approach the case in a particular way. It is important in cases where this procedure is to be used that the Judge has the opportunity to read the papers in advance and to voice any doubts that he has about either the need for disqualification or its length at the earliest possible moment so that the parties can consider whether they or either of them would prefer a full trial.

Disqualification in the Public Interest

Following an investigation by the Department of Trade and Industry, the 25–018
Secretary of State has power to apply to the court for a disqualification order where it appears to be in the public interest that such an order be made. The Court has power to order disqualification under s.8.

The maximum period of disqualification under s.8 is 15 years. The principles concerning the length of disqualification as set out in *Re Seven Oaks Stationary Retail Ltd* (see above, para.25–009) will apply.

Disqualification Following a Declaration of Fraudulent or Wrongful Trading

25–019 S.10 provides that disqualification may also follow a declaration of fraudulent or wrongful trading under ss.213 and 214 of the Insolvency Act 1986 which are covered in chs 26 and 30 respectively.

The maximum period of disqualification under s.10 is 15 years. The principles concerning the length of disqualification as set out in *Re Seven Oaks Stationary Retail Ltd* (see above, para.25–009) will apply.

Disqualification Where an Undischarged Bankrupt Acting as a Director

25–020 Under s.11 it is an offence for an undischarged bankrupt to act as a director or to take part in or be concerned in, either directly of indirectly, the promotion, formation or management of a company except with leave of the Court.

The Consequences of Contravention of an Order for Disqualification

25–021 Under s.13 of the Act, if a person acts in contravention of a disqualification order or of s.12(2), or is guilty of an offence under s.11, he is liable on conviction on indictment, to imprisonment for not more than two years or a fine, or both; and on summary conviction, to imprisonment for a maximum of six months or a fine not exceeding the statutory maximum, or both.

Register of Disqualification Orders

25–022 Under s.18 of the Act the Secretary of State maintains a register which is open to inspection of disqualification orders which remain in force.

Chapter 26

Confiscation of Assets and Compensation

Introduction

Confiscation of the proceeds of crime has two aspects both of which attract popular support and approval; the first is to deprive criminals of the fruits of their criminal activity (a tradition recognised by the common law under which the property of anyone convicted of a felony was forfeit to the Crown until 1870) and the second is to allow for the compensation of the victims of crime. Following the Hodgson Committee report on "Forfeiture of the Proceeds of Crime" in 1984 a number of pieces of broadly parallel legislation were passed—the Drug Trafficking Offences Act 1986 aimed at the removal of the proceeds of drug trafficking, the Prevention of Terrorism (Temporary Provisions) Act 1989 aimed at the removal of the proceeds of terrorism, and Pt VI of the Criminal Justice Act 1988 which introduced confiscation orders aimed at the removal of the proceeds of other areas of lucrative crime. More recently, the legislation has undergone a complete overhaul and it is now contained in the Proceeds of Crime Act 2002 ("POCA"). The new legislation is intended to widen the powers of the Courts to confiscate the proceeds of criminal activity which are not the result of drug trafficking or terrorism. This Act has significant potential application in cases of investor fraud. **26–001**

Procedure

Confiscation Orders

The Crown Court is required by s.6 of POCA to make a confiscation order where a person has been convicted of an offence involving the acquisition of property and the prosecution asks the Court to do so, or the Court itself considers that it is appropriate to do so. **26–002**

As a first step the Court is required to decide whether the convicted defendant has a "criminal lifestyle". If he has, the Court must proceed to decide whether the defendant has benefited from his "general criminal conduct". The amount of the benefit is called the "recoverable amount", and this is the sum in which the confiscation order must be made, unless the defendant can show on a balance of probabilities that the value of the property available to satisfy the confiscation order is less than the amount of the benefit. In this event, the recoverable amount is reduced to reflect the lower figure.

26–003 If the Crown Court decides that the defendant does not have a "criminal lifestyle", the Court must decide whether he has benefited from his "particular criminal conduct", in which event the recoverable amount will be fixed at the amount of the benefit unless, once again, the defendant can show that the value of the property available to satisfy the confiscation order is less than the amount of the benefit.

The significance of a determination by the Court that a defendant has a "criminal lifestyle" must not be under-estimated. Where the Crown makes this determination it has the effect of deeming all the property held by the defendant as obtained a result of his general criminal conduct. There are three other "statutory assumptions" which also apply to the defendant's property in these circumstances.

Against this background, it is necessary to explore in greater detail exactly what is meant by the new notions of "criminal lifestyle", "general criminal conduct", "particular criminal conduct", and the "statutory assumptions".

Criminal Lifestyle

26–004 Under s.75(2) of POCA there are three different ways in which a Crown Court can make a determination that a person has a criminal lifestyle.

The first way is triggered whenever a defendant is convicted of a criminal offence listed in Sch.2 of the Act. Typically, these offences involve drug trafficking, money laundering, counterfeiting, and intellectual property.

The second way occurs where a person commits conduct which is deemed to form part of "a course of criminal activity". Conduct forms part of a course of criminal activity if a defendant has benefited from the conduct and either he has been convicted of at least four offences in the proceedings for which he has been sentenced or he has committed on at least two occasions in the previous six years of an offence constituting conduct from which he has benefited. In order for an offence to qualify for these purposes, the defendant must have obtained a minimum benefit of £5,000 from the offence in question.

The third way in which criminal lifestyle is triggered is where a defendant has committed an offence over a period of at least six months and the defendant has benefited from the offence. Typical examples would be continuing offences such as conspiracy to defraud or fraudulent trading.

The Statutory Assumptions

26–005 The statutory assumptions which must be made by a Crown Court where it has found that a defendant has a criminal lifestyle are draconian. Under s.10 of POCA, the Crown Court must assume that any property held by the defendant at the time at the time of his conviction was obtained by him as a result of his general criminal conduct, and obtained by him at the earliest time in which he appears to have held it. The only exception to this rule is where the defendant can prove that in relation to any particular item of property he obtained the property from legitimate activity or where he can show that "there would be a serious risk of injustice" if the assumption were made.

General Criminal Conduct and Particular Criminal Conduct

The notion of "general criminal conduct" is extremely wide. It embraces all the defendant's conduct, and it is immaterial whether the conduct occurred before or after the passing of the new POCA legislation. Criminal conduct is defined in s.76 of POCA to include not only conduct which constitutes an offence in England and Wales, but also conduct which "would constitute an offence if it occurred in England and Wales". This means that if a defendant is convicted of keeping a brothel contrary to s.33 of the Sexual Offences Act 1956, which is a Sch.2 "criminal lifestyle" offence, his benefit is deemed to include not only the income from the brothel in England and Wales but also the income from his licensed brothel in Amsterdam which he conducts perfectly legally in accordance with Dutch law. **26–006**

By way of contrast, "particular criminal conduct" constitutes the criminal conduct of which the defendant has been convicted in the proceedings in which the confiscation hearing is taking place.

Written Notice by the Prosecution

S.16 of POCA requires the prosecutor to tender to the court a statement containing information relevant to whether the defendant has benefited from general criminal or particular criminal conduct and the value of any such benefit. Where such a statement is tendered the defendant should be asked specifically whether what the prosecution says is true. An admission by the defendant as to the truth of the allegations in the written notice is to be taken as conclusive proof of their accuracy. **26–007**

Provision of Information by the Defendant

S.17 of POCA empowers the court to order the defendant to give it information to assist in carrying out its functions under the new confiscation regime. Failure to comply with such an order would be punishable as a contempt of court. The order may specify such information as may be required by the court. There is no provision in the Act limiting the use to which information received in this way may be put. If the information discloses other criminal offences, there appears to be no reason why the defendant would not be vulnerable to further prosecution. The defendant may only refuse to comply with the order to supply information if he has a reasonable excuse. Refusal to comply with an order without reasonable excuse allows the court to draw such inference as it considers appropriate. Plainly, such inferences will depend to a very large extent on the individual facts of each case but are likely to be adverse to the defendant. **26–008**

Provision for the Review of Cases

26–009 Ss.19 to 22 of POCA allow for the review of cases where the court has either made no assessment as to the proceeds of crime, or where the Court has made an assessment of no benefit or of limited benefit and subsequent evidence comes to light that the defendant has benefited from crime to a greater extent than had originally been put before the Court.

The procedure is broadly the same whether there has been no assessment, an assessment of no benefit or an under assessment. Where further evidence showing benefit comes to light within a period of six years from the date of conviction, it is for the prosecution to apply to the court to consider new evidence. Having considered the evidence and all the circumstances of the case the Court may then proceed to make a confiscation order. The Court is under no duty to make an order and it has discretion as to the amount of any such order. The Court must take into account any fine or order for compensation which was imposed upon the defendant. The Court may take into account any payments or other rewards received by the defendant after he was sentenced. Where there is an upward revision of a confiscation order, the period of imprisonment in default of payment shall also be revised in accordance with s.139 of the Powers of the Criminal Courts (Sentencing) Act 2000.

Enforcement of Confiscation Orders

26–010 Under ss.35 to 39 of POCA, confiscation orders are enforced by the Magistrates' Court as if they were fines. The Court may allow time for payment of an order and it may direct that payment of an order be made in instalments. The Court must make an order fixing a term of imprisonment in default of payment of the confiscation order. S.139 of the Powers of the Criminal Courts (Sentencing) Act 2000 sets out the maximum periods of imprisonment applicable which go up to 10 years imprisonment for orders in excess of £1 million. In the event of a failure to pay the confiscation order, the Court will issue a warrant of commitment specifying the period of imprisonment that the defendant is to serve. This term shall take into account any payment made towards the confiscation order. A term of imprisonment imposed in default of payment will run consecutively to any other custodial sentence, and periods of imprisonment served in default of payment of confiscation order will not extinguish the obligation to pay. This is in contrast with the position as far as fines are concerned where serving a period of imprisonment in default wipes out the fine.

Where a confiscation order has been made, the Crown Court may appoint the Director of the Assets Recovery Agency ("ARA") to enforce the confiscation order. This is likely to occur in the more complex cases, especially where foreign assets are involved.

Restraint Orders

26–011 The new legislation allows for quasi-civil action to be taken in advance of or during trial to ensure that assets which may be the subject of a confiscation order remain available to meet any such order. The Crown

Court has powers to make restraint orders (under s.41 of POCA). In making such an order the Court must be satisfied that the defendant has benefited or may have benefited from the proceeds of crime. In contrast to the position under the old legislation, a prosecuting authority can obtain a restraint order over assets from the moment when a criminal investigation has been started. Previously, a prosecution authority had to wait until a criminal charge had been brought. Since criminal charges tended not to be brought until after search and seizure operations had taken place, defendants were able to take action and move their assets out of the jurisdiction before a restraint order could be obtained. Under the new legislation, the first time that a defendant is likely to hear about the interest of a prosecution authority will be when he receives notice that a restraint order over his assets has been obtained.

Restraint orders are plainly of enormous practical importance in that their use can prevent dissipation of the proceeds of criminal conduct at a very early stage of the criminal process, thereby enhancing the possibility that the victims of crime will recover at least some of their losses.

The Order

A restraint order may be made on the ex parte application of the prosecutor to a Crown Court judge sitting in chambers and must provide for notice to be given to persons affected by the order. Under s.41 of POCA the order will prohibit any person from dealing with any "realisable property", which is defined by s.83 to mean "any free property held by the defendant, and any free property held by the recipient of a tainted gift". A "tainted gift" is a gift made a by a defendant from the proceeds of crime. **26–012**

The provisions of the Act which confer jurisdiction on the Court to make restraint are civil in character. Although the Act does not contain express provisions empowering the Court to order a defendant to make full disclosure of all his assets there is inherent power under s.41(7) of POCA to make any order necessary to make a restraint order effective, including a power to order a defendant to make such disclosure. This power, however, is discretionary and is exercisable subject to certain conditions and exceptions. The Act does not abrogate the common law rule against self-incrimination. Hence, it is customary to insert in a restraint order a clause which indicates that any information disclosed in the course of the proceedings will not be used in evidence in support of a criminal prosecution—*Re O (disclosure order)* [1991] 1 All E.R. 330. Hearsay evidence may be used in obtaining a restraint order under the POCA regime.

The Court may make provision for reasonable living as it thinks fit—see *Re Peters* [1988] 3 All E.R. 46. However, a restraint order is not in all respects equivalent to a freezing order in the High Court, (as to which, see Ch.34). There is no jurisdiction either under the statute or the Court's inherent jurisdiction to provide for the payment of compensation to innocent third parties—see *Re R (restraint order)* [1990] 2 All E.R. 569. **26–013**

Previously, provision could also be made for the payment of legal expenses. However, after a number of occasions where the totality of the restrained funds were utilised for the payment of legal fees, Parliament decided to change the law, and under s.41(4) of POCA the restrained funds must not be utilised to pay legal costs if they relate to an offence in respect of which the criminal investigation has been started.

26–014 A restraint order may apply to all realisable property held by a specified person whether the property is described in the order or not and it also applies to all realisable property held by a specified person being property transferred to him after the making of an order. The restraint order may be varied or discharged on the application of any person affected by it in relation to any property—see, for example, *Re K* (1990) 2 W.L.R. 1224, where a bank was entitled to obtain variation, it having a right of set off where several accounts were restrained including overdrawn ones.

A restraint order must be discharged at the conclusion of proceedings for the offence. Where the Crown Court has made a restraint order and criminal proceedings result in the making of a confiscation order, the Court may appoint an enforcement receiver to take possession of any realisable property and he may manage or deal with such property as the court directs. Property the subject of a restraint order may be seized by a constable for the purpose of preventing its removal from England and Wales.

Management Receivers

26–015 Where a Crown Court has made a restraint order, under s.48 of POCA the Crown Court may appoint a management receiver to take possession of the property and hold it until the conclusion of the criminal proceedings.

Compensation Orders

General Principles

26–016 The power to order compensation is contained in s.130 of the Powers of the Criminal Courts (Sentencing) Act 2000. A compensation order may be made in respect of personal injury, loss or damage resulting from the offence of which the defendant is convicted or from any offence taken into consideration.

Where a Court has power to make a compensation order and does not do so it must give its reasons for not doing so when passing sentence. The amount of a compensation order is the amount that the Court thinks appropriate having regard to any evidence and any representations made by the prosecution or the defendant. Where, for example, property which has been stolen has been recovered undamaged then the Court cannot make a compensation order in respect of the value of the goods.

26–017 In ordering compensation the Court does not have to find that the loss, damage or personal injury was inflicted intentionally—see *R. v Corbett* [1993] 14 Cr. App. R (S.) 101. Nor is it necessary that the loss, damage or personal injury is actionable in the civil courts—see *R. v Chappell* [1984] 6 Cr. App. R(S.) 214.

A compensation order should not be made in conjunction with a custodial penalty unless the Court is satisfied that the defendant has the means from which to pay it. An inability to pay compensation should not be a factor affecting the length of a custodial sentence.

A compensation order made by the Crown Court is enforced like a fine by the Magistrates' Court. The Crown Court has no power to fix a term of imprisonment in default of payment of a compensation order. The Magistrates court has the power to commit a defendant to custody in the event of default of payment, the term of imprisonment is determined from the table in Schedule 4 of the Magistrates' Courts Act 1980. The Crown Court may direct that a longer maximum term of imprisonment in default is available to the Magistrates' Court where the order for compensation exceeds £20,000. The Crown Court may allow time for payment of compensation and it may allow for payment by instalments.

Procedure

In making a compensation order the Crown Court should have before it either an agreed figure as to the amount of the loss or it should hear evidence as to the extent of the loss. However, the Court of Appeal in a series of cases has discouraged the criminal courts from embarking on complicated investigation as to the extent of loss which is more properly the province of the civil courts. A compensation order may include an amount in respect of interest. **26–018**

A compensation order may be made following the application of the prosecution or of the Crown Court of its own motion.

Amount

A separate compensation order should generally be made for each offence, although where there have been a series of offences against a victim forming a course of conduct a single compensation order may be made. Where there is more than one defendant, the level of compensation payable by each must be determined individually for a portion of the loss. Where there are a number of victims and the defendant's means are not enough to compensate each victim in full, the amount of compensation payable to each victim should usually be assessed on a pro rata basis, although there may be circumstances where it may be preferable to pay one victim in full rather than small amounts to a number of victims. **26–019**

The determination of the amount of a compensation order must take into account the means of the defendant and an order should only be made when it is realistic that the defendant will be in a position to pay it following an inquiry into the means of the defendant. However, when considering a defendant's means the Court is not restricted to funds which appear to be the proceeds of crime nor does the Court have to be satisfied that the defendant has derived any profit from his crimes. Where there is a change in the defendant's financial circumstances after the imposition of a compensation order it is open to the defendant to apply to the enforcing court to vary the compensation order accordingly. However, the change must be a genuine and unforeseen one. In the case of *R. v Dando* [1995] Crim. L.R. 750 the defendant, who had given evidence on oath as to his means, claimed his assets were in truth more limited than he had originally claimed. The Court of Appeal held that the defendant could not complain about the amount of compensation order imposed because he had lied to the Crown Court on oath about his means in an effort to mitigate his sentence.

Compensation or Confiscation

26–020 Where the Crown Court has power to make both a confiscation order and a compensation order, the Court must proceed with the confiscation process and then fix the amount of compensation without regard to the existence of the confiscation order. If the Court believes that a defendant will not have sufficient means to satisfy both the confiscation order and the compensation order in full, s.13(5) of POCA requires the Court to order the shortfall in compensation to be paid out of the confiscated sum. See *Mitchell* [2001] 2 Cr. App. R. (S.) 141; Williams [2001] 1 Cr. App. R. 500.

Restitution Orders

26–021 A restitution order may be made where goods have been stolen, obtained by criminal deception or blackmail and the defendant has been convicted of an offence "with reference to" the theft or such an offence has been taken into consideration. The power to make a restitution order is to be found in s.28 of the Theft Act 1968 and s.6 of the Criminal Justice Act 1972.

There are four types of restitution order. The Court may order the defendant to deliver to the victim any other property which he has which directly or indirectly represents the stolen goods. If any money has been taken from the defendant on his arrest, the Court may order an amount not exceeding the value of the property stolen to be given to the victim. If a third party is ordered to return property to a victim which he had purchased in good faith or has made a loan secured against the stolen property, that third party may receive a sum equal to the amount he paid or loaned from any money which was taken from the defendant at the time of his arrest.

Failure to comply with a restitution order will be treated as a contempt of court and will be treated accordingly.

Deprivation Orders

26–022 S.143 of the Powers of the Criminal Courts (Sentencing) Act 2000 empowers a Court to make orders depriving offenders of property used in connection with the commission of an offence. Before making a deprivation order the Crown Court must be satisfied that the property was taken from the defendant at the time of his arrest or that it has been lawfully seized from the offender, or that the property was in the possession of the offender when a summons was issued. The Court must have regard to the likely financial effects on the offender of making the order. A deprivation order may be made in addition to any other form of sentence. A Court which has made a deprivation order under s.143 is empowered to order that any proceeds of sale of the property seized may be paid to the victim of the offence. The Court of Appeal has held that it is inappropriate to make a deprivation order where the property is the subject of multiple ownership—*R. v Troth* [1979] 1 Cr. App. R. (S.) 341.

New Investigation Powers Under POCA

POCA creates three different types of financial investigation which may be **26–023**
variously conducted by ARA, police officers and customs officers. The object of these investigations is directed at the identification of criminal property, which can then be made subject to a restraint order pending the outcome of criminal proceedings and subsequently the making of a confiscation order.

The first type of investigation is called a "confiscation investigation", defined by s.341 of POCA as an investigation into whether a person has benefited from his criminal conduct, or the extent or whereabouts of his benefit from criminal conduct. This type of investigation may be undertaken by the ARA, and also by police officers and customs officers, and it is likely to be the type of investigation most frequently carried out under the Act.

The second type of investigation is called a "civil recovery investiga- **26–024**
tion", defined as an investigation into whether property is recoverable property, or an investigation into the identity of a person who holds recoverable property or the extent of the property or its whereabouts. This type of investigation can only be carried out by ARA and in the early years of ARA's existence there are unlikely to be more than thirty five or so investigations each year. "Recoverable property" is defined in s.304 of POCA as property obtained through unlawful conduct.

The third type of investigation is called a "money laundering investigation", defined by POCA as an investigation into whether a person has committed a money laundering offence. This type of investigation may be conducted by ARA as well as police officers and customs officers. In most cases, money laundering investigations will be undertaken by customs officers, since POCA confers authority on HM Customs & Excise to bring criminal proceedings for money laundering offences. For the purposes of the exercise of their powers, a money laundering investigation is treated as an assigned matter within the meaning of the Customs and Excise Management Act 1979.

Production Order

A production order may be obtained under s.345 of POCA by ARA, a **26–025**
police officer or a customs officer during the course of a confiscation, civil recovery or money laundering investigation. The order requires a person to produce material or allow access to material in his possession or control

within seven days of the date when the order is made. There must be reasonable grounds on the part of the investigation authority for believing that "the material is likely to be of substantial value (whether or not by itself) to the investigation", and that it is in the public interest for the material to be produced, having regard to the benefit likely to accrue to the investigation if the material is obtained. When applying for a production order the application must identify the person holding the material. The application must also describe the material in question. Additionally, there is an over-arching requirement for ARA, a police officer or a customs officer to establish that there are "reasonable grounds for suspecting" that (i) in a confiscation investigation, the subject of the investigation has benefited from criminal conduct; or (ii) in the case of a civil recovery investigation, the property is recoverable property; or (iii) in the case of a money laundering investigation, the subject of the investigation has committed a money laundering offence.

Application to obtain a production order must be made to a Crown Court judge. The investigating authority can chose whether to serve notice on the bank or financial institution holding the material, or apply to the Crown Court *ex parte*. Once an order has been made, any person affected by the order may apply to discharge the order or vary the terms on which the order has been granted. There are specific provisions in POCA conferring power on the Crown Court to require entry to premises in order to obtain access to material, and also to obtain access to material held on computer. POCA does not permit a production order to require access to material which is protected on the grounds of legal professional privilege, although the privilege disappears in cases where the material was created in furtherance of a criminal enterprise.

Search and Seizure Warrant

26–026 In the event that "it is not practicable to communicate with the person against whom the production order is made" and "that the investigation might be seriously prejudiced unless an appropriate person is able to secure immediate access to the material", under s.353 of POCA a Crown Court judge may issue a search and seizure warrant authorising an investigating authority to enter premises to seize and retain any material likely to be of substantial value (whether or not by itself) to the investigation. A search and seizure warrant cannot be granted unless the criteria for obtaining a production order have first been satisfied.

Disclosure Order

26–027 Under s.357 of POCA, ARA may obtain a disclosure order during the course of a confiscation investigation or a civil recovery investigation. The order enables the Director of ARA to give notice in writing to any person requiring him to answer questions, or to provide information specified in the notice, or to produce documents specified in the notice, where information is considered by the Director to be relevant to the investigation.

Customer Information Order

A customer information order is one of the two most radical investigation powers introduced by POCA. A customer information order is defined in s.363(5) of POCA as: **26–028**

> "an order that a financial institution covered by the application must, on being required to do so by notice in writing given by an appropriate officer, provide any such customer information as it has relating to the person specified in the application."

This order may be obtained by ARA, a police officer or a customs officer during the course of a confiscation, civil recovery or money laundering investigation on application to the Crown Court, either on notice or *ex parte*. The criteria for obtaining an order are similar to the requirements for obtaining a production order, in that there must be reasonable grounds for suspecting that the subject of a confiscation investigation has benefited from criminal conduct, or that the property in a confiscation investigation is recoverable property, or that in the case of a money laundering investigation, the subject of the investigation has committed a money laundering offence. However, unlike an application for a production order, the investigating authority does not need to identify the particular material to be produced, except to state that it is "customer information" as defined by the Act. This definition is contained in s.364(1) to (3) of the Act, and is extensive in its reach: **26–029**

> "(1) 'Customer information', in relation to a person and a financial institution, is information whether the person holds, or has held, an account or accounts at the financial institution (whether solely or jointly with another) and (if so) information as to—
>
> (a) the matters specified in subsection (2) if the person is an individual;
> (b) the matters specified in subsection (3) if the person is a company or limited liability partnership or a similar body incorporated or otherwise established outside the United Kingdom.
>
> (2) The matters referred to in subsection (1)(a) are—
>
> (a) the account number or numbers;
> (b) the person's full name;
> (c) his date of birth;
> (d) his most recent address and any previous addresses;
> (e) the date or dates on which he began to hold the account or accounts and, if he has ceased to hold the account or any of the accounts, the date or dates on which he did so;
> (f) such evidence of his identity as was obtained by the financial institution under or for the purposes of any legislation relating to money laundering;
> (g) the full name, date of birth and most recent address, and any previous addresses, of any person who holds, or has held, an account at the financial institution jointly with him;
> (h) the account number or numbers of any other account or accounts held at the financial institution to which he is a signatory and details of the person holding the other account or accounts.

(3) The matters referred to in subsection (1)(b) are—
(a) the account number or numbers;

(b) the person's full name;
(c) a description of any business which the person carries on;
(d) the country or territory in which it is incorporated or otherwise established and any number allocated to it under the Companies Act 1985 (c. 6) or the Companies (Northern Ireland) Order 1986 (S.I. 1986/1032 (N.I. 6)) or corresponding legislation of any country or territory outside the United Kingdom;
(e) any number assigned to it for the purposes of value added tax in the United Kingdom;
(f) its registered office, and any previous registered offices, under the Companies Act 1985 or the Companies (Northern Ireland) Order 1986 (S.I. 1986/1032 (N.I. 6)) or anything similar under corresponding legislation of any country or territory outside the United Kingdom;
(g) its registered office, and any previous registered offices, under the Limited Liability Partnerships Act 2000 (c. 12) or anything similar under corresponding legislation of any country or territory outside Great Britain;
(h) the date or dates on which it began to hold the account or accounts and, if it has ceased to hold the account or any of the accounts, the date or dates on which it did so;
(i) such evidence of its identity as was obtained by the financial institution under or for the purposes of any legislation relating to money laundering;
(j) the full name, date of birth and most recent address and any previous addresses of any person who is a signatory to the account or any of the accounts".

26–030 The requirement in the legislation to produce "such evidence of . . . identity as was obtained by the financial institution under or for the purposes of any legislation relating to money laundering" emphasises the clear obligation on banks and financial institutions to identify the beneficial owner of funds, or, in the language of the European Directive on Money Laundering, "the real identity of the persons on whose behalf those customers are acting". See Council Directive 91/308 [1991] O.J. L166/77, Art.3(5).

A customer information order may be made against all financial institutions, or a particular description of financial institution, or a particular financial institution, depending upon the requirements of the investigation in question. A "financial institution" is defined as meaning "a person carrying on a business in the regulated sector". A person carries on business within the regulated sector if the business engages in any of the activities listed in Sch.9 Pt 1 of POCA. This includes all banks, building societies and money transmitters, as well as any business activity involving dealing in investments as a principal or agent. The scope of the regulated sector expanded dramatically when the Amending European Directive on Money Laundering was implemented. The Amending Directive required member States to re-define the regulated sector to embrace professions and businesses that are vulnerable to money laundering.

Account Monitoring Order

Finally, under s.370 of POCA persons within the regulated sector may be served with an account monitoring order which requires provision of "account information of the description specified in the order". The definition of "account information" is wider than the definition of "customer information" and is expressed in the following terms: **26–031**

> "Account information is information relating to an account or accounts held at the financial institution specified in the application by the person so specified (whether solely or jointly with another)".

This definition embraces all banking records relating to a customer, such as notes of meetings, correspondence and records of instructions.

Once again, an order may be obtained by ARA, a police officer or customs officer during the course of a confiscation, civil recovery or money laundering investigation on application to the Crown Court, either on notice or *ex parte*. The criteria for obtaining an order are similar to the requirements for obtaining a customer information order, in that there must be reasonable grounds for suspecting that the subject of a confiscation investigation has benefited from criminal conduct, or that property in a confiscation investigation is recoverable property, or in the case of a money laundering investigation, that the subject of the investigation has committed a money laundering offence. The order must state the manner in which the account information is to be provided, and the period during which the order runs, which must not exceed 90 days. There is nothing in POCA to prevent an investigating authority from seeking a new order at the expiry of 90 days. **26–032**

Evidence Overseas

Financial institutions with operations abroad may be required to provide access to information located outside the UK in cases where ARA can satisfy a Crown Court judge under s.376 of ARA that there is evidence abroad which discloses that a person has benefited from his criminal conduct. **26–033**

Non-compliance with Order

Non-compliance with the new investigation powers is punishable by criminal sanction. Production orders will have effect "as if they were orders of the court", which means that disobedience is punishable as a contempt of court. Failure to comply with a disclosure order without reasonable excuse will constitute a summary offence punishable by a maximum period of six months imprisonment, and where a person knowingly or recklessly makes a false or misleading statement in response to a requirement imposed on him under a disclosure order he will commit a criminal offence punishable by a maximum of two years imprisonment. Similarly, if a financial institution without reasonable excuse fails to comply with a **26–034** customer information order, the institution is subject to a fine of up to £5,000, and if it knowingly or recklessly makes a false or misleading statement in response to a customer information order, the potential fine is unlimited. As with a production order, an account monitoring order will have the same effect as an order of the Crown Court, and breach will be punishable as a contempt of Court.

Prejudicing an Investigation

26–035 Under s.342 of POCA, a person commits an offence if—

> "(a) he makes a disclosure which is likely to prejudice the investigation, or
> (b) he falsifies, conceals, destroys or otherwise disposes of, or causes or permits the falsification, concealment, destruction or disposal of, documents which are relevant to the investigation".

Additionally, in order to be guilty of an offence, a person must know or suspect that an investigation is being conducted, or is about to be conducted. It will be a defence for a person to show that he did not know or suspect that the disclosure is likely to prejudice the investigation. Additional statutory defences have been included to cover the situation when the existence of an investigation is disclosed to the authorities when a suspicious activity money laundering report is made, and where a professional legal advisor makes a disclosure to a client in connection with the giving of legal advice or representing a person in legal proceedings or contemplated legal proceedings, provided that the disclosure was not made with the intention of furthering a criminal purpose.

Duty of Confidence

26–036 S.348 of POCA expressly overrides any duty of confidence owed by person in the regulated sector to a customer, so that an order will have effect "in spite of any restriction on the disclosure of information".

Chapter 27

Money Laundering

Introduction

At its most basic, money laundering is the concealment of the criminal origins of money by its use in legitimate financial activity. There are usually three stages to money laundering—the placement stage, the layering or agitation stage, and the integration or re-integration stage. Money laundering is an international activity, and increasingly so, with the increase in cross-border financial crime. It is estimated that approximately £200 billion non-drugs related money is laundered each year. An element of money laundering is likely to be found in every serious investor fraud. **27–001**

In an effort to meet this problem there have been a number of initiatives aimed at co-ordinating an international response. These have included initiatives by the United Nations in the form of the United Nations Convention Against Illicit Traffic in Narcotics Drugs and Psychotropic Substances (the Vienna Convention) and the setting up of the Financial Action Task Force under the auspices of the G7 countries. The European Community has responded by issuing Directive 91/308 ([1991] O.J. L166/77) which followed the Council of Europe Convention on Laundering, Tracing, Seizure and Confiscation of Proceeds of Crime (1990). In November 2001 this Directive was supplemented by an Amending Directive 2001/97 ([2001] O.J. L344/76). The provisions of the European Directives have been implemented in the UK by Part 7 of the Proceeds of Crime Act 2002 ("POCA") and the Money Laundering Regulations 2003. The mechanism of regulation is through the creation of a series of criminal offences.

The Principal Money Laundering Offences

The first principal money laundering offence ("concealing etc") under s.327 of POCA may be committed in five different ways, by concealing, disguising, converting, transferring or removing criminal property from the jurisdiction. A person is exposed to liability under this section if he or she handles investor monies in circumstances where the monies are derived from the proceeds of crime. **27–002**

The second principal money laundering offence ("arrangements") raises concerns for solicitors not where they handle client monies, but where they give advice or assist clients in circumstances where the monies funding the transaction derive from the proceeds of crime. S.328 prohibits a person **27–003** from "being concerned in an arrangement which he knows or suspects facilitates (by whatever means) the acquisition, retention, use or control of criminal property by or behalf of another person".

27–004 The third principal money laundering offence ("acquisition, use and possession") set out in s.329 punishes a person who "(a) acquires criminal property; (b) uses criminal property; (c) has possession of criminal property. However, there is a special defence where a person acquires, uses or possesses criminal property for adequate consideration. Although not expressly spelt out, conventional wisdom holds that this defence covers the situation where a person receives criminal property on account of fees, provided the fees are reasonable and related to work which has been done or is about to be done.

Criminal Property

27–005 "Criminal property" is the common denominator between the three principal money laundering offences. Under s.340(3), property is "criminal property" if: "(a) it constitutes a person's benefit from criminal conduct or it represents such a benefit (in whole or part and whether directly or indirectly), and (b) the alleged offender knows or suspects that it constitutes or represents such a benefit". This definition must be read in conjunction with the definition of "criminal conduct" under s.340(2), which is defined as conduct which "(a) constitutes an offence in any part of the United Kingdom, or (b) would constitute an offence in any part of the United Kingdom if it occurred there".

Suspicion

No Suspicion

27–006 At first blush, a person might be forgiven for thinking that many of the problems can be avoided by alighting on s.340(3)(b) which requires an alleged offender to "know or suspect" that the funds constitutes or represents the proceeds of crime". The difficulty with this line of defence is the low threshold attributed to the notion of "suspicion". Facts giving rise to suspicion may be remarkably thin. The Shorter Oxford English Dictionary defines the act of suspecting as:

> "(1) the feeling or state of mind of one who suspects; imagination or conjecture of the existence of something evil or wrong without proof, apprehension of guilt or fault on slight grounds or without clear evidence . . . (2) Imagination of something (not necessarily evil) as possible or likely; a slight belief or idea of something, or that something is the case; a surmise; a faint notion; an inkling . . . (3) Surmise of something future; expectation . . . (4) A slight or faint trace, very small amount, hint, suggestion (of something) . . ."

27–007 The Joint Money Laundering Steering Group ("JMLSG"), established under the auspices of the British Bankers Association, offers the following guidance on the meaning of "suspicion":

> "Suspicion is personal and subjective and falls far short of proof based on firm evidence. Suspicion has been defined by the courts as being beyond mere speculation and based on some foundation *i.e.*:
>
> > 'A degree of satisfaction and not necessarily amounting to belief but at least extending beyond speculation as to whether an event has occurred or not'".

These definitions place the threshold for suspicion rather low, since they contemplate the forming of suspicion where a person has no more than a surmise, faint notion or inkling that a person has been engaged in criminal conduct or benefited from the proceeds of criminal conduct. Support can be found for this low threshold in the Privy Council case of *Hussein v Chong Fook Kam* [1970] A.C. 942 where it was held that reasonable suspicion could not be equated with *prima facie* proof of guilt when considering the circumstances in which a power of arrest could be exercised. During the course of giving the Privy Council's opinion, Lord Devlin said at p.948B that: **27–008**

> "Suspicion in its ordinary meaning is a state of conjecture or surmise where proof is lacking. 'I suspect but I cannot prove'. Suspicion arises at or near the starting-point of an investigation of which the obtaining of prima facie proof is the end".

In *Holtham v Commissioner of Police*, *The Times*, November 28, 1987, where there was an action for false imprisonment, the Court of Appeal established a very low threshold for reasonable suspicion. The trial Judge had ruled that police officers could make a lawful arrest only where they had reasonable grounds for suspicion and in his view this meant "a good deal more than suspicion". The Court of Appeal disagreed with this statement, holding that "reasonable grounds for suspicion" meant nothing more than "suspicion": **27–009**

> "Suspicion . . . might or might not be based on reasonable grounds but it remained suspicion and nothing more. By applying a test of something which was not suspicion but something a good deal more than suspicion, the judge had erred and that error was fundamental to his judgment"—*per* Sir John Donaldson, M.R.

Authorised Disclosure and Appropriate Consent

In circumstances where a person has concerns that monies funding a transaction might be "criminal property", he or she must make an "authorised disclosure" to the National Criminal Intelligence Service ("NCIS"). Making an "authorised disclosure" provides a person with a defence to a money laundering charge, provided that where the disclosure is made before the act mentioned in the offence is one, "appropriate consent" has been obtained. **27–010**

"Appropriate consent" is deemed to have been given under where NCIS has not refused consent to the doing of the act within a period of seven working days starting with the first working day after the person makes the **27–011** disclosure. If NCIS refuses consent to proceed within seven working days, "appropriate consent" is deemed to have been given when the moratorium period expires. The moratorium period lasts for 31 days, starting with the day on which the person receives notice that consent to the doing of the act is refused.

A person will rarely be able to justify not making "authorised disclosure" until after the act has been done. Under s.338 a disclosure will not be authorised unless there is good reason for the failure to make disclosure before the act is done, and the disclosure is made as soon as it is practicable for the solicitor to make it. It is difficult to envisage many circumstances in which a person will be able to satisfy these criteria, particularly in cases where they have performed client identification and due diligence enquiries.

Making a Disclosure Report

27–012 Persons working in investment services must become familiar with the form for making an authorised disclosure to NCIS. The NCIS disclosure form is to be found on the world wide web at *ww.ncis.co.uk/disclosure.asp*.

Failing to Disclose: Regulated Sector

27–013 Much publicity has been generated by the extension of the "failing to disclose" offence, since s.330 of POCA alters the law to criminalise a failure not only where a person knows or suspects money laundering activity, but also where there are reasonable grounds for such knowledge or suspicion. The offence applies where the information comes to a person in the course of a business in the regulated sector, and it imposes a discrete obligation to make a suspicious activity report entirely independently of any need to make a disclosure under any of the three principal money laundering offences discussed above. The Government made clear when introducing this extension that "the introduction of a negligence test was necessary as a deterrent against those in the professions who fail to act competently and responsibly where information before them ought to make them suspect money laundering in keeping with the relevant guidance".

The definition of the regulated sector has traditionally focused on the provision of financial services, but the definition was widened by the Money Laundering Regulations 2003 to implement the Amending EC Directive which requires "vulnerable professions and businesses" to be brought within the regulated sector. These vulnerable businesses include the vast majority of solicitors, all accountants and tax advisors, estate agents, casinos and any trader in high value items where more than €15,000 is accepted in cash.

Reasonable Grounds for Suspicion

27–014 Where a person or business falls within the regulated sector, the consequences are far-reaching. Instead of determining the need to make a disclosure by applying a subjective test (*i.e.* do I suspect that criminal property is involved?), an objective test is employed (*i.e.* are there reasonable grounds to suspect that criminal property is involved?)

In order not to fall foul of the objective test, the JMLSG has indicated that it is likely that staff within regulated firms will need to be able to demonstrate that they took all reasonable steps in the particular circumstances to know the client and the rationale for the transaction or the instruction. This is the origin of the "due diligence" requirement relating to knowledge of the client and the source of funds.

An illustration of the type of the situations that might give rise to reasonable grounds for suspicion in certain circumstances are: **27–015**

- transactions which have no apparent purpose and which make no obvious economic sense;
- where the transaction being requested by the client without reasonable explanation, is out of the ordinary range of services normally requested or is outside the experience of the firm in relation to the particular customer;
- where, without reasonable explanation, the size or pattern of transactions is out of line with any pattern that has previously emerged;
- where the customer refuses to provide the information requested without reasonable explanation;
- where a customer who has entered into a business relationship uses the relationship for a single transaction or for only a very short period of time;
- the extensive use of offshore accounts, companies or structures in circumstances where the customer's needs do not support such economic requirements;
- unnecessary routing of funds through third party accounts;
- unusual investment transactions without apparently discernable profitable motive.

Criminal lawyers are familiar with the notion of "reasonable suspicion" since police powers of search and arrest can be exercised only when this threshold has been crossed (s.1(3), Police and Criminal Evidence Act 1984). Annex A of the Code of Practice on Stop and Search provides that: **27–016**

> "Whether a reasonable ground for suspicion exists will depend on the circumstances in each case, but there must be some objective basis for it".

Assessment of "reasonable grounds" is plainly an objective standard. A person's honest belief is not relevant when considering whether he had reasonable cause for his belief (*Castorina v Chief Constable of Surrey* [1979] R.T.R. 454). The test is simply whether in the light of the information available there are objective grounds for suspecting that the transaction in question involves the proceeds of criminal conduct. A definition of **27–017** "reasonable suspicion" based on objective criteria has been put forward by the European Court of Human Rights in *K-F v Germany* [1997] 26 E.H.R.R. 390 at p. 410 in the following terms:

> "Having a 'reasonable suspicion' pre-supposes the existence of facts or information which would satisfy an objective observer that the person concerned might have committed the offence. However, facts which raise a suspicion need not be of the same level as those necessary to justify a conviction or even the bringing of a charge, which comes at a later stage of the process of criminal investigation"

Tipping Off

27–018 Once a person knows or suspects that a disclosure report has been made, nobody else can be told about it. Indeed, to "tip-off" another person that a disclosure report has been made is a criminal offence under s.333 of POCA and is punishable by a maximum of five years imprisonment. The prosecution would have to prove that the disclosure was likely to prejudice an investigation.

Breach of Confidence

27–019 Under s.337, where there is disclosure of any suspicion or belief that funds represent the proceeds of criminal conduct, the disclosure shall not be treated as a breach of any restriction upon the disclosure of information imposed by statute or otherwise. This section is necessary because, having imposed a positive duty on professional advisors to report suspicious transactions, disclosure might be said to amount to a breach of the duty of confidentiality owed to another.

The protection afforded by s.337 stops short of giving protection against liability of any kind, as was originally suggested in the EC Directive. This might leave the way open for an aggrieved person to bring an action in defamation, although a defence of qualified privilege would almost certainly be raised.

Client Identification Procedures and Anti-money Laundering Training

27–020 Where a person or business falls within the regulated sector, obligations under the Money Laundering Regulations will also have to be satisfied. These include the maintenance of client identification procedures, record keeping procedures and the organisation of staff training.

The Money Laundering Regulations require firms within the regulated sector to provide training for their staff so that they understand the way in which the anti-money laundering law applies to them. In addition, firms must provide training which makes staff aware not only of the firm's anti-money laundering procedures but also how to recognise and handle transactions carried out by any person who is, or appears to be, engaged, in money laundering.

Money Laundering in Practice

It was initially thought that there would be about 250 reports of suspicious transactions a year; however, in 1994, 15,000 suspicious transactions were reported to the National Criminal Intelligence Service Economic Crimes Unit. About one in five was found to have some criminal connection. There is a widespread belief in the financial community that although they are diligently reporting money-laundering activities, they are seeing very little consequential action from the law enforcement agencies. No doubt in response to this perception, a new police fraud unit was established by the City of London police in May 1996, called the Financial Investigation Unit (FIU). The Unit has warned the legal profession that they may unwittingly be representing clients with connections to organised crime. **27–021**

Certainly awareness of the money laundering provisions has increased in recent times. Today, the number of suspicious activity disclosures is running at 60,000 a year, and this is expected to increase to 100,000 in 2004. Investors should remember that requirements to produce identity and information supporting the legitimate source of funds is unexceptional in today's market place. On the June 24, 2003 the government launched a nationwide campaign setting out how the public can help to tackle money laundering and the financing of terrorism. The campaign saw the production of information leaflets informing investors of the reasons why they need to prove their identity to financial services companies. Effective identification of customers using bank accounts and other financial services was said to make it harder for terrorists and other criminals to hide and move "dirty cash".

Whether this increased level of customer identification and due diligence work makes any different in the fight against crime remains to be seen. Although it is certainly true that money laundering rarely takes place though consumer accounts in the High Street, it is an incontrovertible fact that much illicit money has been passed through the United Kingdom, utilizing its investment services. **27–022**

Rarely, problems may occur in practice where a suspicious activity disclosure has been made and the holder of the monies is unsure as to how they should best be handled. For example, if there is a strong suspicion that the monies have been stolen from a third party, should the holder of the funds follow his customer's instructions, or should he seek directions from the Court as to whether the monies should be remitted to the third party in accordance with the principles of constructive trust. For a consideration of the principles to be applied in this situation, see the decisions of the Court of Appeal in *C v S* and others [1999] 1 W.L.R. 1551 and *Bank of Scotland v A Limited* [2001] 3 All E.R. 58, and the decision of the Queens Bench Division in *Amalgamated Metal Trading v City of London Police Financial Investigation Unit* [2003] EWHC 703 (Comm).

Chapter 28

Investor Protection and the Criminal Process

Although consideration of criminal procedure is beyond the scope of this book, there are two particular areas which are worthy of interest in the investor context. The first relates to the special powers given by Parliament to the Serious Fraud Office to obtain information by interviewing witnesses when a serious fraud has been committed. In such cases aggrieved investors will be concerned to know whether they can obtain access to the interview transcripts to use as evidence in support of civil proceedings. **28–001**

The second area relates to the circumstances where an investor can seek relief against a prosecution authority if it decides not to bring criminal proceedings, notwithstanding the perpetration of a serious fraud. For example, this situation occurred in the case of Nick Leeson and Barings Bank, when the Serious Fraud Office declined to bring criminal proceedings on the grounds that it was more appropriate for Mr Leeson to stand his trial in Singapore. Proceedings brought by aggrieved investors for judicial review against the Serious Fraud Office were abandoned before a Court ruling was obtained. In other cases an aggrieved investor may wish to bring proceedings for judicial review against a regulatory body which has decided not to bring disciplinary proceedings or institute an inquiry in the circumstances of his case.

The Serious Fraud Office

Creation

The investigation of serious fraud creates greater problems for prosecuting authorities than the investigation of more straight-forward crimes. In 1976 the Roskill Committee was set up to consider the investigation and prosecution of fraud, and it recommended the establishment of a unified organisation responsible for all the functions of detection, investigation and prosecution of serious fraud cases. (*Fraud Trials Committee Report*, HMSO, 1986). The Committee also recognised that a fraud investigatory body requires more extensive powers of investigation, if it is to be successful, than other investigatory bodies: **28–002**

> "An investigator naturally needs to be able to question witnesses, including suspects. Of even greater importance in fraud cases, an investigator needs

access to the documents which were the vehicle of the fraudulent scheme and which will enable him to understand what has happened and piece together the case for the prosecution. The skilled fraudster is likely to do all he can to prevent the investigator from finding and using the documentation in the case; and a further problem for the investigator may be that some documents are in the hands of banks and other third parties in this country orf abroad." — Fraud Trials Committee Report, para.2.32.

Putting into effect some, but not all of the recommendations made by the Roskill Committee, Parliament established the Serious Fraud Office—by s.1(1) of the Criminal Justice Act 1987--and gave to the Director of the Serious Fraud Office special powers of investigation under s.2 of the Act.

Compulsory Interview and Production of Documents

28–003 S.2(2) of the Criminal Justice Act 1987 confers power on the Director of the Serious Fraud Office to compel witnesses, including an accused, to attend for interview and to answer questions. S.2(3) extends this power to include the production of documents. The draconian nature of these powers is illustrated by the case of *Smith v Director of the Serious Fraud Office* [1992] 3 All E.R. 456 where the House of Lords held that the enactment of ss.2(2) and 2(3) of the Criminal Justice Act 1987 have overridden the common law privilege against self incrimination. The defendant was chairman and managing director of a company which was reported to the Bank of England as being in financial difficulties in 1991. The case was taken on by the Serious Fraud Office. The Director of the Serious Fraud Office issued a notice under s.2(2) of the Criminal Justice Act 1987 requiring the defendant to attend for interview after he had been charged with criminal offences for which he was being investigated. The House of Lords confirmed that the clear words of the 1987 Act showed that Parliament had intended to establish an inquisitorial regime in relation to serious or complex fraud in which the Director of the Serious Fraud Office could obtain by compulsion answers to questions that might be self-incriminating. There was no implied qualification that a person was entitled to invoke the privilege after he had been charged. The privilege against self-incrimination is discussed fully in Ch.34.

The powers of compulsion conferred on the Director of the Serious Fraud Office by s.2(2) and (3) of the Criminal Justice Act 1987 are supported by a number of criminal offences which have been created to deal with non-compliance.

28–004 It is a summary offence to fail to comply without reasonable excuse with a requirement under s.2. This is punishable by imprisonment of up to six months and/or to a fine not exceeding level five (s.2(13)). What may amount to a reasonable excuse for the purposes of a defence to a charge brought under s.2(13) will depend on the circumstances of the case. In the case of *R. v Director of Serious Fraud Office Ex p. Johnson* [1993] C.O.D. 58 the Court held that being the spouse of a person facing criminal charges did not amount to a reasonable excuse which allowed that person to refuse to answer questions posed under the s.2 powers. This contrasts with the position under s.80 of the Police and Criminal Evidence Act 1984 which prevents spouses from being compelled to give evidence against each other. Nor is it a reasonable excuse to refuse to answer questions posed under s.2 because the person being questioned has already been charged with criminal offences—see *Smith v Director of the Serious Fraud Office* [1992] 3 All E.R. 456.

A person who purports to comply with a requirement under s.2, but who **28–005** knowingly or recklessly makes a statement which is false or misleading in a material particular commits an offence which is punishable on conviction in the Crown Court by imprisonment up to a maximum of two years and/or a fine, and if convicted in the Magistrates' Court to imprisonment of up to six months and/or a fine not exceeding the statutory maximum (ss.2(14) and (15)).

Where a person deliberately falsifies, conceals, destroys or otherwise disposes of any documents or causes the same to be done to any document when he knows or suspects that an investigation by the police or Serious Fraud Office is being or is likely to be carried out he commits an offence which is punishable on conviction in the Crown Court by imprisonment up to a maximum of seven years and/or a fine, and if convicted in the Magistrates' Court to imprisonment of up to 6 months and/or a fine not exceeding the statutory maximum (ss.2(16) and (17)).

A person may refuse to produce information requested by the Director of the Serious Fraud Office under his s.2 powers where to do so would breach legal professional privilege or where such disclosure would undermine an obligation of confidence by virtue of carrying on banking business (s.2(9) and (10)).

Use of Information Obtained Under s.2 in Civil Proceedings

S.2(8) of the Criminal Justice Act 1987 restricts the way in which **28–006** information obtained under s.2 powers may be used. Information obtained under s.2(2) or 2(3) may only be used in a criminal trial against a defendant if in giving evidence in the course of a trial, the defendant gives evidence which is inconsistent with the information given in response to a s.2 investigation or where the defendant is being prosecuted for an offence under s.2(14) of the Criminal Justice Act 1987, as to which, see below.

The provision in s.3 of the Act is of more interest to an aggrieved investor. This section concerns the ability of the Director of the Serious Fraud Office to disclose information obtained in the exercise of s.2 powers to other parties. Under this section, information may only be disclosed to other government departments, or to a competent authority (as defined by s.3(6)), or for the purposes of a prosecution and for the purposes of assisting any public or other authority designated by the Secretary of State. The list of competent authorities includes several classes of persons appointed to carry out investigative functions under statutes, such as inspectors appointed under the Companies Act 1985, the Building Societies Act 1986 and the Financial Services Act 1986. The list includes any body having supervisory, regulatory or disciplinary functions in relation to any profession or area of commercial activity.

28–007 The scope of s.3 was considered in *Morris v Director of Serious Fraud Office* [1993] 1 All E.R. 788 which arose in the aftermath of the BCCI collapse. The Serious Fraud Office had obtained documents concerning BCCI under its s.2(3) powers which it had exercised against Price Waterhouse (BCCI's auditors) and other third parties. The liquidators of BCCI applied for disclosure of these documents to use in the course of an investigation under s.236 of the Insolvency Act 1986. Accordingly, the Court had to consider whether the Serious Fraud Office could make disclosure of documents which had come into its possession pursuant to the exercise of its s.2 powers. The Court held that voluntary disclosure could not be made by the Serious Fraud Office since its powers were constrained by the language of s.3. Liquidators and administrators were not included in the list of bodies to whom disclosure could be made; accordingly, no voluntary disclosure could be made. Nicholls V.C. said that:

> "The powers conferred by section 2 are exercisable only for the purposes of an investigation under section 1. When information is obtained in exercise of those powers the SFO may use the information for those purposes as may be authorised by statute, but not otherwise. Compulsory powers are not to be regarded as encroaching more upon the rights of individuals than is fairly and reasonably necessary to achieve the purpose for which the powers were created. That is to be taken as the intention as Parliament, unless the contrary is clearly apparent" (at p.795b).

28–008 The Court proceeded to consider whether the Director of the Serious Fraud Office could be ordered to disclose the transcripts under s.236(2) of the Insolvency Act 1986. The Court came to the conclusion that there was no reason why disclosure should not be ordered, provided that a Court took into account any prejudice that a third party might suffer if disclosure was ordered. Nicholls V.C. held that persons from whom documents were seized or the true owners of the documents were in general entitled to be given an opportunity to present to the Court any objections they might have to the disclosure of the documents.

It is interesting to consider whether, by analogy with this decision, business documents evidencing fraud could be obtained from the Serious Fraud Office if a subpoena were issued by an aggrieved investor in support of an action for damages. Regulatory bodies who fall within the definition of "competent authorities" could, subject to legal professional privilege and public interest immunity concerns, obtain the documents from the Serious Fraud Office by way of subpoena, but what about the position of the aggrieved investor?

28–009 The starting point, perhaps, is a dictum of Nicholls V.C. in *Morris v Director of Serious Fraud Office* (at p.797h) when he said that:

> "There is no sound distinction between production of documents in answer to a subpoena and production of documents pursuant to an order made under section 236".

28–010 Whether this passage is sufficient to open the door to the obtaining of such information by an aggrieved investor remains to be seen. Support for a plaintiff investor's argument can be derived from the decision of the Court of Appeal in *Marcel v Commissioner of Police* [1992] 1 All E.R. 72 where a defendant in a civil action issued a subpoena against the police to produce documents against the police officer in charge of investigations for use in the civil proceedings. The police had no objection to production. The Court of Appeal held that a police officer, like anybody else, is amenable to produce on subpoena any documents in his possession, subject to the true owner having the right to challenge the subpoena, or the production of documents, on any of the grounds on which a subpoena can be challenged. Such grounds would include, of course, legal professional privilege and public interest immunity. Different considerations might apply where an application for production of documents against the Director of the Serious Fraud Office where the documents were made expressly for the purpose of a criminal prosecution. Witness statements, for example, would fall into this category—*per* Nicholls V.C. in *Morris v Director of the Serious Fraud Office* at p.798j and *Re Barlow Clowes Gilt Managers Ltd* [1991] 4 All E.R. 385.

The decision in *Marcel v Commissioner of Police for the Metropolis* was **28–011** applied by Morritt J. in *Hoechst UK Ltd v Chemiculture Ltd* [1993] F.S.R. 270 where the plaintiffs, who had brought an action for passing off and infringement of trade mark, obtained information from the Health and Safety Executive which had been obtained by the Executive under powers conferred by the Food and Environment Protection Act 1985. The defendant sought to set aside an Anton Pillar order which the plaintiffs had obtained in reliance on the information which the Health and Safety Executive had supplied. Morritt J. dismissed the defendants' application, holding that there was no impropriety in disclosure to a person for whom, given the purposes of the statute, the information was of mutual interest and concern. The decision in *Marcel v Commissioner of Police for the Metropolis* was also considered in *Bank of Crete SA v Koskotas* [1992] 1 W.L.R. 919 where Millett J. had to consider the position where material had been disclosed in civil proceedings on the basis of an undertaking which confined the use of the material in support of the plaintiff's claim for misappropriation of funds. The order was varied to permit the plaintiff to disclose the material to an interested foreign party.

Once documents and interview transcripts have been passed from the **28–012** Director of the Serious Fraud Office to another party, it will be much easier for an aggrieved litigant to obtain the documents from that other party. In *Wallace Smith Trust Co Ltd v Deloitte* (unreported) July 10, 1996, the liquidator of a bank brought proceedings in professional negligence against the bank's auditors. The auditors had in their possession transcripts of interviews held with two of the auditor's employees which had been conducted by the Serious Fraud Office in exercise of its s.2 powers. The Court of Appeal held that discovery of the transcripts should be ordered only where the plaintiff can show that production is necessary to dispose fairly of the matter or to save costs. The auditors tried to resist discovery on the basis that the documents were protected by public interest immunity but this was rejected by the Court. The documents were not protected in the hands of the auditors, since they could not be characterised as documents which by their nature would be protected regardless of whose possession they were in.

Most interestingly, on the question of whether the documents would have been protected in the hands of the Serious Fraud Office at the suit of the plaintiff, different views were expressed by members of the Court on this point.

Reviewing a Decision not to Prosecute

Introduction

28–013 The second procedural area to be discussed in this chapter is whether an aggrieved investor can seek to judicially review a decision by the prosecuting authorities not to commence a prosecution in a case of investor fraud.

The decision whether or not to prosecute an individual is a serious step with far-reaching implications for all involved including the accused, the victims and the witnesses. In all cases the prosecuting authority must reach its decision of whether or not to prosecute by applying its prosecution policy to the circumstances of each individual case, in the light of its assessment about the sufficiency of evidence and the competency of criminal proceedings. The Crown Prosecution Service, for example, is bound to approach a decision about the commencement of criminal proceedings within the framework of principles set out in the Code for Crown Prosecutors which was issued in June 1994.

Jurisdiction

28–014 The jurisdiction of the court to judicially review a decision not to prosecute was established by the case of *R. v Metropolitan Police Commissioner Ex p. Blackburn* (No.1) [1968] 1 All E.R. 763. In that case the court drew a distinction between a review of the terms of policy which underlay a decision whether or not to commence criminal proceedings and the review of the way in which the terms of the policy had been applied in a particular case. The court held that there was no jurisdiction to review the terms of a policy but that its application to the facts could be judicially reviewed by the court in a particular case. This distinction between terms of policy and the application of policy has been confirmed in later cases, notably in *R. v Chief Constable of the Kent Constabulary, Ex p. L (a minor)* [1993] 1 All E.R. 756, where the court held that decisions whether or not to pursue a prosecution were reviewable only in as far as the applicant for judicial review could allege that the policy had been wrongly applied in the circumstances of the particular case.

28–015 Stuart-Smith L.J. conducted a review of the contemporary state of the law in this area in *R. v Inland Revenue Commissioners Ex p. Mead and Cook* [1993] 1 All E.R. 772 where two taxpayers had been charged with tax evasion together with their accountant. The accountant was charged with a number of additional offences which named other taxpayers who had not been charged by the Inland Revenue even though it was clear that they had dishonestly benefited from the tax evasion scheme set up by the accountant. Instead, these taxpayers had been made the subject of civil penalties. The two taxpayers who had been charged with criminal offences sought to challenge the decision of the Inland Revenue to bring criminal proceedings against them. The issue for the Court to decide was whether the decision by a prosecuting authority to prosecute an adult was judicially reviewable. In rejecting the application for judicial review, Stuart-Smith L.J. said (at p.782d) that the circumstances in which such jurisdiction would be invoked would be rare in the extreme:

> "Absurd examples, such as a policy only to prosecute black men or the political opponents of an outgoing government, which are virtually unthinkable, do however point to the theoretical existence of the jurisdiction to review. Fraud and corruption are perhaps other examples where the jurisdiction could be invoked".

These principles were applied by the Court in *R. v DPP Ex p. C* [1995] 1 Cr. App. R. 136 and *R. v CPS Ex p. Waterworth* (unreported) December 1, 1995, where it was said by the Divisional Court that it was clear from the authorities that the Court could only be persuaded to act in this case if it could be demonstrated that the CPS had arrived at a decision not to prosecute because they had failed to act in accordance with their own settled policy or because their decision was manifestly unreasonable. **28–016**

Reviewing a Decision not to Commence Disciplinary Proceedings or an Investigation

In addition to prosecutions brought in the criminal courts, investor protection is also achieved by the implementation of disciplinary actions and/or investigations by the regulatory authorities. The decision not to prosecute before a regulatory tribunal is subject to judicial review—see *R. v General Council of the Bar, Ex p. Percival* [1990] 3 All E.R. 137—and the same principles apply with regard to the way this jurisdiction will be exercised. **28–017**

Part 6

Investor Protection in Civil Law

Chapter 29

Investor Protection in Company Law

Introduction

In this Chapter, consideration is given to the provisions of company law which are relevant to the protection of investors in the corporate context. Necessarily, in the context of company law, it is the interests of the shareholder investor which form the focus of attention. **29–001**

The present Chapter is split into six sections. The first focuses on directors' duties. The second discusses the issue of corporate governance. The next three sections deal respectively with minority shareholders' actions, relief for unfair prejudice and winding up on the just and equitable ground. The final section examines the powers of the Department of Trade and Industry (DTI) to investigate companies.

In addition to the provisions of company law which form the subject matter of this Chapter, the Companies Acts impose a number of statutory obligations and restrictions on directors, which are designed to promote fair dealing. These include restrictions as to directors' dealings in shares and options, restrictions on directors' loans, and the disclosure of any interest in contracts, proposed contracts, transactions or arrangements with a company of which he is a director. These are discussed in Ch.23.

Directors' Duties

Every company must have at least one director, and public companies must have at least two directors (Companies Act 1985, s.28). The Companies Act 1985 does not define the term "director", though it does state (in s.741(1)) that, in the Act, the term includes "any person occupying the position of director, by whatever name called", so covering those who act as directors even though not formally appointed as such (*i.e. de facto* as opposed to *de jure* directors). The Act also makes provision for "shadow directors", who are persons in accordance with whose directions the directors of the company are accustomed to act (s.741(2)). The latter term is also used in the Company Directors Disqualification Act 1986. The Court of Appeal recently gave guidance on the circumstances in which a person will be treated as a shadow director, and hence amenable to a disqualification order under the 1986 Act, in *Secretary of State for Trade and Industry v Deverell* [2001] Ch. 340. **29–002**

29–003 Directors manage the company in accordance with the articles of association. Although the company is a separate corporate entity, its directors are often said to be its directing mind and will. The duties of directors in fulfilling the management of the company are therefore of critical importance in practice. Directors' duties may be either (a) fiduciary duties, which are often said to be duties of good faith, integrity and honesty, and which are strictly interpreted by the courts; and (b) duties of skill, care and prudence in conducting the business of the company.

Directors must exercise their duties in such a way as to ensure that the interests of both the present and future shareholders of the company are maintained. It is a fundamental duty of directors not to place themselves in a position where their personal interests conflict with those of the company. The law imposes restrictions on the way in which directors may act which are designed to ensure fair dealing and to guard against directors taking financial advantage of their positions.

29–004 There has been considerable recent discussion about whether the courts should take into account regulatory rules when determining the existence or extent of a fiduciary duty. When regulatory rules are considered to be adequate, a court can be expected to decide that the fiduciary duty has been modified and that compliance with the rules is sufficient to meet the fiduciary obligations. The situation, however, might be different where the court considers that the regulatory rule is too stringent or lax; in this situation there will be a mismatch between the regulatory rules on the one hand and the scope of fiduciary duties on the other. The Law Commission explored these issues in its Consultation Paper on *Fiduciary Duties and Regulatory Rules* (1992), No. 236.

Directors' Fiduciary Duties

29–005 The fiduciary duties owed by directors are usually described as duties of good faith, integrity and honesty. The duties are owed to the company alone. A director is under a duty to promote the interests of the company and must not let his personal interests intrude. A director does not owe a fiduciary duty to any subsidiary or associated company nor is such a duty owed to the individual shareholders of the company. That no fiduciary duty was owed to individual shareholders was established by the case of *Percival v Wright* [1902] 2 Ch. 421, in which directors of a company had purchased shares from a number of shareholders, following an approach from the shareholders. At the time of the purchase the directors, but not the shareholders, were in possession of information which significantly affected the value of the shares. The court held that the directors were not under any duty to disclose such information to the shareholders and that in the circumstances of the case there had been no "unfair dealing". Had the directors approached the shareholders seeking to purchase shares rather than the shareholders approaching the directors seeking to sell, the decision might have been rather different.

Duty to act in Good Faith

The primary duty of a director is to act in good faith (bona fide) in the interests of the company. It was clearly established by the leading case of *Re Smith & Fawcett Ltd* [1942] Ch. 304, that the test of what is bona fide in the interest of the company is subjective and not objective, in the sense that directors are required to exercise their powers "bona fide in what they consider—not what a court may consider—is in the interests of the company" (*per* Lord Greene M.R. at p.306). **29–006**

The Interests of the Company

The interests of the company are usually described as the interests of the company as a commercial entity. Strictly, a company's interests should be judged by reference to the interests of present and future shareholders. Where there are different classes of shareholder, the directors have a duty to act fairly having regard to the interests of all the shareholders. In reality, those running a company are likely to take account not only of the interests of the shareholders, but also the interests of the company's customers, creditors and employees when considering what is in the interests of a company. There is nothing in law which prevents directors from considering the interests of third parties with whom the company has a relationship, provided that the consideration of their interests is not allowed to displace the primacy of the shareholders' interests. Indeed, under s.309 of the Companies Act 1985 the directors of a company are now obliged to have regard to the interests of employees. Additionally, where a company is insolvent or on the brink of becoming insolvent, the interests of creditors become paramount. **29–007**

If directors are found to have exercised a power not bona fide in the interests of the company, the action may be declared void. A transaction entered into with a third party who has notice of the lack of bona fides will be voidable at the election of the company. If the action causes loss to the company, the director responsible may be liable to make good the loss.

Acting for Proper Purposes

Directors must exercise their powers in accordance with the articles of association. An exercise of powers for some purpose other than the purpose for which the power was granted, *i.e.* for some "collateral purpose", lays the conduct of the directors open to challenge. It is not open to a director who has exercised a power for a collateral purpose to argue that he believed he was acting in the interests of the company. **29–008**

In *Hogg v Cramphorn* [1967] Ch. 254, the directors of a company, who were anxious to avoid the company being taken over by a potential acquirer, allotted shares to persons who would support them in office. The court found that the allotment of shares for the purpose of defeating a take-over was not within the purpose of the power of allotment conferred on the directors under the articles of the company, notwithstanding that the directors honestly believed that their action was in the best interests of the company. However, a meeting of the shareholders prior to allotment could have authorised such a course of action.

29–009 In the later case of *Howard Smith v Ampol Petroleum* [1974] A.C. 821, which again arose in circumstances relating to a takeover bid, the Privy Council set aside the allotment of shares to the bidder for the company. The facts of *Howard Smith v Ampol Petroleum* were that two shareholders held 55 per cent of the shares in a company between them. The two majority shareholders indicated that they would not accept any offer which amounted to a takeover bid. The directors allotted sufficient shares to the bidder for the company to reduce the majority shareholders holding to below 50 per cent. That decision of the directors was set aside on the basis that it had been made for an improper purpose even though there was no element of self-interest involved. In giving the opinion of the Privy Council, Lord Wilberforce (at 837) analysed the relationship between the powers of the directors and the interests of the shareholders as follows:

> "The constitution of a limited company normally provides for directors, with powers of management, and shareholders, with defined voting powers having power to appoint the directors, and to take, in general meeting, by majority vote, decisions on matters not reserved for management. Just as it is established that directors, within their management powers, may take decisions against the wishes of the majority of shareholders, and indeed that the majority of shareholders cannot control them in the exercise of these powers while they remain in office . . . so it must be unconstitutional for directors to use their fiduciary powers over the shares in the company purely for the purpose of destroying an existing majority, or creating a new majority which did not previously exist. To do so is to interfere with that element of the company's constitution which is separate from and set against their powers."

The Notion of Trusteeship

29–010 Directors are regarded as trustees of company property under their control. A director is therefore answerable for any misapplication of the company's property in which he participated. The application of trust law in the context of investor protection is set out in Ch.30.

Suffice it to note at this point that a director will be considered to be a constructive trustee where he has received company money to which he is not entitled. In *Guinness plc v Saunders* [1990] 2 A.C. 663, a company director received payment of £5.2 million for services rendered in connection with a take-over bid for another company. The payment was received by the director in breach of s.317 of the Companies Act 1985 and of his own company's articles of association. In the Court of Appeal ([1988] 2 All E.R. 940), the company director was said to hold the money as a constructive trustee of the company and was obliged to account to the company for it. The basis of the constructive trust was, said Fox L.J. (at p.945h):

> "the combination of three factors, namely a fiduciary relationship, a breach of a duty arising in respect of that fiduciary relationship and the receipt, in breach of duty, of property belonging to the person to whom such duty was owed."

The decision of the Court of Appeal was affirmed by House of Lords on other grounds.

Conflict of Interest

It is a well-established principle that a director must not embark on a course of conduct which creates even the possibility of a conflict between his personal interests and his duty to the company. If a court finds that a director has acted in such a way that a conflict arises, the court may order him to account to the company for any profits made. In the case of *Industrial Development Consultants v Cooley* [1972] 2 All E.R. 162, the managing director of a company was asked to undertake work personally by the local gas board. The gas board indicated that it did not wish the work to be performed by the company. In order to take up the offer of work, the managing director obtained his release from his service contract by falsely representing ill-health. The court held that he was liable to account to the company for the profit he obtained from performing the contract, as he had embarked on a course of conduct which put his personal interest in direct conflict with his pre-existing duty as managing director of the company. **29–011**

Secret Profits

Directors are under a duty not to make personal profits while acting as directors. It is a general principal that a director must account to the company for any profit acquired by him as a result of holding the office of director. The leading case on secret profits is *Regal (Hastings) Ltd v Gulliver* [1942] 1 All E.R. 378. The company in this case owned a cinema. The company directors wished to acquire two further cinemas but the company was unable to fund the acquisition. To avoid buying the leases in their own names, the directors formed a new limited company of which they were also shareholders, and this company made the acquisition. The three cinemas were subsequently sold together as a going concern and the directors each received a substantial profit as shareholders of the second company. It was held that the directors had used their special knowledge and opportunities as directors to make a secret profit for themselves and that they were accountable to the company for the profits made. It was irrelevant that the company lacked the resources to acquire the two cinemas itself and could never, therefore, have made the profit for which the directors were held to be accountable. **29–012**

The prohibition on directors receiving secret profits is equally applicable to the receipt by a director of a bribe or secret commission received in the course of negotiating a contract on behalf of the company. In *Attorney-General for Hong Kong v Reid* [1994] 1 A.C. 324, the Privy Council held that when a fiduciary accepted a bribe as an inducement to betray his trust he held the bribe in trust for the person to whom he owed the duty as fiduciary. If property representing the bribe increased in value, the fiduciary was not entitled to retain any surplus in excess of the initial value of the bribe because he was not allowed by any means to make a profit out of a breach of duty. **29–013**

It has yet to be decided by a United Kingdom court whether a director may legitimately take the benefit of business opportunity which has already been rejected by the company. This point came before the Canadian Courts in the case of *Peso Silver Mines v Cropper* [1966] 58 D.L.R. 281. The decision in that case suggests that it might be acceptable for a director to take the benefit of a business opportunity which has been rejected by the company as long as he has not influenced the decision.

Duty not to Compete

29–014 It is now common practice for a director's contract to provide that competition with the company is prohibited. The only decided cases on this point date from the nineteenth century and seem to suggest that a case director is free to compete with his company—see for example *London & Mashonaland Exploration Co v New Mashonaland Exploration Co* [1891] W.N. 165. A modern court would most probably take a different view, at least in a case where a director who has any active involvement with one company becomes involved with a competitor. However, the Court of Appeal accepted in *In Plus Group Ltd v Pyke* [2002] 2 B.C.L.C. 201 that there is no completely rigid rule that a director could not be involved in the business of a competitor. The facts in that case, however, were extreme, in that the director had been effectively excluded from the company for more than six months before setting up his own rival company. The director did not use any of the first company's property for the purposes of the new business, nor did he make use of any confidential information which he had acquired as a director of that company. Sedley L.J. observed that, for all the influence the director had on the first company, he might as well have resigned.

Directors' Duties of Skill and Care

29–015 In contrast to directors' fiduciary duties, the directors' duties of skill and care have traditionally not been held to be onerous. The leading cases in this area were decided at a time when professional directors were unusual, and suggest that the courts will take a lenient view of directors' shortcomings of ability. The seminal review of the old authorities is contained in the case of *Re City Equitable Fire Insurance Co Ltd* [1925] Ch. 407. According to these cases, there is no objective standard of the reasonable director; a director is required only to exhibit that level of skill and care which may reasonably be expected from a person of his knowledge and experience. Applying this principle, a director who is a qualified accountant might be expected to exhibit a greater degree of skill and care in respect of the company's financial dealings than a director who is unqualified.

29–016 In practice, however, the law would seem to be moving towards a more objective standard. In the first place, where the director is employed under a service contract, the court is likely to imply an objective standard of care and skill into the contract, even if none has been expressed by the parties. Secondly, Parliament has instituted an objective test for the personal liability of a director in wrongful trading cases (s.214 of the Insolvency Act 1986, discussed in Ch.33). The courts have also tendency to apply an objective test in cases of disqualification brought under s.6 of the Company Directors Disqualification Act 1986 (as to which, see Ch.25). More generally, there have been cases where the court has indicated its willingness to apply an objective standard when considering the liability of a director: see, for example, the decisions in *Re D'Jan of London Ltd* [1993] B.C.C. 646 and *Re Westlowe Storage and Distribution Ltd* [2000] B.C.C. 851. Reference may also be made to the Australian case of *Daniels v Anderson* (1995) 16 A.C.S.R. 607 (NSW), in which it was held that the directors owed a common law duty of care and skill to the company. The board in that case apparently met only once a month for half a day. It was not thereby excused from taking reasonable steps to monitor the management of the company. If more frequent meetings were necessary for the proper performance of that duty, then those meetings should be held. The court pointed out that neither the law about the duty of directors, nor the law of negligence, had stood still since the decision in the *Re City Equitable* case.

Relieving a Director from Liability

There are a number of ways in which a director may be relieved of liability for breach of duty. The first of these is by ratification by the general meeting. The general meeting may "cure" a breach of duty by a director by the passing of an ordinary resolution. Breaches which may be cured in this way must be ones where the director has acted honestly in what he conceives to be the interests of the company and include a failure to disclose an interest in a contract, obtaining a secret profit (otherwise than through the misapplication of company property), a failure to act with skill and care, and the use of a power for an improper purpose. Breaches which cannot be cured by ratification by the general meeting include any breach which involves a lack of bona fides on the part of the director, any breach which results in the company performing an illegal or *ultra vires* act, any breach which involves the failure to obtain the prior sanction of a special resolution (where this is required by the articles), any breach which infringes the personal rights of individual shareholders under the articles, and any breach involving a fraud on the minority. **29–017**

Alternatively, breaches of duty may be ratified by way of obtaining the consent of all members of the company. Such consent may be given informally, but it is not capable of ratifying a breach if it is *ultra vires* the company or involves a fraud on the creditors of the company. Where the breach of duty results in the company acting *ultra vires* (*i.e.* doing an act which is beyond its corporate capacity), the act may now be ratified by special resolution under s.35(3) of the Companies Act 1985. The directors' breach of duty in causing the company to perform that act may also by ratified under s.35(3), but only by the passing of a separate special resolution. **29–018**

S.727(1) of the Companies Act 1985 gives the court a discretionary power to provide relief in any case where it appears to the court that a director or other officer is or may be liable for negligence, default, breach of duty or **29–019** breach of trust, but that he has acted honestly and reasonably and that, having regard to all the circumstances of the case, he ought fairly to be excused. In such a case, the court may relieve the director or other officer, either wholly or partly, from his liability on such terms as it thinks fit. In seeking relief under s.727(1), the onus rests on the director or other officer to establish that he acted honestly and reasonably and that he ought fairly to be excused in all the circumstances.

29–020 S.310(1) of the Companies Act 1985 renders void any provision (whether or not contained in the articles of association) which purports to exempt any officer of the company or any person employed by the company as auditor from, or indemnifying him against, any liability which by virtue of any rule of law would otherwise attach to him in respect of any negligence, default, breach of duty or breach of trust of which he may be guilty in relation to the company. It is, however, specifically provided that s.310(1) does not prevent a company from purchasing and maintaining insurance for its officers or auditor against any such liability (see s.310(3)(a)).

29–021 *Movitex Ltd v Bulfield* [1986] 2 B.C.C. 99 gives some guidance on the difficult question of the extent to which s.310 invalidates articles which purport to relax the duties imposed on directors under the general law. While, in general, the section will invalidate any provision in the articles which seeks to exclude or restrict the duties which a director owes to the company, it appears that the section will not be infringed by articles which merely limit or exclude disabilities arising from the directors' fiduciary position (such as the principle which prevents fiduciaries placing themselves in a position of conflict between their duty and their interest).

Reform of the Law Relating to Directors' Duties

29–022 The DTI White Paper, *Modernising Company Law*, July 2002, proposes wholesale reforms to company law, building on the recommendations of the independent Company Law Review set up in March 1998. Sch.2 to the draft Companies Bill (in Vol.II of the White Paper) sets out a general statement of the principles by which directors are bound. If enacted in its present form, Sch.2 would rationalise and codify the current law relating to the duties of directors. While the statutory regime would make a number of changes to the existing law (for example, reversing the decision in the *Regal (Hastings) Ltd v Gulliver*, above, and imposing an objective duty of care, skill and diligence on all directors), it would leave intact the main principles which underlie the present law.

Corporate Governance

The Cadbury, Greenbury and Hampel Reports

29–023 The trend for setting standards in corporate governance first emerged in the United States in the late 1980s, prompted by concerns about the reliability of financial reporting, the adequacy of internal control systems and the effectiveness of audit committees. Similar concerns in the United Kingdom were prompted by a series of corporate failures, most notably those concerning BCCI and the Maxwell Communications Group. As a result, the Cadbury Committee on the Financial Aspects of Corporate Governance was set up in May 1991 by the Financial Reporting Council (the FRC), the London Stock Exchange and the accountancy profession. The Committee was chaired by Sir Adrian Cadbury, and produced a Code of Best Practice (the Cadbury Code) in December 1992.

In response to further concerns about unjustified compensation packages in the privatised utilities, a study group chaired by Sir Richard Greenbury was set up to identify good practice in determining director remuneration and to prepare a code of practice for use by large UK companies. The Greenbury Report on Directors' Remuneration was published in May 1995, and made various recommendations intended to strengthen the link between pay and performance in the boardroom.

The next development was the formation of the Committee on Corporate Governance under the chairmanship of Sir Ronald Hampel. The Committee reviewed the operation of the Cadbury Code and the recommendations of the Greenbury Committee, and produced a number of further proposals of its own. Following the publication of its report in January 1998, the Hampel Committee produced a set of principles of good governance and a code of best practice, which combined the recommendations of the Cadbury, Greenbury and Hampel Committees into a single document known as the *Combined Code*.

The Combined Code

The *Combined Code* was published in June 1998. It is divided into two sections, with s.1 being of general application and s.2 being limited to institutional investors. The Code is appended to, but does not form part of, the *Listing Rules* (as to which, see Ch.5). R.12.43A of the *Listing Rules* requires any listed company which is incorporated in the United Kingdom to include in its annual reports and accounts: (a) a narrative statement of how it has applied the principles set out in s.1 of the Code, and (b) a statement as to whether or not it has complied with the provisions of s.1 of the Code throughout the relevant accounting period and, to the extent that it has not complied, a statement of the reasons for its non-compliance. Thus, while it is not obligatory for a listed company to comply with the Code, it is obligatory for a company which chooses not to comply to provide an explanation. **29–024**

S.1 of the *Combined Code* consists of principles and code provisions dealing in turn with (A) directors; (B) directors' remuneration; (C) relations with shareholders; and (D) accountability and audit. In each of these four parts, the relevant principles of good governance are elaborated in more detailed code provisions. **29–025**

As regards directors, principle A.1 provides that every listed company should be headed by an effective board which should lead and control the company. Among other things, this requires all directors to bring an **29–026** independent judgment to bear on issues of strategy, performance, resources (including key appointments) and standards of conduct (code provision A.1.5). Principle A.2 states that there are two key tasks at the top of every public company—the running of the board and the executive responsibility for the running of the company's business. There should be a clear division of responsibilities at the head of the company which will ensure a balance of power and authority, such that no one individual has unfettered powers of decision. As a consequence, any decision to combine the posts of chairman and chief executive in one person should be publicly justified (code provision A.2.1). Principle A.3 states that the board should include a balance of executive and non-executive directors (including independent non-executives) such that no individual or small group of individuals can dominate the board's decision taking. Non-executive directors should comprise not less than one third of the board. In addition, the board should be supplied in a timely manner with information in a form and of a quality appropriate to enable it to discharge its duties (principle A.4); there should be a formal and transparent procedure for the appointment of new directors to the board (principle A.4); and all directors should be required to submit themselves for re-election at regular intervals and at least every three years (principle A.5).

29–027 On the sensitive topic of directors' remuneration, principle B.1 states that levels of remuneration should be sufficient to attract and retain the directors needed to run the company successfully, but companies should avoid paying more than is necessary for this purpose. A proportion of executive directors' remuneration should be structured so as to link rewards to corporate and individual performance. Sch.A to the Code sets out detailed guidelines for remuneration committees to follow in designing schemes for performance-related remuneration (in particular, whether directors should be eligible for annual bonuses and benefits under long-term incentive schemes). It states that payouts or grants under all incentive schemes should be subject to challenging performance criteria, reflecting the company's objectives.

The Code also states that there is a strong case for setting notice or contract periods at, or reducing them to, one year or less (code provision B.1.7).

Principle B.2 states that companies should establish a formal and transparent procedure for developing policy on executive remuneration and for fixing the remuneration packages of individual directors. It also states that no director should be involved in deciding his or her own remuneration. Principle B.3 provides that the company's annual report should contain a statement of remuneration policy and details of the remuneration of each director. Sch.B to the Code sets out provisions which the board should follow in preparing the remuneration report. So, for example, the report should include full details of all elements in the remuneration package of each individual director by name, such as basic salary, benefits in kind, annual bonuses and long-term incentive schemes including share options. The report should also state the pension entitlements earned by each individual director during the year.

29–028 Turning to relations with shareholders, principle C.1 states that companies should be ready, where practicable, to enter into a dialogue with institutional shareholders based on a mutual understanding of objectives. Principle C.2 provides that boards should use the AGM to communicate with private investors and encourage their participation.

On the crucial issue of accountability and audit, principle D.1 states that the board should present a balanced and understandable assessment of the company's position and prospects. Principle D.2 states that the board should maintain a sound system of internal control to safeguard shareholders' investment and the company's assets. The directors should, at least annually, conduct a review of the effectiveness of the group's system of internal control and should report to shareholders that they have done so. The review should cover all controls, including financial, operational and compliance controls and risk management (code provision D.2.1). Companies which do not have an internal audit function should from time to time review the need for one (code provision D.2.3). As we shall see, guidance for directors on principle D.2 and its associated code provisions was subsequently given in the Turnbull Report (discussed in para.29–030, below). **29–029**

Principle D.3 provides that the board should establish formal and transparent arrangements for considering how they should apply the financial reporting and internal control principles and for maintaining an appropriate relationship with the company's auditors. In this regard, the board should establish an audit committee of at least three directors, all non-executive, with written terms of reference which deal clearly with its authority and duties (code provision D.3.1). The duties of the audit committee should include keeping under review the scope and results of the audit and its cost effectiveness and the independence and objectivity of the auditors. Where the auditors also supply a substantial volume of non-audit services to the company, the committee should keep the nature and extent of such services under review, seeking to balance the maintenance of objectivity and value for money (code provision D.3.2). As noted in para.29–035, below, the Smith Report has proposed an expansion and strengthening in the code provisions associated with principle D.3.

The Turnbull Report

In September 1999, the Internal Control Working Party of the Institute of Chartered Accountants in England and Wales produced guidance for directors on implementing the requirements of the *Combined Code* relating to internal control (*viz.* principle D.2 and its associated code provisions, outlined in para.29–029, above). The working party was chaired by Nigel Turnbull and its report, *Internal Control: Guidance for Directors on the Combined Code*, is frequently referred to as the Turnbull Report. **29–030**

The report proceeds on the basis that a company's system of internal control has a key role in the management of risks that are significant to the fulfilment of its business, and should be embedded in the company's operations and form part of its culture. An effective system of internal control not only contributes to safeguarding the shareholders' investment and the company's assets, but also facilitates the effectiveness and efficiency of its operations. The guidance deals first with what is required to maintain a sound system of internal control, secondly with the steps that should be taken to keep the effectiveness of the system under review, thirdly with the content of the board's narrative statement of how the company has applied principle D.2 of the *Combined Code*, and finally with the responsibility of directors to review the need for an internal audit function in those cases where the company does not have one.

Revisions to the Combined Code

29–031 Following the collapse of Enron, and other dramatic corporate failures which occurred in the United States early in 2002, a number of initiatives were taken to review the effectiveness of the *Combined Code* as a safeguard against the risk of similar scandals occurring in the United Kingdom.

29–032 In April 2002, the Government appointed Derek Higgs to lead an independent review of the role and effectiveness of non-executive directors. His report, *Review of the role and effectiveness of non-executive directors*, was published on January 20, 2003, and made a large number of recommendations designed to strengthen the role of non-executive directors, and the accountability of boards generally. The report also incorporated a proposed revision of the *Combined Code* to give effect to the recommendations in the report. The Higgs Report is considered further in paras 29–033 to 29–034, below.

In July 2002, the Government asked the FRC to put in hand the development of the existing guidance on audit committees in the *Combined Code*. That led to the establishment, in September 2002, of an FRC-appointed group, chaired by Sir Robert Smith. The Smith Report, *Audit Committees Combined Code Guidance*, was published on January 20, 2003 (the same day as the Higgs Report), and contains extensive guidance for boards in making suitable arrangements for their audit committees, and for directors serving on such committees. The Smith Report is considered further at paras 29–035 to 29–036, below.

The Higgs Report

29–033 The recommendations of the Higgs Report included the following:

- At least half the members of the board, excluding the chairman, should be independent non-executive directors. The amendments to the *Combined Code* proposed in the report state that a non-executive director will be considered independent for this purpose "when the board determines that the director is independent in character and judgment and there are no relationships or circumstances which could affect, or appear to affect, the director's judgment". The proposed amendments go on to give examples of such relationships and circumstances (*e.g.* that he or she was an employee of the company in the last five years, or has had a material business relationship with the company within the last three years).
- The roles of chairman and chief executive should be separated and the division of responsibilities between the two roles set out in

writing and agreed by the board. The chief executive should not subsequently become the chairman of the same company.

- The non-executive directors should meet as a group at least once a year without the chairman or executive directors present.
- A senior independent director should be identified. He or she should be available to shareholders if they have concerns that have not been resolved through the normal channels of contact with the chairman or chief executive.
- The nomination committee should consist of a majority of independent non-executive directors. While the committee may include the chairman, it should be chaired by an independent non-executive director.
- A comprehensive induction programme, including meetings with major investors, should be provided to new non-executive directors.
- The performance of the board, its committees and its individual members should be evaluated at least once a year.
- A full-time executive director should not take on more than one non-executive directorship, nor become chairman, of a major company. No individual should chair the board of more than one major company.
- The remuneration of non-executive directors should be sufficient to attract and fairly compensate high quality individuals. While non-executive directors should be able to take part of their remuneration in the form of shares, they should not hold options over shares in their company.
- The remuneration committee should comprise at least three members, all of whom should be independent non-executive directors.
- Except in the case of smaller listed companies, no one non-executive director should sit simultaneously on all three principal board committees (*viz.* the audit, nomination and remuneration committees).

Following publication of the Higgs Report, consultations on the proposed amendments to the *Combined Code* were carried out by the FRC (which is the body responsible for the Code). The consultation process brought to light some strong criticism of the proposed changes to the Code. A major focus of criticism has been the role envisaged for the senior independent director, which some critics believe will undermine the authority of the chairman and tend to divide the board into opposing camps. Other areas of concern are the proposal that the chairman of the board should not chair the nominations committee, and the proposal that non-executive directors should not serve for more than two three-year terms. In response to those criticisms, a working group of FRC members (including Derek Higgs himself) has been set up to produce a final draft of **29–034** the revised Code that will build on the approach taken in the Higgs Report and command general support. The FRC currently expects the final draft of the Code to be published in July 2003 and brought into effect by October 2003.

The Smith Report

29–035 As mentioned above, the Smith Report was published on the same day as the Higgs Report and contains guidance relating to audit committees, as well as proposed amendments to the *Combined Code* to expand and strengthen the code provisions associated with principle D.3 (*viz.* the principle that the board should establish and maintain formal and transparent arrangements for considering how they should apply the financial reporting and internal control principles and for maintaining an appropriate relationship with the company's auditors). The importance of the audit committee in averting an Enron-style collapse is highlighted in paragraphs 9 and 10 of the background report:

> "Audit committees have a particular role in underpinning the assurance that boards give to shareholders of the integrity of the company's audit and internal control processes.
>
> If things go wrong, the audit committee also has a role to play in ensuring that they are put right — for example if an audit failure seems to be leading to poor, or even deliberately misleading, financial reporting decisions. This can put the committee into an adversarial relationship with both the external auditors and the executive, and audit committees must be ready to accept that role if necessary. The US corporate failures of 2002 point vividly to the importance of this. We believe that failures on that scale will continue to be rare, but audit committees must be capable of tackling the worst."

29–036 The guidance in the Smith Report includes a number of essential requirements that every audit committee should meet. In order to comply with the *Combined Code*, therefore, listed companies will need either to comply with these requirements or explain why they have not done so. The key requirement is that the board should establish an audit committee, whose main role and responsibilities should be:

- to monitor the integrity of the financial statements of the company;
- to review the company's internal financial control system and, unless addressed by a separate risk committee or by the board itself, its risk management systems;
- to monitor and review the effectiveness of the company's internal audit function;
- to make recommendations to the board in relation to the appointment of the external auditor and to approve the external auditor's remuneration and terms of engagement;
- to monitor and review the external auditor's independence, objectivity and effectiveness; and

- to develop and implement policy on the engagement of the external auditor to supply non-audit services.

Where the audit committee's monitoring and review activities reveal cause for concern or scope for improvement, it should make recommendations to the board on action needed to address the issue or make improvements.

In addition, the audit committee should include at least three members, who should be independent non-executive directors, and the chairman of the company should not be a member of the committee. The audit committee should be provided with sufficient resources to undertake its activities, and at least one of its members should have significant, recent and relevant financial experience, for example, as an auditor or a finance director of a listed company.

Postscript

A speech delivered on June 3, 2003 by Sir Howard Davies, the current **29–037**
chairman of the FSA, casts and interesting and somewhat sceptical sidelight on the recent proliferation of codes relating to corporate governance. He observed at the beginning of his speech that:

> ". . . in the United Kingdom, we have been especially fertile in generating such codes. First there was Cadbury, then Greenbury. And, predictably, once there were two codes, they began to breed. Since then, in quick succession, there have been Hampel, Turnbull and most recently two new ones, Smith and Higgs, appeared on the same day. This is one area in which we can proudly say that the United Kingdom leads the world in productivity."

Later, reflecting on what lessons were to be drawn from the experience of the FSA and its predecessor bodies in the sphere of financial regulation, Sir Howard said:

> "Our experience shows, for example, that a dominant chief executive, or indeed business head, who is not effectively challenged by the Board or his colleagues, is a danger sign. Similarly, a Board lacking in relevant experience is unlikely to act effectively as a constraint on excessive risk taking.
>
> It is also clear, to me at least, that Board which does not display sufficient interest in strategic issues is putting the institution at risk. That is one aspect of the current corporate governance debate which concerns me. The codes of practice often seem to me to encourage Boards to focus attention on risk management and control processes, in a way which can leave strategic thinking as an optional extra. Yet incoherent strategies can be just as potent a source of instability as poor risk management itself.
>
> A related point, which emerges strongly from our experience, is that Boards must be open to external stimulus. It is dangerous for a Board to accept all its information and advice from within the company, and be unprepared to listen to dissenting views."

Minority Shareholders Actions

This section is concerned with the common law remedies available to **29–038**
minority shareholders in cases where the company has suffered loss as a result of a breach of duty by the directors. To set the common law remedies

in context, it should be noted that the Companies Act 1985 creates two additional, inter-related statutory remedies; first, a member of a company may petition the court on the ground of unfair prejudice under the provisions of ss.459 to 461 of the Companies Act 1985, and secondly, the court may be asked to have the company wound up on the ground that it would be just and equitable to do so under s.122 of the Insolvency Act 1986. Both of these remedies can be claimed in the alternative. These remedies are considered in paras 27.048 to 27.059, below.

When considering the existing remedies available to shareholders, it should be noted that the Law Commission's Report on *Shareholder Remedies* (1997) No. 246, recommended reforms to the unfair prejudice remedy, and to the derivative action by which a shareholder may seek to enforce a claim belonging to the company (as to which, see paras 29–044 to 29–046, below). These recommendations have yet to be implemented.

The rule in *Foss v Harbottle*

29–039 The rule in *Foss v Harbottle* (1843) 2 Hare 461 is that, if a wrong is done to a company, only the company may sue for the damage caused to it. A shareholder has no right to bring an action on behalf of the company in order to protect the value of his shares. The rule preserves the rights of majority shareholders against an attempt by a minority shareholder to bring an action where the majority do not wish such an action to be brought. Minority shareholders cannot sue for wrongs done to their company or complain of irregularities in the conduct of the company's internal affairs. The rule rests on two propositions: first, the right of the majority to block a minority action where the majority is in a position to ratify alleged misconduct and secondly, the exclusive right of a company to sue upon a corporate cause of action.

The Exceptions to the Rule in *Foss v Harbottle*

29–040 There are a number of exceptions to the general principal that minority shareholders cannot bring an action. The general rule does not apply where it is alleged that those in control of a company have defrauded it, *i.e.* where there has been fraud upon the minority, or where the action is *ultra vires* or where the action is unfair and oppressive upon the minority.

Fraud on a Minority

29–041 It was established in the case of *Burland v Earle* [1902] A.C. 83, that a minority may bring an action where:

> "the acts complained of are of a fraudulent character or are beyond the power of the company. A familiar example is where the majority is endeavouring directly or indirectly to appropriate to themselves money or property, or

advantages which belong to the company, or in which the other shareholders are entitled to participate."

What behaviour may amount to "fraud" in this context was the subject of consideration in the case of *Daniels v Daniels* [1978] Ch. 406, which shows that the term bears a wider meaning than it does at common law. The court held that "a minority shareholder who has no other remedy may sue where directors use their powers, intentionally or unintentionally, fraudulently or negligently in a manner which benefits themselves at the expense of the company".

Wrongdoer Control

An exception may be made to the rule in *Foss v Harbottle* where the persons against whom relief is sought control the company and are in a position to stifle any attempt to institute proceedings in the name of the company. The case of *Pavlides v Jensen* [1956] Ch. 565, however, illustrates the limitations on this exception. In that case, the directors who were alleged to have harmed the company by their negligence were a majority of the board, although they did not in the strict legal sense control the company. The minority action against them failed because, first, the directors' actions did not amount to fraud or to an *ultra vires* act but instead was merely negligent and thus open to ratification. Secondly, the action failed because the directors were held not to have sufficient control over the company to enable them to prevent the shareholders deciding in general meeting to institute proceedings in the name of the company. **29–042**

It is well established that if directors exercise their powers mala fides or for an improper purpose this is a matter of which the minority are entitled to complain as well as being a breach of duty. For example, if the directors were to use their powers to issue shares to take over majority control, a shareholder might seek an injunction to protect the rights of the existing shareholders. The use of directors' powers for an improper or collateral purpose may also be the subject of a minority shareholder action. Such situations often arise in the context of take-over battles, where the directors issue shares in an effort to thwart the efforts of a potential bidder: see *Hogg v Cramphorn* [1967] Ch. 254. **29–043**

Derivative Actions

Where the case falls within one of the exceptions to the rule in *Foss v Harbottle* (*i.e.* where there has been fraud on the minority or there have been *ultra vires* acts), a claimant shareholder may be entitled to bring a representative, or "derivative", action on behalf of the shareholders to recover damages from the directors for their breach of duty, or to seek restitution of property to the company. The distinctive feature of a minority shareholders' action is that relief is granted not to the claimant but to the company. The defendants to the action will be those who have committed the act complained of and the company itself. The reasons for **29–044** this were set out by Chitty L.J. in *Spokes v Grosvenor Hotel Company* [1897] 2 Q.B. 124 at 128 when he said:

> "To such an action as this the company are necessary defendants. The reason is obvious: the wrong alleged is done to the company, and the company must be a party to the suit in order to be bound by the result of the action and to receive the money recovered in the action If the company were not bound they could bring a fresh action for the same cause if the action failed, and there were subsequently a change in the board of directors and in the voting paper. Obviously, in such an action as this, no specific relief is asked against the company; and obviously, too, what is recovered cannot be paid to the plaintiff representing the minority, but must go into the coffers of the company."

29–045 Minority shareholders' actions must be brought by a present shareholder although the subject matter of the action may have taken place prior to the claimant becoming a shareholder. If the shareholder ceases to be a shareholder, the action may be continued by another shareholder. The claimant shareholder must not have participated in the wrong-doing complained of. The action must be brought in the interests of the company and not for the benefit of a rival company which has indemnified the claimant's costs. However, the courts have recognised that a minority shareholder who brings a derivative suit may have a right to an indemnity as against the company in respect of his costs: see *Wallersteiner v Moir (No. 2)* [1975] Q.B. 373. Rules of court prescribe that, after the claim form has been issued in a derivative action, the claimant must apply to the court for permission to continue the claim, and must not take any other step in the proceedings except where the court gives permission. On the hearing of the claimant's application for permission, the court has power to order the company to indemnify the claimant against liability in respect of costs incurred in the claim (Civil Procedure Rules, r.19.9).

29–046 A minority shareholder must bring the action for the benefit of the company and not for an ulterior purpose (*Nurcombe v Nurcombe* [1984] B.C.L.C. 557). Thus, in *Barrett v Dockett* [1995] 1 B.C.L.C. 243, the Court of Appeal held that a shareholder would be allowed to bring a derivative action on behalf of a company where the action was brought bona fide for the benefit of the company for wrongs to the company for which no other remedy was available but not for an ulterior purpose. Conversely, if the action was brought for an ulterior purpose or if another adequate remedy was available, the court would not allow the derivative action to proceed.

Once a company is in liquidation, redress must be sought from the liquidator; a minority shareholder's action cannot be brought once a company is in liquidation.

29–047 Where a company has suffered loss, whether as a result of a breach of duty by its directors or otherwise, the loss will necessarily be reflected in a reduction in the value of the shareholdings of individual investors in the company. The individual shareholder will not be allowed to bring his own action for the recovery of that loss. To allow such a claim would either expose the defendant to the risk of having to compensate both the claimant and the company separately for the same loss, or (if recovery by the shareholder barred recovery on behalf of the company) result in prejudice to the company and its creditors and other shareholders. If, however, a shareholder can prove that he has suffered a loss which is genuinely distinct from that suffered by the company, he will not be barred from bringing his own action to recover it: *Johnson v Gore Wood & Co.* [2002] 2 A.C. 1.

Unfair Prejudice

The restrictions on minority shareholders' actions imposed by the rule in *Foss v Harbottle* mean that derivative actions do not always lie in cases of minority oppression. The provisions contained in ss.459 to 461 of the Companies Act 1985 go some way towards alleviating this restriction. S.459(1) allows a member of the company to apply to the court by petition for an order on the ground that: **29–048**

> "the company's affairs are being or have been conducted in a manner which is unfairly prejudicial to the interest of its members generally or of some part of its members (including at least himself) or that any actual or proposed act or omission of the company (including an act or omission on its behalf) is or would be so prejudicial."

The procedural rules to be followed in any action brought under this section are now contained in the Companies (Unfair Prejudice Application) Proceedings Rules 1986 (SI 1986/2000). Guidance on the procedural aspects will be found in the practice direction on applications under the Companies Act 1985 (*Civil Procedure*, 2003, paras 2G-53 to 2G57).

The Companies Act 1985 does not define "unfair prejudice." The courts have considered what is meant by "unfair prejudice" in a number of cases. In the unreported case of *Re Bovey Hotels*, July 31, 1981, Slade J. said: **29–049**

> "a member of a company will be able to bring himself within the section if he can show that the value of his shareholding in the company has been seriously diminished or at least seriously jeopardised by reason of a course of conduct on the part of those persons who have had de facto control of the company, which is unfair to the member concerned. The test of fairness must, I think, be an objective, not a subjective one. In other words it is not necessary for the petitioner to show that persons who have had de facto control of the company have acted as they did in the conscious knowledge that this was unfair to the petitioner or that they were acting in bad-faith; the test I think is whether a reasonable bystander observing the consequences of their conduct would regard it as having unfairly prejudiced the petitioner's interests".

The scope of the "unfair prejudice" prejudice was considered by the House of Lords in *O'Neill v Phillips* [1999] 1 W.L.R. 1092. In this case, the company was a private company which provided specialist services for stripping asbestos from buildings. Mr Phillips originally owned all the 100 £1 issued shares in the company. In 1983, the company employed the petitioner, Mr O'Neill, as a manual worker. In 1985, Mr Phillips, having **29–050** been impressed by Mr O'Neill's energy and ability, gave him 25 shares and appointed him a director. Later that year, Mr O'Neill took over the day-to-day running of the business, and Mr Phillips retired from the board, leaving Mr O'Neill as the sole director. Mr O'Neill was credited with half the profits. Between 1989 and 1990, discussions took place between Mr Phillips and Mr O'Neill with a view to Mr O'Neill's shareholding and voting rights being increased to 50 per cent when certain targets were reached. However, no concluded agreement was reached. With the onset of recession in the construction industry in 1991, the company's business began to struggle. Mr Phillips became alarmed about the company's financial position and concerned about Mr O'Neill's management. Accordingly, in August 1991, Mr Phillips, as controlling shareholder, procured his reappointment to the board as managing director, with Mr O'Neill remaining as an ordinary director. In November 1991, an acrimonious meeting took place between them, at which Mr Phillips told Mr O'Neill that he would no longer receive 50 per cent of the profits, but would only be paid his salary and the dividends to which he was entitled on his 25 per cent shareholding. In 1992, Mr O'Neill issued a petition under s.459, claiming that Mr Phillips had been guilty of unfairly prejudicial conduct in terminating the equal profit-sharing arrangement and in repudiating the alleged agreement to increase his shareholding to 50 per cent if the specified targets were reached.

29–051 The House of Lords dismissed the petition. Lord Hoffmann (giving the only reasoned speech) pointed out that, in s.459, the concept of unfairness was being deployed in a commercial context. Thus, a member of a company would not ordinarily be entitled to complain of unfairness unless there had been some breach of the terms on which he agreed that the affairs of the company should be conducted, those terms being contained in the articles of association and sometimes in collateral agreements between the shareholders. There would, however, be cases in which equitable considerations made it unfair for those conducting the affairs of the company to rely on their strict legal powers. Thus, unfairness might consist either in a breach of the rules or in using the rules in a manner which equity would regard as contrary to good faith. In considering the circumstances in which an equitable restraint will be placed on the exercise of a party's legal rights, Lord Hoffmann approved the following formulation by Jonathan Parker J. in *Re Astec (B.S.R.) plc* [1998] 2 B.C.L.C. 556, 588:

> ". . . in order to give rise to an equitable constraint based on 'legitimate expectation' what is required is a personal relationship or personal dealings of some kind between the party seeking to exercise the legal right and the party seeking to restrain such exercise, such as will affect the conscience of the former."

A particular example in which such an equitable restraint will arise is provided by the case in which the parties form a quasi-partnership company. In commenting on such cases in *O'Neill v Phillips*, Lord Hoffmann said (at p.1101F-H):

> "In a quasi-partnership company, [the promises which the parties appear to have exchanged] will usually be found in the understandings between the

> members at the time when they entered into association. But there may be later promises, by words or conduct, which it would be unfair to allow a member to ignore. Nor is it necessary that such promises should be independently enforceable as a matter of contract. A promise may be binding as a matter of justice and equity although for one reason or another (for example, because it is in favour of a third party) it would not be enforceable in law."

Applying the above principles to the facts of *O'Neill v Phillips* itself, Lord Hoffmann's conclusion was that no unfair prejudice had been established. Mr O'Neill had not been removed from participation in the management of the business, since he remained as a director. Nor had Mr Phillips breached the terms of any agreement with Mr O'Neill (no final agreement having been concluded). There was nothing unfair or inequitable in Mr Phillips denying Mr O'Neill a right to additional shares or to a continued 50 per cent profit-share in circumstances where he had made no promise to confer those rights on him. A shareholder who had not been dismissed or excluded could not seek relief under s.459 merely because he felt there had been a breakdown of trust and confidence between the parties. **29–052**

Exactly what will constitute a shareholders' interest which will fall within the scope of s.459 has been the subject of a number of decisions of the courts and has yet to be satisfactorily settled. As a general rule, in bringing a petition under s.459, the petitioner must be seeking to protect his interests as a member of the company and not interests which he may hold in some other capacity (*i.e.* as the freeholder of land). However, there have been some judicial decisions which have allowed a more liberal approach to be taken to the construction of the phrase "interests of some part of its members" in s.459(1). Thus, in the case of a quasi-partnership company, the dismissal of the petitioner from employment may in some circumstances be capable of constituting prejudice to the petitioner's interests as member: compare *Re London School of Electronics Ltd.* [1986] Ch. 211. In *Re a Company* [1986] B.C.L.C. 382, Hoffman J. observed in this connection that: **29–053**

> "the interests of a member who had ventured his capital in a small private company might include the legitimate expectation that he would continue to be employed as a director — so that his dismissal would be unfairly prejudicial to his interests as a member."

In applying the above passage, it should be noted that, in *O'Neill v Phillips*, above, Lord Hoffmann made it clear (at p.1102E-F) that the concept of a "legitimate expectation" should not be allowed to lead a life of its own: it was simply a label to describe the position which arises where an equitable restraint of the kind described in para.29–051, above, would make it unfair for a party to exercise his rights under the articles.

Breaches of directors' fiduciary duties may form the subject matter of a complaint under a petition for unfair prejudice brought under s.459. This may be a practical way of getting round the limitations of the exceptions of the fraud on the minority rule in *Foss v Harbottle.* See in this connection the decisions of Hoffmann J. in *Re a Company* [1986] 1 W.L.R. 281; *Re a Company* [1986] B.C.L.C. 382; and *Re a Company* (1986) 2 B.C.C. 99,171. **29–054**

Remedies for Unfair Prejudice

29–055 The remedies which may be granted by a court hearing a petition for unfair prejudice are set out in s.461 of the Companies Act 1985. S.461(1), which is very widely drawn, allows the court to make such order "as it thinks fit for giving relief in respect of the matters complained of". S.461(2) sets out specific remedies which may be imposed by the court. Under the latter provision, the court may regulate the conduct of the company's affairs in the future; or it may require the company to refrain from doing or continuing an act complained of; or it may order the company to carry out an act which it has omitted to carry out. The court may authorise the bringing of civil proceedings in the name of or on behalf of the company, although this power is little used in practice. Finally, the court may provide for the purchase of the shares of any members of the company by other members of the company or by the company itself. This final power is the remedy most often sought in practice and is known as a "buy-out" order.

29–056 "Buy-out" orders raise a number of practical problems in their implementation which have been subject to consideration by the courts. The first and most difficult problem is how to value the minority's shares. The problem was considered in *Re Bird Precision Bellows* [1986] Ch. 658, in which the Court of Appeal emphasised that the overriding consideration is that the valuation must be fair and equitable. Valuation of shares may be either on a pro-rata basis according to the value of the shares as a whole or, alternatively, on the basis that the price of the shares should be discounted to reflect the fact that the shares were a minority holding. Generally, where shares have been acquired on the incorporation of a quasi-partnership company the pro-rata method of valuations likely to be preferred (an approach supported by Lord Hoffmann, *obiter*, in *O'Neill v Phillips*, above, at page 1107D). The date at which the valuation of the shares is to be made is also subject to what may be considered fair. In practice a number of dates have been utilised for this purpose including the date of the unfair prejudice, the date of the petition and the date when the valuation was made, and the date of a consent order that shares should be purchased.

Just and Equitable Winding up

29–057 Under s.122(1)(g) of the Insolvency Act 1986 a member may petition for a just and equitable winding up. The leading case on the scope of the just and equitable ground is the House of Lords decision in *Ebrahimi v Westbourne Galleries* [1973] A.C. 360. The facts of that case were that A and B set up a business selling Persian carpets, essentially as a partnership. After a time, the business became a company with each partner receiving 500 shares. A's son became a director and shareholder of the company, receiving 100 shares from each partner by way of transfer. The company had only these three directors, all of whom worked full time for the company. Profits were distributed as directors' remuneration. No dividends were ever paid. Relations between the directors deteriorated and B was removed from the board by the other two directors. At first instance, the court, allowing the petition for winding up, held that, although the removal of the director was lawful, it still constituted an "abuse of the power and a breach of good faith which partners owe to each other", in that B's removal represented the exclusion of B from all participation in the business. The case went to the House of Lords which ordered winding up. The mere fact that the exclusion of a director from participation in a company falls within the powers conferred by s.303 of the Companies Act 1985 (as it now is) and the articles of a company is not conclusive. The power to order winding up on the just and equitable ground allows the court to "subject the exercise of legal rights to equitable considerations; considerations, that is, of a personal character arising between one individual and another, which may make it unjust, or inequitable, to insist on legal rights, or to exercise them in a particular way". The court did not however, give an exhaustive definition of the circumstances in which a court would make such a decision.

The primary importance of this decision is the rejection of the view that **29–058** the petitioner must prove that his exclusion was not bona fide in the interest of the company or such that no reasonable man could consider it to be in the interest of the company. The case established that the court may make a winding-up order where the circumstances of the case disclosed an underlying obligation in good faith and confidence that the petitioner should participate in management so long as the business continued.

The application of the decision in *Ebrahimi v Westbourne Galleries* to situations which do not involve expulsion remains uncertain. Any course of dealing which produces a breakdown in mutual confidence may well suffice to justify the making of a winding-up order under s.122(1)(g) unless the breakdown is as a result of the behaviour of the complainant shareholders.

Overlap Between Unfair Prejudice and Just and Equitable Winding up

The circumstances of the particular case will determine whether one or **29–059** other or both the remedies of a just and equitable winding up and relief for unfair prejudice are available. When considering the relationship between these two types of action, attention should be paid to the provisions of s.125(2) of the Insolvency Act 1986, which requires the court, on hearing a just and equitable winding-up petition, to consider whether "some other remedy is available to the petitioners and that they are acting unreasonably in seeking to have the company wound up instead of pursuing the other remedy". There will be many cases in which the relief available under s.459 of the Companies Act 1985 will constitute an alternative and more satisfactory remedy than an order for the winding up of the company under s.122(1)(g).

Powers of the DTI to Investigate Companies

The Companies Act 1985 (as amended by the Companies Act 1989 Pt III) **29–060** gives the DTI powers to appoint inspectors to investigate the affairs of a company. The Secretary of State for Trade and Industry has powers of investigation where fraud or other misconduct is suspected. Investigations into a limited company which is an authorised person may also be conducted (either by the DTI or by the FSA) under FSMA 2000, s.167 or (where there are circumstances suggesting market abuse) s.168. The latter provisions are considered in Ch.14, above.

The object of a Companies Act investigation is to find out what is going on, for which purpose the inspectors may require the production of papers and interview officers of the company and other witnesses. Following investigation, the action that may be taken includes criminal prosecution, winding up the company, the disqualification of directors and the imposition of sanctions by regulators. The ultimate purpose served by the availability of these sanctions is the protection of investors and the promotion of efficient and honest markets.

29–061 Investigations are carried out by officials from the DTI's Companies Investigation Branch (the CIB), or by private sector lawyers, accountants or other specialists. In a typical year, the CIB receives more than 4,000 complaints, resulting in some 800 cases being formally considered for the use of the statutory investigative powers. Approximately two-thirds of the requests for investigation are received from the public and the remainder come from various other organisations working in the regulatory field. The Secretary of State almost always has a discretion to decide which complaints to pursue, and around 250 are ultimately accepted for investigation.

Inspections Under s.447 of the Companies Act 1985

29–062 In practice, the vast majority of DTI investigations are carried out under s.447 of the Companies Act 1985 (as amended by s.63 Companies Act 1989). S.447 confers on the Secretary of State the power to require the production of documents. A s.447 investigation is limited to an inspection of documents and is commonly referred to as a "calling for papers" inquiry. S.447 investigations are confidential, fact-finding inquiries. "Documents" include information recorded in any form, so encompassing electronically stored information (s.47(9)). Where a s.447 investigation produces evidence of corporate misconduct, a full investigation into the company's affairs may be ordered.

Failure to produce documents legitimately required by a DTI inspector is a criminal offence punishable by a fine (s.447(6)). It is a defence for a person charged with such an offence to prove that the documents were not in his possession or control (s.447(7)).

Under s.447(5)(a)(ii), the person producing the documents, and any past or present officer or employee of the company, may be requested to provide an explanation for the contents of documents requested for inspection. It is an offence to furnish false information either knowingly or recklessly in purported compliance with a requirement imposed under s.447 to provide such an explanation. Such an offence is punishable by imprisonment or a fine, or both (s.451).

Powers of Entry and Search of Premises

The Secretary of State may apply to a magistrate for a search warrant if he has reasonable grounds for believing that documents which he requires to be produced under his powers are being held on premises, or that the documents would not otherwise be produced but would be removed, hidden, tampered with or destroyed (Companies Act 1985, s.448(1) and (2)). **29–063**

Investigations Under s.431 or 432 of the Companies Act 1985

The Secretary of State has a discretion to appoint inspectors to investigate and report on the affairs of a company, when asked to do so by the company itself or by a prescribed number of its shareholders (Companies Act 1985, s.431(1) and (2)) Those asking for the inspection must satisfy the Secretary of State that there is good reason for an investigation and may be required to give security for the costs of the investigation (not exceeding £5,000). **29–064**

Inspectors may be appointed under s.431:

- in the case of companies having a share capital, on the application of not less than 200 members or of members holding not less than one-tenth of the shares issued;
- in the case of a company not having share capital, on the application of not less than one-fifth of the company's members; or
- on the application of the company itself.

In addition to his powers under s.431, the Secretary of State must order an inspection into the affairs of a company where there is a court order declaring that the company's affairs should be investigated (s.432(1)). The Secretary of State also has a discretion to appoint inspectors to investigate the affairs of a company under s.432(2) if he suspects: **29–065**

- that the company's affairs are being or have been conducted with intent to defraud its creditors or the creditors of any other person, or for some fraudulent or unlawful purpose, or in a manner which is unfairly prejudicial to some part of its members; or
- that any actual or proposed act or omission of the company (or on its behalf) is or would be so prejudicial, or that the company was formed for a fraudulent or unlawful purpose; or
- that persons concerned with the company's formation or management have been guilty of fraud, misfeasance or other misconduct towards the company or its members; or
- that the members of the company have not been given all the information with respect to its affairs which they might reasonably expect.

29–066 An investigation under s.431 or 432 will normally be conducted by two inspectors, who are usually one senior accountant and a Q.C. or senior solicitor. The inspectors appointed to conduct the investigation may also investigate the affairs of subsidiary or holding companies if they think it necessary for the purposes of their investigation (s.433).

Where a company is under investigation under s.431 or 432, its officers and agents have a duty to produce all documents relating to the company, a duty to attend on the inspectors and to render the inspectors all assistance they are reasonably able to give (s.434(1)). The inspectors may examine a person on oath in the course of an investigation and answers given may be used in evidence against him (s.434 (3) and (5)).

The inspectors carrying out an investigation have a duty to act fairly. Accordingly, if they propose to criticise anyone in their report, they must first inform him of the substance of the criticism and give him the opportunity to respond: *Re Pergamon Press Ltd.* [1971] 1 Ch. 388.

If a person fails to comply with any of the requirements of s.434, the inspectors may certify the fact in writing to the court. The court may then enquire into the case and, after hearing any witnesses for the alleged offender and after hearing any statement offered in defence, may punish the offender as if he had been guilty of contempt of court (s.436).

The Privilege Against Self-incrimination

29–067 During the course of an investigation a person called upon to answer questions by the inspectors must do so. The courts have considered the relationship between the DTI's power of investigation and the common-law privilege against self incrimination. In *Re London United Investments Plc* [1992] 2 All E.R. 842, the Court of Appeal considered whether on a proper construction of the Companies Act 1985 the common law right to refuse to answer questions the answers to which may tend to incriminate had been abrogated. The case arose out of a DTI inspection in respect of London United Investments Plc under s.432(2) of the Companies Act 1985. The inspectors were appointed to investigate the circumstances surrounding the payment of commission on reinsurance contracts relating to a subsidiary company of LUI. The privilege against self-incrimination was held to be impliedly excluded where DTI inspectors have undertaken an investigation, because the circumstances which give rise to the investigation will often include those where fraud is suspected. There is an obligation on those questioned to answer questions, and the inspector's report may lead the Secretary of State to petition for the winding up of the company or to bring civil proceedings in the public interest.

Where, however, statements are made to DTI inspectors under compulsion, the subsequent use of those statements by the prosecution in criminal proceedings against the person who made the statements may contravene his right to a fair hearing under Art.6(1) of the European Convention on Human Rights. That may be so not only where the statements are directly incriminating, but also where exculpatory remarks or statements of fact are later relied upon by the prosecution to contradict other statements of the accused or otherwise to undermine his credibility: *Saunders v United Kingdom* [1998] 1 B.C.L.C. 362.

Subsequent Proceedings

Following an inspection under s.431 or 432, the inspectors make a report to the Secretary of State (s.437(1)). The report may be published (s.437(3)(c)), and it usually will be published if there is a public interest in the case, though publication may be delayed if criminal proceedings are on foot or in contemplation. The report is admissible in legal proceedings as evidence of the opinion of the inspectors and, in proceedings under the Company Directors Disqualification Act 1986, as evidence of any fact stated in it (s.441). **29–068**

On receipt of a report, the Secretary of State may bring civil proceedings which are in the public interest and could have been brought by the company itself (s.438(1)). The Secretary of State may also petition for the company to be wound up where it appears to him from the report that winding up would be expedient in the public interest (see the Insolvency Act 1986, s.124(4)(a)). The Secretary of State may seek relief under s.460 of the Companies Act 1985 where, having received the report, it appears to him that the affairs of the company are being conducted in a way which is unfairly prejudicial to its members or some part of its members.

Investigations into the Ownership of a Company

The DTI has the power to appoint inspectors to investigate and report on the membership of a company, and otherwise with respect to the company, under s.442 of the Companies Act 1985. The purpose of such investigations is to determine who has a financial interest in the success or failure of the company and who is able to control the company or materially influence its policy. An appointment under s.442 may be made at the request of the shareholders in the company, though in such a case the shareholders must satisfy the same requirements as apply to an application for the appointment of inspectors under s.431 (summarised in para.29–064, above). **29–069**

If it appears to the Secretary of State that there is good reason to investigate the ownership of any shares in, or debentures of, a company, but that it is unnecessary to appoint inspectors for the purpose, he may instead require persons whom he reasonably believes to have the relevant information to give such information to him (s.444). It is open to the Secretary of State to take this course in a case where he receives an application from shareholders for the appointment of inspectors under s.442 (s.442(3C)).

If, in connection with an investigation under ss.442 or 444, the Secretary of State considers that there is difficulty in finding out the relevant facts about the shares, he has power to impose restrictions on transfers of shares, on the exercise of voting rights in respect of the shares, and on the making of payments in relation to the shares (s.445).

Investigations Under s.446 of the Companies Act 1985

The Secretary of State has power under s.446 of the Companies Act 1985 to appoint inspectors to investigate suspected share dealings by directors or their families in their own companies or related companies in contravention of the Companies Act, s.323 or 324 and Sch.13. **29–070**

Privileged Information

29–071 S.452 of the Companies Act 1985 provides that nothing in ss.431 to 446 of the Act requires a person to disclose to the Secretary of State or to an inspector appointed by him any information which, in an action in the High Court, he would be entitled to refuse to disclose on grounds of legal professional privilege. A lawyer may, however, be required to disclose the name and address of his client.

Chapter 30

Investor Protection in Trust Law

Introduction

There are three ways in which trusts law may impinge in the area of investor protection. 30–001

In the first instance, there are occasions when an investor passes investment funds to another person in circumstances where the funds are to be used for a specific purpose, such as the purchase of shares, government securities, gold bullion or some other form of property or financial security. In this type of case the funds are held on trust for the investor, so that if the moneys are misapplied by the receiver and/or the receiver becomes insolvent, the receiver's duty to return the funds to the investor is founded not simply in terms of debt but also in breach of an obligation to account in terms of trust. The existence of the trust relationship has considerable significance in this context. In an insolvency the funds will not enter the general pool of assets from which a receiver's creditors will fall to be paid because the funds are "impressed" with a trust and held by the receiver on a different basis, on resulting trust for the investor. This means that if an investor's funds can be identified, the funds will be recoverable and protected from the claims of other creditors. The circumstances in which an investor's funds will be impressed with a trust will be considered in the first part of this chapter.

There is a second area in which trusts law may impinge in the context of investor protection law. In any modern case of investment fraud, persons other than the fraudster will almost certainly handle or assist in handling the misapplied funds, either at the time of misappropriation or during the laundering process. Third parties, such as banks, building societies, stockbrokers, estate agents, solicitors and accountants are potentially exposed in this regard. Where misapplied funds have been handled by a third party or a third party has assisted in the handling of funds, it will be important for an investor to know whether there is any actionable claim against the third party in respect of his conduct. A third party may become personally liable to an investor as a constructive trustee where, with regard to his action or inaction in relation to the investment funds (*i.e.* the trust property), a Court considers it appropriate to order him to make good the investor's loss. Although a professional third party like a bank may not be an accomplice to a fraudulent scheme, this will not be sufficient to absolve the third party from personal liability where there were circumstances which should have put the third party on enquiry. In cases where the fraudster may have fled the jurisdiction, or where he is resident but 30–002 insolvent, the possibility of legal action against a professional third party can sometimes provide the aggrieved investor with his only realistic chance of recovering his lost investment. The circumstances where an aggrieved investor can recover his loss from a third party is the subject of consideration in the second part of this chapter.

Modern trusts law is also significant in procedural terms, because where an investor can establish a claim against a trustee for breach of trust or a third party for assisting in a breach of trust, an investor can utilise the extensive power of tracing monies which has been retained by the Court in the exercise of its ancient equitable jurisdiction. The operation of these tracing remedies is considered in part three of this chapter.

Investor's Funds Held on Trust

Relationship in Contract and/or Trust

30–003 In the ordinary situation, when a person pays over his monies to another, the relationship between the payer and the payee is governed by the terms of the agreement which has been made between them. A contract for banking services is a classic example, where a payer pays money to a banker for the latter to hold on his behalf. The relationship is exclusively contractual, and it is the duty of the payee as debtor to repay the payer as creditor in accordance with the terms of the contract which have been agreed. The debtor's obligation is personal and not proprietary, which means that the obligation to repay arises in debt rather than in any obligation to deal with the money in a particular way. However, in cases where money is paid over for the purposes of investment, the position will probably be different, for in this type of case the purpose for which the money is paid will often be specified. For instance, where an investor pays money to a financial services company for the purchase of some specified form of investment, such as stocks or shares, government securities, bonds, or commodities, the words which are used when the payment is made will probably be capable of being construed as creating an obligation both in terms of contract and also in terms of trust. Indeed, if the financial services company is regulated under the terms of the Financial Services and Markets Act 2000 a relationship of trust will almost certainly be created since the authorised person will be obliged to hold the funds in a designated client account—see Ch.3 on this point.

The essence of a trust relationship is the passing of property by one person (known as the beneficiary) into the possession and control of another person (known as the trustee) for the trustee to deal with the property on behalf of the beneficiary in a particular way. Unlike a contractual relationship, which is exclusively personal, a trust relationship is proprietary, in the sense that it arises independently of agreement and attaches to the property itself. There is no reason why, in terms of law, the relationship of debtor/creditor and trustee/beneficiary cannot co-exist in cases where the circumstances demonstrate that the parties intended to create both forms of obligation.

A good illustration of the confluence between a contractual and a trust relationship occurred in the Barlow Clowes case where the Barlow Clowes group marketed off-shore investment schemes, known as portfolios, for investment in gilt-edged stock. Investors were induced to invest in the portfolios by representations that their moneys would be securely invested in British government securities. The brochure stated that investors cheques were to be paid to the Barlow Clowes groups' international account, which on its face suggested that a relationship of debtor and creditor was to be created between the investor and the financial services company. However, the brochures went on to state that all moneys were to be held in a designated clients account and "the clients are the beneficial owners of all securities purchased on their behalf", which strongly suggested that a relationship of trust between the investor as beneficiary and the financial services company as trustee was to be created as well. In these circumstances the Court of Appeal determined that it was clear from the brochures and the terms of the portfolio investments, construed as a whole, that the Barlow Clowes group had received funds from investors on trust to invest them in British government stocks—see *R. v Clowes* [1994] 2 All E.R. 316. **30–004**

The practical implications of a trust relationship were vividly demonstrated some years ago by a case which was heard in the House of Lords, *Barclays Bank Ltd v Quistclose Investments Ltd* [1968] 3 All E.R. 651. A company needed to borrow a significant sum of money to pay dividends which had been declared on its shares. The company borrowed the money from Quistclose Investments under an arrangement whereby the loan was to be used only for that purpose. The money was paid into a separate account at Barclays Bank, the bank having notice of the nature of the arrangement. Before the dividend was paid the company went into liquidation. Barclays Bank sought to off-set the money against the company's overdraft liability but Quistclose Investments intervened and argued that the company had received the money as trustees and continued to hold it as trustee. The House of Lords held that the money had indeed been received on trust to be applied for the payment of dividends. That purpose having failed, the money was held on trust for the lender. The fact that the transaction was a loan, recoverable by an action at law, did not exclude the implication of a trust. The legal (*i.e.* debt) and equitable (*i.e* trust) remedies could co-exist. As Lord Wilberforce explained in his judgment which continues to govern this area of law: **30–005**

> ". . . when the money is advanced, the lender acquires an equitable right to see that it is applied for the primary designated purpose . . .; when the purpose has been carried out (ie: the debt paid) the lender has his remedy against the borrower in debt; if the primary purpose cannot be carried out, the question arises if a secondary purpose (ie: the repayment to the lender) has been agreed, expressly or by implication: if it has, the remedies of equity may be invoked to give effect to it, if it has not (and the money is intended to fall within the general fund of the debtor's assets) then there is the appropriate remedy for recovery of a loan. I can appreciate no reason why the flexible interplay of law and equity cannot let in these practical arrangements, and other variations if desired: it would be to the discredit of both systems if they could not".

Application in the Investor Context

30–006 The Courts have permitted the "Quistclose trust" principle to apply quite broadly in cases where money has not been paid to a defendant to hold beneficially. In *Carreras Rothmans v Freeman Mathews* [1985] 1 All E.R. 155 the plaintiff lent money to the defendant company for the specific purpose of settling invoices submitted by the plaintiff in the course of its business. The Court, applying *Barclays Bank v Quistclose Investments Limited*, held that a relationship of trust had been created because the money had not been paid to the defendant beneficially. Broadening the category of case to which the Quistclose trust principle will apply, Peter Gibson J. said (at p.165f) that equity fastens onto the conscience of the person who receives property from another person for a specific purpose only and not for the recipients' own purpose:

> "If the common intention is that property is transferred for a specified purpose and not so as to become the property of the transferee, the transferee cannot keep the property if for any reason that purpose cannot be fulfilled".

30–007 The payment of monies into a designated bank account was a significant but not conclusive indication of a common intention to create a trust—*Re Kayford Ltd* [1975] 1 All E.R. 604. The Quistclose trust principle has been applied in other cases, such as *Barclays Bank plc v Willowbrook International Ltd*, The Times, February 5, 1987 and *Re EVTR Ltd, Gilbert v Barber*, *The Times*, June 24, 1987.

The significance of the application of these principles in the investor protection context, where investor's funds are misapplied and/or an investment scheme fails, will be readily appreciated. In *Re Nanwa Gold Mines Ltd* [1955] 3 All E.R. 219 a company issued a share form application to existing shareholders seeking fresh capital to resume its activities. The application contained a statement which said that shares would be issued on condition that a scheme for reduction of capital was approved by the company in general meeting and ratified by the Court. The scheme was formally abandoned after existing members had subscribed for new shares. The Court held that the money was repayable to the members because they had subscribed the money on the faith of a promise to refund the money if certain conditions were not fulfilled.

In a more recent case, *Stanlake Holdings Ltd v Tropical Capital Investment Ltd, Financial Times* 1991, June 25, a businessman lent £70,000 to an investment company in order to assist an off-shore client with a contract to buy tyres in the Ivory Coast. In fact the scheme was a fraud and the director of the defendant company, together with his solicitor, were convicted of obtaining property by deception. £55,000 of the £70,000 was found in a safe at the solicitor's office. Applying the *Quistclose Trust* principle, the Court of Appeal ruled that the money was held in trust for the plaintiff, the purpose of the loan having failed.

Knowing Receipt and Knowing Assistance in Breach of Trust

The General Principle

The foundation of liability in this complicated area of law is rooted in the notion that persons, not appointed trustees, may be liable as if they were so appointed, if they intermeddle with funds which are held on trust. This important principle of trusts law was famously expressed long ago by Lord Selborne L.C. in *Barnes v Addy* [1874] L.R. 9 Ch. App. 244 in terms which continue to express the present state of the law in this area: **30–008**

> "That responsibility [of a trustee] may no doubt be extended in equity to others who are not properly trustees, if they are found . . . actually participating in any fraudulent conduct of the trustee to the injury of the . . . [beneficiary]. But . . . strangers are not to be made constructive trustees merely because they act as the agents of trustees in transactions within their legal powers, transactions, perhaps of which a Court of Equity may disapprove, unless those agents receive and become chargeable with some part of the trust property, or unless they assist with the knowledge in a dishonest and fraudulent design on the part of the trustees."

In this passage Lord Selborne delineated two distinct limbs of potential liability. The first limb, contained in the first sentence of the citation, provided that a third party (*i.e.* stranger or non-trustee) may become liable to account if he "actually participates in any fraudulent conduct" by receiving funds which have been misapplied in breach of trust. The second limb, reflected in the second sentence of the citation, established that a third party may become liable where he "assists with knowledge in a dishonest and fraudulent design", not necessarily where he actually receives the trust funds but where he provides some other form of assistance. The first limb has become known as "knowing receipt", in contrast to the second limb which has become known as "knowing assistance".

Problems

During the last thirty years there has been much litigation directed at defining more precisely the circumstances in which a third party can be held liable as a constructive trustee in application of the principles formulated by Lord Selborne. There have been two main areas of contention. The first area of dispute concerned the degree of dishonest knowledge which had to be imputed to a third party before he could be held liable as a constructive trustee. Was it necessary to prove that the third party was dishonest in a strictly subjective sense, or was a more objective standard sufficient, as where a third party "turned a blind eye" to the breach of trust or where there were circumstances which should have alarmed the third party by "putting him on notice" that he was assisting in the handling of funds in breach of trust? **30–009**

The second area of dispute has focused not on the mental state of the third party's mind but on the state of mind of the trustee. In these cases litigants have sought to argue that a dishonest third party could not be held liable for dishonestly assisting in the handling of trust funds where the breach of trust committed by the trustee was innocent or negligent rather than dishonest. Dishonest conduct on the part of the trustee was, so litigants argued, a condition precedent to the liability of an (albeit dishonest) third party.

The Position Resolved

30–010 After a series of contradictory decisions in both these areas of dispute, the position was resolved by the Privy Council recently in the case of *Royal Brunei Airlines Sdn v Tan* [1995] 3 All E.R. 97. Summarising the Privy Council's conclusion, Lord Nicholls said:

> "Drawing the threads together, their Lordships' overall conclusion is that dishonesty is a necessary ingredient of accessory liability. It is also a sufficient ingredient. A liability in equity to make good resulting loss attaches to a person who dishonestly procures or assists in a breach of trust or fiduciary obligation. It is not necessary that, in addition, the trustee or fiduciary was acting dishonestly, although this will usually be so where the third party who is assisting him is acting dishonestly. 'Knowingly' is better avoided as a defining ingredient of the principle . . ."

Within the formulation put forward by Lord Selborne in *Barnes v Addy*, instead of referring to "knowing receipt" and "knowing assistance", "dishonest receipt" and "dishonest assistance" are more accurate epithets.

Dishonesty

30–011 Exploring the position a little further, the Privy Council considered what was meant by the notion of "dishonesty". Was dishonesty a subjective matter or, as some of the earlier cases had suggested, could dishonesty be established by a more objective standard? The answer, said the Privy Council, lay in keeping in mind that honesty is an objective standard. Irrespective of the position in criminal law, in the context of the accessory liability principle, acting dishonestly, or with a lack of probity, meant simply not acting as an honest person would in the circumstances. This was clearly, said Lord Nicholls, an objective standard.

Whilst it was right that there is a subjective aspect to dishonesty, in the sense that it is a description of a type of conduct assessed in the light of what a person actually knew at the time, honesty could not be measured on an optional scale. "If a person knowingly appropriates another's property, he will not escape a finding of dishonesty simply because he sees nothing wrong in such behaviour". An honest person does not, said Lord Nicholls, deliberately close his eyes and ears, or deliberately not ask questions, lest he learn something he would rather not know, and then proceed regardless:

> "The individual is expected to attain the standard which would be observed by an honest person placed in those circumstances. It is impossible to be more specific. Knox J captured the flavour of this, in a case with a commercial setting, when he referred to a person who is 'guilty of commercially unacceptable conduct in the particular context involved': see *Cowan de Groot Properties Ltd v Eagle Trust plc* [1992] 4 All E.R. 700 at 761 . . . . Ultimately, in most cases, an honest person should have little difficulty in knowing whether a proposed transaction, or his participation in it, would offend the normally accepted standards of honest conduct" (at p.107 c–f).

A Trustee's State of Mind

As regards the second area which had been the subject of dispute, Lord Nicholls explained by use of examples why the trustee's state of mind was not a relevant consideration to a third party's liability: **30–012**

> "Take a case where a dishonest solicitor persuades a trustee to apply trust property in a way the trustee honestly believes is permissible but which the solicitor knows full well is a clear breach of trust. The solicitor deliberately conceals this from the trustee. In consequence, the beneficiaries suffer a substantial loss. It cannot be right that in such a case the accessory liability principle would be inapplicable because of the innocence of the trustee" (at p.101h).

The trustee, as Lord Nicholls pointed out, will be liable in any event for the breach of trust, even if he acted innocently, unless excused by an exemption clause in the trust instrument or relieved by the court. But his state of mind is essentially irrelevant to the question whether the third party should be made liable to the beneficiaries for the breach of trust.

Assessment of the Royal Brunei Airlines Decision

Seen within the context of investor protection, the Privy Council decision is helpful to an aggrieved investor in two respects. The objective standard of dishonesty by which a third party is to be judged is helpful in terms of investor protection because it means that third parties, such as the smaller merchant banks, will no longer be able to "turn a blind eye" and retain "dodgy" business without accepting responsibility to re-imburse the aggrieved investor if his investment is lost. So far as the trustee's state of mind is concerned, whilst it is right that in most cases of investment fraud the trustee, *i.e.* the fraudster to whom the investor paid his funds, will be acting dishonestly in subjective, let alone objective, terms, there will be other cases where, in the financial services arena, an investor may suffer loss at the hands of an honest, but recklessly incompetent, trustee of his funds. In these situations, an action against a third party who handles or assists in handling the funds should not be ruled out. As Lord Nicholls pointed out (at p.108b-c), professional advisors employed by trustees owe a duty to exercise reasonable skill and care. The rights flowing from that duty, in Lord Nicholls' view, form part of the trust property and can be **30–013** enforced by the beneficiaries in a suitable case if the trustees are unable or unwilling to do so.

30–014 The facts of the *Royal Brunei Airlines* case usefully illustrate the application of the constructive trust principle in practical terms. The defendant was the principal shareholder and managing director of a travel company which had been appointed to act as a general travel agent for an airline. From time to time monies were transferred from the company's current account into fixed term deposits held in the name of the defendant. The company current account contained moneys received by the company from sales of airline tickets, in respect of which the company was obliged to account to the airline within thirty days of receipt. The company terminated its agency agreement and became insolvent, whereupon the airline brought an action against the defendant on the basis that he had knowingly assisted in a fraudulent and dishonest design on the part of the company to deal with the funds in breach of trust. The defendant argued that he had acted dishonestly in a subjective sense, and further the company, as trustee of the funds, had not been acting dishonestly. Asserting arguments which are commonly advanced in the context of fraudulent trading, the defendant said that he expected to pay the airline but that the funds had been lost in the ordinary course of a poorly run business with heavy overhead expenses. The Privy Council rejected these arguments, holding that the airline should succeed in its claim.

The Privy Council extensively reviewed the previous cases which had been decided in this area and reference should be made to Lord Nicholls' opinion for references to these cases. Suffice it to note that the circumstances in *Lipkin Gorman (a firm) v Karpnale Ltd* [1992] 4 All E.R. 331 and *Barclays Bank plc v Quincecare Ltd* [1992] 4 All E.R. 363 are of particular interest in the context of investor protection.

The Akindele and Yardley Decisions

30–015 Two important cases followed after the *Royal Brunei Airlines* decision. In *Bank of Credit & Commerce International (Overseas) Ltd v Akindele* [2000] 3 W.L.R. 1423, the Court of Appeal gave a detailed commentary on the controversy surrounding the issue of knowledge, concluding that in order to incur liability as a constructive trustee the state of mind of a recipient who received funds must be such as to make it unconscionable for him to retain the benefit of the receipt. The Court held that dishonesty was not a prerequisite of liability.

Subsequently, in *Twinsectra Ltd v Yardley* [2002] 2 W.L.R. 802, the House of Lords was required to consider whether a deliberate failure to ask questions or consider the implications of embarrassing facts would trigger liability under the principle of a constructive trust. With Lord Millett dissenting, the majority of the House of Lords held dishonest assistance in a breach of trust would only be made out upon proof of a dishonest state of mind, *i.e.* consciousness that one was transgressing ordinary standards of honest behaviour.

A careful reading of the decision of the House of Lords decision in *Twinsectra Ltd v Yardley* reveals a retreat from the more objectively based criterion developed by the Privy Council in the *Royal Brunei Airlines* case. It also represents a departure from the unrestricted notion canvassed in the *Akindele* decision that unconscionable behaviour should be the yardstick by which to judge liability, notwithstanding the inherently imprecise nature of this concept. It remains to be seen whether the lower Courts will run with the subjective baton handed to them by the House of Lords.

Funds Must Have Been Held on Trust

Liability as a constructive trustee will be imposed only where the trustee has "intermeddled" with funds which are held on trust. Of course, a trust does not need to have been formally, or expressly, established. There are many cases where the law imputes a relationship of trust where it can be seen that the parties intended the funds to be held in trust. As noted when considering the application of a *Quistclose* trust, this can usually be demonstrated by an analysis of the purpose for which the money was paid. Generally, investment funds will be received under some obligation to retain or deal with the funds in a particular way, as where, for example, the funds are to be invested in stocks and shares, government securities, unit trusts, bonds, commodities or real estate. **30–016**

In the absence of an obligation on the part of the recipient to retain and deal with funds in a particular way, the principle of constructive trusteeship cannot apply. This requirement was satisfied in *Royal Brunei Airlines* because, albeit not an investment case, the company was obliged under the terms of its general agency agreement to account to the airline for ticket sales within 30 days of their receipt. An example of a case where the position was different occurred in *Goose v Wilson & Sandford* (unreported) April 1, 1996 where the defendant had persuaded the plaintiff to become jointly involved in a venture with a third party who turned out to be a fraudster. The defendant was the accountant of the company in which the plaintiff invested, and on the basis of this relationship the plaintiff brought a claim against him as a constructive trustee as well as a claim in negligence. The Court dismissed the claims because, so far as the constructive trustee allegation was concerned, a person could not be a trustee in the abstract. Since the company was not subject to account for the money which it had received from the plaintiff, there could be no trusteeship. No person can be liable for assisting in the performance of a dishonest design if the alleged trustee does not hold any property for the benefit of another.

Assistance

A third party has to afford some active assistance to the trustee if he is to become liable as a constructive trustee. Mere knowledge of a breach of trust is not enough, some participation in furtherance of the breach must be shown. In *Brinks Limited (formerly Brink's Mat Limited) v Kamal Hassan Abu-Saleh* (unreported) October 10, 1995, the plaintiff sought to hold a defendant liable as a constructive trustee on the grounds that she had **30–017** assisted in furtherance of a breach of trust by accompanying her husband on various journeys from England to Switzerland when her husband had been transporting approximately £3 million in cash. The money had been derived from the sale of melted down gold bullion which had been stolen from Heathrow Airport in a large robbery. The breach of trust had been committed not by the defendant's husband, who plainly assisted in the furtherance of the breach, but by a security guard at Heathrow Airport who, in breach of trust, had passed security information to the robbers. The Court held that the security guard was employed in a position of trust, that he owed a duty not to divulge security information, that he breached that duty by disclosing this information to the robbers, but that the defendant's association with her husband did not amount to "assistance" in furtherance of the breach of trust to hold her liable as a constructive trustee. The plaintiff's claim against the defendant's husband was settled prior to the hearing.

Liability for Breach of Trust

30–018 Where a trustee (or a third party liable as if he were a trustee) is found to be under a liability to a beneficiary, it is necessary to consider the extent of the trustee's liability to compensate the beneficiary for such loss. Traditionally, the trustee is obliged to restore the assets or to pay compensation for the loss but this will apply only where there is some causal connection between the trustee's breach and the loss. There would be liability even if the direct cause of the loss was not caused by the trustee if, but for the trustee's breach, the loss could not have occurred—*Nestle v National Westminster Bank* [1994] 1 All E.R. 118. This is not to say that the Courts will expect a trustee to act as an insurer for the assets held in trust. A trustee will not be liable to compensate the beneficiary for losses which the beneficiary would, in any event, have suffered even if there had been no breach of trust. This was established recently by the House of Lords in *Target Holdings Ltd v Redferns (a firm)* [1995] 3 All E.R. 785 where solicitors acting for a client/mortgagee erroneously transmitted money to mortgagors before the charges were executed over the relevant properties. The properties were later (through no fault of the solicitors) found to be insufficient security for the loans. The purpose of equitable compensation for breach of trust was to make good loss suffered by the beneficiary which, using hindsight and common sense, could be seen to have been caused by the breach.

Tracing Remedies

General Principles

30–019 Whereas an action for breach of contract is personal, in the sense that the action fixes on the liability of the person rather than the asset, an action for breach of trust will fix on the property where the property is capable of identification. The advantage of a proprietary remedy over a personal remedy is that the former does not depend on the defendant's solvency if the property is still in existence. In an investor fraud where funds have been lost, attention is focused on whether the funds are capable of identification for the purposes of the proprietary remedy. The position is relatively clear in a case where a defendant has exchanged one chattel for another, but suppose he has mixed investment funds with his personal monies. How can an investor's funds be traced and identified for the purpose of the proprietary remedy in these circumstances? These questions have been asked many times before, and the relevant principles were established long ago. It is the application of these principles to the complexities of modern commercial life which continue to occupy the time of the Court on a daily basis.

The Court first grappled with the problems engendered in this area by an investor fraud over one hundred and eighty years ago, in *Taylor v Plumer* [1815] 3 M. & S. 562 where a defendant, an investor, paid money to his stockbroker to purchase exchequer bonds. The stockbroker used the funds to buy some American investments and sought to flee to the new country. He was arrested, and on his bankruptcy the plaintiff, his assignee in bankruptcy, tried to recover the American investments. The defendant resisted on the ground that the investments were the ascertainable product of the money which he had given to the stockbroker, and, in terms, they were owned by him. The Court agreed and rejected the assignee's claim. The relevant principles to be applied in this type of case were elucidated by Lord Ellenborough in terms which continue to have considerable relevance today:

> "It makes no difference in reason or law into what form, different from the original, the change may have been made, whether it be into that of promissory notes for the security of the money which was produced by the sale of the goods of the principal, as in *Scott v Surman* [1742] Willes 400, or into other merchandise, as in *Whitcomb v Jacob* [1710] Salk 160, for the product of or in substitute for the original thing still follows the nature of the thing itself, as long as it can be ascertained to be such, and the right only ceases when the means of ascertainment fail, which is the case when the subject is turned into money, and mixed and confounded in a general mass of the same description. The difficulty which arises in such a case is a difficulty of fact and not law, and the dictum that money has no ear-mark must be understood in the same way; ie. as predicated only of an undivided and undistinguishable mass of current money. But money in a bag or otherwise kept apart from other money, guineas, or other coin marked, if the fact were so, for the purpose of being distinguished, and so far ear-marked as to fall within the rule on this subject, which applies to every other description of personal property whilst it remains (as the property in question did) in the hands of the factor [the bankrupt] or his general legal representatives".

The position is more complicated where a trustee has mixed trust funds **30–020**
with other monies. At common law the right to trace is considered to be lost because the funds are no longer identifiable, but equity has sought to overcome this problem by the application of some complex rules. Where trust funds have been mixed, equity has imposed an onus on the trustee to

establish that part of his own money has been mixed with the trust funds. A beneficiary will be entitled to the funds which the trustee cannot prove to be his own. But suppose the trustee has drawn on mixed funds and/or replenished the funds from an outside source. The general rule is that the tracing remedy can be applied against a mixed fund only to the extent that the trust funds can still be shown to be there. If the account falls below that sum, that part of the trust money will be deemed to have been spent—*Roscoe v Winder* [1915] 1 Ch. 62. Later payments into the mixed fund will not be treated as repayments of the trust fund unless the trustee shows an intention to do so. It is essential, therefore, to determine from the accounts the lowest intermediate balance in the fund to see if a tracing remedy is available.

30–021 In cases where funds have been mixed in a bank account, the Courts are sometimes prepared to apply the rule in *Clayton's Case* [1817] 1 Mer. 572 which provides that the first payment into the account is appropriated to the earliest debt which is not statute-barred, in other words "first in, first out". An example of a situation where this rule will not apply, however, is a case where many small investors participated in a collective investment scheme by which their money would be mixed together and invested through a common fund. This is what happened in the Barlow Clowes case where the Court concluded that the presumed intention of the parties must have been that the "first in, first out" rule would not apply and that all the assets available for distribution, whether moneys already invested in British government stocks, moneys awaiting invested and moneys diverted into other assets would be shared *pari passu* in proportion to the amounts due to them. The Court said that the "first in, first out" rule would not apply where it would be impractical or would result in injustice between investors because a relatively small number of investors would get most of the funds. The "first in, first out" rule would be applied in an investor fraud case only where the rule provided a convenient method of determining competing claims where several beneficiaries' moneys had been blended in one account and there was a deficiency or where there had been a wrongful mixing of different sums of trust money in a single account—*Barlow Clowes International Limited (in liquidation) v Vaughan* [1994] 2 All E.R. 22.

The leading trusts law textbooks are replete with further examples of the application of these tracing principles. Suffice it in this context if consideration is confined to some problems which have occurred recently in the investor context.

Recent Applications in Investor Fraud Cases

30–022 The elasticity of the equitable tracing remedy was insufficient to assist the trustees of the hapless Maxwell pension fund after money had been improperly paid into the overdrawn bank account of Maxwell Communication Corporation plc. Equitable tracing, although devised for the protection of misapplied funds, could not be pursued through an overdrawn and therefore non-existent fund. As the Court of Appeal explained, it was only possible to trace in equity funds which had continued existence, actual or notional, and which could be identified at every stage of their journey through life—*Bishopsgate Investment Management v Homan* [1995] 1 All E.R. 347.

At one time it had been thought that the Courts might have been prepared to stretch the tracing remedy to cover all the assets of the trustee, after Lord Templeman had said in *Space Investments Ltd v Canadian Imperial Bank of Commerce Trust Co* [1986] 3 All E.R. 75 (at pp.76–77), a case involving the position of an insolvent bank that had been taking deposits and lending money, that equity would allow the beneficiaries to trace the trust money "to all the assets of the bank". These words were given a wide interpretation by the New Zealand Court of Appeal in *Liggett v Kensington* [1993] 1 N.Z.L.R. 257, where in a case involving a gold bullion company which had become insolvent, non-allocated claimants were permitted to assert a proprietary claim to gold bullion which was held by the company. This decision, however, was overturned by the Privy Council, reported as *Re Goldcorp Exchange Ltd (in receivership)* [1994] 2 All E.R. 806, on the basis that an equitable title could not pass under a simple contract for the sale of unascertained goods merely by virtue of the sale because the buyer could not acquire title until it was known to what goods the title related. These established principles were affirmed by the Court of Appeal in *Bishopsgate Investment Management v Homan*. As Buckley L.J. said in *Borden (UK) Ltd v Scottish Timber Products Ltd* [1979] 3 All E.R. 961 (at p.974), in a passage approved by Leggatt L.J. in *Bishopsgate Investment Management v Homan*:

> ". . . it is a fundamental feature of the doctrine of tracing that the property to be traced can be identified at every stage of its journey through life".

The limitation imposed by this fundamental feature on the efficacy of the tracing remedy in cases of investor fraud is well demonstrated by the *Bishopsgate Investment Management v Homan* decision. **30–023**

It follows from an application of these principles that there can be no equitable remedy over an asset acquired before misappropriation of funds takes place, unless there is a possibility of subrogation, since *ex hypothesi* the funds cannot be followed into property which existed and so had been acquired before the funds were received and therefore without their aid—*Re Goldcorp Exchange Ltd (in receivership)* [1994] 2 All E.R. 806. The relationship between tracing and subrogation was explored by the Court of Appeal in *Boscawen v Bajwa* [1995] 4 All E.R. 769 where the Court noted that the remedies were quite distinct in law.

Application of the Tracing Remedy to a Constructive Trustee

Whilst the issues concerning the ability of a litigant to trace his assets have tended to arise during the course of litigation for breach of trust, the tracing remedy can be utilised against a constructive trustee who dishonestly handles or assists in handling the trust funds. As Millett L.J. said recently in *Boscowen v Bajwa* (at p.776g), in a case where a judgment creditor claimed to be entitled to property over which he had a charging order: **30–024**

> "Tracing properly so called . . . is neither a claim nor a remedy but a process. Moreover, it is not confined to the case where the plaintiff seeks a proprietary remedy; it is equally necessary where he seeks a personal remedy against the knowing recipient or knowing assistant. It is the process by which the plaintiff traces what has happened to his property, identifies the persons who have handled it or received it, and justifies his claim that the money which they have handled or received (and if necessary which they still retain) can properly be regarded as representing his property".

The unhappy experience of the Maxwell pensioners and the gold bullion investors may be contrasted with the experience of a wealthy Saudi Arabian investor who recently succeeded in recovering £2.325 million by an application of the tracing principles in a claim based on constructive trust, albeit after a protracted battle in the courts. The investor's money had been spent by his dishonest agent on the purchase of a large number of worthless shares which had been marketed by fraudulent salesmen in Amsterdam. The profits of the fraud were laundered through an elaborate international system and some of the proceeds eventually came to be represented by part of the interest which ostensibly belonged to the defendant, Dollar Land Holdings plc, a UK property company, in a site at Nine Elms, Battersea. This interest was acquired by another UK property company, Regalian plc, for £4.65 million. Regalian plc had been a joint venture partner of the defendant, Dollar Land Holdings, but had no knowledge of the fraud. The investor sued the defendant to recover his money based on the defendant's knowing receipt of assets traceable in equity as representing his misappropriated funds. The investor had invested approximately US$6.673 in the company and on the strength of this investment he claimed to recover the total sum of £2.325 million, which represented one-half of the purchase price paid when the property was sold by the defendant to Regalian plc. Although the Court at first instance held that the assets were traceable in equity, it rejected the plaintiff's claim on the basis that the knowledge of a former chairman of the defendant company did not amount to knowledge on the part of the company.

30–025 The Court of Appeal reversed this decision and remitted the case to the Chancery Division to determine the assessment of damages—*El Ajou v Dollar Land Holdings plc* [1994] 2 All E.R. 685. Evidence presented before the Dutch court had shown that although the shares had been sold fraudulently to 4,000 investors, the plaintiff, as the largest investor by far, was the only victim whose lost assets could be specifically traceable to the defendant company through the laundering process. In these circumstances the plaintiff argued that his equitable right extended to recovery of the whole of his investment. The defendant company presented a contrary argument, contending that the plaintiff could recover only a fraction of the £2.325 million and that the balance belonged in equity to the other victims. The court held that since there was no other claimant who was seeking to assert a charge ranking rateably with the plaintiff's charge and that there was no realistic possibility of such a claim being made in the future, there was nothing inequitable in permitting the plaintiff to recover the whole of his investment. The Court said that there could be no rigid rule as to whether or not the rights of a third party could be raised as a defence to a tracing claim because each case depended on its individual circumstances—*El Ajou v Dollar Land Holdings (No 2)* [1995] 2 All E.R. 213.

This case is significant in the investor protection context for two reasons. 30–026
First, in terms of imputing dishonesty to a limited company for the purposes of establishing a claim based on constructive trust, the case demonstrates that an aggrieved investor will not be limited to reliance on the conduct of a company officer who holds office at the time of the misappropriation. Rather, the Courts will examine the mind and will of the natural person or persons who manage and control the company. As Nourse L.J. acknowledged in the Court of Appeal (at p.696c), "decided cases show that, in regard to the requisite status and authority, the formal position, as regulated by the company's articles of association, service contracts and so forth, though highly relevant, may not be decisive". Secondly, the decision draws attention to the unavoidable element of randomness which occurs in this type of case where an investor attempts to recover misapplied funds. As Robert Walker J. acknowledged when assessing the amount of damages (at pp.221j and 222b), changes in the "state of investment" of the fund which is being traced may occur in a totally random way, and it is possible for one claimant to lose his right to trace and another claimant may in consequence be preferred through circumstances over which neither has any control. In this sense the position of a claimant in a constructive trust case is different from that of a beneficiary of a properly constituted trust fund. In the latter case the rights between beneficiaries will not alter, whereas in the former case the rights between beneficiaries will alter, depending on changes in the composition of the trust fund.

Jurisdiction

A jurisdictional issue often arises in cases where restitutionary remedies are 30–027
sought in respect of property which is situated outside the jurisdiction. The problem occurred in another aspect of the Maxwell case, in this instance concerning shares in a New York company which had been pledged in England to banks as security for loans without the shareholder's consent. The question arose as to whether the issue of priority of ownership of the shares should be determined according to English law or the law in the United States. The Court of Appeal held that the appropriate law to decide questions of title to shares was the law of the place where the shares were situated which was in the ordinary way the place where the company was incorporated. Since New York was also the place where the share register was maintained, the applicable law for determination of the issue of priority was the domestic law of the State of New York—*Macmillan v Bishopsgate Investment Trust (3)* [1996] 1 All E.R. 585. Each of the three judges, Staughton, Auld and Aldous L.JJ., reviewed the principles which are to be applied in this type of case at some length.

Chapter 31

Investor Protection at Common Law

Introduction

This chapter is concerned with an aggrieved investor's ability to obtain redress through the civil Courts where he has been induced to make an investment and/or his investment funds have been misapplied as a result of another's fraud, or where the investor has suffered loss as a result of another's misrepresentation and/or breach of contract. Other situations where an investor can obtain redress, as where an investment has been made on the basis of inaccurate financial information and/or incorrect investment advice, or where loss can be attributed to some breach of director's duty or breach of trust, are the subject of consideration in other chapters, *viz.* Chs 29 (breach of director's duties and other company law remedies), 30 (breach of trust and constructive trust remedies) and 32 (liability for negligent mis-statement). Readers should bear in mind that the civil remedies discussed in this chapter have been considered in a number of learned works. Reference should be made to these works where necessary. **31–001**

Deceit

General Principle

An action for deceit involves (1) the making of a false representation by the defendant, who either knows the representation to be untrue or who has no belief in its truth or who is reckless as to its truth, (2) an intention by the defendant that the investor will rely on the representation, and (3) actual reliance by the investor on the representation. Each ingredient has to be established before an action for the tort of deceit can succeed. **31–002**

The representation which is necessary to found an action must be a representation as to a past or existing fact. A classic example of a false representation occurred in *Edginton v Fitzmaurice* [1885] 29 Ch. D. 459 where directors issued a prospectus inviting subscriptions for debentures. The prospectus stated that the object of the loan was to enable the company to enlarge its premises and buy additional plant, but in fact the money was needed to discharge trading liabilities. The court held that the misrepresentation of the purpose was sufficient to found an action for deceit. Complicated issues sometimes arise in this area, as for instance where the substance of the representation reflects a person's opinion or concerns some future fact (*e.g.* "in the opinion of the auditors the profits of the company will exceed £5 million in the next accounting year"), or where non-disclosure of a critical fact impacts on the way in which a representation of existing fact may be understood. A detailed examination of the law in this area is beyond the scope of this book.

31–003 As regards the defendant's state of mind, the position was established long ago in the leading case of *Derry v Peek* [1889] 14 App. Cas. 337 where Lord Herschell set out (at p.376) the essential ingredients of an action of deceit:

> "First, in order to sustain an action of deceit, there must be proof of fraud and nothing short of that will suffice. Secondly, fraud is proved when it is shown that a false representation has been made (i) knowingly, (ii) without belief in its truth, or (iii) recklessly, careless whether it be true or false. Although I have treated the second and third as distinct cases, I think the third is but an instance of the second, for one who makes a statement under such circumstances can have no real belief in the truth of what he states. To prevent a false statement from being fraudulent, there must, I think, always be an honest belief in its truth".

Proof of the defendant's lack of honest belief will not be easy to achieve in cases of this nature. In forensic terms an investor will be assisted where the grounds of honest belief are obviously unreasonable, but in the majority of cases it will be difficult to tip the balance of the scales in the investor's favour. The facts of *Derry v Peek* illustrate the point. In that case a private Act of Parliament had provided that cars provided by a tramway company could be propelled by steam power if the Board of Trade consented to this course. The directors, before obtaining consent, issued a prospectus stating that under the terms of the private Act the company had authority to use steam power. In the event the Board of Trade refused to grant consent and the company was wound-up. In an action brought by the shareholders against the directors for deceit, the House of Lords held that the directors, having no intention to deceive, were not liable. The shareholders had not proved that the directors lacked honest belief. Lord Herschell reached this conclusion with reluctance, exhorting directors who seek to raise funds from the public to be vigilant to see that the prospectus contains only such representations "as are in strict accordance with fact".

31–004 The difficulties involved in the proof of fraud are well engrained in the consciousness of the legal profession, and when considering an action on behalf of an aggrieved investor, legal advisers should reflect on the advice given by Hilbery J. in his book, *Duty and Art in Advocacy* (1946), when he wrote (p.6):

> "By a case of fraud a lawyer means a complete cause of action in fraud. A charge of fraud is a charge of dishonesty. A claim for the recovery of money lost through fraud is the criminal charge of obtaining money by false pretences made in civil form, and no more serious charge can be placed upon the Records

of a Civil Court. The Barrister [sic: Advocate] is called upon in this instance to some extent to exercise the judicial function. If the material before him is not sufficient in his view to warrant the allegation he must advise his client that is his view and that he cannot put his signature to the pleading if it is to contain that charge".

The more stringent evidential standard of proof must also be considered when considering the sufficiency of evidence to sustain an allegation of fraud. In *Bater v Bater* [1951] P 35, Denning L.J. said (at p.37) that: **31–005**

"A civil Court, when considering a charge of fraud, will naturally require for itself a higher degree of probability than that which it would require when asking if negligence is established. It does not adopt so high a degree as a criminal court, even when it is considering a charge of a criminal nature; but still it does require a degree of probability which is commensurate with the occasion".

Denning L.J. cited this passage with approval in *Hornal v Neuberger Products Ltd* [1957] 1 Q.B. 247 (at p.258).

Once, however, an action of deceit can be successfully established, compensation for an aggrieved investor will be assessed by the Courts on a generous basis. The purpose of damages in the tort of deceit is to put the claimant into the position he would have been in had the representation not been made to him. The basic assessment will be the difference between the price actually paid and the market value of the property at the time of sale—*Saunders v Edwards* [1987] 1 W.L.R. 1116. Any damage directly flowing from the fraudulent inducement, whether or not such damage is reasonably foreseeable may be recovered unless it is caused by the claimant behaving completely without prudence or common sense—*Doyle v Olby (Ironmongers) Ltd* [1969] 2 Q.B. 158. **31–006**

A recent example of a successful claim brought in deceit for investment losses occurred in *Macdonald v Polaine & Hill Publishing* (unreported) February 11, 2002, where the claimants recovered damages arising from the circumstances in which they were induced to sell their shareholding in a company to the defendants. The principal misrepresentation made by the defendants was that there was no other party interested in purchasing the shares. The claimants' damages were assessed on the basis that they should be entitled to compensation for their actual loss, which was consistent with the principles enunciated by the House of Lords in *Smith New Court Securities v Scrimgeour Vickers (Asset Management) Ltd* [1996] 4 All E.R. 769. In that case, the House of Lords held that the normal method of calculating loss caused by deceit was the price paid less the real value of the subject matter of the sale as at the date of the transaction or acquisition by the victim. **31–007**

Misrepresentation

The practical difficulties in the establishment of a defendant's absence of honest belief were substantially alleviated by the Misrepresentation Act 1967 which artificially extended the scope of an action of deceit by casting **31–008** the onus onto the defendant to establish that he had reasonable grounds for believing, and did believe, that the facts represented were true.

S.2(1) of the Act reads as follows:

> "Where a person has entered into a contract after a misrepresentation has been made to him by another party thereto and as a result thereof he has suffered loss, then, if the person making the representation would be liable in damages in respect thereof had the misrepresentation been made fraudulently, that person shall be so liable notwithstanding that the misrepresentation was not made fraudulently unless he proves that he had reasonable ground to believe and did believe up to the time the contract was made that the facts represented were true".

31–009 In terms, therefore, the Misrepresentation Act 1967 imposes an obligation not to make representations which the representor cannot prove that he had reasonable grounds to believe. It will not be sufficient for a representator to show that he took reasonable care when he made the representation. The legislation requires the representator to go further and establish that he believed that the facts were true, and that there were reasonable grounds for that belief—see *Howard Marine and Dredging v A Ogden & Sons (Excavations)* [1978] Q.B. 574. Where liability can be established under the Act, the measure of damages was the same as the measure of damages in the tort of deceit, with the result that the claimant can recover all losses which flow from the misrepresentation even if the loss could not have been foreseen—*East v Maurer* [1991] 2 All E.R.733 and *Royscot Trust Ltd v Rogerson* [1991] 3 All E.R. 294.

In practice, actions continue to be brought by aggrieved investors in the tort of deceit, with claims for misrepresentation under the Misrepresentation Act 1967 asserted in the alternative.

31–010 Whilst the Misrepresentation Act 1967 has considerably broadened the ability of the Courts to make awards which compensate an investor who has lost his funds, certain limits about the scope of the statutory remedy should be noted. First, it applies only where the misrepresentation induced the investor into entering a contract. In investor loss cases, this requirement can usually be satisfied. Secondly, as with an action of deceit, it remains essential that a representation by assertion is made. Concealment of relevant facts may not be sufficient. Failure to make disclosure in breach of a duty to disclose will not amount to a misrepresentation that full disclosure has been made—*Banque Financiere v Westgate Insurance* [1989] 2 All E.R. 952.

31–011 A recent illustration of the issues which can typically arise in an action for deceit and/or misrepresentation occurred in the case of *Witter Ltd v TBP Industries* [1996] 2 All E.R. 573 where, in management accounts provided to a prospective purchaser of a company, a one-off expense of £120,000 was included which suggested that, in the absence of the one-off expense, the underlying profits of the company would have been higher. An action was brought against the seller of the company in deceit and for misrepresentation in the alternative. The Court awarded damages to the purchaser for misrepresentation in respect of the one-off expense, but in the course of reaching its decision guidance was given on a number of practical issues which tend to arise in these cases. So far as proof of deceit was concerned, the Court confirmed that the essence of deceit was dishonesty and that recklessness was not sufficient. Within the parameters set down by Lord Herschell in *Derry v Peek*, it had to be shown that the defendant was reckless in the sense that he disregarded the truth in a manner which would be regarded as fraudulent. There was also discussion in the case about the scope of remedies under the Misrepresentation Act 1967 where a defendant can establish proof of belief under s.2(1). The case considered whether there was a further remedy for innocent misrepresentation under s.2(2) of the Act which could be exercised in circumstances where a right to rescind the contract had been lost, and whether liability for pre-contractual misrepresentations could be excluded under the terms of the contract. Consideration of these issues fall beyond the scope of this book. Suffice it to note that s.3 of the 1967 Act provides that if a contract contains a term which would exclude or restrict any liability for misrepresentation, the term shall be of no effect except in so far as it satisfies the requirement of reasonableness. In the circumstances of this case the clause was not considered to be reasonable because it sought to exclude liability for all types of misrepresentation, whether fraudulently, negligently or innocently made.

Conspiracy

In the most serious cases of investor fraud, where more than one person is involved, a civil action for conspiracy can be brought. Broadly, a civil conspiracy consists of two forms, a conspiracy to use unlawful means and a conspiracy to injure the interest of another. A conspiracy to use unlawful means is actionable if it causes damage, but a conspiracy to injure the interests of another will not be actionable unless the damage was done with the sole or dominant intention of that other. As Lord Bridge explained in *Lonrho plc v Fayed* [1991] 3 All E.R. 303: **31–012**

> "Where conspirators act with the predominant purpose of injuring the claimant and in fact inflict damage on him, but do nothing which would have been actionable if done by an individual acting alone, it is the fact of their concerted action for that illegitimate purpose that the law, however anomalous it may now seem, finds a sufficient ground to condemn their action as illegal and tortious. But when conspirators intentionally injure the claimant and use unlawful means to do so, it is no defence for them to show that their primary purpose was to further or protect their own interests; it is sufficient to make their actions tortious that the means used were unlawful" (at pp.309j—310a).

When alleging an action against defendants for conspiracy, the Statement of Claim must describe the parties and the relationships between them. The agreement between the defendants must be alleged, together with the purpose of the agreement, and the overt acts performed by each defendant have to be alleged. The conspirators need not all join in the conspiracy at the same time, but it has to be shown that at some stage **31–013** during the conspiracy a defendant must have performed an act which furthered the conspiracy. Where a number of people have been culpably involved in an investment fraud, in relation to each person the aggrieved investor will have to consider whether that particular person, having regard to his knowledge, utterances and actions, was sufficiently a party to the combination and the common design.

31–014 An example of the difficulties associated with an action for conspiracy in the context of fraudulent activity can be demonstrated by a consideration of the case of *Metall und Rohstoff AG v Donaldson Lufkin* [1989] 3 All E.R. 14 where a company and its officers were alleged to have traded fraudulently on the London Metal Exchange. To protect its own position the company seized warrants and closed accounts owned by the claimant. After obtaining an unsatisfied judgment against the company, the claimant issued a writ against the company's American parent company in which it alleged conspiracy to steal the warrants. The claim failed because the predominant purpose of the agreement between the company and its American parent had been to close the claimant's positions in order to advance the parent companies' own commercial interests. There has been some doubt as to whether this case was correctly decided. The decision has been attacked because the Court of Appeal appeared to accept that it was an essential ingredient in the civil tort of conspiracy to establish that the predominant purpose of the conspirators was to injure the claimant, even in a case where the means used to effect that purpose were unlawful. It was against this background that the House of Lords were asked to overrule the *Metall* decision in *Lonrho plc v Fayed*. The House of Lords accepted that the Court of Appeal had erred in its suggestion that the predominant purpose to injure needed to be established in a case where unlawful means were used to effect the purpose, but the House stopped short of saying that *Metall* was wrongly decided.

As Lord Templeman recognised, this complex area of law will inevitably be the subject of further litigation.

> "Without encouraging the continuation or initiation of litigation by the present or any future disputants, I apprehend that the ambit and ingredients of the torts of conspiracy and unlawful interference may hereafter require further analysis and reconsideration by the courts".

It may well be that, in due course, the Courts will come to the view that the *Metall* case was wrongly decided.

Conversion

31–015 At first blush, where an investor swindle has occurred, it might be thought that a civil action could be brought for conversion under the Torts (Interference with Goods) Act 1977. In fact, in many cases no action can be brought because of the limited definition of "goods" in s.14 of the 1977 Act which broadly follows the common law. This section provides that "goods" are to be taken as including "all chattels personal other than things in action and money". This statutory exclusion rules out almost any action in a modern investor fraud where the misapplied funds will have been represented by some form of chose in action. Detailed consideration is given to the definition of chose in action in Ch.16 when considering the definition of "property" which is capable of being stolen under the Theft Act 1968. Suffice it to note that the artificial limitation on the meaning of "goods" in civil law is replicated by the constricted meaning which is applied to "property" in the criminal context. In both civil and criminal jurisdictions, English law is out of step with modern times.

Money Had and Received

The deficiency in the law of conversion is made good by the traditional restitutionary remedies in contract and quasi-contract, which confer wide protection on an aggrieved investor who has suffered at the hands of fraudster. These restitutionary principles can be traced back to a famous judgment given by Lord Mansfield in *Moses v Macferlan* [1760] 2 Burr. 1005 where he set out the principles which underlay an action for money had and received to the use of the claimant in the following terms: **31–016**

> "This kind of equitable action to recover back money which ought not in justice to be kept is very beneficial, and therefore much encouraged. It lies for money which, ex aequo et bono, the defendant ought to refund . . .. It lies for money paid by mistake; or upon a consideration which happens to fail; or for money got through imposition (express or implied); or extortion; or oppression; or an undue advantage taken of the claimant's situation, contrary to the laws made for the protection of persons under those circumstances. In one word, the gist of this kind of action is that the defendant, upon the circumstances of the case, is obliged by the ties of natural justice and equity to refund the money."

For a more modern formulation of the restitutionary principle, see Lord Wright's opinion in *Fibrosa Spolka Akcyjina v Fairbairn Lawson Combe Barbour Ltd* [1943] A.C. 32 at p.61. **31–017**

There have been a number of occasions when the restitutionary principle has been applied in cases of fraud. In *Gurney v Womersley* [1854] 4 E & B 133, where the names of the drawer and the acceptor were forged to a bill of exchange, and the bill was discounted by the claimants for the defendants (who had indorsed it), it was held that, since the genuiness of the acceptance was of the essence of the description of a bill, there was a total failure of consideration entitling the claimants to recover from the defendants the amount paid to them. Five years earlier, in *Vaughan v Matthews* [1849] 13 Q.B. 187, a claimant was allowed to sue a defendant to recover his loss after the defendant had obtained payment of a promissory note payable to the claimant by means of a false or forged representation of authority purporting to emanate from the claimant.

A recent example of the use of money had and received occurred in *Agip (Africa) Ltd v Jackson* [1992] 4 All E.R. 451 where the claimant's employee forged a payment order in favour of a nominee company which had been **31–018** set up and controlled by the defendants. The ability of the claimant to trace this money at common law was also an issue in the case.

A defendant may be liable in a restitutionary action even where the fraud was committed by his partner and agent, and not by him personally. Where payments of premiums on a policy were continued by the claimant because of false representations by the defendant's agent, it was held in *Kettlewell v Refuge Assurance Co* [1908] 1 K.B. 545 that the premiums could be recovered by the claimant in a claim in restitution, although they might also have been recovered in an action of deceit.

The ability of a claimant to hold a defendant responsible for the fraud of his partner and agent has implications where a limited company is involved, and sometimes an application of this principle can allow an aggrieved investor to pursue a director in his personal capacity on the ground that the limited company is liable as his agent. This aspect is explored in more detail in Ch.30.

31–019 The width of the restitutionary principal can also be demonstrated by the case of a defendant who, without intending to pay for it, fraudulently induces the claimant to perform a service for him. The claimant may sue either for the tort of deceit or in restitution for reasonable remuneration—*Rumsey v NE Railway* [1863] 14 C.B., N.S. 641.

An aggrieved investor who has been induced by fraud to enter into a contract must, as soon as he discovers the fraud, elect to rescind the contract and seek to recover his funds. An investor must be careful not to affirm the contract in any shape or form. The right to rescind is lost by affirmation, and it is doubtful whether it would be revived by the subsequent discovery of another incident in the same fraud.

In practice, experience suggests that the Courts continue to apply the spirit of Lord Mansfield's approach in a case where an aggrieved investor has lost some or all of his funds, and in any such case the pursuit of a restitutionary remedy must not be overlooked.

Illegal Transactions

31–020 The Courts have repeatedly held that public policy precludes the bringing of a civil action for redress on the basis of an illegal act. So if an investor suffers loss as a result of dealings with a defendant which are intrinsically illegal, he will not be able to recover damages for his loss, irrespective of whether his loss was caused by a fraudulent representative or breach of contract. The principle has been fully articulated in the leading textbooks on Torts (Clerk & Lindsell) and Contracts (Chitty). Suffice it to mention here a dramatic and very recent application of this principle in the context of investor protection where, following the ruling of the Court of Appeal in the "Titan" case, investors are unlikely to be able to benefit from investments which they made in the scheme. The scheme was based on invitations to become a member of a business club. To take up the invitation, a person had to be interviewed and pay £2,500. The new recruit then had the right to introduce new members. For the first two new members he received £450 from each of the new members. If he introduced a third or subsequent member, he became a "senior partner" and received £1,250. In addition he received £770 for each new member introduced by members who were introduced by him. The balance of the membership fee was distributed amongst the members and the companies involved in the scheme. The scheme was best described as an enormous financial "chain letter". The Court of Appeal held that the scheme was unlawful because it was an unlicensed lottery and the Department of Trade and Industry was correct to bring proceedings for winding-up the scheme—*Re Senator Hanseatische Wertwaltungs Gesellschaft mbh*, [1996] 4 All E.R. 933.

Chapter 32

Liability for Negligent Mis-statement

This chapter focuses on the common law obligations of a person who, in the absence of any contract between the parties which defines their respective obligations, advises an investor or disseminates accounting information to an investor in relation to an investment. How does the law protect the investor against negligent advice or the dissemination of negligently prepared financial information? If negligent advice or incorrect financial information is given, what is the investors' remedy? Often the person giving the advice or disseminating the information will be a professional advisor, such as a financial consultant or intermediary, broker, accountant, banker or solicitor. **32–001**

Background

The ability of an investor to recover financial loss as a result of an accountant's professional negligence was raised directly in *Candler v Crane, Christmas & Co* [1951] 2 K.B. 164, [1951] 1 All E.R. 426. There a potential investor wanted to see the accounts of a company before deciding whether to invest in it. The company accountants were told to complete the company's accounts as soon as possible because they were to be shown to the potential investor. Subsequently, the potential investor discussed the accounts with the accountants and he was allowed to take a copy. The accounts had been carelessly prepared and gave a wholly misleading picture. Not appreciating the errors, the potential investor subscribed £2,000 for shares in the company. The company went into liquidation and the investor lost his money. The Court of Appeal held, after an extensive review of the law, that in the absence of a contractual arrangement between the parties, the accountants did not owe any duty to the potential investor to exercise care in preparing the accounts. In a dissenting judgment, Denning L.J. expressed concern about the position of investors. The accountant, noted Denning L.J., was required to do more than certify accounts for the satisfaction of his client. Accounts were required for the guidance of shareholders, investors, revenue authorities, and others who may have to rely on the accounts in serious matters of business. **32–002**

In a passage which foreshadowed problems which have come to plague this area of the law, Denning L.J. questioned the scope of the duty of care which he wished to establish. Would the accountants be liable to any person in the land who chose to rely on the accounts in matters of business, or would they be liable only if the accounts were prepared for the guidance of a specific class of persons in a specific class of transactions?

It was over 30 years before these questions came to be addressed by the House of Lords, and today the answer to these questions remains far from clear. The law continues to develop on a case by case basis.

Hedley Byrne

32–003 The majority decision of the Court of Appeal in *Candler v Crane, Christmas & Co* was disapproved by the House of Lords in *Hedley Byrne & Co Ltd v Heller & Partners Ltd* [1963] 2 All E.R. 575. This decision is now the foundation of the modern law. In *Hedley Byrne & Co Ltd v Heller* the House of Lords held that a person who made a negligent statement could owe a duty of care to a person who suffered economic loss through reliance upon the statement. The facts of this case did not involve a potential investor but a firm of advertising agents who sought a credit reference on one of their clients. The reference was sought from the client's bankers. A favourable reference was negligently given, and the advertising agents suffered heavy losses on the transactions which they entered in reliance on the reference. Since the credit reference was given "without responsibility", the advertising agents failed in their action for damages against the client's bankers, but as matter of principle the House of Lords was unanimous in holding that there were circumstances where damages could be awarded for financial loss brought about by a negligent mis-statement.

Lord Morris expressed the principles succinctly as follows:

> "My Lords, I consider that it follows and that it should now be regarded as settled that if someone possessed of a special skill undertakes, quite irrespective of contract, to apply that skill for the assistance of another person who relies on such skill, a duty of care will arise. The fact that the service is to be given by means of, or by the instrumentality of, words can make no difference. Furthermore if, in a sphere in which a person is so placed that others could reasonably rely on his judgment or his skill or his ability to make careful inquiry, a person takes it on himself to give information or advice to, or allows his information or advice to be passed on to, another person who, as he knows or should know, will place reliance on it, then a duty of care will arise" (at p.594B).

The law reports are replete with cases in which this principle has been applied during the last 30 years. In this chapter consideration is confined to cases which have arisen in the investment context.

Liability for Negligent Investment Advice or Conduct

The Lloyds Litigation

32–004 The culmination of the litigation concerning the losses suffered by Names at Lloyd's of London are now the seminal cases in this area. The test case actions progressed to the House of Lords and are reported under the leading case of *Henderson and others v Merrett Syndicates Ltd* [1994] 3 All E.R. 506.

The Claimants were Lloyd's Names and were members of syndicates managed by the defendant underwriting agents. The Claimants were either "direct Names", in which case the syndicates to which they belonged were managed by the members' agents (known as "managing agents"), or "indirect Names", in which case the members' agents placed Names with syndicates managed by other agents. Where Names were placed with other syndicates managed by other agents, the members agents entered into sub-agency agreements with the managing agents of those syndicates. Under these sub-agency agreements the managing agents of those syndicates were appointed to act as sub-agents in respect of the Names' business. The relationship between Names, members' agents and managing agents was regulated by the terms of agency and sub-agency agreements which gave the agent "absolute discretion" in respect of underwriting business conducted on behalf of the Name but it was accepted that it was an implied term of the agreements that the agents would exercise due care and skill in the exercise of their functions as managing agents. In the course of preliminary proceedings, notwithstanding the contractual relationship between the parties, legal issues arose concerning the nature and extent of care owed by the member's agents and the managing agents under the sub-agency agreements.

In a robust judgment the House of Lords rejected the defendant **32–005** underwriting agents' contentions. Their Lordships held that the managing agents owed a duty of care to Names. By holding themselves out as possessing a special expertise to advise the names on the suitability of risks to be underwritten and the circumstances in which reinsurance should be taken out and claims settled, the managing agents had assumed responsibility towards the names in their syndicates. The managing agents well knew that the names placed implicit reliance on their advice, and the names gave authority to the managing agents to bind them in contracts of insurance and re-insurance and to the settlement of claims. The discretion given to managing agents in the agreements defined the scope of the agents' authority, not the standard of skill and care required of the agents in carrying on underwriting business on behalf of Names. The assumption of responsibility by a person rendering professional or quasi-professional services gave rise to a tortious duty of care irrespective of whether there was a contractual relationship between the parties.

The implications of this decision are quite far-reaching for investors who **32–006** have suffered financial loss at the hands of a negligent financial advisor. The House of Lords reached its decision by applying the principles set out in *Hedley Byrne & Co v Heller & Partners Ltd*. Their Lordships noted that the underlying principle rested on the assumption of responsibility by one party towards another party, and whilst this assumption of responsibility undoubtedly covered the provision of investment advice and information, it was said that there may be other circumstances in which there will be necessary reliance to give rise to the application of the principle.

As Lord Goff said:

> "In particular, where the Claimant entrusts the defendant with the conduct of his affairs in general or in particular, he may be held to have relied on the defendant to exercise due skill and care in such conduct" (at p.520g).

In the context of investor protection, the same principles will apply to all professional or quasi-professional advisors who advise investors or undertake investment business on their behalf.

32–007 Covering similar ground, the first instance decision in *Brown v KMR Services* [1994] 4 All E.R. 598 is interesting because, unlike the House of Lords ruling in *Henderson and others v Merrett Syndicates Ltd*, the judgment was delivered after the facts of the case had been determined. The Judge, Gatehouse J., concluded that where a Lloyd's Name obtained an assurance from his member's agent that only syndicates constituting a low risk conservative underwriting policy would be recommended, the agent would be in breach of his duty of care (as well as in breach of contract) if he subsequently recommended high risk excess of loss syndicates contrary to that assurance without first obtaining the Name's informed consent. A Lloyd's Name was entitled to expect a warning of the dangers inherent in excess of loss reinsurance syndicates from his members' agent, irrespective of whether he happened to be a sophisticated investor.

Interestingly, whilst this decision was affirmed on appeal, the Court of Appeal said that Gatehouse J.'s assessment of an agent's duty was too restrictive. A members' agent owed a duty to a Lloyd's Name to provide proper advice when recommending that he allocate a percentage of his premium in income limit to high risk excess of loss syndicates. Proper advice involved the giving of information and advice about the character and extra risk of the business underwritten by such syndicates, individually and collectively, as well as advice on maintaining a proper balance between allocation of premiums to such syndicates and the allocation of premiums to syndicates which were not high risk in order to ensure a prudent spread of risk—*Brown v KMR Services Ltd* [1995] 4 All E.R. 598.

Ingredients of a Cause of Action

32–008 It follows that an investor may recover damages for financial losses in circumstances where the investor can show that (i) he relied on a professional or quasi-professional advisor to provide investment advice or to conduct investment affairs on his behalf, and (ii) the professional or quasi-professional advisor realised that the investor was relying upon his skill and judgment in providing investment advice or conducting investment affairs. Establishment of these two elements gives rise to a "degree of proximity" between the parties which the Courts deem sufficient to show that a duty of care is owed to the investor on the facts of a particular case.

In addition to the establishment of this relationship of proximity between the parties, an investor has to prove three further elements before he can recover damages for financial loss in this type of case.

32–009 First, he must show that the professional or quasi-professional advisor acted negligently in the exercise of his skill and judgment.

Secondly, he must show that the negligence caused him to suffer financial loss. The real test of whether the negligence was the effective cause of the loss is a pragmatic one based on common sense. Causation is a question of fact in each case—*Banque Bruxelles Lambert SA v Eagle Star Insurance* (unreported) March 22, 1996. In the context of the Lloyd's litigation, the question of causation was approached by identifying first what advice the Name ought to have received and then what the name could prove, on the balance of probabilities, would have been the consequence of his receipt of such information and advice—*Brown v KMR Services Ltd* [1995] 4 All E.R. 598.

Thirdly, the investor must prove that the loss was reasonably foreseeable in all the circumstances. On the issue of foreseeability of loss, the test for negligence is the same regardless of whether the victim complains of pure economic loss or damage to property. Either way, the victim has to show that the damage was reasonably foreseeable—*Marc Rich & Co AG v Bishop Rock Marine Co.* [1994] 3 All E.R. 686.

In most cases in the investment context, foreseeability of loss will not be **32–010** difficult to prove once the other elements of the cause of action have been established. In *Aiken v Stewart Wrightson Members Agency* [1995] 3 All E.R. 449, another case in the Lloyds litigation, Potter J. held that it was reasonably foreseeable that syndicates would rely on run-off reinsurance for the benefit of names in future years. Those Names were inevitably persons who would be affected if the run-off reinsurance were to be avoided for non-disclosure.

Measure of Damages

The proper measure of damages in a case of where negligent advice had **32–011** been given was the subject of consideration in *South Australia Asset Management Corp v York Montague Ltd* [1996] 3 All E.R. 365, a case involving the negligent valuation of property. During the course of his judgment in which he reviewed the relevant principles at some length, Lord Hoffman confirmed that foreseeability of loss was the test by which recoverability of loss would be determined. A negligent supplier of information is responsible for all the foreseeable consequences of the information being wrong, and a negligent advisor is responsible for all the foreseeable losses which are a consequence of that course of action having been taken. The loss suffered by the claimant is compared with what his position would have been if he had received information which was correct or had not entered into the transaction in respect of which he was negligently advised.

Applying these principles to the facts of the case before it, the House of Lords held that the compensation payable by a valuer who had negligently overvalued property on which a lender had secured a loan was restricted to the difference between the valuation negligently provided and the correct property value at the time of valuation. As Lord Hoffman acknowledged (at p.373j), a different measure of damages is applied where the Claimant has been induced to enter into the transaction by virtue of fraud—see Ch.31 on this point.

32–012 In cases where an incorrect projection of profits is made, there is a prima facie assumption that the most likely forecast would have reflected the actual outcome. The nature of the problem is demonstrated by a consideration of the facts in *Lion Nathan Ltd v CC Bottlers Ltd* (unreported) May 14, 1996, where the vendor of a company made a projected profit forecast of $2.223 million for the remaining two months of the financial year. In the event actual earnings were $1.233 million. The trial Judge held that a properly prepared forecast would have been $1.6 million, but the Court of Appeal of New Zealand thought that a proper forecast would have been $1.2 million. The Privy Council concluded that a proper forecast should be taken as the actual outcome, and this would be taken as the basis for assessing damages. The Privy Council said that the uncertainty inherent in the process of forecasting may have led to reasonable forecasts both higher and lower than the actual outcome but since those uncertainties tended in both directions, the only way to deal with the matter was to regard the unpredictable factors as cancelling each other out.

Sometimes, where an investor is negligently advised not to make a particular investment, he will suffer the loss of a chance. This may occur, for example, where a claimant is negligently advised not to enter into a business venture with a third party, and because of the claimant's lack of support the third party does not proceed with the business venture. The loss of chance will be difficult to quantify in these circumstances. Certainly a claimant will be entitled to succeed if he can establish that there was a substantial, and not a speculative, chance that a third party would have taken action to confer some benefit on him. According to the Court of Appeal in *Allied Maples Group Ltd v Simmons & Simmons* [1995] 4 All E.R. 907, the evaluation of a substantial chance was a question of quantification of damages, the range lying somewhere between something that just qualified as real or substantial on the one hand and near certainty on the other.

32–013 An example of a court's assessment of damages in this type of case occurred in *First Interstate Bank of California v Cohen Arnold & Co*, [1995] TLR 664, where the Court of Appeal considered the position where a bank claimed that it would have taken action to enforce its security if it had known the true facts about the financial state of the borrower. In the event the bank sold the security for £1.4 million when, if it had enforced the security earlier, it would have received between £3.5 million and £4 million. The court concluded on the facts of the case that the bank had lost the opportunity to sell the property for £3 million. The chance should be valued at 2:1; accordingly the bank obtained judgment for £2 million less the £1.4 million actually received.

Contributory Negligence

32–014 Although unusual in an investor related case, there is no reason in principle why, if justified on the facts of a case, a deduction for contributory negligence on the part of a claimant could not be made. The possibility of a deduction for contributory negligence on the basis that a bank had negligently failed to assess the risks of a transaction was rejected in *Cavendish Funding Ltd v Henry Spencer & Sons Ltd* (unreported) March 20, 1996.

Limitation of Action

Under the terms of the Limitation Act 1980 all actions for negligence seeking compensation for economic loss must be brought within six years from the date when the cause of action accrued. This date may sometimes be difficult to determine. The cause of action will accrue when an investor suffers loss, but is the loss suffered at the time of the negligent advice or at the time when financial loss is sustained? The latter date is the date which is usually taken. In *First National Commercial Bank plc v Humberts*, *The Times*, January 27, 1995, bankers alleged that they financed a property acquisition on the basis of a negligent property valuation. The property was valued at £4.4 million when a value of £2.7 million should have been given. The Court of Appeal held that the cause of action accrued on the date when the bankers' loss crystallised, which was the date when the loan security was sold. The date of the advance was the date when prima facie the measure of loss might be established but this was the starting point. It did not follow that the loss occurred at this time since the loss might have been recoverable in other ways. **32–015**

Practical Problems

The practical problems of establishing liability on the facts of a particular case can be quite formidable. First, the element of reliance has to be established. In *Anthony v White*, *Independent*, September 27, 1994, investors who were beneficiaries of a trust failed to establish liability against auditors of a trust because they did not rely on the audit, and in any event the beneficiaries were not sufficiently close to force such a duty on the auditors. To similar effect, in the Canadian case of *Bank Für Handel und Effekten v Davidson & Co Ltd* [1975] 55 D.L.R. (3d) 303, a stockbroker escaped liability after negligently advising the bank as to its clients' investment transactions because the bank had not relied on the advice. In *Eagle Trust v SBC Securities*, [1995] B.C.C. 231, it was held that a financial adviser to an acquiring company did not owe a duty of care to the company to ensure that the sub-underwriters were good for the money necessary for the underwriting. **32–016**

The difficulties of establishing negligence and causation are illustrated by a consideration of the decision in *Stafford v Conti Commodity Services Ltd* [1981] 1 All E.R. 691, where an investor brought proceedings against a commodity broker on the London commodities futures market. Between January and August 1976 the broker had carried out 46 transactions which had resulted in an overall loss of over £19,000 for the investor. Only 10 of the 46 transactions made a profit. The investor argued that the extent of the losses demonstrated that the broker had failed to exercise due care and diligence in the conduct of his affairs. Whilst the Court accepted that the broker may have made an error of judgment in giving advice, the commodities market was unpredictable and a broker could not always be expected to be correct. "Losses in the ordinary course of things do occur even if proper care is used when one is dealing with transactions on the commodities futures market" *per* Mocatta J. at p.698d.

Examples of Successful Cases

32–017 There have been other cases where investors have been successful in recovering damages for financial loss. In *Cornish v Midland Bank plc* [1985] 3 All E.R. 513 the Court of Appeal held Midland Bank liable in negligence for its failure to advise a customer as to the financial consequences of executing a mortgage in favour of the bank (*cf. Barclays Bank v Khaira* (1992) 1 W.L.R. 623). A trust company which advised an investor that a co-operative was 100 per cent insured has been held liable in negligence where the co-operative failed and the money was not insured—*Blair v Canada Trust Co* [1986] 32 D.L.R. (4th) 515. If a bank negligently gives advice as to specific investments, as opposed to referring the customer to a stockbroker, a duty of care will be owed. There is also an old Assize case in which Salmon J. held a bank liable for giving a prospective customer negligent investment advice—*Woods v Martins Bank Ltd* [1958] 3 All E.R. 166. Canadian courts have held a mortgage broker liable for misrepresenting the value of property to an investor—*Herrington v Kenco Mortgage & Investments Ltd* [1981] 125 D.L.R. (3d) 377—and a stockbroker liable for negligently giving the impression that he had inside information on the company which was the subject of his investment recommendation—*Elderkin v Merrill Lynch Royal Securities Ltd* [1977] 80 D.L.R. (3d) 313.

32–018 A recent example of a successful claim occurred in *Verity and Spindler v Lloyds Bank plc* (unreported) September 4, 1995, where the claimant had specifically sought the bank manager's advice on the prudence of a transaction. The manager advised the claimants that the transaction was financially viable and encouraged them to proceed with it. In these circumstances the claimants were not just seeking a loan but asking whether it was "a sensible thing to do" or whether they should "forget it".

The *Verity and Spindler* case can be contrasted with *Bankers Trust International plc v PT Dharmala Sakti Sejahtera* (unreported) December 1, 1995, where it was held that a commercial bank did not owe an investor company any duty to explain the risks and effects of leveraged interest rate swaps. It would seem that unless asked to do so by its customer, a commercial bank owes no duty of care to assess a customer's suitability for the purchase of a derivative or to advise him on the risks involved.

The Duties of a Financial Adviser to Advise its Client on a Takeover

32–019 In recent years questions have arisen concerning the scope of the duty of care owed by a financial adviser who has been instructed to advise on a takeover. To date, these questions remain largely unresolved. Inspectors appointed by the DTI to investigate the affairs of Atlantic Computers plc considered that a merchant bank acting as a financial adviser on a takeover did not impliedly assume a responsibility for giving advice on the question of whether an acquisition was in the best interests of the offer company's shareholders. The inspectors said that the financial adviser's duties were no higher than "to satisfy itself that the company has taken all reasonable steps to enable it to evaluate the target and judge whether the acquisition is in the best interests of shareholders".

Whether the Courts will adopt such a restrictive view remains to be seen. Preliminary indications suggest otherwise. In *Ginora Investments Ltd v James Capel & Co Ltd* (unreported) February 10, 1995, Rimer J. held that a merchant bank had assumed a wide duty of care to the offeror company to advise on the financial implications, suitability, and terms of a proposed acquisition, and also to advise on the tactics to be employed, in particular whether the bid should be a recommended or hostile bid and whether it should be declared unconditional in all respects.

The basis of this extended duty of care rested on the terms of the letter of engagement between the offeror company and the merchant bank, under which the merchant bank expressly assumed an obligation to advise on tactics and strategy. On the facts of the case, however, the Court held that the merchant bank had not breached any of the duties which it owed. Those seeking investment advice can learn from this case about the importance of setting out clearly in the letter of engagement the scope of the duties and obligations which the financial adviser is to assume.

Negligent Statements in Accounts

Duty of Care to Shareholders, Existing and Potential

The House of Lords decided in *Caparo Industries plc v Dickman* [1991] 1 All E.R. 568 that auditors who certified accounts for the purposes of the Companies Act 1985 owed no duty of care to a potential takeover bidder. It was not sufficient that it was foreseeable, even highly foreseeable, that a bidder might rely on the accounts. The House of Lords held that there was no relationship of proximity between auditors and bidder to found a duty of care. In *Caparo* the auditor's certificate had been required by the Companies Act 1985. An analysis of the company's legislation led to the conclusion that the statutory purpose of the auditor's certificate was to provide the shareholders and debenture holders with reliable information to enable them to exercise their rights as such and not to protect investors in the market. The legal limits of investor protection in this context are well demonstrated in the following passage from Lord Bridge's judgment (at p.580j): **32–020**

> "Assuming for the purposes of the argument that the relationship between the auditor of a company and individual shareholders is of sufficient proximity to give rise to a duty of care, I do not understand how the scope of that duty can possibly extend beyond the protection of any individual shareholder from losses in the value of the shares which he holds. As a purchaser of additional

shares in reliance on the auditor's report, he stands in no different position from any other investing member of the public to whom the auditor owes no duty."

This decision caused some consternation in the commercial world which had relied heavily on the accuracy of an auditor's report in relation to a company's accounts.

Duty of Care to Bidders and Potential Lenders

32–021 In *James McNaughten Papers Group Ltd v Hicks Anderson & Co (a firm)* [1991] 1 All E.R. 134, the Court of Appeal held that an accountant did not owe a duty of care to a bidder when preparing draft accounts at the request of the target company for use in takeover negotiations. The Court of Appeal said that the draft accounts were produced for the target company and not the bidder, the accounts were merely draft accounts and the accountants could not reasonably have foreseen that the bidder would treat the draft accounts as final accounts. In any event, the bidder was aware that the target company was in poor financial health and the bidder could reasonably have been expected to consult its own accountants.

The position with regard to a potential lender is the same. In *Al Saudi Banque v Clark Pixley (a firm)* [1989] 3 All E.R. 361, Millett J. held that the auditors of a company owed no duty of care to a bank which lent money to the company, regardless of whether the bank was an existing creditor or a potential creditor of the company. Although the bank had relied on audited accounts when making loans to the company to enable it to finance business operations, there was not a sufficiently close or direct relationship between the auditors and the bank to give rise to the degree of proximity necessary to establish a duty of care. As the Judge noted in that case, the potential liability of the auditors to a creditor was far greater than the potential liability to the company's shareholders. Where the value of a company is negligently overstated or understated in the accounts, the auditor's liability to investors and shareholders would be measured by, or at least related to, the extent of their own negligence. That is not so where creditors are concerned and the company is alleged to have been insolvent. In the case of a subsequent and irrecoverable advance, the auditors' maximum liability would fall to be measured by the amount of the advance, which would be unknown to the auditors and could not be foreseen by them. It would bear no necessary relationship to, and could be many times greater than, the value of the company as shown by its published accounts.

32–022 These decisions may be contrasted with the decision of the Court of Appeal in *Morgan Crucible Co v Hill Samuel Bank* [1991] 1 All E.R. 148, where a profit forecast was issued by financial advisers to a target company in the course of a takeover bid. The Court concluded that if the bidder could show that the financial advisers of the target company had intended the bidder to rely on the profit forecast for the purpose of deciding whether to make an increased bid, a relationship of proximity between the parties would be established. Distinguishing the decision in the *Caparo* case, Slade L.J. noted that in that case the relevant statement by the auditors had not been given for the purpose for which the Claimant takeover bidder relied upon it.

The limits of the decision in *Morgan Crucible* are well illustrated by a consideration of the decision in *Al-Nakib Investments (Jersey) Ltd v Longcroft* [1990] 3 All E.R. 321, where a company had issued a prospectus inviting shareholders to subscribe for shares by way of a rights issue. The shareholder applied for some shares, and some months later bought further shares through the stock market. In an action against the company for negligence following misrepresentations in the prospectus, the shareholder argued that it was reasonably foreseeable that a shareholder might rely on the prospectus when deciding to buy shares on the open market. The Court rejected this argument on the basis of the *Caparo* decision. The prospectus was addressed to shareholders for the particular purpose of inviting a subscription for shares. If the prospectus was used by a shareholder for a different purpose of buying shares through the stock exchange there was not a sufficiently proximate relationship between the directors and the shareholder for a duty of care to arise on the part of the directors.

A different result was achieved in *Galoo Ltd (in Liquidation) v Bright* **32–023** *Grahame Murray (a firm)* [1995] 1 All E.R. 16, where company auditors had provided accounts to enable a purchaser to determine a purchase price of a target company. The purchaser subsequently purchased further shares and made loans to the company and a wholly owned subsidiary company. The Court of Appeal considered the decisions in *Caparo* and *Morgan Crucible*. Glidewell L.J. expressed the distinction between the cases in the following terms:

> "Mere foreseeability that a potential bidder may rely on the audited accounts does not impose on the auditor a duty of care to the bidder, but if the auditor is expressly made aware that a particular identified bidder will rely on the audited accounts or other statements approved by the auditor, and intends that the bidder should so rely, the auditor will be under a duty of care to the bidder for the breach of which he may be liable" (at p.37d).

Glidewell L.J.'s summary of the principles represents a clear statement of the modern law in this area. The position concerning liability to a potential lender or creditor is the same.

An example of a case where subscribing and after-market investors have **32–024** been allowed to proceed to trial against auditors who negligently shared responsibility for misrepresentations in a prospectus occurred recently in *Possfund Custodian Trustee Ltd v Diamond* [1996] 2 All E.R. 774. Rejecting an application to strike out the Statement of Claim as disclosing no reasonable cause of action, the Court held that it was arguable that the auditors owed a duty of care to both subscribing and after-market investors in the light of the way in which the prospectus had been worded. The case involved the flotation of a company's shares on the unlisted securities market, and the prospectus specifically stated that, as part of the exercise of allotment, the facility would be available for shares to be traded on this market. Lightman J. held that if the shareholders could establish that, at the date of preparation and circulation of the original share prospectus, the auditors intended to inform and encourage after-market purchasers, in addition to those investors who relied on the prospectus in making a decision whether to accept the allotment offer, it was at least arguable that the auditors had assumed and owed a duty of care to those investors who relied on the contents of the prospectus in making after-market purchases. The decision in *Al Nakib v Longcraft* was distinguished on the ground that the purpose of the prospectus in that case was limited to inducing investors to take up the allotment of shares in respect of which the prospectus was issued.

Auditing Standards

32–025 It follows that, unless the auditor is made aware that a particular identified bidder or lender will rely on the accounts, no duty of care will arise to the potential equity or creditor investor. In many cases an investor who suffers financial loss as a result of negligently drawn accounting statements will not be able to recover compensation through the Courts, and the most effective practical way to protect investors is to ensure that the standards of the accountancy profession are maintained. In December 1994 the Auditing Practices Board recommended that auditors should be asked to sign their reports on company accounts personally as part of a series of reforms to help re-establish their objectivity and bolster their authority. Whilst the Audit Agenda was careful to say that it did not want to extend auditors' duty to third-party readers of accounts or to potential stakeholders beyond shareholders, the implementation of the Auditing Practices Board recommendations would undoubtedly be welcomed as a step in the right direction.

An interesting case where auditors became liable to a bidder for a company occurred in *ADT v Binder Hamlyn* (unreported) December 6, 1995, when Binder Hamlyn were asked by the bidder to confirm whether they stood by their audit of the company. Binder Hamlyn answered in the affirmative. May J.'s judgment is interesting because it provides a detailed analysis of the standards to be expected in the audit of a substantial group of companies. It identifies the problems which occur in joint audits and the measures which need to be taken if standards are to be met in these circumstances. More work is needed in this area if auditors are to avoid liability when asked to verify their reports personally.

Overlap Between Claims for Negligent Advice or Misrepresentation and Breach of Contract

32–026 This chapter has focused on the circumstances in which the Courts will recognise liability for negligent advice or mis-statement in the absence of a contractual relationship between the parties. Frequently, though, cases occur where claims for breach of contract and liability in tort under the *Hedley Byrne* principle arise concurrently. In most of these cases there will be no difference between the ability of a Claimant to establish his case in contract or tort because the outcome depends upon the Claimant's ability to prove the factual aspects of his case, *i.e.* whether the advice or representation was incorrect, whether the defendant failed to take reasonable care, whether the failure caused reasonably foreseeable damage or damage which was within the reasonable contemplation of the parties.

In some cases, however, the difference can be important. The limitation period within which a cause of action can be brought starts to run at different times, depending on whether the action is brought for breach of contract or in tort. In contract, the limitation starts to run from the date when the breach occurred, whereas in tort the period runs from the date when financial loss has been sustained. Often loss is sustained some time after the breach of contract has taken place, and it is against this background that there have been a number of cases in recent years where Claimants have sought to pursue a claim in tort where the incidents of their relationship has been governed by the terms of a contract made between them. In these situations defendants have been assiduous to challenge the Claimant's ability to make out a concurrent cause of action in tort.

In *Henderson v Merrett Syndicates Ltd* [1994] 3 All E.R. 506 the House of **32–027**
Lords held that where liabilities arose concurrently in tort and contract it was open to a Claimant to assert the cause of action that appeared to him most advantageous, and in the circumstances of that case the House of Lords was satisfied that concurrent liability could be made out. However, this will not always follow; the mere fact that a contractual duty exists does not mean that there is a co-extensive duty owed in tort. As set out in this chapter, liability in tort will depend on the nature of the relationship between the parties. It will be difficult to establish a tortious claim where the claim is derived from an obligation or duty which has been set out in a contract. For a more comprehensive consideration of the issues which arise in this context, see *Banque Financiere de la Cite SA v Westgate Insurance Co* [1989] 2 All E.R. 952 and *Aiten v Stewart Wrightson Members Agency* [1995] 3 All E.R. 449.

Chapter 33

Parties to a Civil Action

When an aggrieved investor considers the commencement of a civil action to recover his loss, it is essential for him to correctly identify the appropriate defendants. There are, of course, a number of different considerations to be taken into account. In cases where investment funds have been handled by a limited company, the investor Claimant has to consider whether the pursuit of the company is worthwhile. Commonly, by the time litigation is envisaged a limited company will be insolvent and any judgment against it will almost certainly be worthless. In these circumstances it is necessary to consider whether any liability can attach to a director personally, because if it can, the chances of recovering the misapplied assets and/or damages will be considerably enhanced. **33–001**

Personal Liability of Directors

The General Principle of Corporate Liability

It is trite law that a limited company duly formed and registered under the companies legislation is a separate legal entity and has to be treated like any other independent person with its own rights and liabilities as distinct from those of its directors and shareholders. This position was firmly established over one hundred years ago in *Salomon v Salomon* [1897] A.C. 22 when the House of Lords refused to allow unsecured creditors to obtain judgment against Mr Salomon personally, even though Mr Salomon was controlling shareholder and the principal secured creditor of the company. As Lord MacNaughton explained in this seminal case: **33–002**

> "The company is at law a different person altogether from the subscribers to the memorandum; and, though it may be that after incorporation the business is precisely the same as it was before, and the same persons are managers, and the same hands receive the profits, the company is not in law the agent of the subscribers or the trustees for them. Nor are the subscribers as members liable in any shape or form, except to the extent and in the manner provided by the Companies Act".

To every rule, however, there are exceptions. In the case of company law there have been a succession of cases throughout the twentieth century in which the Courts have been prepared to "lift the corporate veil" to identify the persons who directed and controlled the activities of the company and to hold these people accountable for their misdeeds. It is not possible to formulate any single principle as to the basis of these decisions, but their direction is reasonably clear. It is the purpose of this chapter to explore the boundaries of these exceptional cases to see when they might assist an investor Claimant who seeks to recover his misapplied funds where those funds have been held by a limited company.

Fraud

33–003 Where a defendant uses a company to raise funds from an investor on a fraudulent basis, a Court will be prepared to look behind the corporate entity and permit the investor to recover his funds. Authority for this proposition can be found in the old case of *Re Darby and Brougham* [1911] 1 K.B. 95 where Darby and Brougham arranged for a company prospectus to represent to potential investors that a corporation owned by the company was making profits from a mining contract when in fact the profits were being passed through the corporation to themselves. Darby and Brougham were prosecuted and convicted of making fraudulent and material misstatements in the prospectus, since they had failed to disclose that the corporation was simply an alias for themselves. The company went into liquidation and the liquidator sued Darby, who had considerable assets, for breach of trust and for return of the undisclosed profits which he had received. Phillimore J. allowed the liquidator's claim. The corporation was merely an alias for Darby and Brougham which they had used as a vehicle for fraud:

> "The fraud here is that what they did through the corporation they did themselves and represented it to have been done by a corporation of some standing and position, or at any rate a corporation which was more than different from themselves".

33–004 This decision has clear implications for an investor who wishes to sue a defendant to recover his loss in circumstances where the defendant has used a limited company for the purposes of fraud. An illustration of the contemporary application of this application can be found in the recent case of *Customs and Excise Commissioners v H* [1996] 2 All E.R. 391 where, albeit in a reverse situation, the Court of Appeal confirmed its willingness to lift the corporate veil in the face of fraud. In *Customs and Excise Commissioners v H* two companies had been utilised by three defendants to import a large volume of alcoholic liquor in breach of the excise duties. The defendants sought to resist an application by Customs and Excise to obtain restraint orders over the assets of the two companies on the basis that the company assets could not be said to form part of the realisable property of the defendants. In rejecting this argument the Court of Appeal said that it was willing to lift the corporate veil so as to treat the assets of the companies as the realisable property of the defendants because the companies had been used by the defendants as vehicles for fraud.

Device to Evade a Contractual or Legal Obligation

Consistent with the approach taken in cases of fraud, the Courts have also been prepared to lift the corporate veil where a company has been used as a device to evade a contractual or other legal obligation. This exceptional category may interest an investor Claimant in a case where a defendant attempts to play "fast and loose" with the civil process. **33–005**

The classic authority here is that of *Gilford Motor Co v Horne* [1933] Ch. 935 where a defendant formed a limited company to carry on business in circumstances where he was prohibited from carrying on this business by virtue of a restrictive covenant. The Court granted an injunction against the defendant on the grounds that the company was not a genuine, independent legal entity. The same principle was applied by the Court in *Jones v Lipman* [1962] 1 W.L.R. 832, where a defendant sought to escape from a conveyancing obligation by transferring the property to a nominee company. The company was, said Russell J, "the creature of the first defendant, a device and a sham, a mask which he holds before his face in an attempt to avoid recognition by the eye of equity". See also *Wallersteiner v Moir (No 1)* [1974] 3 All E.R. 217, *per* Lord Denning M.R. at p.237/8 in this context.

An investor Claimant will be interested in a recent application of these principles to the not uncommon situation where a defendant seeks to avoid liability by transferring his personal assets into a complicated network of offshore companies and trusts. This situation occurred in *Re A Company* [1985] B.C.L.C. 333 where the defendant was sued for fraud and breach of trust. He sought to conceal his true beneficial interests by transferring them into a complex corporate and trust network but the Court of Appeal restrained him from dealing with the assets held by these companies and trusts pending the outcome of the case. In the next chapter the way in which a Claimant can seek to locate the whereabouts of the defendant's assets is addressed. **33–006**

Holding Companies

In some cases the Courts have concluded that a holding company has been carrying on business through the agency of its subsidiary company. There are a number of decided cases which illustrate the relevant principles (see, for example, *D H N Food Distributors Ltd v Tower Hamlets LBC* [1976] 1 W.L.R. 852) but they do not impact significantly in the area of investor protection. Perceived injustice in the face of insolvency will not be sufficient to cause a Court to treat a subsidiary company and a holding company as one economic unit—*Re Polly Peck International plc (in administration) (No.4)* [1996] 2 All E.R. 433. **33–007**

Agency

Exceptionally, as with the relationship between an holding company and its subsidiary, the circumstances of a particular case may permit a Claimant to circumvent the sanctity of the corporate personality by asserting that the **33–008** company has acted as an agent for a director who is a principal. The decision in *Salomon v Salomon* did not exclude the operation of principal and agent in this context but in reality this relationship will be difficult to establish because a Claimant will have to show that, in terms of some tortious liability, the director is the employer or principal of the company. As Tomlin J. explained in *British Thomson-Houston Co Ltd v Sterling Accessories* [1924] All E.R. 294:

> "It has been made plain by the House of Lords that, for the purpose of establishing contractual liability, it is not possible, even in the case of the so-called one-man companies, to go behind the legal corporate entity of the company and treat the creator and controller of the company as the real contractor merely because he is the creator and controller. If he is to be fixed with liability as a principal, the agency of the company must be established substantively and cannot be inferred from the holding of director's office and the control of the shares . . . Any other conclusion would have nullified the purpose for which the creation of limited companies was authorised by the legislature".

Three recent cases where the Courts have applied the agency principle to attach personal liability to a director are worthy of mention because they illustrate the increasing willingness of the Courts to impose personal liability in this area.

33–009 In *Haley v Northington Archives Ltd* (unreported) November 15, 1995, a deputy High Court Judge held that an employee of a company which traded in currency futures owed a non-contractual personal duty of care to the Claimant when he gave investment advice upon which the Claimant acted. Although employed by the company and acting on its behalf, the defendant held himself out as an advisor and specialist, and regarded himself to be a professional man providing services to a client. This was enough to bring him within one of the existing categories where a personal duty of care was owed.

A few weeks later, in *Williams v Natural Life Health Foods Ltd* (unreported) December 1, 1995, Langley J. held a managing director of a company liable for negligent mis-statements made in the name of the company concerning the company's financial projections. The Judge said that the fact that the director controlled the company was not in itself sufficient to make him personally liable, but since he had personally directed the presentation to the Claimant of the financial projections and assumed responsibility for them, personal liability had been established. It was found as a fact that, in considering the financial projections, the managing director had appreciated that the Claimant would rely on his personal experience and expertise.

33–010 Lastly, in *Infante v Charman* (unreported) July 31, 1996 a Court held that the defendant, who was a director of a company with whom the Claimant had placed a building contract, had contracted with the Claimant as principal and not as an agent of the company. The Claimant and the defendant were long-standing friends. All the correspondence had been informal, although it had been written on the company's headed notepaper. The Court said that use of company headed notepaper was not enough in itself to demonstrate that the defendant was contracting as the company's agent. Given the relationship between the Claimant and the defendant, there had to be explicit wording to such effect in the correspondence. Applying *The Swan* [1968] Lloyd's Rep. 5, whether a director contracted as a principal or an agent depended on the objective intention of the parties, as evidence by (1) the nature of the contract, (2) its surrounding terms and (3) the surrounding circumstances.

Wrongful Trading

Until 1986 it used to be the case that directors could hide behind the corporate shelter unless they had been acting fraudulently or in some other way intending to evade a contractual or legal obligation. The enactment of s.214 of the Insolvency Act 1986 made a radical change in this position and today a negligent director of an investment company may be vulnerable where the company has become insolvent. Potentially, this legislative change significantly erodes the inviolability of the corporate entity in the investment context. **33–011**

The Cork Committee recommended the institution of a new remedy of wrongful trading in its report in 1982 (Cmnd 8558) where a company went into liquidation in circumstances where the directors or shadow directors knew, or ought to have known, that the company could not pay its debts. This recommendation was adopted by Parliament in s.214 of the Insolvency Act 1986 which provides that a person will be liable for wrongful trading if: **33–012**

(a) the company has gone into insolvent liquidation;

(b) at some time before the commencement of the company's winding-up that person knew or ought to have known, that there was no reasonable prospect that the company would avoid going into insolvent liquidation;

(c) he was a director or shadow director of the company at that time; and

(d) the court is not satisfied that he took every step that he ought to have taken with a view to minimising the potential loss to the company's creditors (assuming him to have known that there was no reasonable prospect that the company would avoid going into insolvent liquidation).

The last criteria is the most difficult to satisfy. Further guidance on the meaning the requirement is contained in s.214(4) which reads as follows: **33–013**

> ". . . the facts which a director of a company ought to know or ascertain, the conclusions which he ought to reach and the steps which he ought to take are those which would be known or ascertained, or reached or taken, by a reasonably diligent person having both—

(a) the general knowledge, skill and experience that may reasonably be expected of a person carrying out the same functions as are carried out by that director in relation to the company;

(b) the general knowledge, skill and experience that that director has."

33–014 This test represents a curious mix of objective and subjective standards, and where the director or shadow director has particular expertise, for example in financial accounting, the standard will be higher than that required of his less highly trained counterpart. In *Re Produce Marketing Consortium Ltd (No 2)* [1989] B.C.L.C. 520, the Court held that a director or shadow director had to be judged by the standards that might reasonably be expected from somebody fulfilling his functions and showing reasonable diligence in doing so. Certain minimum standards would be assumed, such as knowledge on the part of the directors of information compiled by the company in accordance with its obligation under the Companies Act 1985 to publish annual accounts.

It was said in *Re Purpoint* [1991] B.C.L.C. 491 that the Court is concerned to ensure that the director makes good the depletion in assets attributable to the period after the moment when he knew or ought to have known that there was no reasonable prospect of avoiding an insolvent winding-up. This, then, is the measure of compensation which a director will be required to pay in an appropriate case.

33–015 Initially there was some concern at the scope of persons who might fall into the definition of a shadow director, as where, for example, a bank supported an ailing company with a business plan which the company was obliged to follow. To some extent the point was resolved in *Re MC Bacon* [1990] B.C.L.C. 324 where the Court said a liquidator's claim against a bank had been rightly abandoned. More recently, in *Re Hydrodan (Corby) Ltd* 1994 B.C.C. 161, a Court refused to accept that the directors of a holding company were shadow directors of a subsidiary company.

The most significant limitation on this innovative power is that a liquidator is the only person by whom an application may be made under this section. In a compulsory winding-up the official receiver acts as liquidator by virtue of s.136(2) of the Act, unless a different person is appointed by virtue of ss.139 or 140. In most cases the necessary evidence will be difficult to gather, and the liquidator is likely to be in the best position to decide whether the requirements of the section could be established to the satisfaction of the court. Unfortunately no procedure has been set up to deal with the situation where a liquidator fails to take action in the face of good evidence. Arguably, an aggrieved investor might have sufficient status to bring the matter before the Court in proceedings for declaratory relief. If not, his remedy would be confined to the Parliamentary Ombudsman.

Costs

33–016 There is one further area in which a director may be personally vulnerable where a limited company is involved. This area is exclusively procedural, focusing on the power contained in s.51(1) of the Supreme Court Act 1981 which confers power on the Court to determine by whom and to what extent the costs of any legal action are to be paid. The section contemplates the making of an order against a party who has not been joined as a party to an action, although in *Taylor v Pace Developments Ltd* [1991] B.C.C. 406 the Court said that it would seldom be appropriate to make such an order against a director of an insolvent company.

Chapter 34

Pre-emptive Civil Remedies

The purpose of this chapter is to address an important area of civil procedure which has particular relevance in cases where an investor Claimant brings an action against a defendant to recover his losses following the discovery of an investor fraud. The area concerns the efforts which an investor Claimant can make to identify, locate and freeze the misapplied funds. Reliance by a defendant on the privilege against self-incrimination can operate to thwart these efforts and the scope of the privilege is considered in the second part of this chapter. In the third section of this chapter brief mention is made of the ability of an investor Claimant to obtain summary judgment in an investor fraud case. **34–001**

The Freezing Order and Search Order Jurisdiction

General Principles

In cases where investor losses have been suffered, it is essential for investors to have swift recourse to the civil process so as to ensure that misapplied funds are identified, located and returned to the United Kingdom in cases where (as often occurs) they have been transferred abroad. There are two main ways in which this can be achieved. First, an aggrieved investor can seek to obtain an injunction which freezes the assets of the defendant. This used to known as a "Mareva" injunction. Secondly, an investor can seek to obtain an order which enables him to enter the premises of the defendant and search for specified documents and property which he may then seize. This order is known as a search order. It used to be known as an "Anton Pillar" order. **34–002**

A Claimant can apply for both orders in an appropriate case. Applications for a freezing order and a search order are made *ex parte* since secrecy is essential for the success of the operation. Experience has shown time and again that these pre-emptive remedies provide the only realistic chance for an investor Claimant to recover his loss where he has been a victim of investor fraud. The police, the Serious Fraud Office and the regulatory bodies seem to take an unconscionable time to decide whether to act on information which they receive, and by the time search warrants have been obtained through the criminal process the misapplied monies have often been subjected to the laundering process. There is no other mechanism whereby an investor or a liquidator can require a defendant to disclose the whereabouts of misapplied funds at an early stage in the investigatory process. In a case of investor fraud, although it may be late and perhaps much of the money might have gone, the sooner that steps are taken to try and trace where it is the better. If steps are going to be taken, it is important that they are taken at the earliest possible moment.

34–003 A freezing order will be granted where a Claimant can show that there is a real risk that the defendant has dissipated the investment funds or that the funds have been removed from the jurisdiction. An investor Claimant must show that he has a good arguable case and that there is a real risk that any judgment which he obtains will be unenforceable because of dissipation or secretion of the misapplied funds. It should be possible to satisfy these criteria in almost every serious fraud case. A freezing order can be granted against any defendant in an action, whether inside or outside of the United Kingdom and whether or not the defendant has assets inside or outside the jurisdiction—*Derby & Co Ltd v Weldon (Nos 3 & 4)* [1990] Ch. 65.

There may be occasions where a Claimant will be required to give an undertaking not to make any application to a foreign court without first obtaining leave of the UK Court because the Court was concerned to ensure that the freezing order would not enforced by a multiplicity of actions in different countries throughout the world, but this will not occur in every case. In *Re Bank of Credit and Commerce International SA (9)* [1994] 3 All E.R. 764 the Court of Appeal recognised that it was undesirable for liquidators who were seeking material for the prosecution of fraud and the enforcement of regulatory procedures in international cases to be fettered by undertakings simply because they were seeking worldwide freezing relief in domestic civil proceedings for the benefit of creditors.

34–004 One unresolved issue which is likely to recur in the future is whether a Court can grant a freezing order to restrain a defendant's assets in the United Kingdom where a Claimant has brought proceedings in another jurisdiction and the subject matter of the action has no connection with the domestic jurisdiction. The issue was raised before the Privy Council in *Mercedes-Benz AG v Herbert Heinz Horst Leiduck*, [1995] 3 All E.R. 929, but the point was not decided because the Claimant's claim failed on a different point. Whilst it is right that there is increasing emphasis on the importance of international co-operation in the battle against international fraud, it has to be remembered that the freezing relief takes effect *in personam* and not *in rem*, which means that the injunction is not an attachment and does not confer on the Claimant any proprietary rights in the assets seized. Bearing this in mind, a Court may not find it easy to afford assistance to a foreign investor Claimant where the matters in dispute have no connection with an English court, even though the defendant is present in the United Kingdom, perhaps because he has fled from another jurisdiction. The position is different where the Court is asked to assist in aid of proceedings begun in another jurisdiction. Under s.25 of the Civil Jurisdiction and Judgments Act 1982 an English Court has jurisdiction to give pre-trial or post-trial relief in aid of proceedings commenced in a Brussels Convention country.

An application for a search order will be successful where an investor Claimant can show strong evidence that serious harm or serious injustice would be suffered by him if the order is not granted, and strong evidence that the defendant has in his possession inculpating documents or other property. There must be a strong *prima facie* case that the defendant may destroy or dispose of the documents or property before an *inter partes* application can be made. Again, in cases involving serious fraud, these criteria can usually be satisfied.

Disclosure of Assets

The critical importance of a freezing order in the investor context is that an ancillary disclosure order can be attached to the injunction which requires a defendant to make full disclosure of his assets, confirming by affidavit the existence, location and amount of these assets. This power is derived from s.37 of the Supreme Court Act 1981 which confers jurisdiction (albeit implicitly) to make all such orders as appear to the Court to be just and convenient for the purpose of ensuring that the exercise of the freezing jurisdiction is effective to achieve its purpose. A defendant may have more than one asset within or outside the jurisdiction—for example, he may have a number of bank accounts. A Claimant will not know how much, if anything, is in any of them, nor will each of the defendant's bankers know what is in the other accounts. Without information about the state of each account it is difficult, if not impossible, to operate the freezing jurisdiction properly—see *A J Bekhor & Co Ltd v Bilton* [1981] 1 Q.B. 923, and *A v C (Note)* [1981] Q.B. 956. When pursuing a tracing remedy to recover the misapplication of investor funds, it is vital that a defendant is ordered to disclose details of his foreign assets as well as assets which he holds within the jurisdiction. **34–005**

Bankers Trust Order

In the area of investor fraud in particular, the growth of freezing orders has led to an expansion of the equitable jurisdiction relating to the obtaining of details of a defendant's bank accounts. Frequently an investor Claimant will seek a tracing order in relation to such accounts, in order to recover the misapplied funds. In *A v C* [1981] Q.B. 956 Goff J. confirmed that a Court had inherent jurisdiction to obtain information about bank accounts so as to facilitate the operation of a freezing injunction in this type of case. As Lloyd J. explained during the first instance hearing in *PCW (Under-Claiming Agencies) Ltd v Dixon* [1983] 2 All E.R. 158 (at p.164E-F), the distinction between an ordinary freezing Claimant and the case where a Claimant is laying claim to a trust fund is that in the latter case the whole object of the action is to secure the trust fund itself so that it is available if the Claimant proves his claim. **34–006**

The power to obtain this type of order operates in addition to the powers to inspect bankers books under the Bankers Books Evidence Act 1879. As with the normative Freezing injunction, a bankers order needs to be sought as a matter of urgency. It has been established that a bankers order will be made only if the order is likely to lead to the discovery of misapplied funds or alternatively where it is necessary to preserve such funds—*Arab Monetary Fund v Hashim (No 5)* [1992] 2 All E.R. 911. The investor Claimant must establish that he has a proprietary claim to the funds which he is seeking to locate or preserve—*Lipkin Gorman (a firm) v Cass*, *The Times*, May 29, 1985. In this type of case a bank may be ordered not simply to disclose details of bank accounts held in a defendant's name but also to disclose details of the balances standing in any account and to permit the Claimant to take copies of banking documents which relate to the operation of the account.

34–007 The Court of Appeal upheld the making of such an order in *Bankers Trust Co v Shapira* [1980] 1 W.L.R. 1274, from which "the Bankers Trust order" takes its name. In complicated cases a Court will sanction the appointment of a specified firm of chartered accountants to prepare a schedule setting out the identity and whereabouts of all assets which are held or retained by the defendant. This occurred in the *PCW (UnderClaiming Agencies) Ltd* case.

Documents produced by a bank pursuant to a Bankers Trust order can be used for the purposes of mounting personal claims against other persons and pursuing parallel remedies in other jurisdictions—*Mohamed Omar v Chiiko Aikawa Omar*, *The Times*, December 27, 1994. The Court noted in this case that confidentiality in bankers' documents was broken when there was fraud.

Delivery Up

34–008 In rare cases of serious fraud, a Court can order a defendant to deliver up the misapplied assets to the Court so that the assets can be held pending judgment in the action. This order will not be made unless a Claimant can establish that the assets have been acquired by a defendant as a result of his wrong-doing and that he is likely to dispose of them in order to deprive the Claimant of the fruits of any judgment he may obtain. The Court must be able to specify as clearly as possible the identity of the assets in question—*CBS United Kingdom Ltd v Lambert* [1983] Ch. 37.

Restraining a Defendant's Freedom of Movement

34–009 Rarely a Court may be prepared to take the ultimate step and restrain a defendant from leaving the country if there is a significant risk that he will flee the jurisdiction in order to frustrate an order which requires him to disclose the whereabouts of his assets. This occurred in *Bayer AG v Winter (No 2)* [1986] 1 W.L.R. 540 where, after an order was made for disclosure of certain correspondence and documents in a search order case, the Court of Appeal ordered that the defendant should be restrained from leaving the jurisdiction for a period of two days following service of the order, and that he should deliver up his passport to the solicitor who served the order on him, with a requirement that the passport should be returned on the expiry of the two days in question.

This type of Court order must be distinguished from the ancient Claim of *ne exeat regno* under which a Court can impose a power of arrest. There are four conditions which have to be satisfied before a Claim of *ne exeat regno* can be issued, these being (1) that the action is one in which the defendant would formerly have been liable to arrest at law; (2) that a good cause of action for at least £50 is established; (3) that there is probable cause for believing that the defendant is about to leave England unless arrested ; and (4) that the defendant's absence would materially prejudice the Claimant in the prosecution of his claim—*Felton v Callis* [1969] 1 Q.B. 200. It is the fourth condition which prevents the Claim of *ne exeat regno* being granted as an ancillary order in the freezing jurisdiction.

As Leggatt J. explained in *Allied Arab Bank Ltd v Hajjar* [1988] 22 W.L.R. 942, the primary purpose of a freezing order is to identify assets in relation to which an injunction can operate. That is not part of the prosecution of the claim, and it follows that the fourth condition cannot be satisfied.

Cross-examination

If there are grounds for believing that a defendant has not made full disclosure in response to an order made in freezing or search proceedings, a Court has power to order that the defendant is subjected to cross-examination on his affidavit—*House of Spring Gardens Ltd v Waite* [1985] F.S.R. 173. Once again the jurisdiction to make such an order is derived from s.37 of the Supreme Court Act 1981 and the need for a Court to ensure that its freezing order and search order jurisdiction is efficacious. **34–010**

A judge has to exercise his discretion when deciding whether to make an order for cross-examination of a defendant on the disclosure of his assets. There are no hard and fast rules. As a general rule cross-examination will not be ordered unless a Claimant can show that there are some grounds for believing that there are serious inaccuracies or omissions in a defendant's affidavit, in circumstances where an application for contempt of court might be appropriate.

In *CBS United Kingdom Ltd v Perry* [1985] F.S.R. 421 Falconer J. **34–011** expressed the view that it would not be right to allow a Claimant the opportunity of a roving cross-examination merely because a Claimant harbours suspicions that a defendant has not been entirely open in his disclosure. It is, after all, in the nature of an application for freezing or search relief that a Claimant harbours grave suspicions about a defendant who is served with an order. Also, the power to order cross-examination cannot be used for some ulterior purpose which goes beyond the efficacy of the freezing order and search order jurisdiction. In *Cloverbay Ltd (joint administrators) v Bank of Credit and Commerce International SA* [1991] Ch. 90 the Court refused to allow the administrators oral examination of certain BCCI employees in order to decide whether to bring claims of constructive trust against them. The Court said that the administrators had considerable material, including material obtained in a Bankers Trust order, on which to make this decision. Pre-trial oral depositions would be unduly oppressive for the employees concerned.

Guidance on the making of an order for cross-examination was given by the Court of Appeal in the *House of Spring* case. Slade L.J. explained the approach of the Court in the following terms:

> "I can very well see that on the particular facts of many cases—perhaps most cases—the court might not consider it "just and convenient" to order the cross-examination of a defendant who has filed an affidavit in purported compliance with a Freezing order, in a case where the Claimant has not yet seen fit to issue a motion for contempt and is not seeking an order for the swearing of a second affidavit by the defendant concerned. The court will always seek to be careful to ensure that the Freezing jurisdiction is not used as a weapon to oppress a defendant; it will no doubt be particularly on guard against potential oppression in a case where it considers that there is no immediate issue before it which calls for decision".

34–012 On the other hand, as Slade L.J. went on to acknowledge:

> " . . . cases can . . . arise where, on the particular facts, the court may properly take the view that the calling or recalling of a defendant for cross-examination on his affidavit is the only just and convenient way of ensuring that the exercise of this jurisdiction will be effective to achieve its purpose, by ensuring that all the relevant assets are identified before any opportunity arises for their dissipation. And this may be so even if, procedurally, the only application before it is the application for cross-examination itself (made subsequent and ancillary to the making of the Freezing order) and the Claimant has not yet seen fit to launch a motion for committal".

Cumming-Bruce L.J. agreed with Slade L.J.'s approach, declaring that there are situations where the circumstances demonstrate that it is more sensible, in the interests of speed and urgency, not to order further affidavits in order to fill the vacuum alleged to exist in the affidavits filed pursuant to the original order but to proceed at once to order that the defendant attends for cross-examination on his affidavit.

34–013 The proper scope of cross-examination in this type of case will be two-fold. First, to ascertain whether or not a defendant has fully and properly complied with the obligations imposed on him in the freezing order and/or search order to disclose the location of his assets and his dealings with them. Secondly, in so far as there has not been full and proper compliance, to elicit the missing information which should have been supplied. Under Pt 25 of the Civil Procedure Rules cross-examination can be ordered to take place before a Judge, a Master of the Supreme Court or an examiner appointed by the Court. On a purely practical point, no shorthand note of the cross-examination is taken by the Court, so a Claimant would be well advised to make his own arrangements.

The ability of the Court to order cross-examination of a defendant in these circumstances will almost certainly be the subject of future litigation. The first instance Judge in *House of Spring*, Scott J., came to the view that, notwithstanding the defendant's consent to be cross-examined, no cross-examination should take place because the Claimant had not ascertained or clarified the specific issue which was disputed between the parties. The function of a civil court, said Scott J., was to decide issues between the parties and not to police the court's order. The Court of Appeal, of course, disagreed with this view, holding that Scott J. had taken too narrow a view of the width of the freezing jurisdiction possessed by the Court, but in the subsequent case of *Bayer AG v Winter (No 2)* [1986] 1 W.L.R. 540, Scott J.

was clearly unrepentant. In that case a Claimant had obtained *ex parte* a search order which directed the defendant to disclose certain information relating to the alleged distribution by the defendant of a counterfeit product. The Claimant was dissatisfied with the disclosure which it obtained and sought an order for cross-examination. Scott J. rejected the Claimant's application on the basis, once again, that, in his view, the proper function of a judge in civil litigation is to decide issues between the parties and not preside over an interrogation. "Star Chamber interrogatory procedure", said the Judge, "has formed no part of the judicial process in this country for several centuries".

As regards the decision in *House of Spring*, Scott J. said that it could be distinguished because the defendant in that case had consented to cross-examination. The Judge said that for his part he found it very difficult to envisage any circumstances in which, as a matter of discretion, it would be right to make such an order as was sought in *Bayer AG v Winter (No 2)* and as was made by consent in *House of Spring*. Scott J.'s approach ignores not only the clear spirit of the judgments in the Court of Appeal, but also the protection afforded to a defendant by the privilege against self-incrimination, the operation of which is considered in the second part of this chapter. **34–014**

Procedure

The procedure for a freezing and/or search application is set out in Pt 25 of the Civil Procedure Rules and it is right to record that there is much learning on these pre-emptive civil remedies which extends beyond the scope of this work. Suffice it in the second part of this chapter to focus on the principal impediment to a successful application for a freezing order and/or a search order where a defendant seeks to exercise the privilege against self-incrimination. The successful assertion of this privilege can frustrate an investor Claimant's attempts to locate the whereabouts of his misapplied funds, and since the privilege is commonly asserted in investor fraud cases, it is necessary to consider the matter in some detail. **34–015**

2. The Privilege Against Self-incrimination

The Privilege

The privilege against self-incrimination has been described recently, by Lord Browne-Wilkinson, in *Re Arrows Ltd (No 4) Hamilton v Naviede* [1994] 3 All E.R. 814 as "one of the basic freedoms secured by English law". It has, said Lord Wilberforce in *Rank Film Distributors v Video Information Centre* [1981] 2 All E.R. 76, been too long established in our law as a basic liberty of the subject to be denied. In *Rank Film Distributors* the Claimant sought disclosure from the defendants of information which, if revealed, might expose them to a prosecution for conspiracy to defraud in **34–016** respect of the unauthorised recording and sale of a large number of video cassettes. The question before the House of Lords was whether the defendants could avail themselves of the privilege against self-incrimination in order to resist the Claimant's application for disclosure. Reluctantly, the House of Lords upheld the defendants' right to claim the benefit of the privilege and the Claimant failed in his appeal to obtain disclosure of the incriminating information.

The decision was consistent with the position under Art.6(1) of the European Convention for the Protection of Human Rights and Fundamental Freedoms (Rome, November 4, 1950), which recognises that it is unlawful to render a demand to produce self-incriminating documents (see *Funke v Funke* [1993] 16 E.H.R.R. 297, *Miailhe v France* [1993] 16 E.H.R.R. 332, and *Cremieux v France* [1993] 16 E.H.R.R. 357). Moreover, the European Court of Justice has held that under European Community law an individual cannot be compelled to give incriminating answers to the European Commission since to do so would infringe "the general principles of Community law, of which fundamental rights form an integral part".

34–017 The privilege against self-incrimination is derived from a Latin maxim, "*nemo tenetur prodere seipsum*" and came to be incorporated into English law in the sixteenth century in response to the compulsory interrogations then being conducted by the Star Chamber and the High Commission for Causes Ecclesiastical. The classic statement of the privilege is contained in the judgment of Goddard L.J. in *Blunt v Park Lane Hotel* [1942] 2 K.B. 253, as follows:

> "The rule is that no one is bound to answer any question if the answer thereto would, in the opinion of the judge, have a tendency to expose the deponent to any criminal charge, penalty or forfeiture which the judge regards as reasonably likely to be preferred or sued for".

Asserting the Privilege

34–018 The privilege has to be asserted by the defendant. However, it is not sufficient for him to merely state that his answer or production of documents would in his opinion render him liable to criminal prosecution. Affidavit evidence asserting the privilege will not be conclusive. The specific offence or offences have to be identified. This is not to say that the defendant will be required to set out the details of the incriminating evidence. He must provide sufficient information for the Judge to make his ruling, but no more.

It is for the Judge to satisfy himself that the defendant's claim to rely on the privilege against self-incrimination is properly made. The Court will examine whether, taking into account the circumstances of the case and the nature of the evidence, there is reasonable ground to apprehend some danger if the defendant is compelled to answer the question or produce the documents in question. The privilege will not be available where the defendant is already at risk of prosecution and the risk will not be increased if he were to answer questions or provide information. However, once the danger of self-incrimination is apparent, great latitude will be allowed to the defendant in assessing for himself the effect of any particular question. The cases of *Rio Tinto Zinc Corp v Westinghouse Electric Corporation* [1978] A.C. 547 and *Sociedade Nacional de Combustiveis de Angola v Lundqvist* [1991] 2 Q..B 310 are the seminal cases in point and authorities for these propositions. In *Sociedade* Staughton L.J. set out the test (at p.324E) which is to be applied:

> "The substance of the test is this, that there must be grounds to apprehend danger to the witness, and those grounds must be reasonable, rather than fanciful".

A Court will have regard to the petty nature of any offence and the fact that prosecutions are rare. In *Rank Film Distributors* the House of Lords held that the possibility of charges under s.21 of the Copyright Act 1956 which carried a maximum penalty of a £50 fine could not justify the claim for privilege. **34–019**

By s.14(1) of the Civil Evidence Act 1968, Parliament has confirmed that the privilege against self-incrimination is to be taken to include any answer which would tend to expose the spouse of the defendant to proceedings for a criminal offence. A company, being a legal person, may also claim the privilege. In these circumstances it should be remembered that the privilege belongs to the company and not to its officers, although the officers can claim the benefit of the privilege in their own right. If a defendant elects not to claim the privilege, his answers cannot be recalled.

In recent times, the Courts have moved towards a situation where freezing orders and search orders will not be granted *ex parte* without a provision in the order which informs a defendant of his right to claim the benefit of the privilege against self-incrimination. Lord Wilberforce said in *Rank Film Distributors* that forms should be worked out which will enable the orders to be as effective as practicable whilst preserving the defendant's essential rights. Such a formula of words was incorporated into an Search order by Warner J. in *IBM United Kingdom Ltd v Prima Data International Ltd* [1994] 1 W.L.R. 719, to the following effect: **34–020**

> ". . . before any persons enter [the premises] pursuant to this order the supervising solicitor shall offer to explain to the [defendant] the meaning an effect of this Order in everyday language and shall also advise the [defendant] of his right to obtain legal advice before permitting entry provided that such advice is taken as once (such advice to include an explanation that the [defendant] may be entitled to avail himself of the privilege against self-incrimination) . . ."

This order was executed but the defendant subsequently complained that he had not fully understood the privilege against self-incrimination to which reference had been made. In the course of its judgment the Court approved the use of this formula, noting that defendants are bemused by the appearance of solicitors bearing thirteen page orders in legal language. The Judge, Sir Mervyn Davies Q.C., said that it would have been helpful to have seen cross-examination of the solicitor and the defendant as to exactly **34–021** what was said when the order was executed but neither party had applied to take this course. In the event the Court concluded that since the defendant was a businessman of some experience he must have understood the position which had been explained to him by the solicitor concerned. This type of clause protects the interests of a defendant but at the expense of a Claimant who is seeking to recover losses as a result of an investment fraud.

Freezing Orders

34–022 The privilege is often asserted by defendants in applications for freezing orders where the Court orders the defendant to disclose the whereabouts of his assets and/or attend for cross-examination on the contents of his affidavit. In these circumstances it is sometimes difficult for a Claimant to circumvent the operation of the privilege. The Court of Appeal held in *Sociedade* that a defendant in civil proceedings who is facing allegations of conspiracy to defraud is entitled to rely on the privilege against self-incrimination to resist an order requiring him to disclose the value of his assets overseas where the value of such assets might form a link in the chain of proof against him on a criminal charge. Moreover, it seems that a defendant can seek to rely on the privilege against self-incrimination as a secondary defence in circumstances where he disputes on the facts of the Claimant's claim that he has conducted himself in a way which might expose him to criminal proceedings. It is not open to a Claimant to say that a defendant, because he protests his innocence, he must be lying when he claims potential incrimination. A defendant in such a case may properly claim the benefit of the privilege against self-incrimination—*AT & T Istel Ltd v Tully* [1993] A.C. 45.

In recent times there has been some litigation on whether the operation of the privilege against self-incrimination can be circumvented by an assurance that the disclosed material will not be used in a criminal prosecution. In *AT & T Istel Ltd* the House of Lords sanctioned this approach, deciding that a defendant cannot rely on the privilege where the prosecuting authorities have stated by letter that any disclosure made in civil proceedings will not be used as evidence in criminal proceedings. As Ralph Gibson L.J. pointed out in *Bank of England v Riley* [1992] 2 W.L.R. 840, the question as to whether there was any misuse of information could be determined by a criminal court which was subsequently involved. The position is different, however, in the absence of an assurance from the prosecuting authorities.

34–023 In *United Norwest Co-operatives Ltd v Johnstone*, *The Times*, February 24, 1994, the first instance Judge ordered disclosure of assets in a claim for fraudulent trading but sought to protect the interests of the defendants by ordering that the Claimant was restrained from disclosing the information to any person who was not a party to the action and in particular to any police force or prosecuting authority. The Court of Appeal was unable to approve of this approach because it did not depend on any assurance from a prosecuting authority. It did not follow, the Court of Appeal said, that a Court could withhold its assistance to a prosecuting authority where there had been no assurance given by the prosecuting authority and the Court order had been made without notice to the prosecuting authority, let alone its consent.

It is presently unclear whether the privilege against self-incrimination applies where a defendant is concerned about his exposure to prosecution in another country. S.14(1) of the Civil Evidence Act 1968 provides that the privilege against self-incrimination "shall apply only as regards criminal offences under the law of any part of the United Kingdom", but it is difficult to see how, in these times of trans-border crime, this provision can sit easily with Art.6(1) of the European Convention. The Court of Appeal went some way to recognising to this point in *Arab Monetary Fund v Hashim* [1989] 3 All E.R. 466 when it held that the possibility of self-incrimination in respect of criminal offences in foreign law was a factor to be taken into account by the Court in deciding whether, and in what terms, a disclosure order in support of a freezing order should be made. Where a defendant asserts that he is vulnerable to criminal proceedings in a foreign jurisdiction, it will be necessary for a Claimant to obtain expert evidence on the law in that jurisdiction. **34–024**

In exceptional circumstances the Court has limited jurisdiction to order that the facts required to be disclosed by a defendant should not be disclosed to the Claimant provided that they are disclosed to someone on the Claimant's side (such as the Claimant's solicitor) who can effectively deal with the matter—*Arab Monetary Fund v Hashim*. The propriety of this approach is far from clear. It is unsatisfactory that a Claimant's solicitor should come into possession of information which he cannot disclose to his client.

Search Orders

Similar considerations arise where a Claimant obtains a search order to search and seize documents from a defendant's premises. A Court should not make an order at the *ex parte* stage if it is apparent on the facts alleged by a Claimant that disclosure of documents or the immediate answer to questions might tend to incriminate the defendant on a criminal charge—see *Rank Distributors Limited* and *Tate Access Floors Inc v Boswell* [1990] 3 All E.R. 303. Where a Claimant obtains and executes an *ex parte* search order, a defendant can apply to set aside the order and may obtain return of his documents if he can satisfy the Court that he is entitled to claim the privilege against self-incrimination, provided that the application to set aside the order is made before the documents have been adduced in evidence—*Universal City Studios Inc v Hubbard* [1983] 2 All E.R. 596, on appeal [1984] Ch. 225. **34–025**

Bankers Trust Orders

At present there is no direct authority on whether the privilege against self-incrimination can be raised in answer to a tracing order where details of a defendant's bank accounts are required. Bankers Trust orders are necessarily concerned with the recovery of funds which are alleged to have been **34–026** misapplied, so the same considerations which apply in cases of freezing orders and search orders can be expected to apply.

Bankers Books Evidence Act

34–027 In the course of civil proceedings a Claimant may seek to apply for discovery of a defendant's bank account under the provisions of the Bankers Books Evidence Acts 1876 and 1879. Once again, the privilege against self-incrimination operates to impede an aggrieved Claimant in his attempt to recover his losses where he has been the victim of an investment fraud. In *Waterhouse v Wilson Barker* [1924] 2 K.B. 759 it was alleged that the defendant and her husband had fraudulently taken certain monies belonging to Mr Waterhouse. The Claimant was the executrix of Mr Waterhouse's will and sought inspection of the defendant's bank account. The defendant successfully raised the privilege against self-incrimination to prevent the Claimant's inspection of his bank account.

Exceptional Cases Where the Privilege Against Self-incrimination has Been Abrogated by Statute

34–028 The operation of the privilege against self-incrimination has been embraced by the Courts with some equanimity, particularly in recent times. Whilst in the nineteenth century the Lord Chancellor, Lord Eldon, in *Cossens Ex p., In the Matter of Worrall* [1820] *Cases in Bankruptcy* 53, accepted that the privilege was "one of the most sacred principles in the law of this country", the contemporary approach is more sceptical. As Lord Wilberforce pointed out in *Rank Film Distributors* it was a strange paradox that the worse, *i.e.* the more criminal, the activities of the defendants can be made to appear, the less effective is the civil remedy that can be granted.

Mindful of this paradox, Parliament has intervened in a number of situations to abrogate the operation of the privilege where this has been perceived to be in the public interest. Notwithstanding these statutory interventions, for some members of the judiciary nothing short of abolition would be sufficient. Lord Templeman in *AT & T Istel Ltd* described the privilege against self-incrimination as "an archaic and unjustifiable survival from the past", and said (at p.53B) that:

> "it was difficult to see any reason why in civil proceedings the privilege . . . should be exercisable so as to enable a litigant to refuse relevant and even vital documents which are in his possession or power and which speak for themselves".

Theft

34–029 S.31(1) of the Theft Act 1968 provides that a witness, who may be a defendant in a civil action, shall not be excused from answering a question in proceedings for the recovery or administration of any property, for the execution of any trust or for an account of any property or dealings with property, or from complying with any order made in any such proceedings, on the ground that it would incriminate him or his spouse in an offence under the Theft Act 1968. The abrogation of the privilege is tempered by the fact that the section further provides that no statement or admission made by the witness shall be admissible in criminal proceedings for an offence under the Act. The provision is extended to cover offences under the Theft Act 1978.

Suppose a defendant falls within the scope of s.31(1) but he is liable to be prosecuted for some other offence outside the parameters of the Theft Acts, such as forgery under the Forgery and Counterfeiting Act 1981. Will the privilege be abrogated in these circumstances? The Court of Appeal answered this question affirmatively in *Khan v Khan* [1982] 2 All E.R. 60, where a defendant was obliged to swear an affidavit concerning the whereabouts of money removed from an account. The Court upheld the order notwithstanding that a possible charge of forgery might have been brought as well.

This decision was applied by the Court of Appeal in *Renworth Ltd v* **34–030** *Stephansen* (unreported) December 21, 1995, where the defendant was required to swear an affidavit specifying certain matters in relation to the Claimant's claim for breach of contract and conversion. The defendant claimed the privilege against self-incrimination because there was a risk of prosecution for offences under the Theft Acts and non-Theft Act offences. The correct approach, the Court held, was for the matter to be considered from the point of view of separate claims to privilege in respect of both types of criminal offence. In each case the test was whether to answer the question would tend to expose the defendant to proceedings for the relevant offence by creating or increasing the risk of proceedings for that offence. If the test was satisfied in the case of a Theft Act offence, s.31 applied. In the case of the non-Theft Act offence, the test was whether the question would create or increase the risk of proceedings for that offence separate and distinct from its connection with the Theft Act offence. If the answer was "no", there was no privilege. If the answer was "yes", the privilege subsisted in relation to the non-Theft Act offence notwithstanding the availability of the Theft Act charges.

The prohibition set out in s.31 concerning the use in criminal proceedings of answers obtained in civil proceedings does not extend to cover answers given in proceedings for bankruptcy. In *R. v Kansal*, [1993] Q.B. 244, the Court of Appeal held that evidence given by a bankrupt in bankruptcy proceedings was admissible against him in his subsequent prosecution for offences under the Theft Act 1968. The Court held that s.31 related to civil proceedings, *inter partes*, where a claim was made in relation to property which had been acquired in circumstances of an incriminating nature. The normal privilege against self-incrimination was abrogated by the terms of s.31 in such proceedings.

Copyright

After the decision in *Rank Film Distribution* Parliament intervened and by **34–031** s.72 of the Supreme Court Act 1981 it removed the privilege against self-incrimination in actions for breach of copyright. The Courts have held that this provision is not to be construed restrictively—*Universal City Studios Inc v Hubbard*—but there have been difficulties in establishing what is a "related offence" for the purposes of the section—see *Crest Homes plc v Marks* [1987] 2 All E.R. 1074 *per* Lord Oliver at p.1079b-1081a. Again, however, the abrogation of the privilege against self-incrimination was tempered by a restriction against the use of admissions in criminal proceedings.

Bankruptcy

34–032 The effect of s.290 of the Insolvency Act 1986 is more draconian, in the sense that there is no tempering provision so far as admission of evidence in criminal proceedings is concerned. Where a bankruptcy order has been made and the Official Receiver applies for a public examination of the bankrupt under s.290 of the Insolvency Act 1986, r.9.4(3) of the Insolvency Rules provides that the bankrupt shall be examined on oath and shall answer all such questions as the Court may put to him. In *Re Paget* [1927] 2 Ch. 85, a case decided under earlier legislation, it was held that a witness could not refuse to answer questions on the ground that his answers might incriminate him. Answers given in bankruptcy proceedings will be admissible in evidence against an accused in a criminal case. R.6.175(5) of the Insolvency Rules provides that "the Claimten record may, in any proceedings . . . be used as evidence against the bankrupt of any statement made by him in the course of his public examination".

Business Fraud

34–033 Procedures have been established under s.432 of the Companies Act 1985 and s.236 of the Insolvency Act 1986 for examinations to be conducted by inspectors and/or liquidators in order to elicit the true facts from those who know them. Although the statutory provisions establishing such inquisitorial rights for the purpose of discovering the true facts about the conduct of a company or an individual are silent on the question of whether the privilege against self-incrimination is to apply, the Courts have been ready to hold in recent years that Parliament has impliedly overridden the ancient privilege against self-incrimination by their enactment of these provisions. It has been held that a witness cannot rely on the privilege so as to refuse to answer questions put by inspectors under the Companies Act 1985—*Re London United Investment plc* [1992] 2 All E.R. 842 —or by liquidators on an examination under the Insolvency Act 1986—*In Re Jeffrey S Levitt Ltd*, *The Times*, November 6, 1991 and *Bishopsgate Investment Management Ltd v Maxwell* [1992] 2 All E.R. 856.

34–034 What is more, answers will be admissible against a defendant in any criminal proceedings. In *R. v Saunders* [1996] Crim. L.R. 420, the defendant was interviewed by inspectors appointed to conduct an investigation into the Guinness acquisition of Distillers under ss.432 and 442 of the Companies Act 1985. The defendant was subsequently prosecuted for criminal offences and the trial Judge admitted into evidence the transcripts of interview which the accused had given to the inspectors before he was charged in order to establish his dishonest state of knowledge and to contradict his testimony to the jury. The Court of Appeal, Lord Taylor C.J. presiding, upheld the trial Judge's decision, having come to the view that Parliament intended to override the privilege against self-incrimination in the fields of insolvency and company fraud. The European Commission of Human Rights has, however, taken a different view, saying that the admission into evidence of the interview transcripts offended against Art.6(1) of the Convention. The European Court of Human Rights usually adopts the opinion of the European Commission, and this can be expected to happen in the *Saunders* case.

Whether an unfavourable ruling by the European Court of Human Rights will persuade the Government to intervene and alter the law remains to be seen. Certainly it is right to note that s.31 of the Theft Act 1968 would not fall foul of Art.6(1) of the European Convention because of the tempering provision against the admission of answers into evidence in criminal proceedings. It might be thought that a similar limitation could be applied to the use of interview transcripts obtained under the Companies Act and Insolvency Act powers.

The Effect of Asserting the Privilege

Traditionally, no adverse inference can be drawn from a defendant's assertion of the privilege against self-incrimination. For as Staughton L.J. said in *Sociedade* (at p.319F): **34–035**

> "to comment adversely about a person who claims privilege to avoid incriminating himself is plainly wrong".

The opponents of the privilege have sought to advance a contrary view, exemplified by Templeman L.J.'s comments in *Rank Film Distributors* when the case was heard in the Court of Appeal:

> "The Claimant is not wholly or necessarily defeated and the defendant is not necessarily assisted by the defendant relying on the privilege against self-incrimination. The civil court may draw conclusions where a criminal court may not. If the privilege is raised in connection with an inquiry as to damages the court will be driven to draw conclusions as to the scope and harm caused by the defendant's activities and, in the face of silence and concealment on the part of the defendant, will not be slow to make assumptions and draw inferences which will enable damages to be awarded on a scale which will do justice to the Claimant".

Whether this contrary view can be said to undermine the efficacy of the privilege to such an extent that it contravenes Art.6(1) of the European Convention on Human Rights remains to be seen, but an investor Claimant can undoubtedly contend that the time has now come for the Courts to depart from the traditional position and draw adverse inferences from a defendant's silence. On April 10, 1995 English law was altered by s.35 of the Criminal Justice and Public Order Act 1994 and a criminal court is now **34–036** allowed to draw an adverse inference from the exercise by an accused of his right to silence. In these circumstances an investor Claimant may argue with some considerable force that it is absurd for a defendant to be better protected in a civil Court than a criminal Court.

Whether or not the concomitant effect of s.35 of the Criminal Justice and Public Order Act 1994 has been to allow a civil court to draw an adverse inference of liability in an action where the defendant asserts the privilege against self-incrimination, cases will continue to occur where the raising of the privilege can be used to thwart recovery of misapplied funds. Unless an aggrieved Claimant has knowledge of the whereabouts of the misapplied funds, in all probability any judgment against the judgment will be unenforceable. This begs the question as to whether Parliament should extend the operation of s.31 of the Theft Act 1968 to all criminal offences. As Sir Nicholas Browne Wilkinson observed in *Sociedade*, "if [this] is not done, I fear that the effectiveness of civil remedies designed to redress fraud will be seriously impaired". The s.31 approach is to be preferred to the approach taken by Parliament in the Companies Act 1985 and the Insolvency Act 1986 because it provides protection for the defendant against the admission of incriminating answers in criminal proceedings.

Fear of Physical Violence

34–037 Although it is a factor to be taken into account when deciding whether to set aside a freezing order or a search order, the risk of violence to the defendant by another party whose wrongdoing will be exposed by compliance with a Court order will rarely outweigh a Claimant's pressing need for the information in question. The point arose in *Coca-Cola v Gilbey* [1995] 4 All E.R. 711 where the Claimant obtained a Search order against a defendant in a breach of trade mark case. Documents disclosed the existence of another party against whom the Claimant subsequently obtained a further Search order. This party sought to set aside the order on the basis that his documents would disclose the names of others involved which would place his safety in danger. Lightman J. rejected the submission. "I cannot think that in any ordinary case where the Claimant has a pressing need for the information in question, the existence of the risk of violence against the potential informant should outweigh the interest of the Claimant in obtaining the information".

Summary Judgment

34–038 It is possible to obtain summary judgment in a civil case where a defendant has no defence to the claim. The advantage of the procedure is that it enables a Claimant to obtain a quick judgment without incurring significant costs in the pursuit of a defendant who does not have a bona fide defence.

In order to obtain summary judgment it will be necessary for the evidence of investor fraud to be overwhelmingly clear, and in practice this may occur only after a defendant has been convicted of fraud offences in a criminal court. Nevertheless if a Claimant is successful in securing the freezing of the misapplied funds under the freezing jurisdiction, the summary judgment procedure can be usefully employed as soon as the criminal case has concluded. By s.11(1) of the Civil Evidence Act 1968 a criminal conviction is admissible in a civil court to prove that a person committed the offence in question, and by s.11(2) a person is deemed to have committed the offence unless the contrary is proved. Therefore, if a defendant is to resist an application for summary judgment, he bears a heavy onus to show that he was wrongly convicted by the criminal court.

The summary judgment procedure was successfully utilised in the **34–039** Brinks-Mat bullion case when summary judgment was entered against a total of 57 defendants who had been involved in varying ways with the stolen gold or laundering the stolen gold. Two of the defendants sought to resist summary judgment but without success. Jacobs J. held that before a convicted robber or money launderer could raise a defence under RSC Ord.14 (now CPR r 24.2) he had to raise a real or bona fide defence to the claim. A defence that was "practical moonshine" would not do—*Brinks Ltd v Abu-Saleh and others* [1995] 4 All E.R. 65. The Court also held that delay in making an application for summary judgment was not of itself a relevant matter in determining the application in circumstances where there was no defence to the claim.

In *Brinks Ltd v Abu-Saleh (No 2)* [1995] 4 All E.R. 74, on a different but tangentially relevant point, Rimer J. held that a transcript of a Judge's summing up in criminal proceedings was at least potentially relevant in subsequent civil proceedings as a means of identifying the factual basis on which a defendant was convicted of the offence with which he had been charged. The admission of the transcript would clearly be helpful where a defendant contests the relevance of a criminal conviction on an application for summary judgment under Pt 24 of the Civil Procedure Rules.

Part 7

Conclusion

Chapter 35

The Future

On the day when the manuscript for this book was delivered to the publishers, the Government announced that there would be swift legislation to increase powers to investigate companies and improve the regulation of auditors. Inspectors at the Department of Trade and Industry are to be given a new legal right of access to companies' offices, and new powers to request information including computer records. Companies will be required to give a detailed breakdown in annual reports of the lucrative non-audit services purchased from their auditors, and the Inland Revenue will be permitted to provide details of accounting irregularities to a regulator that deals with companies suspected of breaching financial reporting rules. In addition, companies listed on the London Stock Exchange will be required to publish risk focused information, known as an operating and financial review, in their annual reports. **35–001**

Investor Scandals in America

These proposals are designed to guard against the occurrence of investor scandals similar in nature to those which have recently shaken corporate America to the core. Indeed, almost simultaneously with the Government's announcement about these proposed reforms, Alan Greenspan, the Chairman of the US Federal Reserve, issued a warning that "a pervasive sense of caution" was casting a shadow over the US investment markets, and this has been caused by the rash of scandals that had stunted investment in the corporate sector. **35–002**

The magnitude of these corporate scandals is difficult to grasp. Public dismay has focused on the debacle at Enron, the US energy provider, with mere mention of the company's name conjuring up dark images of staff at the accountancy firm Arthur Anderson shredding documents to obstruct an investigation into the company's affairs. The principal problem with Enron's financial well-being was triggered by the establishment of off-sheet partnerships largely financed by company stock used to hide around $1 billion of debt. The effect was to give the investing public a false impression that the company was financially stronger than it really was. The net result, of course, was to cause significant investor losses for those who owned Enron stock.

In 2002 a multi-billion dollar accounting fraud was identified at the second largest US telecoms company, Worldcom. The mis-statement was far larger in financial terms that Enron's misdeeds, with the US Securities **35–003** and Exchange Commission describing the accounting improprieties as being of "unprecedented magnitude". Worldcom admitted that it had not made the $1.4 million profit it had reported in 2001, nor the $130 million profit stated for the first quarter of 2002. The devious device utilised to achieve these misstatements was relatively simple. Worldcom pretended that $3.8 million expended in normal operating expenses had qualified as an investment by the company, which under US accounting rules permitted the company to spread the cost of the expense over a number of years, instead of having to account for it all at once. Unsurprisingly, the corporate profits looked stronger than they would otherwise have appeared, again, to the obvious prejudice of the investor.

35–004 Worse still for corporate America, the scandals at Enron and Worldcom were not isolated, as one could be forgiven for thinking that the capitalist system was starting to implode. The US media during the spring and summer months of 2002 was replete with headlines trumpeting corporate impropriety of the gravest order. In April 2002, the media reported that a Court had heavily criticised investment bank Merrill Lynch for issuing favourable reports from research analysts who represented the reports to be independent, in circumstances where the reports assisted Merrill Lynch in securing and maintaining lucrative contracts for investment banking services. Merrill Lynch agreed to pay a fine of $100 million to the regulators, and class actions to recover investor losses are expected to follow. Two months after the problems at Merrill Lynch emerged, the media reported an inquiry into high profile investment advisor Martha Stewart, focusing on allegations of insider dealing in relation to a biotech firm called ImClone. Stewart had received word from the founder and chief executive of ImClone that a US regulator was about to reject an experimental cancer drug, and she sold shares on the basis of this inside information. At around the same time the well known company Xerox issued a statement in which it admitted it had overstated sales in its accounts by $6.4 million, and this was swiftly followed by an announcement from another US company, Qwest, that it had also misstated its profits. The latter announcement triggered an 89 per cent drop in the value of share price, at a time when the chairman and the chief executive each drew bonus payments of $1.5 million. Other US companies, such as Charter Communications and Tyco, were also caught up in corporate scandals.

In response to the emergence of these corporate scandals, the US investing public was warned by the investment guru Warren Buffet to beware of other forms of corrupt corporate practices which were beginning to emerge. He spoke of "hollow swops" where companies swap useless commodities with each to artificially generate revenues; "channel stuffing" and "round tripping" where a company floods the market with more products than its distributors can sell, again to boost sales; and "pre-dispatching" where goods are marked as sold as soon as an order is placed but before payment.

35–005 Warren Buffet expressed the view that these devices were being utilised to stem the damage caused by the disasters of the dot-com era. Certainly those well experienced in the investigation and prosecution of fraud would agree with this sentiment, and today there is a feeling that there are many more problems currently masked by the low interest rates which permit a troubled company to borrow its way in the short term. Many more rotten apples will be shaken from the tree when the present economic cycle is broken and interest rates begin to rise.

The American Legislative Response

The US legislature has responded to this spate of financial scandals by enacting the Sarbanes-Oxley Act 2002 which requires chief executive officers and chief financial officers of companies to provide written certification to the Securities and Exchange Commission which states that they have reviewed the financial reports and confirm that to his or her knowledge these reports comply with accounting requirements, and that the information contained in the financial reports "fairly presents, in all material respects, the financial condition and results" of the company. In other words, the onus for making accurate reports no longer rests on the company and its officers, but on the shoulders of the chief executive personally. Additionally, the Sarbanes-Oxley Act requires public companies to establish an Audit Committee comprising of independent directors who have authority to engage independent counsel and establish procedures for the treatment of complaints regarding accounting and auditing matters. The Audit Committee must have amongst its members a person who qualifies as a "financial expert", with experience in the preparation or auditing of financial statements. **35–006**

Further legislative developments aimed at investor protection will be promoted in America in the near future. New rules announced by the Securities and Exchange Commission will be directed at the proxy process by which directors are elected at annual meetings. The rules will force companies to improve their disclosures to shareholders about the selection of board nominees and make it easier for shareholders to push through their own candidates for the board or changes in corporate policies.

Is the United Kingdom Vulnerable to Investor Scandals?

Differing views have been expressed as to whether the UK financial system is vulnerable to the same weaknesses which have precipitated the corporate scandals in America. In July 2002 the House of Commons Treasury and Civil Service Select Committee, which concerns itself with regulatory affairs, backed the idea that companies should rotate auditors every five years, and referring to Enron, the Trade Secretary Patricia Hewitt said that "it would be crazy to say it can't happen here", adding that such scandals had demonstrated a "much too cosy relationship between finance officers or chief executives and their auditors". The head of the City of London Police Fraud Squad Ken Farrow is far from sanguine about any perceived differences between corporate behaviour in London and New York. He **35–007** estimates the cost of corporate in the United Kingdom as running as high as £14 billion a year. One only has to think of the Barlow Clowes investors, the Mirror group pensioners, the BCCI and Barings Bank depositors to appreciate that the UK financial system is not immune from scandal, and as the Fraud Advisory Panel has recently warned, the collapse of Enron and Worldcom had dramatically underlined the damage that even the suspicion of fraud in major companies may cause to share values and therefore to the economy itself.

Whether the reforms proposed by the Government will be adequate to prevent the corporate scandals in the United Kingdom remains to be seen. The Department of Trade and Industry published a White Paper in 2002 which proposed to foster enterprise through the sweeping modernisation of company law by simplifying the governance and financial reporting requirements on small, private companies. Business has been critical of the Goverment's reluctance to introduce such widespread change at the present time, but against the backdrop of the corporate scandals in America this reluctance is perhaps understandable.

35–008 The role of auditors generally has continued to generate much interest. It is noteworthy that, contrary to the wishes of the accountancy profession, the Government has declined to introducing protection against catastrophic investor loss litigation by placing a cap on the extent of their legal liability, and as corporate scandals occur, the trend to launch class actions to recover investor losses will continue. Auditors are a prime target in this regard.

There can be no doubt at all that further significant reforms will have to be made if investor protection is to be effective in the twenty first century. Instead of the re-active recognition of investor interests, it is vital for the law to encourage a pro-active approach. As recent events in America have amply demonstrated, it is no longer acceptable for the legislature to respond to new cases of investor malpractice with swathes of new legislation to close the stable door long after the horse has bolted. The time has come for Parliament to demand that the scope and application of the regulatory system is sufficiently comprehensive to protect the interests of investors so as to ensure the security of their investments in the years to come. It is incumbent on the legislators, and in particular the House of Commons Treasury and Civil Service Select Committee to take the lead in this regard.

Criminal Sanctions for Corporate Misconduct: the Way Forward?

35–009 Finally, the inadequacy of the criminal process in the context of investor protection has been well documented. In 1986 Lord Roskill said in his report on Fraud Trials that:

> "the public no longer believes that the legal system in England and Wales is effectively to book. The overwhelming weight of the evidence laid before us

suggests that the public is right. In relation to such crimes, and to the skilful and determined criminals who commit them, the present legal system is archaic, cumbersome and unreliable".

Consideration of the matters discussed in Part 5 of this book show that the situation has not improved in the ten years which have passed since these words were written, notwithstanding the passing of the Criminal Justice Act 1977 which was designed to make special provision for the speedy trial of serious fraud. The images of the defendants in the *Maxwell* and *Wickes* trials hover over the void which characterises the impotence of the criminal law in this area. As *The Times* recognised in its leading editorial on the January 20, 1996:

> "The Government must initiate a serious inquiry into the laws and regulations which govern financial dealing . . . The common law offences of fraud and theft are simply not appropriate to cover the complicated transactions and chains of contractual relationships which arise in the biggest financial mishaps . . . The idea of creating a powerful financial regulator, modelled on the US Securities and Exchange Commission, is finding growing support even within the City and the Bank of England, which have traditionally insisted on the lightest possible financial supervision, based on self-regulation. Whichever of the many possible options are ultimately enacted, the Government and the City cannot afford to ignore the evidence that the present system of financial regulation has failed".

Since this editorial was published, there have been numerous attempts **35–010** on the part of Government to alter the way in which criminal frauds are conducted, in particular, by abandoning trial by jury in favour of trial by Judge, with or without assistance from lay assessors. These proposals have been strongly opposed by the legal profession, fearful that, in so far as trial by jury is concerned, they represent the "thin end of the wedge", leading to a more wholesale abandonment of the traditional way in which the guilt or innocence of serious criminal offences is determined in the United Kingdom.

Of greater significance, perhaps, is the recommendation made by the **35–011** Law Commission in July 2002 to introduce a general criminal offence of fraud which would simplify the criminal law and make it much easier to prosecute cases in which corporate scandals have occurred. In particular, the Law Commission noted that a single offence of fraud would make the law more comprehensible to juries, especially in serious fraud cases. The recommended fraud offence would make fraud indictments simpler and more self-explanatory, enabling a jury to focus exclusively on the facts of a case. The Government has yet to grasp this nettle. Certainly, in America it is not uncommon for those involved in corporate scandals to face multiple criminal indictments alleging a miscellany of serious offences punishable by long periods of imprisonment. Criminal proceedings have been initiated against Enron's former Chief Executive Officer and former Chief Financial Officer, as well as against former executives in Worldcom and Martha Stewart, to name a few. Sam Waksal, the founder of ImClone who passed inside information to Martha Stewart and acted upon it, became the first executive to be imprisoned in the recent spate of corporate scandal cases in June 2003 when he was sentenced to a period of seven years and three months imprisonment and ordered to pay $4.26 million in fines and restitution. The media reported that the Manhattan courtroom was shocked by the sentence, which will leave Waksal languishing in a federal penitentiary until he is aged 62 with no prospect of parole. At the time of writing, Martha Stewart faces a lengthy period of imprisonment if she is found guilty of the insider dealing offences and Andrew Fastow, the former Chief Financial Officer of Enron, faces an even longer period of incarceration after pleading guilty to 78 counts of fraud, money laundering and conspiracy.

In the interests of investor protection, the UK Government would do well to implement the changes recommended by the Law Commission and follow the American example.

Part 8

Appendix

Appendix

The Companies Act 1985, Sch.24 (as amended)

A–001

Section 730

SCHEDUELE 24
PUNISHMENT OF OFFENCES UNDER THE COMPANIES ACT 1985

Note: [. . .]

Section of Act creating offence	*General nature of offence*	*Mode of prosecution*	*Punishment*	*Daily default fine (where applicable)*
6(3)	Company failing to deliver to registrar notice or other document, following alteration of its objects.	Summary.	One-fifth of the statutory maximum.	One-fiftieth of the statutory maximum.
18(3)	Company failing to register change in memorandum of articles.	Summary.	One-fifth of the statutory maximum.	One-fiftieth of the statutory maximum.
19(2)	Company failing to send to one of its members a copy of the memorandum or articles, when so required by the member.	Summary.	One-fifth of the statutory maximum.	
20(2)	Where company's memorandum altered, company issuing copy of the memorandum without the alteration.	Summary.	One-fifth of the statutory maximum for each occasion on which copies are so issued after the date of the alteration.	
28(5)	Company failing to change name on direction of Secretary of State.	Summary.	One-fifth of the statutory maximum.	One-fiftieth of the statutory maximum.
31(5)	Company altering its memorandum or articles, so ceasing to be exempt from having "limited" as part of its name.	Summary.	The statutory maximum.	One-tenth of the statutory maximum.

A–002

31(6)	Company failing to change name, on Secretary of State's direction, so as to have "limited" (or Welsh equivalent) at the end.	Summary.	One-fifth of the statutory maximum.	One-fiftieth of the statutory maximum.
32(4)	Company failing to comply with Secretary of State's direction to change its name, on grounds that the name is misleading.	Summary.	One-fifth of the statutory maximum.	One-fiftieth of the statutory maximum.
33	Trading under misleading name (use of "public limited company" or Welsh equivalent when not so entitled); purporting to be a private company.	Summary.	One-fifth of the statutory maximum.	One-fiftieth of the statutory maximum.
34	Trading or carrying on business with improper use of "limited" or "cyfyngedig".	Summary.	One-fifth of the statutory maximum.	One-fiftieth of the statutory maximum.
54(1)	Public company failing to give notice, or copy of court order, to register, concerning application to re-register as private company.	Summary.	One-fifth of the statutory maximum.	One-fiftieth of the statutory maximum.
56(4)	Issuing form of application for shares or debentures without accompanying prospectus.	1. On indictment. 2. Summary.	A fine. The statutory maximum.	

A–003

Section of Act creating offence	*General nature of offence*	*Mode of prosecution*	*Punishment*	*Daily default fine (where applicable)*
61	Issuing prospectus with expert's statement in it, he not having given his consent; omission to state in prospectus that expert has consented.	1. On indictment. 2. Summary.	A fine. The statutory maximum.	
64(5)	Issuing company prospectus without copy being delivered to registrar of companies, or without requisite documents endorsed or attached.	Summary.	One-fifth of the statutory maximum.	One-fiftieth of the statutory maximum.
70(1)	Authorising issue of prospectus with untrue statement.	1. On indictment. 2. Summary.	Two years or a fine; or both. Six months or the statutory maximum; or both.	
78(1)	Being responsible for issue, circulation of prospectus, etc. contrary to Part III, Chapter II (overseas companies).	1. On indictment. 2. Summary.	A fine. The statutory maximum.	
80(9)	Directors exercising company's power of allotment without the authority required by section 80(1).	1. On indictment. 2. Summary.	A fine. The statutory maximum.	
81(2)	Private limited company offering shares to the public, or alloting shares with a view to their being so offered.	1. On indictment. 2. Summary.	A fine. The statutory maximum.	

82(5)	Alloting shares or debentures before third day after issue of prospectus.	1. On indictment. 2. Summary.	A fine. The statutory maximum.	
86(6)	Company failing to keep money in separate bank account, where received in pursuance of prospectus stating that stock exchange listing is to be applied for.	1. On indictment. 2. Summary.	A fine. The statutory maximum.	
87(4)	Offeror of shares for sale failing to keep proceeds in separate bank account.	1. On indictment. 2. Summary.	A fine. The statutory maximum.	
88(5)	Officer of company failing to deliver return of allotments, etc., to registrar.	1. On indictment. 2. Summary.	The statutory maximum.	One-tenth of the statutory maximum.
95(6)	Knowingly or recklessly authorising or permitting misleading, false or deceptive material in statement by directors under section 95(5).	1. On indictment. 2. Summary.	Two years or a fine; or both. Six months or the statutory maximum; or both.	
97(4)	Company failing to deliver to registrar the prescribed form disclosing amount or rate of share commission.	Summary.	One-fifth of the statutory maximum.	
110(2)	Making misleading, false or deceptive statement in connection with valuation under section 103 or 104.	1. On indictment. 2. Summary.	Two years or a fine; or both. Six months or the statutory maximum; or both.	
111(3)	Officer of company failing to deliver copy of asset valuation report to registrar.	1. On indictment. 2. Summary.	A fine. The statutory maximum.	One-tenth of the statutory maximum.

A–005

Section of Act creating offence	General nature of offence	Mode of prosecution	Punishment	Daily default fine (where applicable)
111(4)	Company failing to deliver to registrar copy of resolution under section 104(4), with respect to transfer of an asset as consideration for allotment.	Summary.	One-fifth of the statutory maximum.	One-fiftieth of the statutory maximum.
114	Contravention of any of the provisions of sections 99 to 104, 106.	1. On indictment. 2. Summary.	A fine. The statutory maximum.	
117(7)	Company doing business or exercising borrowing powers contrary to section 117.	1. On indictment. 2. Summary.	A fine. The statutory maximum.	
122(2)	Company failing to give notice to registrar of reorganisation of share capital.	Summary.	One-fifth of the statutory maximum.	One-fiftieth of the statutory maximum.
123(4)	Company failing to give notice to registrar of increase of share capital.	Summary.	One-fifth of the statutory maximum.	One-fiftieth of the statutory maximum.
127(5)	Company failing to forward to registrar copy of court order, when application made to cancel resolution varying shareholders' rights.	Summary.	One-fifth of the statutory maximum.	One-fiftieth of the statutory maximum.
128(5)	Company failing to send to registrar statement or notice required by section 128 (particulars of shares carrying special rights).	Summary.	One-fifth of the statutory maximum.	One-fiftieth of the statutory maxiumum.
129(4)	Company failing to deliver to registrar statement or notice required by section 129 (registration of newly created class rights).	Summary.	One-fifth of the statutory maximum.	One-fiftieth of the statutory maximum.

A–006

141	Officer of company concealing name of creditor entitled to object to reduction of capital, or wilfully misrepresenting nature or amount of debt or claim, etc.	1. On indictment. 2. Summary.	A fine. The statutory maximum.	
142(2)	Director authorising or permitting non-compliance with section 142 (requirement to convene company meeting to consider serious loss of capital).	1. On indictment. 2. Summary.	A fine. The statutory maximum.	
143(2)	Company acquiring its own shares in breach of section 143.	1. On indictment.	In the case of the company, a fine. In the case of an officer of the company who is in default, two years or a fine, or both.	
		2. Summary.	In the case of the company, the statutory maximum. In the case of an officer of the company who is in default, six months or the statutory maximum; or both.	
149(2)	Company failing to cancel its own shares, acquired by itself, as required by section 146(2); or failing to apply for re-registration as private company as so required in the case there mentioned.	Summary.	One-fifth of the statutory maximum.	One-fiftieth of the statutory maximum.

A–007

Section of Act creating offence	*General nature of offence*	*Mode of prosecution*	*Punishment*	*Daily default fine (where applicable)*
151(3)	Company giving financial assistance towards acquisition of its own shares.	1. On indictment.	Where the company is convicted, a fine. Where an officier of the company is convicted, two years or a fine; or both.	
		2. Summary.	Where the company is convicted, the statutory maximum. Where an officer of the company is convicted, six months or the statutory maximum; or both.	
156(6)	Company failing to register statutory declaration under section 155.	Summary.	The statutory maximum.	One-fiftieth of the statutory maximum.
156(7)	Director making statutory declaration under section 155, without having reasonable grounds for opinion expressed in it.	1. On indictment. 2. Summary.	Two years or a fine; or both. Six months or the statutory maximum; or both.	
169(6)	Default by the company's officer in delivering to registrar the return required by section 169 (disclosure by company of purchase of own shares).	1. On indictment. 2. Summary.	A fine. The statutory maximum.	One-tenth of the statutory maximum.

A–008

169(7)	Company failing to keep copy of contract, etc., at registered office, refusal of inspection to person demanding it.	Summary.	One-fifth of the statutory maximum.	One-fiftieth of the statutory maximum.
173(6)	Director making statutory declaration under section 173 without having reasonable grounds for the opinion expressed in the declaration.	1. On indictment. 2. Summary.	Two years or a fine; or both. Six months or the statutory maximum; or both.	
175(7)	Refusal of inspection of statutory declaration and auditors' report under section 173, etc.	Summary.	One-fifth of the statutory maximum.	One-fiftieth of the statutory maximum.
176(4)	Company failing to give notice to registrar of application to court under section 176, or to register court order.	Summary.	One-fifth of the statutory maximum.	One-fiftieth of the statutory maximum.
183(6)	Company failing to send notice of refusal to register a transfer of shares or debentures.	Summary.	One-fifth of the statutory maximum.	One-fiftieth of the statutory maximum.
185(5)	Company default in compliance with section 185(1) (certificates to be made ready following allotment or transfer of shares, etc.)	Summary.	One-fifth of the statutory maximum.	One-fiftieth of the statutory maximum.
189(1)	Offences of fraud and fogery in connection with share warrants in Scotland.	1. On indictment. 2. Summary.	Seven years or a fine; or both. Six months or the statutory maximum; or both.	

A–009

Section of Act creating offence	*General nature of offence*	*Mode of prosecution*	*Punishment*	*Daily default fine (where applicable)*
189(2)	Unauthorised making of, or using or possessing apparatus for making, share warrants in Scotland.	1. On indictment. 2. Summary.	Seven years or a fine; or both. Six months or the statutory maximum; or both.	
191(4)	Refusal of inspection or copy or register of debenture-holders, etc.	Summary.	One-fifth of the statutory maximum.	One-fiftieth of the statutory maximum.
210(3)	Failure to discharge obligation of disclosure under Part VI; other forms of non-compliance with that Part.	1. On indictment. 2. Summary.	Two years or a fine; or both. Six months or the statutory maximum; or both.	
211(10)	Company failing to keep register of interests disclosed under Part VI; other contraventions of section 211.	Summary.	One-fifth of the statutory maximum.	One-fiftieth of the statutory maximum.
214(5)	Company failing to exercise powers under section 212, when so required by the members.	1. On indictment. 2. Summary.	A fine. The statutory maximum.	
215(8)	Company default in compliance with section 215 (company report of investigations of shareholdings on members' requisition).	1. On indictment. 2. Summary.	A fine. The statutory maximum.	
216(3)	Failure to comply with company notice under section 212; making false statement in response, etc.	1. On indictment. 2. Summary.	Two years or a fine; or both. Six month or the statutory maximum; or both.	

A–010

217(7)	Company failing to notify a person that he has been named as a shareholder; on removal of name from register, failing to alter associated index.	Summary.	One-fifth of the statutory maximum.	One-fiftieth of the statutory maximum.
218(3)	Improper removal of entry from register of interests disclosed; company failing to restore entry improperly removed.	Summary.	One-fifth of the statutory maximum.	For continued contravention of section 218(2) one-fiftieth of the statutory maximum.
219(3)	Refusal of inspection of register or report under Part VI; failure to send copy when required.	Summary.	One-fifth of the statutory maximum.	One-fiftieth of the statutory maximum.
223(1)	Company failing to keep accounting records (liability of officers).	1. On indictment. 2. Summary.	Two years or a fine; or both. Six months or the statutory maximum; or both.	
223(2)	Officer of company failing to secure compliance with, or intentionally causing default under section 222(4) (preservation of accounting records for requisite number of years).	1. On indictment. 2. Summary.	Two years or a fine; or both. Six months or the statutory maximum; or both.	
231(3)	Company failing to annex to its annual return certain particulars required by Schedule 5 and not included in annual accounts.	Summary.	One-fifth of the statutory maximum.	One-fiftieth of the statutory maxiumum.

A–011

Section of Act creating offence	*General nature of offence*	*Mode of prosecution*	*Punishment*	*Daily default fine (where applicable)*
231(4)	Default by director or officer of a company in giving notice of matters relating to himself for purposes of Schedule 5 Part V.	Summary.	One-fifth of the statutory maximum.	
235(7)	Non-compliance with the section, as to directors' report and its content; directors individually liable.	1. On indictment. 2. Summary.	A fine. The statutory maximum.	
238(2)	Laying or delivery of unsigned balance sheet; circulating copies of balance sheet without signatures.	Summary.	One-fifth of the statutory maximum.	
240(5)	Failing to send company balance sheet, directors' report and auditors' report to those entitled to receive the.	1. On indictment. 2. Summary.	A fine. The statutory maximum.	
243(1)	Director in default as regards duty to lay and deliver company accounts.	Summary.	The statutory maximum.	One-tenth of the statutory maximum.
[. . .]				
[. . .]				
246(2)	Company failing to supply copy of accounts to shareholder on his demand.	Summary.	One-fifth of the statutory maximum.	One-fiftieth of the statutory maximum.
254(6)	Company or officer in default contravening section 254 as regards publication of full individual or group accounts.	Summary.	One-fifth of the statutory maximum	

A–012

[. . .]				
[. . .]				
[. . .]				
288(4)	Default in complying with section 288 (keeping register of directors and secretaries, refusal of inspection).	Summary.	The statutory maximum.	One-tenth of the statutory maximum.
291(5)	Acting as director of a company without having the requisite share qualification.	Summary.	One-fifth of the statutory maximum.	One-fiftieth of the statutory maximum.
294(3)	Director failing to give notice of his attaining retirement age; acting as director under appointment invalid due to his attaining it.	Summary.	One-fifth of the statutory maximum.	One-fiftieth of the statutory maximum.
305(3)	Company default in complying with section 305 (directors' names to appear on company correspondence, etc.)	Summary.	One-fifth of the statutory maximum.	
306(4)	Failure to state that liability of proposed director or manager is unlimited; failure to give notice of that fact to person accepting office.	1. On indictment. 2. Summary.	A fine. The statutory maximum.	
314(3)	Director failing to comply with section 314 (duty to disclose compensation payable on takeover, etc.); a person's failure to include required particulars in a notice he has to give of such matters.	Summary.	One-fifth of the statutory maximum.	
317(7)	Director failing to disclose interest in contract.	1. On indictment. 2. Summary.	A fine. The statutory maximum.	

A–013

Section of Act creating offence	*General nature of offence*	*Mode of prosecution*	*Punishment*	*Daily default fine (where applicable)*
318(8)	Company default in complying with section 318(1) or (5) (directors' service contracts to be open to inspection); 14 days' default in complying with section 319(4) (notice to registrar as to where copies of contracts and memoranda are kept); refusal of inspection required under section 318(7).	Summary.	One-fifth of the statutory maximum.	One-fiftieth of the statutory maximum.
[322B(4)	Terms of unwritten contract between sole member of a private company limited by shares or by guarantee and the company not set out in a written memorandum or recorded in minutes of a directors' meeting.	Summary.		Level 5 on the standard scale.]
323(2)	Director dealing in options to buy or sell company's listed shares or debentures.	1. On indictment. 2. Summary.	Two years or a fine; or both. Six months or the statutory maximum; or both.	
324(7)	Director failing to notify interest in company's shares; making false statement in purported notification.	1. On indictment. 2. Summary.	Two years or a fine; or both. Six months or the statutory maximum; or both.	
326(2), (3), (4), (5)	Various defaults in connection with company register of directors' interests.	Summary.	One-fifth of the statutory maximum.	Except in the case of section 326(5), one-fiftieth of the statutory maximum.

A–014

328(6)	Director failing to notify company that members of his family have, or have exercised, options to buy shares or debentures; making false statement in purported notification.	1. On indictment. 2. Summary.	Two years or a fine; or both. Six months or the statutory maximum; or both.	
329(3)	Company failing to notify [investment exchange] of acquisition of its securities by a director.	Summary.	One-fifth of the statutory maximum.	One-fiftieth of the statutory maximum.
342(1)	Director of relevant company authorising or permitting company to enter into transaction or arrangement, knowing or suspecting it to contravene section 330.	1. On indictment. 2. Summary.	Two years or a fine; or both. Six months or the statutory maximum; or both.	
342(2)	Relevant company entering into transaction or arrangement for a director in contravention of section 330.	1. On indictment. 2. Summary.	Two years or a fine; or both. Six months or the statutory maximum; or both.	
342(3)	Procuring a relevant company to enter into transaction or arrangment known to be contrary to section 330.	1. On indictment. 2. Summary.	Two years or a fine; or both. Six months or the statutory maximum; or both.	

A–015

Section of Act creating offence	*General nature of offence*	*Mode of prosecution*	*Punishment*	*Daily default fine (where applicable)*
343(8)	Company failing to maintain register of transactions, etc., made with and for directors and not disclosed in company accounts; failing to make register available at registered office or at company meeting.	1. On indictment. 2. Summary.	A fine. The statutory maximum.	
348(2)	Company failing to paint or affix name; failing to keep it painted or affixed.	Summary.	One-fifth of the statutory maximum.	In the case of failure to keep the name painted or affixed, one-fiftieth of the statutory maximum.
349(2)	Company failing to have name on business correspondence, invoices, etc.	Summary.	One-fifth of the statutory maximum.	
349(3)	Officer of company issuing business letter or document not bearing company's name.	Summary.	One-fifth of the statutory maximum.	
349(4)	Officer of company signing cheque, bill of exchange, etc. on which company's name not mentioned.	Summary.	One-fifth of the statutory maximum.	
350(1)	Company failing to have its name engraved on company seal.	Summary.	One-fifth of the statutory maximum.	
350(2)	Officer of company, etc., using company seal without name engraved on it.	Summary.	One-fifth of the statutory maximum.	

A–016

351(1)(a)	Company failing to comply with section 351(1) or (2) (matters to be stated on business correspondence, etc.).	Summary.	One-fifth of the statutory maximum.	
351(5)(b)	Officer or agent of company issuing, or authorising issue of, business document not complying with those subsections.	Summary.	One-fifth of the statutory maximum.	
351(5)(c)	Contravention of section 351(3) or (4) (information in English to be stated on Welsh company's business correspondence, etc.).	Summary.	One-fifth of the statutory maximum.	For contravention of section 351(3), one-fiftieth of the statutory maximum.
352(5)	Company default in complying with section 352 (requirement to keep register of members and their particulars.	Summary.	One-fifth of the statutory maximum.	One-fiftieth of the statutory maximum.
[352A(3)	Company default in complying with section 352A (statement that company has only one members).	Summary.	Level 2 on the standard scale.	One-tenth of level 2 of the standard scale.]
353(4)	Company failing to send notice to registrar as to place where register of members is kept.	Summary.	One-fifth of the statutory maximum.	One-fiftieth of the statutory maximum.
354(4)	Company failing to keep index of members.	Summary.	One-fifth of the statutory maximum.	One-fiftieth of the statutory maximum.

A–017

Section of Act creating offence	*General nature of offence*	*Mode of prosecution*	*Punishment*	*Daily default fine (where applicable)*
356(5)	Refusal of inspection of members' register; failure to send copy on requisition.	Summary.	One-fifth of the statutory maximum.	
363(7)	Company with share capital failing to make annual return.	Summary.	The statutory maximum.	One-tenth of the statutory maxiumum.
364(4)	Company without share capital failing to complete and register annual return in due time.	Summary.	The statutory maximum.	One-tenth of the statutory maximum.
[. . .]				
366(4)	Company default in holding annual general meeting.	1. On indictment. 2. Summary.	A fine. The statutory maximum.	
367(3)	Company default in complying with Secretary of State's direction to hold company meeting.	1. On indictment. 2. Summary.	A fine. The statutory maximum.	
367(5)	Company failing to register resolution that meeting held under section 367 is to be its annual general meeting.	Summary.	One-fifth of the statutory maximum.	One-fiftieth of the statutory maximum.
372(4)	Failure to give notice, to member entitled to vote at company meeting, that he may do so by proxy.	Summary.	One-fifth of the statutory maximum.	
372(6)	Officer of company authorising or permitting issue of irregular invitation to appoint proxies.	Summary.	One-fifth of the statutory maximum.	
376(7)	Officer of company in default as to circulation of members' resolutions for company meeting.	1. On indictment. 2. Summary.	A fine. The statutory maximum.	

A–018

380(5)	Company failing to comply with section 380 (copies of certain resolutions etc. to be sent to registrar of companies.	Summary.	One-fifth of the statutory maximum.	One-fiftieth of the statutory maximum.
380(6)	Company failing to include copy of resolution to which section 380 applies in articles; failing to forward copy to member on request.	Summary.	One-fifth of the statutory maximum for each occasion on which copies are issued or, as the case may be, requested.	
382(5)	Company failing to keep minutes of proceedings at company and board meetings, etc.	Summary.	One-fifth of the statutory maximum.	One-fiftieth of the statutory maximum.
[382B92)	Failure of sole member to provide the company with a written record of decision.	Summary.	Level 2 on the standard scale.]	
383(4)	Refusal of inspection of minutes of general meeting; failure to send copy of minutes on member's request.	Summary.	One-fifth of the statutory maximum.	
[. . .]				
[. . .]				
[387(2)	Company failing to give Secretary of State notice of non-appointment of auditors.	Summary.	One-fifth of the statutory maximum.	One-fiftieth of the statutory maximum.]
389(10)	Person acting as company auditor knowing himself to be disqualified; failing to give notice vacating office when he becomes disqualified.	1. On indictment. 2. Summary.	A fine. The statutory maximum.	One-tenth of the statutory maximum.

A–019

Section of Act creating offence	*General nature of offence*	*Mode of prosecution*	*Punishment*	*Daily default fine (where applicable)*
[389A(2)	Officer of company making false, misleading or deceptive statement to auditors.	1. On indictment. 2. Summary.	Two years or a fine; or both. Six months or the statutory maximum; or both.	
389A(3)	Subsidiary undertaking or its auditor failing to give information to auditors of patent company.	Summary.	One-fifth of the statutory maximum.	
389A(4)	Parent company failing to obtain from subsidiary undertaking information for purposes of audit.	Summary.	One-fifth of the statutory maximum.	
[. . .] [391(2)	Failing to give notice to registrar of removal of auditor.	Summary.	One-fifth of the stautory maximum.	One-fiftieth of the statutory maximum.]
[. . .] [392(3)	Company failing to forward notice of auditor's registration to registrar.	1. On indictment. 2. Summary.	A fine. The statutory maximum.	One-tenth of the statutory maximum.
392A(5)	Directors failing to convene meeting requisitioned by resigning auditor.	1. On indictment. 2. Summary.	A fine. The statutory maximum.]	
[. . .] 394A(1)	Person ceasing to hold office as auditor failing to deposit statement as to circumstances.	1. On indictment. 2. Summary.	A fine. The statutory maximum.	

A–020

394(4)	Company failing to comply with requirements as to statement of person ceasing to hold office as auditor.	1. On indictment. 2. Summary.	A fine. The statutory maximum.	One-tenth of the statutory maximum.
399(3)	Company failing to send to registrar particulars of charge created by it, or of issue of debentures which requires registration.	1. On indictment. 2. Summary.	A fine. The statutory maximum.	One-tenth of the statutory maximum.
400(4)	Company failing to send to registrar particulars of charge on property acquired.	1. On indictment. 2. Summary.	A fine. The statutory maximum.	One-tenth of the statutory maximum.
402(3)	Authorising or permitting delivery of debenture or certificate of debenture stock, without endorsement on it of certificate registration of charge.	Summary.	One-fifth of the statutory maximum.	
405(4)	Failure to give notice to registrar of appointment of receiver or manager, or of his ceasing to act.	Summary.	One-fifth of the statutory maximum.	One-fiftieth of the statutory maximum.
407(3)	Authorising or permitting omission from company register of charges.	1. On indictment. 2. Summary.	A fine. The statutory maximum.	
408(3)	Officer of company refusing inspection of charging instrument, or of register of charges.	Summary.	One-fifth of the statutory maximum.	One-fiftieth of the statutory maximum.
415(3)	Scottish company failing to send to registrar particulars of charge created by it, or of issue of debentures which requires registration.	1. On indictment. 2. Summary.	A fine. The statutory maximum.	One-tenth of the statutory maximum.

A–021

Section of Act creating offence	*General nature of offence*	*Mode of prosecution*	*Punishment*	*Daily default fine (where applicable)*
416(3)	Scottish company failing to send to registrar particulars of charge on property acquired by it.	1. On indictment. 2. Summary.	A fine. The statutory maximum.	
422(3)	Scottish company authorising or permitting omission from its register of charges.	1. On indictment. 2. Summary.	A fine. The statutory maximum.	
423(3)	Officer of Scottish company refusing inspection of charging instrument, or of register of charges.	Summary.	One-fifth of the statutory maximum.	One-fiftieth of the statutory maximum.
425(4)	Company failing to annex to memorandum court order sanctioning compromise or arrangement with creditors.	Summary.	One-fifth of the statutory maximum.	
426(6)	Company failing to comply with requirements of section 426 (information to members and creditors about compromise or arrangement.)	1. On indictment. 2. Summary.	A fine. The statutory maximum.	
426(7)	Director or trustee for debenture holders failing to give notice to company of matters necessary for purposes of section 426.	Summary.	One-fifth of the statutory maximum.	
427(5)	Failure to deliver to registrar office copy of court order under section 427 (company reconstruction or amalgamation).	Summary.	One-fifth of the statutory maximum.	One-fiftieth of the statutory maximum.

A–022

[429(6)	Offeror failing to send copy of notice or making statutory declaration knowing ti to be false, etc.	1. On indictment. 2. Summary.	Two years or a fine; or both. Six months or the statutory maximum; or both.	One fiftieth of the statutory maximum.
430A(6)	Offeror failing to give notice or rights to minority shareholders.	1. On indictment. 2. Summary.	A fine. The statutory maximum.	One-fiftieth of the statutory maximum.]
444(3)	Failing to give Secretary of State, when required to do so, information about interests in shares, etc.; give false information.	1. On indictment. 2. Summary.	Two years or a fine; or both. Six months or the statutory maximum; or both.	
447(6)	Failure to comply with requirement to produce [documents] imposed by Secretary of State under section 447.	1. On indictment. 2. Summary.	A fine. The statutory maximum.	
[448(7)]	[Obstructing the exercise of any rights conferred by a warrant or failing to comply with a requirement imposed under subsection (3)(d)].	1. On indictment. 2. Summary.	A fine. The statutory maximum.	
449(2)	Wrongful disclosure of information or document obtained under section 447 or 448.	1. On indictment. 2. Summary.	Two years or a fine; or both. Six months or the statutory maximum; or both.	
450	Destroying or mutilating company documents; falsifying such documents or making false entries; parting with such documents or altering them or making omissions.	1. On indictment. 2. Summary.	Seven years or a fine; or both. Six months or the statutory maximum; or both.	

A–023

Section of Act creating offence	*General nature of offence*	*Mode of prosecution*	*Punishment*	*Daily default fine (where applicable)*
451	Making false statement or explanation in purported compliance with section 447.	1. On indictment. 2. Summary.	Two years or a fine; or both. Six months or the statutory maximum; or both.	
455(1)	Exercising a right to dispose of, or vote in respect of, shares which are subject to restriction under Part XV; failing to give notice in respect of shares so subject; entering into agreement void under section 454(2), (3).	1. On indictment. 2. Summary.	A fine. The statutory maximum.	
455(2)	Issuing shares in contravention of restrictions of Part XV.	1. On indictment. 2. Summary.	A fine. The statutory maximum.	
458	Being a party to carrying on company's business with intent to defraud creditors, or for any fraudulent purpose.	1. On indictment. 2. Summary	Seven years or a fine; or both. Six months or the statutory maximum; or both.	
461(5)	Failure to register office copy of court order under Part XVII altering, or giving leave to alter, company's memorandum.	Summary.	One-fifth of the statutory maximum.	One-fiftieth of the statutory maximum.
[. . .]				
651(3)	Person obtaining court order to declare company's dissolution void, then failing to register the order.	Summary.	One-fifth of the statutory maximum.	One-fiftieth of the statutory maximum.

A–024

652E(1)	Person breaching or failing to peform duty imposed by section 652B or 652C.	1. On indictment. 2. Summary.	A fine. The statutory maximum.	
652E(2)	Person failing to perform duty imposed by section 652B(6) or 652C(2) with intent to conceal the making of application under section 652A.	1. On indictment. 2. Summary.	Seven years or a fine; or both. Six months or the statutory maximum; or both.	
652F(1)	Person furnishing false or misleading information in connection with application under section 652A.	1. On indictment. 2. Summary.	A fine. The statutory maximum.	
652F(2)	Person making false application under section 652A.	1. On indictment. 2. Summary.	A fine. The statutory maximum.	
697(1)	Overseas company failing to comply with any of sections 691 to 693 or 696.	Summary.	For an offence which is not a continuing offence, one-fifth of the statutory maximum. For an offence which is a continuing offence, one-fifth of the statutory maximum.	One-fiftieth of the statutory maximum.
697(2)	Oversea company contravening section 694(6) (carrying on business under its corporate name after Secretary of State's direction).	1. On indictment. 2. Summary.	A fine. The statutory maximum.	One-tenth of the statutory maximum.

A–025

Section of Act creating offence	*General nature of offence*	*Mode of prosecution*	*Punishment*	*Daily default fine (where applicable)*
[697(3)	Oversea Company failing to comply with section 695A or Schedule 21A.	Summary.	For an offence which is not a continuing offence, one-fifth of level 5 of the standard scale. For an offence which is a continuing offence one fifth of level 5 of the standard scale.	£100]
703(1)	Oversea company failing to comply with s. 700 as respects delivery of annual accounts.	1. On indictment. 2. Summary.	A fine. The statutory maximum.	One-tenth of the statutory maximum.
[703R(1)	Company failing to register winding up or commencement or insolvency proceedings etc.	1. On indictment. 2. Summary.	A fine. The statutory maximum.	£100]
[703R(2)	Liquidator failing to register appointment, termination of winding up or striking-off of company.	1. On indictment. 2. Summary.	A fine. The statutory maximum.	£100]
710(4)	[*Repealed by the Insolvency Act 1986, Sched. 12.*]			
720(4)	Insurance company etc. failing to send twice-yearly statement in form of Schedule 23.	Summary.	One-fifth of the statutory maximum.	One-fiftieth of the statutory maximum.
720(3)	Company failing to comply with section 722(2), as regards the manner of keeping registers, minute books and accounting records.	Summary.	One-fifth of the statutory maximum.	One-fiftieth of the statutory maximum.

A–026

Sched. 14, Pt. II, para. 1(3)	Company failing to give notice of location of overseas branch register, etc.	Summary.	One-fifth of the statutory maximum.	One-fiftieth of the statutory maximum.
Sched. 14, Pt. II, para. 4(2)	Company failing to transmit to its registered office in Great Britain copies of entries in overseas branch register, or to keep a duplicate of overseas branch register.	Summary.	One-fifth of the statutory maximum.	One-fiftieth of the statutory maximum.
[Sched. 21C, Pt. 1, para. 7	Credit or financial institution failing to deliver accounting documents.	1. On indictment. 2. Summary.	A fine. The statutory maximum.	£100]
[Sched. 21C, Pt. II, para. 15	Credit or financial institution failing to deliver accounts and reports.	1. On indictment. 2. Summary.	A fine. The statutory maxiumum.	£100]
[Sched. 21D, Pt. 1, para. 5	Company failing to deliver accounting documents.	1. On indictment. 2. Summary.	A fine. The statutory maximum.	£100]
[Sched. 21D, Pt. 1, para. 13	Company failing to deliver accounts and reports	1. On indictment. 2. Summary.	A fine. The statutory maximum.	£100]

AMENDMENTS

A–027 The Note to Schedule 24 was repealed by the Statute Law (Repeals) Act 1993.

The words in square brackets were inserted by Sched. 16 para. 27 of the Financial Services Act 1986.

The words omitted from this Schedule were repealed by the Insolvency Act 1986, Sched. 12, and by the Companies Act 1989, Sched. 24.

The words in square brackets relating to s. 387(2) were inserted by the Companies Act 1989, s. 119.

The words in square brackets relating to ss. 389A(2), (3) and (4) were inserted by the Companies Act 1989, s. 120.

The words in square brackets relating to ss. 391(2), 392(3) and 392A(5) were inserted by the Companies Act 1989, s. 122.

The words in square brackets relating to ss. 394A(1) and (4) were inserted by the Companies Act 1989, s. 123.

The words in square brackets relating to s. 447(6) were substitued by the Companies Act 1989, s. 63(8).

The words in square brackets relating to s. 448(7) were substituted by the Companies Act 1989, s. 64(2).

For the repeal of references to ss. 56(4), 61, 64(5), 70(1), 78(1), 81(2), 82(5), 86(6), 87(4) and 97(4) see S.I. 1986 No. 2246 (para. B–700 below), S.I. 1988 No. 740 (para. B–760, below), and S.I. 1988 No. 1960 (para. B–766, below).

The references to ss. 245(1) and (2) were repealed by the Companies Act 1989, Sched. 24, subject to transitional provisions in S.I. 1990 No. 2569, para. A–3639, below.

The words in square brackets relating to ss. 322B(4), 352A(3) and 382B(2) were inserted by S.I. 1992 No. 1699.

The words in square brackets relating to ss. 697(3), 703R(1) and 703R(2) and to Scheds. 21C and 21D were inserted by S.I. 1992 No. 3179.

The entries relating to s. 652E(1), 652E(2), 652F(1), and 652F(2) were inserted by the Deregulation and Contracting Out Act 1994, Sched. 5.

Index